Developing Areas

Developing Areas

A Book of Readings and Research

Edited by

VIJAYAN K. PILLAI

and

LYLE W. SHANNON

with the assistance of

JUDITH L. McKIM

BERG

Oxford · Providence, USA

Published in 1995 by

Berg Publishers Limited

Editorial offices:
150 Cowley Road, Oxford OX4 1JJ, UK
221 Waterman Street, Providence, RI 02906, USA

© 1995 Vijayan K. Pillai, Lyle W. Shannon

A CIP catalogue record for this book is available from the British Library.

Library of Congress Cataloging-in-Publication Data
Developing areas / by Vijayan K. Pillai and Lyle W. Shannon [editors].
        p.   cm.
    Includes bibliographical references and index.
    ISBN 0 85496 741 9 (HB) 1 85973 002 7
        1. Economic development.   I. Pillai, Vijayan K.   II. Shannon, Lyle W.
    HD75.D485   1993
    338.9—dc20   93-5295
                                                                      CIP

ISBN 0 85496 741 9 (Cloth)
      1 85973 002 7 (Paper)

Printed in the United Kingdom by WBC Book Manufacturers, Bridgend, Mid Glamorgan.

Contents

Preface

POLITICIANS AND RELIGIONISTS from around the world exhort their followers and hopefully would-be followers to action on behalf of this or that political party, or religion, or movement. Each sincerely, sometimes vehemently, believes that their "ism" holds the greatest hope for our salvation from whatever we wish to be saved. We have now seen that none of the "isms" has led to world salvation and the fulfillment of basic needs of its population. Neither conservatism nor radicalism, even though radicalism means "get to the roots," has done what a unified science may accomplish. We do not mean that science should become a religion. We mean that research on how people come to behave the way that they do will, in the long run, be a more successful approach than are political and religious "isms." Research will show us how our human and physical resources may be used to generate higher levels of living and longer life for earth's people.

This volume is not just another reader on developing areas and their problems. It is meant to be a basis for thinking about the unresolved problems of development that may be found in what are considered highly developed areas but which have even more stark and real consequences in lesser developed areas. They are problems and process on a continuum of development that extends from the least developed, in terms of modern industrial society, to the most highly developed, in terms of production based on computer-assisted design and manufacture.

It should be clear to the reader that no invidious comparisons are made. That highly "industrialized" society which has the ability to destroy civilization from afar is not considered superior to a society in which the spear is still considered part of the national dress. But industrial society does have the ability to organize production with available raw materials and human resources to provide longer life and greater human comforts. If that is of value to persons who live in less mechanized and industrialized societies, then what must we and they do to help bring about a transformation in pertinent segments of their society? What must be changed in the structure of their society to facilitate the development of technical skills and the utilization of unharnessed energy?

Unfortunately, we live in a world where billions are spent on weapons of destruction, destruction, and rebuilding – a world in which people bomb each other back into the Stone Age with the belief that something has been accomplished. While research and development of armaments generated by peoples' fears of each other continue without hesitation, the decision to support research in the behavioral and social sciences is usually a luxury that cannot be afforded or, if afforded, is done so at a level that has only permitted us to scratch the surface of what we must know about societal development and human behavior. It is this of which the reader will be aware as article after article concludes with the statement that it is the beginning, that we cannot make a conclusive statement, a generalization of such sophistication to be applicable to the problems of all who are involved in planning for development.

Then what do we have here? First of all, it is an interdisciplinary selection of articles, mostly from the 1960s through the 1980s – thirty years of research and thought on the process of social and economic development and planned efforts to direct it. But it is really more than that, for the authors of many of the articles – the sociologists, the anthropologists, the political scientists, and the economic historians – have built not only upon the work of generation of scholars but also upon the experience of humankind over hundreds of years. By including the citations and references of these scholars we have, in essence, included a representation of what we know about the process of development and the names of those who have been best known for their contributions as well as the titles of hundreds of articles and books on the subject.

The undergraduate will profit from reading this volume and the graduate will be able to go beyond it to the citations and references. Our introductions to the chapters include references to many articles not included in this volume but which we thought had made an important contribution to some of the issues that have been debated in recent years.

The articles included in these thirteen chapters range from summaries of the literature on development and those that have a historical orientation, to those that describe modern experiments in social or economic change. They range from articles that account for economic development in terms of social structure and change in elements of the structure to those that see change as based upon the behavior of an economic man. Some of the articles deal with demographic change and others with demographic characteristics as the determinants of change or lack of change.

Some articles describe how capital must be accumulated for development, others discuss how accumulated capital (saving, loans, grants) is the basis of development, and yet others show how development permits the accumulation of capital. Goverment planning vs. the free market are debated as the mechanisms that facilitate this or that aspect of development or development in general. Quite different articles describe the role of religion or politics at various stages in development or the relationship of economic development to national resources.

This book does not give all the answers but it does permit one to have an informed view of past and present efforts to develop societies that permit people to live longer and better, to have their basic human needs fulfilled. Those who read it will be prepared for an informed discourse on the problems of developing nations and the roles that various social institutions may play in bringing about greater development.

In a sense, this volume should enable us to see the world quite differently, in a social structural and processual manner, rather than as somewhat disjointed accounts of institutional malfunction or individual failings. Although the articles and introductory comments for each chapter were written before the cataclysmic events of late 1991 in Soviet Europe and Asia, the argumentation and research included here is relevant to them. The sweep of past historical event and today's "surprises" become comprehensible as natural phenomena to be studied as a basis for understanding and ultimate control of the future for the benefit of all people.

VIJAYAN K. PILLAI
LYLE W. SHANNON

CHAPTER 1

Definition and Distribution of Developing Areas

Introduction

EVERYDAY CONVERSATION among people who are attuned to the exciting, almost over-powering stream of events in and among ancient nations, many of which are now thought of as developing, has, for the past fifty years, dealt with changes in their political and economic status. Some of these nations are near and familiar but more often are far away and perhaps little known to us.

In recent years television has brought us instant views of what is happening in distant places, but it does not always make events much more comprehensible. Perhaps it has even added confusion in the minds of people who have enjoyed a complacency based on their lack of information. If we are to understand what happens on the international scene, if we are to even commence to predict what will happen in the future (much less control events), we must take a careful look at the past and how social, economic, and demographic factors have contributed to conflict among nations.

It would be very easy to say that this is a book about social factors in economic growth, that it will tell us something about the developing and developed nations, how they have come to be that way, how we might help the developing nations, and how they could help themselves in the process of development. Empirical studies have arrived at contradictory conclusions about how some nations have become so highly developed that their rich farmlands produce the food that feeds much of the rest of the world. These studies have also shown how some less developed nations produce minerals that help more industrially developed nations provide opportunities for the majority of their residents to avoid mass deprivation, even to live at a level that is almost incomprehensible to the poorest of the poor. And they have described how a small segment of some nations live in glittering apartments or in homes that are surrounded by the lushest of gardens, both almost within a stone's throw of mountainside *favelas* (slums) and tidal basin shacks.

We wish to do more than this and point the way to research and policy development that will harness human energy, make the poor more productive, and show that the solution to problems comes from the brilliance of the human mind rather than the muzzle of a

1

gun. The task is not easy but if we build on the knowledge that has come from success and failure in nations around the world, we shall have a basis for scientific social and economic development.

The Problem of Definition and Measurement

Various areas of the world may be characterized as either developing or developed. Organizations such as the World Bank and the United Nations categorize nations as least developed, less developed, newly industrialized, and developed. The United Nations Committee for Development has identified 36 countries as least developed, a large proportion of them in Africa.

Although the 1957 version of this volume was titled *Underdeveloped Areas*, underdeveloped has come to have a pejorative meaning as have undeveloped, less developed, backward, etc. As Myint (1954) indicated, the terms "underdeveloped" and "backward" are not interchangeable, underdeveloped resources being the actual referent for underdeveloped. Whether human resources are part of the total resources that have not been developed or whether their development must be considered separately from natural resources is dealt with at length in Myint's excellent paper. The last word has not yet been written. Be all that as it may, some of the selections included in our volume still use this term and others use Third World. The latter has never appealed to us because they was something remiss in referring to the other worlds (capitalist and communist) as coming before them. All could be placed on the development continuum and there would be considerable overlap depending on which measure or measures of development had been selected.

Before we examine the process of development and the experiences that persons from a variety of applied scientific fields have had in developing areas, we must see where we are, take a brief look at the conditions of nations circa 1950, and then make a more detailed examination circa 1990. This will involve a bit of puzzling over the conceptual basis for classifying nations. Then we shall turn to several scholarly articles from the vast literature on social factors in economic growth and development.

As social science has developed, most researchers have recognized the utility of scales that represent numerous facets of development, thus reducing the number of variables that must be manipulated in analyses. In *Underdeveloped Areas* (Shannon, 1957) we described a number of scales based on as many as 56 different variables. In the end, we determined that a scale with 17 different social, demographic, and economic variables of a per capita or per square mile nature represented development as well as did the larger scales.

When the relationship between developmental status and political status as self-governing or non-self-governing was examined, it was found that a cutting point that placed 147 of the 195 political entities (then on our list) in the underdeveloped (least developed) category best discriminated between self-governing and non-self-governing entities. Dividing two continua into into two dichotomies in such a way that maximizes one's ability to predict one characteristic of an entity from another characteristic is one strategy for objectively determining cutting points. These 147 underdeveloped areas included 63.3 percent of the world's population, close to the statement so often heard that two-thirds of the world is ill-fed, ill-housed, and ill-clothed. Although 49 of these underdeveloped areas were in Africa, they contained 7.7 percent of the world's population while the 26 Asian underdeveloped areas contained 47.5 percent, almost half of the world's population. Thirty-four of the world's forty-eight most developed nations were in Europe and made up only 16.3 percent of the world's population in 1950.

These political entities, self-governing and non-self-governing, were ranked on several development scales and correlated with political status, population, age, and stage of the demographic transition in earlier papers (Shannon, 1961) revealing that there was a dynamic aspect to size, development, demographic changes, and change in political status for the 1940-1960 period. Although we have not included papers from that period in this volume, suffice it to say that neither demography nor social and economic development in themselves completely accounted for political status. We are inclined to believe that distance from controlling powers and the cost of controlling an area when transportation was changing from ocean-going vessels to air transport rendered some non-self-governing countries less valuable to the military and the taxpayer. We shall deal with the relationship of development to political status again in Chapter 2.

The Geographical Distribution of Developing Countries

In Table 1 the 208 political entities of the world as of 1990 are classified as self-governing, new self-governing, or non-self-governing. Those 37 political entities that could be classified as least developed are indicated by an asterisk since they were in the lowest or next to lowest categories on a scale of 1-9 or 1-10 in at least one comparison of the measures included in Table 1. For example, Mali and Chad were in the least developed category for GNP per capita, Literacy, PQLI, and the Index of Suffering. Six comparisons were possible, although countries did not necessarily appear in all six: GNP-LIT, GNP-PQLI, GNP-SUF, LIT-SUF, LIT-PQLI, and PQLI-SUF. Mali was in the least developed category in each comparison and Denmark and Switzerland were in the most developed category.

We shall not worry so much if you disagree with exactly where the Middle East begins and Europe ends or where the Middle East ends and Asia begins. The first two columns of the table indicate the population (Ellen Jamison, *World Population Profile* and *The 1990 Information Please Almanac*) of each political entity, when it obtained self-government, from whom if this happened between 1950 and 1990, and which country still maintains some control if the entity is still non-self-governing.

One can see why the 1960s were referred to as the decade in which there was a great march to freedom in Africa, continuing into the 1970s and 1980s in other parts of the world. Those countries of Africa that were self-governing prior to 1950 make up only 2.8 percent of the world's population today but the new-self-governing countries of Africa constitute 9.5 percent of the world's population. By contrast, the countries of Asia that were self-governing prior to 1950 made up 44.2 percent of the world's population while those Asian countries that received self-government since 1950 make up only 2.2 percent of the population. Southeast Asia has a more balanced proportion of its population in each group.

Note that while the countries of the Caribbean and South America may sometimes be in the spotlight of the world, they make up little more than 1 percent of the world's population. Think about how small countries have so often plunged the world into wars that destroy the development of their own and other countries. Has the optimism shown by Surenda J. Patel (1964), that we too have shared, been somewhat diminished by

Table 1: Political, Population, Social, and Economic Status of Political Entities by Continent: 1990

A. AFRICA		POPULATION CIRCA 1990 IN THOUSANDS	PER CAPITA GNP	PERCENT LITERATE	PQLI	INDEX OF SUFFERING
Self-Governing Prior to 1950						
Egypt		52,805	650	43	43	55
*Ethiopia		49,762	120	35	20	82
Union of South Africa		38,509	2,290	99	53	52
Ciskei		675				
Bophuthatswana		1,300				
Transkei		3,610	42			
Venda		400	390			
*Liberia		2,556	310	20	26	71
		149,317				
Percent of World Population – 2.84						
New Self-Governing, 1950 to 1990						
*Nigeria	(UK–1960)	115,316	290	30	25	80
*Zaire	(Bel–1960)	34,279	170		32	84
Morocco	(Fr–1956)	25,606	750	28	41	66
Tanzania	(UK–1961)	25,206	160	85	31	75
Algeria	((Fr–1962)	24,946	2,450	80	41	67
*Sudan	(UK–1956)	24,476	340	20	36	77
Kenya	(UK–1963)	24,346	360	59	39	77
Uganda	(UK–1962)	17,008	280	52	40	71
*Ghana	(UK–1957)	14,839	400	45	35	87
*Mozambique	(Port–1975)	14,275	100	17	25	95
Ivory Coast	(Fr–1960)	11,619	740	35	28	73
Madagascar	(Fr–1960)	11,430	180	53	41	68
Cameroon	(Gr,Fr,UK–1960)	10,817	1,010	65	27	78
Zimbabwe	(UK–1965)	9,889	660	77	46	69
*Mali	(Fr–1960)	8,918	230	10	15	88
*Malawi	(UK–1964)	8,737	160	20	30	83
*Burkina-Faso	(Fr–1960)	8,707	230	13	16	84
*Angola	(Port–1975)	8,537	600	20	16	91
*Somalia	(UK,It–1963)	8,248	170	60	19	87
Tunisia	(Fr–1956)	7,916	1,230	64	47	56
*Zambia	(UK–1965)	7,875	290	56	28	74
*Senegal	(Fr–1960)	7,506	630	23	25	71
*Niger	(Fr–1960)	7,448	146	21	13	85
*Rwanda	(UK–1962)	7,322	310	49	27	80
*Guinea	(Fr–1958)	7,086	350	28	20	82
*Burundi	(UK–1962)	5,456	230	30	23	77
*Chad	(Fr–1960)	4,949	160	17	18	88
*Benin	(Fr–1960)	4,661	340	29	23	83
Libya	(It–1952)	4,080	5,410	50	45	53
*Sierra Leone	(Fr–1961)	4,064	440	24	27	76
*Togo	(Gr,Fr–1960)	3,449	370	18	27	82
*Central African Republic	(Fr–1960)	2,806	390	33	18	84
Congo	(Fr–1960)	2,228	930	80	27	74
*Mauritania	(Fr–1960)	1,977	480	17	17	81
Lesotho	(UK–1966)	1,711	410	65	48	69
Namibia	(UK–1990)	1,372	1,152			
Botswana	(UK–1966)	1,185	880	59	51	60
Mauritius	(UK–1968)	1,121	1,800	83	71	39
Gabon	(Fr–1960)	1,060	2,970	65	21	
*Guinea-Bissau	(Fr–1974)	974	150	9	12	
*Gambia	(UK–1970)	799	220	12	25	
Swaziland	(Fr–1968)	756	790	68	35	
*Comoros	(Fr–1975)	444	440	15	43	
Cape Verde	(Port–1975)	364	350	37	48	
*Equatorial Guinea	(Sp–1968)	353	350	55	28	
Djibouti	(Fr–1977)	329	1,067	20		

A. AFRICA (continued)		POPULATION CIRCA 1990 IN THOUSANDS	PER CAPITA GNP	PERCENT LITERATE	PQLI	INDEX OF SUFFERING
Sao-Tome and Principe	(Port–1975)	121	340	54		
Seychelles	(UK–1976)	70	3,800	65		
		497,676				

Percent of World Population – 9.48

Non-Self-Governing, 1950 to 1990

Reunion	(Fr)	566	3,695		73	
Mayotte	(Fr)	69	NA			
St. Helena	(UK)	7	NA			
		642				

Percent of World Population – .12

AFRICA: PERCENT OF WORLD POPULATION – 12.32

B. ASIA

Self-Governing Prior to 1950

China		1,112,229	330	77	69	50
India		833,422	330	36	43	61
Japan		123,220	21,040	99	96	11
★Pakistan		110,407	350	26	38	73
Korea, South		43,347	3,530	95	82	44
Korea, North		22,521	910	95		40
Taiwan		20,233	3,640	92	86	
★Nepal		18,700	170	23	25	81
Sri Lanka		16,881	420	87	82	58
★Afghanistan		14,825	220	12	18	88
Mongolia		2,125	880	90		47
		2,317,980				

Percent of World Population – 44.16

New Self-Governing, 1950 to 1990

★Bangladesh	(UK–1974)	114,718	170	29	35	79
★Bhutan	(India–1985)	1,534	218	15		80
Maldives	(UK–1965)	211	410	94		
		116,463				

Percent of World Population – 2.22

Non-Self-Governing, 1950 to 1990

Hong Kong	(UK)	5,700	9,230	75	86	29
Macao	(Port)	436	4,350	88		
		6,316				

Percent of World Population – 0.12

ASIA: PERCENT OF WORLD POPULATION – 46.5

C. ASIA, SOUTHEAST

Self-Governing Prior to 1950

The Philippines		64,907	630	88	71	55
Thailand		54,187	1,000	86	68	47
Myanmar		40,452	310	78	51	61
		159,546				

Percent of World Population – 3.04

New Self-Governing, 1950 to 1990

Indonesia	(Neth–1956)	187,651	430	64	48	62
Vietnam	(Fr–1975)	66,821	200	78	54	69
Malaysia	(UK–1957)	16,727	1,870	65	66	48

C. Asia, Southeast (continued)		Population Circa 1990 in Thousands	Per Capita GNP	Percent Literate	PQLI	Index of Suffering
★Cambodia	(Fr–1953)	6,838	65	48	40	80
Laos	(Fr–1954)	3,936	180	85	31	
Singapore	(UK–1965)	2,674	9,100	86	83	18
Brunei	(UK–1983)	345	10,970	45		
		284,992				

Percent of World Population – 5.43

ASIA, SOUTHEAST, PERCENT OF WORLD POPULATION – 8.47

D. CARIBBEAN AND CENTRAL AMERICA

Self-Governing Prior to 1950

Cuba		10,482	1,800	96	84	31
Guatemala		9,117	880	51	54	64
Dominican Republic		7,106	680	74	64	53
★Haiti		6,322	360	23	36	74
El Salvador		5,125	950	69	64	65
Honduras		5,104	850	56	51	62
Nicaragua		3,503	600	87	54	67
Costa Rica		2,954	1,760		85	40
Panama		2,373	2,290	90	80	47
		52,086				

Percent of World Population – 0.99

New Self-Governing, 1950 to 1990

Jamaica	(UK–1962)	2,485	1,080	76	84	40
Barbados	(UK–1966)	258	5,990	99	89	
Bahamas	(UK–1973)	247	10,570	95	84	
Belize	(UK–1981)	176	1,460	93		
St. Lucia	(UK–1979)	150	1,540	78		
St. Vincent and the Grenadines	(UK–1979)	105	1,100	85		
Antigua and Barbuda	(UK–1981)	84	2,800	90		
Grenada	(UK–1974)	84	1,370	85	77	
Dominica	(UK–1978)	83	1,650	80		
St. Kitts and Nevis	(UK–1983)	40	2,770			
		3,712				

Percent of World Population – 0.06

Non-Self-Governing, 1950 to 1990

Puerto Rico	(US)	3,301	NA		90	
Guadeloupe	(Fr)	341	3,630	70	76	
Martinique	(Fr)	332	3,650	70	83	
Netherlands Antilles	(Neth)	183	6,800		82	
Virgin Islands	(US)	109	6,000+			
Cayman	(UK)	24	NA			
Montserrat	(UK)	12	NA			
British Virgin Islands	(UK)	12	NA			
Turks and Caicos Islands	(UK)	10	NA			
Anguilla	(UK)	7	NA	80		
		4,331				

Percent of World Population – 0.08

CARIBBEAN AND CENTRAL AMERICA, PERCENT OF WORLD POPULATION – 1.15

E. EUROPE

Self-Governing Prior to 1950

Soviet Union		288,742	8,735	99	91	19
Germany		77,682	15,948	99	93	7
Italy		57,558	13,320	93	92	16
United Kingdom		57,028	12,800	100	94	12

E. EUROPE (continued)

	POPULATION CIRCA 1990 IN THOUSANDS	PER CAPITA GNP	PERCENT LITERATE	PQLI	INDEX OF SUFFERING
France	55,994	16,080	99	94	14
Spain	39,417	7,740	97	91	25
Poland	38,170	1,850	98	91	25
Yugoslavia	23,725	2,680	90	84	32
Romania	23,153	6,030	98	90	25
Czechoslovakia	15,658	9,280	100	93	20
Netherlands	14,790	14,530	99	96	7
Hungary	10,567	2,460	99	91	17
Portugal	10,460	3,670	80	80	33
Greece	10,041	4,790	95	89	25
Belgium	9,888	14,550	98	93	9
Bulgaria	8,973	6,800	98	91	20
Sweden	8,401	19,150	100	97	12
Austria	7,586	15,560	98	93	9
Switzerland	6,611	27,060	100	95	4
Denmark	5,130	18,470	100	96	9
Finland	4,964	18,610	100	94	16
Norway	4,203	20,020	100	96	14
Ireland	3,550	7,480	99	93	23
Albania	3,208	906	75	75	47
Luxembourg	366	22,600	100	92	6
Iceland	249	20,160	100	96	16
Andora	50	NA	100		
Monaco	29	NA	99		
Liechtenstein	28	16,500	100		
San Marino	23	8,380	98		
Vatican City State	1	NA			
	786,245				

Percent of World Population – 14.98

New Self-Governing, 1950–1990

Malta	(UK–1964)	371	5,050	83	87	

Percent of World Population -0.01

Non-Self-Governing, 1950–1990

Channel Islands	(UK)	134	6,000+		
Isle of Man	(UK)	65	NA		
Greenland	(Den)	55	8,290	99	
Faeroe Islands	(Den)	47	17,139	99	
Gibraltar	(UK)	30	4,427	99	
Svalbard	(Nor)	4	NA		
		335			

Percent of World Population – 0.01

EUROPE, PERCENT OF WORLD POPULATION – 14.99

F. MIDDLE EAST

Self-Governing Prior to 1950

	POPULATION CIRCA 1990 IN THOUSANDS	PER CAPITA GNP	PERCENT LITERATE	PQLI	INDEX OF SUFFERING
Iran	55,867	1,756	48	43	65
Turkey	55,356	1,280	80	55	55
Iraq	18,074	2,400	55	45	64
Saudi Arabia	16,109	6,170	52	29	56
★Yemen Arab Republic	6,942	650	15	27	78
Jordan	4,420	2,070	75	47	53
Israel	4,371	8,650	92	89	32
Lebanon	3,301	545	75	79	46
Oman	1,305	5,070	20		53
	165,745				

Percent of World Population – 3.16

F. MIDDLE EAST *(continued)*		POPULATION CIRCA 1990 IN THOUSANDS	PER CAPITA GNP	PERCENT LITERATE	PQLI	INDEX OF SUFFERING
New Self-Governing, 1950 to 1990						
Syria	(Fr–1961)	12,011	1,670	55	54	61
*Yemen	(UK–1967)	2,504	430	25	33	74
United Arab Emirates	(UK–1971)	2,115	15,720	68	34	40
Kuwait	(UK–1961)	2,008	13,680	71	74	35
Cyprus	(Greece–1960)	700	6,260	89	85	
Bahrain	(UK–1971)	497	8,110	40	61	
Qatar	(UK–1971)	469	11,670	70	31	
		20,304				
Percent of World Population – 0.39						
Non-Self-Governing 1950 to 1990						
Jordan West Bank	(Isr)	1,015	NA			
Percent of World Population – 0.02						

MIDDLE EAST, PERCENT OF WORLD POPULATION – 3.56

G. NORTH AMERICA

Self-Governing Prior to 1950						
United States		248,231	19,780	96	94	8
Mexico		86,366	1,820	88	73	47
Canada		26,311	16,760	99	95	9
		360,908				
Percent of World Population – 6.88						
Non-Self-Governing, 1950 to 1990						
Bermuda	(UK)	58	19,719			
St. Pierre and Miquelon	(Fr)	6	NA			
		64				
Percent of World Population – 0.001						

NORTH AMERICA, PERCENT OF WORLD POPULATION – 6.88

H. OCEANIA

Self-Governing Prior to 1950						
Australia		16,452	12,390	99	93	16
New Zealand		3,373	9,620	100	94	16
		19,825				
Percent of World Population – 0.38						
New Self-Governing, 1950 to 1990						
Papua New Guinea	(Austrl–1975)	3,736	770	32	37	68
Fiji	(UK–1970)	757	1,540	80	80	
Solomon Islands	(UK–1978)	324	430	60		
Western Samoa	(NZ–1962)	182	580	90	84	
Vanuatu	(Fr–1980)	160	820	15		
Tonga	(UK–1970)	100	1,004	95		
Kiribati	(UK–1979)	69	650	90		
Nauru	(UK, Austrl, NZ–1968)	9	17,973	99		
Tuvalu	(UK–1978)	9	472	50		
		5,345				
Percent of World Population – 0.10						
Non-Self-Governing, 1950 to 1990						
French Polynesia	(Fr)	196	7,647			
New Caledonia	(Fr)	152	6,914			

H. OCEANIA (continued)		POPULATION CIRCA 1990 IN THOUSANDS	PER CAPITA GNP	PERCENT LITERATE	PQLI	INDEX OF SUFFERING
Guam	(US)	138	6,000+			
Federated States of Micronesia	(US)	102	6,000+			
Marshall Islands	(US)	42	6,000+			
American Samoa	(US)	41	6,000+			
Northern Mariana Islands	(US)	21	NA			
Cook Islands	(NZ)	18	NA			
Wallis and Futuna Islands	(Fr)	15	NA			
Trust Territory of the Pacific Isls.	(US)	14	NA			
Norfolk Islands	(NZ)	2	NA			
		741				

Percent of World Population – 0.01

OCEANIA, PERCENT OF WORLD POPULATION – 0.49

I. SOUTH AMERICA

Self-Governing Prior to 1950						
Brazil		150,750	2,280	74	68	50
Columbia		31,945	1,240	88	71	44
Argentina		31,914	2,640	94	85	38
Peru		21,449	980	80	62	61
Venezuela		19,263	3,170	88	79	44
Chile		12,827	1,510	96	77	46
Ecuador		10,262	1,080	85	68	54
Bolivia		6,589	570	63	43	66
Paraguay		4,522	1,180	84	75	53
Uruguay		2,989	2,470	96	87	37
		292,510				

Percent of World Population – 5.58

New Self-Governing, 1950 to 1990						
Trinidad and Tobago	(UK–1962)	1,244	3,350	95	85	21
Guyana	(UK–1970)	765	410	86	85	42
Suriname	(Neth–1975)	401	2,450	65	83	
		2,410				

Percent of World Population – 0.05

Non-Self-Governing, 1950 to 1990						
French Guiana	(Fr)	95	2,292	82		
Aruba	(Neth)	62	6,065	95		
Falkland Islands	(UK)	2	NA			
		159				

Percent of World Population – 0.003

SOUTH AMERICA, PERCENT OF WORLD POPULATION – 5.62

historic events of the 1970s and 1980s which sapped the energy and slowed the progress of new and old nations in Africa and the Mideast? In Chapter 2 we shall investigate the relationship between size, controlling powers, and year of independence.

Comparing Conceptions and Measures of Development

Two research questions that have generated a considerable amount of literature in the field of development are related to the concepts and explanations of development. For some researchers development is indicated by one variable, Per Capita Income; most countries that we eventually characterized as having the lowest development scores also had low per capita income. Other researchers, as we have stated, have used a multiple indicator approach that includes social, economic, and health indicators to measure development. Differences in the approach to the measurement of development have implications for the classification of nations in terms of development. As development measures vary, the development levels of nations also vary.

Economists have usually been comfortable with Gross National Product (GNP), presented in the third column of Table 1, but sociologists and anthropologists believe that there is considerable production on the farms, in the villages, and in hidden sectors of the economy outside of that measured by formal economic activity included in the GNP. GNP also says nothing about the distribution of the fruits of production which usually accrue to a small percent of the population, e.g., the distribution in oil producing and exporting countries, particularly if wells, refineries, and distribution facilities are owned by overseas or multinational corporations. Data for most of the countries were taken from the *World Bank Atlas, 1989* but others were based on data in *The 1990 Information Please Almanac.*

GNP per capita per year ranged from $65 in Cambodia to $13,680 in Kuwait to $27,060 in Switzerland. Thirty-two of 53 African political entities had per capita annual GNPs of $580 or lower. Haiti had the lowest GNP in the Americas, $360, followed by Guyana with $410. Bolivia was next with a GNP of only $570. In Europe only Albania had a comparably low GNP and that was $906. And Lebanon, once known for Beirut's splendors, had a GNP of $545. Suffice it to say that with all of its faults as an indicator of development, GNP is an excellent starting point.

Many investigators believe that percent of the population literate (data from *The 1990 Information Please Almanac*) is a better indicator of development because it evidences how the national wealth is utilized and is a proxy for general well-being. We have included it because we believe that its relationship to GNP per capita tells something about a country. How the relationship between the two measures varies within regions (why does Sri Lanka, whose GNP per capita is similar to that of India, have a high literacy rate, 87 percent, and India a low rate, 36 percent?) raises many questions.

Half of the African countries had less than 80 percent of their population literate, while only Albania in Europe had less than 80 percent of the population literate. Literacy in Africa varies from 9 percent to 85 percent. How does this relate to each country's cultural background, the experiences that its citizens had during the colonial period, and the regimes that have been in place since independence? The articles in this chapter will help us understand at least some of the relationships between education and development.

The first scale that we shall present is one that measures the physical quality of life (PQLI). This scale is based on life expectancy, infant mortality at age one, and adult literacy. Although this measure includes literacy, one of our two single measures of development in the table, we shall see that the two measures are not entirely correlated. M.D. Morris (1979), who developed the PQLI scale for the Overseas Development Council following the basic human needs approach, believes that this measure is based on results, social benefits, rather than input, i.e., how much money has been spent on programs. Morris found the correlation to be .729 for 150 countries, but there was a small inverse relationship for countries with per capita GNP of $2,000 or more. The article in this chapter by

Hicks and Streeten, who also see basic needs as an integrating concept for analyses and policy making (development strategy), is more critical of PQLI than are we. Whether you agree with Hicks and Streeten is not as important as is familiarizing yourself with the argument about measures of development.

Morris' PQLI map of the world reveals (as does our Table 1) that political entities with the lowest PQLIs are concentrated in Africa, the Mideast, and South and Southeastern Asia. PQLI scores range from 12 for Guinea-Bissau and 13 for Niger to 53 for the Union of South Africa, which does not, of course, include the homelands (Ciskei, Bophuthatswana, Transkei, and Venda). But in Japan PQLI is 96; in Hong Kong, to which some of the authors of articles will refer, it is 86 and in Singapore 83.

In most of the Caribbean and Central America, where scores are available, they are higher than the highest in Africa: Cuba 84, Costa Rica 85, Barbados 89, Jamaica 84, Bahamas 84, Martinique 83, and Puerto Rico 90. Almost every PQLI in Europe is above 90, with Denmark 96 and Sweden 97. Of the Middle Eastern continental countries, note that Israel is highest with 89 and Yemen, with 33, and Qatar, with 31, are the lowest. Only Bolivia in South America has a low PQLI.

While GNP and PQLI are highly correlated at the extreme ends of each distribution – for example, 22 African Countries are low on both variables – there are differences. As a matter of fact, all of the variables are highly correlated at the extremes; i.e., there are 10 or 20 political entities at each end of the continuum that have similar scores for each pair of variables, but there is considerable variation in which countries have similar scores from variable pair to variable pair.

The last measure is an International Human Suffering Index (Sharon L. Camp and J. Joseph Speidel, Population Crisis Committee) based on: Per Capita Gross National Product, Average Annual Rate of Inflation, Average Annual Growth of Urban Population, Infant Mortality Rate per 1,000 Live Births, Daily Per Capita Calorie Supply as Percent of Requirement, Percent of Population with Access to Clean Drinking Water, Energy Consumption Per Capita in Gigajoules, Adult Literacy Rate, and Personal Freedom Governance. This, as one would gather, is a complex omnibus scale involving other specialized scales, objective measures, and assessments of many facets of life in 130 countries circa 1986. Although some of these variables capture the average availability of goods, they do not give us a measure of the prevalence of food, clothing, shelter, water, and sanitation or how equally these are distributed among the population. This is a concern upon which we will touch as we progress through the various chapters.

In the International Human Suffering Index, the higher the figure, the greater the suffering. Index scores vary from 11 for Japan to as low as 4 for Switzerland and to 95 for Mozambique and 91 for Angola. The lowest African score is 39 and most mainland scores are in the 70s and 80s. Thirteen of the 15 political entities with low PQLIs (low quality of life) and high suffering indexes are in Africa.

More sophisticated developmental scales have been constructed than the relatively simple measures to which we have referred in this introduction. Berlage and Terweduwe (1988) have constructed scales that permit the classification of countries using cluster and factor analysis. They provide lists that are quite comparable to a list that could be produced from the data included in Table 1 and more or less comparable to classifications utilized by international organizations – for example, the United Nations Committee for Development Planning. The United Nations list of thirty-six countries includes 26 from Africa. Our list of 37 countries includes 29 from Africa.

There are numerous perspectives and ideologies for development, three of which are very popular. The first, the free market perspective, suggests that the factors of economic growth, such as land, labor, capital, and technology, are best allocated by the market free of government intervention. Some of the authors of the papers from a vast literature on economic development have long been aware of the danger of assuming that economic forces alone will result in individual development. As Myint (1954) has stated: "The fundamental assumption of liberal economics is that the free play of economic forces would lead to the maximum development of *individual* talents and abilities, whereas in practise the free play of economic forces in backward countries has resulted, not in a division of labour according to individual abilities, but in a division of labour according to stratified groups." This perspective has also been challenged by the Keynesian position, which supposes a positive role for government regulation. Government regulation is particularly effective in controlling undesirable conditions such as pollution. Finally, the dependency perspective proposes that underdevelopment in certain regions is a product of development in others. A few developed nations enjoy monopoly positions in the world market, controlling the supply of manufactured goods and technology. These nations consume the raw materials produced by the less developed nations. The less developed countries are believed to be locked into their peripheral position in the world economy.

The Articles in Chapter 1

Smith presents a detailed evaluation of two influential theories of political development: developmentalist and dependency models. The developmentalist model makes extensive use of evolutionary and functionalist perspectives. Development is seen as an internal problem and the goal of the developmentalist is to discover a set of conditions and factors that contribute to development. Studies of political development have focussed on the problems of state and nation building. The dependency model is rooted in the conflict perspective and, unlike the developmentalist model, takes into account the external conditions that impinge on socio-political structures. This model suggests that the developed nations play an important role in maintaining poverty and low productivity in developing countries. Smith concludes that an appreciation of the contributions of both perspectives provides a foundation for a unified approach to the investigation of a variety of compelling issues.

Hicks and Streeten provide a detailed account of the shortcomings of the various indices of development. The commonly used indicator, Gross National Product, does not consider inequalities in the distribution of wealth and the extent to which basic needs are satisfied. The social indicators approach attempts to measure the distribution of basic needs deficiencies. These indices tend to be poorly correlated with the GNP index. Another alternative to the GNP index is the Quality of Life index. This index is the best known among a set of composite development indices. The quality of life index, however, suffers from a number a drawbacks. The most pressing need now is to provide for a cross-national data collection system that will improve our ability to measure development.

Notwithstanding the ideological and technical debates on development, the developing countries are becoming more economically heterogeneous. A few countries, such as Singapore and Taiwan, have become highly industrialized. A few others, such as Zambia and Tanzania, have become poorer than they were twenty years ago. The United Nations Committee for Development Planning calls these poor nations the least developed countries. The economic resources and populations of these countries are enormous. Yet they have not been able to organize themselves as a power bloc through sustained economic cooperation. There is also some recognition among the developed nations that the continuing prosperity of the developed world is linked to that of the developing countries.

In sum, in recent decades the concept of development has undergone changes in its theoretical and ideological content. There has been a shift from ballooning the GNP to improving the well-being of the people. Thus, the concept of equality has become closely associated with the concept of development. Current pursuits of development are likely to further intensify as the developing countries continue to emerge as a political and economic force in the international economic system.

Although we have sometimes reduced the number of footnotes during the process of editing the articles included in this volume, we have kept most of them so that the reader will be able to become even better acquainted with the vast sociological, anthropological, economic, historical, political, and other literature on the subject of developing areas.

REFERENCES

Berlage, Lodewijk and Dirk Terweduwe, "The Classification of Countries by Cluster and Factor Analysis," *World Development*, 16(12), pp. 1527–1545, 1988.

Camp, Sharon L. and J. Joseph Speidel, *International Human Suffering Index* (Washington, D.C.: Population Crisis Committee), 1987.

Information Please Almanac, 1990 (New York: Houghton Mifflin), 1990.

Jamison, Ellen, *World Population Profile: 1989* (Washington, D.C.: Bureau of the Census), 1989.

Morris, M.D., *Measuring the Conditions of the World's Poor* (Elmsford, New York: Pergamon Press), 1979.

Myint, H., "An Interpretation of Economic Backwardness," Oxford Economic Papers, New Series, 6(2), June 1954, pp. 132–163.

Patel, Surendra J., "Economic Transition in Africa," *The Journal of Modern African Studies*, 2(3), 1964, pp. 329–349.

Shannon, Lyle W., *Underdeveloped Areas: A Book of Readings and Research* (New York: Harper and Row), 1957.

Shannon, Lyle W., "The Demographic Characteristics of Non-Self-Governing Political Entities," *Planning Outlook*, V(3), 1961, pp. 37–52.

World Bank Atlas, 1989 (Washington, D.C.: World Bank), 1989.

Requiem or New Agenda
For Third World Studies?

TONY SMITH

••••

I. The Developmentalist Model

The field of development studies, which has always been dominated by American academics, was founded in the first years after World War II, when the United States assumed leadership of a ravaged world in which the problems of containing the Soviet Union and dealing with national liberation movements throughout much of Asia and Africa were the country's top foreign policy priorities. From the beginning, the divisions among the academic disciplines and the avowedly eclectic concerns of many working in the field made it difficult to label developmentalism a "school." Area specialization constituted one line of differentiation among these scholars, but formal training in economics and political science – as well as in anthropology, sociology, psychology, and history – tended to create other distinctions in interest and method as well. And yet, a field of study certainly existed. Formal mechanisms such as the SSRC pulled these analysts together as a group, but more informal ties also held them together: their familiarity with each other's work through their association at the country's leading universities, and their conscious effort in a larger sense to see their work as complementary, each cultivating a different vineyard for the sake of a common harvest. Thus, while economists laid out models of how productivity in the late-industrializing world might be stimulated, sociologists and social psychologists studied the group dynamics of change, and political scientists devoted themselves to the problems of state and nation-building. Whatever the rough edges, the result was indeed a unified and cumulative agenda for Third World studies, a "whole" of intellectual discourse both theoretically and empirically.

The life span of the school might be variously dated, but there seems to be some agreement that it began after 1945, that it had what might be called its "Golden Decade" for economists in the 1950s and for political scientists from the late 1950s until the late 1960s, and that it ran out of steam in the early 1970s. Writing in 1975, Samuel Huntington and Jorge Dominguez, two political scientists, professed to find nothing particularly surprising about the fact that "in the early 1970's the initial surge, which had emerged about 1960, in the study of political development had about run its course." It was the fate of any theoretical paradigm, they maintained, to go through a set of phases (note the usage even here of a developmentalist style of reasoning) where an "initial surge" was typically followed by a "pause," "redirection," and a "new surge."[1] In 1983, Gabriel Almond, one of the fathers of political developmentalism, attributed the school's stagnation more to the motivation of those working in it: "Over time as the new and developing nations encountered difficulties and turned largely to authoritarian and military regimes, the optimism and hopefulness faded, and along with it interest, productivity, and creativity abated."[2] The developmentalist economist Albert Hirschman voiced a similar lament in 1980: "As an observer and long-time participant I cannot help feeling that the old liveliness is no longer there, that new ideas are even hard-

Tony Smith. Permission received from *World Politics* and the author. First published in 1985 in volume 37, No. 4., pp. 532-561.

er to come by and that the field is not adequately reproducing itself."[3] Hirschman's explanation of the school's failure was more self-critical than those of his colleagues in political science (reflecting perhaps a professional difference: economists frequently pride themselves on being mavericks, while political scientists are more likely to think of themselves as team players).

••••

Yet the early objectives of the developmentalist school were sensible enough, even if ambitious. They sought first to specify general categories which, despite their universality, would allow analysts to distinguish essential elements of the chief social processes that interested them; or, alternatively, to differentiate various types of social organization and stages, or sequences, in their development. These general categories were to be heuristic tools, "metatheoretical" classificatory schemes, promoted most successfully by Talcott Parsons along the lines of Max Weber's ideal types. Such models or paradigms of social action were labeled "structural-functionalism" in sociology and political science, and were intended to be both basic and comprehensive enough to provide the vocabulary and concepts allowing any society to be described in comparative terms. Thus the individuality and the specificity of the various forms of social life in Africa, Asia, and Latin America would be respected, while these lands would at the same time be recognizable comparatively (in terms of the advanced industrial countries as well as of each other).

Hirschman may have been correct when he maintained that "the compulsion to theorize...is often so strong as to induce mindlessness."[4] But the effort in question must be understood to lie at the heart of the social sciences, concerned as they are to establish general verifiable explanations of human action. Led particularly by sociologists like Parsons, and working on the basis of earlier men of genius such as Durkheim,

Toennies, and especially Weber, the developmentalist school was deliberately doing what was expected of it. And, as we shall see presently, the Marxists in their efforts to offer a better analysis of the Third World than that of the developmentalists were engaged in a strikingly similar heuristic undertaking.

Although the descendants of Weber and Marx were alike in their concern with establishing a general framework for comparative historical analysis, the similarity ended there. For, whereas the Marxists held to a single analytical category in their belief that the force of the class struggle swept all else before it, the followers of Weber were more avowedly eclectic in the variety of theoretical tools they brought to an understanding of the Third World. General heuristic categories provided a common vocabulary, a common set of problems, and the promise of readily exchangeable information, so that an integrated, cumulative understanding of the Third World could proceed; developmentalism intended to apply insights or theories developed independently by the various social sciences to explain the logic of social action in the South. The general categories did not, then, claim the status of scientific theories, but acted instead as intellectual guidelines that assured some connectedness to the host of empirically verifiable theories that were anticipated. The result was a proliferation of books written by teams of specialists, often from different backgrounds or dealing with very distinct issues, whose unity presupposed or confidently anticipated commonly shared models – for instance, Talcott Parsons and Edward Shils, eds., *Toward a General Theory of Action* (1951); Clifford Geertz, ed., *Old Societies and New States* (1963); Max F. Millikan and Donald L. M. Blackmer, eds., *The Emerging Nations* (1961).

In retrospect, it is difficult not to empathize with the excitement of those years. Scholars anticipated not simply a better understanding of the Third World, but the growing unification of the social sciences around their increasingly common understanding of a set of particular issues. The various "cultures" of sociology, anthropology, economics, history, political science, and psychology might keep their separate identities, but their interdisciplinary pursuits would allow them to draw strength from one another, to pull them away from their narrow (often parochial) concerns, to the level of the wholeness of social life. One might even say that a bit of American pluralism was involved here, for no single discipline (much less theorist) was expected to have the answer to the entire puzzle (although some surely came to think they did); instead, the truth would emerge as the result of the collaborative efforts of quite dissimilar kinds of work. The outcome would be a unified social science able not only to criticize but finally to replace Marxism.

The obvious question we must ask of this approach today is whether the products of its labors were at the level of its ambitions. Without denying the importance of some of the work, the answer must surely be negative – even in the minds of those most active in the field. Today, it is rare indeed to see any of these books cited other than critically; library shelves are invariably fully stocked with the numerous (unused) copies of each volume that were once the standard fare of graduate students the country over.

In my opinion, there are two principal reasons developmentalism failed in its efforts, reasons that at first glance might appear contradictory. One problem was that the models in many cases were so formal and abstract that they proved too stifling, too tyrannical, and ultimately too sterile for the empirical work they sought to organize. The other problem was that the models were too loose, too incoherent, and too incomplete to act as adequate guidelines assuring the interconnectedness of research. Let us look at each of these shortcomings in turn.

The most frequently heard, and the bitterest, charge against the developmentalist paradigm is that it was "unilinear" or "ethnocentric" in its concept of change; that is, it projected a relatively inflexible path or continuum of development in which social and political forms would tend to converge, so that the developmental path of the West might well serve as a model from which to shed light on transformations occurring in the South. As a result, developmentalism might be accused of being too "formalistic" in the sense that it sought to reduce the histories of the various countries of Asia, Africa, and Latin America to the terms of models or ideal types and jargon that distorted the true logic of social change in these areas.

••••

In cases where the West was not self-consciously posited as a model of the future the South might come to enjoy, the heuristic models of "modern" and "traditional" societies performed much the same function. Here the work of Talcott Parsons proved to be particularly influential – especially his so-called pattern variables, with their assumption that cultural values are of a whole with economic, social, and political systems in such a fashion that social organization should be conceptualized as a self-reinforcing unity. This kind of thinking resulted in the unfortunate tendency throughout much of developmentalism, first, to exaggerate the congruence of elements within a given a social organization (a preference for static equilibrium models which often classified contradiction and change as "dysfunctional"), and second, to separate "traditional" from "modern" societies as if such a dichotomy made not only heuristic but empirical sense.

••••

The models that emerged were too confining to be of much use in actual empirical investigation. When the past of the West or the model of traditional society was projected onto the Third World, too much disappeared from sight. The formalism of these paradigms often turned out to be as reductionist as Marxism – a turn of events developmentalism had hoped to escape by virtue of its avowed disciplinary eclecticism. There is, then, some justice to the charge leveled by many radical as well as by some conservative writers who felt that the reality of the Third World was simply not being grasped. Reinhard Bendix, for example, formulated some of these charges quite early, Howard Wiarda more recently.[5]

••••

Yet if formalism of the sort described above was a real problem with developmentalism – as the work of Daniel Lerner, Cyril E. Black, and W. W. Rostow suggests[6] – it was not a completely endemic disease. I think there would be wide agreement, for example, that the two most influential books by political scientists on development were Gabriel Almond and James Coleman's *Comparative Politics of Developing Countries* (1960) and Samuel Huntington's *Political Order in Changing Societies* (1968).

••••

For its part, Huntington's book rests on such an explicitly damning criticism of a unilinear approach to the study of history that on this account alone it deserves to be seen as one of the classics of political science during the period. In economics, there is equal agreement that Alexander Gerschenkron's *Economic Backwardness in Historical Perspective* (1962) is a classic statement on the development process similarly free of formalistic bias. In short, some excellent comparative historical work has been free of the problems of formalism. Moreover, it is important to insist that formalism as a reductionist mode in the social sciences must not be confused with the effort to establish general theoretical frameworks for the understanding of change in the fashion of Weber or Keynes. This latter enterprise is the hallmark and the promise of the social sciences; it must not be repudi-

ated simply because some of its practitioners have given it a bad name.

Indeed, rather than lambasting developmentalism for models that were too rigid and writers who were overly concerned with methodology, we might complain that it did not generate stronger general categories to integrate research and that it did not concern itself adequately with producing a set of robust "middle-range" theories of development, or general analytical propositions established empirically, that could serve to organize the field. At the time, prominent developmentalist writers certainly seemed to sense the problem. Thus James Coleman admitted in 1960 that, "Given the array of disparate systems … it is only at the highest level of generalization that one can make statements about their common properties."[7] In 1963, Harry Eckstein offered a much more biting commentary. While he welcomed the return to fundamental questions of comparative study as a healthy event, he nonetheless complained of the "bewildering variety of classificatory schemes" his colleagues had produced, whose "disconcerting wealth" was "almost embarrassing": "The field today is characterized by nothing so much as variety, eclecticism, and disagreement … particularly great in regard to absolutely basic preconceptions and orientations."[8]

••••

Why was the modeling not better? The quickest answer is that no theorist emerged of the status of Weber or Durkheim, a person of genius who could pull the entire field together into a coherent whole. Brave attempts may be cited – the work of David Apter, for example – but they proved unable to impose themselves intellectually on the community of developmentalists. Instead, there was a kind of happy anarchy, where writers seem to have labored to invent jargon and classificatory schemes in the manner of a Freud or a Durkheim – as much to ensure their professional standing as to advance the discipline. And here the highest accolades would be reserved for the theorist who could establish a "general theory of action," to recall the title of a book Talcott Parsons and Edward Shils edited in 1951.

••••

It would be an error to explain the limitations of developmentalism by placing too much emphasis on the skills of the individuals involved. The striking shortcoming of the school was its inability to articulate a unified model of comparative political economy, just as it lacked any broad-based comparative historical perspective into which the problems of mid-20th-century development could be placed. It must be emphasized that the obstacle was not individual mediocrity, but institutional and ideological impediments best studied in terms of a sociology of knowledge. Two sets of factors emerge as important in this respect: the structure of the social science disciplines in American universities, and the place of the academics concerned with it in American political life.

Whatever the attraction, rhetorically, of interdisciplinary studies in the United States, the various fields of the social sciences jealously insisted on their autonomy, on an identity based on a body of theoretical propositions over whose integrity they stood guard. In this context, development studies represented virgin territory, not only for the unification of the social sciences, but more immediately for the carving out of new, discrete domains of analysis. Thus, Gabriel Almond proudly declared in the introduction to *The Politics of the Developing Areas*, "This book is the first effort to compare the political systems of the 'developing' areas, and to compare them systematically according to a common set of categories...." He considered it to be "a major step forward in the nature of political science as science."[9] From the viewpoint of political science, economics in particular represented a threat, for it had an apparent sophistication as a science that

many political scientists long to duplicate. For this reason, for example, the Harvard-M.I.T. Joint Seminar on Political Development, founded in 1963, has always deliberately excluded economists from its membership. The ambition, then, of political scientists was to elaborate the logic of political processes in a manner that would establish their analytical independence and their social importance. At the same time, they would strike a blow against Marxism, which had constantly sought to reduce political factors to reflections of more decisive socioeconomic processes. One can exaggerate the extent or the impenetrability of these barriers between academic disciplines; these scholars knew each other's work and felt themselves to be engaged in a collaborative enterprise.

••••

To derive at a different sociological explanation for the lack of adequate modeling, one may look at the place of the American academics involved in Third World studies in terms of American political life. For example, Irene Grendzier has recently suggested that many of these scholars intended their writing to be policy-relevant, and that their interests included fostering the spread of capitalism and an elitist brand of democracy in the South while blocking the expansion of communism. These concerns limited the agenda and biased the arguments of many developmentalists in a way unappreciated at the time.[10]

••••

In view of the ideological and institutional concerns of those working in developmentalism, it is difficult to see how, as a group, they might have sponsored the kind of work in comparative history or political economy that at one and the same time would have ensured more broad-range model building at the level of heuristic typologies and more robust constructions of theories at the level of aggregate empirical analysis.

••••

Developmentalist paradigms were, then, loose and incomplete at a heuristic level on the one hand, and deficient in genuinely interdisciplinary empirical propositions at the level of comparative theory on the other. Since there was no intellectual center of gravity holding together all the disparate undertakings that characterized the field, specialization proliferated, spin-off leading to spin-off, with some perhaps holding Shils's happy illusion that eventually it would all add up to a unified movement. Instead, however, the focus shifted increasingly to more modest and manageable models targeted on particular issues or areas. In many of these instances, a deeper understanding of the process of change did occur. But as the field became more complex, questions of its unity became more difficult; memories of the common origin of it all, in the Big Bang of trying to establish order amid the chaos of the postwar world, grew increasingly dim. An essential reason for the stagnation of the field around 1970, therefore, was what was coming to be seen as its chaotic diversity. If developmentalism's *formalism* (the reductionist tyranny of its models) was a real problem, it was relatively minor. The major cause of its debilitation lay in its *fragmentation* (the weakness of its models).

This fragmentation emerged as an acute problem when it became evident to many that developmentalism was impotent in the face of many of the terrible trials through which the Third World was passing. The growth of poverty and the attendant human misery; the spread of repressive, authoritarian regimes; the waste and suffering caused by wars both civil and regional – all combined to disillusion those working in the field, especially as the realization began to grow that in fact there was no theoretical, commanding height from which to make sense of these awful realities. The fragmentation made it difficult to get more than a partial understanding of the range of forces at work in the South.

••••

II. The Dependency Perspective

For many, the void left by the demise of developmentalism as a unified theory of change in the Third World was filled in the 1970s with the analytical categories provided by the dependency perspective. The term "dependency" grows out of writing on Latin America; related works dealing with Asia and Africa have until recently been more comfortable using the term "neocolonialism" to describe the world that concerns them. Whatever the preferred nomenclature, these *dependencis-tas*, if we may use their Latin American name, share the view that the power of international capitalism setting up a global division of labor has been the chief force responsible for shaping the history of the South. Originally as mercantilism, then as free trade, later as finance capital, and most recently under the auspices of the multinational corporation, capitalism over the last five centuries has created a world economic system. The profound changes this process has generated in every part of the world offer, then, a common historical experience that is the basis of a *unified comparative* model of social life in the Third World. Dependency literature is therefore properly viewed as a subset of the so-called "world system" approach, whose terms have become increasingly prominent in the United States in the field of international relations. To be sure, as in any broad-based intellectual movement, debates within the dependency school are many and sharp. The clear dominance of Marxism within the literature has not prevented fierce differences over such far-ranging matters as how to establish the identity of classes in widely disparate settings; what degree of autonomy to accord the state as a political institution charged with providing coherence in circumstances typified by rapid domestic change and extensive foreign penetration; and how to argue for typologies of stages or degrees of dependency. However acute these differences, they are overshadowed by the common allegiance of the writers in this school to an approach whose roots run back to the 1920s, even if it was not until the 1970s that the dependency perspective made itself felt in force within American academia. And the fundamental premise of this approach – the uncontested proposition on the basis of which all this writing has been constructed – is that, to understand the chief forces of change in the Third World (or "on the periphery"), one must see them ultimately as a function of the power of economic imperialism generated by the capitalist "core" of world affairs.[11]

Indeed, it is the emphasis on imperialism that constitutes a recognition on the part of many *dependencistas* themselves that their approach cannot claim the status of a theory. For dependency literature studies the *effects* of imperialism, not the *nature* of imperialism itself. Its focus is therefore on a part and not on the whole – the latter providing the "totality" of experience on which sound theory can be based. Traditional matters, such as the character of capitalist accumulation with its "anarchy of production" combined with such modern forces as the logic of multinational corporate competition, must ultimately escape the purview of the dependency approach (only to fall into the domain of the related world system analysis); the primary agent of change in the South thus escapes direct study. As explained by Fernando Henrique Cardoso and Enzo Faletto in a book that has found a wide audience throughout the Americas, "it seems senseless to search for 'laws of movement' specific to situations that *are dependent*, that is, that have their main features determined by the phases and trends of expansion of capitalism on a world scale."[12] Relying on a theory of imperialism proposed by their colleagues doing world system analysis, dependency writers content themselves with explaining the logic of capitalist expansion on the periphery. The result is a powerful, unified theory of imperialism: the world system analysts establish the logic of the "whole" or core of historical change while the dependency scholars lay out the working of these forces on the periphery.

In this undertaking, their most important conceptual tool is the analysis of the dual economy. The notion of the dual economy itself did not originate with these writers, but in their hands it has acquired a character particular to their analysis.[13] In brief, the argument is that – as capitalist penetration has occurred successively in Latin America, Asia, and Africa under the impetus of northern imperialism – one part of the local economies of these regions has come to be a modern enclave. By virtue of these historical origins, the basis of the modern sector is export trade (even if subsidiary manufacturing or service interests grow up to sustain it). Here capital accumulates, skills are learned, and class interests are formed whose innermost needs tie them tightly to foreign concerns. The culture of the modern enclave may be of the periphery; but its economic and political character make it a child of the international system. Root and branch, it is dependent.

Alongside this modern economy, there exists a subsistence sector – whence the term *dual* economy. To some extent, the technology, culture, and social institutions of the subsistence sector are inherited from the past. But this is not a simple traditional world slumbering in a millenary torpor, as writers from the developmentalist school have so often depicted it. Today as yesterday, the modern sector is constantly at work disintegrating this subordinate sector, try as the latter may to preserve its integrity. Thus, cheap manufactured goods destroy the traditional artisanry; the expansion of plantation agriculture displaces large numbers of peasants, forcing them onto poorer land; and elites in the subsistence area invest such capital as they possess in the modern enclave, thereby intensifying the lack of investment funds for projects that might directly benefit the poor. Through the linkages between the two sectors, the modern acts like a leech on the body of the subsistence economy – ever increasing the difficulty of life there, while by its very exploitation it consolidates its own power. In short, the terrible misery of so much of the Third World derives not from a locally generated, traditional resistance to modernity – for example, the lack of appropriate skills, attitudes, or resource endowments of the poor, where developmentalist economics had us look – but from the operating forces of modernity itself, as it has historically implanted itself on the periphery. The misery of the many and the affluence of the few have their common origin in an international division of labor spawned and maintained by the forces of capitalist imperialism.

As the foregoing account implies, economic forces do not live in a social vacuum, but express themselves in class formations on the periphery. Here the key development is the modern sector, where class interests form in symbiosis with the interests of international capitalism. A class alignment thus takes shape in the South wherein the power of the dominant groups derives from their role as intermediaries between the international order run by imperialism and the local peoples over whom they must secure their rule. Although this collaborating class may have local concerns, its reliance on the world economic system ultimately decides its conduct. At different times or in different countries the character of these elites may vary, but their common identity lies in their dependence on the rhythms of the international economic order to ensure their survival as a class. There is an international political dimension to this as well. These local bourgeoisies have struck the main political bargains that concern their well-being not with domestic forces, but with foreign capitalists. The result is that the collaborating class is not only particularly exploitive in historical terms, but it is particularly weak at home as well. For these reasons, it is subject to being overthrown by local revolutions when those in the subsistence sector try to save themselves through force of arms. It is at this point, of course, that the United States intervenes today by suppressing such uprising in the name of anticommunism, when its real interest is to preserve a certain established form of economic organization locally as well as globally. Just as poverty in the Third World must ultimately be understood in terms of the international division of labor, so authoritarian governments there must in the final analysis be seen as products of foreign imperialism.

From the preceding discussion it should be apparent that the dependency school's primary intellectual debt is to Marxism (which is not to say that all Marxists subscribe to this view). First, the division of labor is seen as the prime social reality, the engine of changes that drives all else before it. The originality of dependency writing lies in its tying the dynamic of economic life on the periphery into that of the world system beyond; to see it as *dependent*, that is. The dependency approach thus works on an ambitiously large canvas, linking the pace of life on the periphery to the movements at the core. Second, political activity is understood to take place through social groups or classes antagonistically related to one another around ownership of the means of production. In this respect, the originality of dependency writing lies in its capacity to seize on the function of the collaborating class and to plot the changes in its conflicts and alliances over time, including those that link it to political forces abroad. Finally, the dependency approach shares with Marxism a bias against certain other considerations: that ethnic rivalries may have a life quite their own (hence, for example, the denigration of the term "tribe" in relation to groups in Africa); that the state may play a relatively autonomous and enormously significant role in the process of great historical transformations; and that, in foreign affairs of powerful states, balance-of-power considerations are primary calculation of leaders at critical historical junctures. To be sure, there are individuals who are not Marxists who have contributed to this school: John Gallagher and Ronald Robinson with their idea of the "informal empire" of "free trade imperialism"; Gunnar Myrdal with his descriptions of how dual economies create "backwash effects" that systematically disadvantage the traditional sector; Raúl Prebisch with his work concerning the way in which unequal exchange in international trade acts to handicap the South.[14] Such ideas are not held eclectically by the dependency school, however. They have been adopted it because they strengthen the tools of analysis of an approach that enjoys a fundamental unity of orientation through a reliance on Marxist analysis.

The foregoing sketch of the dual economy was too brief to suggest certain crucial refinements that have added enormously to the sophistication of the dependency approach during the last decade. Three relatively new conceptual qualifications are of particular importance. The first is the argument that the dual economy is not actually as rigid as was once believed. Spurred on especially by the work of Cardoso, many dependency writers have come to see the abundant evidence that a genuine industrial base is being laid in parts of the South, and that economies there are becoming far more diversified, integrated, and advanced than earlier spokesmen of this persuasion had thought possible. For, although both Marx and Lenin had anticipated that the worldwide spread of the industrial revolution would take place under capitalist auspices, the first generation of *dependencistas* talked of "growth without development" and of the way the souther countries would forever be, in their favorite cliché, the "hewers of wood and drawers of water" of the world economic system. But facts are a hard thing, and in due course, dependency analysts had to face the mounting evidence that heavy industry was growing in the Third World; that the manufacturing component of exports was steadily mounting there; and that internal, integrated markets were beginning to pulse with a life of their own. Indeed, statistics are readily at hand to show that the vigor of economic growth in large parts of the Third World is substantially greater than in the North. As Peter Evans describes it, "classic dependency" is giving way to "dependent development."[15]

A second (and related) conceptual innovation made by dependency writers during the last decade lies in their new emphasis on the crucial role of the state in this changing order of things. Whereas *dependencistas* had previously viewed Third World politics as little more than an auxiliary function of the international economic system, they have now begun to argue (and here the work of Guillermo O'Donnell is especially important) that the growing complexity of class and economic relations locally as well as internationally calls for more assertive action on the part of the state on the periphery. As the diversity and integration of these local economies grow, new groups arise that have to be controlled politically, just as some old groups must be divested of their power or find ways to reconstruct it. In a parallel manner, foreign actors have come to be more closely supervised than before. Their investments have been made a part of local plans involving the creation of backward and forward linkages, and their action has increasingly been harmonized with more fine-tuned domestic fiscal and employment measures. In a word, the growing complexity of local economies calls for new demands for a more competent state. In conceptual terms, the result is that the dependency literature now possesses a far richer political vocabulary that has substantially expanded its range analysis.

The two preceding conceptual refinements in turn prepare the ground for a third: the recognition of the diversity of Third World countries and a growing appreciations of the significance of local factors in determining the pattern of long-term development processes. Not all countries on the periphery are industrializing, and not all have states aggressively determined to promote domestic interests. Different natural resource endowments, preexisting lines of class or ethnic group conflict or coalition, political culture and the structure of inherited political institutions – all of these are acquiring a new relevance in analysis. As a consequence, stages or degrees of dependency may now be discussed, whereas previously not much more could be said than that a country was or was not dependent.

••••

At this point, the reader may well anticipate the final trump in the dependency deck: the charge that developmentalism itself was the ideological handmaiden of imperialism and the ruling elites in the Third World. For even if the charge were only implied, it was frequently enough asserted that the very categories with which American academics analyzed the South were – as the quotation from Edward Said suggests – instruments in the subjugation of Africa, Asia, and Latin America.

Such an argument might be constructed along the following lines. In its "classic" form, economic developmentalism posited a modern sector acting as a pole of development from which the industrial revolution would eventually diffuse out to the rest of Third World society. Although the modern sector might initially be in league with the international system, it would invariably turn toward the local market – first for food and labor, later for intermediate manufacturing products, and finally as a source of demand for larger-scale manufacturing. Eventually, an integrated local economy should form, still a part of the world economy producing in line with comparative advantage, but reflecting throughout the characteristics of economic modernity, including a generalized modern skill structure. Where obstacles to development occur, they should be understood as having a nonmarket origin: inadequate resource endowment; a population base that is too small or growing too rapidly; inept government unable to oversee capital formation because of weakness or corruption, or misguided notions about the merits of state planning; inherited ethnic prejudices making the free mobility of economic factors especially difficult. In this light, the job of political development becomes more comprehensible. It is to engineer solutions to these obstacles to economic diffusion through the use of force or by the building of concensus, so that institutions are ultimately created that can make the process of change self-sustaining.

From a dependency perspective, the problem with this diffusionist approach is that it fails to recognize that its alleged solutions to problems in the Third World – the intensification of market relations there – are in fact at the origin of all the difficulties. That is, political instability in the Third World comes not so much from the recalcitrance of the traditional world in the face of change as from the brutality of change inflicted on the traditional world. When peasants are dispossessed of their land and herded into urban slums; when traditional artisans find their means of livelihood destroyed; when old patterns of power that provided at least some security are removed and the nuclear family is left to determine its fate as best it may – then one may indeed expect conflict. But it is modernity, not tradition, that is at the origin of the struggle. From the dependency perspective, therefore, the authoritarian governments typical of a large portion of the Third World are perceived as a necessary concomitant of capital exploitation rather than as the inevitable response to traditional backwardness. As we have seen, the fragility of these authoritarian regimes may be understood in terms of the weakness of the local classes they represent. Since these classes are the product of international economic forces and not the consequence of indigenous development, the political pacts they have made at home are relatively flimsy. The result is a ruling class ideologically unsure of itself ("denationalized") and only shallowly rooted in local social forces. The governments that represent the interest of such classes will of necessity be particularly reliant on the use of force to ensure their rules.

In this undertaking, such Third World governments can usually count on the support of the United States. For just as the international economic system lays down the social bases of much of southern development, so the international political system will attend to shifts in the political balance of power. Where the International Monetary Fund cannot travel, we might say, there the Marines will tread. From a dependency perspective, then, the consistently counter-revolutionary cast of American foreign policy is entirely in line with what one would expect. When the power of collaborating states in the Third World proves unequal to the task of containing the enormous pressures released by capitalist economic development in these areas, Washington will aid them in repressing popular uprisings and so protect the international economic system from the challenge of socialist economic nationalism.

It should thus be understandable that, in the eyes of the *dependencistas*, developmentalists in the United States were responsible for much more than inadequate model building with respect to affairs in the Third World. This very "inadequacy" was nothing more than an ideological smokescreen behind which North American imperialism freely operated. Developmentalist economists presented models of the beneficent spread of the industrial revolution through-

out the world and denounced obstacles to such progress as being caused by backwardness. Their colleagues in political science presented institution building as one of organizational techniques, and often sanctioned the establishment of military governments for periods of "transition." The separation of economics from politics was not an artificial, but rather a logical, expression of the needs of advanced capitalism. So was the developmentalists' failure to credit imperialism with the force it has had. In their work, the developmentalist intelligentsia of American universities had given the lie to all their protestations of academic freedom and value-free or progressive theorizing, revealing instead their true character as apologists for the established international division of wealth and power. The attack was now complete: the dependency school not only had established a paradigm for the study of the Third World, but it had provided an explanation of its rival, developmentalism, powerful enough to complete the latter's disintegration.

••••

The coherence, complexity, flexibility, and self confidence of the dependency approach should be clear. When we add the important consideration that it can serve as a powerful political force uniting Marxism ideologically with Third World nationalism – as is clear in the case of Liberation Theology in Latin America – we must recognize that dependency thinking has established itself as an intellectual force with which we must reckon. Quite unlike developmentalism – which lives on in the wide variety of studies it spawned earlier, but which today lacks a center of gravity in a well-anchored, broad-based theory of change – the dependency school is in its prime.

III. Challenging the Dependency Approach

It is no easy matter to determine from where critical assaults on dependency thinking should come. Because of the fragmentation of the field described in section I, developmentalism by the 1970s lacked the conceptual unity and vigor to mount an attack. Without a broad historical perspective and an integrated study of political economy, what serious hope was there that this school could rally, particularly after a fuller verdict on the Alliance for Progress and the engagement in Vietnam had become available? No wonder, then, that no one closely related with developmentalism has demonstrated an ability to do more than thumb his nose ineffectively at the *dependencistas*.

One possibility is that, like developmentalism, the dependency perspective will over time breed its own undoing. As this approach becomes increasingly sophisticated in its insights and broad in its applications, there is the chance of divergent or rival lines of analysis, or of an alduteration of the basic unity of view that characterized its literature throughout the 1970s. Consider the possible fate of the three recent refinements in the dependency approach discussed in the preceding section: the importance of local factors in determining the course of change in the South; the critical role of the state in development there; and the genuine gains in economic strength that have become apparent there over the last two decades. Could these factors be persuasively combined to suggest that a situation of dependency no longer exists (if indeed it ever did)? Looked at more closely, are these refinements not simply restatements of a version of the diffusion/political modernization models reviewed earlier as the hallmarks of developmentalism? If genuine growth *is* taking place, if the shape and pace of this change *do* reflect in good measure local economic and social circumstances, and if the state *is* especially responsible for how these events transpire, then one quite plausible inference would be that the ability of imperialism to make these areas "dependent" is declining, and that therefore the cardinal reference point of the

dependency approach is fast losing its utility as a lodestar. Ironically, then, *dependencia* as a perspective may be spreading just as the situation that gave rise to it is coming to an end, and the very sophistication of its method can be used as its own cannons turned against itself. Surely to a Marxist there should be nothing paradoxial to such a situation, as the doctrine teaches that ideas reflect the material world around them, usually with a time lag. The judgement of other historians may be more severe; they may hold that dependency theorizing reflected on a transitory moment in the process of Third World change, and that its major contribution was not to give insight to events there, but to be the ideological representation of a triumphing nationalist consciousness in these areas. It might even appear in retrospect that dependency writing represented only the narrow and short-term perspective, while the developmentalist approach proved better able to explain the course of change in the Third World over the long haul. What greater irony than for the dependency school to reaffirm, as the result of its own labors, the established verities of developmentalism!

Intriguing as such speculation may be, there is little reason to think that the dependency approach will founder for these reasons. As we have seen, dependency writing is not a simple-minded affair. It is no surprise, therefore, to learn that it has already generated concepts that enable it to pull back into line any potentially fissiparous tendencies leading toward apostasy.

A key argument in this respect is that the dramatic changes occurring on the periphery essentially leave untouched both the central characteristics of political life in the South and the predominance of northern power in shaping development there. For instance, industrialization to build up import substitution, through which southern countries attempted to become more self-reliant, led to the costly purchase of plants and equipment from abroad, the

increased penetration by multinational corporations of local tariff barriers, and the
development of ventures that catered largely to the ruling class. On the other hand,
export-led industrialization also relied (as its
very name suggests) on foreign know-how,
markets, and financial institutions. In either
case, the rich continued to monopolize the
benefits of growth on the periphery and to
depend on authoritarian governments to
keep the masses in their place.

At the same time, foreign actors retained
their paramount positions. Dependencistas
point out that, while the periphery may be
developing economically, the leading sectors of industry there – the "commanding
heights" or the "pace-setters" – are owned
overwhelmingly by Americans, Europeans,
and Japanese. Moreover, because the local
economy is now far more integrated than it
was previously, it has also become far more
sensitive to economic fluctuations abroad,
as the current Third World debt crisis with
its extreme vulnerability to interest rates in
the United States so dramatically illustrates.
As a result, the international system has
maintained its grip on the periphery despite
the real economic changes that have taken
place there. And with this grip, its various
agents – from multinational corporations to
the International Monetary Fund – are able
to create an environment suitable for the
unimpeded accumulation of capital: a
docile, cheap work force to exploit; favorable taxing regulations for private enterprise; and a fiscally "responsible" state (i.e.,
one that does not engage in "excessive"
social service expenditures). Once again,
the consequences have entailed the impoverishment of a substantial portion of the
population and the need for an authoritarian regime to keep the discontented in line:
the dependency relation itself may even
have been strengthened.

According to the dependencistas, the economic modernization of the periphery has
also affected the international order; but
here, too, the continuity of imperialist con-

trol lies beneath the apparent change. As
countries in the South come to diversify
and integrate their economies, they may
leave the periphery – but not to join the
core, since neither their financial nor their
technical infrastructure is autonomous
enough to play a part in controlling world
economic affairs. Instead, because of their
continued dependence, these countries
come to play the part in the world system
that their middle class plays domestically.
That is, they have little real power, but the
demonstrable privileges they enjoy relative
to those beneath them on the periphery (in
part because of their exploitation of those
less well placed) obligates them to do their
part to keep the system operating. So those
on the "semi-periphery" (sometimes called
the "newly industrializing countries" or
NICs) become junior, collaborating members of the international trading, investment, and financial system – their very
gains serving only to reinforce the system
that binds them on its will. If in appearance
the international economic system is undergoing change, in reality the power of capitalism and the dominance of the northern
imperialists have never been more effective.[16]

Thus, however much the dependency
school may seem to possess within itself
arguments that could lead to its own
destruction, such a forecast takes no
account of the ways in which the doctrine
can maintain its stability despite the changes
it is undergoing. Like other coherent ideologies, the dependency perspective has
self-protecting concepts to deflect all manner of threat and preserve the doctrine's
integrity. More than just an ideology is at
stake here; there are other forces in operation assuring the doctrine's stability. The
dependency perspective is an ideological
"united front" in the Leninist sense: it binds
together Marxists and Third World nation-
alists in their mutual hatred of imperialism.
Just as dependencistas maintain that developmentalist ideas are "ideological" in the

sense of serving political interests, so there is a political urgency to the dependency case as well. In short, for practical political, as well as doctrinal, reasons, we should expect the dependency approach to remain assertive. It will not be undone, as was speculated above, by its own hand.

An adequate criticism of the dependency school must simultaneously provide an account of British and American imperialism since the late 18th century and an account of change in the late-industrializing world. It must demonstrate that economic interests constitute but one motive to imperialism (and not necessarily its most important), and it must establish that the form development has taken in Africa, Asia, and Latin America is only partly (and usually not primarily) the result of imperialism's influence; instead, it represents the outcome of local forces at work. Any such undertaking will confront fully and directly the core propositions of the dependency school: that imperialism works fundamentally to accumulate profits for capitalists, and that the power of this enterprise over the last several centuries has been so great that it has literally molded the economic, social, and political profile of the Third World. One cautionary note: piddling criticism of the dependency school is a waste of time. A perspective as supple and complex as that of *dependencia* will have no trouble explaining away as irrelevant. or as understandable in its own terms, relatively minor points about change in the core, the periphery, or the international system, or demands that its claims be made quantifiable and so readily testable. One must instead go to the heart of the matter, exploding dependency's myth of imperialism at the same time as its myth of the logic of change on the periphery. This is not to say that imperialism does not continue to be of influence in the South, or that Marxism is without its insights into the human condition. It is indeed possible to accept dependency interpretations of history where they seem appropriate. But that is not good enough for the advocates of dependency; like proponents of any holistic ideology, they are intensely suspicious of eclecticism. For the unity of the movement to be irredeemably shattered intellectually, it is not necessary, in short, to maintain that dependency is always and everywhere mistaken, but only that is no better than a partial truth.[17]

The extremeness of the dependency model, its holism, and the way it comes to rest on few simple premises constitute its source of unity and strength, and at the same time its point of greatest vulnerability. Consider, for example, its enormous emphasis on the character of the collaborating class in the Third World context. This group, born of imperialism and serving its interests locally through the power to manage affairs on the periphery, is predominant thanks to its international connections. But if it can be maintained that, for a specific time or place, this class is only one among many, and that other factors, such as inherited political institutions or ethnic cleavages, are equal or even more significant in determining the course of events, the claim that the country is dependent loses its essential meaning. Through the insertion of a collaborating class in the South, imperialism must dominate life there; it is not enough that this be one force among the many, or only triumphant at certain intervals. If it were not dominant, then the country would no longer be shaped primarily by the force of economic imperialism. The tie with world system analysis would snap, the claim to a unified approach to the study of the Third World would be invalid, and the militant accusations that the class struggle and the national struggle in the South are one would be more difficult to sustain. One may find that some countries, at some times, correspond more closely to the dependency model than do others; so it clearly has its value as a paradigm for analysis. But the suggestion that the paradigm is useful only sometimes would be unacceptable to this school. Its ambition requires far more. And, though this ambition is an undeniable source of the dependency movement's strength, it is likewise the point at which the arms of criticism may be used most devastatingly against it.

There is no reason to believe that attacks on the dependency approach will weaken the convictions of its advocates. Like the proponents of any strong model, these writers have ways of deflecting attacks and maintaining their conceptual unity. And, as we have seen, the political interests served by such an ideology will insist on the veracity of this way of understanding the world whatever the objections.

IV. New Agenda for Third World Studies

••••

In future undertakings there is no need to repudiate the important insights provided by either the developmental or the dependency approaches. For whatever the shortcomings of their general categories of analysis as such, each has provided useful empirical and theoretical tools for Third World studies which should on no account be abandonned. Freed of the agendas set by their paradigms, we may nonetheless borrow from their labors.

The problem with developmentalism was that it was too fragmented; with *dependencia*, that is too holistic. Is it nonetheless possible to promote some kind of cross-fertilization that breeds the strengths of each into a new synthesis while leaving the deadwood behind? If we have catalogued the failings of each school, what of their positive legacies? Is some kind of "postmodernist" borrowing possible that moves us forward?

Thanks in good measure to the dependency perspective, those in the "mainstream" must now think more broadly and complexly about the Third World than before, while moral advocacy is no longer

taboo in the name of an "objective" social science. We must think more broadly because the dependency approach obliges us to analyze Third World development globally and historically on a far larger scale than before. We must think more complexly because *dependencia* obliges us to see the interconnectedness of things – especially in the realm of political economy. And we must think in a more normative manner because of the dependency school's insistence that the terrible human problems of change can simply not be put to the side. Indeed, it should be possible to take the dependency lesson one step further, not only by extending its methods to new areas, such as the study of Soviet imperialism in Eastern Europe or examining the ways in which relations with the South actually debilitate and undermine the great powers involved (witness the multinationals exporting jobs and selling the technological patrimony of the West for a pittance), but by expanding our sensitivity to the range of influences apart from the economic that the United States in particular may use to shape the Third World in basic ways. In its greatly exaggerated emphasis on the economic motivations of the United States and the earlier imperialist powers, the dependency school has completely overlooked the political logic of imperialism, both as a reason for American policy and as an active agent of change in the South. Thus, for all its warnings of the threats that imperialism poses to the late-industrializing world, dependency thinking has neglected, ironically enough, one of the chief avenues by which northern influence is exercised.

By contrast, the major accomplishment of developmentalism lies in the variety of analytical tools it brought to the study of change, and in the care with which it used them. The focus of this school was essentially on working out the logic of different social processes in their own terms – political, economic, social and psychological. If God is in the detail – that is, if excellence is apparent in the mastery of nuance and technique – if it is the specificity, the concreteness of social life that brings us closest to understanding it, then developmentalism still has a great deal to teach us by example. It is from developmentalism that we can come to appreciate, for instance, the "laws of motion" of discrete domains; in politics, there are the rich studies done on bureaucracies, parties, and matters of legitimacy, for instance. Eclecticism is sometimes thought of negatively, as if it had an *ad hoc*, superficial character that is of little use analytically. But if eclecticism is thought of instead as the effort to bring a variety of insights to bear on a problem in a patient manner that respects the complexity of the problem studied, then the various analytic tools offered by the social sciences today can continue to have the utility that the developmentalists originally hoped they would have. Thus, current topics – such as ethnicity as a source of solidarity or conflict in development, the character of the state and its role in change, and the varieties of religious cultures and their impact on change – were all subjects of interest to developmentalists a good quarter of a century ago.

From dependency thinking, we may learn a breadth of vision (even if most of these writers used this vantage point to violate the integrity of individual cases). From developmentalism, we can learn how a variety of theoretical tools may be used in harmony to organize the complexity of social life (even if in the hands of most of these writers such an approach did not add up, so that an overly fragmented view was the result). At the same time, Third World studies may work more fruitfully in the case of issue-oriented problems of comparative analysis, without the feeling that such efforts must ultimately vindicate either of those will-o'-the-wisps, a "general theory of action" or the notion that "all of recorded history is the history of class struggle." Simultaneously, there may be a renewed

appreciation of works of art or history that, despite their lack of comparative focus (or indeed, because of it), are able to communicate so well the character of the Third World. In this way, perhaps something of the unity of the field may be resurrected – by the frank admission that the range of issues to be investigated admits of a variety of approaches such that discourse is facilitated, not ended.

••••

ENDNOTES

1. Samuel P. Huntington and Jorge I. Dominguez, "Political Development," in Fred I. Greenstein and Nelson W. Polsby, eds, *Handbook of Political Science*, Vol. 3: *Macropolitical Theory* (Reading, MA: Addison-Wesley, 1975), 90.

2. Gabriel Almond, "Comparative Politics and Political Development: A Historical Perspective," Joint Seminar on Political Development, Harvard - Massachussetts Institute of Technology, October 26, 1983, p. 7.

3. Hirschman, *Essays in Trespassing: Economics to Politics and Beyond* (New York: Cambridge University Press, 1981), 1.

4. Hirschman, "The Search for Paradigms as a Hindrance to Understanding," *World Politics* 22 (April 1970), 329.

5. Wiarda, "Toward a Non-Ethnocentric Theory of Development: Alternative Conceptions from the Third World," paper presented at the meeting of the American Political Science Association, September 1981, p. 25. For a more accessible version of this position, see Wiarda, "The Ethnocentrism of the Social Sciences: Implications for Research and Policy," *The Review of Politics* 42 (April 1981). For an earlier statement of this view by a Weberian, see Reinhart Bendix, *Embattled Reason: Essays on Social Knowledge* (New York: Oxford University Press, 1970), esp. 268 ff., and *Nation Building and Citizenship: Studies of Our Changing Social Order* (Berkeley: University of California Press, 1964), Chap. 8.

6. For example, in the 1964 Preface to *The Passing of Traditional Society: Modernizing the Middle East* (Glencoe, IL: The Free Press, 1958), Lerner writes: "The 'Western model' is only historically Western; sociologically it is global…the same basic model reappears in virtually all modernizing societies of all continents of the world, regardless of variations of race, color or creed" (pp. viii-ix). Two other well-known examples from an abundant literature are Rostow, *The Stages of*

Economic Growth: A Non-Communist Manifesto (New York: Cambridge University Press, 1960); and Black, *The Dynamics of Modernization: A Study in Comparative History* (New York: Harper & Row, 1966).

7. Gabriel A. Almond and James S. Coleman, eds., *The Politics of the Developing Areas* (Princeton: Princeton University Press, 1960), 535.

8. Eckstein, "A Perspective on Comparative Politics, Past and Present," in Harry Eckstein and David Apter, eds., *Comparative Politics: A Reader* (Glencoe, IL: The Free Press, 1963).

9. Almond and Coleman (fn. 9), 3, 4.

10. Grendzier, *Managing Political Change: Social Scientists and the Third World* (Boulder, CO: Westview Press, 1985). For a powerful early attack along these lines, see Noam Chomsky, *American Power and the New Mandarins* (New York: Pantheon Books, 1969).

11. For the debates within the dependency camp, see, among others, Fernando Henrique Cardoso, "The Consumption of Dependency Theory in the United States," *Latin American Research Review* 12 (No. 3, 1977); Richard R. Fagen, "Studying Latin American Politics: Some Implications of a *Dependencia* Approach," *Latin American Research Review* 12 (No. 3, 1977); and Ronal H. Chilcote, ed., *Dependency and Marxism: Towards a Resolution of the Debate* (Boulder, CO: Westview Press, 1981). The most influential writer on world system analysis in the United States is Immanuel Wallerstein; see his *The Modern World System: Capitalist Agriculture and the Origins of the European World-Economy in the Sixteenth Century* (New York: Academic Press, 1974), and *The Modern World System II: Mercantilism and the Consolidation of the European World-Economy, 1600-1750* (New York: Academic Press, 1980).

12. Cardoso and Faletto, *Dependency and Development in Latin America* (Berkeley: University of California Press, 1979), xxiii.

13. For an indication of the history of the concept, see Benjamin Higgins, *Economics Development: Principles, Problems, and Policies,* rev. ed. (New York: W.W. Norton, 1968), chaps. 12 and 14. For a comprehensive application of the notion of the dual economy in

dependency terms, see William W. Murdoch, *The Poverty of Nations: The Political Economy of Hunger and Population* (Baltimore: The Johns Hopkins University Press, 1980), chaps. 8 and 9.

14. Gallagher and Robinson, "The Imperialism of Free Trade," *Economic History Review,* 2d series, 6 (No. 1, 1953); Gunnar Myrdal, *Economic Theory and Underdeveloped Regions* (London: Gerald Duckworth, 1957). On Prebisch, see Joseph L. Love, "Raúl Prebisch and the Origins of the Doctrine of Unequal Exchange," *Latin American Research Review* 15 (No. 3, 1980).

15. Evans, *Dependent Development: The Alliance of Multinational, State and Local Capital in Brazil* (Princeton: Princeton University Press, 1979). An early and especially strong statement on this matter can be found in Bill Warren, "Imperialism and Capitalist Industrialization," *New Left Review* 81 (1973). See also Fernando Henrique Cardoso, "Dependent Capitalist Development in Latin America," *New Left Review* 74 (1972), and Cardoso, "Associated-Dependent Development: Theoretical and Practical Implications," in Alfred Stepan, ed., *Authoritarian Brazil: Origins, Politics, and Future* (New Haven: Yale University Press, 1973).

16. While the term "semi-periphery" appears to have been coined by Immanuel Wallerstein, the earliest use of the concept of which I am aware is in the idea of "go-between countries" as explained by Johan Galtung, "A Structural Theory of Imperialism," *Journal of Peace Research* 8 (No. 2, 1971).

17. See Tony Smith, *The Pattern of Imperialism: The United States, Great Britain, and the Late-Industrializing World since 1815* (New York: Cambridge University Press, 1981), chaps. 1 and 2. Strong attacks on world system analysis — which is the cornerstone of dependency theory — include Theda Skocpol, "Wallerstein's World Capitalist System: A Theoretical and Historical Critique," *American Journal of Sociology* 82 (March 1977); Aristide R. Zolberg, "Origins of the Modern World System: A Missing Link," *World Politics* 33 (January 1981); and Patrick O'Brien,"European Economic Development: The Contribution of the Periphery," *The Economic History Review,* 2d series, 35 (February 1982).

Indication of Development:
The Search for a Basic Needs Yardstick

NORMAN HICKS and *PAUL STREETEN*

Ever since economists have attempted to tackle development problems, the principal yardsticks for measuring economic development have been GNP, its components, and their growth. Despite the many problems with national accounting in developing countries, the national accounts have continued to be the main framework for discussions of growth, the allocations between investment, consumption, and saving, and the relative influence of various sectors in total value added. GNP per head is widely accepted as the best single indicator of development, both historically and for international comparisons....

This paper identifies and reviews four different approaches to the measurement problem: (1) adjustments to GNP, by which standard concepts of national income accounting are modified to capture some of the welfare aspects of development and to improve international comparability; (2) social indicators, which attempt to define nonmonetary measures of social progress; (3) the related social accounting systems, which attempt to provide an organizing framework for some of the social indicators; and (4) the development of composite indexes, which combine various social indicators into a single index of human and social development or of the "quality of life." In addition to these four broad approaches, efforts have been made to design an adequate measure of income distribution and to count the number of people living below a defined poverty line. This is briefly discussed in the following

Hicks, Norman and Paul Streeten. First published in *World Development*, 7(6), 1979, pp. 567-580. *World Development* is published by Pergamon Journals Ltd., Oxford, United Kingdom.

section. The extensive literature on this subject could, however, warrant a separate review.[1]

Adjustments to the GNP Measure

Despite the overwhelmingly attention to growth, the deficiencies of GNP per head as an indicator of economic development became apparent to many, even during the early years. Pigou had pointed out in 1920 that economic welfare comprises not only national income per head but also its distribution and the degree of its steadiness of fluctuation over time.[2] Measurement problems became apparent in the attempt to make intercountry comparisons of GNP per head. Part of the problem arises from the fact that official exchange rates do not measure relative domestic purchasing power, since a large portion of marketed GNP does not enter into world trade. In addition, trade policies often create distortions in nominal exchange rates, so that they fail to reflect the true value of even that proportion of GNP which is traded.

Clark was one of the first to attempt to convert national accounts by the use of purchasing power parities.[3] This means measuring the output of each country at a common price level, usually international prices. The most recent and complete work on purchasing power parities has been undertaken by Kravis and others.[4] The results of this research suggest that the GNP of India, for instance, should be adjusted upward by a factor of 3.5, while that of most other countries would be adjusted by a somewhat smaller margin. Even these kinds of adjustment, however, cannot eliminate all the problems of comparing GNP among countries. For instance, climatic conditions may require greater expenditure for clothings and shelter in the more temperate parts of the world, while dry tropical zones require more expenditure on irrigation and disease control. Evaluations of nontradables, particularly public and other services, are difficult and subject to conceptual problems. In addition, a great deal of work is necessary to cover hundreds of goods and services for an accurate estimate of purchasing power parities. Unless a short cut or a reduced information approach is developed, it would be difficult to make wide use of this method.

Nordhaus and Tobin attempted to adjust GNP so that it would be a better measure of economic welfare (MEW).[5] They substracted from GNP an allowance for defense expenditures and other "regrettable necessities," such as the "disamenities" of urbanization (pollution, congestion, and crime), and added an estimate of the value of leisure and the services of consumer durables. At the same time, Nordhaus and Tobin reclassified health and education expenditures as investment, rather than consumption. The final result produced a MEW for the United States that was about twice as large GNP, mainly because the high value imputed to leisure (the measure of which raises great difficulties) and other nonmarket activities. The growth rate of MEW for the United States between 1929 and 1965 was somewhat lower than that for GNP, mainly because the larger value of leisure and nonmarket activities in the base year (1929) reduced the proportionate rate of growth, and partly because of the growth of defense expenditure and urban disamenities. Denison and others have criticized this approach on the ground that GNP was never meant to measure welfare, and attempts to adjust it only confuse the concept.[6]

GNP adjustments might be able to incorporate some of the items captured by social indicators. Thus, life expectancy could be allowed for by using expected life-time earnings instead of annual income per head or, more crudely, the product of average income per head and life expectancy. The consumption benefits of literacy could be allowed for by imputing the value of services from education as a durable consumer good. (The benefits of literacy as a durable investment good already show in the form of higher productivity.) Distribution could be allowed for by taking the median or the mode rather than the mean income, which gives excessive weight to the few very rich, or by multiplying the mean income by 1 minis the Gini coefficient.[7]

There are certain difficulties in using the Nordhaus-Tobin corrections to indicate the satisfaction of basic needs. "Regrettable necessities" are substracted from GNP because "we see no direct effect of defense expenditures on household economic welfare. No reasonable country (or household) buys 'national defense' for its own sake. If there were no war or risk of war, there would be no need for defense expenditures and no one would be the worse without them." But similar reasoning could be applied to the components of basic needs. Medical services from nurses, doctors, and hospitals are not desired for their own sake; if it were not for disease and accidents, there would be no need to incur this expenditure. The same goes for shelter against the cold, for sewerage, and perhaps for literacy. Even food for under- or malnourished people is a necessity to prevent hunger, disease, or death. A logically consistent application of the Nordhaus-Tobin principle would include in the national income only those items that are not really needed—the inessentials and frills. This paradoxical conclusion would be contrary to the judgement of those who wish to *exclude* all frivolous luxuries from national income accounts.[8]

If it were possible to distinguish precisely between "goods," "bads,"and "anti-bads," one could deduct from national income all "anti-bads": expenditures on defense to combat the "bads" generated by potential enemies, expenditures on heating, shelter, and medicines to offset the "bads") generated by nature – the narrowest definition of basic needs; and expenditures to offset the "bads" generated by the domestic economic system itself, which "artificially" creates wants through advertising, social pressures, and industrial pollution. In fact, it is not possible to distinguish between good and bad artificially created wants without introducing value judgements: the desire for books, art, and music is also artificially created. Nor is it possible to distinguish between "anti-bads" the need for deodorants or anti-dandruff shampoo created by the fear of social ostracism) and "goods" (the need for literature created by the desire to participate in the cultural life of society).

Adjustments to GNP for distributional value judgements can be made by weighting different components of the national income according to who receives them. Such a redefinition would, however, eliminate the distinction between the national income and its distribution. Kuznets and Ahluwalia and Chenery have suggested that the growth rate of GNP in itself is a misleading indicator of development, since it is heavily weighted by the income shares of the rich.[9] A growth of 10 percent in incomes of the richest 20 percent of the population will have a greater effect on the aggregate growth rate that will a 10 percent growth in incomes of the poorest 20 percent. They suggest either the equal weighting of each decile of income recipients or the introduction of "poverty weights," which would place more weight on the growth of incomes for the poorest 40 percent. The result is a revised aggregate growth rate that allows for differences and changes in income distributions.

Another approach would simply use the absolute income level of the poorest 40 percent as the appropriate indicator of the satisfaction of basic needs. This measure has the advantage of shifting the focus from the distribution of income, a politically sensitive subject in many countries, to the level of living of the poor. Progress in reducing poverty can be judged, however, only if the income level of the poor can be compared with some standard minimum which constitutes a poverty line. A common approach is to calculate the cost of a "minimal" nutritionally balanced diet for an "average" person and then to calculate the ratio of food expenditure to total expenditure. The diet costs are multiplied by the reciprocal of this ratio to allow for expenditure on nonfood items. Those families or individuals whose income is insufficient to cover these minimal expenditures are judged to be below the poverty line and in the poverty target group.

Among the many shortcomings of this approach, the examination of family income and food consumption ignores the important problem of distribution of food and other amenities both among different families below the poverty line and within a family. In many countries women (who may work harder than men) and children receive less than an adequate amount of food, although the family's total consumption may be judged to be "adequate." Poverty line measures do not consider how far below the line families may be, nor do they show improvements that take place below this line. They suggest that a "solution" has been found for those brought barely above the line. They therefore conceal the efforts required to reduce poverty. Sen has proposed weighting individuals on the basis of how far below the poverty line they fall, a suggestion combining poverty line and income distribution approaches.[10]

In addition, a nutritionally adequate diet is difficult to define since caloric needs vary widely with climate, body weight, activity, height, age, and other factors, and even for the same conditions between persons and for the same person in the same conditions from day to day. Household income surveys generally show that many families below the poverty line could consume an adequate diet by purchasing a different basket of foods, but the more nutritious foods available are rejected on grounds of taste, variety, habit, and so on. Families living below the poverty line often spend on nonbasic items, such as drink and entertainment. Even with an income above the poverty line, a family may not be able to purchase essential goods and services (such as health, education, water) that are in short supply or controlled by the public sector. It may have to rely on less efficient and more costly alternatives such as traditional healers, private water deliveries, or private schools. The importance of the public sector in these areas derives from the view that these goods and services meet "merit wants," that is, the government judges them to be more important than consumers would judge them to be, and also derives from the "external economies": the benefits accrue not only to the individual consumer but also to others. The basic needs approach, in fact, stems from the experience that raising incomes alone is insufficient because of inefficiencies in the consumption pattern of the poor and the lack of some essential goods and services. Therefore, any measure of poverty income, no matter how carefully derived, will be inadequate for measuring basic needs.

Two final questions are whether the poverty line should move upward with rising average income, and whether the number or the proportion of the poor below the line is the same or a changing group of individuals.

Social Indicators

Another approach is to develop better indicators of human, social, and economic development that cover areas not reflected in most income-based measures. These so-called social indicators attempt to measure the development of health, nutrition, housing, income distribution, and other cultural and social factors. Various agencies –

including the United Nations, OECD, USAID, and Unesco – have put a great deal of work into compiling a set of social indicators.[11]

Social indicators are more useful in cross-country comparisons, since they avoid the problems of exchange rates and valuation. But the statistical basis for comparing these indicators between countries or over time remains very frail. The figures are often unreliable and not comparable because different definitions are used. Many data are based on limited sample surveys or other highly inaccurate methods of data collection. Differences observed in social indicators between countries often reflects these statistical and definitional variations rather than real differences in social development. But this constitutes a challenge to collect better, more comparable data.

Although the pricing mechanism is used to combine heterogeneous items in the national accounts, there is no obvious way to combine different social indicators. Consequently, problems arise in absorbing the content of a large number of socio-economic indicators and in attempting to draw general conclusions. Furthermore, the movement to develop social indicators has lacked a clear sense of purpose. The term "social indicators" itself very loosely encompasses a whole range of human, economic, social, cultural, and political indicators. The need to supplement the GNP as an indicator of economic development has become confused with a search for indicators of other aspects of development as well as of the "quality of life." The latter concept has generally been taken to cover concepts such as security, peace, equality of opportunity, participation, and personal satisfaction, all of which present difficult problems of measurement. It has never been clear whether the search was for an alternative, a complement, or a supplement to GNP.

Even without a unifying conceptual framework, and despite the problems mentioned above, social indicators do have certain advantages over GNP per head. First, they are concerned with ends as well as means, or at least with intermediate ends nearer to the ultimate end of a full and healthy life than are aggregate measures of average production. Even those social indicators that measure inputs (such as hospital beds per thousand population or school enrollment rates) rather than results (life expectancy, morbidity, literacy) attempt to capture inputs that are nearer to the desirable results than GNP per head.

Second, many social indicators say something about the distribution as well as the average, because the upper end is less skewed than it is for income per head. (The mode or the median for income per head can, however, eliminate skewness and reflect some aspects of distribution in the average.) There is practically no limit to how much income a man can receive, but the maximum life span is limited. Any increase in literacy reflects also a rough distributional improvement because the *proportion* of beneficiaries has risen.

Some indicators are better than others for showing the distribution of basic deficiencies since they are based on the presence or absence of certain conditions. Thus, measures of literacy, access to clean water, and primary school enrollment can indicate the percentage of the population with deficiencies in each of these important sectors. Measures such as life expectancy, infant mortality, and average caloric consumption are less informative since they average the statistics of rich and poor alike. There seems to be a clear need to develop more specific measures related to the poor, such as indicators of life expectancy or caloric consumption of those in the lower quintile of the income distribution, of women, of rural dwellers, and so on.

Third, while GNP per head follows an ascending order from the poorest to the richest countries, some social indicators are capable of catching something of the human, social and cultural costs of opulence (such as heart disease, stomach ulcers, or deaths in automobile accidents) as well as of poverty. They can, in principal, register some of the shared global problems, such as pollution and cultural dependence or interdependence, and reduce the false hierarchical and paternalistic impression that may be created by purely economic indicators. As a result, a different meaning can be attached to the so-called gap betwen the developed and developing countries. The GNP measure points to "catching up" and suggests a race. Social indicators can point to common and shared values and problems, to alternative styles of development, to the opportunities for learning from one another. Reducing or closing the international gap in life expectancy, literacy, infant mortality, or morbidity would appear to be a more sensible objective, and can be achieved at much lower levels of GNP per head and therefore much sooner, than reducing the income gap, though even less is known about how to achieve the former than the latter.

Inputs versus Results

Whether indicators of social and basic needs should reflect inputs or results depends on their purpose. For testing performance there is something to be said for choosing indexes that measure results, impact, or outputs, since these are closer to the ultimate objective. Furthermore, measures of inputs can introduce biases toward certain patterns of meeting needs which may not be universal. For instance, a country with fairly acceptable health standards should not be encouraged to acquire the same number of doctors as one with serious health problems: "regrettable necessities" should not be counted as final goods or as social achievements.

Another drawback is that the number of doctors does not measure the distribution of these doctors and of medical services or the degree of their specialization. Resources may be deployed in inefficient ways and fail to benefit the poor. In contrast, measures such as infant mortality and life expectancy indicate the degree to which basic needs have been fulfilled. Similarly, literacy measures the effectiveness of the educational system and is a better indicator than the number of students enrolled or the student-teacher ratio. In general, measures of output are better indicators of the level of welfare and the satisfaction of basic needs.

Most outputs are also inputs. Health, education, and even nutrition are valued not only in their own right, but also because they raise the productivity of present and future workers; higher productivity in turn is valued because it contributes to a better life.

Input measures, such as doctors or hospital beds per thousand population or enrollment rates in schools, also have their uses, however. They may reflect government intention, commitment, and efforts to provide public services. To assess policies and monitor performance, both sets of indicators are necessary. Input measures are useful indicators of the resources devoted to certain objectives (though the resources can be misdirected). To the extent to which inputs can be linked to results, that is, inputs have a known "production function," the connections between means and ends can be traced. Even without knowledge of a production function (as in the case of the links between expenditure on family planning and a decline in fertility rate), the combination of input and output measures presents the raw material for research into the causal links between the two, particularly since, in a social system of interdependent variables, many outputs are also inputs. In addition, when output measures cannot be readily found, it might be necessary to fall back on measures of inputs as useful proxies.

GNP versus Social Indicators

Several studies have suggested that since rankings of countries by GNP and by social indicators are very similar, GNP can be used as a proxy measure of social development.[12] Morawetz found that there was a weak correlation between the level of GNP and indicators of basic needs fulfillment, and even less correlation between the growth of GNP and improvements in basic needs indicators.[13] Sheehan and Hopkins concluded, however, that "the most important variable explaining the average level of basic needs satisfaction is per capita gross national product."[14] These contradictory results appear to arise from the selection of different indicators, sources of data, and country samples, as well as different interpretations of results. Many scholars include in social indicators such nonmonetary measures of economic performance as the consumption of newsprint or energy or the ownership of automobiles and radios. These economic indicators are almost always highly correlated with GNP, and at times they have been suggested as a short cut to estimating internationally comparable income levels.[15] Some authors exclude the developed countries because their high levels of GNP and social development might dominate the sample. Different results are obtained with the inclusion or exclusion of the centrally planned economies, the OPEC countries, and the very small developing countries.

Correlations based on 1970 data from the World Bank's Social Data Bank are shown in Table 1. The results for seven social indicators show a modest correlation with GNP (average $r^2 = 0.50$), while a sample of five economic indicators shows a somewhat higher correlation ($r^2 = 0.71$). When the social indicator data are disaggregated into samples of developing and developed countries, however, the correlation coefficients (technically, the square of the correlation coefficient is called the coefficient of determination) for both groups drop significantly ($r^2 = 0.25$ for developing countries, 0.18 for developed). Similar declines in the correlation are also found when the economic indicators are disaggre-

Table 1. Correlation of Indicators with GNP per Head, 1970

| | COEFFICIENTS OF DETERMINATION (r^2) | | | |
INDICATORS	ALL COUNTRIES	DEVELOPING	DEVELOPED	SAMPLE SIZE
Social Indicators				
Expectation of life at birth	0.53	0.28	0.13	102
Caloric consumption (as				
percentage of required)	0.44	0.22	0.02	103
Infant mortality	0.42	0.34	0.25	64
Primary enrollment	0.28	0.24	0.05	101
Literacy	0.54	0.47	0.16	70
Average persons per room (urban)	0.58	0.08	0.29	34
Housing units without piped				
water (percent)	0.74	0.13	0.36	36
Average	0.50	0.25	0.18	
Economic Indicators per Head				
Newsprint consumption	0.79	0.20	0.46	85
Automobiles	0.85	0.59	0.46	102
Radio receivers	0.43	0.14	0.07	97
Electricity consumption	0.67	0.30	0.24	102
Energy consumption	0.82	0.28	0.49	99
Average	0.71	0.30	0.34	

NOTE: This sample excludes the centrally planned economies and all countries with populations of less than 1 million. Although the total sample includes 106 countries, missing data reduce the sample size for each correlation.

SOURCE: Based on data taken from the World Bank's Social Data Bank.

gated. Apparently studies that examine only social variables for developing countries are apt to discover a poor relation with GNP, while those that consider economic and social variables for all countries are likely to find better relations.

One reason social indicators are not more highly correlated with GNP per head is that the relations are often distinctly nonlinear. Indicators such as life expectancy, literacy, and school enrollment have asymptotic limits that reflect biological and physical maximums. It is impossible, for instance, to have more than 100 percent literacy. These limits are often reached by middle-income countries, so that further increases in income show little gains in social indicators. For instance, life expectancy reaches seventy years of age for countries with income per head (1970) of $2,000, and it does not increase even as incomes increase to $5,000. Most countries have attained close to 100 percent literacy by the time their income per head reaches

the $2,500 level. Conversely, countries below $500 GNP per head demonstrate a wide variety of social development that is largely unrelated to the level of GNP. This can be seen more clearly in figures 1 and 2. The cluster of points along both axes indicates the lack of correlation between GNP and life expectancy and literacy at both the high- and low-income levels (other social indicators show similar patterns). It seems clear that a much better correlation could be developed by using some sort of non-linear relation.[16] A nonlinear function, would, however, obscure the fact that the correlation exists only among the middle-income countries. GNP per head is likely to be a misleading indicator of social development and progress in meeting basic needs, particularly when used in some linear fashion. Yet rankings of countries by social indicators and GNP are likely to be very similar because the ranking process obscures these nonlinearities.

Social Accounting Systems

Some work has been done on developing a system of social accounts to provide a kind of national accounting framework for social indicators. Stone and Seers have proposed the use of lifetime activity sequences, calculated by dividing total life expectancy into segments.[17] Such tables would show the average time a person could expect to spend in various mutually exclusive states. One such matrix might divide lifetime activity between school, work, leisure, retirement, and the like, while another might be built on a marital sequence (single, married, divorced, widowed). Such tables would combine various important social statistics from different fields and

Figure 1. GNP and Life Expectancy, 1970

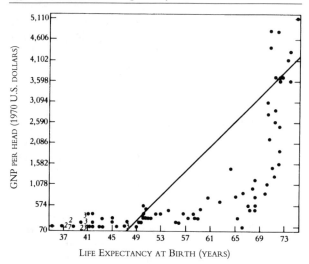

NOTE: Regression line: LE = 47.5 + 0.00689 GNP per head; R^2 = 0.53.
Numbers in the graph indicate points with more than one observation.
Source: World Bank data.

Figure 2. GNP and Literacy, 1970

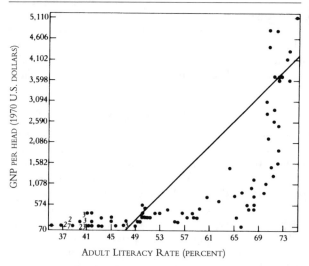

NOTE: Regression line: LIT = 42.15 + 0.0186 GNP per head; R^2 = 0.54.
Numbers in the graph indicate points with more than one observation.
Source: World Bank data.

would indicate changes over time, either actual or planned. But of the system's many problems, not the least is its inability to incorporate fully all aspects of social development. Some indicators (income distribution, security, police protection, pollution) cannot readily be transformed into segments of life expectancies. Furthermore, the system requires more data than are available in most countries and is thus more suited for those that are industrialized. Nevertheless, the concept has some potential for integrating a large variety of social variables and providing the basis for a theory linking policies to results in the area of social planning.

Other ideas have been developed for a more limited social accounting approach. The social accounting matrix (SAM) of Pyatt and Round does not utilize social indicators but expands the traditional input-output table into a matrix of payments made by productive sectors to different income recipients.[18] Recipients can be disaggregated in various ways to indicate the distribution of income between factors, urban and rural households, or income classes. The power of SAM is that it integrates production and income distribution data to give a better view of the economy and of the flows between sectors. It still relies, however, on the use of GNP as a measure of welfare and is limited in its application by the absence of good income distribution data.

Terleckyj has developed a matrix framework for analyzing the impact of government programs on various social goals, as indicated by the appropriate social indicators.[19] Since programs affect more than one social goal, the approach develops a matrix of inputs and outputs and suggests the possibility of defining the most efficient set of programs for achieving a particular set of goals. While this approach provides a useful rational for using different indicators, it does not provide a better measure of growth or development.

Composite Indexes of Development

Relatively more work than has been done on a system of social accounts has gone into developing composite indexes to replace or supplement GNP as an indicator of social, economic, or general development. The U.N. Research Institute for Social Development (UNRISD) during the 1960s undertook to develop better social indicators, including composite indicators. For instance, Drewnowski and Scott developed the Level of Living Index, which was defined as "the level of satisfaction of the needs of the population as measured by the flow of goods and services enjoyed in a unit of time."[20] The Level of Living Index itself, however, goes beyond the provision of goods and services and consider basic needs, subdivided between physical needs (nutrition, shelter, health) and cultural needs (education, leisure, security). "Higher needs" or "surplus over basic needs" is taken as the surplus income over some minimum level. The basic needs part of the index includes items that are very difficult to measure for many countries, such as the amount of leisure time available, the number of people in possession of private saving, and the quality of housing. This makes the index very difficult to apply, and Drewnowski and Scott were forced to use approximations even for their limited sample of twenty countries. Furthermore, the work, once begun, was not continued after 1966 in the same form.

McGranahan and others examined seventy-three indicators of economic and social characteristics and found a fairly high intercorrelation between them.[21] Through a process of elimination, they constructed the Development Index based on eighteen core indicators, which included nine social and nine economic indicators. The resulting index was highly correlated with GNP per head ($r^2 = 0.89$), although the ranking of some countries (Venezuela, Chile, and Japan) was substantially different under the index. In general, the correlation of the index and GNP per head was somewhat lower for developing than developed countries. McGranahan and others concluded that social development occured at a more rapid pace than economic development up to a level of about $500 per head (1960 prices). Some of these results are themselves, however, a product of the method employed, since the eighteen core indicators were selected, in part, on the basis of their high intercorrelation with the other indicators. As a result of the high intercorrelation, the composite index was relatively insensitive to the choice of component variables. McGranahan and others found, for instance, that the country rankings remained virtually unchanged when the number of indicators was reduced from eighteen to ten.

A study by the U.N. Economic and Social Council sought to analyze the development by ranking 140 countries by seven indicators other than GNP.[22] These included two social indicators (literacy and life expectancy) and five economic indicators (energy, manufacturing share of GDP, manufacturing share of exports, employment outside agriculture, and number of telephones). An overall rank for each country was calculated by giving equal weight to the ranks under each separate indicator. When the results were arranged by quintiles and compared with GNP, the overall index was closely associated with the ranking by GNP. The U.N. index was heavily weighted by economic rather than purely social indicators, however, and thus tends to replicate the findings of Beckerman[23] and others that show nonmonetary indicators are highly correlated with GNP. A similar study by the OECD in 1973 used regression techniques for six variables to establish a predicted GNP per head index for eighty-two developing countries.[24] A 1977 paper by the OECD, however, concluded that "per capita GNP still appears to be the best measure" of the level of development.[25]

The use of a composite index has been studied by the Overseas Development Council (ODC), under the guidance of M.D. Morris.[26] Morris's Physical Quality of Life Index (PQLI) uses three simple indicators with equal weights to attempt to measure the fulfillment of "minimum human needs": life expectancy at age one, infant mortality, and literacy. Morris argues that indicators used for judging performance under basic needs criteria should concentrate on outputs or results, rather than inputs. Input measures, he feels do not measure success in meeting the desired goals and may lend an ethnocentric bias to the means employed. The use of only three indicators permits the calculation of the PQLI for a wide range of coutries and facilitates the examination of changes in the index over time. The term "quality of life" is perhaps a misnomer, since what is really being measured is effectiveness in reducing mortality and raising literacy. Life expectancy measures the length, not the quality of life. (These ends also have an ethnocentric bias.) Most important, the weighting system of the PQLI is arbitrary, and there is no rationale for giving equal weights to literacy, infant mortality, and life expectancy at age one. It is not possible to prove that the PQLI gives a "correct" index of progress on human needs, as opposed to some alternative index having different weights or different components. It is not clear what is gained by combining the component indexes with a weighting system that cannot be defended. Analytical work can use the component indexes almost as easily as the composite index, without intro-

ducing the biases of the PQLI. While Morris's index, has received much attention in the popular press and has been incorporated in the 1979 report of Development Assistance Committee of the OECD and in the World Almanac, most serious scholars find it difficult to accept the results of a composite index without a stronger theoretical foundation.

A similar but more complicated index has been constructed by Sivard for the U.S. Arms Control and Disarmament Agency.[27] She gives equal weight to three factors – GNP per head, education, and health – by averaging country ranks. Education and health indicators are themselves composed of an average of five factors each, combining input and output measures. The result is a ranking of countries according to combined economic and social performances that contains all the problems of other composite measures.

Despite the potential attractiveness of having a single index of socioeconomic development, there is little theoretical guidance to govern the choice of indicators, the correct scaling of component indexes, or the appropriate weights. Moreover, an index that relies only on ranking neglects the distance between ranks.

Scaling problems arise when raw data on social indicators are converted into component indexes ranging from 0 to 100. For instance, reasonable values for life expectancy could be either 40 to 75 years, or 40 to 100 years. A country with a life expectancy of 60 years will obviously have a different "score" depending on the scale chosen (57 as opposed to 33; that is, 20 years' superiority expressed as a proportion of the interval 35 to 60 and multiplied by 200) and this will materially change the composite index. Furthermore, the scaling system need not be linear. Drewnowski used "expert opinion" to derive a linear scale system reflecting set levels of basic needs satisfaction. McGranahan and others developed an elaborate system of correspondence points to determine the appropriate scale range and utilized nonlinear (logarithmic) scaling for many indicators. Morris simply took the range of the data for each indicator, with the "worst" country being defined as 0 and the "best" as 100.

An even more difficult problem concerns the proper weights to be used in combining the component indexes into the composite. Drewnowski tried both equal fixed weights and a system of sliding weights under which deviations from the normal were given more weight than indexes close to the normal. The rankings of countries by sliding or equal weights were highly correlated with the rankings of countries by GNP per head or consumption per head, and the shift in the weighting system did not materially affect the rankings. McGranahan's weighting system gave greater weight to the component indicators that had the highest degree of intercorrelation with the other indicators, a somewhat dubious method. The absence of correlation might be thought an equally valid criterion, though it might then be asked why there is no correlation and why the indicators should be integrated. McGranahan also found that moderate changes in the weighting system did not affect the level of each country's index or its ranking. The insensitivity of the general index to the choice of weights is a logical result of having high intercorrelation among the components, since the high correlation implies that any one component is a good substitute for any other. The U.N. ECOSOC study gives equal weight to the country *ranks* of the social indicators, thus avoiding, in a certain sense, the scaling problem. As mentioned above, the PQLI gives equal weight to each of the three components without ascertaining if this implies the correct tradeoff between the various components. None of these studies indicates that much effort was devoted to developing a theoretically sound rationale for the weighting system. If one is ever found, it will have to be based on the rela-

tive preferences of people.

Because of these problems, it might well be argued that a composite index is either unnecessary, or undesirable, or impossible to construct. It is unnecessary if the components are highly correlated with one another, because then any one of the component indicators by itself will serve as an adequate index. If, however, the components move in different directions in cross-country comparisons and time series, averaging would conceal the important issues and would be undesirable. Using the same index for a situation in which mortality is high and literacy low, as for one in which literacy is high and mortality low, implies evaluating the tradeoff between literacy and life expectancy. Unless the basis for such an evaluation can be established, all weighting remains arbitrary and misleading, and composition is impossible. The case for considering the two indexes separately is exactly the same as the case for having an index independent of GNP.

If basic needs were interpreted literally, all needs that were "basic" would have to be met together, and tradeoffs between different basic needs would be ruled out. A composite index would therefore not be necessary. As long as the package of basic needs has not been fully met, no amount of additional satisfaction of any one component could compensate for the slightest deficiency in any other, so that a composite indicator would be ruled out. Once all basic needs had been met, again no composite index would be required, for the indicator for any one need would show that all had been satisfied. But I am not advocating such a literal interpretation of basic needs.

Conclusion

This brief survey has reviewed four alternatives to GNP per head for calculating some of the dimensions of development. The adjustment-to-GNP approach has focused largely on improving GNP as a measure of economic welfare. Attempts to introduce other costs and benefits of development, which would make GNP a broader measure of welfare, lack a logical basis and tend instead to result in a confusion of concepts. Research on social indicators has failed to produce an alternative that is as readily accepted and comprehended as GNP per head, though such indicators are useful for judging social performance. Systems of social accounts, which could integrate social indicators through some unifying concept, have not been able to overcome successfully all the difficult problems encountered.

Efforts to develop composite indexes have ranged from a search for better measures of the physical production of goods and services to a measure of the quality of life, of economic or social welfare, of satisfactions, happiness, and other objectives. The search for a composite index of social welfare, analogous to GNP as an index of production, has been fruitless so far, since it has proven virtually impossible to translate every aspect of social progress into monetary values or some other readily accepted common denominator. The great deal of work devoted to composite indexes, however, suggests the need for a single number which, like GNP per head, can be quickly grasped as a rough indication of social development.

The current discussion of basic needs-oriented development focuses on the alleviation of poverty through a variety of measures other than merely the redistribution of incremental output. Attention to *how much* is being produced is supplemented by attention to *what* is being produced, how, for whom, and with what impact. Obviously, the rapid growth of output will still be important to the alleviation of poverty, and GNP per head remains an important figure. What is required in addition are some indicators of the composition and beneficiaries of GNP and of the results of output growth – indicators that would

supplement the GNP data, not replace them. The basic needs approach, therefore, can give the necessary focus to work on social indicators.

As a first step, it might be useful to define the best indicator for each of the essential basic needs, at present considered to be in six areas: nutrition, primary education, health, sanitation, water supply, and housing and related infrastructure.[28] This list is merely illustrative, not exhaustive, and all needs do not have the same status. A limited set of core indicators covering these areas would be a useful device for concentrating efforts to collect more adequate, standardized, comparable international statistics on basic needs. From the fact that we consider six basic needs, it does not necessarily follow that there be six core indicators. More than one indicator may be necessary to measure adequately progress in any one area, or one indicator may serve more than one basic needs sector. Nevertheless, the basic needs concept can serve to integrate efforts to gather and analyze data.

Once defined, these core basic needs indicators could be important in policy analysis, permitting, for instance, international comparisons of performance and of relative aid levels. Such indicators could be used to view the relative gap between rich and poor countries and the speed with which this gap is widening or narrowing. They would indicate which countries are meeting the basic needs of their citizens and how their policies are related to the growth of output, trade, investment, and so on.

Because work on social indicators has often lacked a sharp focus, a large number of disparate indicators have been collected and tabulated. It might be more fruitful to concentrate work on a few important indicators and to improve their quality and coverage. In particular, it would be useful to add a distributional dimension to indicators now collected as averages. Instead of, for example, average caloric consumption, it would be preferable to compare caloric consumption of the highest income quartile with that of the lowest. The same goes for life expectancy, literacy, infant mortality, school enrollment, and so on. Similarly, distinct figures for males and females would reveal a great deal about the distribution of the goods and services that meet basic needs....

ENDNOTES

1. A fifth method would be to interview a sample of individuals and to ask each to place himself on a happiness or basic needs scale between, for example, zero and ten, and to say whether his basic needs were being met more adequately than at some specified date in the past. But this kind of survey is still rudimentary and does not provide the kind of information needed to monitor a basic needs approach.

2. A. C. Pigou, *The Economics of Welfare*, 1st ed. (London: Mcmillan, 1920).

3. Colin Clark, *Conditions of Economic Progress*, 3d ed. (London: Macmillan, 1951).

4. Irving B. Kravis, Zoltan Kenessey, Alan Heston, and Robert Summers, *A System of International Comparisons of Gross Product and Purchasing Power* (Baltimore, Md.: Johns Hopkins University Press, 1975); and Irving B. Kravis, Alan Heston, and Robert Summers, *International Comparisons of Real Product and Purchasing Power* (Baltimore, Md.: Johns Hopkins University Press, 1978).

5. William D. Nordhaus and James Tobin, "Is Growth Obsolete?" in *Economic Growth* (New York: Columbia University Press for NBER, 1972); see also Wilfred Beckerman, *Two Cheers for the Affluent Society* (New York: St Martin's Press, 1974), chap.4.

6. Edward F. Denison, "Welfare Measurement and the GNP," *Survey of Current Business*, vol. 51, no.1 (January 1971), pp. 13-16.

7. See A. K. Sen, "Economic Development: Objectives and Obstacles," paper presented at the Research Conference on the Lessons of China's Development Experience for the Developing Countries, sponsored by the Social Science Research Council/American Council of Learned Societies, Joint Committee on Contemporary China, San Juan, Puerto Rico, 1976.

8. Since in the absence of desires and wants there would be no need for the goods to satisfy them, the national income might be by definition zero if this line of reasoning were carried to its logical conclusion.

9. Simon Kuznets, "Problems in Comparing Recent Growth Rates for Developed and Less Developed Countries," *Economic Development and Cultural Change*, vol. 20, no. 2 (January 1972), pp. 185-209; and Montek S. Ahluwalia and Hollis Chenery, "The Economic Framework," in Hollis Chenery and others, *Redistribution with Growth* (London: Oxford University Press, 1974), pp. 38-51.

10. A. K. Sen, "Poverty, Inequality, and Unemployment," *Economic and Political Weekly*, vol. 8, special no. 31-33 (August 1973); reprinted as "Poverty: An Ordinal Approach to Measurement," *Econometrica*, vol. 44, no. 2 (March 1976); and *Poverty and Economic Development*, Second Vikram Sarabhai Memorial Lecture, Ahmedabad, December 5, 1976.

11. United Nations, Economic and Social Council (ECOSOC), Committee for Development Planning, "Developing Countries and Levels of Development" (New York, October 15, 1975); Organisation for Economic Co-operation and Development (OECD), Development Assistance Committee, "Socio-economic Typologies or Criteria and Their Usefulness in Measuring Development Progress" (Paris, April 7, 1977); U.S Agency for International Development (USAID), "Socio-economic Performance Criteria for Development" (Washington, D.C., February 1977); and United Nations Educational, Scientific and Cultural Organization (Unesco), *The Use of Socio-Economic Indicators in Development Planning* (Paris, 1976).

12. D.V. McGranahan, Claude Richaud-Proust, N.V. Sovani, and Muthu Subramanian, *Contents and Measurement of Socio-Economic Development* (New York: Praeger, 1972); and ECOSOC, "Developing Countries and Levels of Development."

13. David Morawetz, *Twenty-five Years of Economic Development, 1950 to 1975* (Baltimore, Md.: Johns Hopkins University Press, 1977).

14. Glen Sheehan and Michael Hopkins, *Basic Needs Peformance: An Analysis of Some International Data*, World Employment Programme Research Working Paper, WEP 2-23/WP9 (Geneva: International Labour Office, 1978), p. 95.

15. See Wilfred Beckerman, *International Comparisons of Real Incomes* (Paris: OECD, 1966).

16. For life expectancy, a semilog function increases the r^2 from 0.53 to 0.75.

17. Richard Stone, *Toward a System of Social and Demographic Statistics* (New York: United Nations, 1975); and Dudley Seers, "Life Expectancy as an Integrating Concept in Social and Demographic Analysis and Planning," *Review of Income and Wealth*, ser. 23, no. 3 (September 1977), pp. 195-203.

18. Graham Pyatt and Jeffrey Round, "Social Accounting Matrices for Development Planning," *Review of Income and Wealth*, ser. 23, no. 4 (December 1977), pp. 339-64.

19. Nestor Terleckyj, *Improvements in the Quality of Life* (Washington, D.C.: National Planning Association, 1975).

20. Jan Drewnowski and Wolf Scott, "The Level of Living Index," Report no. 4 (Geneva: U.N. Research Institute for Social Development, 1966), p. 1.

21. McGranahan and others, *Contents and Measurement of Socio-Economic Development*.

22. ECOSOC, "Developing Countries and Levels of Development."

23. Beckerman, *International Comparisons of Real Incomes*.

24. OECD, Development Assistance Committee, "Performance Compendium: Consolidated Results of Analytical Work on Economic and Social Performance of Developing Countries" (Paris, 1973).

25. OECD, Development Assistance Committee, "Socio-economic Typologies or Criteria and Their Usefulness in Measuring Development Progress."

26. M.D. Morris and F.B. Liser, "The PQLI: Measuring Progress in Meeting Human Needs," Communique on Development Issues no. 32 (Washington, D.C.: Overseas Development Counsil, 1977).

27. Ruth Sivard, "World Military and Social Expenditures, 1979" (Leesburg, Va.: World Priorities, 1979).

28. Paul Streeten and Shahid Javed Burki, "Basic Needs: Some Issues," *World Development*, vol. 6, no. 3 (March 1978), pp. 411-21.

ABOUT THE AUTHORS IN CHAPTER 1

Tony Smith is currently Jackson Professor of Political Science at Tufts University and is also associated with the Minda de Gunzburg Center for European Studies of Harvard University. His *The Logic of Marx's Capital: Replies to Hegelian Criticisms* was published by the State University of New York Press, Albany, a part of the SUNY Series in the Philosophy of Social Sciences.

Norman L. Hicks is Principal Economist for Latin America and the Caribbean in the Regional Office of the World Bank in Washington, D.C. He has written numerous articles on social and economic development.

Paul Streeten is Director of the World Development Institute at Boston University. Among the more than a dozen books of which he is the author is *First Things First: Meeting Basic Human Needs in Developing Countries,* from which the paper in this chapter was taken in its revised form.

CHAPTER 2

The Role of the State in Developing Areas

Introduction

SINCE 1950 THE POLITICAL MAP OF THE WORLD has undergone dramatic changes, the most noteworthy of which was the transition of many nations from non-self-governing to self-governing status. Forty-four nations at various stages of development became independent between 1950 and 1960. Others have followed. As a result, the association that existed between political status and development in the 1950s became weaker in the 1980s. The question of whether or not development lays the foundation for the transition from non-self-governing to self-governing status is no longer an issue. Instead, the effect of types of political systems on development has become more pertinent.

In the first chapter of this volume we presented data on the population and social and economic status of 208 political entities in the world as self-governing or non-self-governing by continent. We also indicated which could be classified as developing or developed on the basis of the data included in the table but made it clear that other measures might produce a slightly different arrangement. The Hicks and Streeten article included in the first chapter went into the problem of measurement and classification in great detail. Our attention will now be more sharply focused on changes in the political status of these entities between 1950 and 1990.

Table 1 in the introduction to this chapter builds upon (and summarizes) the data in Table 1 in the introduction to Chapter 1. Eighty-two entities were self-governing prior to 1950. Eleven of these countries were in Asia and included China and India, over 46 percent of the world's population. The Soviet Union, although area-wise more in Asia than Europe, was included in Europe, which contained thirty-one self-governing countries and 15 percent of the world's population. Of those eighty-two countries that were self-governing prior to 1950, only seven are still considered to be developing (the least developed thirty-seven political entities) based on the data in the introduction to Chapter 1.

What many people have forgotten is that eighty-eight non-self-governing entities received self-government between 1950 and 1990, forty-four of them (exactly half) between 1960 and 1970 as chronologically arrayed in Table 2. Forty-eight of the eighty-eight were in Africa, comprising 9.48 percent of the world's population. The ten from Asia and Southeast Asia made up 7.65 percent of the world's population. Since the twenty-six

45

Table 1. Distribution of World's Political Entities and Population by Political Status and Continent: 1950 and 1950–1990

	SELF-GOVERNING PRIOR TO 1950		NEW SELF-GOVERNING 1950–1990		NON-SELF-GOVERNING 1990		TOTAL	
	NUMBER OF ENTITIES	% OF WORLD'S POPULATION	NUMBER OF ENTITIES	% OF WORLD'S POPULATION	NUMBER OF ENTITIES	% OF WORLD'S POPULATION	NUMBER OF ENTITIES	% OF WORLD'S POPULATION
Africa	4	2.84	48	9.48	3	.12	55	12.44
Asia	11	44.16	3	2.22	2	.12	16	46.50
Asia, Southeast	3	3.04	7	5.43	—	—	10	8.47
Caribbean and Central America	9	.99	10	.06	10	.08	29	1.13
Europe	31	14.98	1	-.01	6	.01	38	14.99
Middle East	9	3.16	7	.39	1	.02	17	3.57
North America	3	6.88	—	—	2	-.01	5	6.88
Oceania	2	.38	9	.10	11	.01	22	.49
South America	10	5.58	3	.05	3	-.01	16	5.63
TOTAL	82	82.01	88	17.74	38	.36	208	100.10
% of Political Entities	39.42		42.31		18.27		100.0	

entities from the Caribbean, the Middle East, and Oceania that received independence contained only .55 percent (about one-half of one percent) of the world's population, their impact on world events comes not from their size but from their strategic location, resources, or disruptive behavior at a time when it was not overshadowed by even more disruptive actions of the great powers.

Those thirty-eight political entities that continue to be non-self-governing make up only .36 percent (about one-third of one percent) of the world's population. It is interesting that they still constitute over 18 percent of the world's political entities.

In order to present the changes that took place between 1940 and 1990, a fifty-year period of violence and rapid change throughout the world, we have chronologically arranged (see Table 2, pp. 48–49) those political entities that obtained independence during this period by population size as of 1990. A similar chronological table with each entity arranged by population size at the time of independence was also prepared. The relationship between year and independence was essentially the same.

Between 1940 and 1950 only eleven entities received self-government, of which three were ancient Middle East (Lebanon, Jordan, and Israel), all part of what westerners have called the Holy Land. Eight larger Asian countries were "born" during this period, and most had been controlled on one basis or another by Great Britain. Between 1951 and 1960, ten entities received self-government, eight of which were African and five with French "tutors."

The period from 1960 to 1970 brought self-government to forty-four political entities, as we have said, thirty-three of which were African and eighteen of which are still classified as least-developed. Most had been controlled by France or Great Britain. As the "march to freedom" progressed from Nigeria to Nauru, the population of these entities, i.e., those receiving independence, decreased from nearly 100,000,000 to less than a million. Most entities that achieved self-government between 1970 and 1980 also had populations of one and a half million or less. Although nine of the twenty-seven were African, the Middle Eastern oil emirates, United Arab Emirates, Qatar, and Bahrain were among those that received independence. This was also the period of independence for the Caribbean, Central America, and Oceania. Since 1980, seven additional entities have obtained self-government.

Research on the relationship between political status and development has produced several perspectives or models of the process of political development. Within a systemic model (Kumar, 1978) the latter is seen as an inseparable dimension of overall social change and is marked by political stability, institution building, and modernization. As a component of social change, all changes that occur in the socioeconomic strata of the society are relevant to the study of political development. This orientation is, for many, quite recent but was presented in considerable detail by others in the 1950s and 1960s, the political scientist Deutsch (1961) and Shannon (1958, 1959, and 1962), for example. Several decades ago the focus was on the traditional vs. modern dichotomy. This is no longer the case. The political status of developing nations is now analyzed in terms of a number of characteristics such as the core/periphery status, the nature of the government (democratic vs. non-democratic), the interests of the elites in the country, and the nature of political change.

There is a large literature that deals with the political bottlenecks to development in Africa. Sandbrook (1986) has described how state strength plays an important role in stimulating economic development. While in countries such as Korea and Singapore development is state supported, many African states experience state sponsored economic decline. In many African countries dictators and one party systems encourage mismanagement, corruption, and inefficiency to ensure the survival of the regimes. Over half of the African states are military and the political survival of these regimes depends upon foreign powers who support their defense sector. In the long run, these regimes become irrelevant to the social and economic security of the common people.

The effect of the state on development is complex. External and internal social and economic conditions must be considered to understand the nature of political institutions and their impact on development. Political institutions that encourage rational use of scarce resources are more likely to facilitate capital growth. The articles in this chapter examine the relationship of political institutions to economic development in its historical and theoretical context and then in a more recent empirical framework.

THE ARTICLES IN CHAPTER 2

Potekhin provides a description of the historical conditions that have influenced the political development of African states. African and Asian countries experienced prolonged periods of colonization with borders having little relationship to language or tribal boundaries. As they emerged as independent nations, new borders were drawn with continuing disregard for the socio-demographic composition of the borderlands. As a result, linguistically and

Table 2. Political Entities and Year of Self-Government 1941–1990 by Population in 1990

Year		UNDER 375,000	375,000 TO 749,000	750,000 TO 1,499,999	1,500,000 TO 2,999,999	3,000,000 TO 5,999,999	6,000,000 TO 11,999,999	12,000,000 TO 24,999,999	25,000,000 TO 49,999,999	50,000,000 TO 99,999,999	100,000,000 AND ABOVE
1941	Lebanon					X ME					
1944	Iceland	X EUR									
1945	Mongolia				X ASIA						
1946	Jordan					X ME					
	Philippines									X AS, SE	
1947	India										X ASIA
	Pakistan										X ASIA
1948	Sri Lanka							X ASIA			
	Myanmar								X AS, SE		
	Israel					X ME					
1949	Taiwan							X ASIA			
1952	Libya					X AFR					
1953	Cambodia						X AS, SE				
1954	Laos					X AS, SE					
1956	Morocco								X AFR		
	Sudan							X AFR			
	Tunesia						X AFR				
	Indonesia										X AS,SE
1957	Ghana							X AFR			
	Malaysia							X AS,SE			
1958	Guinea						X AFR				
1960	Nigeria										X AFR
	Zaire								X AFR		
	Ivory Coast						X AFR				
	Madagascar						X AFR				
	Cameroon						X AFR				
	Mali						X AFR				
	Burkina-Faso						X AFR				
	Senegal						X AFR				
	Niger						X AFR				
	Chad					X AFR					
	Benin					X AFR					
	Togo					X AFR					
	Cent. Afr. Rep.				X AFR						
	Congo				X AFR						
	Mauritania				X AFR						
	Gabon			X AFR							
	Cyprus		X ME								
1975	Mozambique							X AFR			
	Angola						X AFR				
	Comoros		X AFR								
	Cape Verde	X AFR									
	Sao Tome & Principe	X AFR									
	Vietnam									X AS,SE	
	Pappau New Guinea					X OC					
	Suriname		X SA								
1976	Seychelles	X AFR									

Year	Country	Region
197?	Djibouti	X AFR
1978	Dominica	X CCA
	Solomon Islands	X OC
	Tuvalu	X OC
1979	St. Lucia	X CCA
	St. Vincent & Gren.	X CCA
	Kiribati	X OC
1980	Vanuatu	X OC
1981	Belize	X CCA
	Antigua & Barbuda	X CCA
	Brunei	X AFR
1983	St. Kitts & Nevis	X CCA
1985	Bhutan	X ASIA
1990	Namibia	X AFR
1961	Tanzania	X AS,SE
	Sierra Leone	X AFR
	Syria	X ME
	Kuwait	X ME
1962	Algeria	X AFR
	Uganda	X AFR
	Rwanda	X AFR
	Burundi	X AFR
	Jamaica	X CCA
	Western Samoa	X OC
	Trinidad & Tobago	X SA
1963	Kenya	X AFR
	Somalia	X AFR
1964	Malawi	X AFR
	Malta	X EUR
1965	Zimbabwe	X AFR
	Zambia	X AFR
	Maldives	X ASIA
	Singapore	X ASIA
	Lesotho	X AFR
1966	Botswana	X AFR
	Barbados	X SA
1967	Yemen	X ME
1968	Mauritius	X AFR
	Swaziland	X AFR
	Equatorial Guinea	X AFR
	Nauru	X OC
1970	Gambia	X AFR
	Fiji	X OC
	Tonga	X OC
1971	Guyana	X SA
	United Arab Em.	X ME
	Bahrain	X ME
	Qatar	X ME
1973	Bahamas	X CCA
	Guinea-Bissau	X AFR
1974	Bangladesh	X ASIA
	Grenada	X CCA

KEY: AFR – Africa; ASIA – Asia; AS,SE – Southeast Asia; CCA – Caribbean and Central America; EUR – Europe; ME – Middle East; OC – Oceania; SA – South America ethnically homogeneous regions continued to be split apart and heterogeneous social groups were combined to form nations. The political development of many countries has continued to be hampered by ethnic unrest during the past decade. The current scene indicates that it will become an even greater obstacle to development in Europe and Asia.

Weede had earlier (1983) examined the effect of democracy on economic growth in developing countries but goes even further in his more recent 1988 article in this chapter.

Many articles have suggested that there is a "dynamism" associated with authoritarianism that promotes economic growth. Historically-oriented analyses of selected countries may suggest as much. However, the historical development of the East Asian "Gang of Four," South Korea, Taiwan, Singapore, and Hong Kong, described by Bruce Cummings (1984) indicates that the idea of authoritarianism as a driving force is an oversimplification. Does authoritarianism facilitate low wages and dreadful working conditions? This article, although not included in the chapter, is another of the numerous historically-oriented articles that should be helpful to those who are interested in what lies behind events of the day.

This finding has several political implications. One would be that international aid might best be channelled to authoritarian governments. Weede finds very little support for the claim of these previous studies. He concludes that democratic governments do no worse economically than repressive regimes and that repression today cannot be justified by the possibility of benefits tomorrow.

REFERENCES

Cummings, Bruce, "The Origins and Development of the Northeast Asian Political Economy: Industrial Sectors, Product Cycles, and Political Consequences," *International Organization*, Vol. 38, 1984, pp. 1–40.

Deutsch, Karl W., "Social Mobilization and Political Development," *The American Political Science Review*, LVX(3), 1961, pp. 493–514.

Kumar, Sushil, "The Concept of Political Development," *Political Studies*, 26(4), 1978, pp. 423–438.

Sandbrook, Richard, "The State and Economic Stagnation in Tropical Africa," *World Development*, 14(3), 1986, pp. 319–332.

Shannon, Lyle W., "Is Level of Development Related to Capacity for Self-Government?" *The American Journal of Economics and Sociology*, July 1958, pp. 367–381.

——, "Socioeconomic Development and Political Status," *Social Problems*, Fall 1959, pp. 157–169.

——, "Socio-Economic Development and Demographic Variables as Predictors of Political Change," *The Sociological Quarterly*, January 1962, pp. 27–42.

Weede, Erich, "The Impact of Democracy on Economic Growth: Some Evidence from Cross-National Analysis," *Kyklos*, Vol. 36, 1983, pp. 21–39.

Legacy of Colonialism in Africa

I. POTEKHIN

The discrepancy between state frontiers and ethnic boundaries is part of the burdensome legacy of colonialism in Africa. It is the cause of territorial disputes, tension in relations between states and, in some areas, threatens military clashes. Nearly all African states are faced with this problem, and the continent would be steeped in blood if they tried to settle the resulting territorial disputes by attacking their neighbours.

••••

Most African states are young. They emerged on the ruins of the colonial system of imperialism, within boundaries established by the European imperialist Powers in their division of Africa. Of the 34 African states, only five – Ethiopia, Egypt, Tunisia, Algeria and Morocco – were in existence when the imperialists began to carve up the continent. Names like the Upper Volta, Gabon, or Kamerun, appeared on the map of Africa for the first time.

This does not mean that there had been no states in tropical Africa before the arrival of the European colonialists. We find many great and small states on the map of Africa at the time of the Middle Ages in Europe. The mighty Empire of Ghana existed on the vast expanses of West Sudan from the 4th to the 13th century. It gave way to the Mali Empire, which in face of an armed Moroccan invasion in the 16th century broke up into a great many petty states. To the south of these territories, a number of Hausa states had existed from the 8th to the 10th century; somewhat later came the states of the Congo basin, etc.

I. Potekhin. From *International Affairs*, March 1964, pp. 15-20.

As was the case on other continents, the development of the African peoples was uneven; in the Middle Ages a considerable part of them continued to live under a primitive-communal society, without being organised into states. But on the whole the Africa of that period could not be considered a backward continent.

The end of the European Middle Ages coincided with a great expansion of the African slave trade. In Europe, developing capitalist relations gave a mighty boost to the productive forces and led to the formation of nationalities and nations, and the establishment of a system of bourgeois states which were, as a rule, uninational. Meanwhile, Africa was greatly retarded in its development by the slave trade, which continued for more than four centuries.

The end of the slave trade and the start of European colonialisation found Africa "atomised". The slave trade involved more than just the export of slaves. The hunt for slaves bred endless wars; the chiefs of one tribe sought to capture men from others, village attacked village, neighbour fought neighbour. *Such a state of affairs ruled out the possibility of the tribes merging into nationalities and nations and forming large centralised states.*

When the conditions for the formation of such states in some areas did eventually arise in the 1820s – 1840s their emergence was blocked by the troops of the European colonialists. Let us take a few examples. In the 1820s, Zulu Chief Shaka united all the tribes inhabiting the present province of Natal in the South African Republic and set up a United Zulu state. Bryant, a specialist in the history of the Zulus who spent many years among them, summed up the results of Shaka's activity as follows: the independent tribes ceased to be so and became part of a vast amalgam which could be called the Zulu nation headed by Shaka.[1] In the late 1820s, Shaka led a campaign into the lands of the Tembu, Pondo and Xhosa tribes, with the aim of integrating them in his state.[2] These are the very territories on which the Verwoerd Government has set up the Transkei, the first Bantustan, in furtherance of its reactionary plan for setting up phoney Bantu states.

Shaka's campaign could have led to the formation of a vast state, including, at the very least, the whole of the south-eastern coast of Africa between the Limpopo and the Great Fish River. But the British authorities in Cape Colony sent their troops against the bold African chief and drove him back. Ten years later, the Zulu state fell under the combined blows of the Anglo-Boer colonialists.

Another state was being set up in the mountains of modern Basutoland in the thirties and forties of the last century by the efforts of chief Moshesh of the Bakwena tribe. The French missionary, Casalis, who settled in Basutoland in 1833, testified that these tribes were "all looking to the one who stood for their common interests;...the idea of the tribes uniting to resist the foreigners is gaining ground among them from day to day". Casalis reported his conversation with a Bakwena chief who spoke about the need for unity. "Pointing to the windows of the room in which we sat, he added: 'If you break one window the cold will come into the house, even if the other window remains intact.'"[3] This rings very true even for our own day.

Moshesh set up a state (the present British protectorate of Basutoland) but the greater part of the territory inhabited by the Basuto tribes remained in the hands of the Anglo-Boer colonialists, and was not included in the state. The Basuto people now number 1,800,000, but only 685,000 of them live in Basutoland, the rest inhabiting the adjacent areas of South Africa.

Let us look at another part of the continent, West Africa. The south of modern Ghana, bounded by the Volta River on the east and the north and by the Tana River in the West, is inhabited by the Akan people, whose main elements are groups of the Fanti tribes on the coastal strip, and the Ashanti, who live in the hinterland to the north of them. The Ashanti tribes united in a state in the late 17th century, and in the the first half of the 19th century repeatedly tried to extend its boundaries to include the Fanti coastal strip.

This was an attempt to heal the tribal and feudal divisions among the Akan people and to set up a united national state. But the British, who were already entrenched on the coast, frustrated all these attempts, and the Akan people never really succeeded in setting up a national state, while the Ashanti state fell in the late 19th century under the blows of the British colonialists.

There are any number of similar examples in various parts of the continent. The peoples of Africa were going through the same processes of overcoming tribal and feudal divisions and the establishment of large centralised states, but these were taking place at a later period than similar processes in Europe. This natural historical development was violently disrupted by colonialist intervention.

The imperialist powers completed their final division of Africa at a rapid pace. In 1876, the territories seized by the European Powers constituted only 10 percent of the African continent and were mere bases dotting the coast. By the end of the 19th century, only two African countries – Ethiopia and Liberia – remained independent, the latter only nominally until quite recently.

Commenting on the events in the final quarter of the 19th century, Lenin said that it was in this period "that the tremendous 'boom' in colonial conquests begins, and that the struggle for the territorial division of the world becomes extraordinarily keen".[4] Britain, France, Germany, Portugal, Belgium, Italy and Spain took part in the carve-up of the African continent. By then the U.S.A. had control of Liberia.

Each Western Power was afraid to be late, and tried to seize as much territory as possible. The African peoples fought the invaders heroically, but the forces were unequal. The imperialists literally tore the continent apart. The territory of Africa is striped and checkered by artificial and arbitrary boundaries, Emperor Haile Selassie told the Conference of African Heads of State and Government of independent African countries which was held in Addis Ababa in May 1963.

The political map of Africa just before the collapse of the colonial system shows 52 territorial units with political boundaries on the continent proper, not counting the various offshore islands. Of these Britain held 20; France, 18; Portugal, 5; Spain, 4; Italy, 3; and Belgium, 2. The population of most of these territories was extremely small: 16 had a population of less than one million; and 22, from one to five million.

France got the lion's share. Her colonial possessions with the exception of a part of Somali territory, lay in a single unbroken tract from which the other imperialist plunderers tore hunks of various sizes.

Here is a picture of Africa's Atlantic seabord in the early 20th century. First, there was French Morocco, with the tiny Spanish enclave of Ifni (1,500 sq. km.; 1960, population 54,000) in its side; the Spanish Sahara, or Rio de Oro; and the French possessions of Mauritania and Senegal. Britain had secured a footing on the banks of the Gambia, which flows through Senegal, and there set up her colony of Gambia (10,400 sq. km.; 1960, population 284,000). Then came French Guinea, in which Portugal had an enclave with the offshore islands (36,100 sq. km.; 1960, population 571,000). British Sierra Leone, Liberia, the French Ivory Coast, The British Gold Coast, German Togo, British Nigeria, German Kamerun, French Gabon, in which Spain had the enclave of Rio Muni (together with the offshore islands it is part of the colony known as Spanish Guinea); Portugese Angola, cut by the Congo River corridor with a broad riparian strip belonging to Belgium; German South-West Africa, and the British Cape Colony.

Thus was Africa divided in the heyday of colonialism, and thus it remained when the present sovereign African states were set up. They have no natural geographic, economic or ethnic justification. They sprang from the balance of power among the imperialist states of Europe in the last quarter of the 19th century, and were inherited by Africa as she threw off the chains of colonialism.

A look at the physical map of West Sudan will show that the boundaries of climatic and floral zones run from the west to east: tropical forest, savannah, and arid plain. Ethnic boundaries in the main coincide with these zones, but the boundaries of all African colonies run from north to south, cutting right across ethnic bodies.

As a result, the Mandingo people, numbering several million, found themselves in Senegal, French Guinea (now the Guinean Republic), the French Sudan (now the Republic of Mali), the Ivory Coast, Gambia, Sierra Leone, Portugese Guinea and Liberia. Upon the other hand, the population of each colony, and now of each state, was a kind of ethnic sandwich: the coastal strip is inhabited by tribes or nationalities speaking languages of the same family or dialects of the same language; to the north of them live nationalities or tribes belonging to another language family, and further north, those of a third.

No modern African state is linguistically uniform. The ethnic sandwich is illustrated by the following table showing a number of neighbouring countries on the Guinean coast.[5]

Things were made much worse by the fact that the colonialists prevented the for-

Table 1. Language Groups in Countries on the Guinean Coast [6]
    (,000)

LANGUAGES	LIBERIA	IVORY COAST	UPPER VOLTA	GHANA	TOGO	DAHO-MEY
Semito-Hamitic group	—	—	10	—	—	—
Hausa group	—	1	1	35	6	2
Central Bantu group	—	710	3,036	1,372	555	420
Songhai	—	—	85	—	—	16
Western Bantu group	185	1	265	14	10	110
Mandé group	985	1,650	332	30	—	17
Guinean group	800	1,710	—	3,378	525	1,155

mation of nations in their colonies, for it was in their interest to preserve the tribal divisions. "If the system breaks down and tribal discipline disappears, native society will be resolved into its human atoms, with possibilities of universal Bolshevism and chaos. Such a break-down should be prevented at all cost,"[7] Field-Marshall Jan Smuts told future colonial officials in his lecture at Oxford University. The division of peoples into small tribal communities or groups of tribes was preserved artificially.

While preventing the formation of wider ethnic entities, the colonialists denied their peoples the right to independence on the plea that the colonies were an ethnic patchwork. An ex-governor of a French colony in Africa, Hubert Deschamps, said "political chaos" had existed before the arrival of the colonialists in Africa, and declared that, "independence in Africa may lead to disintegration into tribes – that is return to chaos".[8]

The British author of a book on Kenya argues that because "the native population consists of many quite distinctive races", it was almost impossible to unite it into a single "democratic community", so that a

colonialist withdrawal from Kenya would amount to "great shameful betrayal of the backward race".[9] Many more such statements are available but there is no sense in quoting them all because the peoples of Kenya, like those of other former colonies, have already given a practical demonstration that sovereign states can exist even within artificial boundaries.

Let us return, however, to our main topic: the question of frontiers and territorial disputes in modern Africa.

Let us examine one example taken from the northeastern part of the continent. In 1891, Britain and Italy signed a protocol demarcating their spheres of influence in Eastern Africa.[10] Under it, the line of demarcation ran from the Indian Ocean along the Juba River to the point of intersection with latitude 6° N., then on along this parallel to longitude 35° E., and farther on along this meridian to the Blue Nile. This line split the territory inhabited by the Somalis, with Britain getting that part which later became the Northern Province of the British colony of Kenya, and which is now a bone of contention between the Government of Somalia and Kenya. This line ran along territory which now is part of Ethiopia.

By the time of the Anglo-Italian Protocol, Ethiopia, surrounded by colonial plunderers on every side, had twice to take up arms to beat them back (Britain in 1867 – 1868, and Italy in 1887 – 1888). Emperor Menelik II and the people of Ethiopia were naturally concerned over their country's security. On April 10, 1891 a fortnight after the signing of the Protocol, Menelik sent a letter to the heads of a number of European states (Britain, France, Germany, Italy and Russia) in which he defined his country's frontiers, and announced his intention to restore Ethiopia within her ancient frontiers, from Khartoum in the west to Lake Nyanza (Lake Victoria) in the south.[11]

Hardly anyone knows the exact line of Ethiopia's ancient boundaries. She is the successor of Askum, which is generally recognised as one of the largest states of antiquity. It is known that in 350 A.D. the Aksumite King Esana conquered the Meroë kingdom which lay in the valley of the Nile on what is today the Republic of the Sudan. In the 8th–7th century B.C. an Ethiopian dynasty ruled Egypt (the XXV dynasty). It should be emphasised in this connection, as N.S. Krushchov said in his message to All Heads of State (Government), that, "if we were to take as a basis for solution of a boundary problem the history of several thousand years, then, evidently, everyone will agree that in many cases we would come to no solution at all".

Take another example in West Africa, namely, the boundaries of the Federal Republic of Cameroun, Kamerun, using the German name, was seized by Germany. To the east of it lay the French colonies of Gabon, and Ubangi Shari, now the central African Republic, and to the west the British colony of Nigeria. Its boundaries with the French possessions were established by the Franco-German agreements of 1885, 1894 and 1908. The first of these defined the frontier as follows: the mouth of the Campo River, along the Campo River to its intersection with longitude 10° E. (7°40' east of Paris) and further on along the parallel until its intersection with longitude 15°(12°40' east of Paris).[12]

The colonialists were not in the least concerned with what this line did to the peoples living in those parts. As a result, 750,000 of the Fang people found themselves in Kamerun and 120,000 in Gabon; 210,000 of the Maka people in Kamerun, and 10,000 in Gabon.[13] The frontier line between Kamerun and Nigeria was demarcated in a similar way. In fact, almost all

boundaries were drawn this way: a point of reference was taken on the coast and a line traced on the graticule.

During the first World War, British troops from Nigeria and French troops from Gabon and Ubangi Shari moved into Kamerun. The German colony was divided between the victorious Powers and the boundary between the British Cameroons and the French Cameroun was established along the line of meeting of their troops. Of what ethnic value was this new frontier?

The British ethnographer, Meek, who had a good knowledge of this part of Africa and had for many years been Government anthropologist in Nigeria's colonial administration gives the following picture: 1. A group of Higi tribes inhabit a number of villages on either side of the boundary line. 2. The villages of Maiha, Paka, Hudu, Ligudira, Nguli, Furkawi and Ndeekwe in the British Cameroons are inhabited by the Njai people, the bulk of whom live in French Cameroun across the border. 3. The villages of Muvi, Muda, Gela, Kwoja and others in the British Cameroons are inhabited by the Cheke people; across the border, in French Cameroun, they live in the villages of Bukura, Zakura, etc. 4. The population of the villages of Woga, Wemgo and Vizik in the British Cameroons belongs to a tribe, the bulk of which lives in French Cameroun.[14]

Let us see what the Cameroonians themselves think of this boundary.

Here is an excerpt from a petition submitted by the National Federation of the Cameroons to the U.N. Trusteeship Council on December 9, 1949. It says: No greater injustice has been perpetrated by the European rulers in respect of the Cameroonian people than the division of the Cameroons between Britain and France, which was carried out without consulting the people immediately affected by this division ... tribal and even family ties were severed by this division. ... The frontiersman has to travel dozens of miles to the headquarters of the Administering Power to obtain a passport making it legal for him to visit a relative or friends who lives across the border a few yards away from his home.

The Cameroonian people fought long and hard to reunite the two parts of their country in a single Cameroon state and were supported in their just cause by the progressive forces of the world. The part of the Cameroons which was under French rule became a sovereign state on January 1, 1960. The British Cameroons was divided into two parts, Southern and Northern Cameroons, and the latter was illegally integrated as an administrative part of Nigeria when she was still a colony.

Under a decision of the 14th U.N. General Assembly, a referendum was held in both parts of the British Cameroons on February 11 and 12, 1961, to decide either for joining Nigeria, which had by then become a sovereign state, or the Republic of Cameroun. There was a separate count in the two parts. In the southern part, where the national-liberation and unity movements were especially strong, the majority were in favor of joining Cameroun. In the northern part, the majority opted for Nigeria.

The Government of the Republic of Cameroun questioned the correctness of the returns in the northern part of the British Cameroons. On May 31, President Ahidjo issued the following statement: "On June 1, a part of the Cameroun nation will be separated from the motherland contrary to the will of her inhabitants. We express our profound regret to our brothers in the Northern Cameroons and assure them that we shall do everything to end this brutal separation.[15] On October 1, 1961, Cameroun became a Federal Republic; it filed a complaint, with the International Court of Justice at The Hague, which the latter refused to examine.[16]

To get a correct understanding of the essence of this issue of Cameroun's bound-aries, we must look at the one established between the northern part of the British Cameroons and Nigeria. The most numerous people in the northern part of the British Cameroons is the Bura (665,000), of whom 275,000 live in Nigeria, 315,000 in the northern part of the former British Cameroons, and 75,000 in the Republic of Cameroun. Another people, the Kanuri, numbering 1,994,000, is divided as follows: 1,503,000 in Nigeria, 135,000 in the northern part of the former British Cameroons, 21,000 in the Republic of Cameroun, and the rest in Niger and Chad. The Fulbe people and several other peoples are dismembered in a similar way.

It follows that integration either with Nigeria or Cameroun could not in itself settle the problems arising from the discrepancy between political frontiers and ethnic boundaries. Any arbitrary north-south line is bound to cut across the body of a people.

The boundaries between former French colonies show how the colonialists ruled Africa. I said above that these French colonies stretched in one unbroken tract. On the coast, French possessions alternated with the possessions of the other colonial Powers, which prevented France from changing boundaries arbitrarily, but she certainly made up for it in the hinterland. Here are a few examples.

The Upper Volta colony was separated from the Ivory Coast colony only in 1919 and became a separate administrative entity in the vast colonial federation known as French West Africa. The federation did not yield enough profit and during the world economic crisis of 1929–1933 it was decided to abolish the Upper Volta as an independent entity; a part of its territory went to the Ivory Coast and the rest, to French Sudan. In 1947, the Upper Volta was reconstituted as a separate colony.

In 1900, the colony of Niger was called "military district" and constituted a part of the so-called Upper Senegal-Niger area. A few years later, the district of Gao in French

Sudan (the eastern part of the present Republic of Mali) was joined to the colony, but in 1911, Gao was returned to Sudan, and in 1922 Niger became a separate colony.

The boundaries between the present Republic of Mali and Mauritania were repeatedly altered at the whim of the colonialists. The line between Morocco and Algeria was never defined at all. Only along the short stretch of 165 km. from the Mediterranean coast to Teniet-El-Sassi was the border precisely defined and fixed by the Lalla-Marina Treaty in 1845.[17]

There is no point in going over the whole history of boundaries in France's colonial possessions in Africa but it should be stressed that most of them were the product of arbitrary administrative decisions and have now become the state frontiers of young sovereign states.

The artificial lines have given rise to two acute problems: relations between neighboring states, and relations between peoples within the boundaries of a single state. The first of these is especially acute. The artificial boundaries have already led to armed clashes between Morocco and Algeria, Somalia and Ethiopia, and tensions in relations between Morocco and Mauritania, Somalia and Kenya, and Ghana and Togo; they may lead to dangerous tensions in other parts of the continent as well; they hamper the strengthening of African unity. The most serious obstacle to African unity, President Aden Abdullah Osman of the Somali Republic said at the Addis Ababa conference, was the artificial political boundaries forcibly established on vast areas of the continent by the colonial Powers.

This question of artificial boundaries has long worried political leaders in Africa. The first All-African Peoples' Conference in 1958, that is, when the disintegration of the colonial system in the tropical part of the continent was just beginning, devoted a great deal of attention to the problems of frontiers. A special resolution said that boundaries separating peoples of the same origin were unnatural and their preservation did not lead to peace. The conference urged the neighbouring Governments to co-operate in seeking a final solution of the problem of frontiers.

The conference recommended the establishment of regional federations as a radical means of eliminating this burdensome legacy of colonialism. This would undoubtedly be a great step towards the solution of this thorny problem and would have a beneficial effect on the solution of many other problems. But as N. S. Krushchov justly pointed out, "The peoples, especially if they have but recently rid themselves of foreign domination, take a very jealous attitude to their sovereign rights." The idea of federation remains unrealised.

The Charter of the Organization of African Unity adopted at a conference of African Heads of State and Government in May 1963 provides for the peaceful settlement of all outstanding issues through negotiation, mediation, reconciliation or arbitration.

••••

Armed clashes between African states may open the door to armed intervention by the imperialist Powers and may result in the loss of the independence they won at such great cost. That is why N. S. Krushchov's proposal for an international agreement which would include "an undertaking to resolve all territorial disputes exclusively by peaceful means" is of especial importance to Africa.

The problem of relations between various African peoples who find themselves within the boundaries of a single state goes beyond the framework of the present article, but I must stress that the difficulties this may produce could also give rise to armed conflicts and imperialist interference in the affairs of African countries. A successful solution of this problem could mitigate the frontier problems, and eliminate them altogether in the future. There is only one way to this goal: it is all-round help in bringing different peoples within one state closer together and merging them in one or several national entities.

A revision of existing state frontiers in Africa is, I think, possible only in some areas, but not for the continent as a whole. In West Africa, for instance, it would require the elimination of all existing states and the establishment of new ones, with boundaries running along parallels instead of meridians.

In the long run new ethnic entities, nationalities and nations, may take shape within existing state boundaries. In the light of this historical prospect, solution must be found for this other question of state system: are the states to be unitary or federal? This was the subject of a keen exchange of opinion in many countries during their transition from colonial status to sovereign state.

In spite of the ethnic patchwork in most of the countries of tropical Africa, I think, all tribes and groups of tribes could merge in single nations, in which case the establishment of unitary states would be fully justified and would promote national consolidation. But in such a big country as Nigeria, which had several national entities even in the colonial period (Yoruba, Ibo, etc.), the establishment of a unitary state could harm good relations between peoples and lead to national strife.

Whatever the solution of this question of relations between the various peoples within a single state, the *sine qua non* is free will and inadmissibility of any coercion in respect of peoples, whether great or small.

ENDNOTES

1. A. T. Bryant, *Olden Times in Zululand and Natal*, London, 1929.

2. Together with the Zulus these tribes actually constituted one people, and spoke dialects of one language known as Nguni, the name by which these tribes were known among the Tsonga, their neighbours in the north. See A. T. Bryant, *A Zulu-English Dictionary*, Moritabarg, 1905, p. 430.

3. Eugene Casalis, *Les Bassoutos*, Paris, 1860, p. 267.

4. V. I. Lenin, *Selected Works*, Vol. I, Part 2, Moscow, 1952, p. 512.

5. There is as yet no generally accepted scientific classification of African languages and the reader may find different classifications in other sources.

6. Б. В. Андрианов, Насепекце Афрцкц. Прциожекце к карте кародов, М., Иэдательсьство восточнй лит-ературы, 1960, стр. 62–63

7. J. C. Smuts, *Africa and Some World Problems*, Oxford, 1930, p. 87.

8. *New Commonwealth*, Jan. 24, 1955, p. 59.

9. Christopher J. Wilson, *One African Colony*, London, 1945, pp. 4–6.

10. Protocol between the British and Italian Governments for the demarcation of their respective spheres of influence in Eastern Africa, from the River Juba to the Blue Nile. Signed at Rome, March 24, 1891. *The Somali Peninsula: A New Light on Imperial Motives*. Published by the Information Services of the Somali Government, 1962, pp. 87–88.

11. Ibid., p. 86.

12. "Protocol Relating to the German and French Possessions on the West African Coast", Berlin, December 24, 1885. E. Hertslet, *The Map of Africa by Treaty*, Vol. II, London, 1909, p. 653.

13. Б. В. Андрианов, Населеище Афрцкц, стр. 64–66.

14. S. Ch. Meek, *Tribal Studies in Northern Nigeria*, Vol. I, London, 1931, pp. 252, 282, 293, 320.

15. *Afrique Nouvelle*, June 7, 1961.

16. *West Africa*, Dec. 14, 1963, p. 140.

17. Anthony S. Reyner, "Morocco's International Boundaries: A Factual Background". *The Journal of Modern African Studies*, Vol. I, No. 3, p. 316.

Price Distortion, Democracy or Regime Repressiveness and Economic Growth Rates among LDCs, 1973-1983

ERICH WEEDE

Theoretical Perspective

For years the Republic of Korea has enjoyed some of the highest economic growth rates in the world. South Korea is now no longer a less-developed country. Instead it is an *almost* developed country.

••••

To the extent that a gap exists between South Korea and the more economically and technologically developed societies of the world, the Republic of Korea has been reducing it with amazing speed. Among the high foreign debt countries, South Korea's performance is similarly unique. The country cannot only easily service its debtload, but reduce it – again with amazing speed.

It is often maintained that democracy cannot work, unless a country has previously surmounted poverty and achieved at least moderate, if not a high level of economic development.[1] Viewed from this perspective, it can be said that the predemocratic governments of the Republic of Korea have laid the foundations of democracy by their economic achievements. Recently, South Korea had a presidential election that almost all unbiased foreign observers regard as fair and truly democratic in process as well as in outcome. Given the country's solid economic base and the vivid interest of the Korean people in democracy, the prospects of democracy in South Korea are certainly much better than in the poor Latin American countries where American as well as indigenous pres-

sure has time after time lead to short-lived democratic experiments. Of course, it is still too early to judge the viability of South Korea's experiment with democracy. The history of Weimar Germany certainly illustrates the point that democracy can fail among economically well-developed nations.

Be that as it may, the Korean economic miracle and the recent democratic transition of South Korea provide an opportunity to reconsider the relationship between regime types and economic growth rates. In social science literature, one often finds the proposition that, at least in the LDCs, democracy and high economic growth rates are incompatible with each other. Stanislav Andreski has argued this point forcefully and well: "Democracy is compatible with rapid economic growth only in countries which already have enough resources to make heavy investment a relatively painless process. There is no case of a democratic government breaking through the vicious circle of misery and parasitism."[2]

••••

Is the incompatibility proposition true? Strangely, there are not many empirical investigations of the regime type-growth rate relationship. Except for my own previous efforts,[3] there are only four empirical studies. Adelman and Morris,[4] Huntington and Dominguez,[5] and Marsh[6] support the view that authoritarianism tends to promote economic growth, whereas democracy tends to retard it. Dick[7] contradicts these conclusions. My own previous studies did not find any support for the simple incom-

Eric Weede. Reprinted with permission from *Pacific Focus*. First published in Volume 3, No. 2, 1988, pp. 23-29.

patibility proposition, but suggested a more complicated relationship. In general, authoritarianism and democracy were unrelated to economic growth rates. Nonetheless, among a certain subset of nations – the high tax states – democracy and economic growth indeed appeared to be incompatible.[8] According to my research, democracy per se did not retard growth, but democracy combined with high levels of taxation did.

This set of findings is puzzling. Three studies claim superior economic performance lies with authoritarian or repressive regimes, two studies deny it. One study[9] questions a general relationship between democracy and reduced growth, but supports a conditional one. Moreover, all studies suffer from serious technical short-comings. Because these studies have been criticized elsewhere,[10] I shall only summarize the main points here. First, these studies often used crude classifications and simple bivariate modes of data analysis. Second, their data analysis was little informed by theory. And third, control variables in multiple regressions did not contribute to explaining cross-national growth patterns.

••••

Since price distortions themselves figure in some theoretical arguments why democracy should retard economic growth rates, the reasoning behind the proposed incompatibility between democracy and rapid economic growth needs some more discussion. In essence there are three ways by which democracy may reduce economic growth rates. First, democracy might favor consumption over investment in poor countries.[11] If you ask hungry people whether they want food or investment, they might well chose more food. By definition, democracies cannot avoid listening to the people's preferences. Second, democracy may encourage a politicized process of economic decision-making.[12] Instead of placing a new factory close to its sources of raw material or to its markets or wherever

the prospects for maximizing profits are best, vote-maximizing politicians might make their decisions dependent on expected political rather than economic returns. For example, district A might get a factory to win a marginal seat for the ruling party; whereas district B might get another factory in order to maintain the regional or tribal balance. Both of them might produce losses and require public subsidies. In a democracy political conflicts may be waged by economic means. Too much thinking about scoring electoral points might produce too little thinking about comparative advantage, economies of scale and related topics.

The third reason why democracy might retard economic development is a corollary to the one just mentioned. Where politicized decision-making results in economically unwise decisions and unviable enterprises, governments tend to interfere with markets and distort prices.[13] Subsidization of infrastructural services like power or transportation might make an otherwise unviable enterprise viable. Protection of the domestic market against foreign competition may be carried out. Capital prices might be kept artificially low. Access to foreign exchange may be biased in favor of particular industries, projects or enterprises. Whatever the details of government-sponsored price distortion, the result is less efficiency in resource allocation and, ultimately, reduced economic growth.

Among the less-developed countries the most frequent type of price distortion found is called urban bias.[14] In most LDCs, the rural agrarian population is larger and poorer than the urban population. Since urban interests are better organized than rural interests – this is true for both urban employers and urban workers – they have more political clout. This leads to some distortion of the urban-rural terms of trade for the benefit of city-dwellers. While this distortion, like other distortions, depends on government action and support, and although it reduces efficiency and equality at the same time, it seems politically unavoidable. Politicians have to respond to organized interest groups and they may neglect unorganized ones.

In my opinion, the reasoning why democracy might damage economic development sounds rather plausible. But it is opened to one serious, if not devastating countercharge. Why should we assume that authoritarian and repressive rulers do better than elected politicians? An authoritarian ruler enjoys more decision-latitude to divert money to his Swiss bank account than elected politicians do. If authoritarian rulers behave as kleptocrats[15], as occurs rather often in Africa or Latin America, it is not clear that repressive regimes would invest more than democracies. Moreover, with regard to the consumption-investment question, while one can argue that feeding the poor might contribute to the formation of human capital, pampering an authoritarian ruling class does not. Second, politicized decision-making need not be restricted to competitive democracies. Among repressive regimes the politicization process might involve the military services, bureaucratic organs, influential capitalists, religious and, in some places, tribal leaders. It is not clear, why democratic politicization should be worse than other types of politicized decision-making. Finally, price distortions are a likely result of politicized decision-making and might be used by authoritarian decision-makers to enrich themselves and their cronies. While it is easy to point to the pressures which make for unwise economic decision-making in democracies, it is almost impossible to explain why authoritarian or repressive regimes should do better.

••••

An Empirical Investigation

The dependent variables in my study are either GNP or GNP per capita (henceforth GNPC) growth rates for the 1973-1983 period.[16] Since there is no theoretically compelling reason why democracy or regime repressiveness should affect GNP or GNPC growth rates differently, I shall treat equations with either dependent variable as equivalent tests of the incompatibility proposition. Should both types of equations result in a similar verdict on the democracy – growth linkage, we can place more confidence in the findings than if they should be less robust.

Yearly data about regime characteristics were compiled from Freedom House for the period from 1973 to 1982.[17] There is one rating for political rights and another for civil rights. Political rights are the rights of ordinary citizens to influence the composition and policies of their government. Civil rights refer to the protection of individuals against arbitrary decisions by the authorities. The better the endowment of the population with civil and political rights, the more democratic the regime is. Where both sets of rights are very weak, the regime is classified as authoritarian or repressive. Yearly ratings for nations on civil and political rights are given on a seven-point scale, where 7 is the most repressive score. For purposes of this paper, I took the average of the civil and political rights scores and called the result regime repressiveness.[18]

Because some nations may have changed their political regime within the period of growth observation, effectively distorting the relationship between the democratic or repressive characteristics of the regime on the one hand and its growth rate on the other, regime stability had to be taken into account. As a result, three different scales of regime repressiveness were devised: average, stable and nearly stable.

The average regime repressiveness scale simply averaged the yearly regime repressiveness ratings. Although the problem of instability was neglected using this method, a repressiveness score for each nation was obtained. The stable regime repressiveness scale is nearly identical to the average regime repressiveness scale except that on this scale the averages were disqualified and missing values scored if a single yearly value for regime repressiveness deviated by one or more from the average for the entire 1973-1982 growth period. The nearly stable regime repressiveness scale somewhat relaxed the stability requirement of the previous scale. Deviations larger than one were tolerated, but only in the corner years of the period under observation, thus in 1973 or 1982. In contrast to the first scale, the last two scales assess only the degree of regime repressiveness of those states which have maintained their degree of democracy or repressiveness more or less throughout the period of growth observation.

From a methodological perspective, one should hope that the average repressiveness, nearly stable and stable repressiveness ratings will all show similar relationships vis-à-vis the growth rates. Then we would have confidence in the findings derived from the better sample coverage provided in the average repressiveness scale and the confidence derived from dealing with regime stability in the other two indicators. If there are major discrepancies in the findings, we at least get some warning.

According to the theoretical reasoning outlined above, price distortion may be regarded as a control variable or as an intervening variable. Because there is evidence that price distortions reduce growth rates, the relationship between regime repressiveness (or democracy) and growth should control for the effects of price distortions. Furthermore, because one of the three reasons why democratic regimes might grow more slowly than repressive regimes is the assumed proclivity of democracy toward price distortion, we should expect some causal chain running from democracy (or low degree of repression) to price distortion and, ultimately, to reduced growth rates.

Unfortunately, World Bank data[19] on price distortions cover only 31 less-developed nations – among them South Korea which is much less afflicted with them than most of the other nations in the sample. According to the World Bank, the measure "concentrates on distortions in the prices of foreign exchange, capital, labor, and infrastructural services (particularly power)." Overvalued domestic currencies, trade restrictions, negative interest rates, faster increases in real wages than in productivity, and underpricing by public utilities are the components of the index. Data availability on this measure constitutes more of a problem than that of other variables, thus the maximum sample size of this study is determined by data constraints on price distortions.

••••

Although I do not want to repeat the arguments made and published elsewhere,[20] the military participation ratio needs to be controlled, if nations which put a major part of their working age population into military service indeed perform better than others. The data source is the Third edition of the World Handbook[21] and the reference year is 1975.

Often it is argued that the economic growth rate depends on the level of economic development.[22] In global samples including developed as well as less-developed economies, we often observe a curvilinear relationship between the level of economic development or average incomes and growth rates, with countries at intermediate levels of development like Korea and Brazil doing better than either much poorer or richer countries.[23] Since my sample here does not include truly developed economies, there is little trace of a curvilinear relationship in the data presented here. Nonetheless, the linear effects of the level of economic development need to be controlled. Thus the natural logarithm of GNPC in 1975, again from the Third edition of the World Handbook of Political and Social Indicators,[24] serves as another control variable.

We are now prepared to look at the regressions of either GNP or GNPC growth rates on price distortions, the level of economic development, the military participation ratio,[25] and a variety of regime repressiveness indicators. Some of the control variables perform as expected. The higher the military participation ratio, the higher economic growth rates are. The worse the price distortions, the lower economic growth rates are. Contrary to expectations and my own previous findings, the lower the level of economic development, the higher economic growth rates are. These findings held for per capita and other growth rates. Insofar as problems of significance arise at all, they were concentrated in the smallest sample where regimes, either repressive or democratic, suffering from instability were eliminated.

With regard to the six relationships between the three indicators of regime repressiveness and economic growth rates, the results are both surprising and unambiguous at the same time. In contrast to the incompatibility proposition which claims that democracies do worse than repressive regime in fostering economic growth, we find that more repressiveness is correlated with lesser rather than higher growth rates. Although the strength of all of these relationships is rather weak and only one out of the six coefficients is of borderline significance (jumping the ten percent, but not the five percent threshold), the consistently negative relationship between regime repressiveness on the one hand and economic growth rates on the other certainly rejects the proposition that authoritarian regimes outperform democratic ones economically.

Part of the reasoning behind the incompatibility proposition, which is refuted above, makes price distortions into an intervening variable between low repressiveness (or democracy) and retarded economic growth rates. The regressions provided in Table 1 confirm the second part of this presumed causal chain. Price distortions did indeed reduce growth rates in the 1973-1983 period. However the bivariate correlations between average, nearly stable, or stable repressiveness on the one hand and price distortions on the other vary between -0.05 and -0.15. None of these correlations comes even close to the ten percent threshold of significance. If repressive regimes do not significantly succeed in avoiding or reducing price distortions, one should not be surprised to find that they entirely lack economic advantage.

The most serious shortcoming of Table 1 is that it refers to only 31 countries. The small number of observations was the price to be paid for controlling the effects of price distortions. However, in 1970 Lipton[26] published data on the urban-rural disparity in terms of output-per-person, in which he suggested that the urban-rural gap largely results from politicized decision-making and price distortions. Lipton's disparity can be regarded as a specific measure of some type of price distortion, namely price distortions favoring the cities over the countryside. If Lipton[27] is right in his view that urban bias is the "main explanation of why poor people stay poor in post-colonial LDCs," replacing the more broadly based World Bank measure of price distortions with Lipton's more specific measure makes sense. Moreover, the data base can be expanded by another 20 less-developed countries.[28]

While Lipton's disparity never affects economic growth rates as strongly in Table 2 as price distortions did in the first and fourth columns of Table 1, the effects of disparity seem less affected by the elimination of less stable regimes than the effects of price distortions in the smaller sample on which Table 1 was based. By and large, Lipton's disparity does rather well. Price distortions in favor of the cities at the expense of the countryside are clearly related to slower economic growth. The military participation ratio still has a rather strong relationship with growth rates. Probably, the smaller, but still highly signif-

Table 1. Regressions of Economic Growth 1973–83 on Price Distortion, Economic Development, Military Participation and Regime Repressiveness

	GNP GROWTH			GNPC GROWTH		
	(1)	(2)	(3)	(4)	(5)	(6)
Price distortion	-3.73	-2.94	-2.07	-3.76	-2.74	-2.24
	0.00	0.03	0.17	0.00	0.01	0.06
	-0.59	-0.43	-0.28	-0.60	-0.41	-0.30
ln GNPC	-1.46	-1.41	-1.21	-1.19	-1.21	-1.16
	0.00	0.05	0.12	0.01	0.04	0.06
	-0.46	-0.49	-0.41	-0.38	-0.43	-0.39
Military participation ratio	1.62	1.99	2.18	2.04	2.59	2.73
	0.00	0.01	0.01	0.00	0.00	0.00
	0.45	0.67	0.70	0.58	0.90	0.88
Average regime repressiveness	-0.14			-0.34		
	0.63	—	—	0.23	—	—
	-0.06			-0.15		
Nearly stable regime		-0.30			-0.54	
repressiveness	—	0.44	—	—	0.09	—
		-0.17			-0.31	
Stable regime repressiveness			-0.19			-0.50
	—	—	0.64	—	—	0.13
			-0.11			-0.29
Constant	17.76	16.44	12.91	13.72	12.35	10.80
N	31	20	18	31	20	18
Adjusted percentage of variance explained	52.6	40.9	39.4	57.9	61.7	63.9

Except for the last three rows, first cell entries are unstandardized regression coefficients, second cell entries are significance levels of regression coefficients in two-tailed tests, and third cell entries are standardized regression coefficients.

icant effects based on the larger sample deserve more credibility than the exaggerated effects based on the smaller sample above.[29] Much of the deterioration one sees in moving from Table 1 to Table 2 has to be blamed on logged GNPC values. In the larger sample, its effects are no longer significant.

Turning finally to the effects of the regime repressiveness measure, we see that none of them ever comes close to significance; the positive and negative coefficients nearly balance each other. Thus Table 2 reinforces the principal conclusions from Table 1: Democracy or regime repressiveness does not significantly affect growth rates. Price distortion in general and urban bias as a specific form of it reduce growth rates. High military participation ratios contribute to high growth rates. Only the effect of the level of economic development seems unstable.

In another attempt to expand the data base and to investigate the robustness of the uncovered relationship between democracy or regime repressiveness and economic growth rates, Lipton's own measure of the urban–rural disparity has been replaced by estimates based on World Handbook data[30] and Bradshaw's[31] formula:

$$\text{Disparity} = \frac{\text{percent non-agricultural GDP} \ | \ \text{percent agricultural GDP}}{\text{percent non-agricultural labor} \ | \ \text{percent agricultural labor}}$$

The results in Tables 2 and 3 are rather similar. Urban bias, as assessed by the

Table 2. Regressions of Economic Growth 1973–83 on Lipton's Disparity, Economic Development, Military Participation and Regime Repressiveness

	GNP GROWTH			GNPC GROWTH		
	(1)	(2)	(3)	(4)	(5)	(6)
Lipton's disparity	-0.13	-0.15	-0.15	-0.14	-0.16	-0.16
	0.01	0.00	0.00	0.01	0.00	0.00
	-0.34	-0.44	-0.49	-0.36	-0.47	-0.53
ln GNPC	-0.48	-0.76	-0.29	-0.56	-0.90	-0.46
	0.36	0.26	0.63	0.29	0.18	0.44
	-0.15	-0.23	-0.09	-0.17	-0.28	-0.15
Military participation ratio	1.56	1.74	1.66	1.50	1.69	1.56
	0.00	0.00	0.00	0.00	0.00	0.00
	0.43	0.50	0.52	0.42	0.50	0.50
Average regime repressiveness	0.12			-0.06		
	0.68	—	—	0.84	—	—
	0.06			-0.03		
Nearly stable regime repressiveness		0.06			-0.15	
	—	0.87	—	—	0.67	—
		0.03			-0.09	
Stable regime repressiveness			0.28			0.05
	—	—	0.38	—	—	0.87
			0.17			0.03
Constant	3.98	6.21	2.80	2.80	5.49	2.43
N	51	39	36	51	39	36
Adjusted percentage of variance explained	24.7	37.3	48.4	23.7	36.2	46.1

Except for the last three rows, first cell entries are unstandardized regression coefficients, second cell entries are significance levels of regression coefficients in two-tailed tests, and third cell entries are standardized regression coefficients.

urban-rural disparity, reduce the economic growth rate. The level of economic development hardly matters. High military participation ratios contribute to economic growth. And whether one examines average regime repressiveness or stable regimes only, the degree of repressiveness never significantly affects growth rates. Concerning the main topic of this paper, the results are unequivocal. Repressive regimes do not outperform democratic ones in the economic sphere of life.

Conclusions

This cross-national study could not support the proposition that repressive regimes achieve better economic growth rates than democratic ones. While none of the correlation or regression coefficients was significant at conventional thresholds, the sign of the relationship pointed as often to a democratic advantage as to a democratic disadvantage in the growth and development race. Of course, this finding is conditional on the underlying study and its limitations. In order to control for the effect of price distortions or urban bias and to find out whether price distortions mediate the relationship between regime repressiveness (or democracy) and growth, the sample had to be restricted to somewhere between 31 and 72 nations. In addition the findings refer only to the period from 1973 to 1983. Moreover, they are contingent on an almost certainly incomplete list of control

Table 3. Regressions of Economic Growth 1973–83 on Urban-Rural Disparity Economic Development, Military Participation and Regime Repressiveness

	GNP GROWTH			GNPC GROWTH		
	(1)	(2)	(3)	(4)	(5)	(6)
Urban-rural disparity	-0.09	-0.13	-0.14	-0.11	-0.16	-0.17
	0.10	0.01	0.01	0.04	0.00	0.00
	-0.20	-0.32	-0.35	-0.24	-0.39	-0.43
In GNPC	-0.80	-0.70	-0.27	-0.60	-0.48	-0.09
	0.08	0.07	0.59	0.16	0.19	0.84
	-0.27	-0.24	-0.10	-0.21	-0.16	-0.03
Military participation ratio	1.49	1.80	1.74	1.52	1.68	1.55
	0.00	0.00	0.00	0.00	0.00	0.00
	0.43	0.52	0.53	0.44	0.49	0.49
Average regime repressiveness	0.09			0.03		
	0.74	—	—	0.91	—	—
	0.05			0.02		
Nearly stable regime repressiveness	—	F-level insufficient —			F-level insufficient —	
Stable regime repressiveness			0.17			0.16
	—	—	0.54	—	—	0.55
			0.10			0.10
Constant	5.77	5.92	2.97	2.41	2.41	-0.14
N	72	51	47	72	51	47
Adjusted percentage of variance explained	16.1	33.8	40.8	19.7	37.9	45.0

Except for the last three rows, first cell entries are unstandardized regression coefficients, second cell entries are significance levels of regression coefficients in two-tailed tests, and third cell entries are standardized regression coefficients.

variables, such as price distortions or urban bias, the level of economic development, and the military participation ratio. Although the small number of observations ruled out a much longer list of control variables (at least for Table 1), my rather short list implies the possibility that the inclusion of further determinants of growth might greatly affect the results.[32]

The results produced here should be put in perspective. This paper is part of a necessary counterweight to earlier papers which seem to support the notion of faster growth under authoritarian regimes. By now there are as many studies that deny any general advantage of repressive over democratic regimes in promoting economic growth. Indeed, if one controls for variables like the level of economic development, investment, school enrollment, military participation ratios, price distortion and urban bias, thereby reducing the risk of finding spurious relationships,[33] the balance of the evidence suggests that democratic regimes do no worse economically than repressive regimes.

Empirical investigations of the relationship between regime type and economic performance have obvious political implications. If repressive regime did generally outperform democratic ones, then LDCs would face a cruel choice between promoting civil, human, and political rights today and feeding their hungry masses tomorrow, then one may be tempted to justify repression today by claiming benefits tomorrow.[34] According to the findings of this study, LDCs do *not* face this choice. Repression today cannot be justified by the presumed creation of benefits tomorrow. Whereas repression is an immediate burden, benefits are future and tend never to materialize.

The findings of this paper show that South Korea needs not fear reduced economic performance as an inevitable result of its recent moves towards democratization. The two blessings of democracy and growth appear to be available simultaneously. Furthermore, there is no reason why formerly authoritarian-ruled societies should lose their dynamic economies merely because of a democratic transition. Some dictatorships outperform others, some democracies outperform others.

ENDNOTES

1. Evidence in favor of linkage between economic development or average incomes and the viability of democracy is provided by Seymour M. Lipset, "Some Social Requisites of Democracy: Economic Development and Political Legitimacy," *American Political Science Review* 53 (1959), pp. 69–105; Deane E. Neubauer, "Some Conditions of Democracy," *American Political Science Review* 61 (1967), pp. 1002–1007. Recently this view has been challenged by Edward N. Muller, "Dependent Development, Aid Dependence on the United States, and Democratic Breakdown in the Third World," *International Studies Quarterly* 29 (1985), pp. 445–469.

2. Stanislav Andreski, *Parasitism and Subversion. The Case of Latin America* (New York: Schocken 1969), p. 266. Similar points have been made elsewhere. Peter T. Bauer, *Equality, the Third World, and Economic Delusion* (London: Weidenfeld and Nicholson 1981), pp. 187–190; Samuel P. Huntington and Joan M. Nelson, *No Easy Choice, Political Participation in Developing Countries* (Cambridge, MA: Harvard University Press), pp. 23–26; Herman Kahn, *World Economic Development* (London: Croom and Helm 1979), pp. 38–471.

3. Erich Weede, "The Impact of Democracy on Economic Growth," *Kyklos* 36, No.1 (1983), pp. 21–39; "Democracy, States Strength and Economic Growth in LDCs," *Review of International Studies* 10 (1984), pp. 297–312.

4. Irma Adelman and Cynthia T. Morris, *Society,*

Politics, and Economic Development (Baltimore: Johns Hopkins University Press, 1967).

5. Samuel Huntington and Jorge I. Dominguez, "Political Development" in Fred I. Greenstein and Nelson W. Polsby (eds.), *Handbook of Political Science, Vol. 3: Macropolitical Theory* (Reading, MA: Addison-Wesley, 1975), pp. 1–114.

6. Robert M. Marsh, "Does Democracy Hinder Economic Development in the Late-comer Developing Nations?" *Comparative Social Research* 2 (1979), pp. 215–248.

7. William G. Dick, "Authoritarian versus Nonauthoritarian Approaches to Economic Development," *Journal of Political Economy* 82 (1974), pp. 817–827.

8. These were operationally defined by 20% or more of general government revenues/GDP.

9. Since my earlier studies (quoted in note 3 above) are quite similar to each other, I count them as a single one here.

10. *Op. cit.*, note 3.

11. Stanislav Andreski, *op. cit.*, note 2, is an adherent of this view.

12. Peter Bauer, *op. cit.*, note 2, seems to subscribe to this view.

13. While there are traces of this line of thought in Huntington and Nelson as well as in Bauer, *op. cit.*, note 2, you often find the problem discussed with little reference to democracy. For example, Charles R. Frank and Richard C. Webb (eds.), *Income Distribution and Growth in Less Developed Countries* (Washington, D.C.: Brookings, 1977). Robert H. Baters, *Essays on the Political Economy of Rural Africa* (Berkeley: University of California Press, 1983).

14. See Michael Lipton, *Why Poor People Stay Poor* (London: Temple Smith, 1977); York W. Bradshaw, "Urbanization and Underdevelopment," *American Sociological Review* 52, No. 2 (1987), pp. 224–239; Erich Weede, "Urban Bias and Economic Growth in Cross-National Perspective," *International Journal of Comparative Sociology* 28 (1, 2), pp. 29–41.

15. This is Stanislav Andreski's term, *op. cit.*, note 2.

16. The data source is the *World Bank Atlas 1986* (Washington, D.C.: World Bank), pp. 6–9.

17. Raymond D. Gastil, *Freedom in the World, Political Rights and Civil Liberties 1983–84* (Westport, CT: Greenwood Press), pp. 457–465.

18. Since I apply the same operational procedure as Muller, I also use the same label for the scale, i.e., regime repressiveness. See Edward N. Muller: "Income Inequalities, Regime Repressiveness and Political Violence," *American Sociological Review* 50, pp. 47–67.

19 World Bank, *World Development Report 1983* (London and New York: Oxford University Press), pp. 57–63.

20. Erich Weede, "Rent-Seeking, Military Participation, and Economic Performance in LDCs," *Journal of Conflict Resolution* 30, No. 1 (1986), pp. 291–314 and Erich Weede and Wolfgang Jagodzinski,

"National Security, Income Inequality, and Economic Growth," *Social Science and Policy Research* 3, No. 3 (1981), pp. 91–107; Erich Weede, "Military Participation, Human Capital Formation, and Economic Growth," *Journal of Political and Military Sociology* 11, No. 1 (1983), pp. 11–19.

21. Charles L. Taylor and David A. Jodice, *World Handbook of Political and Social Indicators* 3rd edition (New Haven, CT: Yale University Press).

22. For example, Banko Horvat, "The Relationship between Rate of Growth and Level of Development," *Journal of Development Studies* 10 (1974), pp. 382–394; Simon Kuznets, *Modern Economic Growth,* 7th ed. (New Haven, CT: Yale University Press).

23. See World Bank, *World Development Report 1981* (New York and London: Oxford University Press), pp. 134–137, or Weede, *op. cit.*, note 20.

24. *Op. cit.*, note 21.

25. In order to reduce the skewness of the distribution on the military participation ratio, the variable has been replaced by its natural logarithm, i.e., $\ln(MPR+1)$.

26. *Op. cit.*, note 14, pp. 435–437.

27. Michael Lipton, "Urban Bias Revisited," *Journal of Development Studies* 20, No. 3 (1984), pp. 139–166, quote from p. 139.

28. The appendix lists the nations on which the tables are based.

29. This judgement is based on my other work on the effects of military participation ratios, *op. cit.*, note 20.

30. *Op. cit.*, note 23.

31. York W. Bradshaw, "Overurbanization and Underdevelopment in Subsaharan Africa," *Studies in Comparative International Development* 20, No. 3 (1985), pp. 74–101, especially p. 83.

32. But I did also include a squared term of logged GNPC (in order to control for a curvilinear relationship between economic development and growth rates), gross domestic investment as a percentage of GDP, and the primary school enrollment ratio. None of these additional variables improved the fit of the equations.

33. This has only been done in my own work, *op. cit.*, note 3, and here.

34. Kahn, *op. cit.*, note 2, comes rather close to this position.

Appendix: List of Nations Included in

	TABLE 1	TABLE 2	TABLE 3
Haiti		x	x
Dominican Republic		x	x
Jamaica	x	x	x
Trinidad		x	x
Mexico	x	x	x
Guatemala			x
Honduras		x	x
El Salvador		x	x
Nicaragua		x	x
Costa Rica		x	x
Panama		x	x
Colombia	x	x	x
Venezuela		x	x
Ecuador			x
Peru	x		x
Brazil	x	x	x
Bolivia	x	x	x
Paraguay		x	x
Chile	x	x	x
Argentina	x		x
Uruguay	x		x
Spain			x
Portugal			x
Yugoslavia	x		x
Greece			x
Mali			x
Senegal	x		x
Benin		x	x
Mauritania			x
Niger		x	x
Ivory Coast	x	x	x
Guinea			x
Burkina Faso		x	x
Liberia		x	x
Sierra Leone		x	x
Ghana	x		x
Togo		x	x
Cameroon	x	x	x
Nigeria	x	x	x
Central Africa			x
Congo			x
Zaire		x	x
Uganda		x	x
Kenya	x	x	x
Tanzania	x	x	x
Burundi			x
Rwanda			x
Ethiopia	x	x	x
Zambia		x	x
Zimbabwe		x	x
Malawi	x	x	x
South Africa		x	x
Madagascar		x	x
Morocco		x	x
Algeria			x

Appendix *(continued)*: **List of Nations Included in**

	TABLE 1	TABLE 2	TABLE 3
Tunisia	x	x	x
Sudan		x	x
Turkey	x	x	x
Egypt	x		x
Syria		x	x
Jordan		x	x
South Korea	x	x	x
India	x	x	x
Pakistan	x	x	x
Bangla Desh	x		
Burma		x	x
Sri Lanka	x	x	x
Nepal		x	x
Thailand	x	x	x
Malaysia	x	x	x
Singapore			x
Philippines	x	x	x
Indonesia	x	x	x

ABOUT THE AUTHORS IN CHAPTER 2

I. Potekhin was a professor in the USSR when this article was published in 1964.

Dr. Erich Weede, Professor, Forschungsinstitut fur Soziologie, Universitat zu Koln, is author of *Wirtschaft, Staat und Gesellschaft: Zur Soziologie der Kapitalistichen Markwirtschaft und der Demokratie* (Tubingen: J.C.B. Mohr, 1990) and "Ideas, Institutions and Political Culture in Western Development," *Journal of Theoretical Politics*, 2(4), 1990.

CHAPTER 3

The Process of Economic Development

Introduction

DEVELOPING NATIONS are characterized by inefficient labor, massive unemployment, and poorly diversified systems of trade. These are the consequences of a slow and long-standing process of growth which has created external and internal barriers to development. As Hauser and others have stated, the cultural and social obstacles to economic development stem from the colonial heritage and/or the indigenous cultures of people in the developing areas as well as a shortage of human and physical resources.

The literature on obstacles to development has been varied and lengthy since the end of World War II, much of it by sociologists and anthropologists (Hauser, 1959, Schnore, 1961, Nash, 1964, and Belshaw, 1964) as well as historians and economists. Although economists such as Hoselitz (1957) and Hagen (1957) led the way in turning attention to non-economic factors, more attention has been paid in the literature to traditional economic explanations with only passing references to the cultural and social aspects of development. This chapter deals with the several socioeconomic processes that create barriers to development. Two processes, the growth characteristics of economic forces and the nature of the economic distribution system, are central to this analysis.

The importance of a free market for economic development has been emphasized by Peter T. Bauer and other advocates of this perspective. The free market view conflicted, however, with that of Gunnar Myrdal and others in the 1970s, whose position was that developing world situations make central planning and market controls necessary. More recently, the free market view has resurfaced with perhaps greater popularity. Many economists see market interferences as the principal cause of underdevelopment and the governments of developing countries as large bureaucracies that kill private initiatives and absorb foreign aid to further empower the elites.

The Articles in Chapter 3

Economic development is a slow and difficult process. Some of the obstacles to development are war, mismanagement, and corruption, all of which constrain the market mechanism from being a dynamic growth mechanism contributing to development. *Landes* points out that, in addition, governments in the developing countries impose restrictions on the market. Historically, these policies are believed to have brought about extreme inequalities between nations and retarded the growth of the lesser developed. The gap between the rich and the poor has continued to widen and the more the gap widens, the harder it becomes for developing countries to catch up with developed countries. A highly stratified world creates nation behavior that makes the world an even more dangerous place in which to live. It is therefore in the interest of the developed world to actively engage in the task of helping poor countries improve their economies. This also involves the cooperation of the poor nations in an effort to ensure their own survival.

Solomon categorizes markets in the developing countries in terms of their structure. He identifies five different market structures: the personal services market, the perishable produce market, the agricultural staples market, the manufactured consumers' goods market, and the capital goods market. The most important of these is the agricultural staples market and the least important is the capital goods market. Transformation of the latter is an essential aspect of development.

Olson takes what we would call a middle-ground position, pointing out that the role of the government in developing countries should be kept to a minimum. Governments should be involved in providing for the public good, e.g., in such activities as safeguarding property rights and providing for good communication systems.

Morris and *Adelman* examine the relationship between religion and level of socioeconomic development in seventy-four non-communist, underdeveloped countries. The authors conclude that the strong positive association between religion and economic development is a result of complex historical influences associated with the early spread of commercial and industrial capitalism. This becomes apparent when the countries in their study are arrayed by the Adelman-Morris classification from Mixed Christian and Jewish to various mixtures of non-literate/literate and non-Christian/Christian groups, i.e., from countries in which the predominant religion emphasizes individual responsabilities to those that have what some term a more fatalistic world view. It is also apparent that most of the countries with a less individualistic world view and a Gross National Product of $200 per year per person are found in Africa and Asia.

A scattergram for Level of Socioeconomic Development, based on their data, indicated an ever closer relationship of development to predominant religion categories. Such provocative arrangements of the nations raise the question of the exact interplay of religion and events so as to produce diverse levels of development in some parts of the world but with more uniformly low levels of development in others. Additional scholarship on the subject might commence with an extensive analysis of existing volumes on each nation's historical development.

Other Issues in the Process of Development

The effect of foreign investment on developing countries is even more controversial than the role of foreign aid on economic development. This concern has developed as multinational corporations have moved from their headquarters in highly industrialized nations to the developing countries in search of cheap labor. Whatever their advantages in terms of fostering development, Evans and Timberlake (1980) find that foreign investments cause high levels of inequality by rapidly increasing the growth of the tertiary sector.

Other issues related to the process of economic development have also been generated by the development debate. Some focus on external barriers imposed by the developed nations, such as Japan's post-war protectionism (Weiss, 1986). Others focus on the domestic policies that retard growth, cause inequality, extravagant government spending, and corruption. These are not new issues. For over 30 years it has been apparent that industrialized agricultural systems operate in such a manner as to foster inequity, thus indicating that development along these lines may increase per capita productivity at the expense of the larger agricultural population (Grant, 1973). The controversy over basic needs vs. economic growth has probably been put to rest by research that shows that the attainment of basic needs is followed by higher rates of future growth (Hicks, 1979).

Religion or ideological motivation may also be a force for economic development within a social system (Hansen, 1963) but has often been seen as a conservative force in social action. While the post-World War II influences of the Catholic church in Latin America and the Muslim clergy in the Islamic societies were supportive of the conservatives and traditional regimes, their unquestioned support of authoritarian regimes has changed in recent decades.

A new theology called liberation theology has emerged in Latin America (Bruneau, 1985) and a new Muslim fundamentalism swept across the Muslim world in the 1980s (Ayubi, 1980). These new religious ideologies have often involved conflict between the Christian denominations and within denominations as in the Nicaraguan case (Dodson, 1986) and between the Muslim groups. These ideologies are less supportive of the traditional institutional barriers that perpetuated inequalities. In some cases religious figures have turned from theology to active roles in what they perceive as liberation movements. Liberation theology has called for improvement in the conditions of the poor through social and political revolutions while Muslim fundamentalism has attempted to eradicate economic and social inequalities by returning to the Koranic principles. While many persons have thought of the Gulf states as having the wealth of kings, this wealth has not been distributed evenly and social and income inequalities have increased over time. Fundamentalism is a growing expression of discontent against these growing inequalities and, even though the fundamentalists are not unified, it provides a new force in challenging traditional regimes. This movement confronts establishment Islam but, at the same time, establishment Islam supports the fundamentalist movement by shaping a social and religious system according to Koranic principles and by building mosques (Bill, 1984).

The many problems of development planning, procedures, and strategies cannot be covered in a volume of this size but have been extensively dealt with in other places, e.g., Sagasti (1988). Several scholars in the field of development studies have concluded that the negative effect of poor domestic policies (planning) on economic development is greater than the effect of external barriers on development.

Erich Weede, whose work was included in Chapter 2, in a more recent article (1986), attributes inequality, both domestic and international, to rent-seeking behavior. Monopolies control a giant share of the market. Domestically, groups that can organize (such as the urban dwellers) also wield power by manipulating governments to distort the market by reducing the cost of urban living. He concludes that price distortions and elite politics must be curbed in order to achieve equality and development.

REFERENCES

Ayubi, Nayih N., "The Political Revival Of Islam: The Case of Egypt," *International Journal of Middle East Studies*, Vol. 12, 1980, pp. 481–499.

Belshaw, Cyril S., "Social and Cultural Values as Related to Economic Growth," *International Social Science Journal*, 16(2), 1964, pp. 217–228.

Bill, James A., "Resurgent Islam in the Persian Gulf," *Foreign Affairs*, Vol. 63, 1984, pp. 108–127.

Bruneau, Thomas C., "Church and Politics in Brazil: The Genesis of Change," *Journal of Latin American Studies*, Vol. 17, 1985, pp. 271–293.

Dodson, Michael, "The Politics of Religion in Revolutionary Nicaragua," *Annals of the American Academy of Political and Social Science*, Vol. 483, January 1986, pp. 36–49.

Evans, Peter B. and Michael Timberlake, "Dependence, Inequality, and the Growth of the Tertiary: A Comparative Analysis of Less Developed Countries," *American Sociological Review*, Vol. 14, 1980, pp. 531–552.

Grant, James P., "Development: The End of Trickle Down?" *Foreign Policy*, Vol. 12, 1973, pp. 43–85.

Hagen, Everett E., "The Process of Economic Development," *Economic Development and Cultural Change*, 5(3), April 1957.

Hansen, Niles M., "The Protestant Ethic as a General Precondition for Economic Development," *The Canadian Journal of Economics and Political Science*, 24(4), 1963, pp. 462–474.

Hauser, Philip M., "Cultural and Personal Obstacles to Economic Development in the Less Developed Areas," *Human Organization*, 18(2), Summer 1959, pp. 78–84.

Hicks, Norman L., "Growth vs. Basic Needs: Is there a Trade-Off?" *World Development*, Vol. 7, 1979, pp. 985–994.

Hoselitz, Bert F., "Economic Growth and Development: Noneconomic Factors in Economic Growth," *The American Economic Review*, XLVII(2), May 1957, pp. 28–41.

Nash, Manning, "Social Prerequisites to Economic Growth in Latin America and Southeast Asia," *Economic Development and Cultural Change*, 12(3), April 1964, pp. 225–242.

Sagasti, Francisco, "National Development Planning in Turbulent Times: New Approaches and Criteria for Institutional Designs," *World Development*, 16(4), 1988, pp. 431–448.

Schnore, Leo F., "Social Problems in the Underdeveloped Areas: An Ecological View," *Social Problems*, 7(3), Winter 1961.

Weede, Erich, "Rent-Seeking or Dependency as Explanations of Why Poor People Stay Poor," *International Sociology*, 1(4), 1986, pp. 421–441.

Weiss, John, "Japan's Post-War Protection Policy: Some Implications for Less Developed Countries," *The Journal of Development Studies*, Vol. 22, 1986, pp. 395–406.

Why Are We So Rich and They So Poor?

DAVID S. LANDES

At the risk of tipping my hand, I shall argue that most answers to the question posed by my title fall into one of two lines of explanation. One says that we are so rich and they so poor because we are so good and they so bad; that is, we are hard-working, knowledgeable, educated, well-governed, efficacious, and productive, and they are the reverse. The other says that we are so rich and they so poor because we are so bad and they so good: we are greedy, ruthless, exploitative, aggressive, while they are weak, innocent, virtuous, abused, and vulnerable. It is not clear to me that one line of argument necessarily precludes the other, although most observers and commentators have a strong preference in the matter. What is clear is that, insofar as we may want to do something about the gap between rich and poor, each of these explanations implies a very different strategy.

I

In the beginning was Adam Smith, and he told us not to worry about economic growth: it would take care of itself. Left alone, people would sort things out, do what they did best, make appropriate choices to maximize return. The market would take care of the rest, rewarding reasons and quickness and knowledge and punishing the opposite. All of this, moreover, would work to the general advantage, augmenting the wealth of nations and leading them through a natural progression of stages from agriculture to industry to

David S. Landes. Permission to reprint granted by the author and The American Economic Association for the *American Economic Review*, originally apperared in 80(2), pp. 1–13, in 1990.

commerce. Long live the invisible hand!

To be sure, this sense of immense possibilities of improvement did not last. Malthus and Ricardo in particular developed theses of limits to growth that did much to earn for economics the name of dismal science. Malthus stressed the tendency in the long run for population to increase to and beyond the limits of subsistence, and linked this unhappy outcome to the inexorable operation of arithmetic. For Malthus, natural and man-made disasters – famine, disease, war – were the necessary winnows of a biosphere in disequilibrium. He was not a complete pessimist and recognized the small possibility that self-imposed restraint in reproduction might solve the problem, but given the force of human nature and the prevailing contraceptive technology (to say nothing of the absence of television and other compensating diversions), he was not very hopeful.

Ricardo took the stick from the other end: the limits to the extension of cultivation. As demand for food increased, he argued, ever-poorer land would be brought into cultivation, thereby raising the cost of food and wages, reducing profits, inflating rents, and crowding out other uses for capital. The motor of growth would simply seize up. The result would be the stationary state.

It would be rash to argue that Malthus and Ricardo were not an integral part of the classical paradigm. Yet their pessimistic lessons were in fact dismissed or, more precisely, were put away to be revived another day. In the heady days of nineteenth-century expansion, they seemed at best misguided. It is true that population was growing faster than before (although there were any number of misconceptions about what had passed before), but food was apparently no problem. On the contrary, the famines of yesteryear disappeared, for many reasons: new staple crops (the potato, maize); the application to the soil of outside nutrients; better rotations; virgin lands in and out of Europe; improved transport. And those regions where population pressed on subsistence were able to export their surplus eaters: the opening of frontier areas overseas seemed to provide an indefinite solution to the Malthusian dilemma.

As a result, the theme of limits to growth simply receded from the intellectual consciousness. Occasionally a lonely voice like that of Jevons was heard, warning of the exhaustion of the coal supply, but his anxieties were dismissed as parochial, especially after the technological innovations of the Second Industrial Revolution (liquid and gaseous fuels, electricity) transformed the economics of energy.

II

This "growth is natural" model (though no one would have called it that) remained for well over 100 years the dominant paradigm; so much so, that it became an invisible given of economic thought in general, and more or less disappeared as a subject of inquiry. Insofar as some nations had trouble following this path – doing what comes naturally – the explanation was as Smith himself understood it: man and politics had gotten in the way. In particular, the intervention of the state, however well meant, worked to hobble initiatives, distort the market, and cripple the invisible hand.

The same sense of complacency prevailed in regard to distribution. Clearly some nations were richer than others. But that was all right because it was in the nature of things. Of the three factors of production – land, labor, and capital – it was the first that made the difference. Land

(which included resources under the land and climate above) was unequally distributed. That was God's work. Those nations more richly endowed with resources were, other things equal (the saving proviso of economic thinking), bound to be richer. As for the other two factors, labor and capital, the assumption was that, in the long run, these were homogeneous and equal. People were rational maximizers or could like putty be shaped to the role; and money was money, subject to appropriate rates of exchange. Both factors were assumed to be mobile and/or elastic, ready to move to opportunity – labor by migration or population change, capital by transfer or saving. Even knowledge and know-how were there for the buying. Only land was different, and there, given this natural inequality, it was in the interest of each nation to make the best of what it had. Here the Ricardian analysis of comparative advantage reinforced the Smithian model and the contentment that went with it.

And the discontent. It should not be hard to understand that those countries dissatisfied with their place in the economic order were not prepared to accept this inequality as God-given, that is, to take the message of the economic pundits as gospel. The wealth of nations was also the power and place of nations. Very early on, then, indeed from the eighteenth century, those countries such as France that could reasonably presume to rival Britain understood that Britain's lead in technology was a source of potential dominance as well as wealth and sought to follow suit. To this end, they sent emissaries to look and learn; and where these were barred by business secrecy, they sent spies. They also did their best to lure British workers and mechanics, and to import machines for use but, above all, for copying. The British in turn, who clearly did not believe in the assurances of their best and brightest about the virtues and rewards of laissez-faire (at least not where exports were concerned) issued laws and decrees to bar the sale of machines and the emigration of artisans. To no avail: in the long run, like love, the market laughs at locksmiths.

Sad to relate for sound economic policy, the would-be follower countries were not content to confine themselves to importing and stealing knowledge and hardware. Unwilling as they were to allow cheaper British goods to swamp their own industries, they threw up trade barriers, and these proved more enforceable and effective than British export embargoes. (To limit fraud, for example, the French made use of outright prohibitions: that way, any piece of foreign cloth had to be contraband and was ipso facto subject to seizure.) The British, in turn, who had their own long history of protection and interference with trade, deplored this perturbation of the natural order and regretted the unwillingness of other countries to join them in a spirit of shared freedom and international cooperation.

••••

Even this was not enough. These follower countries, determined to help themselves, began taking steps to hasten the adoption of the new techniques. They recognized perfectly that backwardness had its servitudes and exigencies. They understood, for example, that they needed more capital than the British to pay for newer vintages of machinery and would have to invent institutions to mobilize these resources; and that they had to take deliberate measures to train technicians and engineers to deal with technologies they had not grown up with at the bench and in the shop.

••••

In all fairness, their ability to catch up was the result as much of preparedness as of deliberate preparation. The cultural and intellectual distance that separated them from Britain was relatively small; in some important areas of science, chemistry for example, they were well ahead; and their

own technical and commercial experience was far from trivial. They had their own history of invention and manufacture, their own specialties, their own areas and niches of market dominance. And what they did not have, they could get from one another. The history of British, then French and Belgian and Swiss, then German export of capital and enterprise in the nineteenth century would have rejoiced the heart of any practitioner of marginalist economics.

By the end of the nineteenth century, then, the Industrial Revolution that had begun in Britain had diffused throughout Europe and to European offshoots overseas. Not to Latin America, whose monied elites were long content to trade primary products for overseas manufactures (in those days, such things as wheat, meat, coffee, and copper; today much the same, plus cocaine); nor to European colonies or even free countries in Asia. Africa, especially sub-Saharan Africa, lay beyond the pale of awareness. And if one had asked a European economist about this, he would have described it once again as the natural order of things. The international division of labor had been modified by the diffusion of the new technologies. Britain was no longer the Workshop of the World, which had expanded to include Europe and the United States. But specialization remained, and no European would have seen it as anything but rational and logical, inscribed in geography and, for many in that era, in the racial endowment.

III

It should be said that the Marxian mode of analysis, which presented itself as a dissent, did not reject or seek to alter this paradigm. Marx accepted the naturalness of growth and the positive link between technical advance and wealth. His primary concern was with distribution and the class relations implicit in or derived from the ownership and use of the means of production. In this regard, he never asked questions about the reasons for or determinants of technology or the mode of production – and this for the very simple reason that he did not think there was anything to explain.

The pursuit of productivity was a perfectly natural effort to enhance relative surplus, thereby increasing the rate of exploitation and promoting the accumulation of capital. Besides, for Marx, technological innovation was typically the work of science, and as such, the gratuitous fruit of what he called social labor. The capitalist was a taker. The first to take (to innovate) generally went broke, and the legacy was culled by the jackals of enterprise. "It is, therefore, generally the most worthless and miserable sort of money-capitalists who draw the greatest profit out of all new developments of the universal labour of the human spirit and their social application through combined labour." So much for innovation.

What Marxists (as opposed to Marx and to mainstream economics) did come to concern themselves with was the distribution of wealth among nations. (One can see the analogy to his preoccupation with the question of distribution within the economy.) Specifically, they raised the issue of the economic consequences of imperialism and likened the workers of colonial countries (what we would now call Third World countries) to an external polemical exploited by the capitalists of imperial states. This analogy, which offered polemical advantages in the attack on the old order, had the additional merit for some Marxists of explaining in politically congenial terms such evidence of improvement as they were willing to concede in the standard of living of workers under capitalism. The argument ran that the capitalists were buying off their own workers and thereby buying peace at home by squeezing these outsiders – in effect, by draining their surplus. At the same time, the imperial powers were said to be deliberately holding back these subject countries, blocking their industrial development for the benefit of capitalists at home.[1]

••••

Intellectually, however, the Marxist anti-imperialist thesis remained in the master's tradition by accepting the classical paradigm; that is, it saw growth as natural and interpreted colonial poverty and backwardness as products of political exploitation and the wrong kind of interference. It assumed, therefore, that once the burden of captivity removed, the liberated colonies would be free to pursue their own destiny and develop economically as had their rich oppressors.

IV

When non-Marxist, "mainstream" economists belatedly began looking at the question of growth and development in what we now call the Third World, they were no more inclined than the Marxists to jettison the classical paradigm. The Western experience was proof of what could be done, even by countries that seemed destined to serve as sources of primary products. Canada and Australia, even Argentina and Brazil: there was no reason why a nonindustrial country could not eventually create a balanced, diversified modern economy. What it needed was good government and good markets, and resources would flow to the areas of highest return. If some of these went to industry, say, food processing, why that was just fine, especially if such movement reflected true marginal rates of return and not distorted rewards. Staples theory (vent for surplus) was invented to explain this process, and it seemed to work well with a variety of economies in time and space, ranging from Canada (furs, timber, grain, minerals), to the United States (tobacco, cotton, grain), to Sweden (timber, copper, iron ore), and perhaps eventually to Argentina (hides, grain, frozen meat), and Brazil (gold, sugar, hardwoods, coffee), and even to medieval

England (wool).

The trouble was that once the development bug bit, the poor countries of the twentieth century had no patience for the slow, selective, and contingent success of staples growth. On the contrary, they saw It as a trap. In this they were really no different from the follower countries of Europe in the eighteenth and nineteenth centuries. Like them, they were in a hurry and if anything in a greater hurry, because they were poorer and, thanks to the demonstration effect, hungrier. (If, you ask any of the follower countries today whether they are prepared to wait 100 years to catch up, they will express outrage. Yet that is how long it took Japan.) The primary producers of the twentieth century found that most staples were easily substitutable and subject to fierce competition in world markets; hence that staples income was uncertain and beyond their control. They also found, as nineteenth-century exporters had, that private revenue from staples exports enriched disproportionately a small fraction of the society, who more often than not were self-indulgent consumers of luxury imports, who preferred rents to the risks of market competition, and who therefore avoided engagement in a broader pattern of development.

At the same time, these would-be developers were not prepared to eschew industrialization, that is, to accept the apparent dictates of comparative advantage, because industry, especially heavy industry (above all, coal, steel, and machines), spelled power and Marxist theory told them that there could be no modernization without what Marx called Modern Industry. (In all this, they had the example of such earlier developers as the United States and Japan, which may have built their earliest gains on light industry but then shifted resources into such branches as metallurgy.)

The result was Third World development economics, which bore a strong resemblance to its intellectual predecessors of the nineteenth century (Hamilton, List et al.), but modified, first by Marxian notions of the primacy, indeed the indispensability, of industry; of the superior if not sole legitimacy of government or collective ownership of the means of production, including peasant land; and of the importance of state planning and intervention; and second, by post-Marxian concepts and grievances of international exploitation and the penalties of inequality.

V
••••

The experience of the twentieth century, and especially of the period since World War II, is that development is neither natural nor easy. We have seen that, on the basis of the conventional wisdom, whether classical, neoclassical, or Marxist, it ought to be. Certainly the incentive is there: the gap between what is and what can be is enormous. And the opportunity. Once (here fill in the appropriate condition) the burden of colonialism is lifted, the government sets growth as the objective, the plans are drawn up, and the requisite resources are mobilized, growth and development should follow as the night the day. Only it has not.

To be sure, it is not hard to find grounds for encouragement. There has been staple growth of the classical variety in some of the oil-producing countries, specifically those with large deposits and small populations. More important, there are some instances of incipient but highly promising industrial growth. The best examples here are the East Asian little dragons (Hong Kong, Singapore Taiwan, and Korea), but coming up behind are lesser beasties such as Thailand and perhaps Malaysia, and one should not overlook those awakening giants such as Brazil, India, or Turkey that have now passed from the Third to the Second-and-a-half

World (or is it the First-and-a-half World?). Any repeated visitor to these countries can cite gains in the material standard of life, in the buildup of social overhead capital, in the provision of health care and welfare, in life expectancy.

But these achievements are not unmixed or unambiguous. Things may be better than they were, but they leave much to be desired, especially in those countries that are still in between. Just look at the morbidity data; or better yet, the people and the way they live. Even the showcase examples give cause for anxiety. Take the new rich. Staples booms in wasting assets such as oil are of their nature ephemeral. Even while they last, they bring in windfall wealth that may or may not be a boon, depending on what one does with it.

••••

As for the instances of industrial growth, which as often cited as harbingers, they vary widely in character and scope. The evidence shows that industrialization has been a heavy and not always support- able strain on resources; that it has been a source of serious disamenities (pollution in particular, nowhere worse than in the Second and Third Worlds) that do not show in the income data; that it has pro- duced societies that are deeply split between old standards and new, old ways and new (in some respect, things seem to get worse before they get better).

Much of this development, moreover, is externally rather than internally generated. It is based on a marriage of foreign capital and know-how (multinationals, joint ven- tures, offshore production) with cheap domestic labor. To be sure, capital has always been drawn to cheap labor, and much of early European industrial devel- opment can be accounted for in similar fashion. (This was particularly true of the diffusion of new technologies.) But such imports must be precarious and superficial until they are absorbed by the host society and converted into indigenous initiatives.

Otherwise they remain a kind of industrial plantation.

Finally, we should note that the growth experience is still relatively short, and this in countries where the fragility of political structures is an invitation to reversal. We should be cautious, then, in our conclu- sions.

And these are the winners. Against them one can cite a large number of exam- ples of countries that are not keeping up, that are losing ground relatively and often absolutely, and this in spite of large inflows of capital and other resources. Some of this is obviously the consequence of man-made affliction: civil war; intertribal massacre; political mismanagement. But much of it is deeper and more enduring than the haz- ards of events. Sub-Saharan Africa and parts of Asia live day in and out with hunger, disease, and natural disaster so constant as to be endemic. Africa in partic- ular, the region of most rapid population increase, is a heart-breaker, and there is as much reason to believe that its people are losing the battle for improvement as that they are winning it.[2]

VI

So the picture is mixed; to the point where it is now a commonplace to note that the Third World is a heterogeneous congeries of nations, rich and poor. Some of the dis- tinction is based on the localized distribu- tion of windfall staples wealth; some of it on real differences in the ability to absorb new technologies and grow. Whatever the source of the distinctions, one has the sense of a conceptual unity in course of dissolu- tion. It is coming apart. Some countries arc being "promoted," as it were, into the ranks of the advanced, industrial nations. Others are trying very hard and are still in midstream. Still others are for the moment getting nowhere.

••••

What are the implications? Is it merely a question of optimists versus pessimists?

The question needs to be reformulated. We are talking about late development, of semi-industrial and preindustrial nations that want to catch up with a process of growth that began over 200 years ago. Well, does it make any difference to be a late developer? Or, to put it differently, does it pay to be late? (One proviso by way of circumscribing the question: I shall not concern myself with the losses in potential income incurred by lateness, i.e., by the difference between what has been and what might have been. Instead, I shall focus on the character and extent of the gains that follow on the inception of the development process.)

The conventional wisdom has always been that lateness is an advantage; that the gap between what is and what can be is a tremendous opportunity; that the follower country can profit from the experience and knowledge of its predecessors and avoid their mistakes; and that by mobilizing resources and allocating them energetically to the right uses, it will in fact grow faster than its forerunners. This was the argument made by Alexander Gerschenkron in his seminal articles of 1951-52 on "Economic Backwardness in Historical Perspective." Gerschenkron based his analysis on the European experience, on the comparison and contrast among Britain, Germany, and Russia in particular, and offered a "spurt" model of late growth.[3] He noted, to be sure, that such spurts, when driven from above (i.e., by the state), could impose a heavy burden on the population, to the point of exhaustion; hence the Russian pattern of alternating surges and collapses. But given good judgment and management, there was no reason why a follower country could not catch and even surpass its predecessors.

(And yet the European experience already gave grounds for pause. Russian growth was spotty, with large areas of persistent backwardness; and the experience of a socialist economy has only hardened this unbalanced pattern. Eastern Europe in general, in spite of advanced regions and local centers, was and remains a mixed story. The same has been true for Mediterranean Europe, where the more successful industrializers such as Italy suffered and indeed continues to suffer from dualistic contrast in performance – and this in spite of extensive and deliberate efforts to promote the development of backward regions. We have in effect a pattern of incomplete modernization that has since become a commonplace.)

••••

On the other hand, the moderate success of others and failure of still more have led some to argue that lateness is now a growing handicap. The reasons for such a judgment are not far to seek:

1) The size of the gap. It is now a gulf and keeps widening. By the older paradigm, that only means bigger potential gains to change. On the other hand, the threshold costs are higher. Capital is not the biggest problem. Knowledge and know-how are more esoteric, even opaque, hence harder to come by. Two possibilities present themselves: (a) hire people; (b) train one's own people. The former is expensive, and the best usually have better things to do. So one makes do with less than best (LTB), which may be less than enough. The second is also expensive, not so much for the cost of training as for the permanent loss of talent. How ya gonna keep 'em down on the farm after they seen Paree, London, Cambridge, Berkeley, or what have you? Again, the best are the ones with the least incentive to return; again, one can settle for LTB, which may or may not be enough.

2) Staples are not what they used to be. The same technology that has produced this inequality of nations works to limit the market power of primary products by making them more substitutable. Take sugar, a commodity of unusual potency in

economic history. There was a time, in the eighteenth century, when this luxury-become-necessity could provide the basis of French commercial prosperity and of the industrial growth of the western half of the country: fleets, ports, *fabriques*, all hanging on the cane crop of one island, Saint-Domingue. By the beginning of the nineteenth century, however, that was over: France had been cut off by war from overseas supplies and had learned to make sugar from beets; while other centers of cane cultivation had developed to replace what was now Haiti, lost to sugar and to France as a result of the world's first successful slave revolt.

One could tell similar stories about rubber, food crops, even rare minerals.

3) Lateness makes for bad politics. It creates uncomfortable pressures, which conduce to poor answers. This has always been true, but at one time these pressures were the exclusive concern of governing elites: the ordinary Frenchman of the late eighteenth or early nineteenth century was not aware of and could not have cared less about industrial and technological changes across the Channel. In the twentieth century, however, awareness has been enhanced by the demonstration effect, itself much reinforced by new media of communication; and political urgency has been aggravated by ideological conviction and commitment. Governments are expected to deliver, to their own members to begin with, to the populace thereafter.

Hence great haste, with much waste. Lateness is the parent of bad government. Economists have been quick to point to the adverse effects of bad government on development (indeed, some would call it the primary cause of development failure), but have said little about the sources of bad government itself, which they see as properly the matter of other disciplines. Yet bad government – or for that matter, any kind of government, good, bad, or indifferent – is not unrelated to economics.

(To be sure, some of it is: most of the Third World countries are new, inexperienced excolonial nations, inheritors of irrational, accidental boundaries and of immemorial tribal or ethnic hostilities; also of authoritarian imperial structures that often flout older tribal patterns of discussion and consensus and facilitate obstinate error and abuse; heirs also of capital installations that they were not always in a position to maintain [there is nothing so demoralizing and demeaning as decay and abandonment]. So historical accident has played a role.) (Compare George Ayittey, 1989.)

Government is clearly part of a larger social system that includes economic structures and relations. (Marxists, indeed, would go farther and say that it is the creature of class relations and interests.) Good government is not there for the wanting, or even for the knowing. It is not an act of will or fiat. It will not come about because someone appoints good counselors, even good economists – who may well be our students and who, like us, may or may not agree. (And even if they did, most politicians would say that business and the economy are too important to be left to the economists.) It takes time to create an effective, functional bureaucracy; also to establish a commitment to a larger national identity and purpose. European countries took centuries to do this; new nations have tried to establish the whole panoply of institutions in a matter of years or decades. It is no accident that the success stories of East Asia are of relatively homogeneous societies with a strong sense of historical and cultural identity.

For new nations, moreover, the process has been immensely complicated by the grievances stored up over years of subordination and humiliation; by egalitarian ideologies that deprecate private success while justifying public privilege; by the impatience to set things right and catch up ... quickly, NOW; by the choice of the fast and meretricious over the slow and steady; by the ubiquity of the state, which distorts the reward pattern and makes it easier to get rich by politics than by industry, by connections than by performance; and by the interplay or private, rent-seeking interests that are only too quick to exploit these possibilities.

4) Misdiagnosis and mistreatment. There's nothing that succeeds like success, and conversely. Lateness ideologized is like a malady that invites, even seeks out, bad therapy.

When Gerschenkron wrote about this problem, he offered the undisprovable thesis that nations would leap the gap between backwardness and development when they were ready. Today, by one definition, every nation is ready; and when things do not work out, they do not console themselves with the thought that they have been untimely. Rather they look for villains, whom they characteristically find outside themselves. (They can hardly be expected to blame themselves; besides, it would be morally wrong to blame the victim.)[4]

I need not go into the detail of these alleged sources of failure. They are familiar to all of us: colonialism or neocolonialism, unequal trade, underdevelopment (a noun derived from a newly invented transitive verb, to underdevelop), peripherality, dependency. There is some truth in all of these and with will and good will, there is much that can be done to eliminate or mitigate their effects. On the other hand, they are more the symptoms than the explanation of development failure. There are few of these alleged sources of backwardness, for example, that do not apply to Korea or Taiwan, both formerly Japanese colonies, both deliberately pastoralized by their rulers. And many of them apply to the British colonies in North America, even to the early American republic, and to Meiji Japan. All of them reflect circumstances of inequality that yield to sover-

eignty and to performance: make a better, cheaper radio, TV, watch, etc., and the world will be happy to do business with you on equal terms.

What's more, even if this bill of indictment were true, it would not pay to dwell on it. It leads to self-pity, myopia, and counter-productive policies. At the extreme, it would suggest complete delinking and economic isolation. Also, there is nothing so self-defeating as the transfer of responsibility and blame to others, if only because there are limits to altruism. After an initial surge of guilt, generosity wanes; it is a wasting asset. Indeed, the greater the benefit to others of unequal arrangements, the less likely they are to surrender them. The market, like God, best helps those who help themselves.

5) Cultural factors. Values are an especially thorny problem for would-be developers, partly because, insofar as they are an impediment to growth, they are strongest in "traditional" societies; and partly because they tend to be reinforced by economic failure. To be sure, economists do not like these. They lie outside the purview of the discipline, and they always seem to get in the way. (Historians, on the other hand, to say nothing of sociologists, have often cited them as explanations for exceptional economic performance in earlier periods [compare Max Weber and *The Protestant Ethic*]; or for Japanese achievements today.) They are often rejected as implicitly immutable, almost congenital (hence racist), although there is nothing to that effect in the argument. Or they are rejected for just the reverse, as epiphenomena that will yield easily to interest (in both senses of the word) and reason.

The truth, as so often, lies somewhere in between. Values and attitudes do change, but slowly, and their force and influence vary with circumstances. Many religious values operate, for instance, to impede the mobility and openness conducive to efficient allocation of resources and rational economic behavior. Worse yet, insofar as economic development entails changes in social structures and relations, vested cultural values, like vested material interests (they are in effect interests), can become a potent force for resistance, to the point of overturning governments and reversing the course of development.

••••

VII

In the meantime, the struggle to pass from preindustrial to industrial, from "backward" to "advanced," goes on. By that I do not simply mean growth in income per head. That would be too easy. "Intensive growth," as it is sometimes called, can come about because nature has been kind, because new crops are more productive than old, because new land (including resources) becomes available, because relative prices change, because of outside developments and a free ride. But sustained growth is not possible without technological progress and gains in productivity. And that, history tells us, requires sooner or later the creation or assimilation of new kinds of knowledge and organization, which in turn depends on transformations within the society. External, enclave development will not do.

Such transformations require not only the absorption and adoption of new ways, but also, for many societies, the creation and acceptance of a new ethic of personal behavior. New ways demand and make new people. Time consciousness must become time discipline; the organization and character of work, the very relations of person to person, are transformed. These changes do not come easy. Historically they were often achieved by building on the more docile members of the society, the ones who could not say no, that is, on women and children, and that way creating a new labor force over a period of generations. This is still true. They have been

most readily effected in those societies, like the Japanese, which had already developed appropriate time and work values before the coming of modern industry. Selection, then, is not a matter of chance or need or desire.

So the transition to modernity is necessarily a case-by-case process. Many try but few are chosen. Insofar as the transition is adventitious, superficial, or forced, moreover, it proves to be discouragingly fragile, at least in the early stages. (This is especially true of windfall staples growth: witness the experience of Cote-d'Ivoire.) Small wonder that development is full of mistakes and disappointments, or that what seems like a break-through often slows or aborts.

Which raises another question: if promotion is slow and if the gap between rich and poor keeps growing, especially for the hind-most, and with it the obstacles, do we not have to change the paradigm? Are we not in fact facing, not a general and inevitable life process of maturation, however protracted, but rather a partially stochastic process of selection with diminishing chances of success? As time passes those most qualified make it; but those who do not make it lose ground and become less and less qualified. They are the hard cases. They may, like the poor of the Bible, always be with us.

Where does that leave us? We are not going to give up, for that would go against one of the deepest values of our civilization: the Faustian urge, indeed the need, to shape our destiny, and everyone else's. For their good, of course. As for those who are not moved by altruism, they should recognize that it is not in their interest to allow extreme differences to subsist. We want to, we also have to improve the condition of the laggards. In the long run, of course, it is cheaper to do so by helping them to help themselves, but in the meantime, we must do for them. (As the old proverb puts it, it is better to teach a man to fish than to give him fish; but the quickest way to put fish on the table is to put it there.) They may not catch up, they may continue to lag, but they can become much better off. So long as we do not succeed in this, as now for example, we shall find that they export violence and people (i.e., their substance) instead of good and services.

There is a popular children's book called *The Phantom Toll Booth* (by Norton Juster) that tells the story of a young boy engaged in a heroic quest. Before he sets out, he is told that there is one thing he ought to know, but it were best he be told after his return. So the lad sets forth, accompanied by friends, and after terrible dangers returns with mission accomplished. At which point he is told what he should have known all along, that the task was impossible.

We have the task. It is ours as well as theirs. It is impossible. But we must act as if it were not, for the reward is in the trying. They must too, for more is better than less. It may no longer pay to be late, but better late than never.

ENDNOTES

1. This is a condensed, homogenized version of a diverse literature. Marxist critiques of imperialism range from simple land-drain arguments – it is a system or growing the cash crops and emptying the mines with cheap, forced or semiforced labor of a kind one could not employ at home – to conspiracy theories about capitalist unwillingness to help colonies develop industrially in competition with the mother country. For a guide to some of this diversity, much of which takes the form of rediscovering old news, see Keith Griffin and John Gurley (1985). Note, of course, that this criticism of imperialism was system-specific; that is, it applied only to capitalist or bourgeois government, not to socialist regimes. (Most Marxists would describe socialist imperialism as a contradiction in terms.) In this regard, the Marxists, as collectivists, were far closer to the Tories than to classical economic liberals. Compare S. M. Lipset (1988, p. 30).

2. The region of most rapid population increase: the implications for growth and development are not necessarily negative. Population is like raw capital: its value depends on what one does with it. Used well, it can be an asset, an incentive to investment, the human material of industrialization. Used badly it can be a crushing burden, a seedbed of emergencies and hasty improvisation, a source of political instability. It would be unwise to prejudge these matters, but the historical experience does tell a very different story for Europe (and Japan, for that matter), where rates of growth were never so high (a third perhaps), where the birth rate in the most advanced countries varied in response to the demand for labor (i.e., jobs chased people); and where the areas of population surplus were able easily and legally to export people elsewhere. Europe effected its population transition during its industrial transformation. The Third World today is growing more populous in advance of development, and most rapidly in the regions of slowest development.

3. Although himself politically conservative, Gerschenkron's spurt model has close similarities to the Soviet economic plans of the 1920s and 1930s and their ideological premises. Compare Stalin's emphasis on high-speed growth, on "overtaking and outstripping the advanced capitalist countries." "...the tempo must not be reduced. On the contrary, we must increase it. ..." The same for the 20th National Congress of the CPSU in 1961: "...efforts must be made to augment the industrial output by 2.5 times in the next decade and surpass the level of the industrial development of the United States." The same for Communist China, which aimed at "catching up with and surpassing Britain in the output of steel and other major industrial products" in 15 years or less. Similar parallels between the Soviet emphasis on heavy industry and the Gerschenkron model. (See the article by Dong, pp. 235-36.)

4. This pattern of explanation goes back to the earliest industrialization efforts of what we now call Third World countries. I'm thinking, for example, of what was surely the first push of its kind, that of Mohammed Ali in Egypt in the period from about 1820 to 1848. Mohammed Ali was determined to bring Egypt into the modern world by effecting an industrial revolution. To this end he hired foreign specialists, imported equipment that he had copied as well as installed, established schools to train a cadre of technicians and professionals – the whole project conceived in the largest terms on the basis of European models. But the society was not ready for this leap. Mohammed Ali was unwilling to pay the necessary premiums to attract voluntary wage labor. (The Europeans, facing similar reticence, found the answer in using women and children, the people who could not say no; but a Muslim society was severely limited in this regard.) He began by recruiting slaves and, when too many of these died, moved on to corvée labor. Forced labor is unhappy labor, and soon sabotage became a serious drain on productive capacity;

the favorite instrument of complaint was arson. Machines lay idle for want of maintenance and lack of parts. The whole system was breaking down by the time Britain, in 1839, succeeded in defeating Mohammed Ali's military ambitions and imposed a trade regime that limited Egypt to a modest revenue tariff. No protection. Subsequent generations of Egyptian historians have wanted to place the blame for the Mohammed Ali experiment on this constraint.

REFERENCES

Ayittey, George B.N., "The Political Economy of Reform in Africa," *Journal of Economic Growth*, Spring 1989, 3, 4-17.

Bober, M. M., *Karl Marx's Interpretation of History*, 1st ed., 1927; Cambridge: Harvard University, 2nd ed., rev., 1968.

Craft, N.F.R., *British Economic Growth during the Industrial Revolution*, Oxford: Clarendon, 1985.

Dong, Fureng, "Development Theory and Socialist Developing Economies," in Gustav Ranis and T. Paul Schultz, eds., *The State of Development Economics: Progress and Perspective*. Oxford: Basil Blackwell, 1988.

Evans, F.T., "Wood since the Industrial Revolution: A Strategic Retreat?," *History of Technology*, 1982, 7, 37-56.

Fagerberg, Jan, "Why Growth Rates Differ," in Giovanni Dosi et al., eds., *Technical Change and Economic Theory*, London and New York: Pinter, 1988.

Greenberg, Dolores, "Reassessing the Power Patterns of the Industrial Revolution: An Anglo-American Comparison," *American Historical Review*, December 1982, 87, 1237-61.

Griffin, Keith and Gurley, John, "Radical Analyses of Imperialism, the Third World, and the Transition to Socialism: A Survey Article," *Journal of Economic Literature*, September 1985, 23, 1089-1143.

Jones, Eric L., *Growth Recurring: Economic Change in World History*, Oxford: Clarendon, 1988.

Lipset, S. M., "Neoconservatism: Myth and Reality," *Society*, July-August 1988, 29-37.

McCloskey, Donald, "The Storied Character of Economics." *Tijdschrift voor Geschiedenis*, 1988, 101, 643-54.

Marx, Karl, *Capital: A Critique of Political Economy*, Vol. III, F. Engels, ed., Moscow: Foreign Languages Publishing, 1894/1962.

O'Brien, Patrick K., Keyder, Caglar, *Economic Growth in Britain and France 1780–1914: Two Paths to the Twentieth Century*. London: Allen & Unwin, 1978.

Patel, Surendra J., " Rates of Industrial Growth in the Last Century, 1860-1958," *Economic Development and Cultural Change*, April 1962, 9, 316-30.

Roehl, Richard, "French Industrialization: A Reconsideration," *Explorations in Economic History*, July 1976, 13, 233-81.

_____, "British and European Industrialization: Pathfinder Pursued?" *Review* (Fernand Braudel Center, SUNY-Binghamton), 1983, 6, 455-73.

Smith, Adam, *An Inquiry into the Nature and Causes of the Wealth of Nations,* 1st ed., 1776, New York: Modern Library, 1937.

Smith, Thomas, "Peasant Time and Factory Time in Japan," *Past & Present*, May 1986, 111, 165-97.

Wrigley, E.A., *People, Cities and Wealth: The Transformation of Traditional Society*. Oxford: Basil Blackwell, 1987.

The Structure of the Market in Undeveloped Economies

MORTON R. SOLOMON

This paper attempts an examination of the market structure in the economically backward countries of the world today.

The dearth of written material on the market structure of undeveloped economies has compelled the writer to draw primarily upon his personal observations over a period of four years in the Middle East, but he has been encouraged and justified by two considerations into extending his analysis to the entire belt of densely populated undeveloped economies stretching from Southeastern Europe through the Middle East and India to China. First the few empirical studies of the economies of Southeastern Europe, India, and China yield data regarding the size and organization of production units (both agricultural and nonagricultural), customary marketing practices, distributive margins, spatial and temporal price differentials, etc., which are remarkably similar to the writer's observations in the Middle East, and therefore a theoretical analysis of market structure based on these observations appears to be valid for this entire geographical belt. Second, a preliminary theoretical consideration of the over-all problem makes one realize that the organization and structure of the market are probably a function of certain economic variables like the size of the market, the nature of the goods, the size of the production units, the degree of specialization, etc. And these are the variables which show a basically similar pattern throughout the densely populated undeveloped economies, because they, in turn, are the products of a certain stage of economic develop-

Morton R. Solomon. Previously published in *The Quarterly Journal of Economics*, Vol. 62, pp. 519-537, 1948.

ment and technological advancement and relative factor supplies expressing itself in a production function varying little throughout this area. Expressed more concretely, it is the writer's belief that a definite type of market structure is to be found throughout this area, whose basic uniformity is eventually ascribable to a certain relationship of factor supplies – i.e. low capital *and* low natural resources per capita. In contrast, those undeveloped economies possessing large natural resources per capita – the sparsely populated undeveloped economies – have a market structure distinctly different, and are not treated in this paper. The sparsely populated undeveloped economies are characterized by specialized plantation farming, primarily for export to industrialized economies, with very little development of industry, urban life or local markets, while the densely populated economies – the subject matter of this study – reveal a peasant system of agriculture, nonspecialized farming, a large measure of foreign trade among themselves, and a considerable development of secondary industry, town and local markets.

The Personal Services Market

The problem of market structure is, in the first instance, a problem in classification. Sharply different marketing methods and market structures suggest the following five-fold classification for goods and services: personal services, perishable produce, agricultural staples, manufactured consumer's goods, and capital goods.

The personal services market occupies a much more minor role in an undeveloped than in an advanced economy. In rural areas it is largely non-existent, for each peasant family, through a household division of labor, itself satisfies in a crude fashion the bulk of its limited service requirements. The remaining and usually more skilled requirements (such as the blacksmith's and religious elder's services) that cannot be rendered within the family grouping are supplied within the village grouping. In these cases, the supplier of the service has a nominal monopoly within the village; other members of the village may be equally capable, but tradition and custom tend to dictate the choice of a particular person for each type of service. However, our village monopolist can rarely maximize his earnings, since just as tradition and custom give him his monopoly, so do they limit his fees to a narrow range. This conventional limitation of fees does not exclude, however, a certain amount of price discrimination based more upon the social than upon the financial status of the buyer.

In the towns aud cities the subsistence existence of the bulk of the population does not permit them to resort to the personal services market; their needs are either met within the family, or very infrequently by charitable institutions, or – the usual case – ignored. Only the members of the middle and upper classes – probably less than 10 per cent of the population – resort to the organized personal services market. This market typically consists of a few artisans who occupy small shops but who also frequently work in the homes of their more important customers. They are often organized in some sort of guild or association, but the functions and strengths of these vary enormously. It can be safely stated, however, that these associations are just as much concerned, if not more so, with political lobbying on a municipal level to protect themselves against what they consider excessive police aud tax burdens as they are with wage and price policy.

The degree or generality of collusive wage and price fixing is unknown; that there is a remarkable uniformity of wages and prices in each local area is undeniable, but it may be explainable on two other grounds: (1) a strong wage and price rigidity through time is the tradition of this market; it encourages price conformity among suppliers, which in turn tends to reenforce the tradition-created rather than policy-created rigidity; (2) a preference for non-price forms of competition that is only natural in personal service oligopolies, and that is also present in the more developed economies of the world. However, the non-price forms of competition among personal service suppliers typical in undeveloped economies are not as much manifested in giving additional or better quality services as they are in creating psychological relationships with customers which will attract and maintain their patronage. An illustration of this phenomenon is the very prevalent custom of competitive flattery of one's patrons, an understandable tradition in a society where personal status in the local community is all-important. Price discrimination similar to that in the rural areas is prevalent in the towns, although it should be noted that in the towns it is even more of a conventional price discrimination than that which arises from a monopolistic position. Entry into the personal services trades is very difficult for outsiders, since the business units are invariably small and, therefore, selection of apprentices tends to be confined to family circles.

The structural rigidity and price inflexibility of the personal services market is reenforced by a surprising degree of government regulation. Government, on the municipal level, generally exercises more control over the personal services market than over any other type of market. Licensing, excise taxation, and even price fixing by government are prevalent in this sector of the economy to an extent unapproached in the other sectors. Government price fixing in this area is not an emergency device to combat inflationary pressures, but a permanent practice which seems to serve no real function, since the municipal price-list simply recognizes the *de facto* situation when the infrequent changes do occur.

The Perishable Produce Market

The perishable produce market (fruits,vegetables, meat and dairy products) also occupies a considerably less important place in the undeveloped than in the developed economy. Perishable produce farming is rarely specialized in the undeveloped economy; typically it represents a part, usually a small part, of each peasant farmer's total output. Produce, unlike cereals and other staples, belongs entirely to the peasant, since even tenant peasants do not share their perishable produce production with landlords. On a rough average, less than half is consumed by the peasant producer, even though his output is very small; the bulk is marketed, since perishable produce is considered a semi-luxury. Marketing is direct by the peasant farmer to the retailer, or to the final consumer in his home or at the market-place. There is no wholesaling or jobber class in perishable produce. Nor is there any speculation in this market for the same reason-the impossibility of inventory holding due to the lack of suitable storage facilities.

Prices are determined by individual bargaining, whether with the retailer or the consumer; they are extremely flexible, since the daily supply is inelastic, the farmer being unwilling to cart his produce back to the farm. Seasonal price variations are, of course, very wide, owing to the lack of storage facilities and feasible transportation from climatically different areas. These individual bargaining transactions between peasant and retailer, or peasant and consumer, approach the nature of isolated exchange, with the exact location of each transaction's price depending upon the two parties' indifference curves and bluffing abilities; but this is only within a narrow range limited by a knowledge of probable competitive offers if either party waits a while.

Analysis of the elasticity conditions of demand and supply in this market give these results. The fairly elastic nature of consumer demand schedules and the slight tendency of the peasant producers to vary somewhat their own consumption of produce inversely to price are price stabilizing factors; but the purely local nature of the market, which prevents supply movements to and from other areas in response to price, the variations in the quantity of produce transported to the market from day to day, and the necessity of disposing of the entire day's supply, once it has been transported, are factors of greater weight making for extreme short-run price variations. The individual peasant producer is confronted by a horizontal demand curve, in that variation in his output will not affect market prices, but it is important to note that owing to his unquestioning submission to custom, he does not vary his output (i.e. reallocate his resources) in response to market price movements. If the function of a price system is the proper allocation of productive resources, as well as the rationing of goods, it is apparently not performing that function in the perishable produce market of the undeveloped economies. This relative constancy from year to year in the proportion of the peasant producer's resources allocated to perishable produce production implies that long-run or secular price trends in this market of the undeveloped economy must be explained primarily through studies of shifting demand conditions.

The regional pattern of supply flows in this market is extremely well defined and invariant. Unless situated more or less centrally between two towns, the peasant farmer almost invariably transports his perishable produce to the nearest town, which is usually serviced from a 10 to 30-mile radius. Although the lack of any marketing organization here is wasteful, in that each farmer has to act as transporter, it seems probable that the elimination of the generally very large profits of wholesaling merchants probably results in lower priced produce for the consumer. Given the exclusively local nature of this market, the price differentials among the local market areas are, naturally, extremely wide. Wide spatial price differentials are, of course, an outstanding feature in all markets of an undeveloped economy, but they are greatest in the perishable produce market. Only high-priced produce, such as some fruits, will ever be reshiped from a local market (i.e. the town that is the center for the surrounding peasant villages in a 10 to 30-mile radius). The tendency in these low-standard-of-living undeveloped economies to consider all perishable produce a semi-luxury, plus the relative unimportance of the market, probably explain the lack of government intervention   Municipal price control has been applied in some areas, but apparently for formal reasons of consistency with price control in other types of markets, since enforcement in this sector is rarely attempted.

The Agricultural Staples Market

The third in our category of markets, that of agricultural staples, consisting primarily of cereals and rice, is not only relatively more important in the undeveloped than the developed economy, unlike the two preceding markets, but is overwhelmingly the most important market judged by any economic criterion. In a sense, it is the most typical in market organization and structure, for these directly reflect the essential features of an undeveloped economy *qua* undeveloped – little real capital formation, subsistence standard of living, importance of the middleman, network of local market areas, etc.

The most significant fact for the agricultural staples market is that the individual peasant, whether he be tenant or proprietor, cultivates such a small acreage that after meeting his needs and obligations he has little or no crop to dispose of on the market. Home consumption (since staples supply the main diet), seed required for next year's sowing, and, if a tenant, the landlord's share of the crop account for 70 to 100 per cent of the peasant's output. The result is that the bulk of the staples reaching the market is owned and disposed of by large landlord's, whether share-receiving landlords or large-scale active agricultural entrepreneurs. Since the large landlords; holdings are customarily contiguous, or at least tend to be in the same locality, the number of important market suppliers in each local producing-marketing area is very small. The local market is thus characterized in the producer-middleman transaction by a small group of big sellers (landlords) and a large varying number of unimportant sellers (peasants). The large landlords may sell on a fixed-price contract basis to merchants or wholesalers at harvest time, or they may gradually sell their stocks at the currently quoted local market prices over the course of the year to the same or other wholesalers all of whom are located in the local town market of the producing area. The small peasant producers having surpluses usually sell to the wholesalers at the local market quotation, rather than on fixed-price contract. Neither landowners nor peasants sell staple crops directly to retailers, primarily because landowners are reluctant to engage in commercial activity, and because neither peasant nor retailer has the capital to enable him to carry the stocks required to maintain a regular flow of trade.

Each large landlord is very conscious of the size of his large competitors' crops, any contractual sales they may have made, the rate at which they are offering supplies to the market, and of the effect on the price quotations in the local town market of any large amounts he may offer. He does not react by curtailing his output, either independently or in collusion, and therefore his sales over a long period of time are not curtailed either, partly because he may have no control over the total quantities grown by his peasant tenants. Instead, he attempts to maximize his profits by creating favorable local market price movements through variations in the supply flows that he controls. Although collusion among landlords in this type of control would certainly pay, there is apparently very little – probably due to an even greater degree of the same type of mutual distrust that often breaks up an industrial cartel. Peasants also go in for hoarding when they see an upward price movement and their landlords withholding supplies from the market, but their reactions are usually constrained by the pressure of debts and the immediate need for cash. This local market manipulation, which is reenforced by the interests and activities of the speculative middlemen, results in relatively wide swings in the price quotations of the very thin local market. The meagreness of the market naturally facilitates manipulation, but makes the sudden disposal of large inventories very difficult.

The output of agricultural staples in undeveloped economies is very inelastic with respect to price, especially in an upward direction. The peasant producer has severely limited land and labor resources, cannot increase his productivity because he lacks capital equipment, and lives so close to the subsistence level that the amount of seed he can sow is a direct function of the size of last year's crop. A good crop the preceding year may have meant a lower price but, more important, it also provided for a large quantity of seed to be sown the following year. It is interesting to note that just as the competitively determined prices in the perishable produce market do not seem to influence the allocation of resources, so the locally manipulated prices in the agricultural staples market do not seem to influence the allocation of resources. The heavy hand of peasant tradition creates a price inelasticity of output that is apparent even in the long run, for

long-run shifts over the decades in the agricultural allocation of resources appear, on specific examination, to be due to non-price factors.

The merchants, like the landlords, are very conscious of each other's buying and selling policies. This could conceivably result in intense rivalry, but in practice there seems to be a recognition of their common interests in manipulating the local market. If a leading merchant begins large-scale hoarding, other merchants find it to their advantage to help the price movement along by withholding also, for it is the size of the profit margin on a given inventory rather than the expansion of business that means profit maximization under these conditions.

In their routine distribution to retailers (and, in the case of the few inedible staples, to secondary industry), the wholesalers' margins are markedly high, even though here increased selling volume is presumably an objective and thus the competitive process might be expected to reduce these extremely high margins.

The middleman stands at the crossroads of economic life in the undeveloped economy, and thereby occupies an unusually powerful position. The theoretical justification for the middleman is that through specialization he performs more efficiently and cheaply the function of linking the producer with a market demand increasingly distant in time and space. But the middleman in the undeveloped economy does not appear to service a large enough market, either in time or space, to derive these economies. It seems unquestionable that his exaggerated position arises primarily from his control of the only capital available to carry inventories.

Considered in its spatial and temporal framework the agricultural staples market, like the perishable produce market, reveals a network of price differentials through space and time. But although the costs and risks of transportation through space and the costs and risks of storage through time are sufficiently large to create an essentially local and manipulable market in each area, they are nowhere as large as the price differentials in perishable produce.

The Manufactured Consumers' Goods Market

The manufactured consumers' goods market is supplied in undeveloped economies by all of the following: rural industries, urban handicrafts, the putting-out or domestic system, factories, and imports. The evolutionary development of the first four of the "stages" which the advanced industrialized economies experienced has been varied in the undeveloped economies through imitation of the factory mode of production. This early adoption of factory production, plus an increasing reliance upon imports, may account for the less important role that the putting-out or domestic system is playing today in the undeveloped economies than it did in the historical evolution of the industrialized economy, and certainly explain the decline of rural industries and handicrafts. To a large extent, rural industries, such as weaving, have become a factor in the market on the initiative of the merchant who commissions the work, and thus they are identified to some extent with the domestic putting-out system. The merchant operating a domestic system in either rural or urban areas does not appear to possess any particular control over the market, because even if he is the sole employer in the area he must compete with local handicrafts and the imports and domestic factory goods that find their way into the most remote areas. However, he receives a large return on his capital – even larger than that customarily received by the merchant wholesaler in agricultural staples – which judged by an advanced economy, might misleadingly indicate some control over the market.

Urban handicrafts are largely sold by the craftsmen themselves, who operate under conditions of fairly constant costs and very little overhead. Total unit costs vary little from area to area within an undeveloped economy, as a result of the generally equalized distribution of the production factors needed for this output, and thus there is little area specialization. Given constant costs more or less similar in the various market areas of an undeveloped economy, an improvement in transportation facilities would not widen the essentially local nature of the handicraft market. It would simply abolish it, once production units were established capable of achieving large-scale economies through extension of the market. Handicraftsmen in the undeveloped economies are frequently organized in guilds, but the price fixing abilities of the guilds are limited by the competition of imports and domestic factory output.

Factory production of manufactured consumers' goods is found to some extent in all the undeveloped economies, customarily beginning with textiles, whose successful development is primarily due to the use of the inexpensive unskilled labor made available by the low labor productivity in densely populated undeveloped economies. Factory units vary considerably in size, the smaller plants servicing only their local markets, while the few large plants enter many local markets. But whether small or large, the factory plant are predominantly located in or near urban market centers; there they have direct access to markets, a larger labor supply (since there is little labor mobility in these countries), and less risk of damage or pilferage in transporting the finished goods (the risks of transporting their raw materials being less, and usually resting on raw material sellers). Furthermore, the types of raw materials used in the light consumers' goods manufacturing of undeveloped economies are neither bulky nor limited to special areas. Finally, and possibly most important, there is the greater security of an urban center for the protection of physical property. This concentration of factories, like handicrafts, near urban markets increases price differentials among local markets; they are still not as large as in perishable produce or agricultural staples markets.

There seems to be little or no vertical integration or horizontal combination among factories manufacturing consumer goods, vertical integration not being very meaningful in this type of simple consumers' goods manufacturing, and horizontal combination of little use where a factory rarely has other factory competitors in the same local market and competition comes chiefly from imports and handicrafts. As far as other local market areas are concerned, factory owners tend to be reluctant to make investments where they are not residents and cannot watch those investments.

Considerable differences appear in the crudity and quality of the products of different factories, but little product differentiation is attempted. Advertising and other non-price forms of competition designed to obtain a larger share of the market are negligible. Although the lone factory producer in a local market is sometimes loosely referred to as a local monopolist, the competition of imports in most market areas and the luxury nature of manufactured consumers' goods in a subsistence economy confronts him with a more or less horizontal and elastic demand curve. Even in the more inaccessible areas where large transportation costs give the small local producer control over the market within certain price limits, he customarily will not curtail output in order to raise price, because he can usually dispose of his entire output at the maximum price – that is, the local price of the import. The great importance of imports on the operations of domestic factory producers of consumers' goods is indicated by the fact that in the period before the war those undeveloped economies geographically nearer to the industrailized exporting countries operated their consumers' goods factories at lower percentages of capacity.

The manufatured consumers' goods market, unlike the perishable produce and agriculture staples markets, is characterized by a considerable degree of price stability, due to very rigid wage rates, the constant cost conditions in the handicrafts trades, and the practice of fixing prices to meet the competition of industrial imports subject to administered pricing in industrialized countries. This price stability, as is evident, is not a manifestation of monopolistic rigidity

On the retailing end, price competition is dominant. In fact, the tendency to vary prices within a certain range as a result of individual bargaining between the consumer and the retailer intensifies the importance of price to the average consumer, who tends to do more comparative shopping as a result.

Government intervention in the manufactured consumers' goods market frequently takes the form of direct investment – i.e. the building and operation of large factories – and infrequently the sponsoring of cooperatives. Operation of the government factories has been on a commercial basis, prices conforming to the market, but has generally not been profitable, due to a more than customary degree of nepotism and inefficiency. Profit-margin fixing on mass consumption articles, especially imports such as sugar and tea, is not uncommon but rarely effective.

Perhaps the most significant type of government intervention – and one I believe peculiar to the undeveloped economies – is the unwitting creation of uncertainty and risk for the factory owner and importer through the government's willingness to legislate and act, inconsistently and haphazardly, on any and all matters. Government has no laissez-faire conception of a clearly defined free economic sphere distinct from its own province, nor on the other hand does it have a planned economy conception of its responsibilities. Therefore, its intervention takes the form of spasmodic and inconsistent sallies into various sectors of the economy. Without warning, and depending upon the ideas of whoever is in power, the free import of a particular commodity may be succeeded by a total ban which may then be replaced by a succession of tariff rates, or by the active encouragement of private capital investment to manufacture the commodity, which may then give way to the granting of a private monopoly and/or the construction and operation of government factories. Price fixing often *alternates* with a free market, and the increasing necessity of adopting import quotas permits even greater scope to the arbitrariness and unpredictability of government policy. The undeveloped economies have thus contrived to obtain all the disadvantages of an economy lacking both vigorous enterprise and central planning. The facetious expression, "neither free nor enterprise," is a correct description of the undeveloped economy.

The Capital Goods Market

The capital goods market, the fifth and last of our market classifications, is naturally the least developed in the undeveloped economies, but its structure and future development will have important directional effects upon the economic development of these countries. At present, these countries find it necessary to import the bulk of their relatively small capital goods requirements, partly because of the economic handicaps (unskilled labor, lack of know-how, etc.) that were also present in the early stages of the development of Western economies, but also partly because of the insecurity generated by a political philosophy of economic life that is neither laissez-faire nor paternalistic, and has no discernible principles of what is a proper role for government and what is not. So great, for this reason, has been the reluctance of capital-possessing merchants and landowners to immobilize their liquid and semi-liquid assets (paper money, precious metals, stocks of goods, etc.) through real

capital formation that an increasing proportion of the relatively small capital goods importation and production is being undertaken by the governments themselves, who are also tending to replace foreigners' direct investments in this field. The latter are finding that, except where direct political ties and therefore control exist, their investments are increasingly threatened by rising nationalistic feeling and political insecurity. The extent of direct government importation of capital goods for public projects and for the construction of government-owned consumers' goods and capital goods factories is startling to the Western observer, who tends to assume that government ownership and administration of factories is a concomitant of very advanced economies and sophisticated governments. Governmental dominance in the field of capital goods production is particularly evident when a rapid rate of industrialization is being forced on the population, which typically wants industrialization but is not prepared to reduce immediate consumption or do anything else to help obtain it.

Whatever *private* capital goods production there is (e.g. some iron and steel, some cement, etc.) definitely enjoys positions of monopoly and is usually not controlled as to price, in spite of similar governmental intervention in other markets. Its only competition comes from very expensive imports (due to transport costs), or to the equally expensive output of government operated factories.

Before closing the analysis of the market structure in undeveloped economies a few words about the nature of the money market seem advisable, since its peculiarities help to explain the business behavior and market structure we have been examining. First, there is no long-term money market to speak of in these countries; the general desire for liquidity is so strong that neither individuals nor private banks will lend money for more than a year or two, not even to the government. This inability of government to sell securities to its own people is the primary reason for the establishment of national central banks in virtually all of the undeveloped economies, for it is only from this source that governments can obtain credits. Governments are increasingly trying to improve the long-term agricultural credit situation by setting up special farm banks and sponsoring rural credit cooperatives designed to supply credit at lower rates, but to date they service very few of the farmers. Second, private banks, frequently branches of large European banks, concentrate on short-term lending to merchants at interest rates of 10–15 per cent a year. Those merchants and farmers unable to establish credit lines with the banks are forced to obtain short-term loans from the numerous individual money lenders at interest rates of 25 to 35 per cent a year, and sometimes higher. Third, there is no evidence of collusive control or monopoly over the money market. However, the existence of competitive conditions in the money market has apparently not been a sufficient condition for restraining interest rates from exceeding even those high levels understandable in an economy characterized by capital scarcity; the competitive process offers no solution for the problem of a "liquidity complex."

It is this reluctance to sacrifice liquidity or, if you prefer, it is the high productivity of capital that explains huge profit margins, even in those few sectors of the economy not characterized by any apparent market control. It also explains, along with what I have called the "government generated insecurity," the paradoxical failure to meet the crying need for real capital formation for the production of consumers' goods and capital goods when there are available considerable quantities of liquid capital and other resources, for the merchant-capitalists can play safer by lending out their money, or engaging in the agricultural staples trade, or in the importation of consumers' goods, all at rates of return which they would have difficulty in obtaining as manufacturers of consumer and capital goods. They are behaving like true economic men and applying their resources in the "best" (i.e. most productive) of the possible uses for their capital – but the result is by no means best for the economy as a whole.

Diseconomies of Scale and Development

MANCUR OLSON

Introduction

Those readers who are not only familiar with Lord Bauer's work but also have some acquaintance with my writings probably would not have expected that I would be among the contributors to this Festschrift. Many people know that Lord Bauer's work has been distinguished by its high scientific quality, as well as by a steadfast adherence to a somewhat conservative (or at least classical-liberal) point of view. A few readers may also know that my writings are not inspired by quite the same conviction; I believe that neither left-wing nor right-wing ideologies provide an adequate understanding of the problems of our time. I have even gone so far in some recent essays as to argue that the ideological debate that occupies many leading economists and other intellectuals often confuses rather than clarifies our thinking.[1]

••••

In this essay I offer a reason why I believe Lord Bauer's general policy recommendations are of *greater* pertinence and value to developing countries than to developed ones. The argument that competitive markets will greatly help to solve the problems of underdeveloped countries is, in my opinion, far stronger than the contention that advanced countries should rely on such markets; the poverty problem that still afflicts a small but significant minority of individuals in the most developed nations is, for example, a better candidate for activist governmental programs than is the problem of promoting economic growth in societies that have so far failed to develop economically. The optimal role for government is actually smaller in developing countries than in advanced ones.

••••

To say that most people in most cultures on which there is available information appear to respond to market incentives in the predicted way does not, of course, deny that some cultural groups may be better prepared than others to respond to these incentives or that in other contexts cultural factors could have a profound significance. At a minimum, an advanced culture must bequeath a considerable amount of human capital to those who are raised in such a culture. One hypothesis of this essay, moreover, is that in one crucial extramarket context, culture is critically important, as will be evident from the constructive argument that follows.

A Nonimportable Requirement for Development

One problem with the once prevalent explanations of underdevelopment is that they overlook the possibility that any single factor of production whose scarcity prevents development usually can be imported. Both tangible capital and highly educated manpower can be imported. If the productive factor is especially scarce, it should – if the institutions, organizational structure, and policies of the country are appropriate – bring exceptionally high returns simply because it is so scarce. Thus it should be surprising if any single factor (or any pair or triplet of factors) that can readily be imported would by itself prevent economic growth. It is to factors of production or growth-causing forces that cannot be

Mancur Olson. The Cato Institute granted permission to reprint this article from *Cato Journal*, 7(1), pp. 77-96, 1987.

imported that we should look for the fundamental difficulties of development.

Cultural habits are not so readily imported as physical capital or educated specialists. There is admittedly some tendency for societies to imitate cultures that are deemed to be successful, and thus a certain amount of cultural importation occurs. But it is more often the superficial and less subtle cultural characteristics of successful countries that are imported initially; acquisition of the subtler features of an alien culture can take a very long time as well as considerable investments in learning.

••••

The one political attitude that most uniformly categorizes developing countries in recent times is "anti-imperialism." Although the expression often is used loosely, and sometimes means opposition to any relationship with a more developed country, its initial and core meaning is resistance to being governed by citizens of another country – to taking orders from foreigners. Virtually without exception, the people of poor areas (no less than rich ones) have wanted "independence." Independence in this context is not synonymous with "freedom"; resistance to various home-grown autocracies has not in general been so widespread as the opposition to foreign administration. Although subordination to a foreign government is the main concern, some loosely define imperialism to include direct investment by foreign or multinational firms, or foreign control of universities, schools, and other major institutions. Opposition to ideas and products that originate abroad may also surface, but this is countervailed by the imitativeness and readiness for cultural change mentioned above. Thus, control by a foreign government is almost always ruled out in modern developing countries.[2]

It follows that one of the elements needed for economic development – a stable government that reliably provides law and order, impartially protects private property,

and enforces contracts – usually is not being "imported" into or imposed upon developing countries, and ordinarily could not be without at least profound and violent resistance. Such "importation" is defined as imperialism and is ruled out, and (in my opinion) usually for good reasons. Moreover, no evidence or promise of high "marginal productivity" from better government will normally overcome resistance to imperialism – better government is a "factor of production" that will not be obtained from abroad even when importing it could bring a considerable increase in income.

There is also today considerable resistance in less developed countries to admitting multinational firms, even though foreign firms are not inherently a form of imperialism. A foreign firm that can only obtain labor and other inputs by paying enough for the owners of these resources to sell them voluntarily, and that can only sell its product to willing buyers on a free market, cannot be coercive. Such a firm should therefore not be equated with a colonial government that rules by force. Nonetheless, most developing countries discriminate more against foreign-owned firms (if they allow them to enter at all) than do most developed nations. Thus, in practice, large foreign-controlled corporate hierarchies are also relatively rare in the poorer countries.

The Special Difficulties of Large-Scale Organizations in Underdeveloped Areas

The objection to importation of foreign hierarchies suggests that *developing countries will be especially short of effective large-scale organizations* – unless this factor of production is something they would have in relatively great supply because of their indigenous characteristics (that is, unless it was a factor of production in which they were intensive, so that under conditions of free trade they would tend to export products for which this factor was especially important). This essay attempts to show that the indigenous characteristics of poor countries are strikingly inhospitable to effective large-scale organization, especially to large-scale organizations that have to operate (as governments do) over a large geographical area. This is true both of poor countries today and preindustrial Western nations.

There are several reasons why the indigenous characteristics of underdeveloped areas are unfavorable to effective large-scale organization. One reason is that capital is relatively scarce in poor countries. This scarcity is not, as was argued earlier, a sufficient explanation of underdevelopment, because in the absence of other problems the needed capital would be imported. Nonetheless, the wage-rental ratio in most poor countries tends to reflect their relatively low rate of savings and their enmity toward foreign capital. A scarcity of capital tends to prevent large-scale production; it is often machines and other capital goods that come in large, indivisible units that give rise to economies of large-scale production, not land or labor.[3]

A primitive level of technology also tends to prevent large-scale production, because simple methods, even when they are capital intensive, normally offer no incentive for large-scale production. The development of steam power and the invention of new textile machinery that could not be powered by hand gave rise to the first modern factories. Factories are relatively large-scale establishments, and they became a general and important way of organizing industrial production only during the Industrial Revolution (Ashton 1948, pp. 71-77). Small-scale, or "cottage," industry prevailed when textile machinery was hand powered. It is difficult to think of many types of capital equipment embodying primitive technology that must for efficiency be used in large, indivisible units, and which would therefore give rise to significant economies of large-scale production. Some irrigation works, mining operations, and transport canals in primitive

societies were relatively large scale because of the size of the rivers involved or other geological and geographical conditions, but these were exceptional. In most cases, primitive technologies have been associated with relatively small-scale operations.

The low level of per capita income in poor countries also tends to foster small-scale enterprise. The lower the level of per capita income, other things being equal, the smaller the size of the market. Advocates of balanced growth, such as Rosenstein-Rodan and Nurkse, based their case mainly on the fact that in poor countries the small size of the market limits the inducement to invest. But the small market also limits the scale of the enterprise, because when the market is small the demand will not be great enough to sustain a large enterprise even if the shape of the average cost curve is such that it gives a larger enterprise lower costs.

Market size depends not only on the level of per capita income but also on the costs of transportation and communication. The costs of transportation and communication will, however, be closely associated with the level of per capita income. The same shortcomings that keep a poor country from having a modern, low-cost manufacturing sector will usually keep it from having modern, low-cost transportation and communication systems. Obviously, many underdeveloped nations today have imported some modern transportation and communication devices from advanced societies. Most underdeveloped countries have a few modern roads and railroads linking major cities, but transportation systems in rural areas still are often quite primitive. The cost of modern transportation in poor countries is so great that it cannot be provided to the mass of the population. This is also basically true of such modern communication devices as the telephone and television. Many of the people simply cannot afford them.

Such emphasis on the relative backwardness of the transportation and communication systems of poor countries may seem unnecessary, since this backwardness would perhaps nowhere be denied. If it is accepted, however, two further reasons why poor countries should be expected to have relatively little experience with large-scale organization follow inexorably from it. First, poor transportation and communication tend to force a firm to rely mainly on local factors of production. When a firm's scale increases, it will have to go farther afield to obtain factors of production, and the poorer the transportation and communication systems the faster these factor costs will rise with expanding output.

The second and more important reason why poor transportation and communication systems work against effective large-scale enterprise is that they make it far more difficult to coordinate such enterprises effectively. This is particularly true for large-scale enterprises whose activities are relatively far-flung or space-intensive. A large retail establishment, for example, will have a chain of stores scattered over a wide area. And a large manufacturing organization, even if it has but one factory, will often need to be represented throughout the wide area in which it must buy factors of production and sell its product.

Culture and Organizational Size

If the foregoing reasons why large-scale organizations have usually been uneconomical in poor societies with primitive technologies are valid, we should expect that large-scale organizations would not have been as common in either contemporary developing countries or in historical times as they are in rich countries today. To the extent that market forces operated, these forces would make it difficult and disadvantageous for most firms to expand. Resource scarcities would tend to limit somewhat the size of organizations even in the absence of markets.

A systematic survey is needed before we

can be certain, but my reading and observation suggest that, as the foregoing arguments would predict, the average size of productive enterprise has been far smaller in poor than in prosperous societies. In each country that has industrialized, moreover, the average size of enterprise appears to have increased enormously since industrialization began.

If small-scale enterprise has been indigenous and generally optimal in less developed societies, and large-scale enterprise has not. we would expect the skills, attitudes, and expectations of most people in these societies to be derived from and geared to small institutions rather than large ones. Since the adaptation to small-scale activities presumably goes back to the beginning of social life, and any experience with large-scale organizations is relatively recent in developing areas, we would expect that the cultural attitudes in these areas would be appropriate only to small-scale enterprise. In addition, because low per capita incomes and primitive transportation and communication also foster smaller markets, and (as Adam Smith first showed) the "division of labour is limited by the extent of the market," we would also expect less specialization – and cultural characteristics less suited to detailed specialization – in poor societies.

If the above is true, we should expect that the characteristic institutions of traditional societies would be both small and unspecialized. The prevalence of extended families, tribes, clans, manors, and communal village organization tentatively suggests that this prediction is correct. As Joseph Schumpeter (1954) pointed out, even a separate and specialized government financed by taxes is a post-medieval development. The cultures of underdeveloped societies, including Western societies in preindustrial times, would again presumably also be adapted to these institutions rather than to the specialized and large-scale enterprise of modern developed countries.

We should, for example, expect that the cultures of poor societies would not produce the "organization man," but rather the "extended family man" or the "tribal man." I hypothesize that such cultures would produce far more loyalty to relatives outside the nuclear family, and more "tribal" loyalty, than is evident in developed countries. On the other hand, we also would predict more nepotism and other forms of corruption in those few large-scale organizations that do exist in poor countries than among corresponding organizations in rich countries. These predictions appear to be true.

It should not be surprising that cultural forces should be more significant in large-scale bureaucracies than in individual behavior in markets. Except possibly when the degree of uncertainty is extraordinarily great, the incentives facing the individual in the market are relatively clear-cut and obvious. No extensive indoctrination or particular ethic is needed to convince the peasant that if he can produce a larger output at the same cost, or the same output at lower cost, he will get more money to spend in the local market. The incentives facing a bureaucrat in a large organization may not be so easily discerned. One's superior must be appeased, of course, but often it is not simply effective work in the interest of the organization as a whole that will best achieve this result. The leader of a large bureaucracy cannot know what each individual is doing and therefore cannot reward precisely the behavior he wants to encourage.

••••

The Exceptional Difficulties Facing Large Governments in Poor Societies

In any country, the largest organization is usually the government. Would the foregoing arguments apply to it? Most of them clearly ought to, but there may be reservations in some quarters about whether the diseconomies of very large-scale activities that seem to be present in firms in poor countries would also apply to governments. It would, however, be a serious methodological error to allow the conclusions about government to rest on a mere analogy with firms producing marketable goods. It is therefore necessary to consider governments explicitly.

Governments are differentiated from firms and firmlike institutions in developing countries above all by the fact that they produce the collective or public goods that the private sector characteristically cannot produce in optimal quantities. In most cases, public goods have two properties. First, if the good goes to anyone in some area or group, it goes to everyone in that area or group. Second, consumption is largely nonrivalrous, in that additional consumers can enjoy the good without substantially diminishing the consumption of those who are already consuming the good. Defense, pollution control, and law and order are classical examples of public goods that have these properties.

••••

I hypothesize that governments are not only naturally affected by the general difficulties facing large-scale organizations in developing countries,[4] but are even more seriously affected than the average large-scale enterprise, for two distinct and cumulative reasons.

First, governments govern territory, and (as was argued earlier) activities that take place over large areas are particularly difficult to coordinate, especially without modern transportation and communication. It is likely that the small scale of most agricultural enterprises (except in Soviet-type countries) is largely due, even in the most developed countries, to the difficulties of coordination over large areas. If one worker per square mile is required, a farm with 1,000 employees – not many by the standards of modern industry – would, of course, have to coordinate its activities over 1,000 square miles. It is therefore not surprising that the large corporate structure typical in manufacturing has not also spread to farming, or that the big "bonanza farms" of the late 19th-century Great Plains, and the huge collective farms of the Soviet bloc countries, have been failures.

In underdeveloped societies with poor transportation and communication, the problems of coordinating activities over wide areas are far worse. By governmental standards, moreover, 1,000 square miles is merely a microstate or manorial domain. Thus a government in a developing area that has typical modern dimensions and wants to insure that common policies are followed in all parts of its domain must have tens or hundreds of thousands of functionaries, many of whom are in locations that have only tenuous transportation and communication connections with the national capital.

••••

The second reason why governments are particularly disabled by the problem of large-scale organization in poor countries is that their single most important function is providing public goods, and it is far more difficult to assess the performance of bureaucracies (and bureaucrats) who provide collective goods than of organizations of equal size that produce market outputs. The greater difficulty of measuring outputs of public goods, and of estimating the social production functions that would determine how much output ought to be attainable from given value of inputs, derives in turn partly from the fact that experiments or experiences with the production of collective goods are inevitably on a "group scale," so that experiments are more costly and the experience per unit of time is less informative.

This difficulty reduces the technical efficiency of public goods production. Though the special problems of assessing performance and attaining technical efficiency hold in both developed and developing countries, limited information about performance is a far more troublesome prob-lem when cultural attitudes (which especially affect "unobserved" actions) are unsuited to large organizations and when transportation and communication costs limit a leader's access even to such information as is available on the spot.

The fact that the per-capita cost of providing a given level of military capacity would fall as the number of people receiving the public good increased would (as indicated above) tend to make governments expand to the point of world government. The hypothesis that, in poor and primitive societies, the cost of providing law and order and administering common policies rises with the size of the area governed, however, tends to set severe limits on the amount of "government" an underdeveloped government can provide. These limits must restrict either the total area governed or the quality of public goods provided for a given area. Thus, in poor and truly underdeveloped areas, the government must usually be either very small (as were medieval governments of individual manors or the governments of various primitive tribes) or else relatively ineffective, corrupt, or even merely nominal, as many governments in underdeveloped regions now appear to be.

Political Instability and Guerrilla Warfare

The prevalence of corruption, nepotism, and manifest ineffectiveness in large-scale organizations and especially in governments, both in developing countries today and in the West before the 19th century,[12] is surely consistent with the argument offered here. Evidence from World Bank reports and other sources also confirms that the comprehensive economic planning that developing countries often want usually results at best in a publication, rather than in a series of actions that are in fact implemented. So, too, is the evidence that public services arc extremely poor in most developing countries: mail often fails to reach its destination, government schools and universities often do not conduct honest examinations, telephones and electric power systems do not work well, and so on.

Political instability and the failure of governments to prevent guerrilla warfare also provide evidence for my argument. If governments of poor countries are not effectively administered and the rural areas are governed only nominally, then those who plan a coup are less likely to be caught, and guerrillas have a good chance of operating in the rural areas. The instability of governments in underdeveloped areas is well known, but the striking facts of guerrilla warfare have been overlooked.

Though terrorism of a newsworthy kind has been common, there has not yet been a successful, or even a significant and sustained, guerrilla movement – one that could control and tax significant areas, even temporarily – in a highly developed country, even when the regime imposed upon a people was profoundly repugnant to the subject population. In the relatively developed and urbanized areas conquered by the Nazis in World War II, the subject peoples usually hated the Nazi occupation, which combined political insensitivity with brutality. But despite the depth of this hatred, despite the fact that most of the German Army was fully occupied at the front lines, despite the fact that for much of the war Germany appeared to be a likely loser, despite the outside support available from the Allies, and despite the gallantry of the resistance movements, the Nazis confronted no large-scale guerrilla movements in their occupied territories until the very eve of their departure. Only in backward, rural, and mountainous Yugoslavia were guerrillas able to capture and hold any large areas.

••••

Why is it that in some cases the most despised of regimes can silence all opposition, whereas in other cases even relatively responsive governments cannot avoid guerrilla warfare for years on end? If the Soviet Union could subdue Hungary in a matter of days, why could the United States not pacify South Vietnam even over a longer period? It would be morally gratifying to suppose that the explanation is simply that some governments are ruthless and others are gentle. But this could hardly be the whole story.

••••

A better explanation of these anomalies is that guerrilla warfare is not feasible in economically advanced nations with established and purposeful governments. Such warfare is, however, often politically profitable in rural areas of economically backward societies. Successful guerrilla movements usually start in the most rural areas and attack the more modern areas only if they have raised a stronger army than the incumbents, or have cut the cities off from reinforcements or supplies.

••••

Some Policy Implications

If the argument in this essay is correct, it follows that the current policies of most international organizations of most countries giving foreign aid are questionable. Most countries giving aid and most international lenders encourage patterns of development that are relatively intensive in large-scale organization, both in the public and the private sectors. If large-scale organizational capacity is relatively scarce in developing areas, and it is not feasible or desirable to import this particular input, then this scarcity should affect both the composition of output and the factor proportions used in producing particular products. There is also a greater need for investment in large-scale organizational capacity than is generally recognized. If a crucial factor needed for development is especially scarce, alleviation of this scarcity will be especially valuable. There is a need for better training and exchange programs for managers in both the private and public sectors, more training in accounting and other techniques of administrative oversight for the development of decentralized and self-policing incentive systems, and for better communication and transportation systems.

Most notably, the argument offered here, if it is right, should affect the policies of the developing countries themselves, and in a way that reminds us of Lord Bauer's writings. I have already noted that many people have assumed that the economic theory that emerged in advanced capitalistic countries of the West, showing that markets do allocate resources efficiently, is not applicable to the very different cultures and conditions of developing countries. These countries are allegedly better served by economic planning and protection against imports of industrial goods and against exploitation by multinational companies. Lord Bauer, by contrast, has long emphasized that the underdeveloped countries as well as the developed ones should rely on market mechanisms, both domestically and in international trade.

The general principles that I believe should inspire decisions about the appropriate role for the market and for government in any society are those provided by modern economic theory, which includes the theory of collective choice. Modern economic theory illuminates the circumstances in which markets are the most efficient form of economic organization and also the circumstances in which markets will fail to generate rational results. Some ideologically inspired popularizations of economic theory leave the impression that market failure is relatively rare, if it occurs at all. This impression does not survive a careful scrutiny of either the theoretical or the empirical results: market failure is commonplace, and perfect markets are the exception rather than the rule.

Yet market failure does not necessarily imply that government action would be better: we know from the study of collective choice that governments are also imperfect, and that governments, whatever the institutions and voting rules, will produce optimal allocations only in special circumstances. Those who suppose that, because a market is imperfect, it should be supplanted by government action are (as George Stigler has pointed out) like the Roman emperor judging a musical contest with two contestants and who, having heard only the first, gave the prize to the second. In practice, societies must choose between imperfect markets and imperfect governments. Which instrumentality is the better in a particular situation depends on the circumstances: it depends on how badly the market fails and on whether the government at issue will fail to a lesser extent.

••••

This essay has argued that individuals from different cultural backgrounds are broadly similar in response to unambiguous market incentives: behavior in the bazaars and market squares of the developing world is not vastly different from behavior in the markets of the economically advanced nations. Tangible capital and certain kinds of education are rarer in developing countries, which implies that if institutions and government policies are appropriate, these factors of production will fetch a higher price in developing than in developed areas. This relative price will influence not only the pattern of comparative advantage and trade, but also generate a flow of these factors of production as needed to underdeveloped areas. Thus neither shortages of tangible nor human capital need prevent rapid economic development.

••••

Law and order are needed for economic progress under any system of economic organization. It is evident that at least in rural areas some governments of underdeveloped countries find it difficult to provide even this elemental public service. If a country's full economic potential is to the realized, it must enforce contracts and adjudicate disputes about property rights in impartial and predictable ways.

••••

In some developing countries, even property rights in land are often ambiguous, and squatters, who do not have secure, marketable, and mortgageable rights needed for efficient development, are commonplace. In such circumstances, governments should devote such capacity as they can muster to providing law and order. If they have any effectiveness left over, it should be devoted to the most glaring externalities. Overambitious economic planning and detailed regulation are not likely to be coherently carried out. The wide-ranging governmental intervention that is compatible with high standards of living in some countries of Western Europe should not be expected to work (and has never worked) in any pre-industrial society.

ENDNOTES

1. See, for example, Olson (1986).

2. To refer to this constraint and to emphasize its intensity and generality is not, of course, to attack the constraint. Subordination of a country to a foreign government in which the colonial people have no voting rights not only opens up the possibility that the imperial power will be used exploitatively, but it also may perpetuate feelings of self-hate, inferiority, and bitterness on the part of the subordinate group.

3. Industries with no capital goods (apart from inventories) would be less likely to achieve economies of large-scale production; there might be some gain from increasing specialization of labor as an enterprise grew larger, but it would be hard to think of a marketable product, made without the use of extensive capital equipment, that would involve so many separate operations that a very large work force would be needed to exhaust the gains from the division of labor. There can also be economies of scale in distribution and marketing, but these economies are usually not as important in developing countries with their poor systems of transportation and communication.

4. The view that effective large-scale government is unlikely in poor countries is not new. It would take some searching to determine when and how the notion first took shape. One important and stimulating statement of this view is in the paragraphs on the "administrative revolution" in Hicks (1969). I put the notion forth in Olson (1965), especially pp. 551-54,

and in the mid-1960s paper out of which this presentation grew. Very probably the point was first made long ago.

REFERENCES

Ashton, T. S. *The Industrial Revolution, 1760-1830*. New York: Oxford University Press, 1948.

Bloch, Marc. *Feudal Society*. London: Routledge and Kegan Paul, 1961.

Hicks, John. *A Theory of Economic History*. Oxford: Clarendon Press, 1969.

Kautalya. *Arthasastra*. 8th ed., 2d book. Mysore, India: Mysore Publishing House, 1967.

Laslett, Peter. *Household and Family in Past Time*. Cambridge: Cambridge University Press, 1972.

Nurske, Ragnar. *Problems of Capital Formation in Underdeveloped Countries*. Oxford: Oxford University Press, 1953.

Olson, Mancur. "Some Social and Political Implications of Economic Development." *World Politics* (April 1965): 512-16.

Olson, Mancur. "Evaluating Performance in the Public Sector." In *The Measurement of Economic and Social Performance*. Edited by Milton Moss. New York: National Bureau of Economic Research, distributed by Columbia University Press, 1973.

Olson, Mancur. "Supply Side Economics, Industrial Policy, and Rational Ignorance." In *The Politics of Industrial Policy*, pp. 245-69. Edited by Claude E. Barfield and William A. Schambra. Washington, D.C.: American Institute for Public Policy Research, 1986.

Pollard, Sidney. *The Genesis of Modern Management*. London: Edward Arnold, 1965.

Schultz, Theodore W. *Transforming Traditional Agriculture*. New Haven: Yale University Press, 1964.

Schumpeter, Joseph. "The Crisis of the Tax State." *International Economic Papers*, No. 4, pp. 5-38. Translated by W. F. Stolper and R. A. Musgrave. London: Macmillan, 1954.

Wraith, Ronald and Simpkins, Edgar. *Corruption in Developing Countries*. New York: Norton, 1974.

Von Vorys, Karl. *Political Development in Pakistan*. Princeton, N.J.: Princeton University Press, 1960.

The Religious Factor in Economic Development

CYNTHIA TAFT MORRIS and IRMA ADELMAN

1. Introduction

In this paper we re-examine the positive relationship between religion and socio-economic development that we obtained in 1966 for a sample of 55 non-communist underdeveloped countries.[1]

••••

Our re-examination of our 1966 factor analytic study is designed to see whether a cross-country aggregate analysis can throw any light on the relationship between religion and modernization.[2] In the sections that follow, we recall the methodology that we applied, give our classification system for predominant type of religion, present the results of the statistical analysis, and discuss possible explanations for the cross-sectional relationships among type of religion, socio-cultural concomitants of industrialization and urbanization, and *per capita* GNP. We conclude that the strong statistical association between level of socio-economic development and predominant religion is the outcome of complex historical influences associated with the early spread of commercial and industrial capitalism. This complexity of influences operating over several centuries largely accounts for the world geographical pattern of the major religions as well as the geographical distribution of institutional conditions strongly affecting current socio-economic achievements.

Morris and Adelman. This article was previously published in *World Development*, published by Pergamon Journals Ltd., Oxford, United Kingdom, from whom we received permission to reprint it. It appeared in that journal's Vol. 8, No. 7/8, in 1980 on pages 491-501.

2. The Technique and Variables

Our purpose in selecting the technique of factor analysis and a set of interrelated social and political indicators was to study a domain where widely accepted *a priori* propositions were lacking. To quote Thurstone, who pioneered the use of factor analysis in psychology:[3]

> Factor analysis has its principal usefulness at the border line of science. It is naturally superseded by rational formulations in terms of the science involved. Factor analysis is useful, especially in those domains where basic and fruitful concepts are essentially lacking and where crucial experiments have been difficult to conceive. The new methods have a humble role. They enable us to make only the rudest first map of a new domain. But if we have scientific intuition and sufficient ingenuity, the rough factorial map of a new domain will enable us to proceed beyond the exploratory factorial stage to the more direct forms of psychological experimentation in the laboratory.

The data for the study were classification systems constructed so that judgmental information could be combined with statistical data to obtain reliable assignments of countries to from three to five major categories. Details on our procedures and a discussion of methodological issues are given in the prefatory chapter of *Society, Politics, and Economic Development* (revised edition).[4]

We included a quite large number of variables to summarize characteristics of nations during the period 1957-1962. A number of these described social aspects of urbanization and industrialization: indicators of the character of basic social organization,[5] the size of the traditional subsistence sector and the strength of traditional elites: measures of the modernization of communication, education and outlook; other indicators of the social transformation accompanying industrialization such as the strength of the labour movement, the extent of social mobility and the degree of social tension; and the crude fertility rate.

Indicators of political structure and administration were selected to represent leading characteristics of the emergence of modern nation states. Several of these summarize basic differences in the character and stability of political systems: the strength of democratic institutions, the predominant basis of political parties, the extent of factionalization of political parties, the degree of freedom of political opposition and press, the extent of centralization of political power and the extent of political stability. Four indicators of the caliber and orientation of government administration and leadership were included in the study: the degree of administrative efficiency, the extent of leadership commitment to economic development, the intensity of nationalism and the extent of government participation in economic activity. The domestic influence of significant power groups is depicted by an indicator of political strength of the military, as well as by two characteristics already cited: the strength of the labour movement and the strength of the traditional elite.

A final characteristic included in the study is the classification of countries by type of religion which we will discuss in more detail in the next section.

3. Classification of Countries by Predominant Type of Religion

The primary basis for our classification by type of religion was *A Cross-Polity Survey* by Banks and Textor, raw characteristic No. 15, Religious Configuration.[6] Banks and Textor classified 107 countries into 14 types which are listed in the note to Table 1. We combined these into four principal

categories which we felt we could rank in a manner appropriate to our purpose.[7] Since the focus of our 1966 paper was on fertility rates, and thus on individual choices to limit families, we ranked the categories by the degree to which the predominant religion favoured or was consistent with the concept of individual control over personal fate. Our expectation was that fertility rates would be lower where the predominant religion viewed individuals as having significant influence over their destiny. We also expected less fatalistic attitudes to be positively associated with higher levels of economic development.

The broad lines of the classification scheme are as follows:

A. Countries in which the predominant religion emphasizes the individual's responsibility for his actions and his ability to influence his environment.

B. and C. Countries in which the predominant religion promotes moderately fatalistic attitudes toward man's capacity to alter his destiny.

D. Countries in which the predominant religion teaches that man is subject to the power of his physical and social environment.

The detailed Adelman-Morris classification provides for countries of mixed religion as follows:

A+ Mixed Christian; Jewish
A   Catholic; Eastern Orthodox
A- Mixed: Christian, literate non-Christian
B+ Mixed: Christian, non-literate
B   Muslim
C+ Mixed literate non-Christian
C   Buddhist; Hindu
C- Mixed: literate non-Christian, non-literate
D   Mixed: non-literate, literate non-Christian, Christian

••••

The final classification scheme has several attributes which should be noted because they limit its use. First, the degree of discrimination is not great with, for example, all countries that were predominantly Christian in the top category and all that were predominantly Muslim in the second category. In fact, there is considerable diversity within major religions. Second, in a number of countries, no single religion predominated; *A Cross-Polity Survey* assigns these to 'mixed' categories. Where the different religions within a country were in adjacent categories in our scheme, we applied an intermediate score; where the categories were not adjacent, no such solution was available.

Our decision to rank predominant types of religion by the degree to which, in general, they favoured individual choice also limits our analysis of the relationships between religion and development. Religious attitudes toward individual control over the environment capture only one broad aspect of religion which we assumed was important to fertility. For example, interactions between religion and the political system in the Third World can influence significantly the course of national development. As has occurred recently in the Moslem world, religious faiths which, historically, have proved quite capable of absorbing a rich variety of individual and cultural behaviour can in a setting of nationalistic anti-colonial fervour reinforce greatly state actions designed to reestablish traditional values and limit the growth of Western-type individualism.[8] Our crude classification scheme cannot capture these interactions. It cannot be presumed, even on the average, that, where religions are more favourable to individualism, the ties between religion and the state are weaker or the political influence of religion less strong.[9] Our classification by religions is thus limited by its stress on individualism .

Furthermore, to rank religions by the degree to which they favour individual choice is a controversial procedure. Most sociologists of religion maintain that, because of great heterogeneity within major religions, judgments regarding religion and individualism can only be made for small homogeneous communities. In opposition to this view, one can point out that, whether by historical accident or intrinsic characteristics of the religion, some religions have fostered or absorbed a diversity of behavior which appears, in the aggregate, to have been more favourable to individualism than the usual influence of other religions. We have based our classification scheme on broad judgments regarding this aspect of major religions.

4. The Factor Analysis: Results and Interpretation

Table 1 presents the matrix of common factor coefficients, or 'factor loadings', that summarizes the results of factor analysis. Each factor loading (a_{ij}) gives the weight of factor j in explaining socio-political indicator i; that is, it indicates the strength of the linear relationship between each factor and the observed variables .

The common factor coefficients may more easily be understood by reference to the squares of the entries in the factor matrix. Each $(a_{ij})^2$ represents the proportion of the total unit variance of variable i which is explained by factor j, after allowing for the contributions of the other factors. It can be seen, for example, from the first row of Table 1 that 64% of intercountry differences in predominant type of religion are 'explained' by factor 1, another 3% by factor 2 and an additional 3% by factors 3 and 4. The sum of the squared factor loadings for each variable, or its 'communality', may be found in the right-hand column of the table. The communality for type of religion may be stated as follows:

$$(0.80)^2 + (-0.16)^2 + (-0.18)^2 + (-0.02)^2 = 0.696.$$

The matrix of factor loadings not only indicates the importance of each factor in explaining the observed variables, but also provides the basis for grouping the variables into common factors. Each variable is allocated to that factor in which it has the highest loading, i.e. that factor with which it is most closely correlated. In Table 1, the variables are grouped according to the factor in which they have their highest loadings. The highest loading for each indicator is boxed.

After the variables have been assigned to common factors, the next step is to 'identify' each factor by providing a reasonable interpretation of the underlying forces which it may be construed to represent. To quote Thurstone, 'The derived variables are of scientific interest only insofar as they represent processes and parameters that involve the fundamental concepts of the science involved.'[10] In the following sections, we, therefore, proceed to identify the factors which are specified in the results of our statistical analysis and to discuss their relationship with the predominant type of religion. In so doing, we treat only factor 1 in detail since factors 2 and 3 each explain only about 3%, and factor 4 less than 1% of intercountry variations in predominant type of religion.[11] In contrast, factor 1 explains 64% of variations among countries in predominant type of religion.

(a) The first factor

Nine characteristics have their highest loadings in factor 1: the size of traditional sector, the character of basic social organization, crude fertility rate, the extent of literacy, the extent of mass communication, the degree of cultural homogeneity, the significance of indigenous middle class, the degree of modernization and *per capita* GNP. Clearly, this factor summarizes the social and cultural changes associated with urbanization, industrialization and the raising of *per capita* GNP.

To be more specific, factor 1 may be interpreted to represent the transformation of values and institutions accompanying the breakdown of traditional social organization. Social change may be viewed as taking place through the mechanism of differentiation and of integration of social structure. Differentiation involves 'the establishment of more specialized an autonomous social units'; integration is the process that coordinates and fuses the interactions of specialized social entities.

The process of social differentiation is portrayed by three variables with high loadings in this factor: the basic character of social organization classifies countries with respect to the degree of differentiation of nuclear family unit from extended kinship, village and tribal complexes; the size of traditional sector groups countries according to the extent to which self-sufficient family-community economic units have broken up. The strength of an indigenous middle class is a measure of the importance of a specialized group whose economic activities are removed from traditional socio-economic environments.

The process of social integration is also depicted by several country characteristics. Increases in the extent of mass communication, extensions of literacy and increases in linguistic homogeneity may all be viewed as contributing to the evolution of modern mechanisms that tend to weld together relatively diversified social units.

The two final variables composing factor 1 are degree of modernization and the crude fertility rate. The modernization variable represents changes in social attitudes that typically accompany urbanization and industrialization. It is an overall indicator of the extent to which attachments to traditionalism and traditional society had lost their strength in the period under study. The inclusion of fertility in factor 1, negatively associated with the measures of social differentiation and social integration, is not surprising, given the well-known tendency for fertility rates to be lower where the breakdown of traditional social organization, participation in the market, industrialization and the spread of mass communication have proceeded further.

Table 1. Rotated Factor Matrix for 24 Social and Political Variables and *Per Capita* GNP★

| | ROTATED FACTOR LOADINGS h_i^2 | | | | |
SOCIAL AND POLITICAL INDICATORS	F_1	F_2	F_3	F_4	(R^2)
1. Type of religion	0.80	-0.16	-0.18	-0.02	0.696
2. Size of traditional agricultural sector	-0.86	0.25	-0.19	0.04	0.836
3. Basic character of social organiztion	0.83	-0.13	0.04	-0.02	0.716
4. Extent of literacy	0.87	-0.22	0.04	0.09	0.820
5. Extent of mass communication	0.90	-0.24	0.07	-0.02	0.870
6. Degree of cultural and ethnic homogeneity	0.76	0.37	0.01	0.14	0.736
7. Significance of indigenous middle class	0.64	-0.33	0.37	0.10	0.665
8. Degree of modernization of outlook	0.67	-0.47	0.25	0.12	0.745
9. Crude fertility rate	-0.69	0.23	-0.11	-0.14	0.566
10. *Per capita* GNP	0.69	-0.40	0.19	0.06	0.684
11. Effectiveness of democratic institutions	0.44	-0.79	0.07	0.23	0.873
12. Degree of freedom of political opposition and press	0.35	-0.80	-0.19	0.06	0.805
13. Degree of factionalization of political parties	0.39	-0.66	-0.20	-0.41	0.793
14. Basis of political party system	0.49	-0.53	0.06	-0.22	0.571
15. Strength of labour movement	0.37	-0.66	0.27	-0.04	0.639
16. Political strength of the military	0.32	0.65	-0.26	-0.33	0.700
17. Degree of administrative efficiency	0.30	-0.64	0.30	0.30	0.676
18. Degree of centralization of political power	-0.09	0.84	-0.20	-0.01	0.755
19. Extent of social mobility	0.44	-0.10	0.54	0.26	0.565
20. Strength of traditional elite	0.09	0.28	-0.77	-0.19	0.713
21. Extent of nationalism and sense of national unity	0.60	0.09	0.62	-0.06	0.755
22. Degree of leadership commitment to economic development	0.01	-0.32	0.68	0.32	0.664
23. Extent of government participation in economic activity	0.16	0.38	0.63	-0.44	0.758
24. Degree of social tension	-0.16	-0.05	-0.03	-0.87	0.790
25. Extent of stability of political system	0.08	-0.17	0.30	0.82	0.795

★Boxes indicate the factor to which each variable is assigned.

The final variable, *per capita* GNP in 1961, is a crude measure of level of economic development which proved to have a negligible effect on the pattern of associations among the 24 social and political variables. When the analysis was run omitting this variable, the results were not significantly affected. [12]

The direction of the relationship between our ranking of types of religion and the socio-cultural and economic characteristics grouped in factor 1 is consistent with our expectations. On the average, the predominant religion was more favourable to individual control over the environment where the socio-cultural transformations usually accompanying industrialization and urbanization were further advanced, that is, where tribal and extended-family bonds were less strong, strong attachments to traditional society less common, the non-commercial subsistence sector less important, literacy and mass communication more widely spread, the indigenous middle class larger and fertility rates lower.

The inclusion of religion with a high loading in factor 1 is also consistent with the views expressed by some sociologists of religion regarding the nature of religious evolution. We have interpreted this factor to portray a process of social differentiation among specialized, relatively autonomous social units and a process of social integration through modern mechanisms for bonding together relatively diversified social units. Religious evolution has also been regarded as a process in which religion becomes increasingly differentiated and complex. To quote Bellah in *Beyond Belief*.[13]

> ...The central focus of religious evolution is the religious symbol itself. Here the main line of development is from compact to differentiated symbolism, that is, from a situation in which world, self, and society are seen to involve the immediate expression of occult powers to one in which the exercise of religious influence is seen to be more indirect and "rational". This is the process of the "disenchantment of the world" that was described by Weber. Part of this, process is the gradual differentiation of art, science, and other cultural systems as separate from religious symbolism. Furthermore, changes in the nature and position of religious symbolism effect changes in the conception of the religious actor. The more differentiated symbol systems make a greater demand on the individual for decision and commitment. To support this growing religious individualism, specifically religious group structures are required, whereas at earlier stages religion tends to be a

dimension of all social groups. Finally, the capacity for religion to provide ideals and models for new lines of social development increases with the growing symbolic, individual, and social differentiation.

The inclusion of religion with measures of socio-economic modernization is also consistent with the view expressed by Bellah that the essence of religious evolution is the increased freedom of the personality and of society relative to environing conditions.

The pattern of intercorrelations in factor 1 says little about the institutional mechanisms or channels through which religion and socio-cultural change interact in the process of social and economic development. The literature on Western Europe suggests a set of complex causal interactions. Historically, the spread of rationalist and individualist thinking in the Hellenist tradition contributed to transformations of both religious and socio-economic institutions. Protestant religious reformation reinforced the conjunction of economic, social, cultural and political influences in promoting the spread of capitalism and the growth of a capitalist middle class. Capitalism in turn promoted individualist behavior in the economic arena, thereby contributing to the eventual revolution in the individual's view of her relationship to both her environment and religious authority.[14] However, one cannot transfer reasoning about Western Europe to the underdeveloped world of the early 1960s.

Can we reason that the inter-country differences in religious configuration summarized by our indicator of predominant type of religion are accounted for in part by economic and social modernization? For the most part, the religious configurations in our sample predate by decades and even centuries the start of modern socio-economic development. Thus, causation from the social and economic sphere (as measured by our variables) to the religious sphere does not seem to provide a plausible explanation for our results.

Can we reason that causation runs from religious type to differences in the timing and success of modern development? Neither the literature on the sociology of religion nor recent experience supports such an interpretation. Studies of such countries as Japan and India provide some evidence that religious reforms can favour economic and social change in a manner similar to their operation in Western Europe.[15] However, our classification scheme does not discriminate sufficiently to capture these individual group and country experiences. Recent experience with tribal societies also casts doubt on easy generalizations about the unfavourableness of individual tribal customs and values to modern economic development. Tribal societies have often proved quick to enter into market relations where economic opportunities were consistently favourable.

A third possible explanation for our results is that common influences operated to produce both inter-country differences in religious configurations and variations among countries in social and economic characteristics. A marked coincidence of regional identifications, predominant religions and levels of socio-economic development lends some support to this possibility. Table 2 gives the regional identification of each country, the score on religion and a measure of socio-economic development derived from a factor analysis for 74 non-communist underdeveloped countries.[16] Latin American countries have most of the high scores on religion, African countries most of the low scores, and Near Eastern and Asian countries most of the intermediate scores. With respect to socio-economic development (measured considerably more broadly than by per capita GNP), most Latin American countries fell in the 'high' group, most African countries in the low group, and most Near Eastern and Asian countries in the intermediate group. There were, of course, some striking exceptions.

Given the information in Table 2, can we argue that common historical influences produced the geographical distribution of both religions and levels of socio-economic development reflected in our sample? Clearly, an explanation along these lines would involve explaining several centuries of economic and political change. It would include the colonial origins of the religious characteristics of Latin America as well as the historical spread of Islam and Christianity in Africa and the Middle East. A long-term historical explanation of our results would have to answer the questions why the net impact of colonial influences in Latin America proved, on the average, more favourable to economic change than elsewhere and why the Islamic countries along the Mediterranean proceeded further towards a start on socio-economic modernization than did those of Central Africa.

We will not pursue here the details of a possible long-term historical explanation of the positive relationship between religion and socio-economic development. Such an explanation need not be inconsistent with the proposition that religious attitudes conducive to individualism acted favourably on the socio-economic environment; nor need it be inconsistent with the generalization that socio-economic transformations accompanying the spread of capitalism in turn altered religious perceptions of individual choice. On the contrary, levels of socio-economic development represent the sum of country achievements over very long periods and the religious characteristics of underdeveloped nations have often been extremely persistent over time; consequently, we would expect long-term interactions between religion and development to play a role in accounting for the geographical distribution of religious and socio-economic characteristics evident in our results.

(b) The second factor

The variables most closely associated with factor 2 are the strength of democratic insti-

Table 2. Regional Identification, Type of Religion and Level of Socio-economic Development*

	REGIONAL IDENTIFICATION†	PREDOMINANT TYPE OF RELITION‡	PER CAPITA GNP IN 1961§	LEVEL OF SOCIO-ECONOMIC DEVELOPMENT‖	
Algeria	N. Africa	B	281	0.18	(I)
Argentina	LA	A	379	1.91	(H)
Bolivia	LA	B+	113	-0.35	(I)
Burma	S. Asia	C	58	-0.41	(I)
Cambodia	S. Asia	C	101	-0.55	(L)
Cameroon	Africa	D	86	-1.34	(L)
Ceylon	S. Asia	C+	137	0.35	(I)
Chile	LA	A	453	1.39	(H)
Columbia	LA	A	283	0.66	(H)
Costa Rica	LA	A	344	0.78	(H)
Cyprus	N. East	A-	416	1.08	(H)
Dahomey	Africa	D	40	-1.54	(L)
Dominican Republic	LA	A	218	0.81	(H)
Ecuador	LA	B+	182	0.54	(I)
El Salvador	LA	A	220	0.71	(H)
Gabon	Africa	B+	200	-0.83	(L)
Ghana	Africa	D	199	-0.01	(I)
Greece	N. East	A	431	1.47	(H)
Guatemala	LA	B+	175	0.35	(I)
Guinea	Africa	D	60	-1.47	(L)
Honduras	LA	A	207	0.26	(I)
India	S. Asia	C	80	-0.28	(I)
Indonesia	F. East	B	83	-0.40	(I)
Iran	N. East	B	211	0.09	(I)
Israel	N. East	A+	814	1.77	(H)
Ivory Coast	Africa	D	184	-0.98	(L)
Jamaica	LA	A+	436	1.06	(H)
Japan	F. East	C+	502	1.63	(H)
Jordan	N. East	B	184	0.16	(I)
Lebanon	N. East	A-	411	1.44	(H)
Malagasy	Africa	B+	75	-1.31	(L)
Mexico	LA	A	313	0.75	(H)
Nepal	S. Asia	C+	53	-1.36	(L)
Nicaragua	LA	A	213	0.88	(L)
Niger	Africa	C-	40	-1.86	(L)
Nigeria	Africa	D	82	-0.91	(L)
Panama	LA	A	416	0.84	(H)
Paraguay	LA	A	130	0.97	(H)
Peru	LA	B+	181	0.68	(H)
Philippines	F. East	A	117	0.56	(I)
Rhodesia	Africa	B+	215	0.14	(I)
Senegal	Africa	B	175	-0.52	(L)
Sierra Leone	Africa	D	70	-1.39	(L)
South Africa	Africa	B+	427	0.62	(I)
South Korea	F. East	C	73	0.85	(H)
Surinam	LA	A-	310	0.54	(I)
Taiwan	F. East	A-	145	1.05	(H)
Tanzania	Africa	D	59	-1.22	(L)
Thailand	F. East	C	97	0.50	(I)
Trinidad	LA	A-	594	1.15	(H)
Uganda	Africa	B+	68	-1.22	(L)
United Arab Republic	N. East	B	120	0.73	(II)
Uruguay	LA	A	450	1.59	(H)
Venezuela	LA	A	692	1.37	(H)
Zambia	Africa	B+	170	-0.89	(L)

†   LA = Latin America.
‡   Adelman-Morris classification scheme
§   I. Adelman and C. T. Morris, *Society, Politics and Economic Development*. Rev. ed. (Baltimore: Johns Hopkins Press, 1971), p. 88. The source is the Agency for International Development, Statistics and Reports Division.
‖   Adelman and Morris (1971), *op. cit.*, p. 170. The factor scores are derived from the first factor of a factor analysis of 74 underdeveloped non-communist countries. This factor combines *per capita* GNP and 10 measures of social change which we interpret to represent level of socio-economic development. On the basis of factor scores. we divided the 74 countries into three groups: low, intermediate and 'high'. The assignment of countries to groups is given in parentheses in the last column. See Adelman and Morris (1971), *op. cit.*. Chap. 4 for details.

tutions, the freedom of political opposition, the degree of factionalization of political parties, the predominant basis of political party systems, the strength of the labour movement, the political strength of the military, the degree of administrative efficiency and the degree of centralization of political power. The associations in this factor are strongly suggestive of broad historical and contemporary differences between the political organization of the countries of Western Europe and the North Atlantic and those of the rest of the world. An increase in this factor may be interpreted to represent a movement along a scale which ranges from centralized authoritarian political forms to Western-type parliamentary systems. Historically, it was in Western Europe that a pattern of change occurred in which effective parliamentary institutions were associated with strong labour movements, weak political strength of the military and decentralization of political power. This factor, therefore, may be interpreted to represent the extent of political westernization.

The coefficients resulting from the factor analysis indicate that a typically Western configuration of political traits is weakly associated with religions that favour the idea of individual control over personal destiny. The positive association of religious evolution (in the sense defined by Bellah) with political westernization is consistent with historical experience of Europe and the North Atlantic. However, the weakness of the association suggests that European analogies do not provide a great deal of help in understanding the relationship between religion and political aspects of national development in contemporary underdeveloped countries.

(c) *The third factor*

Factor 3 (whose association with types of religion is small) consists of five socio-political indicators of leadership characteristics: strength of traditional elite, extent of na-

tionalism, degree of leadership commitment to development, extent of government participation in economic activity and extent of social mobility.[17] The nature of leadership and of leadership strategies are the common bond for these variables. A movement along the scale of this factor involves a waning of the power of traditional elites and an increase in the power of nationalistic 'industrializing elites'.[18]

The signs of the loadings in factor 3 indicate a weak tendency for religions more favourable to the idea of individual control over destiny to exist in countries characterized by stronger traditional leaderships. This relationship is contrary to our expectation. It may be a consequence of country observations (for example, Japan and South Korea) where the power of traditional elites had waned considerably by 1962, even though their predominant type of religion, on the average, did not stress a large scope of individual decision-making. A more differentiated scheme based on the *actual* favourableness of religion to individualism might have scored them differently.

(d) *The fourth factor*

As might be expected, factor 4 shows a negligible relationship between type of religion and social and political stability.

5. Conclusion

In this paper we have re-examined a 1966 factor analytic study in order to see what insights it gives into the relationship between predominant type of religion and social and economic characteristics of nations. We found a strong association between a partial ranking of religious configuration by favourableness to individualism and a factor summarizing the socio-cultural concomitants of the industrialization-urbanization process. We found a very weak association between religion and the westernization of political institutions. Factor 1 explained statistically 64% of inter-country variations in predominant religion and factor 2 less than 3%. As expected, the predominant religion in countries that had proceeded further in the modernization process, on the average, stressed more the view that individuals have significant control over their fates.

We concluded that the cross-sectional association between religion and modernization could *not* be interpreted to reflect direct interactions between religion and the influences summarized by our measures of socio-economic development. Rather, it reflects marked regional differences in both religious configuration and levels of socio-economic development which are the outcome of common historical influences operating over several centuries. Of great importance among these are colonial patterns of expansion and the attendant spread of Catholicism in Latin America, the historical characteristics of the spread of Islam and of European economic expansion in the Mediterranean, and the impact of European imperialist expansion on the tribal societies of the African continent. The important historical influences most probably include interactions between religious attitudes and socio-economic characteristics of the early spread of capitalism. However, it is also likely that complex common historical influences helped determine the operation of religious attitudes and actions as well as the phenomena of socio-economic change.

ENDNOTES

1. I. Adelman and C. T. Morris, 'A quantitative study of social and political determinants of fertility', *Economic Development and Cultural Change,* Vol. 14 (January 1966), pp. 129–157.

2. In factor analysis, each of the variables included in the study is treated as dependent and independent in turn. Thus. by contrast with regression analysis, which is a study of dependence, factor analysis is a study of mutual interdependence.

3. L. L. Thurstone, *Multiple Factor Analysis* (Chicago: University of Chicago Press. 1961), p. 56.

4. I. Adelman and C. T. Morris, *Society, Politics, and Economic Development*, Rev. ed. (Baltimore: Johns Hopkins Press, 1971).

5. This indicator classifies countries according to the strength of extended family and tribal ties along a spectrum in which the prevalence of the nuclear family is ranked highest, the extended family is intermediate along the spectrum and the prevalence of tribal societies is ranked lowest.

6. A. Banks and R. Textor, *A Cross-Polity Survey,* Cambridge, Mass.: MIT Press, 1964), pp. 70–71.

The typology of *A Cross-Polity Survey* is, to quote p. 70:

. . . designed to afford approximate, yet meaningful, religious identification for each polity for which relevant information is presently available. In general, we have adhered to a rule of 80 to 85 percent predominance. This means, for example, that a polity coded as 'Muslim' could have a non-Muslim religious minority of as much as 15 to 20 percent, but no greater. The lack of a more precise cutoff point is due to a lack of reliability in religious statistics generally.

The details of the typology are as follows:

A. Protestant.	P. Jewish.
B. Catholic.	Q. Mixed literate non-Christian.
G. Eastern Orthodox.	R. Mixed: Christian, literate non-Christian.
H. Mixed Christian.	S. Non-literate.
I. Hindu.	X. Mixed: Christian, non-literate.
J. Buddhist.	Y. Mixed: literate non-Christian, non-literate.
K. Muslim.	Z. Mixed: Christian, literate non-Christian, non-literate.

7. There is, of course, no unique principle for ranking the categories of a nominal classification such as type of religion or occupation.

8. For a case study of the diverse experience of Morocco and Indonesia with the capacity of the Moslem faith to absorb varied cultures and attitudes, see C. Geertz, *Islam Observed: Religious Development in Morocco and Indonesia* (New Haven: Yale University Press, 1968).

9. At an early stage in our work on fertility, we attempted a five-way classification of countries by the political strength of religious authorities which showed an unexpected quite strong *negative* association with fertility and little or no relationship with the remaining social and political indicators. Because of conceptual difficulties and our inability to determine the influences for which this classification was apparently acting as a proxy, we did not pursue it and shifted our attention to the area of religion and individual choice. Our *statistically* most successful effort to explore the meaning of the preliminary classification by political strength of religions suggested that it was a proxy for climatic influences!

10. Thurstone (1961), *op. cit.*, p. 61.

11. Since the scores of countries on the classification scheme by predominant type of religion are based on an arbitrary linear scoring scheme, estimates of variance explained give only a general order of magnitude. Experiments with alternative scoring schemes that preserve ranks indicate that factor analysis results with our kind of data are surprisingly insensitive to alternative scoring schemes. See the Appendix to Adelman and Morris (1971), *op. cit.*

12. For the results without *per capita* GNP, see Adelman and Morris (1966), *op. cit.*, pp. 129–157.

13. R. Bellah, *Beyond Belief: Essays on Religion in a Post-Traditional World* (New York: Harper & Row, 1970), p. 66.)

14. These generalizations remain controversial.

15. Bellah (1970), *op. cit.*, Chap. 3.

16. See Adelman and Morris (1971), *op. cit.*, pp. 167–171, for an explanation of the derivation of these scores. The factor scores are derived from the first factor of a factor analysis of 74 underdeveloped non-communist countries. This factor combines *per capita* GNP and 10 measures of social change which we interpret to represent level of socio-economic development. On the basis of factor scores, we divided the 74 countries into three groups: low, intermediate and 'high'. The assignment of countries to groups is given in parentheses in the last column. See Adelman and Morris (1971), *op. cit.*, Chap. 4 for details.

17. The reason for the high loading of the indicator of extent of social mobility in the factor that groups together leadership characteristics is that an important element in the definition of this indicator is the degree of openness of access to membership in the leadership elite.

18. The concept of an industrializing elite is discussed in C. Kerr, *et al.*, *Industrialism and Industrial Man* (New York: Oxford University Press, 1964), Chap. 2.

ABOUT THE AUTHORS IN CHAPTER 3

David S. Landes is in the Department of Economics at Harvard University in Cambridge, Massachusetts. He is author of *Revolution in Time: Clocks and the Making of the Modern World* (Cambridge, Mass.: Belknap Press of the Harvard University Press), 1983, and of *The Unbound Prometheus: Technological Change and Industrial Development in Western Europe from 1750 to the Present* (London: Cambridge University Press), 1969.

At the time that this article was published, Morton R. Solomon was writing *A General Theory of Underdevelopment*. He was Director-General of Finance of Southwest Persia from 1943 to 1946.

Mancur Olson is a Professor in the Department of Economics at the University of Maryland, College Park, Maryland. Among his professional contributions is *The Rise and Decline of Nations: Economic Growth, Stagflation, and Social Rigidities*, (New Haven: Yale University Press), 1982.

Cynthia Taft Morris is the Charles N. Clark Professor of Economics at Smith College. She is a former Vice President of the Economic History Association and is currently doing research in the role of the state in the early phases of capitalistic economic development. Morris and Irma Adelman co-authored *Comparative Patterns of Economic Development, 1850-1914*, published in 1988 by Johns Hopkins University Press in Baltimore.

Irma Adelman holds the Thomas Forsyth Hunt Chair in the Department of Agriculture and Resources Economics at the University of California, Berkeley. Her special interests in development are income distribution and poverty, quantification of social and political phenomena, agricultural development, and economic planning.

CHAPTER 4

The Antecedents and Consequences of Declining Fertility

Introduction

One crucial aspect of population growth in developing countries is that fertility rates continue to be higher than death rates. Consequently, rates of natural increase remain high. The demographic transition (reduction of birth, death, and natural increase rates) has been a topic of concern to sociologists, economists, and other demographers for over fifty years. While the major urban, industrial nations of the world made this transition earlier in the century, developing countries were still in various stages of the transition in the 1960s and many are only beginning to make the change. Although it was possible to produce an estimate of economic development based on demographic indicators earlier in the century, this is now not always a reliable indicator (Stockwell, 1960, 1963; Hauser, 1959).

Population growth in developing countries is supported by traditional high fertility norms and values that are being challenged by western small family norms and values. The most important vehicle of westernization in developing countries is the institution of formal education rather than simply the attainment of literacy. Christian missionaries who brought western education consciously taught European values and introduced European clothing and food. In addition, the western school system instilled independence and weakened the parental influence in the process of socialization. Such changes altered the traditional familial roles of children and their economic and familial roles as adults.

The Articles in Chapter 4

Thus, *Caldwell*, in "Mass Education as a Determinant of the Timing of Fertility Decline," proposes that mass education for males and females is the most important factor contributing directly and indirectly to fertility decline in the developing countries. In another article (1979), not included in this volume, Caldwell links mortality and fertility decline to changes in the family. He also finds that mother's education is of much greater significance than father's education in accounting for mortality decline.

This leads us to the next question then, why does high fertility persist in developing countries? In an even lengthier article than the first one in this chapter, "A Theory of Fertility: From High Plateau to Destabilization," *Caldwell* proposes an explanation of high fertility based on modes of family–centered production. As long as a two–tiered, work related arrangement that favors the males, particularly the older males, is in place, fertility will remain high. He argues that when the pattern of material advantage changes, a reversal in the intergenerational flow of wealth will precipitate fertility decline. As long as the net flow of wealth over a generational period favors the parents, they have an incentive to maintain high fertility. The spread of western values through mass education, as he stated in the first article, will weaken familial norms of old age support. Thus, westernization and social development will generate further fertility decline in high fertility societies.

The demographic problem of an aging population has been brewing in the developing countries, the impact of which will be visible by the middle of the next century. *Brown* illustrates the nature of the aging population problem by using Swaziland as an example. The pace of aging is hastened by increasing fertility rates and life expectancies. In Swaziland, while there will be a 248.2 percent increase in the total population between 1980 and 2025, the aged population will have increased by 304.4 percent during the same period. With the burgeoning of the aged population, the traditional system of care–giving is likely to be over–stretched. New policies, new approaches to the provision of shelter, employment and income security, and health care for the elderly will be called for.

Some of the current debates in population research are related to the institutional factors associated with the onset of fertility declines in the twentieth century. For a long time economic development was seen as the only force that would precipitate a fall in fertility. This view is losing ground as new evidence suggests that mass education plays a crucial role in the emergence of small family size. At the same time, a steady decline in fertility will lead to a steady increase in the proportion of aged, a group for whom problems will best be solved by reintegrating them into society.

REFERENCES

Caldwell, John C., "Education as a Factor in Mortality Decline: An Examination of Nigerian Data," *Population Studies*, 33(3), 1979, pp. 395–413.
Hauser, Philip G., "Demographic Indicators of Economic Development," *Economic Development and Cultural Change*, 7(2), January 1959, pp. 95–116.
Stockwell, Edward G., "The Measurement of Economic Development," *Economic Development and Cultural Change*, 7(4), July 1960, pp. 419– 432.
———, "Socio–Economic Differences Among Underdeveloped Areas," *Rural Sociology*, 28(2), 1963, pp. 165–175.

Mass Education as a Determinant of the Timing of Fertility Decline

JOHN C. CALDWELL

The Argument

The greatest impact of education is not direct but through the restructuring of family relationships and, hence, family economies and the direction of the net wealth flow. It is postulated here that education has its impact on fertility through at least five mechanisms:

First, it reduces the child's potential for work inside and outside the home. This occurs not merely because certain hours are subtracted from the day by school attendance and homework, but, perhaps more importantly, for two other reasons. The child is frequently alienated from those traditional chores that he feels to be at odds with his new learning and status. Parents, other adults, and even siblings may share some of these feelings and either fail to enforce traditional work or positively discourage it. Parents may feel that the child should retain all its energies for succeeding at school; they may feel that traditional familial work does not befit a person who is headed for nontraditional employment and status; they may be apprehensive of alienating the affection of a child who is so demonstrably going to be successful in the new, outside world.

Second, education increases the cost of children far beyond the fees, uniforms, and stationery demanded by the school. Schools place indirect demands on families to provide children with better clothing, better appearance (even extending to feeding), and extras that will enable the child to participate equally with other school children.

John C. Caldwell. Permission to reprint this article was received from The Population Council, which publishes *Population and Development Review*. It originally appeared in 1980, 6(2), pp. 225–255.

But costs go beyond this. School children demand more of their parents than do their illiterate siblings fully enmeshed in the traditional family system and morality. They ask for food and other things in the house in a way that is unprecedented, and they ask for expenditures outside. Their authority is the new authority of the school, and their guides are the nontraditional ways of life that have been revealed. Parents regard the school child as a new and different type of child with greater needs, and fear alienating him. Parents are aware that such alienation has been made likelier because the educated child is less likely to need familial employment, and the new morality from the school (and from the outside world to which the school has provided an introduction and a feeling of membership) makes it less likely that he will as completely heed the teachings of family morality.

Third, schooling creates dependency, both within the family and within the society. In the absence of schooling, all members of the family are clearly producers – battlers in the family's struggle for survival. Children may get a disproportionately small share of the returns, but that is because they must have patience and wait, and they owe something for parental guidance and even for the gift of life. With schooling, it becomes clear that the society regards the child as a future rather than a present producer, and that it expects the family to protect the society's investment in the child for that future. Family relationships tend to adjust to this expectation. Reinforcing changes occur in the wider society: legislation to protect children typically accelerates in the first years of universal schooling. All these changes make children less productive and more costly both to the family and to the society. These changes also mean that children no longer really share responsibility for the family's survival in the present.

Fourth, schooling speeds up cultural change and creates new cultures. In the West, values of the school were clearly middle-class values, and the schools imposed as many of these on the working class as they could. However, schools induced changes in all classes, partly because, by their nature and their very existence, their agenda was so obviously that of the broad society and its economy – its capitalist economy – and not that of family production and the morality that sustained that production.

Fifth, in the contemporary developing world, the school serves as a major instrument – probably the major instrument – for propagating the values, not of the local middle class, but of the Western middle class. Little is taught or implied that is at odds with Western middle-class values, while traditional family morality is disdained or regarded as irrelevant and as part of that other nonschool, preschool – even antischool – world.

The first two postulates are widely accepted, partly because they can be seen to operate even without the recognition of a major restructuring of family morality. But it is probably the last three that have the most impact in changing family economies from a situation in which high fertility is worthwhile to one in which it is disastrous. Indeed, the significance of the changes in terms of altering the impact of fertility on parental prerogative may well be in ascending order as listed.

Several points about the nature of education should be made. The important engine of demographic change seems to be formal schooling rather than the widespread attainment of literacy without mass schooling, as occurred in the West prior to the mid-nineteenth century. Furthermore, demographic change is unlikely if the movement toward mass schooling is confined largely to males, as has been the case in parts of the Middle East. The impact of education in the West was not identical with its impact in the contemporary developing world; in the former, the importation of a different culture was a far less important aspect (and so education may have taken longer to reverse the wealth flow and required greater economic change to do so). Finally, the first generation of mass schooling usually appears to be enough to initiate fertility decline. If it does not, the second generation should prove conclusive. Educated parents tend to concede that the demands of educated children are fundamentally right, even if irritating and impoverishing. Educated mothers usually see to it that their children obtain a larger share of the family pie, and justify this to their husbands or the older generation. It seems improbable – and has yet to be demonstrated – that any society can sustain stable high fertility beyond two generations of mass schooling.

Before considering historical and contemporary evidence for education's role in initiating fertility decline, let us review the arguments of the recent literature.

Although there is a vast literature on the relationship between education and fertility, very little is strictly relevant to the argument advanced here, for three main reasons. First, most of the literature fails to concentrate on the onset of fertility transition, but confuses this issue with fertility differentials at other times, usually well on in the course of fertility decline. The examination of post-transitional fertility differentials may be of importance for predicting population growth, or even for demonstrating the different economic-demographic calculuses employed in the various social classes, but is of little value in analyzing the nature of a change that has already affected all social classes. Second, the literature fails to concentrate on the onset of universal education, but usually employs indexes of the proportion of educated or literate persons across a wide age range (or even includes measures of the duration of education). Third, the literature tends to concentrate far more in terms of data, and almost wholly in terms of theory, on the impact of education on the parental generation rather than on their children. It is possible to justify the standard approach by arguing that the parents, during the early period of compulsory education, can control not only their own fertility but also the regularity with which their children attend school. Such an argument ignores the impact that compulsory schooling regardless of level of daily attendance has on creating dependency and on changing social and economic relationships within the family.

Two recent reviews of the literature on the relation between education and fertility, by Harvey Graff and Susan Cochrane, largely fail all three tests (partly, of course, because it is not their explicit or sole aim to concentrate on the onset of fertility transition).[1] Graff's work is largely an attack on his predecessors, although he does briefly make three points of his own: the evidence for a negative relationship between the education of individuals and their fertility is not nearly as general or as strong as has often been stated; the impact of education is often specific to the society to which it is applied; education usually does not cause demographic change directly but mediates the change caused by more basic forces, apparently largely economic ones. The first argument finds support from the Australian evidence: once the Australian fertility transition was underway, the lag by level of education in reducing family size appears to have been only a year or two at most.[2] Indeed, the fertility change appears to affect the whole society as a result of an educational transformation among all the children of the society. Graff's second argument probably does not hold good if it can be taken so far as to imply that a society can withstand the fertility transition. The historical evidence so far is all to the contrary.

His third argument is not as restrictive as it first appears, and could be taken to support fully the thesis that, while the ability to erect a system of universal education and the fact of a major change in the relations of production are both products of fundamental economic change, the timing of the *onset* of fertility decline (in terms of decades, and perhaps, sometimes, generations) is more determined by the timing of the establishment of universal education – indeed education plays a mediating role.

Historians of demographic change have shown greater interest in pinpointing the beginnings of educational and demographic movements. Coale observed, "Every nation in the world today in which no more than 45 percent of the labor force is engaged in extractive industry, in which at least 90 percent of the children of primary school age attend school, and which is at least 50 percent urban has experienced a major decline in fertility. But France reduced its fertility before attaining any of these characteristics, and England had most of them before its marital fertility fell at all."[3] The measure of education is one with which this paper sympathizes – it is certainly superior to most of the aggregate measures of education. However, it is argued below (with evidence from the studies of Coale's Princeton group) that the timing of France's fertility transition is not necessarily at odds with its achievement of universal schooling, and that the timing of the English transition is not at odds at all if we concentrate on the educational measure. Tilly, while arguing that the relationship between education and fertility decline is not necessarily as close as this paper posits, nevertheless includes a quotation from Thabault about the history of his own French village, which is very much in the spirit of wealth flows analysis: "The respect for knowledge … was not strong enough around 1850 [30 years before compulsory education] to push the peasants to shake off their old habits, to give up the labor of their children, or to impose on them the necessary discipline, at the cost of paying constant attention to their performance."[4]

A contemporary observer of the early Australian fertility decline recorded the views of women of reproductive age and reported that these early innovators took for granted that it was the move to universal schooling that changed the economic situation of the family and the position of children in it.[5] There has also been a series of studies of relative educational and fertility differences within a single country.[6] Their evidence – usually inconclusive – is not very relevant to the argument here, partly because most use aggregate educational or literacy data across many age groups, and partly because the argument here is that the attainment of universal schooling across a single nation or culture group is the force that changes intergenerational attitudes and hence economic relationships.

One study, published 40 years ago, did attempt to link the cost of education to the declining birth rate in England, but focused attention on direct costs rather than on the much more massive rises in children's cost occasioned by the transformation of economic relations within the family that accompanies mass education.[7]

Two points are of basic importance when distinguishing between the case put here and those found in the literature. First, the new sets of family relationships and obligations, created by the fact and ethos of universal education, owe much, at least in the timing of the change, to the advent of education. However, this does not mean that the new familial culture, in which the wealth flows are downward, is adopted in each successive generation in proportion to the educational level attained. Once the change has taken place, it tends to become universal, and educational differentials are of little importance (and where they show up as modest fertility differentials, they may rather reflect an educational differential in

the innovational adoption of new and more efficient methods of birth control). Second, form a historical point of view (and in terms of whether global fertility decline ultimately takes place or not) the pauses and apparent slight reversals in the path of fertility decline are not very important. Too many of the widely quoted economic-demographic analyses are derived from the experience of the United States during the last half-century. This was a period three-quarters of a century after nearly universal schooling had been achieved and during which the birth rate never exceeded 25 per thousand. Furthermore, a central feature of the period (and an even more central feature of the economic-demographic analyses) was the so-called baby boom, a misleading label that conveys messages that in fact are probably not real at all. The problem is that the baby boom rise in fertility was largely a compound of earlier and more nearly universal marriages in a period of imperfect contraception, of overlapping cohort reproduction with each birth cohort marrying earlier, of the fertility of some Depression and wartime marriages being delayed until after the war, and of the apparent beginning of the boom being silhouetted against the preceding lower-than-trend fertility arising from the family crises of the Depression of the 1930s.[8] It was not a good period from which to derive general historical lessons, and in retrospect it was only a bump in the long US, and Western, fertility decline.

••••

The Contemporary Developing World

Mass schooling, also as the spread of an idea, has come to much of the developing world at an earlier stage, in terms of economic structure, than it did in much of the West. It has probably much greater implications for changing family relationships and declining fertility than it had in the West. In the latter, a somewhat different culture was transmitted from one part of society to another, and ultimately certain aspects of middle-class culture were intensified and taught to the whole society. In the developing world, not only is a foreign culture being imported, but this is being done at a time when that culture has moved far toward egalitarianism within the family and toward numerous adjustments to low fertility.

The two major strains in developing-world education – the objective of instilling moral values and the importation of these values from Western culture – have their origins in the earliest colonial efforts to provide such education. In early British India, views on the role of education were often very explicit. In 1792 Charles Grant wrote that education should be used "to improve native morals."[9] Macaulay, in his 1835 *Minute*, asserted, "We must at present do our best to form a class who may be interpreters between us and the millions whom we govern – a class of persons Indian in blood and color, but English in tastes, in opinions, in morals and in intellect." Marx in the same year wrote, "England has to fulfill a double mission in India: one destructive and the other regenerating – the annihilation of old Asian society and the laying of the material foundations of Western society in Asia."[10]

In Africa there was even less doubt about promoting new moralities, for missionaries, who formed the backbone of the schooling system until the 1960s, "had come to Africa primarily to convert and civilize the heathen and to stop the slave trade."[11] A more sympathetic observer of the missionaries comments, with regard to initiation and other *rites de passage* that were the hallmark of family morality in that they established differentiations by age and sex: "The age at which children went to school, the prevalence of mission boarding schools, and features of the initiation rites which were dangerous to health and objectionable on Christian moral grounds caused the missionaries to clash with this

traditional training. The result was that it was largely abandoned by Christians." And again, more generally: "When the former training of children and young people in African societies is compared with the modern school systems now operating, certain features of the traditional patterns appear to have been abandoned, notably those which showed the close correlation between the training of personality and character and the integration and cohesion of family, clan and tribal units."[12] Sutton explained the "civilizing" role of education: "This missionary impulse made education in Western forms ancillary to religious purpose. Enough had to be taught to make Christian ideas comprehensible and to combat practices and beliefs that were regarded as barbarous or heathenish."[13] Ogunsheye, reporting somewhat ruefully on the schooling of his own people, the Yoruba of Nigeria, noted an "inevitable emphasis on English traits and individuals"; the "British put the foremost emphasis on character training."[14] Clearly, neither the character nor the traits were those found in traditional familial roles.

Musgrove reported of the school in which he taught in Uganda following World War II that it consciously taught European values and that it saw as part of this process the adoption of European clothing, food, and habits of punctuality. Giraure reported of the school at which he was a pupil during the 1960s in Papua New Guinea that a thoroughgoing effort was made to change his culture.[15] He was given a new European name in the mission school and then required to speak only English while attending the government school. Ultimately, "we looked with horror upon the village life ... the children returned ... having little in common with the people among whom they were to live. The result was and still is chaos ... juvenile delinquency ... the breakdown of village traditions and life."[16] Quotations of this kind, detailing the dismantling of the preexisting system of family relationships, would not be so telling if any participants ever told a different tale. One might anticipate the different tale with independence, but it is not so, for new nations see prosperity being built on the foundation provided by the destruction of traditional society. In modern India, where the educated are identified by "their dress, speech and manners," schooling "is now intended as a prime means of innovation, rather than as the great instrument for conservation."[17] In its crudest form, this goal is stated approvingly by a Westerner: "In Burma the object of education is not in doubt: Education is to serve as one of the means of social transformation from a raw material producing society where the bulk of the people had a narrow, peasant, traditional view to a diversified, somewhat industrialized society able to absorb and use the most modern of scientific knowledge: it is to build a modern nation of responsible citizens."[18]

There has always been some resistance or doubt. In India in the late eighteenth century, Warren Hastings and others in the East India Company banned missionary education on the grounds that it was unsettling to society. In post-World War II Uganda, schoolboys remained suspicious of European motives in providing education.[19] There is, in fact, an interesting question of why the demand for the schooling of children exists, given that it destroys a family structure of which the older generation has always approved and a family economy that brought them benefits in proportion to the number of children they had. Is education seen as a means to further social justice and mobility, the stability of the political order, and national strength, as it was in the West, or are there other attractions?

The earliest attractions toward Western education were varied. One element was virtue, because education had traditionally been a training for priestly duties. This element remains a potent force in India, where the trends toward more education

and toward Sanskritization can have similar roots and appearance. Another was magical power – the ability to transcribe words into marks on paper that someone else could convert back again in another place and time. In the villages of western Uganda in the 1950s, where literacy was greatly respected, the description " 'reader' and 'Christian' [were] still convertible terms."[20] In a more down-to-earth sense, Africans wanted education in order to learn and manipulate the European secret of power.[21] Jobs became increasingly important, first because they brought cash, or extra revenue, to supplement the family economy; then because individuals were deserting that economy and fending for themselves rather than for relatives; and finally because the family economy could not stand either this desertion or the competing forms of production and collapsed.[22] Pride in children's achievements can also play a significant role,[23] although in India a father with an unmarriable educated daughter "may be accused of sacrificing his daughter's chances in life to a mistaken whim intended to glorify his own name."[24] On the other hand, in South Asia and even in Southwest Asia, there is a growing awareness that only an educated daughter can secure that desirable addition to the family – an educated son-in-law with a job in the modern sector – and that a large dowry on its own may no longer be sufficient. In South Asia even a rural family often feels the need for one educated son simply to cope with the bureaucrats.[25]

The present position of education is complex and uncertain. While traditional family morality persists and the wealth flow is from the younger to the older generation, and while the educated are paid far more or have far greater access to power than the uneducated, the temptation for parents to educate their children and so obtain access to the wealth of the economy's modern sector can be immense. Yet the same education may clearly destroy the moral system that alone can guarantee the older generation large and continuing returns. It does not necessarily do so in one generation in the absence of universal education. The traditional morality can show surprising resilience, as among the Yoruba,[26] and the education of children can bring parents high rewards and can buttress high fertility.

How education can endanger the traditional system is clear enough even from the syllabuses and textbooks, and has been shown vividly by a study of infant and primary school textbooks in Ghana, Nigeria, and Kenya.[27] These books are important because they are used in schools attended by a much larger proportion of the community than are secondary schools. They are important also because they are first read when the children are young and impressionable, and when they most uncritically accept the teacher and school as new authority figures and often as superior ones with regard to knowledge about the modern world that many of the pupils will increasingly aspire to join. The messages are all the more potent because they are most often found in reading primers, where the substance or attitudes are taken for truth, rather than in specialized books on society, which might be expected to point to some areas of controversy or doubt.

In the books that we studied, we found no support for such basic African traditional institutions as polygamy, unstable marriage, the condemnation of sterile women or women who repeatedly lose children, bewitchment, and, most importantly, the attitude that the needs of the family have priority over those of the community.

There was in Kenya alone, in a new series of tales form a traditional viewpoint,[28] some support (at least in stories of the past) for bride price, arranged marriage, initiation, and violence in tribal warfare. However, concessions are made to the traditional family authority structure and to the age-old upward direction of the wealth flow. Where arranged marriage and bride

price exist, they merely confirm a love match already in existence – rather like the expression of parental approval of an engagement. And where a tribal conflict is plotted and carried out, it is the young man who does it while leaving his father in ignorance rather than disobeying him.[29] Initiation is handled by laying stress almost solely on the joy of attaining manhood.

The school reading books generally assume that children are dependents; that the husband must farm (or work in an office) while his wife undertakes the domestic work and the children give first place to their schoolwork; that priority should be given to nation-building, citizenship, and honesty in the larger society; that children should do jobs at home to be "good" rather than as an enforceable duty to the family; that fathers are kindly and understanding rather than distant and awesome; and that parents are closer to children, and that husbands are usually closer to wives, than they are to other relatives. Children are portrayed at play; nuclear families are portrayed eating together. Drumming and traditional dance, if covered, are divorced from traditional religious rites. Extended family residence, when mentioned, coexists with nuclearization.[30] An East African first reader unintentionally brings out the magnitude of the changes with its portrayal of a family in a traditional setting behaving like members of the Western middle class: children with toys, father entertaining his young daughter, mother dapper in a clean dress. The chief thrust of school books in independent countries is exemplified by the introductory "Note to the Teacher" in a widely used Ghanaian series: "The chief aim in teaching citizenship education is to help young people become well-informed, hard-working, selfless, honest and responsible citizens. With citizens such as these, a nation will be sufficiently equipped to achieve success and moral prosperity."[31]

These messages – often presented as

African traditions – are remote from the family morality and lifestyle still practiced by the great majority of citizens. Yet the textbooks never give any indication that this is so: African names are used for persons, objects, and ceremonies; the illustrations show African huts, animals, and bush. But the message is contemporary Western and, if fully acted out, would certainly mean that high fertility would prove economically oppressive and that family size would eventually decline.[32]

It should be noted that syllabuses with Western messages were not merely imposed by colonialists. There has always been a strong local demand for colonial educational systems and for syllabuses identical with those in the metropolitan centers; it is partly a question of not accepting the second-best and partly one of students gaining unchallenged access to further education in the metropolises. Newly independent nations felt competitive pressures for closely paralleling the West in the nature and message of schools, and their efforts were strongly supported by international organizations. Carnoy claims, "In the non-industrialized country, the school is an institution that not only keeps the individual from self-definition, but keeps the entire society from defining itself. The schools are an extension of the metropole structure."[33] That definition will in fact never hold, for schools are a mechanism for creating a Westernized global society. They do this largely unwittingly, for most educationalists take learning to be virtue, and do not distinguish the various brands of virtue. In any case, really new workable institutions are extremely difficult to create. The West has an educational model that will inevitably be used, partly because it exists and is widely known; partly because it produces usable textbooks or textbook prototypes, syllabuses, teachers, and organizational models; and partly because it is associated with successful economic development.

The Impact of Schooling on the Developing-World Family System

The main message of the school is not spelled out in textbooks. It is assumed by teachers, pupils, and even parents. They all know that school attendance means acceptance of a way of life at variance with the strictly traditional. Many school children no longer realize just how great that variance is or just what strictly traditional behavior is.

Masemann reported that the hidden syllabus in the Ghanaian girls' school where she taught was the Western way of life, and said of the typical pupil: "She learns how to play marital, parental and occupational roles through experiencing many aspects of school life that are never made explicit in a formal curriculum." "When the students write about the kind of life they expect to lead after marriage, they mention co-operation between husband and wife in financial matters, solidarity of the married couple in conflict with kin, shared responsibility for children...." "They feel ... competent to 'live a modern life' and they have every intention of doing so."[34] Several points should be noted. First, if they achieve the degree of solidarity and cooperation within marriage that they anticipate, and if they focus this on their children to the relative exclusion of their kin, then the upward wealth flow to their own parents will be greatly diminished, and the net flow over a lifetime almost certainly reversed. Second, although it is not discussed by Masemann, these students may already be making ever-stronger demands for financial support from their parents (and possibly other kin) over the strict minimum needed to keep them at school. Third, these changes in family emotional and economic relationships have not been economically determined; the economic effects – profound ones for the society and its fertility – have been purely the result of attitudinal changes arising from the intentional and unintentional Westernizing impact of their schooling.

Most developing-world societies are very much aware that schooling leads to profound social change. At early stages this is usually anticipated with apprehension.[35] Although tempted by the money and influence following in the wake of education, traditional families often remained justifiably apprehensive of schooling, especially for girls. In the Congo Free State during the late nineteenth century, "local people objected strenuously to sending children to the mission station because they 'came back changed.'" Among the Dinka of the Sudan, over half a century later, "girls' education was especially abhorred because that implied turning them into town–women, immoral and unsuited for marriage."[36] The Dinka are not Muslim in religion, but their views are still echoed over much of the Islamic world and beyond it into village India.

There is widespread agreement that schooling at advanced levels is first and foremost a process of Westernization. Tilman wrote of the Malay College in Kuala Kangsar, Malaysia, that "by the time of graduation, its students had been thoroughly socialized into an upper-class English cultural environment," while Kirk-Greene reported much the same for the highly educated Hausa elite of northern Nigeria, and Sutton more generally for those receiving higher education in Africa.[37] However, the same process, although less extreme, occurs from the first days at school; the Wisers observed the effects of vestigial elementary schooling in a small village on India's Gangetic Plain 50 years ago: "The boys who know nothing beyond village routine are content. Those who have gone to school are restless. They have disassociated learning from the work their fathers have to offer them." They also reported a landowner chasing an Untouchable boy, obligated to do him services under the jajmani system, away from their classes, not because the boy had anything else to do at that time of night, but because

the jajman was well aware of the alien influences transmitted by schooling and the likelihood that new attitudes would begin to change ancient lines of authority and obligation.[38] In Latin America, the Westernizing influence of schooling is likely to make Indian students adopt as models the lifestyles of the mestizos or ladinos. This was the major conclusion of Epstein's research in rural Peru and of Redfield's in rural Guatemala. The latter, reviewing a long period of contact with the same village, wrote: "As I look at the school in the little village where I once was resident, it appears to me to play a greater part in changing the culture of the people than in handing it on from one generation to the next, although its influence in the direction of change is indirect."[39]

In one sense, the attack on family morality begins with, or is paralleled by, an attack on the theology that supports and justifies it. This is obvious and widely felt in Muslim societies. An imam in southern Thailand explained that "education made a man unreligious; literacy enables a man to disobey God. Civilization is antireligious."[40] "Civilization" in this sense is Westernization, culturally as well as theologically. This is less obvious in the case of more ancient religions, although these are more intimately connected with ancestral spirits and the morality of gerontocratic control. Greenfield and Bruner found that illiterate children in West Africa, like their ancestors, explained a wider range of phenomena in "magical" terms – as being ordained by persons other than those present at the experiment. However, "the school suppresses this mode of thinking with astonishing absoluteness. There is not one instance of such reasoning among either bush or city Senegalese children who have been in school seven months or longer."[41]

Schools destroy the corporate identity of the family, especially for those members previously most submissive and most wholly contained by the family: children and women. In Mexico, "Going to school has in addition awakened new desires in children by removing them from the limited sphere of parental influence. They are no longer content to stay within patio walls at the beck and call of their mother; they urgently want to be with friends and to play after school. Play always has been, and still is, considered a possible source of danger and a waste of time by parents."[42] These problems are widespread in the developing world, with concern over the danger to the family system outweighing concern over the specific loss of time. Playing is but a symptom of a greater assault on the family's corporate identity. Literate culture often lays stress on behavioral patterns inimical to the family system, such as in its encouragement of differentiation and solitariness, whereas the oral tradition does not.[43] Indeed, in West Africa the main limitation on the extension of rural housing seems to be not lack of labor or capital, but the lack of demand in nonliterate households for space peripheral to the center of family activities. In India, too, education, especially when it is extended, can provide an "initial psychological impetus: a sense of individuality with a desire for greater independence .... [However,] the initiative for leaving the joint family often comes from the wife, whereas psychological conditioning sometimes prevents the husband from himself contemplating such a move."[44] The wife (the daughter-in-law in the joint family) has, of course, much more to gain by such a move, and may attempt it less because she has acquired a feeling of individuality than because she has received from education a new cultural backing and a new cultural status that justifies her break with family tradition both in her own eyes and in those of her relatives-in-law. Education in India may place a man at a distance not only from his family but also from its alliances and the factions to which it adheres, thus eroding another of the values of high fertility.[45]

Schooling means revolt against non-Western family relationships, although research has tended to concentrate much more on the erosion of agreement on the wife's role than on that of the child – perhaps partly because the latter is taken so much for granted. Omari, surveying secondary school pupils in Ghana over 20 years ago, found that 1 percent of girls desired a traditional marriage, while 86 percent "thought polygamy definitely backward" and 94 percent believed "love in marriage most important." Only 45 percent were certain that they would obey their parents' arrangements for marriage. "With increase in education the women fail to see the need for sharing a husband with another – apart from the fact that the thought runs anomalous to the Western ideas they have imbibed at school and abroad."[46] The strongest reaction against the education of girls in the Congo Free State and the Belgian Congo arose from the fear that girls who had been to school would revolt against arranged marriage and marriage to polygamists.[47] The Christian church everywhere has battled polygyny, making it clear in Africa, when protesters pointed to the fact that the Old Testament recorded the institution without condemning it, that modern Christian morality means Western morality. In India there is the "fear that [a woman] will not make a proper, dutiful wife because of her schooling."[48] This paper has concentrated on the direct impact of schooling on child-parent emotional and economic relationships whether or not husband-wife relationships have changed. Nevertheless, in the most traditional families the position of the wife of the younger generation (i.e., the mother of nonadult children) is not very different from that of the children; a change in her role is almost certain to effect a change in theirs (although the fact that children have been to school usually does not affect the role of an illiterate mother).

Fundamentally, the school attacks the

traditional family's economic structure by weakening the authority of the old over the young (and of the male over the female). In Africa, where the mission and the school were for long almost indistinguishable, Yates said of the Congo that, "of course, missionary dominance meant a decrease of African political authority" and quoted the Prefect Apostolic as reported in 1905: "They [the Chiefs] sense as if by instinct that if we are successful it will mark the end of their despotic domination … they do not want us to speak of God, of Christ and especially of monogamy." Clignet argues that this was inevitable because of the extent to which, both in the West and in the developing world, schools have been expected to act *in loco parentis*. Schools attacked parental authority partly by providing new authority models from the West or from Westernized local people who seemed to epitomize the cultural patterns taught or implied. Indeed, the models, by their behavior, provided much of the implicit teaching. In Burma, "The teacher is the repository of knowledge…. They would never challenge [him]"; in Masemann's school in Ghana, the teacher was the role model; throughout Africa when schools first appeared, "the newly educated looked to Europeans … for advancement and for models of behavior."[49] The real position is more complex even than this, for a major stabilizing force in traditional society has been the superior wisdom of the old, both occult and from long experience. The school provides the young with knowledge and skills that the old do not possess, while usually also attacking the value of traditional knowledge. This alone, during the attainment of mass schooling in the nineteenth-century West and the contemporary developing world, weakens family authority.

A Synthesis

In spite of much sophisticated analysis of "the global economy," we have hardly begun to discuss the parallel and related creation of a "global society." The movement toward a global economy makes the movement toward a global society inevitable, but such social movements as the spread of mass schooling can greatly accelerate economic change at every level from the family to the nation. With these changes will come demographic change.

The major change of demographic significance – and perhaps the most significant economic and social change – has been that from family production to capitalist production within a labor market external to the family. In the system of family production, high fertility was no disadvantage, whereas low fertility could be destructive. Family production was controlled by family morality, which gave power to the old and usually to the male, and which frequently sharply differentiated production and consumption roles by age and sex. Family morality formed the greater part of the culture (or super-structure) and often had strong religious underpinnings. The advantages that powerful family members obtained form high fertility did not pass quickly as capitalist production grew, partly because the age-old morality ensured them of more than an equal fraction of consumption and partly because family production of domestic goods and services by wives and children has waned slowly even in the most industrialized societies. Thus high fertility may continue in spite of a major decline in nondomestic family production, as long as family morality does not decay – in other words, as long as the wealth flow continues from the younger to the older generation. Family morality could hardly have decayed anywhere if family production had remained the dominant form of production worldwide. But once it began to lose its dominant position, as in the West, the new societal or capitalistic morality could develop and could be exported. It is quite possible that such a morality can be at least partly grafted onto a society with a high level of family production and that it can be an element in a premature (by the precedents of Western history) fertility decline.

There have long been threats to family morality, quite apart from the development of capitalist production. These include any form of religion that is not family-centered (and even ancestral) and any form of law that is external to the family – anything, in fact, that belongs to the Great Tradition rather than the Little Tradition.[50] The least dangerous type of religion is one that enshrines the family as a necessary unit, such as Hinduism, and especially one that enshrines the sex and age segmentation of family production and addresses itself chiefly to the patriarch, as in Islam. But even these religions can become more interested in the individual, as did Buddhism in splintering from Hinduism. The greatest danger developed in the West: Judaism addressed itself to the individual as well as the family; Catholicism did not only that but did so from a huge extrafamilial, institutionalized base; Protestantism appealed almost solely to the individual (and could hardly have developed if there had not been sufficient capitalist production to have modified family morality). Any type of state organization and authority – certainly the raising of troops – offered potential danger to the uniqueness and unity of the family. This was particularly so with regard to the law, especially in the case of both the Roman law of the Republic and Empire and English common law.

The school has a very complex relation with these Great Traditions. It is another of the extrafamily institutions. But much of its impact on the family lies in the fact that it serves as a medium for these other institutions – for religion, state morality, state legal tradition, and national cultural and historical traditions. In most developing-world villages, the usual way that the first generation of school children explain the impact of education is that it makes them part of a much larger world – often they

just say "of the world." Governments have always been in competition with the family for loyalty; governments that were unable to maintain a share of this loyalty ceased to function. This is particularly true in the developing world. The survival of governments depends on competition with families, and, as is clear from our analysis of school textbooks, governments regard schools as their chief instruments for teaching citizenship – for going over the heads of the patriarchs and appealing directly to the children. In doing so, they inevitably emphasize the importance of the new generation and so strike yet another blow at family morality and family economics.

Nevertheless, family morality can prove remarkably resistant to change. The history of the West proves that: fertility did not fall in Britain until it was an advanced industrialized economy with only 17 percent of its population working in primary production and contributing less than 10 percent of gross national income, and with 25 percent of its population living in centers with more than 100,000 inhabitants. However, that pattern is unlikely to repeat itself; the existence of the Western model and its spread – even when inadvertent – by national educational systems will see to that. The only exception may be the Muslim countries, where religion supports family role segmentation and where, in many cases, levels of female education are likely to remain low. The tropical African family system has so far also proved resilient, and wealth flows have continued upward even in the middle class because of a strong cultural emphasis on what the young owe to the old (partly perhaps because respect for ancestors is still prevalent).[51] In fact the traditional family expects to remain intact, and so eventually overreaches itself. It has always taken risks and has always attempted to maximize its income and resources. Hence, when an outside labor market develops, children are encouraged to earn income and bring it into the household.

They are even sent to school to ensure that they can eventually earn higher incomes. Some traditional families have used their younger people to earn outside incomes for millennia (in the Middle East and the Mediterranean) while retaining control of them and their income and spending relatively little on them. This situation may disappear everywhere within the next half-century; if it does pass as quickly as this, mass schooling rather than mass industrialization will have been responsible.

The family system of morality and production has been little described and has begun to pass without even the circumstances of its passing being noted precisely because it was so all–embracing. It was not *a* morality; it was *the* morality, and hence commonsensical and unremarkable. When it does pass, within a generation or two the old morality is remembered with nostalgia; the respect for the old is remembered as childhood humility, not as the rigid system that it was. The first generation of school children who emerged from it were usually treated differently from the way earlier generations had been treated. Because of their schooling, many expected the kind of treatment they received without realizing this was an innovation, while their parents and grandparents moved, often awkwardly, to accept and engineer this new status without realizing just how irrevocable the step was. To the researcher and to some of the teachers and other citizens, this transition was visible in the towns of Ghana 20 years ago, when many families were composed of a mixture of children who went to school and those, often somewhat older, who had not been and would never go.[52] Most parents treated school children quite differently from the way they treated their illiterate siblings, and few of the school children seemed in any way aware of this. In later life, even as social scientists, they will probably be unable to recall the transition.[53]

One can generalize further. Those who have participated in the affairs of state or the church have always been at least partly outside the confines of the system of family production, and they have had to modify its morality. This is also true of soldiers, scholars, migrants, large merchants, and anyone who employs others. Almost by definition, those who have interpreted, written, read, and challenged historical records have long been members of these numerically marginal groups. As family production and its determining morality passes, the very memories of it pass. Later generations, who live outside the system, do not regard those who were involved in family production as having been in the mainstream of history.

This brings us to an important point in the analysis of the change in relative child-adult status (and also wife-husband status) effected by education. The magnitude of the change is so great because it rests not only on what the school teaches, but also on how the educated child sees himself (especially relative to uneducated parents or siblings) and how his other relatives (especially uneducated parents or siblings) see him. These different perspectives are crucial elements in permanently changing relative intergenerational status. They are, for instance, the greatest factors in altering the relationship between an educated daughter-in-law and an uneducated mother-in-law to a point where the former can intervene individually to care for her children and to change the traditional balance of consumption and treatment within the family, with dramatic effects on child mortality.[54]

There remain two problems and one essential statement.

The first problem is the distinction between the impact of education on the first generation and on subsequent generations. It has been argued here that the change resulting from education in terms of the increased cost of a child and decreased lifetime return is sufficient to cause falling fertility from the onset of mass education. This appears to have been the case in the West; within a decade of the introduction of compulsory schooling, the fertility of all occupational groups was declining.[55] The pattern in the developing world may be different. In the West, a moderately high level of family morality remained so long after the development of the nonfamily labor market that a point was reached at which the chief value of children may have been their low consumption rather than their high production or return: under these conditions it may have taken very little to disturb the equilibrium. This family morality itself was, moreover, relatively weak compared with what is still found in the Middle East, Africa, or South Asia. It was already being challenged by societal morality: in spite of a proportion of parents of the generation of the 1870s and 1880s being unschooled, there was a level of literacy, numeracy, and outward-looking citizenship that affected nearly everyone. There was little equivalent in the West to the illiterate and completely traditional mothers of some of the school children in the contemporary developing world. This female illiteracy and an unquestioning, total immersion in family morality enable the patriarch to treat his wife (or wives) as one of the children and, through dominance over her, to solidify his dominance over his schooled children. A school child can falter in feeling part of a new, wider world if the father, whether educated or not, maintains his patriarchal role and the mother remains unwaveringly traditional. In this case the wealth flow may not turn downward until the second generation of mass education, when mothers as well as children are educated, and may not turn down at all if only fathers are educated and the tradition of illiterate wives persists.

A second and related problem is the distinction between education of males and females. In this regard, the key issue to explore is whether the education of the wife has a separate, interacting and compounding effect on changing family morality. Contemporaries thought such a separate effect was important in the nineteenth-century West, and it is probably important in the contemporary developing world.[56] In the traditional patriarchal family, there is undoubtedly a net wealth flow from wife to husband (and also to mother-in-law and father-in-law), which is reduced if an educated wife demands more equitable treatment or is awarded it because of the way the society views the educated. Even more important, education often leads to a strengthened bond between wife and husband, which renders the traditional family structure and its morality exceedingly difficult to maintain.[57] Finally, educated wives, even when the child-parent wealth flow is still upward, may dislike repeated pregnancies and periods with infants and may attempt to prolong the interval between births, with a consequent impact on fertility.

The essential statement is that the coincidental timing of the attainment of mass education and the onset of fertility decline is probably neither fortuitous nor due to a third factor dictating the exact timing of both. There are ample mechanisms to explain why mass education should have such a powerful impact on family economics. Nevertheless, the education of only half the community does not have the same effect on that half of the population, nor half the effect on the whole population. One reason is probably that, when only a fraction of the population has been to school, there remain strong forces to maintain family morality as the basic morality of the society (this may be less true in a highly stratified society). Probably a more important reason is that in such a divided society there remain very marked differentials in wages and salaries by education (especially in a highly stratified society), and an educated family can prosper. Probably these two reasons interacted in the mid-nineteenth-century West to maintain high fertility, and probably the same applies to urban Nigeria today. In Ibadan in 1973, about 40 percent of mothers under age 60 had been to school, while the great majority of their children – over 90 percent of even their dependent daughters – had attended school. Fertility was not yet falling, but this was partly explained by steep declines in the period of postnatal sexual abstinence.[58] It seems highly unlikely that these daughters will be as fertile as their mothers.

There are mechanisms that can directly relate schooling to fertility decline. They are not identical in the contemporary developing world and the nineteenth-century West. The contemporary developing world has all the influences experienced by the nineteenth-century West, plus the huge force of twentieth-century Westernization, especially with regard to family relationship, as taught by schools, Western example, films, newspapers, magazines, radio, and television. My earlier statement of this brought protests, especially from the developed world, that developing-world schools transmitted not culture but the three Rs needed for economic development. That is why is has been necessary to document at some length in this paper the findings of researchers who have noted the impact of schooling. Although the evidence is scattered, the impressive point is that this long search for evidence has unearthed no findings to suggest that there was little Westernizing influence in developing-world schooling, and none to suggest that this influence was not potent in the area of family relations. Furthermore, the evidence suggests that the most potent force for change is the breadth of education (the proportion of the community receiving some schooling) rather than the depth (the average duration of schooling among those who have attended school).

ENDNOTES

1. Harvey J. Graff, "Literacy, education, and fertility, past and present: A critical review," *Population and Development Review* 5, no. 1 (March 1979): 105–140; Susan H. Cochrane, *Fertility and Education: What Do We Really Know?* (Baltimore, Md.: Johns Hopkins University Press, 1979) (originally World Bank Staff Occasional Paper, No. 26). Geoffrey Hawthorn, *The Sociology of Fertility* (London: Collier-Macmillan,

1970), in a more general treatment of fertility decline, also fails these three tests.

2. L.T. Ruzicka and J.C. Caldwell, *The End of Demographic Transition in Australia* (Canberra: Department of Demography, Australian National University, 1977), pp. 171–174. The occupational evidence for urban areas suggests that the educated led the least educated or uneducated by about three years early in the transition but that this gap subsequently widened to as much as seven years, later narrowing.

3. Ansley J. Coale, "The decline of fertility in Europe from the French Revolution to World War II," in *Fertility and Family Planning: A World View*, ed. S.J. Behrman, Leslie Corsa, and Ronald Freedman (Ann Arbor: University of Michigan Press, 1969), p. 18.

4. Roger Thabault, "L'ascension d'un peuple: Mon village, ses hommes, ses routes, son école, 1848–1914," Paris, 1945, cited in Charles Tilly, "Population and pedagogy in France," *History of Education Quarterly* 13, no. 2 (1973): 123.

5. J. Ackerman, *Australia from a Woman's Point of View* (London: Cassel, 1913), pp. 91–93.

6. On the United States, see Richard A. Easterlin, "Factors in the decline of farm fertility in the United States: Some preliminary results," *Journal of American History* 63 (1976): 600–615; Don R. Leet, "The determinants of the fertility transition in Antebellum Ohio," *Journal of Economic History* 36, no. 2 (1976): .359–378; Maris A. Vinovskis, "Socio-economic determinants of interstate fertility differentials in the United States in 1850 and 1860," *Journal of Interdisciplinary History* 6, no. 3 (1976): 375–396. This problem is also encountered in all studies of Princeton University's Office of Population Research project on the historical decline of European fertility, because concentration on differences between the districts of individual countries is the basic methodological approach.

7. Grace C. Leybourne and Kenneth White, *Education and the Birth-Rate: A Social Dilemma* (London: Jonathan Cape, 1940), pp. 17–28.

8. John C. Caldwell and Lado T. Ruzicka, "Australian fertility transition: Destablizing a quasi-stable situation," Working Paper in Demography, No. 7 (Canberra: Department of Demography, Australian National University, 1977).

9. Martin Carnoy, *Education as Cultural Imperialism* (New York: Longman, 1974), p. 96.

10. Richard Lannoy, *The Speaking Tree: A Study of Indian Culture and Society* (London: Oxford University Press, 1971); quotations from Macaulay and Marx are from pages 238 and 237, respectively.

11. Carnoy, cited in note 9, p. 130.

12. Margaret Read, "Education in Africa: Its pattern and role in social change," in *From Child to Adult*, ed. John Middleton, Studies in the Anthropology of Education, American Museum Sourcebooks in Anthropology (New York: The Natural History Press, 1970); quotations are from pages 275 and 274, respectively.

13. Francis X. Sutton, "Education and the making of modern nations," in *Education and Political Development*, ed. James S. Coleman (Princeton, N.J.: Princeton University Press, 1965), p. 61.

14. Ayo Ogunsheye, "Nigeria," in Coleman (ed.), cited in note 13, p. 130.

15. F. Musgrove, "A Uganda secondary school as a field of culture change," *Africa* 22, no. 3 (1952): 234–249; Nelson Giraure, "The need for a cultural programme: Personal reflections," in *Education in Melanesia*, ed. J. Brammal and Ronald J. May (Canberra: Research School of Pacific Studies, Australian National University; Port Moresby: University of Papua New Guinea, 1975), pp. 101–104.

16. Giraure, cited in note 15, pp. 103–104.

17. David G. Mandelbaum, *Society in India* (Berkeley: University of California Press, 1970), vol. 2: *Change and Continuity*; quotations are from pages 508 and 414, respectively.

18. Manning Nash, "Education in a new nation: The village school in Upper Burma," in Middleton (ed.), cited in note 12, pp. 301–302.

19. On India, see Carnoy, cited in note 39, p. 89; on Uganda, see Musgrove, cited in note 15, p. 248.

20. On India, see Mandelbaum, cited in note 17, pp. 500–520. On education as magical power, see Barbara A. Yates, "African reactions to education: The Congolese case," *Comparative Education Review* 15, no. 2 (1971): 161–167, on the Congo Free State and the Belgian Congo; and Francis Mading Deng, *The Dinka of the Sudan* (New York: Holt, Rinehart and Winston, 1972), pp. 153–154, on the Dinka of southwestern Sudan. On Uganda, see Musgrove, cited in note 15, p. 244.

21. Sutton, cited in note 13, p. 62.

22. Yates, cited in note 20, pp. 161–167.

23. Hani Fakhour, *Kafr El Elow: An Egyptian Village in Transition* (New York: Holt, Rinehart and Winston, 1972), p. 100.

24. David G. Mandelbaum, *Society in India* (Berkeley: University of California Press, 1970), vol. 1: *Continuity and Change*, pp. 108–109.

25. Mandelbaum, cited in note 24, pp. 109 and 247.

26. John C. Caldwell, "Toward a restatement of demographic transition theory," *Population and Development Review* 2, nos. 3 and 4 (September/December 19767): 321–366; John C. Caldwell, "Fertility and the household economy in Nigeria," *Journal of Comparative Family Studies* 7, no. 2 (1976): 250; J. C. Caldwell, "The economic rationality of high fertility: An investigation illustrated with Nigerian survey data," *Population Studies* 31, no. 1 (1977): 25.

27. John C. Caldwell and Pat Caldwell, "The partially hidden syllabus in infant and primary school textbooks in Ghana, Nigeria and Kenya: The family message" (in preparation, and being supplemented to include South Asia).

28. The original impetus came from sessions for secondary school children written by Kenyan playwrights at the request of Radio Kenya. Other works of this type are published by Longman.

29. J. N. Mbugua, *Mumbi's Brideprice* (Nairobi: Longman Kenya, 1971).

30. As a Nigerian textbook about a Yoruba family puts it: "My grandparents live in the compound with us but in a separate house. Their house is where the elders in our village meet from time to time."

31. J. A. Olayomi, "My family," in *Civics and Social Studies for Young Nigerians* (London: Collins, 1970); The New Peak Reading Course, *New Link Reader* (Nairobi: Oxford University Press, East African Branch; first published 1963; ninth reprint, 1973), p. 64; Issac Dankyi Mensah, "Note to the teacher," in *Citizen Education for Schools*, Books 1–6 (Accra: Afram Publications, 1975).

32. The message is the same among the Indians of rural Peru, where "the curriculum was oriented … to life in an urban metropolis, which had little meaning to the Indian child other than, perhaps, to alienate him from an agrarian existence … the impact the school has had seems to be in the direction of creating a hiatus between the values of the Indian child and his parents." See Erwin H. Epstein, "Education and Peruanidad: 'Internal' colonialism in the Peruvian Highlands," *Comparative Education Review* 15, no. 2 (1971): 192–193.

33. Compare Carnoy, cited in note 19, p. 72.

34. Masemann continued: "She is also expected to bring up her children with scheduled meal-times and bed-times, quite unlike the more relaxed demand-feeding and sleeping times of the more uneducated mothers. This attitude to schedule is part of the constellation of values attached to a modern industrial society, and students are expected to be socialized into valuing time as a commodity which can be wasted or put to good use and which can be turned into money." Vandra Masemann, "The hidden curriculum of a West African girls' boarding school," *Canadian Journal of African Studies* 8, no. 3 (1974): 479–494; quotations are from page 483, 486, and 494.

35. However, Margaret Mead presented a different picture of the situation on Manus Island half a century ago: "When people did not understand, when the old women shrieked at each other in the style of long ago, when middle-aged men beat their wives, when there was a poor attendance at church, when discussion in meetings was rambling and petty, the enthusiasts for the New Way would comfort themselves and each other, saying, 'When the schoolboys grow up it will be different.' These others, they grew up in the old bad ways. It is not their fault that they fly into rages, they do not know how to speak in a meeting or how to treat their wives and children. But when the children grow up it will be different.'" The rages had, of course, been a method whereby the aged retained their ancient authority; the beatings of wives and children ensured patriarchal rights; but the family as the main organizational unit could be said to be waning

when it was more important to exert influence in meetings or to attend church. See Margaret Mead, *New Lives for Old: Cultural Transformation-Manus, 1928–1953* (New York: William Morrow, 1956), pp. 421–422.

36. On the Congo, see Yates, cited in note 20, p. 170; on the Dinka, see Deng, cited in note 20, p. 153.

37. Robert O. Tilman, "Education and political development in Malaysia," in L'Institute de Sociologie, *Education and Development in Southeast Asia: Symposium held in Brussels from April 19 to 21, 1966* (Brussels: Collection du Dentre D'Etude du Sud-East Asiatique, Universite Libré de Bruxelles, 1967); Anthony J. M. Kirk-Greene, "Bureaucratic cadres in a traditional milieu," in Coleman (ed., cited in note 13, pp. 372–407; Sutton, cited in note 13, pp. 51–74.

38. William H. and Charlotte Viall Wiser, *Behind Mud Walls, 1930–1960; with a sequel: The Village in 1970* (Berkeley: University of California Press, 1971), pp. 98 and 42.

39. Epstein, cited in note 32, pp. 193–198; Robert Redfield, "Culture and education in the midwestern highlands of Guatemala," in Middleton (ed.), cited in note 12, pp. 287–300; the quotation is from page 289.

40. Thomas M. Fraser, *Fishermen of South Thailand: The Malay Villagers* (New York: Holt, Rinehart and Winston, 1966), p. 84.

41. Patricia Marks Greenfield and Jerome S. Bruner, "Culture and cognitive growth," *International Journal of Psychology* 1, no. 2 (1966): 84.

42. Oscar Lewis, *Tepoztlan: Village in Mexico* (New York: Holt, Rinehart and Winston, 1960), p. 76.

43. Compare Jack Goody and Ian Watt, "The consequences of literacy," *Comparative Studies in Society and History* 5 (1963): 336–337.

44. Lannoy, cited in note 20, p. 125.

45. John C. Caldwell, "The mechanisms of demographic change in historical perspective," *Population Studies* 34, no. 3 (1980), p. 247.

46. T. Peter Omari, "Changing attitudes of students in West African society toward marriage and family relationships," *British Journal of Sociology* 11, no. 3 (1960): 203–205, 208.

47. Yates, cited in note 20, pp. 168–169.

48. Mandelbaum, cited in note 21, p. 108.

49. Yates, cited in note 20, p. 170, quoting Prefect Apostolic Leon Derikx at Gumbari, 30 July 1905, reported in *Mouvement des Missions Catholiques au Congo*, March 1906, p. 83; Remi Clignet, "The liberalizing and equalizing functions of schools: An overview," *Comparative Education Review* 19, no. 1 (1975): 89. On Burma, see Nash, cited in note 18, p. 307; Masemann, cited in note 34, pp. 492–493. On Africa, see Sutton, cited in note 13, p. 66.

50. The Great Tradition is comprised of the religious and cultural values found throughout the society and handed down as the common possession of the culture. The Great Tradition is known to the more

educated or urbanized and is the tradition found generally in literature. The Little Tradition is confined to populations outside the central tradition – above all to villagers – is concerned with local gods and beliefs, and varies greatly from place to place. Robert Redfield and colleagues of the Chicago anthropology school originally applied the term to Latin America, but it is now widely used in the analysis of Indian society and is even more generally used as an analytical tool for all traditional societies.

51. John C. Caldwell, "The mechanisms of demographic change in historical perspective," *Population Studies* 34, no. 3 (1980); "Toward a restatement of demographic transition theory," *Population and Development Review* 2, nos. 3 and 4 (September/December 1976): 348–349; John C. Caldwell, "A theory of fertility: From high plateau to destabilization," *Population and Development Review* 4, no. 4 (December 1978): 553–577; John C. Caldwell, "Fertility and the household economy in Nigeria," *Journal of Comparative Family Studies* 7, no. 2 (1976): 250; J. C. Caldwell, "The economic rationality of high fertility: An investigation illustrated with Nigerian survey data," *Population Studies* 31, no. 1 (1977): 25; John C. Caldwell and Pat Caldwell, "The achieved small family: Early fertility transition in an African city," *Studies in Family Planning* 9, no. 1 (January 1978): 1–18; of Yoruba women of completed fertility interviewed in Ibadan in 1973 and 1974–75, only 1.4 percent deliberately had "small" families of five or fewer live births.

52. John C. Caldwell, *Population Growth and Family Change in Africa: The New Urban Elite in Ghana* (Canberra: Australian National University Press, 1968), pp. 197–209.

53. Of school-age children in Western Nigeria in 1973, 28 percent of those who did not go to school were taken to a doctor when sick, compared with 55 percent of school children. Changing African Family Project, Survey 2.

54. John C. Caldwell, "Education as a factor in mortality decline: An examination of Nigerian data," *Population Studies* 33, no. 3 (1979): 395–413.

55. Ruzicka and Caldwell, cited in note 2, pp. 171ff.

56. For the nineteenth-century West, see Pat Caldwell, file on the *Australasian* newspaper, Melbourne, 1865–1900; for the contemporary developing world, see Caldwell, cited in note 45.

57. Caldwell (1976) and Caldwell (1978), both cited in note 56.

58. J.C. Caldwell and Pat Caldwell, "The role of marital sexual abstinence in determining fertility: A study of the Yoruba in Nigeria," *Population Studies* 31, no. 2 (1977): 206–207; J. C. Caldwell and Pat Caldwell, "Cause and sequence in the reduction of postnatal abstinence in Ibadan City, Nigeria," in *African Traditional Birth Spacing*, ed. Hilary Page and Ron Lesthaeghe (in preparation), Table 2.

A Theory of Fertility: From High Plateau to Destabilization

JOHN C. CALDWELL

If the object is to understand and predict the onset of fertility transition, then study should be focused on the conditions of stable high fertility and on the nature of destabilization. In earlier papers I advanced a series of propositions in order to elucidate the nature of demographic transition from high to low fertility.[1] The fundamental thesis is that fertility behavior in both pretransitional and post-transitional societies is economically rational within the context of socially determined economic goals and within bounds largely set by biological and psychological factors. Two types of society can be distinguished: one of stable high fertility, where there would be no net economic gain accruing to the family (or to those dominant within it) from lower fertility levels, and the other in which economic rationality alone would dictate zero reproduction. The former is characterized by "net wealth flows" from younger to older generations, and the latter by flows in the opposite direction. These flows are defined to embrace all economic benefits both present and anticipated over a lifetime.[2]

I have also argued that the conditions of stable high fertility, and of subsequent destabilization, lie largely in the nature of economic relations within the family. The family that determines economic advantage and demographic decision is not synonymous with the coresidential family, usually identified imperfectly in censuses and surveys and often subsequently analyzed with scant regard for the definitions employed in data collection. Rather it encompasses those

John C. Caldwell. Permission to reprint this article was received from The Population Council, which publishes *Population and Development Review*. It originally appeared in 1978, 4(4), pp. 553–577.

groups of close relatives who share economic activities and obligations. Within this larger and demographically more significant entity, the locus of economic and fertility decision-making is of prime importance, but has not as yet been adequately investigated.

These premises suggested the need for investigation of the family both in historical situations of high fertility immediately before fertility decline and in contemporary situations of high fertility in which indexes of economic and social change suggested that the family structure and the high-fertility system might be under strong pressure. Accordingly, my recent research has been directed largely at study of a western society, namely Australia, in the nineteenth century, immediately before the onset of fertility decline;[3] and more sustained study of the agrarian extended family of the high-fertility belt extending from Morocco to Bangladesh.[4] The emphasis here is on the latter, and particularly on the Islamic groups studied, since they do not present the complexities of caste and of the nature of work and lifestyle implied by caste in Indian society. This research is supplemented by some further work on Sub-Saharan Africa.[5]

General Propositions

The following propositions arise from the study of the family – particularly the traditional, rural, extended family – of North Africa and Southwest and South Asia, an area containing over a quarter of the population of the world, one-third that of the developing world, and half that marked by continuing high fertility. The region is characterized by some of the world's highest and most stable fertility.[6]

Six propositions are advanced as a basis for describing the relations between economic and reproductive behavior in this region.

1. The traditional peasant economy is a familial-based economy, fundamentally different from the non-familial-based capitalist economy. The major difference between the distinct economies of the world lies in the organization of production, or the mode of production.[7] Each mode of production has its own economic, and dependent demographic, laws.

2. Familial modes of production are characterized by relations of production between kin that give the more powerful or the decision-makers material advantage. The struggle of the decision-makers to maintain their advantage is normally seen as the assertion of natural rights and as proper behavior; nevertheless, family economic relationships are exploitative and there is potential for conflict and change.

3. High fertility is advantageous to the peasant family as a whole and to its most powerful members. As long as the internal relations of the familial mode of production remain intact, marital fertility will not be restricted for the purposes of limiting family size.

4. Although the familial mode of production is typically found in circumstances of subsistence production, it can adapt for at least a time to urban life and to the market economy without fully succumbing to the rules of the market and, indeed, while allowing that market to operate in a highly specialized way. Thus, the economic and demographic structure of the familial mode of production may dominate in a society with a limited market economy.

5. In general, modes of production in a society do not change quickly from one to another but may exist in parallel for long periods, and families may participate in more than one mode of production. Familial modes of production other than the peasant economy include hunting and gathering, shifting cultivation, nomadic herding, and feudal.

6. A familial mode of production has long persisted within the capitalist mode of production, as an (at least temporarily) more efficient method of producing part of the family's needs, while giving material advantage to the male head of household as the dominant decision-maker. Post-transitional fertility decline arises from the continuing disintegration of this submode and its reproductive relationships, as capitalist production successfully competes with domestic production and as social change transforms the relations of production.

These propositions will be examined roughly in the order in which they are listed, focusing first on the conditions of stable high fertility and then on the nature of destabilization.

Familial Modes of Production

In familial modes of production, different family members enjoy different advantages according to their position in the family structure. Such situational advantage is characterized by both material advantage and advantage in terms of power, but even the latter is significant largely in its potential for securing material advantage. Material advantage, broadly defined, includes advantages in type and amount of labor activity, in services rendered, in security, in guarantees, and so on. The direction and magnitude of the net wealth flow determine the recipients of material advantage. There are nonintergenerational flows, such as that form wife to husband, but the intergenerational flow is of most importance in assessing the utility of fertility. As will be seen, potential conflict, antagonism, and opposed interests are inherent in the relations of production, but this does not mean that such conflict is necessarily apparent to those involved. Rather it means that there are inherent tensions (or antagonisms) that may be a vehicle for change and that indicate the direction change is likely to take.

An important aspect of material advantage is relative work inputs. Work traditionally has largely been a matter of *drudgery* (Thorner's term for Chayanov's Russian version[8]), and human beings have always been oppressed by the long hours of toil involved in farming and primitive domestic work.[9] In these circumstances, a significant factor in material advantage lies in the nature and amount of work undertaken. A comparison of work inputs of different family members is difficult, however, for a number of reasons. The peasant family of North Africa and South Asia still produces largely for subsistence, and the growing of food in the field, the processing of it in the yard, and the cooking of it in the house cannot be assigned varying productivity values (indeed, processing and cooking cannot always be distinguished). The distinction frequently made between "productive work" and "household work" tends to obscure the value of some forms of work. Indeed, the whole subject of peasant labor inputs is so obscured by conventional wisdoms, convenient to the powerful, that it is difficult to interpret research or to discount the prejudices of researchers. The following are merely selected examples, but each is an important consideration in comparing the real value of different kinds of work.

First, there is a mystique of the plough. This is so pervasive that peasants equate ploughing, done by men, with work and thus contend that men do the real work. In reality, ploughing requires the sudden use of strength, especially on turns, but it is pleasanter and requires less constant effort than the use of digging sticks. Yet almost everywhere cultivation seems to have changed from a female to a male prerogative with conversion from digging stick to plough.

Second, there is a continuous downgrading of the value of women's work that misrepresents its significance. Those peasant households with insufficient female inputs are in just as reduced a condition as those with insufficient male inputs. The downgrading serves to keep women submissive, even grateful, and, when wage labor is employed, to keep their pay far below that of males. There is an incongruity about the whole situation: daughters are less important than sons, as any patriarch will aver, because, at an early age, they marry out into another family; yet the most hardworking labor input within the family (which largely determines living comfort) comes from daughters-in-law, brought in from other families who have conditioned them to be a submissive and hence valuable and economical labor force, precisely because of their under-valuation. Social scientists are likely to accept the obvious preference for sons as evidence that male labor must be more valuable than female. Much work done by both women and children, such as the collection of water, fuel, and manure, is thought of by men as menial, and, in truth, they are loath to do it, although describing it as comparatively easy work. (Similarly, in capitalist production, many men who work outside the home, in occupation that do not involve real drudgery, are loath to share the woman's work within the house.)

Third, nonphysical occupations, especially white-collar and professional ones, are everywhere honored above physical or manual pursuits, in spite of being pleasanter and much less onerous. In developing countries, such occupations are often little more than graceful role playing, and are in no way as productive as the almost dishonored drudgery going on all around.

Another important point is that the peasant household, like those in all modes of production, is not an unguided vehicle moving with frictionless momentum along straight rails provided by societal norms. Decision-making mechanisms operate in both economic and demographic areas; and their investigation, which has hardly been attempted, is absolutely necessary for a complete understanding of fertility transition.

Power in economic decision-making usually means power in demographic decision-making. Fertility may be influenced by decisions in such areas as the practice of premarital sex, the practice of premarital contraception, whether marriage takes place, the age at marriage, the frequency of sexual relations during marriage, the practice of contraception during marriage, and the practice of abortion before or after marriage. In peasant societies none of these decisions is totally within the province of the conjugal pair, and some of them are largely or almost wholly decided by other persons. The older generation (father alone, parents, parents plus others) usually decide upon marriage and upon the age at which it will occur; they are probably the dominant influence, except in transitional economic and social circumstances, in deciding whether fertility will be controlled; and they often influence the level of sexual activity. This influence on reproductive behavior tends to be obscured by its negative nature, which may be interpreted, usually wrongly, as laissez faire. Most residents of this region know of the availability of contraception, and most could practice some form of fertility control if the family wished it. Probably the great majority of adults in extended families see no gain in restricting fertility. Certainly, in three-generational joint families the older decision-makers correctly see no personal advantage from fertility restriction by their children and children-in-law. When this younger generation perceives advantage and acts upon it, the relationships that constituted the peasant mode of production are already dissolving.

The Traditional Extended Family

In the rural areas of the region the great majority of people still live in extended families, in that they live either with or in close proximity to relatives and share land, budgetary arrangements, or at least mutual obligations and guarantees against disaster.[10]

There is no absolute distinction between living close to each other and living as a joint family in the same residence, although coresidence probably makes it less likely that the authority of the older generation will be eroded and that the younger (or intermediate) generation will form sufficiently strong conjugal links to encourage them to attempt to share in economic and demographic decision-making. The families of the Middle East have been described as "extended, patrilineal, patrilocal, patriarchal, endogamous and occasionally polygynous,"[11] a description that, with the exception of endogamy, fits well enough from Morocco to Bangladesh and even, until recently at least, across China. These characteristics go far to explain how the economy of the family works and why its fertility remains high. The extended family is the dominant economic and security unit in this region. Help is usually unobtainable (except among minority groups) from such larger units as the clan, lineage, village, or tribe, all of which are important in Sub-Saharan Africa and exist to a greater or lesser extent throughout the region. The explanation probably lies in fixed land areas with family tenure and a long history of state power, which reduced the level of local physical conflict.

A key question is whether the type of family molded by the peasant mode of production is merely one of the types of family found in the region or whether it is culturally dominant. After all, there have been considerable urban populations for millennia, and for an equally long time there have been landlords as well as peasants, wage earners as well as family helpers, and marketed as well as subsistence food.[12] Nevertheless, subsistence production is still the norm; probably two-thirds of India's food is eaten by its producers.[13] Moreover, the pyramidal family, hallowed by time and enthusiastically sanctioned by religion, prevails even in conditions other than subsistence farming. Except among the modernized urban middle class, it has managed to keep its structure largely intact. Merchant and artisan families, even in cities, retain the agrarian household organization with its unified budgetary and authority structures. Wage earning is most frequently regarded not as an alternative economy to the familial one, nor as a path to liberation from family authority, nor even as a means of accumulating individual property, but as a method for supplementing total family income or wealth. Indeed, Meillassoux argues that capitalism has frequently contributed to this end, paying wages too small for the worker to set up a nuclear family but only enough for him to supplement the income of an extended family.[14] And Wolf maintains that increasing outside opportunities have reinforced the residential joint family and contributed to its survival.[15] Thus indexes of urbanization, or even of the proportion of produce reaching the market, are not good measures of change in the familial economy or of the approach to demographic transition thresholds.

It is the internal economy and the relations of production of the peasant family that are dominant in terms of production and central in terms of demographic decision-making. The economic and social structure of the peasant family is focused on the control of familial labor and consumption. Its demography can be fully and satisfactorily explained in these terms. Why, then, have the economists and anthropologists told us so much that is marginal, while ignoring the essentials?

The major reason seems to be the sanctity of the family. Marx and his successors pointed to the existence of different modes of production, and indeed described capitalism as the last of a series of modes characterized by antagonistic relations of production and by the exploitation of man by man. Yet, Marxists preferred to recognize the peasantry either as a class exploited by landlords and rulers or as incipient capitalists. Even when actual, as well as potential,

antagonisms within the Russian peasant families were documented in the 1920s, these were employed merely as political evidence against the continued existence of this way of life.[16] Chayanov, also employing data on the Russian peasantry, argued that there was a distinct peasant economy that could not be analyzed in terms of the classical factors of production, but he always referred to the family and its labor as a unit.[17] Sahlins, who concluded that "a material transaction is usually a momentary episode in a continuous social relation," described the domestic economy as a setting in which "decisions are taken primarily with a view toward domestic contentment. Production is geared to the family's customary requirements. Production is for the benefit of the producers."[18] Elsewhere, the importance of family relationships in "primitive" economies has been taken to demonstrate the dominance of social goals rather than the essence of the organization of production. Herskovits examined the family without analyzing its internal forces; Polanyi concluded that "man's economy is submerged in his social relationships ... the economic system will be run on non-economic motives"; the Thorners identified the noncapitalist nature of peasant farming but left the family as an atomistic unit: "Peasant farming ... is inextricably woven into the fabric of peasant family life. To rip cultivation out of its family context and pretend that it is a family business, is to distort rural reality"; the women's movement also puts a gloss on the agrarian family, as shown by Mitchell: "The peasant family works together for itself - it is one. The family and production are homogeneous.... Under capitalism, each member of the family is supposed to be an 'individual.'... No wonder there are tensions."[19]

Redfield and Wolf, the leading anthropologists of the peasantry, exhibit somewhat contrasting approaches. The former makes few references to economic activities, and none to production.[20] The latter, essentially economic in his approach, nevertheless equates exploitation solely with the removal of the peasant surplus production by the politically powerful, and decides that "economic relations of coercion and exploitation and the corresponding social relations of dependence and mastery are not created in the system of production."[21] There is a real aversion to even considering the nature of intrafamilial economic relations. Schultz treads carefully even when analyzing the modern American family: "I anticipate that many sensitive, thoughtful people will be offended by these studies of fertility because they may see them as debasing family and motherhood. These highly personal activities and purposes of parents may seem to be far beyond the realm of economic calculus."[22]

The all-important internal economics of familial production has been almost entirely ignored, while great (and demographically misleading) emphasis has been placed on the marketable surplus, on the marginal production being exchanged, and on nonfamilial economic relationships.[23] One can speculate that this emphasis arose because these less important economic relationships were closer to those of capitalist society; therefore they were easily recognizable, could be analyzed with the techniques developed by economists to explain the capitalist economy, and gave reassuring promise that development toward a "modern" economy was inevitable. Production hardly seemed to fit into the picture, so it was conveniently forgotten, leaving economic anthropologists to concentrate largely on exchange. Another reason was that the surplus was commonly identified as the origin of civilization itself in that it supported non-farming populations.[24]

We are not likely to be able to understand stable high fertility in agrarian societies, however, unless we analyze the peasant family in terms of the material advantages arising from production and reproduction.[25]

The Relations of Production in the Peasant Family

Many, often subtle differences in material advantage favor the old and the male in the extended family. They include consumption: the kind and amount of food eaten, precedence in feeding, the clothing customarily worn, use of house space and facilities, and access to transport. They include power and access to services: who can tell whom to do what; the right to be pampered and have the little services performed that make life graceful; the guarantee of support in argument, danger, or a bid for social or political power; and the right to make unchallenged decisions. They include labor: the amount of work done, the kind of work done, the right to control one's own working time, and access to leisure or to activities (such as bargaining) that give real pleasure.

Except when the society and economy are undergoing fundamental change, these differences in privileges and rights are accepted with little or no bitterness. This does not mean, however, that they are not recognized as conferring distinct levels of material advantage and are not valued as such. This is proved by the tenacity with which such rights are held and by the animosity with which the privileged react to any threats of change.

So entrenched is the system that it is difficult to find researchers from within it to evaluate the real distinctions. The usual reaction is that expressed by an observer, trained in the British school of anthropology, of a Chinese village in the 1940s: "If the father or mother eats better food, it is not because he or she has the privilege of claiming it but because the children want to favour the parent in this way.... It is true that women, especially young women, usually have less choice food than their men have, but the difference is by no means significant, and the women usually take it for granted."[26] Much the same description is repeatedly given in rural Bangadesh; yet these privileges, usually taken for granted, are almost certainly the major factor in raising female mortality to almost 50 percent above that of males for the first three decades of life.[27] Consumption privileges begin early: in the Middle East boys are frequently weaned at twice the age of girls. It is difficult in the North Africa – South Asia region to find field workers who will agree that female household processing or preparation of food involves labor inputs comparable to those of the men in selling the surplus, let alone in ploughing the field. Usually only direct observation,[28] not report, reveals that middle-aged men spend much of their time managing or talking or drinking in the coffee shop while their sons take over the heavier field work, or that the effort mothers-in-law put into direction and management is decreasingly onerous and usually pointless since their daughters-in-law can hardly err in carrying out the usual repetitious tasks.[29] Islam, it should be noted, enjoins the young to take over the harder labor.

The task of measuring labor inputs (as well as relative consumption) should be attempted, although the results will always be unsatisfactory and debatable. Chayanov calculated that Russian peasant women and girls worked 1.21 times as many hours as men and boys, respectively, while Fei and Chang calculated a similar ratio in terms of the sex division of labor inputs per acre, although the former seems to have underestimated household labor and the latter to have ignored it.[30] Societies in which women are largely secluded or confined to the household almost invariably appear to arrange tasks so that a high proportion are undertaken in or around the house. In such societies children have two additional values: to deliver the messages and do the carrying and marketing that their mothers cannot do; and, in the case of sons, to help their fathers in the field from a very early age because the woman cannot do field work.

It is probable that larger peasant families would generally be more prosperous than smaller ones even if the individuals shared production and consumption alike. Where, as is usual, the advantage lies with the old and the male, the material advantages of these decision-makers would tend to be undermined by limited fertility resulting in smaller families with a less broadbased pyramidal structure. Large families facilitate division of labor, permitting specialization and enabling the family to send off one or more members to areas of greater opportunity. The larger the family, the less often it must have recourse to paid labor, even for the heaviest, most awkward, or most labor-intensive activities. The seasonality of agricultural work is also an important consideration because it produces periods of intense labor demand occurring simultaneously on all farms;[31] the extra labor demand can be accommodated easily only by the large families who neither have to leave things undone nor pay scarcity-level wages. It also appears probable that larger numbers mean that cooperative tasks are done better, and certainly more cheerfully. Even the drudgery assumes a different air when undertaken with a son or daughter: the help is of use, the company cheering, and there is a satisfaction, and probably a value, in the training imparted. The older person may also get the younger one to do the greater share of the work, or at least the more menial and annoying tasks. "A young wife works harder than anyone else in the family and she lives more thriftily ... she must see that her children do their share towards building up the family's economy."[32] Yang concluded from his study of a Chinese village:

> When a son is born, even to a poor family, he is not looked upon as someone who will further divide the family's land, but as one who will add to it. When a second son is born, the parents do not worry that their small piece of land will be divided into two parts. Instead, they begin to hope that when their sons are grown up, one will be a hired

labourer, another a mason, and they will earn not only their own living but add fifty dollars or so to the family every year. In two or three years, they can buy one more *mou* of land with their savings. Thus, when the parents are old, they will be better off than they are now.[33]

Chayanov concluded that, where there is land available, the crop, and eventually per capita consumption, rise as the family increases; and Sahlins transformed this (without pointing out that Chayanov's data and discussion were focused on the life cycle of the family) into Chayanov's Rule: "the greater the relative working capacity of the household, the less its members work."[34]

Whether, as most people in the region believe, highly fertile families also prosper more over time than less fertile ones is a question for which adequate longitudinal or retrospective measurement is lacking. No existing data seem to show, however, that high-fertility families are at present poorer on a per capita basis.

A key question in times of social change is how stability is maintained in productive relations (and in reproductive relations). Certainly, old men claim traditional knowledge and the traditional hallowing of their power over family members, and they claim to be either the owners or the stewards of ancestral family property.[35] Old men and women also claim to have greater knowledge of day-to-day affairs because of their long experience. They claim ultimate responsibility, and gratitude, for having arranged marriages and for having granted the precious gift of life itself. They claim, correctly, the support of religion in urging veneration for the aged and obeisance to them, and they sometimes claim to be closer to the ancestors. Similarly, with regard to male domination over females, claims to ownership of land and residence and to control over the means of production are important. The greater physical strength of males and the relative vulnerability of females because of parturition also play a

role. So – and this is demographically important – does the fact that wives in the region are usually much younger than husbands and have traditionally married very young. This has been reinforced both by arranged marriage, whereby the wife's duty not to rebel is a duty she owes to her own relatives as well as to her husband's, and by patrilocality, whereby the wife is cut off from any support her own relatives might have offered.

Nevertheless, these observations are insufficient to explain why the young and strong do not revolt or why women fail to band together to protect themselves from exploitation (including reproductive exploitation). Socialization from infancy to conform to the traditional roles, and reinforcement of these roles by Moslem and Hindu family teachings, are of course part of the explanation.[36] So is the fact that a break with relatives can mean social ostracism and economic impotence, the latter determined also by civil laws governing inheritance and land tenure. Yet there are other factors of great importance. One is the life cycle element in all familial modes of production: if one bears one's present situation a little longer, then the system that has been oppressive can yield rewards instead. Sons become fathers and daughters-in-law mothers-in-law. Perhaps the most effective stabilizer is peer rivalry. Just how badly the outside observer can misinterpret the stabilizing influence of rivalry is shown by Wolf's treatment of tensions within the extended family.[37] He regards as signs of family weakness quarrels between women, which in fact strengthen male authority, and those between siblings, which powerfully buttress parental control. The unequal and difficult relationship between mother-in-law and daughter-in-law is probably the single most significant element in the subjection of women, as is the rivalry between brothers in preventing them from competing with fathers. This rivalry and indeed most forms of rivalry are powerfully supported by high fertility. More generally, age and sex dominance are fostered by assigning great importance to age gradations and to the specialization of occupational, consumption, and ceremonial patterns by age and sex; hence the stress that traditional societies lay not merely on such relationships as being "brothers" but on being "senior brothers" or "junior brothers." The larger the family, the more apparent and effective are these distinctions and gradations.

The Demographic Aspects of the Peasant Family

For the purposes of this paper, this essentially economic analysis of the extended family is of interest only in the sense that it determines the demographic nature of the family. Indeed, this nature cannot be understood without the economic analysis. Several demographic aspects should be separately considered.

The most basic matter is that of demographic priorities, an area that existing literature shows to be almost universally misunderstood. The peasant family does not aim at reproducing as quickly as possible, with generations following close upon each other and the number of relatives within the household being maximized. If such were the case, then sons would marry at puberty or the family would be matrilocal. The truth is very different. Priority is given to preserving the structure of discipline and work within the family. Daughters in the North Africa – South Asia – China region are married out,[38] so that the generational structure of the family depends upon the marriage age of sons. In the Middle East, men usually marry for the first time after 25 years of age,[39] and male marriage elsewhere in South and East Asia has not traditionally been early. The major aim has been to retain a five-to-ten-year age gap between spouses, which, together with patrilocality, has ensured male dominance. The price, in terms of reproduction within the household, has been considerable. If the wife begins childbearing when the husband is around 25 years of age, the average length of generation *within* the household is about 36 years – an extraordinary period in countries where life expectancy at birth is still often no more than 50 years (and was much less a few decades ago).

As soon as the young bride enters the household, there is much interest in her reproduction. Her husband may be 25 years old, and his father will probably be between 50 and 75, depending on whether the husband was the first or last child. The old couple will urge the young couple to have many children as soon as possible: if young children mean work, that work will no longer fall upon the old people's shoulders; if somewhat older children run messages and do services, that is precisely the help the old prize. In the traditional family, the young have little option but to be fertile. Even for them there are advantages. Only by bearing children can the young wife establish her position, work a little less hard, enjoy a somewhat larger share of food and other consumption items, and, ultimately, achieve a major breakthrough with regard to all these matters by becoming a mother-in-law. The young husband can have helpers in the field within 10 or 12 years and can shift some of the harder work off his shoulders by the time he is 40 years of age.

Several aspects of the continuous supply of children are important. A frequent pattern – perhaps the anticipated pattern – is that when a husband and wife become the major decision-makers of the family (through the death of the husband's father), the supply of adolescents will be a major factor in easing their lives. Thereafter, those who live most comfortably will be the parents who have a continuing supply of children of both sexes growing up: to meet the need of having persons of different ages to do the age-specific tasks, to engender sibling competition in providing labor during their parents' maturity and comprehensive aid during their decline, and to supply successive new daughters-in-law, who probably work harder than anyone else. Descendants are the most valued protection that a couple can have against destitution in old age. Throughout the region this consideration is paramount; the fear of land fragmentation appears everywhere to be minimal (perhaps, in part, because there is a growing nonagricultural labor market). Where land is not divided until the old die, they seem, in most societies, to be more interested in advantages during their lifetimes than in any disadvantages to their descendants. Fear of land subdivision seems to be an obsession only of western observers.[40]

From the point of view of the decision-makers, probably the most important aspect of high fertility is that it stabilizes the family. It keeps it in the expected mold. Daughters-in-law with many children will be forced to undertake the work women have always done and will need to fit themselves and their progeny into the framework of the larger family. Sons with many siblings can hardly revolt if there are rivals for the inheritance. Numerous grandchildren may provide an extra source of security to whom direct appeal can be made if children are found wanting.

Decision-Making and Fertility Control

While the economic structure of the peasant family holds, fertility everywhere in the region remains high and contraception is rarely practiced. There has been a tendency in some population studies to overstress traditional contraception and to imply that practices that were occasionally employed to prevent socially unacceptable conceptions or to avoid pregnancy during a subsistence crisis were also used to limit ultimate family size. The evidence for the latter contention is poor everywhere in Asia and Africa and almost nonexistent in the regions concentrated upon here.

This lack of fertility control within marriage has often been taken to be a sign of ignorance of contraception or of easy acceptance of the inevitable. There is little to support this view: high fertility is valued, especially among the decision-makers, often as a central aim of societies throughout the peasant cultures of the region. Not only are fertility decisions made, but they are stronger and occasion fewer misgivings than in most low-fertility societies. They merely happen to be for high fertility and against contraception and are undetectable in terms of trends and differentials because they maintain past patterns. It is this maintenance that gives the traditional decision-makers such strength; they could not as easily lead a fertility or contraceptive innovational trend among the younger generation.

Who are the reproductive decision-makers? Usually, they are the old, especially males. Reproductive decisions are not really separable from economic decisions, because the reproductive pattern is needed to support the economic one and to maintain the existing gradations of material advantage within the family. The patriarch, because of his ownership or stewardship of the means of production, is almost unchallenged in economic decision-making. His control of reproductive decision-making is less direct and potentially less certain, but, traditionally, the economic power has provided him with sufficient reproductive control.

This patriarchal control is more one of situation than of personality. Peasant society abounds with scandals about families in which the wife has too much say or the elder son really makes decisions; but these family members are usually powerful only if they support the traditional situation, indeed if they exhort a weak or backsliding patriarch to fulfill his duties. An attempt at economic or reproductive decision-making innovation by the patriarch's wife would probably be countered by the eldest son, or all the sons, chiding their father. A like attempt by an eldest son would probably confront a coalition of his brothers and mother. Few adequate studies of the situation have been made; such studies as exist suggest that encroachments on patriarchal power are highly exceptional.[41] This is not to deny that, even in many patriarchal societies, exhortations to reproductive conformity are made more often by the patriarch's wife to their sons and daughters-in-law, but nearly always within the moral framework approved by her husband.

Perhaps the most important question is why these decisions are obeyed. Certainly the economic power of the patriarch, the family's ability to ostracize and disinherit a son, and the possibility of forcing a divorce against a daughter-in-law are all important. Nevertheless, the strongest control against deviance in peasant society is talk – scandal-mongering, ridicule, and stronger expressions of derision and even anger and disgust – and, less often, violence. In the area of economic decision-making the villagers watch for the weak father, the overmighty son, and the disrespectful or lazy daughter-in-law; they all feel threatened by continuing behavior of this type. In the area of fertility decision-making such vigilance is even stronger because deviation and indiscretion trespass on sensitive areas where instincts or emotions have long been suppressed. Contraception is highly suspect both because of its likely impact on fertility and because of its implications about the wife's attitude toward sexual relations; over much of the region, even involuntary infecundity or subfecundity is taken to be a personal failing justifying contempt and divorce or polygyny.

Just as the peasant family structure has long formed the pattern for many non-peasant segments of the society – the landless laborers and wage earners, the artisans, the urban commercial classes, even traditional rulers and other nonmodern elites – so the peasant pattern of decision-making, and society's backing for these decisions, have operated in a similar fashion among these other groups.

Economic and Demographic Transition

Modes of production do not just replace each other; they usually coexist for long periods, and individuals, families, and tribes may participate in more than one system at a time.

Precapitalist modes of production other than the peasant mode include shifting cultivation, hunting and gathering, and nomadism. Although the basic units in these modes are generally networks of relatives, they usually involve economic and decision-making groupings larger than the family. In many of these groups, children are considered to belong to the group rather than to the individual parents. Further, net intergenerational wealth flows are less specifically directed from children to parents than from younger to older generation in general. Little research has been conducted comparing economic-fertility relationships in these societies with those in peasant societies, but one may speculate that the pressures for high fertility would be significantly lower in them than in the smaller units of the peasant family.

From the point of view of a demographer interested in fertility decline, the transition of most importance is that from familial to capitalist production. This transition is the most complex both economically and demographically – so complex that it has been largely misunderstood – in that it is the only transition from familial to nonfamilial production.

The term capitalist production has been used throughout this paper, instead of industrialization or modern economy or highly developed economy, because it is contended that the real reproductive divide lies between modes of production based largely on networks of relatives and those in which the individuals may sell their labor to complete strangers.[42] It is not factories and steel mills that count in the reduction of fertility; it is the replacement of a system in which material advantage accruing from production and reproduction flows to people who can control or influence reproduction by a system in which those with economic power either gain no advantage form reproduction or cannot control it. This usually occurs only with the collapse of familial production, although it can follow fundamental changes in the balance of material advantage and decision-making within the family.

The transformation from familial to capitalist production is a process rather than a sudden change. What is formed first and is sustained for long periods of time is a two-tiered system in which the two forms of economies coexist. To learn something of the nature of the transition and its implications for fertility, one can look to the historical experience of Western Europe.

Economic and Demographic Transition in the West

Capitalist production as the dominant form of production outside the home first developed in Europe, where there is some evidence that the residential joint family, and even the extended family of mutual obligations, was already collapsing, perhaps because of direct productive relations between the feudal lords and the male heads of conjugal families. Certainly, under capitalism, the ability of the husband to secure employment with adequate remuneration outside the family was decisive in the erosion of the extended family. At the early stages, however, only the husband participated in the capitalist mode of production; services within the house were provided on a subsistence basis by a familial mode of production not very different from that found in the peasant household.

To understand the nature of the supports for high fertility and of fertility decline where it has occurred, it is necessary to ana-lyze this two-tiered system correctly. The failure to do so is, once again, primarily an unwillingness to disturb the mystique of the family. The familial system in the West depended on a sharp division of labor: the husband worked outside the home for wages or profits and almost all his input of labor was into these activities, while a wide range of activities (clothing, feeding, providing a clean and comfortable environment, child rearing) was undertaken by the wife with the help of the children (especially the daughters). In effect, then, the husband ran his own highly efficient family-based subsistence system for producing services. Fundamentally, this was a second (and at least equally important) mode of production in the society; the relations of production in the first mode were between employer and employee, but in this second mode they were between a husband and his wife and children.[43]

Originally this familial mode of production worked cheaply and well (at least from the husband's viewpoint). The cheapness was achieved by the women and children consuming less than the husband. Very real differentials in material advantage were maintained by emphasizing the importance of the husband's work compared with the familial production, by distinguishing between productive and domestic work and between paid and unpaid work, and by stressing that husbands had to have a certain standard of dress and of living to hold their jobs and that they deserved to spend some of their earnings on themselves outside the home. This discrimination between men's and women's work had another effect. Many women (and, especially early in the Industrial Revolution, children) had always worked outside the home. However, the prevailing attitudes allowed women to be paid much less than adult males, and allowed society, their employers, and the women themselves to regard their work as marginal and "temporary," even when the work continued for years.[44]

Demographically, this two-tiered mode of production can sustain high or moderately high fertility.[45] As long as children consume relatively little and boys start earning early (and even contribute to the family budget), then high fertility is no disadvantage. This is especially the case under two conditions: first, where the wife and children can offer a great range of household productive services without effective competition from the market; second, where the wife is uneducated or little educated, where she is not affected by ideologies urging her to demand a greater place in the sun, and where she accepts her place in the household with its implications for low consumption, hard work, and responsibility for keeping child-care problems away from her husband. This is the explanation for high fertility among the urban middle class in much of the developing world,[46] as it was in mid-nineteenth-century Europe.

When this two-tiered system is at its height, large family size remains desirable. Yet, the two-tiered mode of production was inherently unstable in Western Europe for a number of reasons. It depended on competing successfully with capitalist production in the provision of household services, on wives and children remaining hardworking producers and low-level consumers, on economic and fertility decision-making remaining largely with the male household head, and on household production being augmented more by women's activities in the home than by services purchased with their outside earnings. All these conditions were to be challenged by the spectacular growth in capitalist production and by ideological change, rooted in the society but fuelled by economic growth.[47]

Probably the decisive change in Western Europe was a fairly sudden rise in the cost of children and a decline in their labor inputs into household production. The major cause was the spread of education, together with a rise in its duration and cost. This was a product partly of the needs of the industrial system and partly of public awareness that the economy would now bear the cost. School children needed and demanded more expenditure, had less time for household chores, and were more resistant to working – the phenomenon is currently visible throughout the developing world.[48] Growing parental wealth and the waning influence of religious creeds proclaiming virtue in child austerity and child labor reinforced the tendency to spend more on children and demand less from them. Consequently the net intergenerational flow of wealth changed direction from upward to downward.

At much the same time, the industrial system began a massive onslaught on home production, by offering commodities in the market that had been made at home, by offering gadgets that reduced domestic labor inputs, and by tempting the family to raise its capital input into the home. As consumption aspirations rose, the kinds of services that could be performed by dependent members of the family were devalued compared with purchased commodities. Subsistence production declined and the monetized sector of the economy expanded.

There was another source of basic instability in the system: the egalitarian strain in the modern European ideology, powerfully augmented by the spread of education. Girls were educated too (although usually not as much as boys), partly because of the demands of the egalitarian ethic, but partly because educated husbands want to talk to educated wives (an important destabilizing influence in the contemporary Middle East and South Asia) and educated fathers want to talk to educated daughters. Both consumption and decision-making became more democratic. The sex differential in wages narrowed, and married women gained greater acceptance in the workforce (as the more highly capitalized economy increasingly demanded their labor). In the family, the impact of pregnancy or motherhood on the wife began to be taken into account in reproductive decisions. As the wife's income became more important, the reproductive decision became a significant immediate economic decision as well as a long-term one. The fall in fertility was also partly the product of the continuing contraceptive revolution – one of familiarization with a different conjugal relationship as much as changing technology, and one that itself both was a product of changes in family relations and accelerated those changes.

The fall in fertility was protracted as the familial subsistence mode of production, although ever more eroded, showed remarkable resistance to extinction or even to becoming insignificant.[49]

The Conditions of Fertility Change: The Developing World

Fertility in the developing world will decline as the decision-makers no longer secure decisive material advantage from high fertility – which means changes both in the identity and authority of those gaining material advantage and making decisions and in the way in which fertility affects material advantage. These changes will be a product of economic change – of capitalist production outpacing even industrialization – and of largely imported social change (broadly speaking, westernization).[50]

In the modern world the peasant familial system of production is not stable. Wage employment is increasing and the young family member who takes up employment is ever more likely to receive sufficient income to support a separate conjugal family. Urban populations are growing disproportionately. The economic underpinning of the patriarchal joint family in urban areas has never been secure, and has been increasingly susceptible to disintegration with economic and social change. In rural areas, both pressure on the land and government land-redistribution schemes tend to disperse the patriarchal family and so to remove young couples from patriarchal authority, leading to more diffusion of economic and fertility

decision-making. Ultimately the changeover to capitalist or socialist production will terminate the economic system that benefits from high fertility.

Nevertheless, it is social and ideological change that is likely to have the greatest immediate impact. In most of the developing world the familial production of household services and the authority of the family head are even more stably based than was the case in nineteenth-century Europe. However, existing differentials in advantage by age and sex are under attack from the same forces that brought change in nineteenth-century Europe: education of children, relative rise in the position of females,[51] and the lure of household consumption goods. The original position was more stable than in Europe, but the attack is stronger too, largely because of the European example and because of the development of a global economy and global ideologies. The messages from the media and educational systems are largely western and tend to teach age and sex equality. So do the new ideologies both of the left and of those stressing modern capitalism. Furthermore, the discussion of sexual relations and contraception is increasingly legitimized by essentially western influence. This, and the availability of contraceptives, may well make the initial fertility decline more rapid than in the West. The very discussion of contraception and reproductive decisions almost certainly does something to lessen sex differentials and hence male material advantage. This is probably also true in terms of the publicizing of the pleasures of sexual relations. As the conjugal bond becomes closer, or more sentimental, and as the mother's maternal feelings play a greater role in family decision-making, the sex and age differentials in material advantage are likely to be increasingly eroded.

Summary Note

The essence of all precapitalist modes of production was kin-based production, and the relations of production were those between relatives. These relations were unequal and gave material advantage to the elders. Thus high fertility yielded economic advantage. But high fertility was not the sole demographic aim of the family decision-makers; the stability of the relations of production was more important, because continuing material advantage was most important.

A complete capitalist mode of production makes high fertility economically disadvantageous. But long after capitalist production is general in a society, household services continue to be produced by a precapitalist, familial mode of production, which may involve the majority of all labor inputs in the society. It was the persistence of this mode of production, and the unequal relations of production within it, that buttressed moderately high fertility in Europe until a century ago.

Fertility ultimately fell in the West when the pattern of material advantage, and hence the net intergenerational wealth flow, decisively changed within the household mode of production – a result of social change made possible by economic change. Fertility has continued to fall as that pattern has continued to shift.

In high-fertility societies, further economic change will inevitably produce this two-tiered mode of production. Economic and social change will ultimately make high fertility uneconomic in the working of both tiers, a process that will occur faster than in the West because of the import of ideas, ideologies, and educational systems (and child labor laws) that reduce age and sex differentials in material advantage and ultimately make high fertility uneconomic.

Social scientists feel compelled to prove what members of different societies know to be the indisputable truth: high fertility in an advanced capitalist society (especially one in which the domestic mode of production has been curtailed because a large proportion of household needs are provid-ed by the market) reduces a family's potential standard of living, while in a peasant society it does not.

ENDNOTES

1. John C. Caldwell, "Toward a restatement of demographic transition theory," *Population and Development Review* 2, nos. 3–4 (1976): 321–366; "The economic rationality of high fertility: An investigation illustrated with Nigerian survey data," *Population Studies* 31, no. 1 (1977): 5–27; and "Fertility and the household economy in Nigeria," *Journal of Comparative Family Studies* 7, no. 2 (1976): 193–253. See also the collected papers and comparative findings of other researchers in John C. Caldwell, *The Socio-Economic Explanation of High Fertility: Papers on the Yoruba Society of Nigeria*, Monograph 1, Changing African Family Project, Department of Demography, The Australian National University, Canberra, 1976; John C. Caldwell, ed., *The Persistence of High Fertility: Population Prospects in the Third World*, Monograph 1, Family and Fertility Change: Changing African Family Companion Series, Department of Demography, The Australian National University, Canberra, 1977; and L.T. Ruzicka, ed., *The Economic and Social Supports for High Fertility*, Monograph 2, in the same series, 1977.

2. Including goods and money, labor and services, protection and guarantees, and social and political support. Despite problems in measuring the totality of these flows in each direction and their components, it is possible to secure reasonably good evidence of the recent direction of wealth flows in individual societies (e.g., in Nigeria in 1977 and Bangladesh in 1978).

3. John C. Caldwell and Lado T. Ruzicka, "The Australian fertility transition: An analysis," *Population and Development Review* 4, no. 1 (1978): 81–103; Lado T. Ruzicka and John C. Caldwell, *The End of Demographic Transition in Australia*, Monograph 5, Australian Family Formation Project Series, Department of Demography, The Australian National University, Canberra, 1977.

4. Islamic and Indian components of this study are being reported separately. See John C. Caldwell and Pat Caldwell, "Fertility transition with special reference to the ECWA region," forthcoming in a volume on demographic change in the Middle East to be published by the Economic Commission for West Asia, Beirut; Pat Caldwell, "Egypt and the Arab and Islamic worlds," in *The Persistence of High Fertility*, cited in note 1, pp. 593–616; a paper on India is in preparation.

5. John C. Caldwell, "Measuring wealth flows and the rationality of fertility: Thoughts and plans based in the first place on African work," in *The Economic and Social Supports for High Fertility*, cited in note 1, pp. 439–453.

6. The peasant economy observed in these societies also obtained in China until mid-century. See, for example, Fei Hsaio-Tung, *Peasant Life in China* (London: Routledge and Kegan Paul, 1939); Martin Yang, *A Chinese Village: Taitou, Shantung Province* (London: Kegan Paul, Trench and Trubner, 1948); Fei Hsiao-Tung and Chang Chih–I, *Earthbound China: A Study of Rural Economy in Yunan* (London: Routledge and Kegan Paul, 1949).

7. *Modes of production* and *relations of production* were terms first employed by Karl Marx (see *Capital: A Critique of Political Economy* [Harmondsworth: Penguin, 1976], passim) and are suited to the analysis in that they are used in the sense that "the relations of production define a specific mode" (Barry Hindess and Paul Q. Hirst, *Pre-Capitalist Modes of Production* [London and Boston: Routledge and Kegan Paul, 1975], p. 9), although such relations were not equated by Marx, and have rarely been equated by Marxists, with family relations in precapitalist production, as they are in this paper. Capitalist economy is used here to describe any economy in which there is a market for labor beyond kinship or other traditional obligations to work; the industrial economy is treated as a recent manifestation of this economy.

8. Daniel Thorner, "Chayanov's concept of peasant economy," in A.V. Chayanov, *The Theory of Peasant Economy*, ed. Daniel Thorner, Basile Kerblay, and R.E.F. Smith (Homewood, Ill.: The American Economic Association, Richard Irwin, 1966), passim; and A.V. Chayanov, "On the theory of non-capitalist economic systems," in *The Theory of the Peasant Economy*, p. 6, where the term drudgery is preferred by the editors over laboriousness or irksomeness for Chayanov's Russian term, *tyagostnos*.

9. Accordingly, the Sahelian cultivators face the risk of starvation every few years rather than increase the annual level of their drudgery in order to create food buffer stocks. See John C. Caldwell, *The Sahelian Drought and its Demographic Implications*, Overseas Liasion Committee, American Council on Education, Paper no. 8, Washington, D.C., 1975, p. 74. Chayanov argued that the Russian peasantry consciously and necessarily indulged in "self-exploitation" until reaching an equilibrium between drudgery and consumption, beyond which "continuing to work becomes pointless, as further labour expenditure becomes harder ... to endure than is foregoing its economic effects" (see *The Theory of the Peasant Economy*, cited in note 8, p. 6).

10. Throughout this paper, groups of close relatives living in close proximity with mutual obligations and economic interests are described as extended families. Coresident families containing not only husband, wife, and their children but also additional relatives are described as joint families. Thus a joint family is one type of extended family, distinguished by residence in the same household. This usage is in keeping with that set out in Raymond T. Smith, "Family: I, comparative structure," in *International Encyclopaedia of the Social Sciences,* Vol. 5, ed. David L. Sills (New York: Macmillan and Free Press, 1968), pp. 301–313.

11. Raphael Patai, *Society, Culture, and Change in the Middle East* (Philadelphia: University of Pennsylvania Press, 1971), p. 84.

12. For the argument that peasants are a minority, see André Béteille, "The concept of peasant society," in *Six Essays in Comparative Sociology* (Delhi: Oxford University Press, 1974), pp. 40–57.

13. Daniel Thorner and Alice Thorner, *Land and Labour in India* (Delhi: Asia Publishing House, 1962), p. 206.

14. Claude Meillassoux, "From reproduction to production: A Marxist approach to economic anthropology," *Economy and Society* 1 (1972): 102.

15. Eric R. Wolf, *Peasants* (Englewood Cliffs, N.J.: Prentice-Hall, 1966), pp. 66–67.

16. M. Kubanin, "The process and causes of the division of peasant households," in *A Systematic Sourcebook in Rural Sociology*, Vol. 2, ed. Pitirim A. Sorokin, Carle C. Zimmerman, and Charles J. Galpin (New York: Russell and Russell, 1931), pp. 104–114.

17. Chayanov, *The Theory of Peasant Economy*, cited in note 8.

18. Quotations from Marshall D. Sahlins, "On the sociology of primitive exchange," in *The Relevance of Models for Social Anthropology*, ed. M. Banton (London: Tavistock, 1965), p. 139; and Sahlins, *Stone Age Economics* (London: Tavistock, 1964), p. 77.

19. Melville J. Herskovits, *Economic Anthropology: A Study in Comparative Economics* (New York: Knopf, 1952); Karl Polanyi, *Primitive, Archaic, and Modern Economies*, ed. George Dalton (New York: Doubleday, 1968), p. 7; Thorner and Thorner, *Land and Labour in India*, cited in note 13, p. 206; and Juliet Mitchell, *Woman's Estate* (Harmondsworth: Penguin, 1971), p. 157.

20. Robert Redfield, *The Little Community and Peasant Society and Culture* (Chicago: University of Chicago Press, 1960).

21. Wolf, cited in note 15, p. 3.

22. Theodore W. Schultz, "The value of children: An economic perspective," *Journal of Political Economy* 81, no. 2, Pt. 2 (March–April 1973): S2–S3. See also Theodore W. Schultz, "Fertility and economic values," in Theodore W. Schultz, ed., *Economies of the Family: Marriage, Children, and Human Capital* (Chicago: University of Chicago Press, 1974), p. 4.

23. See Raymond Firth, ed., *Themes in Economic Anthropology* (London: Tavistock, 1967); George Dalton, *Studies in Economic Anthropology* (Washington, D.C.: American Anthropological Association, 1971); Scarlett Epstein, *Economic Development and Social Change in South India* (Manchester: Manchester University Press, 1962).

24. See, for example, V. Gordon Childe, *What Happened in History* (Harmondsworth: Penguin, 1964), pp. 30–31.

25. The necessity for analyzing the relations of production in pre-capitalist societies has been pointed out by Meillassoux in the work cited in note 14 and also in his article "The social organization of the peasantry: The economic basis of kinship," *The Journal of Peasant Studies* 1, no. 1 (October 1973): 81–90; but he, rather curiously, did not analyze relative advantage and the role played by the relations of production in maintaining such relativity. Instead he emphasized the priority of reproduction and of the role of male dominance in organizing female marriage and childbearing, and produced a tortuous argument explaining the power of the aged in peasant society in terms of the need of the young cultivator to be sustained through his initial season until he reaped his harvest. This may have been the influence of Levi-Strauss. See Claude Levi-Strauss, "The family," in *Man, Culture and Society*, ed. Harry L. Shapiro (New York: Oxford University Press, 1971). Firth confirmed precapitalist awareness of economic advantage, but identified it solely in terms of interfamilial relations, usually of the exchange type. Raymond Firth, "Themes in economic anthropology: A general comment," in Firth, cited in note 23, p. 6.

26. Yang, cited in note 6, p. 77.

27. Lado T. Ruzicka and A. K. M. Allauddin Chowdhury, *Demographic Surveillance System-Matlab*, Vol. 3, *Vital Events and Migration*, Cholera Research Laboratory, Dacca, 1977–78, Reports for 1974, 1975, 1976.

28. Direct observation has been attempted in Bangladesh by several researchers: Mead T. Cain, "The economic activities of children in a village in Bangladesh," *Population and Development Review* 3, no. 3 (September 1977): 201–227; Barkat-e-Khuda, "Labour utilization in a village economy of Bangladesh" (Ph.D. thesis, Department of Demography, The Australian National University, Canberra, 1978); A.K.M. Jalaluddin, "The value of children in Bangladesh" (current Ph.D. thesis, Department of Demography, The Australian National University); and by the author and Pat Caldwell.

29. Similar work has also been undertaken in Indonesia by Benjamin White and in Nepal by Robert Peet: see Moni Nag, Robert C. Peet and Benjamin White, "Economic value of children in two peasant societies," in *The Proceedings of the International Population Conference: Mexico, 1977*, Vol. 1 (Liege: International Union for the Scientific Study of Population, 1977), pp. 123–139.

30. A.V. Chayanov, "Peasant farm organization," in *The Theory of the Peasant Economy*, cited in note 8, p. 180; and Fei and Chang, cited in note 6, p. 33.

31. Khuda (see note 28) has measured seasonal labor demand in Bangladesh, showing the tendency during the peak season to exceed available labor in the average-sized household.

32. Yang, cited in note 6, p. 73.

33. Yang, cited in note 6, p. 84.

34. Chayanov, "Peasant farm organization," cited in note 30, pp. 67–68; and Sahlins, *Stone Age Economics*, cited in note 18, p. 87.

35. Veneration for the aged will be examined in depth in John C. Caldwell, in press, "The reversal of the veneration flow: The true context of the reversal of the intergenerational wealth flow."

36. The same teachings are deeply embedded in traditional Chinese culture and can be found in gentler versions in Buddhism and Christianity.

37. Wolf, cited in note 15, p. 68.

38. All these societies are patriloca, so traditionally the bride moved into the house of the bridegroom's family. In Islamic areas, however, and especially in the Arab Middle East, the practice of endogamy means that the bride is not likely to leave her particular locality; indeed parallel–cousin and other kin marriages may mean that she does not leave the household.

39. United Nations Economic Commission for Western Asia, *Demographic and Related Socio-Economic Data Sheets for Countries of the Economic Commission for Western Asia*, no. 2, Beirut, 1978.

40. The actual position is more complex in many developing societies. Those without sufficient sons fear losing land to others through physical duress. See Mead T. Cain, "The household life cycle and economic mobility in rural Bangladesh," *Population and Development Review* 4, no.3 (September 1978): 421–438. This conclusion is also borne out by work undertaken in another rural area of Bangladesh by A.K.M. Jalauddin, cited in note 29.

41. Kubanin reported that, in early twentieth-century Russia, neither long-term nor day-to-day economic decisions were ever made against the wishes of the family head, and that the head heeded advice in only 8 and 42 percent of households, respectively, in these two types of decisions. Indeed, he had punitive powers over all members of the household in two-thirds of families and over all children in five-sixth. Kubanin, cited in note 16, pp. 108–109.

42. Familial production may be found in the area of money and large-scale production: for instance, where a whole family act as a firm or as the employers in a firm, or where some members of a peasant family offer their labor for wages without really leaving the traditional family (in that they funnel some or all of their money to it and receive guarantees and other benefits in return).

43. Some women's-movement and Marxist writers have failed to identify these relations of production because of their desire to indict the capitalist system for exploiting the family as a whole or for maintaining a reserve army of female labor. This is less true in the case of Margaret Benston, "The political economy of women's liberation," *Monthly Review* 21, no. 4 (September 1969): 13–27, and Peggy Morton, "A woman's work is never done," *Leviathan* 2 (1970): 32–38, but is generally true of Mitchell, cited in note 19, and Eli Zaretsky, *Capitalism, The Family and Personal Life* (London: Pluto, 1976), although the last

focuses more on historical understanding. Some writers lay stress on the eternal male achievement of material advantage rather than on the domestic mode of production under capitalism – for example, Shulamith Firestone, *The Dialectic of Sex: The Case for Feminist Revolution* (London: Jonathan Cape, 1971); and Eva Figes, *Patriarchal Attitudes* (London: Faber and Faber, 1970). The women's-movement classics also place emphasis on the achievement and maintenance of male advantage, not always even material advantage – for example, Simone de Beauvoir, *The Second Sex* (Harmondsworth: Penguin, 1972); and Kate Millett, *Sexual Politics* (London: Rupert Hart-Davis, 1971).

44. This was the exact counterpart to the outside work done by the younger members of the peasant family, even down to the handing over of most of the earnings without thereby achieving a major role in economic (or, usually, reproductive) decision-making.

45. It cannot as easily sustain early age at marriage. As I have argued elsewhere, the increasingly accepted requirement that a man have a secure job and savings before embarking on marriage led to widespread postponement of marriage in nineteenth-century Europe. Rising age at marriage moderated fertility levels in Europe prior to the major period of demographic transition, but there is little evidence that – as others have claimed – this was its intent. Contemporary evidence suggests it was the rising cost of marriage not the rising cost of children that led to marriage postponement. By postponing marriage, a man built up the necessary savings to capitalize the domestic system of production he would create by marriage. See John C. Caldwell and Lado T. Ruzicka, "The Australian fertility transition: An analysis," *Population and Development Review* 4, no. 1 (March 1978): 83–84.

46. Note John C. Caldwell and Pat Caldwell, "The achieved small family: Early fertility transition in an African city," *Studies in Family Planning* 9, no. 1 (January 1978): 2–18, in which the stability of high fertility in the Ibadan middle class is documented, together with the nature of the very small number of families in which fertility had been restricted.

47. Fertility in Western Europe has been shown to have remained high in those areas where the censuses reported the most use of family labor. See R. Lesthaeghe and C. Wilson, "Productievormen, stemgedrag en vruchtbaarheidstransitie in Westeuropeen perspectief, 1870–1930," *Interuniversity Programme in Demography, Vrije* Universiteit Brussel, Brussels, 1978. Lesthaeghe has subsequently pointed out in a private communication that evidence of this kind

remains least satisfactory for France and that perhaps the most severe test for the approach presented in their paper will be provided by the analysis of changes in family authority and decision-making patterns and in the nature of the family economy an family production in that country.

48. John C. Caldwell, *Population Growth and Family Change in Africa: The New Urban Elite in Ghana* (Canberra: The Australian National University Press, 1968), pp. 96–114, especially pp. 104–110.

49. These issues are touched upon in Heidi Hartmann, "Capitalism, patriarchy, and job segregation by sex," *Signs* 1, no. 3, Pt. 2 (1976): 137–169. Hartmann does not discuss the domestic mode of production in modern industrial society as the most efficient method of producing such goods and services from the standpoint of the chief decision-maker, the male household head. She focuses on the period before the market begins an increasingly successful attempt to compete in producing these goods and services.

50. It can be argued that labor is of paramount value and its control of surpassing importance in economies with very low levels of technology and hence of capital inputs into farming, and that the necessary condition for both economic and demographic change, as well as increased market orientation, is technological advance in farming. In terms of the timing of demographic change, it is doubtful whether this is the case. In India, technological change has been greater in Punjab and social change in Kerala; the demographic breakthrough occurred in the latter. Even the move from subsistence to capitalistic farming is often more related to the appearance of a market for the product than to a change in technology; this was certainly the case in the Central Plain of Thailand from the 1870s, when the Southeast Asian rice market developed, and the extra production was achieved at first by greater family labor inputs under patriarchal direction. See J.C. Caldwell, "The demographic structure," in *Thailand: Social and Economic Studies in Development*, ed. T.H. Silcock (Canberra: Australian National University Press, 1967), p. 28.

51. In both western and Middle Eastern Mediterranean families, the different interests of women have been identified as having the greatest potential of any factor for destroying the patriarchal family and its political, economic, and demographic structure. See J.G. Peristiany, "Introduction," in *Mediterranean Family Structures*, ed. J. G. Peristiany (Cambridge: Cambridge University Press, 1976), p. 2.

Aging in Swaziland:
Accentuating the Positive

C. K. BROWN

Aging Trends

••••

According to United Nations projections for the period 1980–2025, the population aged 60 and over in Swaziland is estimated to rise by a factor of 4.0 from 27,000 in 1980 to 110,000 in 2025, an increase larger than that projected (3.4) for the total population (UN, 1980). However, the aging of the population will not get under way until well after 2025. Continued high rates of fertility coupled with slowly declining mortality rates has in fact resulted in a high gross reproduction rate and an improved survival of its large birth cohorts. Only after the year 2020, when fertility rates are projected to fall quite rapidly, will the conditions be given for the aging of the population.

The changing age structure of the population can also be shown by tracing trends in the median age. It is the median age which divides the population into two equal parts: one older, the other younger. The median age of the population decreased from 18.4 years in 1960 to 17.3 in 1980 and is estimated to decrease further to 16.8 years in 2000, apparently due to the reduction of infant and child mortality rates. However, by 2020, the median age is estimated to be 20 years and is projected to increase to 21.8 years by 2025.

Furthermore, the current trend of decreasing age is reflected in a slight decline of the persons aged 60 and over in the total population from 4.8% in 1980 to its projected 4.7% in 2000. Even by the year 2025, this proportion is only expected to

C. K. Brown. This article appeared in 1988 in *Social Development Issues*, 12(1), pp. 56–70 and is reprinted with their permission.

rise to about 5.7%. Long term projections suggest that it will take until about 2075 for fertility declines ultimately to bring the weight of the 60 plus age group to a situation comparable to what is to be found in many developed countries today (UN, 1985, p. 99).

••••

As could be realized, the total number of the elderly will increase from 16,000 persons in 1960 to an estimated 48,000 by 2000 and will more than double to 108,000 in the year 2025. Indeed, between 1960 and 2025, the older population is projected to increase by a factor of 6.8. The magnitude and pattern of increases in the older population could be seen by the fact that between 1960 and 1980 there was an increase of 68.8% with more rapid increases during the periods 1980–2000 (81.5%) and 2000–2020 (87.8%).

The main reason for the steady increase in numbers of elderly persons in Swaziland is that the cohorts of children who will become the elderly population over the next 40 years will be successively larger. This will result from the high fertility rates of recent decades, coupled with increased life expectancy, especially among the young, but affecting older age groups as well.

••••

The dynamics of population growth in Swaziland will not produce much change in their relative numbers, despite the considerable numerical increases in the elderly population projected for the next 40 years. As has already been pointed out, between 1980 and 2025, the weight of the population aged 60 and over is to be found in the continuing relatively high fertility. Although there have been declines in the birth rate since the 1970s, the most substantial declines are projected to occur only after 2000. Those relatively late reductions in fertility will have an initial effect of increasing the proportions of the adult populations aged 15–59 after the turn of the century. But because of the time lag, before declines in fertility show their full impact on the population age structure, the relative weight of the elderly will only manifest substantial increases after 2025.

The policy implications of the rapid numerical growth in the elderly population in Swaziland during the period 1980–2025 becomes clearer if one compares the growth in the elderly population to that in the population as a whole. ... While the total population will increase by 248.2% between 1980 and 2025, the elderly component will increase by 307.4% during the same period.

It is also worthy of note that within the elderly population, the females have consistently outnumbered the males since the 1960s and will continue to do so even after 2025.

With regard to changes in the overall age structure, an examination of the relative size of other age groups over time indicates that declines in fertility will start to show an impact on the country's age structure only after the year 2000. By 2025, however, the weight of this group is projected to drop to 35.0%. Concurrently, the population of working age (15–59) will account for an almost stable 50% of total population between 1980 and 2000, but will jump to 59.3% by 2025. Indeed, this pattern of a decline in the weight of children and of a substantial increase in the relative size of the population of working age between 2000 and 2025 is typical of most countries in the Africa region. ... The total dependency ratio (defined as the ratio of persons aged 0–14 and 60-and-over, to the population of working age, 15–59) was estimated to be fairly stable during the period 1960–2000. However, by 2020 and up to 2025 and possibly beyond, the total dependency ratio for the country is expected to decline substantially. As can be seen in the table, the decline in the total dependency ratio after 2000 may be explained by the decrease in the child age dependency ratio (brought about by the decline in the fertility rate) and the fairly constant aged dependency ratio during the period 2000–2025.

To conclude this section, we would note that the process of population aging will get under way in Swaziland only after the turn of the century, in the sense that the population as a whole will become older. In the initial phase, the aging trend will be concentrated predominantly in the young and middle-aged adult group. Only after 2025 will progressive aging become manifest in the increasingly relative weight of the oldest segment of the population. However, this is the right time to evolve a comprehensive program which should provide health and other social service infrastructure for the population aged 60 and over in Swaziland.

Developmental Implications of the Aging Trends

There is no doubt that the large numerical increases in the population of older people in Swaziland over the next several decades will have a number of developmental implications and socio-economic consequences. In this place, however, we shall limit the discussion to the following: a weakening of traditional family and community support systems for the elderly; age selective migration from rural areas; and reduced opportunities for older persons to remain economically active.

In the first place, as in most countries in Africa, state-based social security systems are not well developed. Indeed, the homestead, the extended family, and the community still constitute the primary sources of care for the elderly. The aging trend, however, suggests that unless family, homestead, and community traditions of mutual aid can be strengthened, a vast service infrastructure will be required to replace and expand previous informal care-giving. Given the scarcity of economic resources and the competing demands from a large population of the youth, it will be extremely difficult to develop a social security system providing full coverage to the population. A possible solution to the problem will be to strengthen the resources of traditional caregivers, rather than creating new institutions. Such a family-oriented policy should include: channeling financial support to families caring for elderly relatives; legal action; implementation of public education programs; and the promotion of rural development schemes.

Another impact of the aging trend will be the migration of young people from rural communities (Swazi Nation Land R.D.A.s and non-RDAs, and ITF) to urban areas (gazetted and non-gazetted towns, company towns and estates) in search of employment and education and the resulting loss to the agricultural community of a key source of labor and support. At the operational level, rural development may therefore be seen as a policy area with key implications for averting the negative socio-economic consequences of rural-urban migration and youth unemployment. Indeed, by providing employment opportunities, technological support and a service infrastructure, it acts as an inducement for young people to remain in or return to the rural areas.

Finally, the impact of the aging trend in Swaziland may be seen in the reduced opportunities for older persons to remain economically active. Such factors as increasing literacy of the young, the introduction of wage economics, and mechanization of production will decrease their traditional function. The challenge to planners and policy makers in Swaziland is to devise programs and policy measures which will promote the continued activity of older workers to the limit of their capacities and thereby increase the productive potential of the economy as a whole.

Research and Policy Directions

As the population aged 60-and-over in Swaziland quadruples during the period 1980–2025, individual and collective needs will also increase for family and community support, health care and adequate nutrition, housing and a wholesome environment, social welfare services, employment, income security, and educational and other training opportunities. In formulating policies and in undertaking research in these spheres, decision-makers and researchers must work within several parameters of tradition and social change. Since in Swaziland the family and community have traditionally constituted a strong social support network for the elderly, and because of the high social and economic costs of creating new government-based social services, a primary focus should be on strengthening existing family and community resources. At the same time, policy makers and researchers should take cognizance of the extent to which such factors as migration, urbanization, and industrialization have weakened traditional social structures and bonds of family solidarity. Basically, policies should emphasize both coordinated research efforts to determine the magnitude of unmet needs and the provision of necessary services at the community level, avoiding the removal of older persons from their familiar environments (Okojie and Brown, 1987).

Research

In order to determine the actual conditions and needs of the aging in Swaziland, there will be the necessity of conducting periodic in-depth research on aging, the results of which should facilitate the formulation and implementation of plans and programs for the aging and facilitate linking them to development planning. Furthermore, to ensure an integrated approach to the problem of aging, an interdepartmental mechanism could be set up not only for the purpose of monitoring and evaluation but also for the coordination of all activities relating to aging in the country. Such a mechanism should facilitate the retrieving and dissemination of information.

The Role of the Family

Given the central role of the family in providing social protection to the elderly and the great social and economic cost in creating large-scale alternative support systems, policy-makers in Swaziland should place primary emphasis on strengthening family and community resources. In this connection, the important role being played by spouses, children, and relatives in caring for the elderly should be recognized. Important ways and means should be found to protect and strengthen their resources to enable them to discharge their obligations satisfactorily. This may be done by paying older people's allowances to families below certain income levels which maintain elderly members, and granting income tax relief to such families.

Furthermore, the introduction of a viable rural development program in the country will serve as a bulwark for preserving traditional sources of support for the elderly. For example, by providing an economic and service infrastructure, young people will be encouraged to remain in the rural areas and thus maintain the close proximity needed for continued support of older relatives.

Health and Nutrition

The available evidence indicates that the elderly population is a great consumer of basic health care facilities in Swaziland – both modern and traditional–medical. However, owing to the paucity of existing data, there is little certainty concerning the actual health status of older persons in the country. There is therefore the urgent need

for not only systematic research and epidemiological studies on the health status of the elderly, but also systematic collection of medical, demographic and socio-economic data on the elderly for the identification of premature as opposed to normal patterns of aging, and for the analysis of the aging process.

Furthermore, the primary concern of policy makers in the health sphere should be the collection of information on the health needs of the elderly and the provision of and effective network of primary health care at the community level. Emphasis should also be placed on preventative health measures, health education campaigns, removal of financial barriers to health service utilization, and training of primary and specialized health workers in the principles of geriatric medicine and precepts of traditional medicine.

Housing and Environment

With regard to housing and environment, one of the main policy concerns would be to provide a public service infrastructure and to strengthen resources available to families for sheltering older relatives. In this connection, specific strategies should include: the expansion of public housing in general; halting the proliferation of uncontrolled settlement; construction of larger housing units with cheaper materials in urban areas; upgrading of rural housing in the context of self-help and rural development; provision of subsidies and other financial assistance to households accommodating older relatives; and the promotion of the mobility of older persons within their home communities through easy access to available transportation.

Social Welfare

In Swaziland, the Ministry of Home Affairs is responsible for social services. Welfare assistance is provided by the Ministry's social workers who are based in the offices of District Commissioners. Through the public assistance system, some of the elderly receive monthly financial allowances and material help.

However, as in most developing countries, the level of social welfare coverage is quite low, thus suggesting the need for a greater provision of social welfare services. Rather than establishing state-run welfare systems on a large scale, policy makers should focus social welfare services at the community level within the family system, the traditional source of support. The preference for community and home aid should be reflected in an emphasis on home visitation and counselling services, household help, community casework, and expanded social and cultural activities within the community.

As a means of strengthening the community base of support for the elderly, there will be the need to channel social welfare assistance through existing local level organizations, such as community-based self-help and voluntary groups. The resources of these organizations should therefore be improved to enable them to continue their traditional social welfare work with the elderly.

Finally, social welfare services should not be designed to function in isolation from other community services. They should all be effectively integrated and coordinated at the community level to reach their target population.

Employment

The major employment policy concern should seek to increase opportunities for continued participation of both the rural and the urban elderly in productive work. Efforts should be made to encourage the elderly to take to self-employment which would enable them not only to do things at their own pace but also encourage them to introduce innovations. In this connection, cooperatives and production centers for handicrafts, run and self-managed by the elderly themselves, could be set up to encourage independence and self-reliance.

Retraining programs should be initiated to re-educate the elderly and update their knowledge of modern techniques and skills so that they can continue in their present occupation or take up a new one. The upgrading of traditional tools, for example, might relieve agricultural workers of laborious tasks and enable them to remain productive.

Income and Social Security

Even though Swaziland has adopted legislation covering income security benefits, coverage is thus far confined almost exclusively to wage-earners and urban dwellers. Thus, the rural agrarian population, which includes the great majority of elderly persons, remains outside the formal social security system.

There is no doubt that the ideal should be the establishment of comprehensive social security schemes covering all older persons, with particular focus on the rural population. However, in light of the financial implications of broad-scale income security programs and the decreasing ability of traditional social networks to continue to provide support in some contexts, it is suggested that the income security policy of the government should focus on real income security rather than just monetary income security. In this connection, the measures that should be undertaken will include helping other persons support themselves through the introduction of labor-saving agricultural tools, strengthening rural cooperatives, and establishing small-scale village industries.

In view of the difficulty in setting up comprehensive social security schemes, in the interim, at least, emphasis should be placed on providing social welfare aid on a case-by-case basis. For example, it would be more meaningful to strengthen social welfare programs to help aged persons with marginal income.

Education and Training

Given the low level of formal education and literacy of the current generation of the elderly in Swaziland, it will be essential to initiate country-wide adult literacy programs.

In addition to basic literacy and educational programs, there is the need to provide vocational training to the elderly for several purposes: to upgrade the technical skills of older workers (including farmers), and to equip them to undertake new occupations later in life in order to participate fully and effectively in the total development effort. Other aims should include informing the elderly of the availability of social services, proper health care and nutrition in old age, and, in the case of persons employed in the formal or public sector, counselling anticipation of retirement.

Finally, the scope of educational activities in the field of aging should extend beyond to the persons with whom they live and who care for them. In this larger context, the central educational objectives should be to eliminate negative stereotypes about aging, to promote intergenerational contacts, and to make the general public and professional caregivers aware of the specific problems and needs of older persons as well as their productive potential. It is therefore imperative that the existing National Committee on Aging should not only study the problems and needs of older persons but also promote programs that will encourage them to participate in decision-making relating to policies and programs which will affect their own mode of living, environment and welfare.

Conclusion

There is the need to take an active interest in the older generation and strive to improve their lot, namely, to make it possible for them to live out there lives in dignity. After all, we all have a real stake in the welfare of the elderly. If we survive long enough, *we* will be the elderly of the future.

REFERENCES

Okojie, F. & Brown, C.K. (1987). Aging in Sub-Saharan Africa: Towards a redefinition of roles, needs and research directions. Paper presented at the Annual Meeting of the Association for Gerontology and Human Development, Jackson, Mississippi, February.

Swaziland Government, Ministry of Health (1983). Report from the Ministry of Health on the aging. In C.M. Magagula (Ed.), *A report on the proceedings of the Seminar on the Aging* (53–57). Kwaluseni: University of Swaziland.

UN Department of International Economic and Social Affairs (1980). *Demographic Indicators of Countries, Estimates, and Projections as Assessed in 1980*, UN Publication, Sales No. E82.X 111.5.

UN Department of International Economic and Social Affairs (1985). *The World Aging Situation: Strategies and Policies*, UN Publication, Sales No. E85.1V.5.

ABOUT THE AUTHORS IN CHAPTER 4

John C. Caldwell is Director of the Health Transition Center at the Australian National University in Canberra, Australia. He has written or edited numerous books, the most recent of which is *The Causes of Demographic Change: Experimental Research in South India*, Madison, WI: University of Wisconsin Press, 1988, which was edited with P. H. Reddy and Pat Caldwell.

C. K. Brown is with the Social Science Research Unit of the University of Swaziland in Kwalusand. In 1986 his edited volume, *Rural Development in Ghana*, was published by Ghana Universities Press, Accra.

CHAPTER 5

Population Growth and Development

Introduction

World population will reach ten billion by the year 2050. India will have emerged as the most populous nation on earth. Population growth is the most important development issue of this decade and high population growth is considered one of the major obstacles to economic growth in developing countries. Debate about population growth and development over the past thirty years has led to increasingly sophisticated research, e.g., Adelman (1963), and some excellent scholarly overviews by individuals, e.g., Keyfitz (1989), and national and international organizations, e.g., The National Research Council and the World Bank. Population growth has been the topic of addresses and papers by many distinguished demographers, among them Demeny's presidential address to the Population Association of America in 1986.

Research on the relationship between population change and economic development provides very divergent viewpoints, which may be classified into two categories. The first category suggests that population growth impedes economic development. Population growth causes hunger in the short run and poses a threat to the survival of the human race in the long run. The other category suggests that population growth contributes to economic development in the long run. People are seen as innovators. A large number of people are more likely to generate contributions toward the production of social and physical technologies that are likely to improve human welfare.

There are also a few countries in Africa such as Gabon (Newman, 1987) that experience low fertility rates indicative of a quite different population problem. In Gabon and in parts of Cameroon, Zaire, and Zambia, very low fertility rates have wiped out several ethnic groups. The reasons for low fertility are not well known but it is speculated that sterility caused by venereal and other diseases is one of the main factors. Gabon's health and fertility problems are compounded by a pronatalist policy that prohibits the importation of contraceptives. A change in this policy would also assist in the control of disease.

Population growth increases income inequality and the likelihood of starvation for some. A second concern, related to population growth, is the depletion of natural resources and the effect this has on economic development. Although there is disagreement about which are the most important causes of natural resource depletion and scarcity, there is general

158

agreement that population growth is a major cause. Finally, it is argued that population growth has a weak negative effect on savings, therefore constraining capital-intensive investment in development projects.

Szymanski (1974) and others have, however, led many to conclude, after a careful analysis of international economic data for the 1960s, that the Neo-Malthusian analyses are incorrect. Their position has been that our attention would better be turned to the organization of society, the structural causes of high fertility, for when they are removed the birth rate will fall – this was the position of Caldwell in the previous chapter. Even more recently Franke (1981) has analyzed demographic data from West Africa to conclude that it is the mode of production that plays a crucial role in fertility rates. This suggests that there are several policy options available to bring about the "demographic transition."

The Articles in Chapter 5

The selections presented in this and the preceding chapter are only an introduction to a subject that has often been the focus of world attention. The negative effect of population growth on development is well documented on the African continent but many parts of Africa continue to experience increasing growth and will do so throughout the century. *Huth* describes the social and economic consequences of population growth. Per capita food production has declined in Sub-Saharan Africa over the past twenty years. Against mounting population pressures, there is an increase in the scarcity of farm land. The labor force size is likely to expand rapidly, creating serious unemployment problems. There are widespread basic needs deficiencies. The status of women has deteriorated over time as a result of competition for scarce resources and unfavorable government policies. Given these conditions, governments have a role to play in promoting antinatalist policies and promoting family planning. Currently very few African states have official population policies.

The strong emphasis on population growth as the most important cause of hunger, natural resources depletion, and poor savings ratios has been reexamined by *Simon* (1988), criticizing the tendency in population research to emphasize the negative effect of population growth on economic development. Although the short run effects of population growth on development tend to be negative, some of the long term effects may be positive. Population growth may actually stimulate social and technological innovations that improve productive efficiency and the supply of resources.

Simon's contribution to this chapter, "Population Growth, Economic Growth, and Foreign Aid," presents extensive empirical data to support the hypothesis that although additional people generate problems in the short run, there are greater benefits in the long run. This, of course, raises the question of how much immediate suffering may be tolerated without such extensive repercussions as to make the long run view intolerable to those who are absorbing the immediate costs of policy. At the same time, as *Simon* contends, aid programs may also have almost immediate repercussions on the economies whose problems they are attempting to ameliorate. Having read the first three articles in this chapter, one will be ever more conscious of the complexity of the population/development problem.

The relative importance of family planning and social development on fertility decline is central to the theoretical and policy related population issues. Some argue that family planning is far more influential in inducing fertility decline than is socioeconomic development.

Poston and *Gu* examine the effects of development and family planning variables on fertility in China, where a family planning program is strongly administered and implemented through large centralized bureaucracies. In general, Chinese family planning programs have been credited with inducing fertility transition. For details on factors influencing variation by region, see Poston (1986). However, *Poston* and *Gu* show that socioeconomic development variables have a negative effect on fertility net of the effect of family planning programs.

Their results are similar to a number of other studies that show that it is the combination of social development and family planning that induces fertility decline. The government may be seen as having a crucial role to play in providing support to antinatalist policies that facilitate and educate people about birth control.

Lapham and *Mauldin* demonstrate that the strong relationship between socioeconomic predictor variables (some of which are demographic corollaries of SES) and contraceptive prevalence is increased by family planning efforts. Family planning programs that are an essential part of the overall development program are more likely to succeed than are those that are not part of such a program.

Although conflicting opinions on the population and economic development relationship continue to influence national as well as international efforts on population control, that is only part of the issue. As Ozzie G. Simmons (1988) has concluded in his volume on development and population growth in the Third World, there has been increasing concern about *equity or at least improving equity in the distribution and consumption of goods* commensurate with economic growth. He, among others, sees increasing fertility decline as an immediate step toward equity and meeting basic needs.

REFERENCES

Adelman, Irma, "An Econometric Analysis of Population Growth," *The American Economic Review*, 53(3), June 1963, pp. 314–339.

Demeny, Paul, "Population and the Invisible Hand," *Demography*, 23(4), November 1986, pp. 473–487.

Franke, Richard W., "Mode of Production and Population Patterns: Policy Implications for West African Development," *International Journal of Health Sciences*, 11(3), 1981, pp. 361–387.

Keyfitz, Nathan, "The Growing Human Population," *Scientific American*, September 1989, pp. 119–126.

National Research Council, *Population Growth and Economic Development: Policy Questions* (Washington, D.C.: National Academy Press), 1986.

Newman, John G., "Gabon: A Demographic Anomaly," *Association of Pacific Coast Geographers Yearbook*, Vol. 45, 1987, pp. 79–85.

Poston, Dudley L., Jr., "Patterns of Contraceptive Use in China," *Studies in Family Planning*, 17(5), September/October 1986, pp. 217–227.

Simon, Julian L., "On Aggregate Empirical Studies Relating Population Variables to Economic Development," *Population and Development Review*, 15(2), 1988, pp. 323–332.

Simmons, Ozzie G., *Perspectives on Development and Population Growth in the Third World* (New York and London: Plenum), 1988.

Szymanski, Albert, "Economic Development and Population," *Studies in Comparative Economic Development*, 1974, pp. 53–69.

Population Prospects for Sub-Saharan Africa: Determinants, Consequences and Policy

MARY JO HUTH

Despite significant progress in sub-Saharan African countries during the 1960s and 1970s – improved living standards, a substantial decline in mortality rates, impressive expansion of educational opportunities, and continued urbanization – the fertility rates in this part of the world remain at extraordinarily high levels. It is not surprising, therefore, that the pace of economic and social development has already slowed down considerably; and moreover, that, since fertility rates are expected to remain high throughout the remainder of this century, prospects for a resurgence in the rate of development within the near future remain bleak. The World Development Report of 1982,[1] for example, predicted that during the subsequent years of the 1980s economic growth rates would be only 1.9 percent and 2.8 percent per annum in sub-Saharan Africa's low and middle-income countries, respectively.

Population Growth Prospects, 1980–2020

Having outlined the macro-economic forecast as a background, let us now examine four different sets of population growth-rate projections for the thirty-five-year period, 1985 to 2020. These figures encompass nine sub-Saharan African countries – Ethiopia, Ghana, the Ivory Coast, Kenya, Nigeria, the Sudan, Tanzania,

Mary Jo Huth. The African Institute of South Africa gave permission to reprint this article from the *Journal of Contemporary African Studies*, 5(1–2), 1986, pp. 167–181.

Zaire, and Zimbabwe – which together currently support 225 million people, or 62 percent of the total population of the area (see Table 1).

The first set of population growth-rate projections is based upon the very optimistic assumption that fertility in the selected countries will decrease by about 45 percent between the years 1985 and 2020. The second set of projections (see Table 1) draws upon the high variant of the United Nations' population growth-rate estimates for each of the nine countries, which assumes that the composite crude birth rate of these countries will decline by approximately 25 percent between 1985 and 2020. Underlying the third set of population growth-rate projections is the assumption that fertility rates in the nine sub-Saharan African countries will remain at the 1980 to 1985 level of 49.8 births per 1000 of the population. And although the fourth set of projections is based upon the same supposition, the impact of another relevant variable – the mortality rate – is considered. Briefly, this anticipates that income stagnation in the nine African countries may retard progress in the area of health and life expectancy, thus causing mortality rates to improve less dramatically than is assumed in the first three sets of projections – from around 23 per 1000 between 1980 and 1985, to around 11 per 1000 between 2015 and 2020.

According to the population growth-rate projections presented in Table 1, by the year 2000 the combined population of these nine sub-Saharan African countries

Table 1: Projections of Increase in Total Population, Working-Age Population, and Women of Reproductive Age for Nine Sub-Saharan African Countries, under Alternative Assumptions, 1985–2000 and 2000–2020

FERTILITY/MORTALITY ASSUMPTIONS		PROJECTED AVERAGE ANNUAL RATES OF GROWTH (IN PERCENTAGES)					
		TOTAL POPULATION		WORKING-AGE POPULATION		WOMEN OF REPRODUCTIVE AGE	
		1985–2000	2000–2020	1985–2000	2000–2020	1985–2000	2000–2020
I	45 Percent Fertility Decline; Mortality Decline from 23/1000 to 11/1000	3.11	2.38	3.26	3.14	3.29	2.83
II	25 Percent Fertility Decline; Mortality Decline from 23/1000 to 11/1000	3.36	3.26	3.27	3.63	3.29	3.64
III	Fertility Rate Remaining Constant at 49,8/1000; Mortality Decline from 23/1000 to 11/1000	3.43	3.95	3.26	3.81	3.29	3.84
IV	Fertility Rate Remaining Constant at 49,8/1000; Mortality Rate Improving Less Dramatically than in Assumptions I to III	3.29	3.48	3.19	3.44	3.22	3.48

SOURCE: Faruqee, R. and R. Gulhati, *Rapid Population Growth in Sub-Saharan Africa: Issues and Policies* (Staff Working Paper No. 559), World Bank, Washington, DC, 1983, p. 21.

will lie somewhere between 416 and 442 million. However, irrespective of the various fertility assumptions made in Table 1, the dramatic effect of the long history of high fertility in these countries is reflected in the fact that between the years 1980 and 2000 the number of women falling within the reproductive age group will increase by an average of 91 percent. Moreover, since this population growth momentum is now built into the demographic structure of sub-Saharan African countries, the impact of any future declines in fertility will be blunted. For example, during the subsequent twenty-year period (2000 to 2020) in the countries under examination, the number of women within the reproductive age group will increase by at least 75 percent – resulting in a combined population increase of about 60 percent to between 666 and 707 million, even when assuming that fertility rates will indeed decline.[2]

Fertility rates in sub-Saharan Africa have declined much more slowly in response to increases in per capita income than in any other region of the world. Indeed, the recent World Fertility Survey of twenty-nine developing countries, which examined total fertility rates (defined as the aver-age number of children per family), revealed that Africa averages 6.7 children per family – this compared to an average of 4.5 children per family in Asia and the Pacific, and 4.7 children per family in Latin America. In part, this can be seen as a reflection of the fact that the average desired number of children per family in Africa is 7.1; whereas in Asia and the Pacif-ic it is 4.0 and in Latin America 4.3.

What factors, then, explain Africa's unusually high fertility rates and the pre-vailing preference for large families, espe-cially as compared to other developing regions of the world? From a study of the available socio-anthropological literature, two working hypotheses are suggested. First, the notion exists that in fragmented, traditional societies – whose governments have not yet established rule by law and an effective police force to implement this – large numbers of people in a family or clan may be the only guarantee of security. Thus, as Caldwell suggests, the fact that African societies have many – and frequent-ly conflicting – tribes may have strength-ened the norm of unrestricted fertility. Moreover, because sub-Saharan Africa's family institution is characterized by strong descent lineages rather than by close conju-gal ties, land (the principal form of wealth) is usually communally owned. Hence, power and fortune have been derived almost solely from control over a large number of people.[3]

In the second hypothesis, Africa's high fertility is interpreted in terms of the predicament of its female population. Boserup points out that during Africa's pre-colonial history, the distinctive characteris-tic of its women was the dominant role that they played in agriculture. This he ascribes to several factors; namely, concentration on subsistence food crops, low population density, the widespread practice of shifting cultivation, and minimal technology.[4] Sub-sequent European colonial policy, howev-er, did not cater for the prevailing female farming system in Africa. Instead, some males were recruited for wage-jobs on European-owned plantations, whilst others were encouraged to grow cash crops for export to Europe on their own small plots. This resulted in an increasing gap develop-ing between the output of food and cash crops; and, of course, between the produc-tivity of female and male farmers. For, while men acquired cash to improve their cultivation of export crops, women contin-ued to use traditional, low-input, low-yield methods for their food production – a trend which led to a deterioration in the relative position of women. Eventually colonists appropriated all the best lands for the culti-vation of cash crops, thus leaving women responsible for domestic food production on inferior lands while their sons and hus-bands left home to gain an education or to earn wages in the modern sector. However, because women failed to produce enough food on their plots, they became increas-ingly economically dependent on their hus-bands' cash earnings. Furthermore, their already considerable workload was increased thereby: in addition to child-rear-ing, and domestic and food-growing duties, women were expected to take over the responsibility for cash-crop production from their absent sons and husbands.[5]

The damage that the status of women suffered in colonial Africa has unfortunately not been redressed during the two and a half decades of socio-economic develop-ment since independence. After the mid-and late- 1970s, agricultural productivity – both in terms of cash and food crops – has slowed down, as the internal terms of trade have shifted in favour of the cities. Waves of men migrated to urban areas in search of more lucrative job opportunities, while women increasingly head farm households. Nevertheless, the dominant role in family decision-making is still played by the male; on his return-home visits, he must give his consent to such matters as employing a share-cropper, or securing a loan from a local credit union.[6]

••••

Sub-Saharan Africa is the *only* region in the world in which per capita food production has *declined* over the past twenty years. Only a few countries – Burundi, the Ivory Coast, Malawi, Rwanda, Swaziland, and more recently Zambia – have maintained or improved upon the per capita food production level that they achieved in the early 1960s. All other countries – but notably Angola, Botswana, Ethiopia, the Gambia, Ghana, Mozambique, Niger, Somalia, and Uganda – have experienced declining per capita food production. While the annual rate of population growth in Central Africa has been 2.3 percent in recent years, food production has increased by only 1.0 percent per year; the corresponding annual population growth and food production rates for West Africa have been 2.6 percent and 1.1 percent, and for East and southern Africa, 2.8 percent and 1.9 percent, respectively. It is not surprising, therefore, that the volume of cereal imports has been increasing by 10 percent a year in sub-Saharan Africa. The current situation can be attributed to the fact that, while – according to Buringh and Van Heemst – 33 percent of land is potentially arable, only 6 percent of the total land area of sub-Saharan Africa is actually under cultivation. By comparison, out of 20 percent of potentially arable land in Asia, 16 percent is being cultivated. Furthermore, in sub-Saharan Africa average yields of staple crops, such as roots and tubers, cereals and pulses, are much lower than in both Asia and Latin America.[7]

It is obvious that accommodating the food needs of sub-Saharan Africa's rapidly expanding population will require major improvements in the agricultural sector – and involve massive public investment in the development of more farmland, in the acceleration of crop productivity, and in the construction of transportation networks and other relevant infrastructure. The dilemma which sub-Saharan Africa's nations must face, however, is that, while such measures would undoubtedly yield large long-run payoffs in terms of important economic, social and political objectives, they may be too expensive to implement in the immediate future. In this context, for example, due to the necessity of clearing dense vegetation and installing extensive drainage and soil conservation systems, 87 percent of the arable land in sub-Saharan Africa could be developed only at high cost. Moreover, less than 20 percent of the land in sub-Saharan Africa receives sufficient rainfall to produce large crop yields, without employing costly farm machinery, fertilizers and pesticides.[8]

Another difficulty frustrating efforts to improve agricultural output in several sub-Saharan African countries, including Burundi, Kenya, Malawi, Mauritius, and Rwanda, is the increasing scarcity of farmland. In Kenya, for example, Mbithi and Barnes found that migrant squatters had done irreversible damage to much of the country's marginal land, by depleting water catchments, by destroying forests, and through using improper cultivation methods. However, even in relatively fertile areas, excessive fragmentation of ownership on farms held by groups of co-operatives has resulted in less-than-optimum output. In these situations, each family may be given five to seven acres of land on condition that children will seek their livelihood elsewhere when they become adults. Nevertheless, since in many instances grown children do not leave their parents' farm, the land is parceled out further among them, thus engendering ever-increasing productivity declines.[9] Scarcity of cropland in sub-Saharan Africa has led, in turn, to deforestation, thus reducing the supply of firewood in this region – where percent of the people depend upon this source of fuel – to critical levels, and also contributing to soil erosion.[10]

In addition to its impact upon land productivity and food supply, the rapid population growth which has already occurred in sub-Saharan Africa portends a marked acceleration in the size of the labour force, and serious employment problems. Compared to an average annual increase in the labor force of 2.1 percent during the 1970s, an increase of 3.3 percent is expected during the next fifteen years in the nine countries whose population growth prospects were discussed earlier. If African development policy fails to accommodate such unprecedented expansion in the labour force, economic instability and social demoralization will most certainly ensue. Prospects for Africa's labour force in the twenty-first century are much more unpredictable. If fertility rates continue at current levels during the next fifteen years in these nine countries, the annual rate of growth in the labour force will average 3.8 percent during the period 2000 to 2020. On the other hand, a low fertility projection would mean that the annual rate of growth could average about 3.2 percent during this twenty-year period. Thus, depending upon official as well as unofficial decisions regarding fertility issues between now and the end of this century, the combined labour force of these nations (Ethiopia, Ghana, the Ivory Coast, Kenya, Nigeria, the Sudan, Tanzania, Zaire, and Zimbabwe) could number between 304 and 345 million by the year 2020. While such a large labour force can be an economic asset if it is healthy, well trained and fully equipped with capital requirements and infrastructure, this is not likely to be the case given the prevailing financial and management constraints and the formidable obstacles to institutional reform in most countries of sub-Saharan Africa.[11]

That the challenge posed by rapid population growth in this part of Africa has not yet led to a commensurate government response in the form of technological or organizational progress, is also evidenced in the area of basic needs services, where the difficult problem of "keeping up" the quantity and quality of existing coverage has compounded the long-standing problem of "catching up". Despite considerable progress in recent years in the provision of clean water, as well as nutritional, health and educational services, the situation is still unsatisfactory. Infant and child mortality remain at fairly high levels; the coverage of primary education has risen to an average of 70 percent, but that of secondary education remains very low at 9 percent; and sanitary water supplies are available to only 20 percent of the population.[12] The relevance of the fertility issue to a government's ability to satisfy the basic needs of its population is well illustrated in the case of Kenya, which allocated 32 percent of its total budget to education, health, housing, and water supplies during the period 1975 to 1980. However, if fertility continues at about the current rate (51 per 1,000), Kenya will have to increase its expenditures for these services by 878 percent up to the period 2015 to 2020 – just to maintain present coverage and quality. By contrast, if fertility levels declined to about 41 per 1,000 of the population over the next thirty years, the required expenditure increase would be only 269 percent, thus freeing substantial resources with which Kenya could improve both the coverage and quality of its basic services.[13]

Thus, the scale and complexity of sub-Saharan Africa's development problems will be influenced by future fertility trends. If fertility begins to fall in the coming decades, the resulting slower population growth should provide more living space, reduce the rate of increase in food demand (facilitating the attainment of self-sufficiency and moderating pressures on the balance of payments), and relieve pressure on government budgets (facilitating faster expansion of coverage and improvement in the quality of basic needs services). Moreover, a deceleration of population growth should not only reduce the inflow of entrants into the labour force, but should also improve the productivity of each new employee by permitting a more rapid increase in the amount of physical capital with which he/she is supplied on the job. The economies of Africa would also have a better prospect of generating a sufficient number of attractive earning opportunities for the growing number of white-collar workers. Finally, it is to be hoped that a healthier, more educated, and better technically equipped population will be a major factor effecting a gradual change of attitudes and values towards those favouring reduced fertility.[14]

Population Policies: Present and Future

In 1981, the United Nations Economic Commission for Africa conducted a study of population policies in forty-two countries of sub-Saharan Africa. Only eight of the countries (or 19 percent) have[15] an official policy to reduce their population growth rate. These are Botswana, Kenya, Lesotho, Mauritius, South Africa, Uganda, Ghana, and Senegal. Twenty others (or 48 percent) have an official policy supporting family planning for health reasons but not for demographic purposes. The remaining fourteen (or 33 percent) neither have an official policy to reduce their population growth rate, nor do they support family planning for health reasons. It is obvious, therefore, that the great majority (81 percent) of sub-Saharan African countries do not have any official policy to restrict rapid population growth. Moreover, those which do have such a policy are not strongly or consistently committed to its implementation.

Kenya, for example, was the first sub-Saharan African country to adopt an official family planning programme, but – while this was done in 1967 – the programme has received substantial financial support only during the Third Five-Year Plan (1975 to

1979). A 1977/78 Kenyan fertility survey revealed that, although 42 percent of the sampled ever-married women knew of a place to secure family planning services, only 12 percent had ever visited such a facility and a mere 5 percent of women in the reproductive age group were practising family planning. Two major factors explain this situation. First, 80 percent of Kenya's women would have to travel over 4.8 kilometres to reach the nearest facility offering family-planning services, and most of them either lack access to, or cannot afford, the necessary means of transportation. Second, because medical centres are overburdened with demands for therapeutic treatment, because their preventive services are underdeveloped and because their outreach programmes are poorly co-ordinated, many women of reproductive age remain outside the health delivery system. Furthermore, due to staff shortages, family-health field educators reach only a small percentage of the women.[15]

Other, more broadly focused factors which explain sub-Saharan Africa's predominantly negative or ambivalent posture towards the control of population growth, are as follows: first, low population density in most countries contributes to the widespread perception of vast amounts of empty space and unutilized natural resources; second, since concern about Africa's population problems comes mainly from the technologically advanced nations of the West, it is dismissed as politically motivated; third, religious and tribal beliefs and customs make population control an extremely sensitive issue; fourth, newly independent African governments have been giving top priority to nation-building and economic development via foreign aid; and finally, the increasing financial difficulties of African governments in recent years have diverted the efforts of policy-makers towards the tackling of urgent, short-term problems, rather than longer-term ones such as population growth.[16] Consequently, a prerequisite for strengthening or introducing population-control policies in sub-Saharan African countries is a recognition by their own opinion-formers and policy-makers that such efforts are in their respective national interests.

Furthermore, designing effective population policy must be a highly individualized process – one which identifies and assesses factors conducive to changing fertility patterns, as well as those contributing to the *status quo* in each country. This process would involve asking questions such as the following: how does the system of land tenure affect women's sense of security?; does the intra-family division of labour impose an onerous burden on women?; do agricultural extension services, credit agencies and co-operatives discriminate against women?; are women deprived of income-earning opportunities?; do norms regarding family size differ by sex and by generation?; what kinds of individuals, households, kinship groups and social organizations are trying to break away from traditional values and norms?; and what is the nature and extent of opposition to deviant behaviour? In addition – since a key factor affecting the use of family–planning services is *accessibility* – it may be desirable to supplement existing clinic-based programmes, linked to the public health delivery system, with programmes offered through a variety of other outlets, such as community self-help schemes, commercial channels, women's organizations, and rural development agencies. New instruments for propagating the family planning message should also be utilized, including nation-wide adult literacy campaigns and youth recreation programmes, family-life education courses in secondary schools and colleges, and the mass media.[17]

Thus, building enthusiasm for, and commitment to, population control in sub-Saharan Africa will not be an easy task. It will require a thorough grasp of the underlying economic, social and political issues, the ability to project the case for government policy-making in a difficult area, and the capacity to define what is acceptable intervention – taking into account the range within which social and cultural change is feasible in each country. Despite the difficulty of the task, however, realization of the fact that sub-Saharan Africa's long-term economic and social development is contingent upon its achieving control over future population growth, makes the effort imperative as well as challenging.

ENDNOTES

1. See World Bank, Economic Analysis and Projections Department, Comparative Analysis and Data Division, *World Development Report, 1982,* Johns Hopkins University Press, Baltimore, Maryland, 1982.

2. See Faruqee, R. and R. Gulhati, *Rapid Population Growth in Sub-Saharan Africa: Issues and Policies* (Staff Working Paper No. 559), World Bank, Washington, D.C., 1983.

3. See Caldwell, J.C., "The Mechanisms of Demographic Change in Historical Perspective", in *Population Studies* (Vol. 35, No. 1, 1981), pp. 5–27.

4. See Boserup, E., *Women's Role in Economic Development,* St. Martin's Press, New York, 1970.

5. See Salilios-Rothschild, C., "The Role of the Family: A Neglected Aspect of Poverty", in Knight, P.T. (ed.), *Implementing Programmes of Human Development* (Staff Working Paper No. 403), World Bank, Washington, D.C., July 1980, pp. 311–372.

6. See Kossoudji, S. and E. Mueller, *The Economic and Demographic Status of Female-Headed Households in Rural Botswana* (Discussion Paper No. 81–49), World Bank, Washington, D.C., 1981.

7. See Buringh, P. and H.D.J. van Heemst, *An Estimation of World Food Production Based on Labour-Orientated Agriculture,* Centre for World Food Market Research, Wageningen, The Netherlands, 1977.

8. See Faruqee, R. and R. Gulhati, *Rapid Population Growth in Sub-Saharan Africa: Issues and Policies* (Staff Working Paper No. 559), World Bank, Washington, D.C., 1983.

9. See Mbithi, P.M. and C. Barnes, *The Spontaneous Settlement Problem in Kenya,* East African Literature Bureau, Nairobi, 1975.

10. See Brown, L.R., *Global Economic Prospect: New Sources of Economic Stress* (World Watch Paper No. 20),

United Nations Publishing Division, New York, 1978, pp. 1–56.

11. See Faruqee, R. and R. Gulhati, *Rapid Population Growth in Sub-Saharan Africa: Issues and Policies* (Staff Working Paper No. 559), World Bank, Washington, D.C., 1983.

12. See *ibidem*.

13. See Faruqee, R. *et al. Kenya: Population and Development,* World Bank, Washington, D.C., July 1980.

14. See Cassen, R., Wolfson, M. and G. Ohlin (eds.), *Planning for Growing Populations,* Development Centre, Organization for Economic Co-operation and Development, 1978.

15. See Faruqee, R. and R. Gulhati, *Rapid Population Growth in Sub-Saharan Africa: Issues and Policies* (Staff Working Paper No. 559), World Bank, Washington, D.C., 1983.

16. See *ibidem*.

17. See *ibidem*.

Population Growth, Economic Growth, and Foreign Aid

JULIAN L. SIMON

Introduction

It is a great honor, as well as a great pleasure, for me to contribute to this Festschrift honoring Peter Bauer and his pathbreaking work on economic development.

••••

The main points of my paper are the following: First, it is the processes that Bauer emphasizes that account for the speed of a country's economic development. I will adduce some data on three pairs of countries that I think are strong added evidence for that view: North and South Korea, East and West Germany, and China and Taiwan. Second, the rate of population growth does *not* determine the rate of economic development; the same data set supports this point. A corollary is that a more dense population does not hamper population growth; this is attested to by the same data as well as by other data that I will mention. Third, though intentions may be benign (though they certainly are not always so), some aspects of U.S. foreign aid programs for "family planning" are not just wasteful, not just fraudulent, not even just politically dangerous for the United States; but they may well be extremely damaging on net balance by offering a palliative that distracts from the all-important issue of the economic system of the country receiving the aid.

All three points can be subsumed under the single lesson that Henry Hazlitt (1962, p. 17) tried to teach in *Economics in One Lesson:* "The art of economics consists in looking not merely at the immediate but at the

Julian Simon. Permission to reprint this article was granted by the Cato Institute, publishers of the *Cato Journal* in which it appeared in 1987, 7(1), pp. 159–193.

longer effects of any act or policy; it consists in tracing the consequences of that policy not merely for one group but for all groups."

The Role of Population Size, Growth, and Density in Economic Progress

Tables 1–5 compare pairs of countries that have the same culture and history, and had much the same standard of living when they split apart after World War II: North and South Korea, East and West Germany, China and Taiwan. The tables make it abundantly clear, despite the frequent absence of data for the centrally planned countries, that the market-directed economies have performed much better economically, no matter how economic progress is measured. Income per person is higher. Wages have grown faster. Key indicators of infra-structure, such as telephones per person, show a much higher level of development. And indicators of individual wealth and personal consumption, such as automobiles and newsprint, show enormous advantages for the market-directed enterprise economies compared to the centrally planned, centrally controlled economies. Furthermore, birth rates fell at least as early and as fast in the market-directed countries as in the centrally planned countries.

The first line in Table 1 shows that in each case the centrally planned communist country began with less population "pressure," as measured by density per square kilometer, compared to the paired market-directed noncommunist country. And the communist and noncommunist countries in each pair also started with much the same birth rates and population growth rates.

There is certainly no evidence here which suggests that population growth or density influences the rate of economic development.

The most important evidence on the relationship between the rate of population growth and the rate of economic growth is the global correlations, the data that first shook my conventional belief that population growth was the twin of war as the world's great evils. There now exist perhaps a score of competent statistical studies, beginning in 1967 with an analysis by Simon Kuznets covering the few countries for which data are available over the past century, and also analyses by Kuznets and Richard Easterlin of the data covering many countries since World War II. The basic method is to gather data on each country's rate of population growth and its rate of economic growth, and then to examine whether – looking at all the data in the sample together – the countries with high population growth rates have economic growth rates lower than average, and countries with low population growth rates have economic growth rates higher than average. Various writers have used a variety of samples of countries, and have employed an impressive battery of ingenious statistical techniques to allow for other factors that might also be affecting the outcome.

The clear-cut consensus of this body of research is that faster population growth is *not* associated with slower economic growth. Of course one can adduce cases of countries that seemingly are exceptions to the pattern. It is the genius of statistical inference, however, to enable us to draw valid generalizations from samples that contain wide variations in behavior. The exceptions can be useful in alerting us to possible avenues for further analysis, but as long as they are only exceptions, they do not prove that the generalization is not meaningful or useful.

••••

In the very short run, additional people are an added burden. But under conditions of freedom, population growth poses less of a problem in the short run, and brings many more benefits in the long run, than under conditions of government control. To illustrate, compare China with Singapore.

China's coercive population policy, including forced abortions, is often called "pragmatic" because its economic development supposedly requires population control. For example, typically in a recent *Washington Post* supplement (in the context of an article on an eight-year-old Chinese dancer; every writer an expert on population!) the author tells us that "China strictly enforces a policy of one child per family [which] seems unnecessarily harsh and dispiriting. ... [But] then one encounters the reality. ... What does one do in a country that has 1.3 billion people, 27 percent of the world's population, to be fed from only 7 percent of the world's arable land?"

Contrast Singapore. Despite its very high population density, Singapore suffers from what it considers a labor shortage and imports workers. The country is even considering incentives for middle-class families to have more children, in contrast to its previous across-the-board anti-natality policy. This raises the question whether there are economic grounds for China to even *ask* people to have only one child.

Tables 1–5 include data on Hong Kong and Singapore for additional comparisons with China. The experience of these countries, whose people largely share with China their language, history, and culture, give additional proof that China's problem is not too many children but rather a defective political-economic system. With free markets China might soon experience the same sort of labor shortage as found in Singapore, which is vastly more densely settled and has no natural resources. (This does not mean a "free" system such as China is talking about now; it is quite unlikely that a truly free market can coexist with a totali-

Table 1: Population Density and Growth, Selected Countries, 1950–83

	EAST GERMANY	WEST GERMANY	NORTH KOREA	SOUTH KOREA	CHINA	TAIWAN	HONG KONG	SINGAPORE	USSR	USA	INDIA	JAPAN
Population per Sq. Km., 1950	171	201	76	212	57	212	2236	1759	8	16	110	224
% Change in Pop., 1950	1.2	1.1	-7.8	0.1	1.9	3.3	-10.4	4.4	1.7	1.7	1.7	1.6
% Change in Pop., 1955	-1.3	1.2	3.5	2.2	2.4	3.5	4.9	4.9	1.8	1.8	1.9	1.0
%Change in Pop., 1960	-0.7	1.3	3.0	3.3	1.8	3.1	3.0	3.3	1.8	1.7	2.0	0.9
%Change in Pop., 1970	-0.1	1.0	3.0	2.4	2.4	2.2	2.2	1.7	1.0	1.1	2.2	1.3
% Change in Pop., 1983	-0.3	-0.2	2.1-2.6	1.4-1.6	1.3-1.6	1.8	1.5	1.2	0.7-0.9	0.9	2.1-2.2	0.6

SOURCES: Population per square km.: United Nations Educational, Scientific, and Cultural Organization, *UNESCO Yearbook* (1963, pp. 12–21). Percentage change in population: U.S. Department of Commerce, *World Population* (1978); United Nations, Report on *World Population* (1984).

Table 2: Real Income Per Capita, Selected Countries, 1950–82

	East Germany	West Germany	North Korea	South Korea	China	Taiwan	Hong Kong	Singapore	USSR	USA	India	Japan
Real GDP per capita, 1950[a]	1480	1888	n.a.	n.a.	300	508	n.a.	n.a.	1373	4550	333	810
Real GDP per capita, 1960	3006	3711	n.a.	631	505	733	919	1054	2084	5195	428	1674
Real GDP per capita, 1970	4100	5356	n.a.	1112	711	1298	2005	2012	3142	6629	450	4215
Real GDP per capita, 1980	5532	6967	n.a.	2007	1135	2522	3973	3948	3943	8089	498	5996
Real GNP per capita, 1950[b]	Same as WestGerm.	2943	Same as S. Korea	193	n.a.	417	1053	n.a.	n.a.	7447	217	649
Real GNP per capita, 1960	n.a.	3959	n.a.	473	n.a.	429	979	1330	n.a.	8573	220	1403
Real GNP per capita, 1970	6584	6839	556	615	556	868	1807	2065	4670	10769	219	4380
Real GNP per capita, 1982	9914	11032	817	1611	630	2579	5064	5600	5991	12482	235	9774

[a]Figures for real gross domestic product (GDP) per capita are based on 1975 international prices.
[b]Figures for real gross national product (GNP) per capita are based on 1981 constant U.S. dollars.
SOURCES: Real GDP per capita: Summers and Heston (1984). Real GNP per capita: International Bank for Reconstruction and Development (IBRD), *World Tables* (1980), GNP deflator: Council of Economic Advisers (1986, Table B–3).

Table 3: Life Expectancy and Infant Mortality, Selected Countries, 1960–82

	EAST GERMANY	WEST GERMANY	NORTH KOREA	SOUTH KOREA	CHINA	TAIWAN	HONG KONG	SINGAPORE	USSR	USA	INDIA	JAPAN
Life Expectancy at Birth, 1960	68	69	54	54	53	65	65	64	68	70	43	68
Life Expectancy at Birth, 1982	73	74	65	68	67	73	76	73	69	75	55	77
Infant Mortality, 1960	39	34	78	78	165	32	37	35	33	26	165	30
Infant Mortality, 1982	12	12	32	32	67	18	10	11	28	11	94	7

SOURCE: IBRD, *World Development Report* (1985, pp. 260–61).

Table 4: Industrialization and Urbanization, Selected Countries, 1960–82

	EAST GERMANY	WEST GERMANY	NORTH KOREA	SOUTH KOREA	CHINA	TAIWAN	HONG KONG	SINGAPORE	USSR	USA	INDIA	JAPAN
% Labor Force in Agric., 1960	18	14	62	66	n.a.	n.a.	8	8	42	7	74	33
% Labor Force in Agric., 1980	10	4	49	34	69	37 (1978)	3	2	14	2	71	12
% Urbanized, 1960	72	77	40	28	18	58	89	100	49	70	18	63
% Urbanized, 1982	77	85	63	61	21	70 (1980)	91	100	63	78	24	78

SOURCES: Labor force in agriculture: IBRD, *World Development Report* (1985, pp. 258–59). Urban population: IBRD, *World Development Report* (1985, pp. 260–61).

Table 5: Education adn Consuption, Selected Countries, Various Years

	East Germany	West Germany	North Korea	South Korea	China	Taiwan	Hong Kong	Singapore	USSR	USA	India	Japan
Higher Education Enrollment, 1960	16	6	n.a.	5	n.a.	n.a.	4	6	11	32	3	10
Higher Education Enrollment, 1982	30	30	n.a.	22	1	n.a.	12	10	21	56	9	31
Newsprint per Person, 1950–54	3.5	5.1	n.a.	0.6	n.a.	0.9	4.3	n.a.	1.2	35.0	0.2	3.3
Newsprint per Person, 1982	9.6	21.5	0.1	5.8	1.2	n.a.	16.4	32.1	4.5	44.1	0.4	24.0
Telephones per 100 Pop., 1983	20.6	57.1	n.a.	14.9	0.5	25.8	38.2	36.7	9.8	76.0	0.5	52.0
Autos per 100 Pop., 1960	0.9	8.2	n.a.	0.1	0.005	0.1	1.0	4.2	0.3	34.4	0.1	0.5
Autos per 100 Pop., 1970	6.7	24.1	n.a.	0.2	0.018	n.a.	2.8	7.2	0.7	43.9	0.1	8.5
Autos per 100 Pop., 1984	18.9	41.3	n.a.	1.1	0.010	3.1	4.6	9.3	3.9	55.5	0.2	22.8

SOURCES: Higher education: IBRD, *World Development Report* (1985, pp. 266–67). Newsprint: *UNESCO Yearbook* (1963, pp. 400–409). Telephones: U.S. Department of Commerce, *Statistical Abstract* (1986, p. 845). Automobiles: Motor Vehicle Manufacturers Association of the U.S. Inc., *World Motor Vehicle Data* (various years).

tarian political system, because a free economy is too great a political threat.)

It is said, however: Hong Kong and Singapore are different because they are city-states. But what does that mean – that if large hinterlands were attached to those "city-states" they would then be poorer, as China is?

At this point the question frequently arises: If more people cause there to be more ideas and knowledge, and hence higher productivity and income, why are not India and China the richest nations in the world? Let us put aside the matter that size in terms of population within national boundaries was not very meaningful in earlier centuries when national integration was much looser than it is now. But there remains the question of why so many human beings in those countries have produced so little change during the last few hundred years. In earlier writing I suggested that low levels of education of most people in China and India prevented them from producing knowledge and change, though noting the very large (in absolute terms) contemporary scientific establishments in those two countries. But though education may account for much of the present situation, it does not account nearly as well for the differences between the West and the East over the five centuries or so up to, say, 1850.

William McNeill (1963), Eric Jones (1981), and others have suggested that over several centuries the relative instability of social and economic life in Europe, compared to China and India, helps account for the emergence of modern growth in the West rather than in the East. Instability implies economic disequilibria, which, as Theodore Schultz (1975) reminds us, imply exploitable opportunities that then lead to augmented effort. (Such disequilibria also cause the production of new knowledge, it would seem.)

The hypothesis that the combination of a person's wealth and opportunities affect the person's exertion of effort may go far in explaining the phenomenon at hand.

Ceteris paribus, the less wealth a person has, the greater the person's drive to take advantage of economic opportunities. The village millions in India and China certainly have had plenty of poverty to stimulate them. But they have lacked opportunities because of the static and immobile nature of their village life. In contrast, villagers in Western Europe apparently had more mobility, less stability, and more exposure to cross-currents of all kinds.

Just why Europe should have been so much more open than India and China is a question that historians answer with conjectures about religion, smallness of countries with consequent competition and instability, and a variety of other special conditions.

••••

Most, if not all, historians of the period (for example, Nef 1958; Gimpel 1976) agree that the period of rapid population growth from before AD 1000 to the beginning of the mid-1300s was a period of extraordinary intellectual fecundity. It was also a period of great dynamism generally, as seen in the extraordinary cathedral building boom. But during the period of depopulation due to the plague (starting with the Black Death cataclysm) and perhaps to climatic changes from the mid-1300s (though the change apparently began earlier at the time of major famines around 1315–17, and perhaps even earlier, when there also was a slowing or cessation of population growth due to other factors) until perhaps the 1500s, historians agree that intellectual and social vitality waned.

Henri Pirenne's magisterial analysis ([1925] 1969) of this period depends heavily on population growth and size. Larger absolute numbers were the basis for increased trade and consequent growth in cities, which in turn strongly influenced the creation of a more articulated exchange economy in place of the subsistence economy of the manor. And according to Pirenne, growth in population also loosened the bonds of the serf in the city and thereby contributed to an increase in human liberty (though the causes of the end of serfdom are a subject of much controversy).

A corollary, of course, is that once the people in the East lose the shackles of static village life and get some education, their poverty (absolute and relative) will drive them to an extraordinary explosion of creative effort. The events in Taiwan and Korea in recent decades suggest that this is already beginning to occur.

••••

Contemporary Africa is cited as an example of population growth hampering economic development. ... Lester Brown's recent statement that Africa "is losing the ability to feed itself.... Slowing population growth, conserving soils, restoring forests and woodlands, and enhancing subsistence agriculture are sure to be cornerstones of successful efforts to reestablish working economies in Africa" (Brown and Wolf 1985, p. 7). Changing the economic and political system is not mentioned.

We ought to learn from the fact that exactly the same dire assessments were heard in the past, and have proven false. For example, in 1965 Brown applied virtually the same words to Asia: "The less-developed world is losing the capacity to feed itself.... Only in Africa ... has a downward trend been avoided" (as quoted in Tierney 1986, p. 38). Population growth did not prevent Asia and the rest of the less-developed world from "feeding itself" better and better with the passage of years (though self-sufficiency is not a sensible economic goal in a world where trade is possible). Of course, Asia's development might conceivably have been even faster with slower population growth, but no evidence supports such speculation.

The Role of Foreign Aid for "Family Planning"

I wish to say as loudly and clearly as possible: I believe that a couple's ability to have the family size the couple chooses is one of the great goods of human existence. And I am not in principle against a government's giving "family planning" assistance to its own citizens or to citizens of another country if they so desire. I especially cheer efforts to strengthen commercial organizations that provide such assistance through market channels. I emphasize this even though it should not even require saying, because many persons in the population "movement" disingenuously and maliciously assert that people who hold such views as expressed here are against "family planning." But it does *not* follow from being in favor of informed, responsible parenthood that the United States should automatically give foreign aid to organizations that request funds in the name of "family planning," on the grounds that *some* good will be done by the funds even if they are largely wasted or used perversely.

If you ask the population "establishment" why we should and do give such "aid," the answer almost invariably is a masterpiece of doubletalk, arguments made out of both sides of the mouth. On the one hand, the United Nations Fund for Population Activities (UNFPA) and such congressional population-control enthusiasts as James Scheuer and Sander Levin say that their aim simply is to supply "family planning" in order to help people achieve the family size that they wish. Everyone that I know of – including the Vatican, as I understand it – agrees with the aim that families should have the number of children that they wish and believe they can raise well. If family planning were all there is to the matter, we could all easily agree on a one-page statement of goals and means (putting aside the troublesome but obfuscating issue of abortion), and we would not need multi-million dollar conferences and reams of documents and bushels of expensive research reports and fancy organizational publications financed directly and indirectly by the American taxpayer. We could simply say that as an act of plain helpful generosity, we recommend that governments do what they can to provide contraceptive information and devices through private and public channels, and we will do what we can to help.

The arguments of the population organizations are another matter, however. They wring their hands over population growth rates, economic development, natural resource availability, unemployment, social conflict, and the like. A typical example is from a January 1986 cover letter to the annual report from Bradman Weerakoon, the secretary general of the International Planned Parenthood Federation (IPPF): "IPPF believes that knowledge of family planning is a fundamental human right and that a balance between the population of the world and its natural resources and productivity is a necessary condition of human happiness, prosperity and peace." It is clear, especially in the UNFPA statements, that their aim is not simply to help individuals achieve the family size that the individual couples would otherwise like. Rather, these organizations aim at population growth-rate goals – more specifically, at zero population growth – that the leaders of these organizations have decided are desirable for the world.

Furthermore, even the most "moderate" group, the recent NAS Committee on Population, is prepared to go beyond simple provision of information and devices: "When a couple's childbearing decision imposes external costs on other families – in overexploitation of common resources, congestion of public services, or contribution to a socially undesirable distribution of income – a case may be made for policies that go 'beyond family planning' " (NAS 1986, p. 93). The policies discussed include persuasive campaigns to change family size norms as well as combinations of incentives and taxes related to family size.

Cynical observers have suggested that talk about population growth rates is just eyewash to obtain more support for the laudable goal of effective family planning. There are two things wrong with this argument. First, how do we know that these cynics are not manipulating the family-planning appeal to obtain the goal of population reduction rather than vice versa? Second, and more important, can false rhetoric be justified if the end is thought to be good? What about the terribly costly ill effects of the false forecasts of resource gloom and doom over the past two decades? For example, our airlines, airplane manufacturers, and automobile industries have lost tens of billions of dollars in design and manufacturing expenses because they relied on – or were forced by government regulation to rely on – forecasts that the price of gasoline would soon be three dollars a gallon. The banks that lent money to oil ventures now find they are eating tens of billions of dollars in bad loans made on the basis of those forecasts of increasing scarcity. The U.S. agriculture industry, and therefore Congress and the taxpayers, are now suffering greatly because farmers believed that population growth would push up prices for food and increase demand and prices of farm land; former Secretary of Agriculture John Block is a prominent example. Many U.S. paper manufacturers came crying to the federal government for relief from contracts they bid on with the assumption that wood prices would rise, as the U.S. Department of Agriculture had foretold to them – on grounds that it was the government's responsibility because of its faulty forecasts. And so on.

Many of the young people in the Western world – I saw this most recently in a survey of high school students in Australia, of all places – have been thrown into despair by the belief that the world is running out of resources and must inevitably get poorer, a course supposedly exacerbated by selfish consumption in the countries they live in. Should we consider such spirit-destroying rhetoric as acceptable because it leads to a reduction some wish in the number of brown, black, yellow, and – yes – white human beings on the face of the earth, justified by the false belief that such a reduction has on balance positive economic effects? And should we assume no cost to the impact of false propaganda on public credibility and belief in the political process?

Those who call for aid to family planning have usually assumed that poor couples in poor countries do not have their fertility rates under reasonable control as a result of sensible decision making, and need guidance from Western population-planning experts. But couples tend to recognize that in the short run an additional person – whether a baby or an immigrant – inevitably means a lower standard of living for everyone. And the parents who carry almost all the burden, as well as the communities that also carry a small part of the burden, at some point say "enough," even while recognizing that more children would be good to have in the longer run.

Parents in poor countries may overshoot, having more children than they would if they knew that the infant mortality rate had fallen as fast as it has, and that education is accessible but also expensive. If there were a superbeing who knew the present and future with perfect prescience, and also understood perfectly the preferences and feelings of each set of parents, perhaps such a superbeing could choose an "optimum" level of childbearing for each couple and country better than they will achieve by themselves. But such a superbeing does not exist. And to think that, say, the UNFPA is such a superbeing, and that its "recommendations" – always well circumscribed with pious statements about "voluntarism," "sovereignty," "individual human rights," and the like, but clearly intended to influence the practices of parents and countries – will be closer to such an "optimum" than will decisions arrived at independently by individual couples and countries, is both arrogant and ridiculous.

••••

Criteria for Giving Foreign Aid

What are reasonable grounds for giving foreign aid, or charity in general? Economics does not supply the criteria. "There is *no generally accepted economic rationale for foreign aid*," wrote Schultz (1981, p. 124). And, in an essay labeled "a systematic reexamination of aid and its role in development," Anne Krueger (1986, p. 58) referred only to "the rationale for aid, 'aid effectiveness' – that is the degree to which different types of aid are conducive to accelerating development." Nor have I found a set of criteria in the literatures of other disciplines. Therefore, I hazard the following test: Charity is appropriate when the following conditions are present: First, *the recipient person or nation "needs" the help*. (The caveat here is that the presence of need is not always clearcut. The "need" of a bleeding child for medical assistance is not arguable, but the "need" of an unconverted person for religious salvation depends on the values and worldview of the potential giver.) Second, *the recipient wants the help*. Third, *the gift will not have bad effects* in the long run on the recipient or others. Fourth, *the charity will be used more-or-less efficiently* rather than largely wastefully or simply to obtain more money in a pyramid scheme. Fifth, *the charity will not produce hate toward the giver*. Let us test foreign aid to family planning against these criteria.

Do LDCs "Need" Family Planning Assistance?

In ordinary welfare programs, the criterion of need usually involves a means test. A person who owns a yacht is thought not to be an appropriate recipient for welfare, and a similar test might be applied to countries. In this spirit let us look at Table 6, which contains data on public expenditures for education, defense, and family planning in various countries, as well as public expenditures on family planning that include foreign donations, for those countries for which I could find data. In no case is the public expenditure for family planning, with or without foreign funds, more than a tiny fraction of spending for education. The implication is that if family planning is a high priority item, it is within the discretion of governments to redirect needed

funding from other educational expenditures. Lest one worry about the social loss involved in shifting funds from other educational uses, in almost every case the large sizes of the "defense" budgets relative to the education budgets make clear that there is a pool of public expenditures into which countries could dip without causing social loss by reducing education expenditures. It would seem that the potential recipients own gunboats if not yachts, and therefore

Table 6: Defense, Education, and Family Planning Expenditures for 25 Countries

COUNTRY	DEFENSE $/PERSON (RANGE 1978–81)	EDUCATION $/PERSON	FAMILY PLANNING DOMESTIC $/PERSON	FOREIGN $/PERSON (MOST RECENT ESITIMATE)	
Bangladesh	1–2	2	0.06	0.12	(1976)
Bolivia	27–34	29–35	0.00	0.02	(1977)
Brazil	14–17	61–64	0.00	0.05	(1985)
Colombia	9–16	21–34	0.13	0.13	(1983)
Dominican Republic	17–23	19–26	0.18	0.20	(1977)
Egypt	61–78	25(1977)	0.06	0.25	(1983)
El Salvador	16–28	23–30	1.25	0.38	(1980)
Ghana	13–26	33	0.13	0.02	(1977)
Hong Kong	n.a.	83–140	0.10	0.20	(1983)
India	6–7	7	0.46	0.06	(1983)
Indonesia	16–19	7–12	0.34	0.12	(1983)
Iran	202–456	75–198	0.92	0.00	(1977)
Kenya	10–16	21–24	0.15	0.39	(1978)
Korea, South	87–103	32–61	0.42	0.04	(1980)
Malaysia	54–102	108–117	0.60	0.19	(1980)
Mauritius	1–6	72–77	0.66	0.25	(1982)
Pakistan	16–17	5–6	0.12	0.10	(1979)
Philippines	14–16	12–13	0.25	0.18	(1983)
Rwanda	3–4	4–6	n.a.	n.a.	
Singapore	234–304	84–207	0.76	0.00	(1983)
Taiwan	n.a.	n.a.	0.33	0.00	(1983)
Tanzania	7–27	n.a.	0.00	0.03	(1976)
Thailand	24–28	17–28	0.18	0.09	(1983)
Tunisia	7–16	49–73	0.10	0.26	(1980)
Zimbabwe	16–57	28	0.25	0.00	(1978)

SOURCES: Defense per person: U.S. Arms Control and Disarmament Agency (1985, Table 1). Educational expenditure: United Nations Statistical Office, *Statistical Yearbook* (various years); United Nations Educational, Scientific, and Cultural Organiztion, *UNESCO Yearbook* (various years). Population: Nortman (editions 9–12). Family Planning Expenditures: Nortman (editions 9–12).

flunk the means test for charity.

Another standard criterion of need is that the good or service being provided be something that is thought by the giver to be of a nature that will improve the life of the recipient. Agricultural know-how has this nature. Birth-control capacity might be another. One might then wonder whether or not *individual* women and couples need assistance and have no way to pay for it, even if their governments could afford to provide it. Perhaps there are some such cases. But the actual cost of contraceptive information and devices is exceedingly small (which is, incidentally, a major problem in commercial distribution). The funds devoted to "family planning" programs overwhelmingly are spent for things other than "hardware" and straightforward services. What is called "information" and "education," but which is to a considerable degree persuasion, accounts for a large proportion of the expenditures that actually reach the field.

••••

If a true family-planning program were to provide information and devices to some couples to whom they would not otherwise be available, this might be seen as filling a true social need. And the program might be viewed as passing this test.

Do the Potential Recipients Want the Assistance?

One test of whether people "want" something is whether they allocate their resources to that good. Table 6 does not indicate any massive allocation of countries' own funds to family planning.

But do not foreign politicians, and persons involved in family planning activities abroad, often express the desire for these funds? Of course they do. We must ask what these expressions mean, however. To a politician, any foreign dollar coming into the country is another dollar to allocate to one constituency or another, or even to be turned to personal use. (Does anyone doubt that some foreign aid dollars went to buy

shoes for Imelda Marcos?) Therefore, more such dollars are always welcome. And for those who work for family-planning organizations, cutting aid funds breaks their rice bowl, and removes such perks as trips to Mexico City for a UNFPA conference.

Does the Assistance Do Harm?

Economic thought contains few apparent contradictions. One such contradiction, however, is between the fundamental assumption (actually a definition) that an increase in assets ("endowment") increases welfare,[1] and the common-sense observation that giving gifts sometimes harms recipients in the long run by changing their attitudes and habits.[2]

Resolving the apparent contradiction requires the recognition that a person's propensity to exert effort is a function of that person's wealth (as well as of the opportunities facing him or her).[3] General foreign aid programs may have this ill effect on recipients by reducing their propensity to exert effort (for example, the compensation to the natives of Bikini and the payments to certain Native American tribes), but the funds for family planning assistance surely are too small to have this sort of ill effect.[4]

Another ill effect that may flow from foreign aid is damage to a key industry. The dumped food aid of P.L. #480 apparently damaged the agricultures of India, Egypt, and South American nations by lowering prices and reducing incentives for farmers to produce crops (Schultz 1981 and citations therein). But again this sort of harm is not relevant to family planning assistance.

Foreign aid programs can also do damage by directing policymakers' attention away from the fundamental mechanism of economic growth, and away from the obstacles to growth that may exist in a society. This is the gravamen of Bauer's charge (1984, ch. 5) that the Pope and the proponents of a New International Economic Order caused people to dwell on envy and redistribution rather than on personal hard work together with societal changes that would promote liberty and enterprise. And here I think that concern about population growth, and for family planning programs that are intended to reduce population growth, have caused great damage.

For 25 years our institutions have misanalyzed such world development problems as starving children, illiteracy, pollution, supplies of natural resources, and slow growth. The World Bank, the State Department's Aid to International Development (AID), the United Nations Fund for Population Activities (UNFPA), and environmental organizations have asserted that the cause is population growth – the population "explosion" or "bomb" or "plague." This error has cost dearly. It has directed our attention away from the factor that we now know is central in a country's economic development: its economic and political system.

For a recent example, consider this sentence in the press release from the National Research Council about the NAS report: "[T]he recent widespread famine in Ethiopia and other African nations and similar food shortages in China during 1959–61 can be attributed in part to 'very badly functioning markets combined with rapid population growth.'" That sentence leaves a very different impression than a report that food shortages were caused by dictatorial governments that beggared farmers by appropriating their land and heavily taxing their output, together with denying them the right to move freely to wherever they wished to work and live. That sentence sounds as if "market failure" is being used to justify more government interference and control of the activity in question rather than calling for reduction in interference that would allow markets to function more effectively. And such a sentence in the press release contradicts statements in the report that properly emphasize the ill effects of food subsidies, credit market distortions, and

even the property rights mentioned elsewhere in the release. Even worse, it suggests that attention be paid to population growth rather than to fighting tyranny and working for economic freedom.

Another ill effect of foreign aid for population control is suggested by Alan Rufus Waters (1985, p. 3): "Foreign aid used for population activities gives enormous resources and control apparatus to the local administrative elite and thus sustains the authoritarian attitudes corrosive to the development process." This sort of effect is difficult to demonstrate statistically, but Waters's vantage point as former Chief Economist for the U.S. Agency for International Development (USAID) gives him credentials as an expert witness on the subject.[5]

I have my own candidate for the title of worst harm from foreign aid: the advice that goes along with it. The root of the damage lies in the idea that artful manipulation by clever economists is the way to produce economic development. International organizations such as the World Bank have finally realized that prices matter in influencing economic activity. And they have proceeded from this realization to the proposition that countries should "get the prices right." But for them this does not mean that markets should be allowed to set prices, but rather that governments should set the prices with the help of the World Bank and its expert economists.

••••

Under the stewardship of Robert MacNamara and A. W. Clausen, the World Bank – along with USAID – has been the strongest force pushing population-control programs.[6] In the name of "getting the prices right," persons who work for the World Bank advise governments – backed by the threat that recipient countries could lose Bank funds – about the appropriate set of prices to stimulate production and generate economic growth. The "experts" at the Bank, in other words, substitute their judgments for the free market's most important function: automatically producing the prices that give the correct signals to producers. That is, the advisers at the Bank believe they know better than a freely operating market what the "right" prices should be. The implicit grounds for this belief, I would guess, are faith in their own cleverness and the assumption that markets will fail to do the job correctly.

This phenomenon particularly horrifies me because in the name of economics, these persons deny the birthright of Western economists since Mandeville, Hume, and Smith, of whom the present-day prophets are Hayek, Bauer, and Friedman – the vision of the hidden hand that spontaneously produces benign results which central planning cannot accomplish. And the continuation of this practice of advising countries about appropriate prices seems inexorable as long as organizations such as the World Bank exist and (inevitably) employ economists who must find something to do. Giving the advice that governments should stop interfering with markets does not require time-consuming and expensive research, with "missions" from Washington to the capitals of benighted poor countries. But advice to free up markets would render unnecessary many jobs, and therefore it has no chance of coming about as long as the World Bank exists.

The belief that population growth slows economic development is not a wrong but harmless idea. Rather, it has been the basis for inhumane programs of coercion and the denial of personal liberty in one of the most valued choices a family can make – the number of children that it wishes to bear and raise. Also, harm has been done to the United States as donor of foreign aid, over and beyond the funds themselves, by way of money laundered through international organizations that comes back to finance domestic population propaganda organizations, and so on (see Simon 1981, chaps. 21–22).

One of the reasons the population-bogey idea stays in currency is that this has been the rare issue upon which everyone in this ideologically divided world could agree. I ran into this perverted amity not long ago at a meeting in India on population economics, which was attended by many employees of international agencies. During four days, there was not a single mention of the role of the economic system, whether market-directed or state-controlled. When I suggested that the subject should at least be aired, I was met by silence in the formal meeting and was told informally that the issue simply was outside the scope of attention. ("It's like talking about religion," someone said.)

What Kinds of Foreign Assistance Are Most Beneficial?

Lest the reader think that I am against any foreign aid in principle, a few unoriginal words seem in order about programs that can make economic sense. Agricultural research, including the organization and development of foreign agricultural research, has the great advantage that it puts no fungible funds or goods into the hands of bureaucrats, and causes no distortions in prices or other disruptions in markets. And the benefit/cost ratios have been calculated to be high. The provision of education in the United States to talented foreigners, especially if they are chosen by objective test, has many of the same advantages, as well as the advantage of making bright students familiar with the United States, and leaving them with impressions and ideas that they can take home with them. This also provides the opportunity for the United States to recruit valuable young persons of skill, energy, and imagination as temporary or permanent immigrants.

Conclusion

If we apply Hazlitt's central lesson on economics to the nexus of population growth and economic development, and take account of the indirect and lagged effects of economic freedom as well as the most obvious Malthusian effects that occur in the very short run, we can see that on net balance, additional persons being born are not a drag on progress in the long run. And foreign aid given for "family planning" programs may have more ill effects than good effects, and should not simply be viewed as a charitable act that improves the situation of poor people in poor countries.

ENDNOTES

1. An example in the context of foreign aid: "Clearly, a recipient's potential welfare could always be increased by a grant" (Krueger 1986, p. 63).

2. The famous mathematician Mark Kac wrote in his autobiography (1985, pp. 7–8): "My great-grandfather ... amassed what in those days must have been a sizable fortune and at his death, sometime early in the century, he left every one of his eighty grandchildren enough money to relieve them of any need to work for a living. All of them, with the exception of my father, chose a life of idle leisure until the First World War, when their inheritance was wiped out."

3. This is the subject of my latest book, *Effort, Opportunity, and Wealth* (Simon 1987).

4. Doug Bandow (1985) made a similar point in his introduction to *U.S. Aid to the Developing World*, which contains much interesting discussion on the general subject of foreign aid.

5. It is of some interest that other persons who have been involved in USAID activities have also come out strongly against programs of "family planning" aid. These include Peter Huessey, author of a Heritage Backgrounder, and Nicholas Demerath, who wrote *Birth Control and Foreign Policy* (1976).

6. Baum and Tolbert (1985, pp. 213, 217) provide the following up-to-date statement of the World Bank's policy position: "Rapid population growth slows development... For population, the principal objective of most developing countries should be to slow the rate of growth."

REFERENCES

Bandow, Doug, ed. *U.S. Aid to the Developing World,* Washington D.C.: Heritage Foundation, 1985.

Bauer, Peter T. *Reality and Rhetoric.* Studies in the Economics of Development. Cambridge: Harvard University Press, 1984.

Bauer, Peter T., and Yamey, Basil S. *The Economics of Underdeveloped Countries.* Chicago: University of Chicago Press, 1957.

Baum, Warren C. and Tolbert, Stokes M. *Investing in Development: Lessons of World Bank Experience.* Oxford: Oxford University Press, 1985.

Brown, Lester R., and Wolf, Edward C. "Reversing Africa's Decline." Worldwatch Paper 65. Washington, D.C.: Worldwatch Institute, June 1985.

Council of Economic Advisers. *Economic Report of the President.* Washington, D.C.: Government Printing Office, 1986.

Demerath, Nicholas J. *Birth Control and Foreign Policy.* New York: Harper and Row, 1976.

Gimpel, Jean. *The Medieval Machine.* New York: Penguin, 1976.

Hazlitt, Henry. *Economics in One Lesson.* 2d ed. New York: Arlington House, 1962.

International Bank for Reconstruction and Development. *World Development Report 1984.* New York: Oxford University Press, 1985.

International Bank for Reconstruction and Development. *World Tables, 1980.* Baltimore: Johns Hopkins University Press, 1980.

Jones, Eric L. *The European Miracle.* Cambridge: Cambridge University Press, 1981.

Kac, Mark. *Enigmas of Chance.* New York: Harper and Row, 1985.

Krueger, Anne O. "Aid in the Development Process." *World Bank Research Observer* 1, January 1986, p. 57–78.

McNeill, William H. *The Rise of the West.* New York: Mentor, 1963.

Motor Vehicle Manufacturers Association of the U.S. Inc. *World Motor Vehicle Data.* Detroit, Mich., various years.

National Academy of Sciences (NAS), National Research Council, Working Group on Population Growth and Economic Development. *Population Growth and Economics Development: Policy Questions.* Washington, D.C.: National Academy Press, 1986.

Nef, John V. *Cultural Foundations of Industrial Civilization.* Cambridge: Cambridge University Press, 1958.

Pirenne, Henri. *Medieval Cities.* 1925. Reprint. Princeton: Princeton University Press, 1969.

Schultz, Theodore W. "The Value of the Ability to Deal with Disequilibrium." *Journal of Economic Literature* 13, September 1975, pp. 827–46.

Schultz, Theodore W. *Investing in People*. Chicago: University of Chicago Press, 1981.

Simon, Julian L. "The Concept of Causality in Economics." *Kyklos* 23, fasc. 2, 1970, pp. 226–54.

Simon, Julian L. *The Ultimate Resource*. Princeton, N.J.: Princeton University Press, 1981.

Simon, Julian L. "The War on People." *Challenge*, March/April 1985a, pp. 50–53.

Simon, Julian L. "Why Do We Still Think Babies Create Poverty?" *Washington Post*, 12 October 1985b, op-ed.

Simon, Julian L. *Effort, Opportunity, and Wealth*. Oxford: Basil Blackwell, 1987.

Simon, Julian L., and Gobin, Roy T. "The Relationship between Population and Economic Growth in LDCs." *Research in Population Economics*. Edited by Julian L. Simon and Julie daVanzo. Greenwich, Conn.: JAI Press, 1980.

Summers, Robert, and Heston, Alan. "Improved International Comparisons of Real Product and Its Composition: 1950–1980." *Review of Income and Wealth*, June 1984, p. 207–62.

Tierney, John. "Fanisi's Choice." *Science* 86, January/February 1986, pp. 26–42.

United Nations Department of International Economics and Social Affairs. *Concise Report on the World Population Situation in 1983: Conditions, trends, prospects, policies*. New York: United Nations, 1984.

United Nations Educational, Scientific, and Cultural Organization. *UNESCO Yearbook*. Paris: UNESCO, various years.

United Nations Statistical Office. *Statistical Yearbook*. New York: United Nations, various years.

U.S. Arms Control and Disarmament Agency. *World Military Expenditures and Arms Transfers*. Washington, D.C.: ACDA, 1985.

U.S. Department of Commerce. Bureau of the Census. *World Population 1977: Recent Demographic Estimates for the Countries and Regions of the World*. Washington, D.C.: Government Printing Office, 1978.

U.S. Department of Commerce Bureau of the Census. *Statistical Abstract of the United States, 106th edition, 1986*. Washington, D.C.: Government Printing Office, 1986.

Waters, Alan Rufus. "In Africa's Anguish, Foreign Aid Is a Culprit." Heritage Backgrounder No. 447. Washington, D.C., 7 August 1985.

World Bank. *World Development Report 1984*. Washington, D.C.: World Bank, 1984.

Socioeconomic Development, Family Planning, and Fertility in China

DUDLEY L. POSTON, JR. and BAOCHANG GU

In recent years the People's Republic of China has experienced a pronounced and rapid fertility decline; the total fertility rate has fallen from 5.8 in 1970 to 2.6 in 1981 (Chen, 1984), a rather dramatic reduction in only 11 years. Analysts of this decline, both inside and outside of China, have suggested that socioeconomic factors may have played only a minor role (Bongaarts and Greenhalgh, 1985:585; Mauldin, 1982). China's recent success in reducing its fertility while maintaining family planning programs initiated and directed by the government has been hailed by some as representing an "induced fertility transition." It is felt that the "determinative factor that has fostered the birthrate reduction has been the government's birth planning policy" (Mauldin, 1982:119) and not necessarily the kinds of socioeconomic factors shown to be instrumental in the fertility declines of other developed and developing countries. Tien (1984) observed, however, that given the significant variability in fertility among China's subregions, it is likely that those areas experiencing the greatest reductions in fertility may also be characterized by "profound changes in socioeconomic structure... [If true] the Chinese accomplishments should not be regarded [solely] as a success for administratively induced family planning programs, because they could have been caused, at least in part, by development" (Tien, 1984:385; see also Birdsall and Jamison, 1983; Poston and Gu, 1985). Recently, demographers and

social scientists in China have articulated similar views (e.g., see *Beijing Review*, 1985; Wu, 1985:17).

This paper endeavors to widen this discussion by examining the relationships between socioeconomic development, family planning, and fertility among the 28 subregions of China, circa 1982. Most studies of Chinese fertility patterns have concentrated on the country as a whole and not on its subregions. With but few exceptions – notably, Birdsall and Jamison (1983), Tien (1984), and Poston and Gu (1985) – demographers have devoted little if any attention to fertility trends and variations in the country's subregions. There are at least two good reasons, however, for studying fertility among China's subregions, particularly if one is interested in understanding its variability within the context of subregional variability in socioeconomic development and family planning behavior and programs.

One reason is the recent release of extensive socioeconomic, family planning, and fertility data for the subregions. The Chinese issued detailed socioeconomic and fertility data from the 1982 census (State Statistical Bureau, 1983a); detailed family planning data are available from the National Family Planning Commission of China (Zhongguo Renkou Ziliao Zhongxin, 1983); and finally, through the same commission, detailed information on government expenditures for family planning is available (Guojia Jihua Shengyu Weiyuanhui, 1983). No historical data set as extensive as this cross-sectional data set for subregions is available at the national level.

A second reason is the considerable vari-

Dudley Poston and Boachang Gu. The senior author and the Population Association of America granted permission to reprint this article from *Demography*, 24(4), pp. 531–557, 1987.

ability in fertility, socioeconomic development, and family planning behavior among the provinces. Total fertility rates in 1981 ranged from a low of 1.3, equivalent to that of West Germany or Denmark, to a high of 4.4, close to that of Mexico or Indonesia. There is also considerable variability among the subregions in levels of socioeconomic development and family planning behavior circa 1982 (Poston, 1986). We believe that viewing the nation as a composite of highly divergent regions is a particularly advantageous way to investigate Chinese fertility patterns.

The data available for this cross-sectional study, however, are far from perfect. With one exception, they pertain to a single year (c. 1982). We do not have subregional data on development and family planning behavior for prior time periods. Moreover, as will be noted, although we have rather detailed subregional data on family planning behavior, we have only a single variable on family planning expenditures. Many cross-national studies of development, family planning, and fertility (e.g., see Cutright, Hout, and Johnson, 1976; Cutright and Kelly, 1981; Hernandez, 1984; Mauldin and Berelson, 1978; Tsui and Bogue, 1978) have examined changes in these relationships by lagging the development and family planning variables 5–10 years prior to the fertility variables. They have conceptualized and measured family planning in terms of both program expenditures and behavior. The degree to which we will be able adequately to address these relationships will of course be influenced by our imperfect data.

Finally, there are methodological reservations about the extent to which an essentially diachronic relationship, like the one we propose to address, may reasonably be studied with cross-sectional data (Alker, 1969; Hage, 1975; Lieberson and Hansen, 1974). These data problems and issues must be kept in mind in the discussion of the results and implications of our study. It is nonetheless hoped that the analyses reported here will provide some insight into the mechanisms of Chinese fertility change in general and the degree to which socioeconomic factors and family planning behavior play roles in the change and decline.

Rationale

The analytic question motivating this analysis concerns the extent to which socioeconomic development and family planning factors affect fertility among the subregions. This question has received extensive empirical attention cross-nationally and in numerous individual countries (e.g., Cutright, 1983; Hernandez, 1984; Kelly and Cutright, 1983; Lapham and Mauldin, 1985; Mauldin and Berelson, 1978, Tsui and Bogue, 1978). To our knowledge, it has not been addressed empirically for China.

The theoretical model guiding most of this research focuses on factors of socioeconomic development and their direct effects, and indirect effects through family planning, on fertility. Development is viewed as providing an aggregate setting that influences fertility directly. Blake (1965), for instance, noted that socioeconomic structures and institutions tend to influence reproductive motivation and fertility, by specifying the reward structures associated with childbearing (see also Hernandez, 1984:11–13). With respect to fertility change in China, Tien observed that among those subareas experiencing the greatest fertility decline, "profound changes in socio-economic structure may have occurred at the same time" (1984: 385).

••••

Socioeconomic development may also influence fertility indirectly through family planning programs and behavior. Hernandez wrote that development generates "the demand for and use of [family planning] program means of limiting births ... [Land] represents the infrastructure and the sociopolitical context that influence the extent to which family planning programs can and

will be implemented by political leaders...
The socioeconomic setting encompasses
the transportation, communications, and
administrative/bureaucratic infrastructures
that influence the magnitude of the [family
planning] program effort that can be mount-
ed in a particular country" (1984:101–102).

••••

Since family planning programs operate
within a broad spectrum of socioeconomic
development and modernization contexts,
their effects on fertility should coincide
with and overlap the effects of the development and modernization influences. Nortman noted an important synergistic association between development and family
planning variables and the "facilitating role
of family planning programs in providing
access to modern contraceptives" (1985:
782). Since family planning programs and
efforts are "part and parcel of mutually
reinforcing socioeconomic development
policies and projects" (1985:781), we deem
it inappropriate to ask whether development or family planning has the most profound effects on fertility. Instead we
endeavor to identify the individual and collective associations that socioeconomic
development and family planning have
with fertility. We give particularly close
attention to the variability in these associations given differences in the conceptualization and operationalization of development and family planning.

Family planning behavior, of course, is
only one of a number of important proximate variables related to fertility. Others,
such as age at first marriage, breastfeeding,
and abortion, are not included in the
model, however, because of data unavailability.

To summarize, both socioeconomic development and family planning are hypothesized to have negative direct effects on fertility. Regarding the indirect effects of
socioeconomic development on fertility
through family planning, the effects of
development per se on family planning

should be positive. Coupling these effects
with the negative effects of family planning
on fertility, we hypothesize indirect negative effects of socioeconomic development
on fertility.

Data

This paper analyzes the fertility patterns of
28 major provinces, municipalities, and
autonomous regions of China, circa 1982.
(The autonomous region of Tibet has been
excluded because detailed fertility data are
not available for the area. Taiwan has also
been excluded because we do not have all
of the detailed socioeconomic and family
planning data that we have for the other
provinces.) The dependent variable is the
total fertility rate in 1981. The 17 development variables include many of the social,
economic, and demographic factors shown
in earlier studies to be influential in
accounting for fertility among the Chinese
subregions (Birdsall and Jamison, 1983;
Poston and Gu, 1985; Tien, 1984) and
among countries (e.g., Cutright and Kelly,
1981; Easterlin, 1983; Mauldin and Berelson, 1978). Unlike prior studies, with one
exception, the family planning variables
pertain to behavior and not to program
effort.

••••

The 17 development variables represent
various aspects of the social and economic
structure of the subregions. Three reflect
the sustenance organization: One deals
with per capita industrial productivity
(INDUSTRY), defined as the value in
1982 of industrial output (measured in
Yuan) divided by the 1982 population.
This variable has an average value of
Y788.5, with a rather high standard deviation. A second sustenance variable, per
establishment industrial productivity
(PROD), is the 1982 value of industrial
output in the area (in Yuan) divided by the
number of industrial establishments in the
area in 1982. The third sustenance variable
measures industrial diversification (DIVER)

and refers to the number of industrial activities in an area and the distribution of the work force among these activities. The greater the number of activities and the more even the distribution of workers in them, the higher the measure of industrial diversification. This measure is based on an index developed by Gibbs and Martin (1962) and elaborated by Gibbs and Poston (1975). It is computed with population data from 14 industrial categories and has an average value here of 0.465. Based on previous socioeconomic analyses of fertility, we hypothesize that among the 28 subregions, the higher the values of the three sustenance variables, the lower the fertility rates.

Four socioeconomic variables refer to urbanization, literacy, and population density. Urbanization (URBAN) is the percentage of the subregion's total population living in municipalities and towns (municipalities are usually places over 100,000 in population; towns are places under 100,000 and larger than 3,000). URBAN has an average value of 25.8%. Two literacy variables are used, one showing the literacy level for all persons in the province aged 12 and over and the other the literacy of females only. A literate person knows at least 1,500 Chinese characters, is able to read simple books and newspapers, and can write simple messages (*Beijing Review,* 1984b:22). The literacy variable for the total population (TLIT) has an average value of 68.4%, and that for females (FLIT) has an average of 55.8%. DENSITY refers to the number of persons per square kilometer in 1982. The mean value for this variable is 297.9. We expect negative relationships between the URBAN, TLIT, FLIT, and DENSITY variables and the total fertility rate.

Two variables refer to health facilities: the number of hospital beds in the area in 1982 per 100,000 population (BEDS) and the number of medical doctors per 100,000 population (DOCTORS). BEDS has an average value of 230.4, and DOCTORS, a

value of 158.3. Given our expectation that the better the health facilities, the lower the fertility, we anticipate negative relationships between the BEDS and DOCTORS variables and the total fertility rate.

Our study also includes four quality of life variables; they pertain to the peasant or rural populations of the subregions. These are particularly meaningful in the case of the Cc index developed by Bongaarts and Potter (1983) and is based on data on contraceptive prevalence and use effectiveness. Unlike Bongaarts and Potter's development of the index, we use it to measure contraceptive effectiveness rather than ineffectiveness. Table 1 shows an example of the CPE index for Beijing, with a computed value of 0.75. The average value among the subregions is also 0.75, with highs of 0.85 in Heilonjiang and 0.83 in Jiangsu and lows of 0.51 in Qinghai and 0.55 in Yunnan.

The final family planning measure refers to annual costs and expenditures incurred by the province for all family planning activities. This is the only variable in our study for which data are available for years prior to 1981, and it is the only nonbehavioral family planning variable. We developed the measure for 1971 because this was the year in which the "Wan, Xi, Shao" family planning campaign – the first effective campaign – was initiated in China (Tien, 1983). The numerator is family planning costs and expenditures for 1971 (in Yuan). The denominator is the estimated number of women in 1971 in the age group 15–49. We calculated the denominator for each province by multiplying its 1971 total population estimate (as provided by Guojia Jihua Shengyu Weiyuanhui, 1983) by the proportion of its 1982 population that was female between the ages of 15 and 49. This measure (FPCOST) has an average value of Y0.26 per woman, with highs of Y0.56 in Hebei and Y0.55 in Shanxi and lows of Y0.08 in Guizhou and Y0.10 in Yunnan. For all 11 family planning variables, we expect that among the

Table 1: Computation of Contraceptive Prevalence/Effectiveness (CPE) Rate: Beijing, 1981

TYPE OF CONTRACEPTION	% MARRIED FECUND WOMEN AGED 15–49 CURRENTLY CONTRACEPTING (u)	CONTRACEPTIVE USE– EFFECTIVENESS RATE (e)	$u \times e$
IUD	20.79	0.963	20.02
Pill and injections	29.49	0.949	27.99
Condom	14.28	0.616	8.80
Male sterilization	1.41	1.000	1.41
Female sterilization	11.30	1.000	11.30
External methods	1.98	0.798	1.58
Other	5.32	0.700	3.72
Total	**84.57**		**74.82**

CPE = 74.82/100 = 0.75

SOURCES: Laing (1978); Bongaarts and Poner (1983); Zhongguo Renkou Ziliao Zhongxin (1983).

subregions, the higher the value, the lower the fertility rate.

Results

In an earlier section we set forth a theoretical rationale supporting the development of three general hypotheses. We hypothesized that among the Chinese subregions in this period, socioeconomic development variables should be negatively related with fertility and family planning variables should also be negatively related with fertility. Socioeconomic development variables should also have indirect effects on fertility through the family planning variables. In the preceding section, we provided descriptive information on the socioeconomic development and family planning variables, hypothesizing that each should be negatively associated with fertility. Table 2 presents zero–order correlation coefficients indicating the relationship between the TFR and each variable for the 28 subregions. All variables show the expected negative relationship with fertility.

However, the relative effects of the variables on fertility vary considerably. Four of the family planning variables have the highest correlations: the first-birth rate (–0.92), the contraceptive use rate (–0.86), the birth planning rate (–0.83), and the one-child certificate holder rate (–0.82). Eight socioeconomic development variables have correlations with fertility of –0.60 or higher, and an additional five have correlations between –0.50 and –0.60.

These independent variables are, however, highly collinear (correlation matrix not shown), as one would expect given the theoretical and conceptual linkages between and among many of the socioeconomic variables and many of the family planning variables. Moreover, a number of socioeconomic variables are highly associated with certain family planning variables. This too is not unexpected, since family planning programs and the resulting behaviors tend to be "part and parcel of mutually reinforcing socioeconomic development policies and projects" (Nortman, 1985:781).

Owing to issues of multicollinearity as well as the multifaceted nature of modernization, we focused on specific aspects of socioeconomic development to be better able to analyze its association with fertility. Goldscheider noted that "the key to understanding modernization begins with the process of structural differentiation ... of major social structures, roles, and organization ... including specialization and separation of economic, family ..., and stratification systems" (1971:93). Because of the

Table 2: Zero–Order Correlation Coefficients Between Total Fertility Rate and Socioeconomic and Family Planning Variables: 28 Provinces, Municipalities, and Autonomous Regions of China (c. 1982)

VARIABLE	CORRELATION COEFFICIENT
SOCIOECONOMIC VARIABLES	
Per capita industrial productivity (INDUSTRY)	−0.580
Per establishment industrial productivity (PROD)	−0.576
Industrial diversification (DIVER)	−0.680
Percentage urban (URBAN)	−0.586
Percentage total population literate (TLIT)	−0.631
Percentage female population literate (FLIT)	−0.600
Population density per square kilometer (DENSITY)	−0.544
Hospital beds per 100,000 population (BEDS)	−0.365
Doctors per 100,000 population (DOCTORS)	−0.478
Per peasant annual food expenses (FOOD)	−0.398
Per peasant annual clothing expenses (CLOTHES)	−0.612
Per peasant annual fuel expenses (FUEL)	−0.114
Per peasant annual housing expenses (HOUSE)	−0.570
Female life expectancy at birth (FLIFE)	−0.642
Total life expectancy at birth (TLIFE)	−0.674
Infant survival rate (SURV)	−0.697
Percentage employed females in nonagriculture (FNOAGR)	−0.650
FAMILY PLANNING VARIABLES	
Contraceptive use rate (BCRATE)	−0.859
Birth planning rate (BPRATE)	−0.826
Percentage of one–child certificate holders (ONECERT)	−0.821
First–birth rate (FIRST)	−0.916
IUD use rate (IUD)	−0.177
Pill use rate (PILL)	−0.054
Condom use rate (CONDOM)	−0.472
Male sterilization rate (MSTER)	−0.041
Female sterilization rate (FSTER)	−0.246
Contraceptive prevalence/effectiveness rate (CPE)	−0.703
Annual family costs per woman in 1971 ((FPCOST)	−0.326

Table 3: Matrix of Zero–Order Correlation Coefficients Between 4 Development Indexes, 2 Family Planning Indexes/Variables, and the Total Fertility Rate: 28 Subregions of China (c. 1982)

	1	2	3	4	5	6	7
1. Structural development	−	0.829	0.874	0.741	0.245	0.018	−0.664
2. Female status		−	0.969	0.753	0.416	0.240	−0.747
3. Quality of life			−	0.717	0.410	0.269	−0.761
4. Rural quality of life				−	0.279	−0.054	−0.555
5. Contraceptive prevalence/effectiveness					−	0.374	−0.703
6. Family planning costs 1971						−	−0.326
7. Total fertility rate							−

multidimensional nature of the modernization process, we decided against attempting to develop a single summary measure of development (e.g., see Lapham and Mauldin, 1985).

Many of the socioeconomic development variables described previously may be grouped and indexed into at least four of the conceptually distinct components of modernization suggested by Goldscheider. We have indexed *structural development* with the three sustenance variables (INDUSTRY, PROD, and DIVER) and the two variables dealing with urbanization (URBAN and DENSITY). The five variables are combined additively into a single index with a high degree of reliability (Cronbach's alpha = 0.94). We have also developed a *female status* index, using the three female-specific measures dealing with life expectancy, literacy, and nonagricultural employment (FLIFE, FLIT, and FNOAGR). This index also possesses a high degree of internal consistency (Cronbach's alpha = 0.80). We developed a third index pertaining to *quality of life* and a fourth focusing specifically on *rural quality of life*, since nearly 80 percent of the population of China in 1982 lived in rural areas. The general *quality of life* index is based on the literacy, hospital beds, doctors, infant survival, and life expectancy variables (TLIT, BEDS, DOCTORS, SURV, and TLIFE) and has a Cronbach's alpha of 0.80. The *rural quality of life* index is based on the four per peasant expenditures variables (FOOD, CLOTHES, FUEL, and HOUSE) and is internally consistent, with a Cronbach's alpha of 0.76.

Regarding the family planning variables, we first set aside the one pertaining solely to expenditures (FPCOST). We then examined the zero-order correlations of the behavior variables with fertility and with each other. Based on these results and the importance of contraception per se as a family planning behavior, we restricted the family planning behavior index to the *contraceptive prevalence/effectiveness* (CPE) rate. This measure is highly correlated with most of the other family planning variables, especially BCRATE, BPRATE, ONECERT, and FIRST.

Table 3 presents the zero-order correlation matrix for the four modernization indexes, the two family planning indexes/variables, and the total fertility rate. All six development and family planning indexes/variables show the hypothesized negative relationship with fertility. As reported in Table 2, the family planning behavior measure (CPE rate) has a correlation with fertility of −0.70. The four modernization indexes also have high correlations with fertility: quality of life index, −0.76; female status index, −0.75; structural development index, −0.66; and rural quality of life index, −0.56. The family planning costs variable has the lowest correlation with the TFR, $r = -0.33$.

Three of the four development indexes are highly related with each other. This collinearity argues against the use of all of the development indexes in the same multiple regression equation, even though they represent four conceptually distinct dimensions of modernization. In our tests of the proposed theoretical model, we will use only two of these indexes in a model at any one time.

Path analysis, a form of multiple regression, is the statistical approach used for testing the theoretical model. As noted previously, we expect the socioeconomic development and family planning variables to have direct negative effects on fertility, the socioeconomic variables to have direct positive effects on the family planning variables, and the family planning costs variable to have a direct positive effect on the family planning behavior variable.

Figure 1 presents the first empirical model for testing, a path model of the effects of two development indexes (structural development and rural quality of life), a family planning behavior measure (the

CPE rate), and family planning costs in 1971 on the TFR among the subregions. The two development indexes, the two family planning variables, and the total fertility rate are the measured variables. The path coefficients are the standardized partial regression coefficients (betas) from multiple regression equations. Each path coefficient represents the amount of standard deviation change in the dependent variable of a 1-standard-deviation change in the independent variable (holding other independent variables constant). As Duncan noted, path analysis is a model where "each dependent variable [in this case family planning and fertility] must be regarded explicitly as completely determined by some combination of variables in the system... [In those instances] where complete determination by measured variables does not hold [as is the case in our study of China], a residual variable uncorrelated with other determining variables must be introduced" (1966:3). These residual paths are also represented in Figure 1.

Table 4 reports the total, direct, and indirect effects of these independent variables on the fertility rate for all models. The total effect of a variable on fertility (col. 1) is the zero-order correlation coefficient. The direct effect (col. 2) is the path coefficient between the independent variable and the TFR. The total indirect effect (col. 3) is the difference between the total effect and the direct effect. We have decomposed this into the following components: the indirect

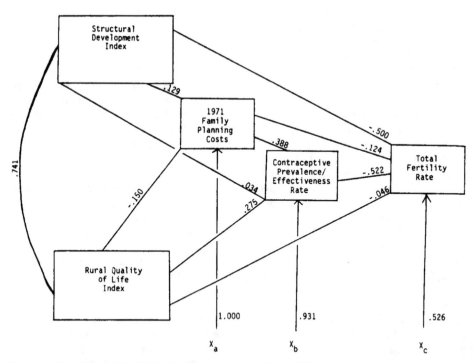

Figure 1: Path Model 1 of Total, Direct, and Indirect Effects of Development Indexes, Family Planning Costs, and Family Planning Behavior on Fertility: 28 Provinces, Municipalities, and Autonomous Regions of China, c. 1982.

Table 4: Effects of Development Indexes, Family Planning Costs. and Family Planning Behavior on Fertility: 28 Provinces, Municipalities, and Autonomous Regions of China, c. 1982

MEASURE	TOTAL EFFECT, r (1)	DIRECT EFFECT, p (2)	TOTAL INDIRECT EFFECT [(1)–(2)] (3)	EFFECT VIA FAMILY PLANNING BEHAVIOR (4)	EFFECT VIA FAMILY PLANNING COST AND FAMILY PLANNING BEHAVIOR (5)	JOINT EFFECT (6)
Model 1						
Development (INDUSTRY + PROD + DIVER + URBAN + DENSITY)	−0.664	−0.500	−0.164	−0.018	−0.026	−0.120
Rural Quality of Life (FOOD + CLOTHES + FUEL + HOUSE)	−0.555	−0.046	−0.509	−0.144	0.030	−0.395
Family Planning Costs in 1971	−0.326	−0.124	−0.202	−0.203	N.A.	0.001
Family Planning Behavior (Contraceptive Prevalence/ Effectiveness Rate)	−0.703	−0.522	N.A.	N.A.	N.A.	N.A.
Model 2						
Development (INDUSTRY + PROD + DIVER + URBAN + DENSITY)	−0.664	−0.345	−0.319	0.084	0.073	−0.476
Female Status (FNOAGR + FLIFE + FLIT)	−0.747	−0.238	−0.509	−0.244	−0.091	−0.174
Family Planning Costs in 1971	−0.326	−0.079	−0.247	−0.126	N.A.	−0.121
Family Planning Behavior (Contraceptive Prevalence/ Effectiveness Rate)	−0.703	−0.490	N.A.	N.A.	N.A.	N.A.
Model 3						
Quality of Life (TLIT + BEDS + DOCTORS SURV + TLIFE)	−0.761	−0.540	−0.221	−0.107	−0.095	−0.019
Rural Quality of Life (FOOD + CLOTHES + FUEL + HOUSE)	−0.555	−0.038	−0.517	−0.062	0.076	−0.531
Family Planning Costs in 1971	−0.326	−0.007	−0.319	−0.150	N.A.	−0.169
Family Planning Behavior (Contraceptive Prevalence/ Effectiveness Rate)	−0.703	−0.469	N.A.	N.A.	N.A.	N.A.

effect on fertility via the family planning behavior measure (col. 4), the indirect effect on fertility via the family planning behavior measure and the family planning costs variable (col. 5), and the indirect effect on fertility through all other independent variables in the model (col. 6). We refer to this last effect as the spurious component of the total indirect effect, or the joint effect.

In model 1, the structural development index has a sizable direct negative effect on fertility ($p = -0.500$); it is rivaled only by the direct effect of the CPE rate on fertility ($p = -0.522$; see col. 2). The second development index, rural quality of life, has a trivial direct effect on fertility and only a slightly higher indirect effect on fertility through family planning behavior (the CPE rate). The family planning costs variable also has a modest indirect negative effect on fertility through family planning behavior (see col. 4). Finally, given the rather low direct effect of the family planning costs variable, the two development indexes have trivial indirect effects on fertility through family planning behavior and family planning costs (see col. 5).

A second model (not shown) substitutes the female status index for the rural quality of life index. All other variables were the same as in model 1. When the female status index is entered, the sizable direct effect of structural development on fertility observed in model 1 is reduced considerably ($p = -0.345$; see Table 4). Also unlike model 1, a development index, the female status index, now has a modest indirect effect on fertility via family planning behavior of -0.244 (see Table 4). The indirect effect of family planning costs on fertility through family planning behavior is reduced in model 2 to -0.126 from the effect of -0.203 in model 1 (see Table 4). A third model (not shown) presents yet another combination of two development indexes. Here we have entered the quality of life index and the rural quality of life index. All other variables remain the same. Like the

patterns in model 1, the direct and indirect effects of rural quality of life on fertility are trivial (see Table 4). Quality of life has a sizable direct effect on fertility ($p = -0.540$), larger than that of structural development in model 1. In model 3 the family planning costs variable now has no direct effect at all on fertility. The CPE rate maintains the strong direct effect on fertility shown in previous models.

Depending on the pairs of development indexes used in the empirical models, indexes of development have strong direct effects on fertility in certain models (structural development in model 1 and quality of life in model 3) and modest to weak direct effects in others (rural quality of life in models 1 and 3 and structural development and female status in model 2). The only development index with a reasonable indirect effect on fertility through family planning behavior is the female status index in model 2. In all three models the family planning behavior variable (the CPE rate) has strong direct effects on fertility, and in all models the family planning costs variable has either trivial or rather low direct effects on fertility.

The theoretical model set forth in figure 1 posited the existence of direct and indirect negative effects of development variables on fertility. The indirect effects were hypothesized to operate through family planning. Family planning variables were also hypothesized to have direct negative effects on fertility. In this paper we have conducted three empirical tests of this theoretical model. Some of the results are consistent across all models. Other results vary, depending on the particular model chosen for examination.

In all models, the family planning behavior has strong negative direct effects on fertility. In all models, the family planning costs variable has much weaker direct effects on fertility than the family planning behavior measures. And in all models, the development indexes have trivial indirect effects on fertility via the combined path through family planning costs and family planning behavior.

When indexes of structural development and rural quality of life are entered into the same model (model l; see fig. 1), structural development has a very strong negative direct effect on fertility, whereas the direct effect of rural quality of life on fertility is trivial. The direct effect of structural development on fertility is greatly reduced when an index of female status is introduced into the model instead of rural quality of life (model 2). In this model, however, female status has a fair indirect effect on fertility through family planning behavior. There is little overall change in the patterning of effects when quality of life is substituted for structural development and entered into a model with rural quality of life.

The path coefficients shown in model 1, along with the effects data shown in Table 4, indicate the dual influences of the development indexes and family planning behavior and family planning costs variables on fertility. Family planning programs and family planning behavior, particularly the latter, function among the provinces of China within a broad spectrum of development contexts. Note that their effects on fertility tend to coincide with and overlap the effects of development and modernization. If anything, our empirical results support a synergistic interpretation of the association between development and family planning variables and fertility (Nortman, 1985).

Note that it would have been ideal to conduct still another test of the general model, one involving the impacts of changes in development and family planning on fertility change. One usually has more faith in the kind of cross-sectional model investigated in this paper when it is possible to examine variation not only in the levels of the independent and dependent variables but in their changes as well. We were able to obtain estimates of the

crude birth rates (CBRs) for the subregions for 1970 and 1981 from the National Family Planning Commission (Guojia Jihua Shengyu Weiyuanhui, 1983), which could have been used to develop percentage change CBR scores for each of the subregions. We did not have available, however, development and family planning data for time periods earlier than 1981–1982. Thus we were not able to lag the development and family planning variables to earlier time periods (say, 1960 or 1970) or to calculate change scores for these variables.

Because of these problems, we opted against regressing the CBR change scores on the 1981–1982 development and family planning variables. In the first place, such an equation would be plagued with extreme simultaneity bias, since the dependent variable would be measuring change over a period of time terminating in the year of measurement of the independent variables. In addition, such an analysis would suffer from specification error because of the inability to assume that the 1981–1982 levels of the independent variables were independent of error in the equation. Owing to the unavailability of development and family planning behavior data for other than the 1981–1982 periods, such an equation would not be able to take into account levels of development and family planning at earlier time periods. We realize that our study would be greatly improved were we able to include an analysis of the impacts of changes in development and family planning on fertility change. Unfortunately, the required data are not available.

Conclusion

This paper was concerned with assessing the degree to which development and family planning variables are related to fertility rates among the 28 provinces, municipalities, and autonomous regions of China circa 1982. This is an important issue, given current studies of Chinese fertility patterns. Some recent investigations of national-level declines have attributed the reductions principally to the government's birth control programs, assigning little if any effect to socioeconomic development. Other analyses, principally the subregional studies of Birdsall and Jamison (1983), Tien (1984), and Poston and Gu (1985), have stressed the importance of socioeconomic factors. To our knowledge, however, no previous studies of subregional Chinese fertility patterns have investigated the influences on fertility of both socioeconomic development and family planning variables. Our paper endeavored to fill this void.

For each of the 28 subregions, we obtained data on 17 socioeconomic development variables and 11 family planning variables. The dependent variable was the total fertility rate. Examination of the zero-order correlations of the independent variables with fertility indicated a high negative relationship in almost all instances. We next grouped the 17 development variables into four conceptually distinct indexes pertaining to structural development, female status, quality of life, and rural quality of life and restricted the family planning variables to the CPE rate and a measure of family planning costs in 1971. Because of collinearity among the four development indexes, we employed only pairs at any one time in our tests of the cross-sectional theoretical model of Chinese fertility patterns. This model (fig. 1) posited direct negative effects of development and family planning on fertility and indirect negative effects of development on fertility through family planning.

Three separate tests of the theoretical model indicated consistently strong negative direct effects of family planning behavior on fertility and weak direct effects of family planning costs. Structural development had strong negative direct effects on fertility when it was introduced in an equation with rural quality of life, but it had reduced effects when used in an equation with a development index gauging female status. The direct negative effects of quality of life on fertility were about the same as those of structural development, although the two development indexes were not used in the same equation because of high collinearity. Regarding indirect effects of development on fertility, only the female status index had high negative indirect effects through family planning behavior. All four development indexes had trivial indirect effects via the combined path through family planning costs and family planning behavior.

These findings are in many ways congruent with analyses conducted elsewhere. Our results, like those of Tien (1984) and Birdsall and Jamison (1983), indicated strong direct effects of certain features of development on fertility. As Tien observed, "differences between rates of natural increase in different provinces [may well be reflecting] ... differences in socioeconomic conditions" (1984:398). We are reminded in our analysis of the high negative direct effects of structural development, female status, and quality of life on fertility.

Our results are also in line with the findings of numerous cross-sectional studies of development, family planning, and fertility among the countries of the world (e.g., Cutright and Kelly, 1981; Mauldin and Berelson, 1978; Tsui and Bogue, 1978). These studies have consistently found very strong direct negative effects on fertility of family planning programs and behavior. Our analysis demonstrated very strong direct negative effects of contraceptive behavior on fertility, although the effects of family planning costs on fertility were weak.

Our results also parallel those of others reporting that certain effects of development on fertility tend to operate through contraceptive behavior (see Kelly, Poston, and Cutright, 1983; Mauldin and Berelson, 1978; Srikantan, 1977). Kelly and his colleagues argued that "the motivating effect of development on fertility should be mediated by more proximate variables"

(1983:92), such as family planning behavior. (See also Davis and Blake, 1956; Bongaarts, 1982; Kelly and Cutright, 1983.) In our study the strong negative indirect effects of female status on fertility through family planning behavior is a case in point. Among the Chinese subregions, levels of female status are positively associated with levels of contraceptive behavior, which are in turn negatively associated with fertility levels.

Nortman noted that family planning programs and efforts are "part and parcel of mutually reinforcing socioeconomic development policies and projects" (1985:781). The results in our paper that indicate a high degree of association between some of our indexes of development and family planning behavior are congruent with Nortman's observation. Indeed her notion of a synergistic association between development, family planning, and fertility is supported by our data. Development and family planning are both highly associated with fertility among the Chinese subregions.

To the degree that our cross-sectional study of subregional patterns of development, family planning, and fertility has application to the analysis of fertility change in China over time, it suggests that the recent fertility declines should not be seen as due solely to successful family planning programs. Although the implementation of programs and their resulting effects on contraceptive behavior have certainly been influential, it is our contention that attempts to assess the Chinese achievements in fertility decline must take into account as well the direct and indirect effects on fertility of socioeconomic development.

Accordingly, we are inclined to echo Tien's conclusion that the " 'induced fertility transition' of the recent past certainly deserves to be acclaimed as a population planning success *sui generis*, but its results up to now cannot, and as the present findings suggest should not, be divorced from socioeconomic change, both in the past and the present" (1984:400).

REFERENCES

Alker, H. R., Jr. 1969. A typology of ecological fallacies. Pp. 69–86 in M. Dogan and S. Rokkan (eds.), *Quantitative Ecological Analysis in the Social Sciences*. Cambridge, Mass.: MIT Press.

Beijing Review. 1984a. Birthrate of women of child-bearing age. 27(March 12):22–23.

——— . 1984b. Educational level of population. 27(April 2):22–23.

——— . 1985. Success crowns population policy. 28(November 4):18–19.

Birdsall, N., and D. T. Jamison. 1983. Income and other factors influencing fertility in China. *Population and Development Review* 9:651–675.

Blake, J. 1965. Demographic science and the redirection of population policy. Pp. 41–69 in M. C. Sheps and J. C. Ridley (eds.), *Public Health and Policy Change*. Pittsburgh, Penn.: University of Pittsburgh Press.

Bongaarts, J. 1982. The fertility-inhibiting effects of the intermediate fertility variables. *Studies in Family Planning* 13:179–189.

Bongaarts, J., and S. Greenhalgh. 1985. An alternative to the one-child policy in China. *Population and Development Review* 11: 585–618.

Bongaarts, J., and R. G. Potter. 1983. *Fertility, Biology and Behavior: An Analysis of the Proximate Determinants*. New York: Academic Press.

Chen, S. 1984. Fertility of women during the 42 year period from 1940 to 1981. Pp. 32–58 in China Population Information Centre, *Analysis on China's National One-per-Thousand Population Sampling Survey*. Beijing: China Population information Centre.

Cutright, P. 1983. The ingredients of recent fertility decline in developing countries. *International Family Planning Perspectives* 9:101–109.

Cutright, P., M. Hout, and D. Johnson. 1976. Structural determinants of fertility in Latin America: 1800–1970. *American Sociological Review* 41:511–527.

Cutright, P., and W. R. Kelly. 1981. The role of family planning programs in fertility declines in less developed countries, 1958–1977. *International Family Planning Perspectives* 7:145–151.

Davis, K., and J. Blake. 1956. Social structure and fertility: An analytic framework. *Economic Development and Cultural Change* 4:211–235.

Duncan, O. D. 1966. Path analysis: Sociological examples. *American Journal of Sociology* 72:1–16.

Easterlin, R. A. 1983. Modernization and fertility: A critical essay. Pp. 562–586 in R. A. Bulatao and R. D. Lee (eds.), *Determinants of Fertility in Developing Countries* (Vol. 2). New York: Academic Press.

Gibbs, J. P., and W. T. Martin. 1962. Urbanization, technology and the division of labor: International patterns. *American Sociological Review* 27:667–677.

Gibbs, J. P., and D. L. Poston, Jr. 1975. The division of labor: Conceptualization and related measures. *Social Forces* 53:468–476.

Goldscheider, C. 1971. *Population, Modernization* Goldscheider, C. 1971. *Population, Modernization and Social Structure.* Boston: Little Brown.

Guojia Jihua Shengyu Weiyuanhui [National Family Planning Commission]. 1983. *Quanguo Jihua Shengyu Tongji Ziliao Huibian [National Family Planning Statistics Data Collection]*. Beijing: Guojia Jihua Shengyu Weiyuanhui.

Hage, J. 1975. Theoretical decision rules for selecting research designs: The study of nation-states or societies. *Sociological Methods and Research* 4:131–165.

Hernandez, D. J. 1984. *Success or Failure? Family Planning Programs in the Third World.* Westport, Conn.: Greenwood Press.

Jiang, Z. 1984. Mortality Data From China's Population Census. Paper presented at the Workshop on China's 1982 Population Census, East-West Population Institute, Honolulu, December 2–8.

Kelly, W. R., and P. Cutright. 1983. Determinants of national family planning program effort. *Population Research and Policy Review* 2:111–130.

Kelly, W. R., D. L. Poston, Jr., and P. Cutright. 1983. Determinants of fertility levels and change among developed countries: 1958–1978. *Social Science Research* 12:87–108.

Laing, J. 1978. Estimating the effects of contraceptive use on fertility. *Studies in Family Planning* 9:150–175.

Lapham, R. J., and W. P. Mauldin. 1985. Family Planning Program Effect: Measurement and Application. Paper prepared for the Annual Meeting of the International Union for the Scientific Study of Population, Florence, Italy, June.

Lieberson, S., and L. K. Hansen. 1974. National development, mother tongue diversity, and the comparative study of nations. *American Sociological Review* 39:523–541.

Mauldin, W. P. 1982. The determinants of fertility decline in developing countries: An overview of the available empirical evidence. *International Family Planning Perspectives* 8:119–127.

Mauldin, W. P, and B. Berelson. 1978. Conditions of fertility decline in developing countries. *Studies in Family Planning* 9:89–147.

Nortman, D. L. 1985. Review of D. J. Hernandez's *Success or Failure? Population and Development Review* 11:781–782.

Poston, D. L., Jr. 1986. Patterns of contraceptive use in China. *Studies in Family Planning* 17:217–227.

Poston, D. L., Jr., and B. Gu. 1985. Socioeconomic Differentials and Fertility in the Provinces, Municipalities, and Autonomous Regions of the People's Republic of China. Paper prepared for the Annual Meeting of the International Union for the Scientific Study of Population, Florence, Italy, June.

Srikantan, K. S. 1977. *The Family Planning Program in the Socioeconomic Context.* New York: Population Council.

State Statistical Bureau. 1982. *The 1982 Population Census of China (Major Figures).* Hong Kong: Economic and Information Agency.

——— . 1983a. *Ten Percent Sample of the 1982 Population Census of the People's Republic of China.* Beijing: State Statistical Publishing House.

——— . 1983b. *Statistical Yearbook of China, 1983.* Beijing: State Statistical Publishing House.

Tien, H. Y. 1983. China: Demographic billionaire. *Population Bulletin* 38(2):1–42.

——— . 1984. Induced fertility transition: Impact of population planning and socioeconomic change in the People's Republic of China. *Population Studies* 38:385–400.

Tsui, A. O., and D. J. Bogue. 1978. Declining world fertility: Trends, causes, implications. *Population Bulletin* 33(4):1–42.

Wu, C. 1985. Family planning meets social progress. *Beijing Review* 28(Nov. 11):15–17.

Zhongguo Renkou Ziliao Zhongxin [Center for Chinese Population Information]. 1983. *Zhongguo Renkou Ziliao Shouce 1983 [Handbook of Chinese Population Statistics 1983]*. Beijing: Zhongguo Renkou Ziliao Zhongxin.

Contraceptive Prevalence: The Influence of Organized Family Planning Programs

ROBERT J. LAPHAM and W. PARKER MAULDIN

Since the 1960s, there has been a substantial increase in the number of countries that have organized efforts to provide family planning supplies and services. These efforts have involved both public and private channels – more often the former, but with significant and growing emphasis on the latter. Also during this period, fertility has declined in many places – substantially in a number of Asian and Latin American countries, and somewhat in a small number of Middle East and North African countries (though by and large not at all in sub-Saharan Africa and in a good many Arab countries). Moreover, there is a strong positive association between fertility declines and increased use of contraception. The purpose of this paper is to analyze factors that affect the use of contraception – or contraceptive prevalence – in developing countries. What are the relationships between increases in prevalence and organized family planning programs? What are the relationships among socioeconomic development, family planning, and fertility change? During the post-World War II period, significant improvements in socioeconomic conditions have occurred in a number of developing countries, especially, but not only, in parts of Asia and Latin America. Donor agencies, private groups, and national governments expend much energy and effort, including modest shares of development budgets, in a number of

Robert J. Lapham and W. Parker Mauldin. Reprinted with permission of the Population Council, from Robert J. Lapham and W. Parker Mauldin, "Contraceptive Prevelence: The Influence of Organized Family Planning Programs, 1985," *Studies in Family Planning*, 16(3), (May/June 1985), pp. 117–137.

countries; altogether, by some estimates, over US$1 billion a year is spent on population programs. Therefore, such questions are significant in the policy arena.

A particular impetus for the current work is the availability of a new set of data on family planning program effort collected by the authors during the period July 1983 to October 1984 with the help of several hundred population specialists around the world. In addition, there is wide interest in contraceptive prevalence and a growing set of prevalence estimates for recent years.

••••

Data and Methods

With regard to data quality, most of our variables lack the preciseness desired.[1] Although better informed now than several years ago, we do not possess unarguable values for the dependent variable – contraceptive prevalence for 1977 and later. Likewise, socioeconomic measures for developing countries are subject to error. The third major data set, measures of family planning program effort, includes several items based on the judgments of knowledgeable family planning program senior personnel and observers, rather that on the reported results of counting and sorting operations.[2] Therefore, with this data set, two broad sources of possible error must be considered: first, the validity of the participant or observer judgments, for example, about the quality of training programs or logistic systems; and second, the validity of the authors' interpretations of inconsistent respondent judgments on a given country's program. However, further work currently underway suggests strong consistency among different categories of respondents, with one exception – program personnel from many countries – whose responses tend to be more favorable than others regarding the service delivery elements of programs (Lapham and Mauldin, 1984a).

Another problem is circularity, or the assignment of responses by observers based on their knowledge of what has happened to prevalence and fertility. Given the consistency of responses just indicated, and the fact that some countries have higher scores but low prevalence (e.g., Bangladesh) and other countries have just the opposite (e.g., Brazil), we believe that the problems of circularity in this study do not seriously affect the findings and conclusions. Also relevant is the fact that the respondents completed questionnaires that ask about many specific aspects of programs; respondents were not asked to do any scoring, which was done by the authors, using a set of scoring rules.

There are other conceptual and analysis problems. How, for example, should the social and economic setting of a country be defined? Moreover, it may be posited that, following the work of Tolnay and Christenson (1984) and Cutright (1983), it is better not to try to classify countries by summary socioeconomic measures, but rather to search for individual variables that have the most effect on the dependent variable under study. In the analysis presented here, we do the former and a variation on the latter, on the grounds that the common measures of socioeconomic status are highly intercorrelated, and this supports the use of summary measures. Similarly, how should family planning program effort be defined and then measured? Recalling our earlier discussion on the concept of program effort, the assignment of objective criteria to distinguish between good and poor programs is no small task, and one not often attempted by researchers. In this article, a new measure of program effort is presented. Although we believe it is improved over our 1972 measure, further improvement is still needed. For example, we believe that for a small number of countries (e.g., Brazil), the new program effort scale does not fully represent the private sector. This is not to suggest that the scale misses the private sector entirely in these countries, but rather to indicate how future studies might benefit from scale improvements.

One of the analysis problems includes the limitations of multiple regression; for example, the program effort scores are heavily skewed toward zero. Also, there are problems with multicolinearity among variables, even with the parsimonious data sets described below. In addition, treating countries as units of analysis masks within-country differences in socioeconomic status and program effort, and in contraceptive prevalence. For example, considerable within-country prevalence differences exist among regions or ethnic groups, and between urban and rural areas in a number of countries. In Egypt in 1980, for instance, there was 40 percent prevalence in urban areas versus 15 percent in rural areas (NAS, Panel on Egypt, 1982, p. 23).

Similarly, cross-tabulational analysis has limitations. Countries that fall in a particular cell are not identical, first because each cell includes a range, and second because the socioeconomic conditions combine in various ways to produce each category, for example, "high" or "low" socioeconomic setting. Nevertheless, when supported by other techniques, cross-tabulational analysis can clearly illustrate broad relationships.[3]

Previous exercises along the present lines have generated considerable interest within the population community. Therefore, despite certain data problems, we proceed on the grounds that the data sets used are of sufficient quality to warrant analysis, that the questions addressed are important, and that any discussion or debate generated by this exercise will contribute to the existing knowledge on the subject. In addition, whereas previous studies have used fertility measures as the dependent variables

(Lapham and Mauldin, 1984b and Mauldin and Lapham, 1985), in this study the conditions of contraceptive prevalence are analyzed.

Socioeconomic Variables

Our aim is to select the socioeconomic variables that are closely related to, and presumably are to some considerable extent causes of, the prevalence of use of fertility regulation measures. To select a parsimonious set of predictor socioeconomic variables, we followed the same procedure used by Mauldin and Berelson (1978), which is similar to the procedure used by others (e.g., Cutright, 1983). Data centered around 1970, for about 50 variables assessed as being relevant, were entered into a data bank, and a large number of multiple regressions were run to sort out the variables that best predicted crude birth rate (CBR) declines. The best predictors, which are used in the analyses below, are:

1 adult literacy
2 primary and secondary school enrollment
3 life expectancy at birth
4 infant mortality rate
5 GNP per capita (log)
6 proportion of males 15–64 years of age employed in nonagricultural work
7 proportion of total population living in cities of 100,000 or more.

To develop a summary socioeconomic variable, we used two procedures. The first was the common approach of ranking countries according to the values for each variable, and then summing or averaging those values. Although this is a simple procedure, it has the disadvantage of assigning equal weights to each variable, with the result that the summary variable has less explanatory power overall than that of the individual values for a set of variables in a regression analysis. The second procedure was to construct a summary measure by using each variable multiplied by its β-coefficient; the latter was obtained in a multiple regression that uses the value of each socioeconomic variable, with prevalence as the dependent variable. (In a regression, the β-coefficient is the amount of change in the dependent variable associated with one unit of change in the independent variable.)

In the cross-classification analyses below, the first approach described above is used – summing the country rankings on each variable and then using these sums as the basis for dividing countries into the four socioeconomic groups of high, upper middle, lower middle, and low. In the correlation analyses, we use the second approach – multiplying the value for each variable by its β-coefficient.

The Measurement of Program Effort

The measurement of family planning program effort in 1982 is based on a new scale developed for this study and applied to 100 countries. This new 30-item scale is a revised and expanded version of a 15-item scale developed by the authors in 1972 and applied at that time to 20 countries (Lapham and Mauldin, 1972). The earlier scale has since been applied to larger numbers of countries – first to 46 by Freedman and Berelson (1976), and then to 94 by Maudlin and Berelson (1978) – in studies of the relationships among socioeconomic setting, program effort, and fertility change. In these studies, all program effort scores refer to 1972. More recently, these 1972 program effort data have been used in various analyses (for example, Cutright and Kelly, 1981; Tolnay and Christenson, 1984; Cutright, 1983; Kelly and Cutright, 1980 and 1983), and a debate about the utility of the scale has developed (Hernandez, 1981). The new scale follows from the framework described earlier in this paper. There are eight items for policy and stage-setting activities, 13 for service and service-related activities, three for record-keeping and evaluation, and six for the availability and accessibility of fertility regulation supplies and services. Throughout this report, each of these four groups of items is referred to as a component of program effort.[4]

One aspect of this scoring process must be emphasized: the reported scores represent the authors' best judgment as to the score indicated by the data received. Specifically, instead of taking the average of all answers on the questionnaires received for each country, we tried to ascertain the most appropriate score for each item for each country using all of the information provided and otherwise available. For example, marginal notes and comments at the end of the questionnaire often provided clues; for some items, such as policies, we used other documents (e.g., Nortman and Fisher, 1982; Tietze, 1983) and the United Nations Monitoring Reports (United Nations, 1982 and 1985). In some cases, a respondent whose answers were very different from the others tended to be discounted.[5]

The score range for each scale item is from zero to four, with four indicating a strong policy or much activity on an item. However, a score of four does not mean that the maximum possible is being accomplished in the country. For example, a score of four on the training item can be obtained by having "very good" answers on training for two categories of personnel, and "moderately good" on training for four other categories. Such a country might have poor training for a seventh category of personnel; in any case, the four "moderately good" situations could be improved.

With 30 items, the scoring range is from zero to 120. We divided the range into four levels of program effort: Strong 80+, Moderate 55–79, Weak 25–54, and Very Weak or none 0–24.

••••

Among the countries with 50 million or more people, eight have strong or moderate program effort, three have weak effort, and one (Nigeria) is in the very weak or none category; the total scores range from

101.1 for China down to 9.0 for the Sudan. (The full report includes more detail on program effort in these and other countries, including discussions of component differences, change between 1972 and 1982, and regional differences.)

How "good" is a score of 90 or more on this scale, with a possible maximum of 120? We suggest that 90 or more is excellent, and scores in the 80s are very good. For example, in Colombia, the scores on the four components are: (1) 19.5 out of a possible 32 on policy and stage-setting activities, (2) 34 out of 52 on service and service-related activities, (3) 11 out of 12 on record-keeping and evaluation, and (4) 20.8 out of 24 on availability and accessibility. Colombia has a maximum score of 4 on ten of the 30 items, and 3 or better on seven others.

A procedure similar to that described for the socioeconomic variables was followed to determine a smaller number of program effort items that could be used as predictors of contraceptive prevalence. There are 30 items in the program effort measure, too many for convenient analysis. We wished to construct three summary measures: first, a single summary measure of program effort items for 1982; second, a summary measure of the four components of program effort – policy and stage-setting activities, service and service-related activities, record-keeping and evaluation, and availability and accessibility of fertility regulation methods; and finally, a combined 1972–82 score.

The first measure is simply the sum of the score values on the 30 items. To construct the second measure, we combined the constructed summary measures for the four components of program effort into a single measure by multiplying each summary variable by its corresponding β-coefficient, obtained in a multiple regression using the four summary measures as predictors of the prevalence level. Finally, the combined 1972 and 1982 program effort score was obtained by doubling the 1972 score and halving the 1982 score. This gave equal weights to the 1972 and 1982 scores, since the maximum for the 1972 score was 30, and for the 1982 score, 120. The same score ranges as those previously established for the 1982 score were used to characterize programs as strong, moderate, weak, and very weak or none.

Contraceptive Prevalence, 1977–1983

We define contraceptive prevalence as current use of a means of fertility control, including male and female sterilization, pills, injectables, IUDs, condoms, spermicides, foams, and diaphragms, as well as traditional methods such as withdrawal, rhythm, and abstinence. For the 47 countries in our sample for which method breakdowns are available, traditional methods account for 28 percent of total prevalence.

••••

Because data on prevalence of contraceptive use are not collected routinely by central statistical offices or other government agencies, our data set is less complete for prevalence than for fertility measures. However, there has been increased interest during the past several years in measuring the prevalence of contraceptive use, and a series of Contraceptive Prevalence Surveys has added to available information. In addition, the World Fertility Survey collected data on prevalence; however, several of these studies were carried out in the mid-1970s, and we have limited our data set to estimates for 1977 or later. Note that the analysis is based on one estimate for each country, for the latest year in which data were available since 1977. To indicate the range of years to which the estimates refer, the terms *prevalence 1977–83* or *prevalence since 1977* are used; however, we are talking about levels of prevalence, not trends.

A key assumption (with which we feel comfortable) is necessary in the analysis of prevalence presented below: in the countries for which prevalence estimates are used, prevalence has not declined between the date of the estimate and 1983. Thus, in the analysis, the prevalence data represents prevalence in 1983 for comparison with the 1982 program effort scores. We believe that this assumption is conservative, and therefore acceptable. In general, prevalence rates have increased with time in developing countries; since some of the rates shown were collected several years prior to 1983, our data set probably underestimates the rates as of 1983 for a number of countries. We do not, however, have any valid way of making an adjustment to these rates.

Results

Our hypothesis is that the relationship between socioeconomic setting and program effort on the one hand, and contraceptive prevalence on the other, is positive.

Table 1 presents our findings with contraceptive prevalence as the dependent variable; we selected a smaller number of predictor variables by starting with a larger set and then successively dropping the variable with the smallest standardized β-coefficient. The values produced with this procedure are shown in columns one through six of Table 1. All seven variables give a coefficient of determination (r^2) of .83. Note that an even smaller number of predictor variables gives the same or nearly the same r^2 value. Indeed, using just two predictors (life expectancy and percent males aged 15–64 years in nonagricultural activities), the r^2 is .79, just .04 less than the r^2 with seven predictor variables.

The next step is to add program effort to the predictor variables. We use the second summary measure for 1982, constructed in the manner described earlier. (Recall that this variable combines the four component measures by multiplying each summary variable by its corresponding β-coefficient, obtained in a multiple regression using the four component measures as predictors of prevalence.) This summary measure of program effort, used here under the key assumption of no decline in prevalence

Table 1: 1970 socioeconomic and program effort variables as predictors of contraceptive prevalence in 1977–83

ITEM	1	2	3	4	5	6	7	8	9	10	11	12	13
	MULTIPLE REGRESSION												
Multiple													
r	.89	.90	.91	.91	.91	.91	.94	.94	.95	.95	.95	.95	.95
r^2	.79	.81	.82	83	.83	.83	.89	.89	.90	.90	.90	.90	.90
	BETA COEFFICIENTS												
Socioeconomic variable													
Life expectancy	74	.79	.69	.72	.78	.77	.43	.54	.58	.48	.53	.52	.52
Males aged 15–64 in non–agricultural work (%)	.18	.30	.28	.18	.18	.17				.11	.14	.12	.12
Log GNP per capita		−.22	−.18	− 18	−.18	− 18					−.07	− 07	− 07
Literate population (%)			.13	.12	.13	.11			.12	.13	.13	.14	−.07
Population in cities of 100,000 + (%)				.10	.10	.10						.03	.03
Infant mortality					.07	.06		.13	.22	.20	.22	.21	.21
Primary and secondary school enrollment						.04							.01
Program effort							.56	.57	.52	.51	.49	.49	.49
Number of cases	76	75	70	69	69	69	75	75	71	71	70	69	69
Degrees of freedom	73	71	65	63	62	61	72	71	66	65	63	61	60
F–ratio for regression	136.7	88.7	75.5	60.2	49 6	41.9	280.5	187.4	141.8	116.0	94.0	77.0	66.3
Significance level (p $\leq$)	.01	01	.01	.01	01	.01	.01	.01	.01	.01	.01	.01	.01

noted above, is highly correlated with prevalence: the correlation coefficient between the two variables is .91 and the r^2 is .82. Thus, this summary measure captures a large proportion of the variance in prevalence. When this summary measure is added to the socioeconomic variables and these are treated as independent variables, the r^2 for prevalence is .90, higher than the .83 obtained with the socioeconomic vari-

ables alone. Indeed, in social science research, an r^2 value of .90 for a set of preclictor variables is remarkably high.

From the information noted above and the data shown in Table 1, the following indicates the percent of contraceptive prevalence associated with socioeconomic variables and program effort; the numbers are actually the percents of variation (r^2) in prevalence:

1 Percent of prevalence associated with socioeconomic setting considered alone (the multiple regression with the parsimonious set of seven socioeconomic indicators) = 83

2 Percent of prevalence associated with socioeconomic setting and program effort together (seven socioeconomic indicators and the summary program effort measure) = 90

3 Net effect of program effort [(2) – (1)]1 = 7

The conclusion to be drawn is that socioeconomic setting is associated with much of the variance in contraceptive prevalence, and that socioeconomic setting and program effort combined are associated with a greater amount of the variance in prevalence. We will return to these relationships in the path analysis described below.

It is also useful to present the prevalence findings in cross-tabulational form. Table 2 classifies the prevalence estimates for 73 countries by 1970 socioeconomic setting and 1982 program effort (summary measure based on the total score). The grand mean is 26 percent for all 73 countries, with the range from 4 to 55 percent between the low and high socioeconomic groups of countries, and from 7 to 59 percent between the very weak or none and strong program effort groups. These means are based on unit weights for each country. It is also possible to weight the data by population size, although we must recognize that the prevalence estimates for countries with large populations will dominate the resulting row and column total means. The mean prevalence estimates for the 16 cells of Table 2 are compared in Table 3 against the values obtained with population size weights. With unit weights, prevalence increases in a regular manner as one moves from very weak or none to strong program effort, and from low to high socioeconomic setting. For example, among the high socioeconomic setting countries, mean prevalence increases from 36 to 60 percent between the very

weak or none and strong program effort countries. Among the upper middle socioeconomic setting countries, the range on program effort is striking: from 11 to 63 percent, a difference by a factor of almost six. The range is considerable also among the lower middle socioeconomic setting countries – from 6 and 8 up to 27 and 48 percent. Even among the low socioeconomic setting countries, the progression is monotonic, but with a smaller range – 3 to 19 percent in the three cells with countries. Note that among these low socioeconomic setting countries, none has a strong program, and only one, Bangladesh, has moderate program effort.

The importance of socioeconomic setting can also be seen in Tables 2 and 3. For example, note the second and third columns under unit weights in Table 3. Among countries with moderate program effort, prevalence ranges from 19 to 58 percent between the low and high socioeconomic setting countries. Among countries with weak program effort, the range is 4 to 50 percent. Among countries with very weak or no program effort, prevalence is low in all socioeconomic categories except the one high socioeconomic setting country, Paraguay.

The trends with population-size weighting are affected by the high prevalence rate in China (69 percent) and the much lower rate in India (32 percent). China's rate leads to an unusually high prevalence rate in the upper middle socioeconomic setting/strong program effort cell (Sri Lanka's population is about 1 percent of China's), while India's value dominates the lower middle socioeconomic setting/moderate program effort cell. Note also that the countries with large populations in the high/strong cell, with their prevalence rates between 40 and 58 percent, pull down the weighted mean in this cell. Similarly, the cell for moderate program effort and high socioeconomic setting contains four small-population countries, plus Cuba at 10 million; thus,

Table 2: Contraceptive prevalence rates (%), by 1970 socioeconomic setting index and 1982 program effort index, in 73 developing countries

1970 SOCIO-ECONOMIC SETTING	STRONG		MODERATE		WEAK		VERY WEAK OR NONE		MEAN
	COUNTRY	%	COUNTRY	%	COUNTRY	%	COUNTRY	%	
High	Hong Kong	80	Cuba	79	Costa Rica	66	Paraguay	36	
	Singapore	71	Panama	63	Brazil	50			
	Taiwan	70	Jamaica	55	Venezuela	49			
	Korea	58	Trinidad/Tobago	54	Peru	43			
	Colombia	51	Fij	38	Chile	43			
	Mauritius	51							
	Mexico	40							
		(60)		(58)		(50)		(36)	55
Upper middle	China	69	Thailand	58	Ecuador	40	Iran	23	
	Sri Lanka	57	Philippines	45	Turkey	40	Syria	20	
			Dominican Republic	43	Honduras	27	Ghana	10	
			Malaysia	42	Egypt	24	Nicaragua	9	
			El Salvador	34	Morocco	19	Zaire	3	
			Tunisia	31	Guatemala	18	Zambia	1	
					Algeria	7			
		(63)		(42)		(25)		(11)	30
Lower middle	Indonesia	48	India	32	Haiti	19	Bolivia	24	
			North Vietnam	21	Zimbabwe	14	Nigeria	6	
					Kenya	7	Lesotho	6	
					Pakistan	6	Burma	7	
					Papua New Guinea	5	Cameroon	2	
					Senegal	4	Uganda	1	
					Liberia	1	Kampuchea	0	
		(48)		(27)		(8)		(6)	12
Low			Bangladesh	19	Nepal	7	Benin	18	
					Tanzania	1	Sudan	5	
							Sierra Leone	4	
							Ethiopia	2	
							Somalia	2	
							Yemen	1	
							Burundi	1	
							Chad	1	
							Guinea	1	
							Malawi	1	
							Mali	1	
							Niger	1	
							Burkina Faso	1	
							Mauritania	1	
				(19)		(4)		(3)	4
Mean		**59**		**44**		**23**		**7**	**26**

1982 PROGRAM EFFORT

NOTE Mean prevalence, at each level of program effort and socioeconomic setting, shown in parentheses.

Table 3: Mean contraceptive prevalence rates (%) by 1970 socioeconomic setting index and 1982 program effort index, with unit weights and population-size weights

1970 Socioeconomic Setting	Mean prevalence (%) by 1982 Program Effort				
	Strong	Mod–erate	Weak	Very weak or none	Total
Unit weights					
High	60	58	50	36	55
Upper middle	63	42	25	11	30
Lower middle	48	27	8	6	12
Low	—	19	4	3	4
Total	59	44	23	7	26
Population–size weights					
High	49	70	49	29	50
Upper middle	69	48	26	14	58
Lower middle	48	34	7	5	29
Low	—	19	4	3	9
Total	64	35	27	7	43

NOTE: A dash indicates that there were no countries in that category.

Cuba's 79 percent prevalence dominates this cell. However, the general picture on this population-weighted basis is not different from that with the unit weights: for all countries, contraceptive prevalence rates increase as one moves from very weak or none to strong program effort and from low to high socioeconomic setting.

It is worth noting the relationship between the 1977–83 prevalence levels and the combined 1972–82 program effort measure, under 1970 socioeconomic conditions. Although lag problems exist (e.g., program effort centered on 1977 compared with prevalence in 1982 or 1983 for some countries), this approach avoids the need for assuming that prevalence did not decline between the years of the estimate and 1982.

••••

The progressions on socioeconomic setting and program effort are smooth except for the cell containing China, and the range for all countries on mean program effort is a bit greater than with unit weights – 6 to 67 percent versus 7 to 59 percent between the very weak or none and the strong program effort countries.

We turn next to the simplified versions of the framework, using path analysis. In Figure 1 the arrows indicate the assumed direction of effect, with the vertical arrows indicating unexplained or residual effects. According to this model, socioeconomic setting (in version one) has slightly more *direct* effect on contraceptive prevalence (.53) as compared with the effect of program effort (.46). But this understates the total effect of socioeconomic variables inasmuch as they also operate through program effort. Their indirect effect is estimated by multiplying the path value from socioeconomic setting to program effort (.78) by (.46), or .36. Thus, the combined direct and indirect effect of social setting is .53 + .36, or .89.

In version two, we assume that availability and accessibility are determined by socioeconomic setting and by the three other program components: policies and stage-setting activities; service and service-related activities; and record-keeping and evaluation. We then assume that prevalence of contraceptive use is determined by socioeconomic variables (socioeconomic setting) and availability and accessibility.

The correlation between socioeconomic setting and the program effort components of policy, service, and record-keeping and evaluation is modest, .62. Thus, the r^2 between those two variables is .38, which means that socioeconomic setting explains a significant part of those components of program effort, but the large majority of program effort remains unexplained. Those components of program effort, however, are highly correlated with availability and accessibility, a coefficient of correlation of .89, and an r^2 of .79.

The path coefficient of socioeconomic setting to prevalence is .56, and that of availability and accessibility to prevalence is .44. Socioeconomic setting affects availability and accessibility directly with a path coefficient of .36, and indirectly through a path coefficient of .62 to program policies, activities, and evaluation, which in turn has a path coefficient of .67 to availability and accessibility. Therefore, the indirect effect

of socioeconomic setting on contraceptive prevalence is [.36 + (.62 x .67)] x .44, or .34. This added to the direct influence of .56 gives the total effect of socioeconomic factors of .90. The corresponding direct effect of availability and accessibility is .44. Thus, both social setting and availability and accessibility are important, with program components having a strong effect on availability and accessibility. This latter point is underscored by comparing the multiple regression as shown in Table 1 with contraceptive prevalence as the dependent variable ($r^2 = .889$) with a multiple regression in which program policies, activities, and evaluation is almost zero

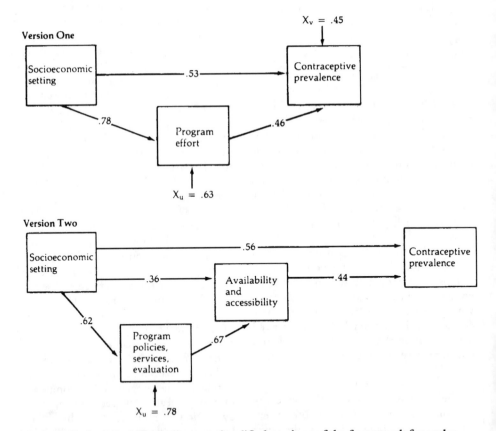

Figure 1: Path analysis applied to two simplified versions of the framework for understanding the effects of program effort on contraceptive prevalence

NOTE: Vertical arrows indicate unexplained or residual effects.

(.005). This indicates that the effect of program policies, activities, and evaluation is added as a third independent variable. The r^2 value is unchanged at .889, and the standardized β-coefficient for program policies, activities, and evaluation is almost zero (.005). This indicates that the effect of program policies, activities, and evaluation on contraceptive prevalence works almost entirely through availability and accessibility. The path coefficients of unexplained variance for availability and accessibility and prevalence are modest, .50 and .46, but relatively large for program policies, activities, and evaluation, .78.

••••

Conclusions

Any analysis of the influence of organized family planning programs on contraceptive prevalence involves a number of pitfalls – in quality of data, the establishment of summary measures or scores, the selection of analysis techniques, and the interpretation of findings. We have tried to point out and deal with some of these pitfalls, but this study does not resolve all of them. Nevertheless, we believe that the exercise is useful and we hope that it will generate further efforts to resolve the pitfalls. In addition, a few conclusions can be drawn for both the analyst and the policymaker.

A Summary for the Analyst

This study of the conditions of contraceptive prevalence shows that socioeconomic setting is important; it is strongly associated with 1977–83 contraceptive prevalence in the countries studied. Family planning program effort strengthens these associations. It is the combination of improved socioeconomic conditions and greater program effort that leads to the strongest associations with increased use of contraception. This finding has important policy implications. Primarily, it demonstrates to economic and social development policymakers that con-

sideration of the best ways to initiate or improve family planning delivery systems should be an integral part of any development strategy. Such policy implications lead to a general summary for the policymaker, one that draws upon the summary in the 1978 study by Mauldin and Berelson.

A Summary for the Policymaker

In presenting the summary below, we claim a number of important caveats, including concerns about the adequacy of the data used.

Our measures of program effort, for 1982 and centered on a period between 1972 and 1982, are based on two sources. The first, collected in the early 1970s, is essentially the subjective judgments of knowledgeable people, but judgments made on 15 different aspects of the program, some of them objective measures. The second source is a study conducted in the last half of 1983 and early 1984, in which some 400 population specialists around the world provided information on 30 items related to family planning programs, and covering four components: policies, resources, and stage-setting activities; service and service-related activities; record-keeping and evaluation; and availability and accessibility of fertility regulation supplies and services. We are confident that programs with higher scores are relatively better programs, and that those with low scores are not as good. In the empirical event, a dichotomy of program effort captures the major discrimination.

The data were examined in a variety of ways: simple cross-tabulations of 1982 (and 1972–82) program effort and an index of socioeconomic setting, simple correlations between the variables, multiple regression analysis using the 1970 values of socioeconomic setting variables and a measure of program effort in 1982, and path analysis. For both the socioeconomic setting variables and the program effort measures, parsimonious sets of variables were developed for use in the analysis.

CONTRACEPTIVE PREVALENCE

Our analysis of contraceptive prevalence is limited to 73 countries because acceptable estimates are not available for the rest. Prevalence is very high in some of the smaller East Asian countries and in Cuba; above 50 percent or more of married couples of reproductive age practice contraception in a substantial number of large and medium-sized countries — China, Thailand, Brazil, Colombia, and the Republic of Korea. Except for Mauritius, which is located off the coast of sub-Saharan Africa, the highest prevalence rates on the mainland of this region are 18 percent in Benin and 14 percent in Zimbabwe. In the Middle East and North Africa, Turkey has the highest prevalence rate at 40 percent, followed by Tunisia at 31 percent.

THE KEY CONCLUSION

Probably the key conclusion is that the two conditions — socioeconomic setting and program effort — work most effectively together. Countries that rank high on both socioeconomic setting and program effort generally have higher contraceptive prevalence than do countries that rank high on just one, and still more than countries that rank high on neither. Furthermore, the path analysis suggests that program effort components are strongly associated with the availability and accessibility of family planning. The policy implication is clear: if a government wants its citizens to use effective means of fertility regulation, it should seek a high level of economic development (which of course all countries do, with considerable cost and difficulty) and it should implement an aggressive family planning program. Moreover, the chances of achieving increased contraceptive prevalence by means of an aggressive family planning program range from good to very good among all but the lowest socioeconomic setting countries. On the other hand, for countries that are the least well off in terms of socioeconomic conditions, the effects of program effort on increased contraceptive prevalence would be more modest, and of course program implementation in these settings is much more difficult. To date, only a handful of countries has been able to implement a strong program effort in a deprived setting.

To conclude, we believe that this study demonstrates the utility of a family planning program as one element in the armamentarium of development programs.

ENDNOTES

The study has been carried out with primary support from The Rockefeller Foundation, including a grant to Robert Lapham for research on the measurement of family planning program effort. Additional support necessary for the study was received from three other sources: the Agency for International Development, The World Bank, and The William and Flora Hewlett Foundation. This support is gratefully acknowledged.

We also received assistance from personnel in the Agency for International Development, The World Bank, The United Nations Fund for Population Activities, The International Planned Parenthood Federation, and several other institutions. For example, these individuals helped with the identification of persons knowledgeable about family planning programs in each of about 100 developing countries. In addition to expressing thanks for this support and assistance, we want to note with particular appreciation some 400 population specialists around the world who took the time and effort to respond to the questionnaire designed for this study.

1. There are three major sources for the socioeconomic setting and contraceptive prevalence data presented in this study. They are (1) international volumes, including the United Nations (UN) yearbooks, publications of the UN Population Division, and selected data tapes from UN organizations; (2) major data banks compiled during recent years, principally those of the Population Council and the US Bureau of the Census, supplemented by that of the World Bank, which incorporate published and new unpublished estimates judged to be acceptable; and (3) Contraceptive Prevalence Survey (CPS) and World Fertility Survey (WFS) reports. The program effort data were obtained from two sources. The 1982 family planning program effort scores come from a study initiated by the authors in mid-1983. The analysis here is based on 433 questionnaires on 100 countries. The 1972 program effort data are from studies published by the authors (Lapham and Mauldin, 1972) and by Mauldin and Berelson (1978).

2 A long-form questionnaire has been designed by the authors in an attempt to address this issue, but it would not be feasible for the large number of countries necessary to carry out a macro-level analysis such as that presented here.

3 The full report on which this paper is based (Lapham and Mauldin, 1984c) contains more detail on some of these methodological problems and also a detailed summary of relevant literature. The latter is based on articles by Tolnay and Christenson (1984) and by Cutright (1983). This report also contains the questionnaire and the scoring rules.

4 A few words about the program effort data are in order here. In May 1983, a draft version of the questionnaire was pretested among population experts in the United States, Indonesia, and Thailand. At the same time, lists of potential questionnaire recipients, including persons knowledgeable about family planning programs in various countries, were compiled from a variety of sources, including the authors' files, donor agencies and foundations, private sector groups, and individuals in the population field with experience in Third World population programs. Based on the results of the pretests, the questionnaire was revised and translated into French and Spanish. In July and August 1983, it was sent to some 630 potential respondents in an attempt to gather information on 105 countries; respondents were guaranteed confidentiality. In the early fall of 1983, the authors sent a reminder to individuals who had not yet responded, and a third request was sent in January 1984. A small number of population specialists responded for more than one country.

5 For example, take an item such as training and a country with five questionnaires: if the application of the scoring rules (questionnaire answers converted to scores) produced four scores around 2, and one score at the maximum 4, we would score this item as the average of all five. In the questionnaire, the question on training is in fact a table listing various categories of staff, for each of which respondents checked boxes labelled very good, moderately good, mediocre or poor, and nonexistent. More details on the application of procedures like this are found in the full report by Lapham and Mauldin (1984c).

REFERENCES

Bulatao, R.A. and R.D. Lee (eds.). 1983. *Determinants of Fertility in Developing Countries*. New York: Academic Press.

Cutright, P. 1983. "The ingredients of recent fertility decline in developing countries." *International Family Planning Perspectives* 9, no. 4 (December): 101–109.

Easterlin, R.A. 1978. "The economics and soci-

ology of fertility: A synthesis." In C. Tilly (ed.), *Historical Studies of Changing Fertility*. Princeton: Princeton University Press.

Freedman, R. 1961–62. "The sociology of human fertility: A trend report and annotated bibliography." *Current Sociology* 10/11, no. 2: 35–121.

Freedman, R. 1975. *The Sociology of Human Fertility: An Annotated Bibliography*. New York: Irvington Publishers, Inc.

Freedman, R. and B. Berelson. 1976. "The record of family planning programs." *Studies in Family Planning* 7, no. 1 (January): 1–40.

Hernandez, D. 1981. "A note on measuring the independent impact of family planning programs on fertility declines." *Demography* 18, no. 4 (November): 627–634.

Kelly, W.R. and P. Cutright. 1980. "Modernization and the demographic transition: Cross-sectional and longitudinal analysis of a revised model." *Sociological Focus* 13, no. 4: 315–330.

Kelly, W.R. and P. Cutright. 1983. "Determinants of national family planning effort." *Population Research and Policy Review* 2, no. 2 (May): 111–130.

Lapham, R.J. and W.P. Mauldin. 1972. "National family planning program: Review and evaluation." *Studies in Family Planning* 3, no. 3 (March): 29–52.

Lapham, R.J. and W.P. Mauldin. 1984a. "The measurement of family planning program effort: Who wears the rose-colored glasses?" Paper presented at the 1984 annual meeting of the American Public Health Association, 13 November 1984.

Lapham, R.J. and W.P. Mauldin. 1984b. "Family planning program effort and birthrate decline in developing countries." *International Family Planning Perspectives* 10, no. 4 (December): 109–118.

Lapham. R.J. and W.P. Mauldin.1984c."Conditions of fertility decline in developing countries, 1965–1980." Paper presented at the 1984 annual meeting of the Population Association of America.

Mauldin, W.P. and B. Berelson. 1978. "Conditions of fertility decline in developing countries, 1965–75." *Studies in Family Planning* 9, no. 5 (May): 89–148.

Mauldin, W.P. and R.J. Lapham. 1985. "Measuring family planning program effort in LDCs: 1972 and 1982." In Nancy Birdsall,

The Effects of Family Planning Programs on Fertility in the Developing World. World Bank Staff Working Paper No. 677. Washington, DC: The World Bank.

National Academy of Sciences, Panel on Egypt. 1982. *The Estimation of Recent Trends in Fertility and Mortality in Egypt.* Washington, DC: National Academy Press.

Nortman, D. L. and J. Fisher. 1982. *Population and Family Planning Programs: A Compendium of Data Through 1981,* 11th edition. New York: The Population Council.

Panel on Fertility Determinants. 1983. "A framework for the study of fertility determinants." In R. Bulatao and R. Lee (eds.), *Determinants of Fertility in Developing Countries.* New York: Academic Press.

Srikantan, K. 1977. *The Family Planning Program*

in the Socioeconomic Context. New York: The Population Council.

Tietze, C. 1983. *Induced Abortion: A World Review,* 1983 5th edition. New York: The Population Council.

Tolnay, S.E. and R.L. Christenson. 1984. "The effects of social setting and family planning programs on recent fertility declines in developing countries: A reassessment." Unpublished paper, Sociology Department, The University of Georgia. Forthcoming in *Sociology and Social Research.*

United Nations. 1982. *World Population Trends and Policies: 1981 Monitoring Report.* New York: The United Nations.

United Nations. 1985. *World Population Trends and Policies: 1983 Monitoring Report.* New York: The United Nations.

About the Authors in Chapter 5

Mary Jo Huth teaches in the Department of Sociology and Anthropology at the University of Dayton in Dayton, Ohio. She is the author of *The Urban Habitat: Past, Present, and Future,* (Chicago: Nelson Hall), 1978.

Julian L. Simon is Professor of Business Aministration in the College of Business Management at the University of Maryland, College Park, Maryland. Of particular interest among his many books is *Population Matters: People, Resources, Environment & Immigration,* (New Bruswick, N.J.: Transaction Publishers), 1990.

Dudley L. Poston is Professor of Sociology in the Department of Rural Sociology at Cornell University, Ithaca, New York. W. Parker Frisbie and Dudley L. Poston, Jr., are authors of *Sustenance Organization and Migration in Nonmetropolitan America,* The Social Organization of the Community Series, Iowa Urban Community Research Center, University of Iowa, March 1978, 104 pp.

Baochang Gu teaches in the Department of Sociology at Peking University in Beijing, China.

Robert Lapham (deceased) was Director of Demographic and Health Surveys at Westinghouse Public Applied Systems in Columbia, Maryland. *Research on the Population of China: Proceedings of a Workshop,* by Rodolfo A. Bulatao and Robert Lapham, was published in 1981 by the National Academy Press of Washington, D.C.

W. Parker Mauldin is with the Rockefeller Foundation in New York City. John A. Ross and W. Parker Mauldin edited *Berelson on Population* (New York: Springer-Verlag), 1988.

CHAPTER 6

Women and Development

Introduction

THE TYPICAL LIFE of one of millions of African farm women was described in the United Nations on the eve of a special General Assembly session on Africa. The session was to honor Eremina Mvura in behalf of the women of Africa. They produce nearly eighty percent of all sub-Saharan African food. The *New York Times,* May 16, 1986, p. 23, reported that Ms. Mvura stated: "A woman's day begins at 3 A.M. in Eremina Mvura's village in Skiaobvu in Zimbabwe. That is the hour she awakens to pound grain into flour in a mortar.

" 'At sunrise one has to go to the river to fetch water.' Mrs. Mvura said, 'then go to the fields for weeding.'

" 'If you have a baby, you breast-feed while you work.' she said. 'And we must climb into the watchtower to chase crop raiders such as buffalo and elephants away – and chase lions, which are dangerous because they eat people.'

"At sunset the woman prepares supper, gathers more water and wood, and, 'if she has energy, bathes herself and her children,' Mrs. Mvura said.

" 'And all night we listen for wild animals,' she added shyly, just in case anyone thought she slept at night."

How much change has occurred since the colonial period is difficult to measure. The early post-colonial period and problems arising from rapid movement of women from rural to urban Africa South of the Sahara have been described by Bunbury (1961). During the 1940s and 1950s, patterns of female participation in metropolitan labor forces have varied in different broader social contexts, from highly industrialized countries to Latin America, the Caribbean, and in Muslim populations in the Middle East (Collver and Langlois, 1962). Although West African women have always been involved in commerce, this is not the same as overall equality in the world of work or in other social institutions. More recent data indicate that not much has changed.

No development program can succeed that overlooks the desires and needs of the population of women, yet it is unfortunately the case that women's issues seldom get the attention they deserve at the level of development planning. These issues have only begun to be thoroughly researched. Questions about even such basic concerns as differences in reproductive goals have not been answered (Mason and Taj, 1987).

213

Powerful cultural values, patriarchal institutions, and some forms of modernization have weakened women's status economically, socially, and politically. The results are beginning to show. Farm productivity is falling where women's role in agriculture has been over-looked. The consequences of women's lack of access to land in India and South Asia, except through male family members, has recently been documented in an extensive liter-ature and an authoritative article by Bina Agarwal (1988). Fewer females are going to school because schools do not address their special needs. These trends are emerging in spite of evidence to show that investment in women's education and employment are a key to social development and population control. Development cannot come about without empowering women.

The Articles in Chapter 6

El-Bakri and *Kameir* suggest that the inferior colonial economic and political statuses of women in Sudan have not been greatly improved during the post-independence period. The colonists' policies isolated Southern Sudan from Northern Sudan. The North has experienced capitalist development while the South still retains its traditional pastoralist culture, both continuing to produce subordinate status for women. Young men migrate on short or long term bases to the North for employment. Women are overworked, the sub-sistence agriculture being left to women who must perform agricultural tasks without the help of men. Women are left with little time for education or political activities.

In Northern Sudan, the development of the capitalist economy has adversely affected the lives of women. Cheap imported goods have replaced the traditional female handicrafts and educated women remain in subordinate roles as a result of religious ideologies and family norms. Working women are concentrated in low paying jobs and they continue in their disadvantaged positions economically and politically in spite of modernization.

Ahmad stresses the need for grass roots level rural women's organizations to enhance women's participation in development. Rural women are involved in a wide range of income generating activities but their full participation in the market is restricted by a lack of access to factors of production such as land and capital. Most women are in very poorly paid jobs and their labor is exploited by their employers. Women's organizations, women's networks, governmental programs targeted toward increasing women's participation, and trade unions are necessary to empower women to resist injustices and discrimination against women at home and in the market place.

Kelkar points out the negative effects on women of technological innovations in the agri-cultural sector. The green revolution in India lowered the proportion of women in the agricultural sector, leaving them with the manual and non-technical positions and, of course, lowering their wages. Indian women in agriculture are now generally paid 40 per-cent to 60 percent of the males' wages and thus have become more and more dependent on men for their livelihoods. *Kelkar* suggests that women must become involved with and trained to use new technologies of production. In order to increase women's participation, new organizations that will represent the collective interests of women will have to emerge.

Kelly suggests that in order to increase women's participation in production, keen atten-tion must be paid to investment in their education. General educational policies may not, however, improve the educational participation rates of boys and girls equally because females are constrained by a number of factors such as distance to school and activities at home such as taking care of younger siblings. Activities that girls perform at home should be taken into consideration in formulating special educational development policies for them. This involves addressing discrimination in employment and wages for women in order that they may have greater incentive for educational attainment.

REFERENCES

Agerwal, Bina, "Who Sows? Who Reaps? Women and Land Rights in India," *The Journal of Peasant Studies*, 15(4), July 1988, pp. 531–581.

Bunbury, Isla, "Women's Position as Workers in Africa South of the Sahara," *Civilizations*, Vol. 11, 1961, pp. 159–168.

Collver, Andrew and Eleanor Langlois, "The Female Labor Force in Metropolitan Areas: An International Comparison," *Economic Development and Cultural Change*, 10(4), July 1962, pp. 367–385.

Mason, Karen Oppenheim and Anju Malhotra Taj, "Differences between Women's and Men's Reproductive Goals in Developing Countries," *Population and Development Review*, 13(4), December 1987, pp. 611–637.

Aspects of Women's Political Participation in Sudan

Z. B. EL-BAKRI and E. M. KAMEIR

The Concepts of the 'Political' and of 'Participation': A Critical View

One of the most widely held assumptions to be found in the literature discussing the political significance and role(s) of women in society is that decisions which women take have no effect on a very wide range of institutions. Furthermore, Middle Eastern societies in particular (although this argument can be extended to many Third World societies) are viewed as being constituted of dual and separate spheres for men and women, the former being public and the latter private. The private sphere is seen as domestic, narrow and restricted, whereas the public sphere is considered to be 'political', broad and expansive. The concerns of women are seen to lie in the domestic and not the political sphere, which raises the question of the nature of power and of the political and why this should be linked to such notions as private (domestic), and public (political) spheres.[1]

Through such conceptions Western social scientists have imposed their own cultural paraphernalia, allowing discussions of power and the political to be greatly influenced by their understanding. Thus, power is viewed in the classic functionalist tradition, with the political system being defined as the maintenance or establishment of social order within a territorial framework by the organized exercise of coercive authority through the use, or potential use, of physical force.[2] Power is therefore not seen as a special kind of social

relation but as a quality embodied and institutionalized in certain types of social structure.[3] Needless to say these social structures are ultimately thought to approximate those of Western-style liberal democracies.

The concept of 'participation' can also be critically analyzed. It has recently come into vogue, concomitantly with attempts at generating 'development' by various Third World governments. Since it was thought that a more 'participatory' attitude towards development was what Third World societies really needed, the ends were to be achieved through the 'participation' of men and women in the process. Such a view was based on two crucial assumptions.

First, the participation envisaged in Third World countries (with the aid of 'foreign experts') is that of the type developed in Western Europe and North America, where individuals participate by voting and/or by working for established political parties or by forming pressure groups to influence the direction of policy. Levels of participation are sometimes measured by personal levels of knowledge of how the system works or who holds public office. In most cases these indices depend on the prior existence of formal organizations and regularized procedures for choosing leaders and the transference of power. For this reason, they only give an incomplete picture of 'participation', especially in Third World situations where elections are only one factor among many in constituting the various groups which impinge upon the state and policy choices, and where in many situations informal political networks rather than functional interest groups are the major actors in the political arena.[4] The

El-Bakri, Z. B. and E. M. Kameir. This article from the *International Social Science Journal*, 35(4–1), 1983, pp. 605–634, is reproduced with the permission of Unesco.

most obvious problem in any attempt to measure female political participation simply by studying voting and official organizational membership is the fact that much of Third World politics occurs outside conventional political institutions. Indeed, electoral politics, when they occur, are only one element of a much broader spectrum of more or less legal or legitimate political activities including strikes, coups, demonstrations, and behind-the-scenes bargaining between the state, however constituted, and key groups in society. Thus, any attempt to measure female political participation that concentrates on conventional political institutions, and a Western model of how a 'democratic' system should function, is doomed to superficiality.[5]

The second assumption on which the Western view of participation is based is that participation in the political system is considered somewhat independently of participation in the sphere of production. Thus, although women have always played a role in the economy, their participation in this sphere has gone largely unmeasured because of its frequent concentration in family and domestic production. As analysed by Tucker, the separation into 'public' and 'private' spheres and its associated notions of participation tend to obscure the continuum of women's economic activities in the cycle of capital accumulation. It obscures the linkage between women's role in the reproduction of labour, on the one hand, and the rate of their absorption into the wage-labour market, on the other.[6] Hence, participation of women is viewed piecemeal, voting being the chief criterion of political participation as working for wages in the capitalist sector was the chief criterion of economic participation.

It was only natural for such views to have appealed to many Third World governments following political independence. Later, there came the realization that, although women struggled together with men for national liberation, once the liberation struggle was over, their position and power in society has remained small, despite officially declared equal rights.[7] Even these concern the superstructural level, few attempts having been made to change the material day-to-day reality that maintains women's oppression. Attempts to change material and economic reality have occurred mainly by drawing women into social production. These have been made with little corresponding attempt to draw men into household production or to socialize housework where the latter remains unpaid. Continuation of the sexual division of labour, which begins in the home, and its transference to factory, office, and the field, whether ideologically or structurally, makes the promises mere words.[8]

The first point we wish to emphasize is that the separation of society into private and public, or domestic and political, spheres is unfounded, as is the view that somehow the effective political participation of women can only be achieved by drawing them out of the private sphere and into public political structures. Rather, we agree with Margaret Stacey that the question of 'women and power cannot be addressed from the public domain alone; it is a question of the relationship of that domain and the private domain of the family between which for many years the men were the mediators'.[9] If we follow this argument to its logical conclusion then we have to assert the necessity of a radical restructuring of entire societies ending the dichotomy of public and private spheres in order for true political participation of women to occur.

Secondly, political participation remains only a superstructural matter unless directly linked with the economic roles of women and their participation in the economic sphere, and an adequate evaluation of both. It is our contention, therefore, that only if these two points are fully taken into account can concepts of participation be profitably fused in the analysis of the behaviour and lives of women, especially in developing societies.

Against this background, the rest of this article analyses the extent to which women have participated or currently do participate politically in Sudanese society, with particular emphasis on the need to look at this comparatively in the northern and the southern regions of the country.

••••

Women in Pre-colonial and Colonial Times

According to Rhoda Reddock: If we were to analyze the whole political psychology of imperialist, class and racial oppression, one common point of contention would be that of control over women. To some the bad thing about colonialism was not only that it took away the land: many of the more heated battles occurred when the colonizers or oppressors appeared to be taking control over the women.[10]

This meant that in effect women were subject to a double form of exploitation. The first they shared with the rest of the population under oppressive systems of colonial administration and the various policies pursued by colonizers to further their aims. The second form of oppression was that arising from the specific position of women within the 'private domain', that of the family. Colonial policies directed at women were intended either to preserve their subordinate positions within the family or to create such subordinate positions. Both forms will be further explored below as we compare the position of women in both pre-colonial and colonial times beginning with the case of the south.

Information on the position of women in the pre-colonial south is obviously scant and even that which is available is primarily provided by male observers, casting some doubt on its validity. Generally, however, it can be argued that both women's and

men's rights and responsibilities were conceived and institutionalized as parallel rather than hierarchical and furthermore that the activities and organizations of each sex cut across both public and private domains.[11] More specifically, we find that Millgis observes that women are the prime movers in all things except wars.[12]

In relation to the Nuer tribe Sharon Hutchinson makes the following interesting statement:

The dependence of men upon the reproductive and nurturing powers of women assures the latter an important source of control; mutual dependence implies mutual independence. Women have an exclusive reason of activity and hence an exclusive domain of control and influence. Moreover, they can subvert political alliances and aggravate divisions within the male hierarchy through the manipulation of their children's loyalties.[13]

In the pre-colonial north, meanwhile, we find that the situation of women was somewhat different. Here it is useful to compare urban and rural (especially nomadic) women. In the few urban centres that existed, women were generally confined to the home, heavily governed by the rules of Islamic segregational behaviour and hence completely isolated from the public domain. Nomadic women, in contrast, were in a far better position, as reported by Ian Cunnison.[14] He observed that they tended to lead an open, unsegregated life in which they were able to influence the public domain through certain informal measures. Although deprived of formal political rights women were able to influence decisions concerning the occupation of specific political offices primarily through spread of reputations (whether favourable or unfavourable) about potential candidates. Women thus played an important role in nomadic society as the arbiters of men's conduct.

The next question to ask is to what extent the advent of colonization influenced the position of various groups of women, especially in matters of education and employment. Political and economic considerations were most important in the colonial attitude towards education and educational institutions. This is especially true in regard to women's education. None of the fairly large number of policy declarations and memoranda exchanged on the question of education during the early years of colonial rule even mentioned the education of women. It was not until 1920 that the first controller of girls' education was appointed in the Sudan, and the first teacher-training college was opened in the north in April 1921. There were only five elementary girls' schools at that time, all in the northern region.[15]

The colonial apology for this retarded development of women's education was based primarily on the maintenance of Islamic traditions. Its real explanation, however, sprang from a limited conception of education designed to serve administrative and political ends in which women played no role. It is furthermore interesting to note that the colonial authorities rationalized educational policy in the north by exploiting and even strengthening dominant male ideologies that helped to subordinate women.

Moreover the content and programs of girls' schools were different from those for boys, of a lower academic standard and included substantial instruction in homecrafts, needlework and the like. Even when it was felt necessary to establish a small midwifery school in 1921, no attempt was made to teach illiterate girls to read or write during their training. Instead much effort was directed at training the girls to differentiate between drugs by sight and smell![16]

In the south, meanwhile, Christian missionaries dominated education. They were given a free hand by the colonial government to engage in medical work, establish a network of schools, make converts but above all to retard, however possible, the

incursion of Arab and Islamic culture. Prior to the mid-1920s no schools at all existed for girls, but by the early 1930s a handful of elementary schools had been established by the missionaries. It was not until after the Second World War that a British inspector of schools in the south was appointed, which meant that education continued until that time to be under control of the missionaries. By the time the British withdrew from Sudan in 1956 no girls' secondary schools existed in the south, and only one girls' intermediate school had been established.

If colonial educational policy in the north aimed at maintaining women's traditionally inferior status, in the south its main aim was to further their isolation. The imposition of Christian values in particular actually worked to change women's traditionally high status and degree of political participation because it meant the importation of Western, bourgeois values concerning the position of women. Specifically, it brought with it the separation into public and private domains which, as we have shown, had not previously existed in the south.

The overall effect of such policies was to enhance the political isolation of women and to reduce the chances of their participation in any sustained political movement. It was clearly in the interests of the colonial powers to keep practically half the subject population outside the political arena.

Naturally, women's opportunities for wage employment were severely limited by lack of education, training and necessary skills. Even such limited opportunities were further curtailed by unfair and unequal labour legislation, an example being the temporary employment status given to women upon marriage.

Women in the Post-independence Period

Essentially similar policies have been followed by the independent state (especially as regards economic matters). Hence, the

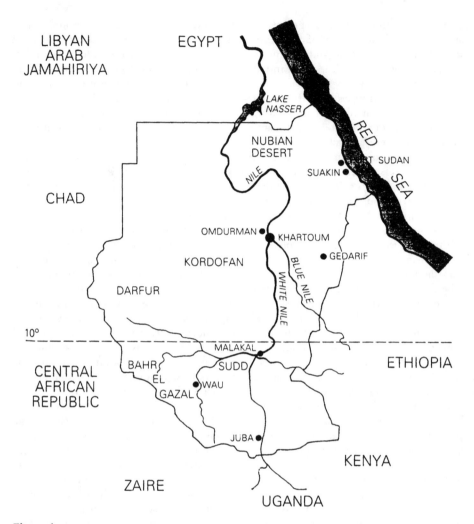

Figure 1.

subordinate position of women has by and large been maintained rather than altered in any radical way. Various national programmes on economic and social development submitted by successive governments since independence in 1956 do not fully recognize the importance of women's participation in the development process. None of the development plans, including the extended Five-Year Plan of Economic and Social Development (1970–77), include projects with specific targets for the improvement of women's lot. Likewise, the Six Year Plan (1977–83) had ignored the issues and is not expected to change the qualitative situation of women.[17]

Official wisdom as regards economic development and women's role in it sees production (and society in general) as divided into 'modern' and 'traditional' sectors. Increases in national income occur only through expansion of the modern sector, especially since it depends upon the utilization of modern technology. Increasing the participation of women in the modern sector is therefore a major aim of development efforts, since the future of the country is thought to depend upon production within the modern sector.[18]

In line with these views only 10 per cent of Sudanese women were perceived to be economically active in 1967–68. Such an estimate clearly overlooks women's work in agriculture, animal husbandry, marketing and other economic activities – to say nothing of activities such as water and fuel porterage and the grinding of grain which would be considered economic activities if performed in urban areas or technologically.[19]

Such views have been strongly criticized on many grounds. Their excessively dualistic emphasis neglects the fundamental interrelations of both sectors of the economy. Furthermore, they lack historical analysis to explain why these sectors developed initially and understanding of their true nature. The problem is not one of technological difference but rather of the nature of relations of production. The traditional sector is based on non-capitalist production relations, whereas the modern sector is based on capitalist production relations. Here, we are arguing that, rather than increasing the participation of women and improving their position, the effect of the expansion of the capitalist modern sector has been the reverse – the continued subordination of women. We will demonstrate below how this occurred, as we consider the contemporary situation of women in both southern and northern Sudan, beginning with the former.

The people of southern Sudan are mainly agriculturalists, though some pastoral communities exist. Women's activities are generally similar throughout the region. While, as we pointed out earlier, non-capitalist systems of production dominate it is wrong to assume that the southern people continue to form the independent and isolated societies which anthropological classics like those of Evans-Pritchard depicted.

These people are intimately connected to labour markets in other areas of the country through the capitalist mode of production by various linkages, especially through the mass exodus of large numbers of young men from the area.[20]

Agriculture is largely of the subsistence type. Maize, sorghum, millet, cassava, groundnuts, sesame, potatoes, sweet potatoes and beans are all grown. Cash crops include cotton and tobacco. Most women are involved in the cultivation of both food and cash crops. Under ordinary circumstances the produce of all members of the household is used communally and is in fact shared over a wide network of family and neighbours (both as cooked food and as grain) through hospitability and sharing in time of need.[21] Family structure and patterns of residence have developed in such a way that there is a tendency for households to operate in subunits, which allows for increased individual control over the disposal of crops. Thus, particularly after good harvests, a woman may make her own decision about using a portion of her grain in some way other than direct consumption, for example to brew local beer, called *merissa*, for sale.[22]

For the most part, however, women are overworked. They begin working early in life and continue through to old age. As is usually the case where there is a system of shifting cultivation, a considerable part of the agricultural work is done by women and, not surprisingly, the most exhausting and tedious work. Generally the work done by men is intermittent (though often more strenuous). Women do most of the day-in, day-out sowing, weeding, cultivating, harvesting and the converting of harvested crops into food.[23]

Like agriculture, animal production is primarily for subsistence, though in some cases animals, dairy products and hides may be sold to fulfil urgent cash needs. The division of labour in pastoral production is generally flexible, the allocation of tasks varying with household consumption, seasonal changes in population and composition of camps and villages.[24]

Traditional 'housework' tasks are primarily the responsibility of women, including food preparation, cleaning and child-care. Cooking is done once or twice a day.[25] All houses depend on open fires, the fuel for which is gathered from the forests. In most cases women make three journeys a day over considerable distances to bring water; some make as many as four.[26]

Women also dominate the various processing activities, such as making liquid butter, or *semn,* or pounding and grinding grain. In addition to these tasks women take part in various building and manufacturing activities. [27]

The extent to which individuals partake of cash-earning activities, if at all, varies considerably and is influenced by several factors, such as the need for cash, opportunities for spending and availability of markets for local products. A noticeable trend, however, is for women to engage in cash activities which are outgrowths of their usual subsistence and domestic tasks.

Tobacco production is important not only for local consumption but as a source of cash. The income from each person's tobacco is his or her own, though since it is usually men who travel to do the selling they will receive a bit more in view of their expenses and travel.[28]

Thus southern women play dominant roles in economic production activities, further increased by the mass exodus of males to work in different parts of the country, especially in the north, where development efforts and therefore opportunities for wage employment are concentrated.

There are three basic types of wage-labour situation in which a person can engage while maintaining economically significant roots in the countryside – seasonal labour, long-term migrant labour and relatively permanent employment. Seasonal labourers are typically young adult men who go north to work on agricultural schemes for two to four months or more during the dry season, earning enough to pay their own taxes and perhaps those of one or two relatives.

The long-term migrant labourer leaves for a whole year or more to work in industry, usually in the towns. His goal in this case is a larger sum of money for investment, usually to buy cattle or perhaps to set up a business. The third type of migrant also maintains significant structural links with the countryside.[29] The significant features of these types of migrant labour is that wages can be maintained at a much lower level than would be necessary if the worker had to feed, clothe and house his family out of what he earns. The existence of the subsistence sector in which such workers are rooted provides for the subsistence of the worker when he is not actually employed in wage labour and it bears the social and economic costs of the reproduction of labour powers.[30] The important point in relation to the phenomenon of migrant labour is that it is a mechanism which is being reproduced due to the continued pattern of capitalist development benefiting the north rather than the south. This is logical since the south continues to be viewed as 'unprofitable' especially in the short term.

The effects on the lives of women and their political participation include the following:

Women in the south have to undertake both domestic and agricultural tasks, in addition to taking care of children and dependants. As a result normal family life is disturbed in the absence of the male figures of fathers, brothers, uncles, etc.

Women are left with very little time for themselves, which they might use profitably for their own activities, income generation or education. Thus, less than 0.5 per cent of rural women in the Bahr el Ghazal area have ever attended school.

There is a lack of formal groupings at the village level, which might serve as vehicles of participation or struggle for women's needs and an improvement of their lives. Thus men, though frequently absent, still play an important role in the public domain of administration and aspects of decision-making.

While women produce within the non-capitalist mode of production, the expansion of the capitalist mode raises certain difficulties, which explains why women are increasingly involved in cultivating cash crops, selling livestock and brewing beer for sale for cash.

Women in Northern Sudan

The status and position of women in the north in the post-independence era makes it necessary to differentiate between categories of women. The so-called 'modernization' of agriculture has led to a decline in women's general position despite rising rates of participation in production. Marginalization, the trend towards wage employment as opposed to self-employment and the exploitation of women as a source of cheap labour marks, the development of capitalism in agriculture. Further the hiring of impoverished women among the poorer stratum of the rural population to work for richer tenants causes the accelerated growth of classes and wage-labour processes under capitalist relations. Also, women have been adversely affected by the arrival of cheap imported goods replacing traditional female handicrafts, thus lessening income opportunities, especially of nomadic women.[31]

In northern urban areas, furthermore, it becomes necessary to distinguish between bourgeois women and working-class women, who constitute the large majority. A large number of the former compose the educated and those employed in government bureaucracies. Their position is heavily influenced by their membership of the urban middle class with its various institutions, most notably that of the extended family. While educated the positions of these women remain subordinate owing to the structure of the family and various religious ideologies which advocate the confinement of women to the private domain.

Working-class urban women, on the other hand, are forced to seek wage employment (besides undertaking domestic chores) in order to supplement meagre family incomes, especially given the low wages and rising inflation in urban areas. These incomes however do not allow women a significant measure of economic independence but go wholly in support of the family; they have little discretion regarding their distribution or use. While the jobs these women fill are generally manual or unskilled, requiring no training, they are even being deprived of these because much investment (especially of foreign capital) goes towards the importation of high technology, which tends to undercut the chances of female employment since, when jobs are scarce, they naturally tend to go to the men.

Women and Political Participation

The first specialized women's organization developed in 1946 when the Sudan was still under colonial rule.

An organization called Rabitat al-Nisa al-Sudaniyyat (League of Sudanese Women) was formed in Omdurman by several educated women, notable among them Dr Khalda Zahir and Fatma Talib, who became president and secretary, respectively. The aim of this early organization was 'to raise the standard' of Sudanese women in pursuit of which the league founded a night school for literacy classes and teaching of sewing, home economics and a nursery which later developed into a girls' primary school. A series of weekly lectures were also planned on women's social problems and disseminating information relating to their health.

Membership was open only to the educated which meant that it remained small and was concentrated in the urban areas. The work of this organization was linked to general trends of the time, particularly the growing political schisms and the general questioning of the extent to which various alliances truly represented different class interests. Such questions began to arise within the organization's leadership and some of its members left to join the Jamiyat Taruiyat al-Mar'a (Society for the Prosperity of Women), founded in Omdurman in 1947. The rise of this organization also cannot be isolated from developments of the time, notably the struggle between the Mahadi family and its political organizations and other political associations.[32] The Mahadist's organizations represented the interests of the Sudanese feudal land-owning aristocracy and generally supported colonial policy. The development of this women's organization was part of their attempt to influence the educated middle classes by appearing to champion the cause of women. The organization thus made numerous, though unsuccessful, attempts to co-opt the Union of Teachers, which resisted, preferring to develop into a full-scale, legal trade union instead.

Activities were limited to organizing lectures on the history and geography of Sudan, literacy classes, founding a library and conducting general lectures. However, due to the marked isolation of the leadership, especially the rift between the leaders from the Mahadi family and their poor followers, the organization was not able in any significant way to increase women's political participation or to influence their position.

The creation of the Union of Nurses in 1948 and the membership of it of most female nurses had the greatest effect in helping to raise women's consciousness and organizing them to fight directly for their rights, taking an active part in demonstrations, strikes, etc. In 1955, one of the nurs-es even won a seat on the union's Executive Committee.[33]

In 1948, a group of primary-school teachers approached the colonial authorities for permission to create a trade union. The response was a refusal, warning the teachers against such activity and stressing that it was not appropriate for Sudanese women, since it would mean mixing and being in contact with male trade-unionists. Thus, under the pretext of the 'protection' of Sudanese values and traditions the teachers were only allowed to operate a union for cultural purposes. Again conflicts arose among the teachers' leadership, some continuing to press for the transformation of the cultural union into a properly functioning and fully fledged trade union; while others called for amalgamation with the Mahadi family's organization. The teachers were finally successful in establishing a trade union in 1949 under the leadership of Nafisa al-Mileik.

This union was constantly harassed by the colonial body in charge of female education, which was able to put various pressures on its leadership. Their principal gain was in 1957 when the Ministry of Education dismissed several married teachers in accordance with the colonial law that stated that women were to be transferred to temporary employment on marriage. The firm stand of the union led to repeal of this law in 1960. Subsequently, the union's activities continued to decline until its winding up in 1968.

The rise and fall of organizations during the final decade of colonial rule paralleled the formation of political parties and the beginning of intense rivalry between them. These parties largely represented different class interests, primarily those of the large landowning class and the educated urban middle classes. Generally, the withering away of various early organizations can be attributed to the lack of any clear conceptualization of women's position and the real causes and dynamics of that position.

The basis of these organizations lay largely in the urban middle classes, which meant a general lack of understanding of the real needs of rural women or even of poor urban women, let alone women in remote parts of the country such as the south. They were relatively isolated also from other political groups, such as trade unions, which represented different interests from those of traditional political associations, and which did have specific tactics for change. By the 1950s and with the intensification of the nationalist movement a need was once again felt for a new organization for women which would raise their standard and promote their participation. Thus the Itihad al-Nisai, (Women's Union) was founded in 1952, again by a group of educated women, some of whom had helped found the earlier organizations. The Union began with 500 members in Omdurman and its charter initially specified literacy as a condition for membership. However, after some time this condition was dropped since it was realized that it would greatly limit membership. Nevertheless, most members tended to be teachers, nurses, students and government officials, only a minority being housewives.

The Union extended branches spearheaded by primary-school teachers, most of them single with plenty of time on their hands. In the south, branches were established by northern women in the principal towns of Malakal, Wau and Juba. Furthermore, specialized committees were formed, some temporary, to execute the decisions and projects of the Union which was very active between 1952 and 1956.

The year 1958 saw the first military coup (after independence in 1956) and a general trend towards curbing the activities of unions and other special-interest organizations. All forms of election were suspended.

In 1959 the government suspended the activities of the Union under different pretexts, which, however, did not bring its activities to a complete halt. It continued to operate informally especially through the magazine *Sawt al-Mar'aa* (Women's Voice) one of the pioneering women's magazines of that period, which was one of the few platforms for free exchange of ideas and debates. This situation continued until 1964, when a multi-party system was installed.

Subsequently, the Union continued to be active in the promotion of nationalist issues, especially the struggle for the establishment of democratic government, its first generation of leaders being the active vanguard. This led to the further drifting away of the Union leadership from its base, as the kind of issues the Union was struggling for were no longer of any interest to the younger generations or urban women. Thus the late 1960s witnessed a decline in its popularity.

The year 1968 was the first in which women used their right to vote in a general election. Generally (especially in rural areas) polling was conducted on separate days for men and women. Women did not attend political meetings and rallies in rural areas and many complaints were received by officials about men preventing women from casting their votes. Women constituted a voting force which could swing the election results. But many were not alert to this potentiality and they had no formal organization (apart from the Women's Union) which could give them an awareness of their significance in the political arena. Meanwhile women in the south suffered from the effects of the civil war which continued until 1972, disrupting normal life since it led to the flight of thousands of southerners either to neighboring countries or into the bush. The struggle of the southern people for autonomy was backed by numerous organizations with women members, but no specifically women's organizations existed. Thus, what happened in the north was quite cut off from developments in the south, especially regarding the situation of women.

The situation largely continued until the

advent of the present military government in May 1969. Originally, the regime was supported by communists, leftists and other progressive elements. Disillusioned with the failure of traditional party politics it sought to effect radical changes in the structure of Sudanese society by means of a series of 'popular organizations' and a popular system of local government. Popular organizations were supposed to change the position of the oppressed groups in society (including women and youth) by increasing their participation. The new local government system was intended to change the traditional pattern of local leadership (based on the colonial system of native administration) in both rural and urban areas by setting up a large number of popularly elected local councils to which a sufficient amount of functions and duties would be decentralized. To ensure their participation, 25 per cent of all local council memberships were reserved for women.

After the regime's turn to the right in 1971, it dissolved the Women's Union and purged most of its politically radical leaders. In its place the government installed a new organization, the Sudan Women's Union (SWU), whose leadership came primarily from certain women co-opted from the leadership of the previous union.

The SWU was expected to mobilize support for the regime, and to encourage the entry of women into the modern capitalist sector. Several high government positions became open to women who supported the regime.

The union opened branches in different parts of the country which also concentrated on mobilizing support for the regime. These mainly attracted those urban and rural petty-bourgeois elements having vested interests in the stabilization and continuity of the regime, while many educated women have reacted against the SWU as being excessively conformist.

As for the 25 per cent female representation on local councils it is widely held to have failed to establish women within the decision-making structure. In many (especially rural) councils, the 25 per cent level has never been reached; indeed, several rural councils have requested a repeal of this stipulation, also rationalized on the basis of protecting Sudanese values which do not allow women to participate in the public arena. A study conducted in the town of Omdurman in 1978–79 reported that female councillors constantly complained that their male counterparts were using certain tactics in order to keep them out of council affairs and politics. Female councillors were manipulated by male councillors who wanted them to vote in their favour on certain issues and women were always urged to vote on the basis of family, ethnicity and the political allegiances of fathers, brothers, husbands, etc.[34]

Three main reasons can be put forward to explain this situation:

First the assumption, especially on the part of men, that only disreputable women would enter the political arena discourages many respectable women from taking part and adversely affects the social standing of those who do take part.

Secondly, the local government system's general reputation of being corrupt discourages large parts of both the male, but especially the female, population.

Thirdly, women are not fully aware of the opportunities offered by the system. They underestimate their influence on decision-making. Thus issues such as the siting of water-pumps or health facilities of vital concern to women tend to be decided by reference to men's needs, and all women can do is to complain among themselves after the event.[35]

In a study conducted in 1979 in the southern region it was found that initiatives were usually started when a government official visited a village and encouraged the women to organize themselves into a group and elect a leader on the spot. In villages where this occurred no follow-up meetings were ever held by the elected leader, the main reason given by the leaders being that they did not quite understand the purpose of the SWU, in addition to feelings of uncertainty and inadequacy in performing their role due to the lack of briefing or supervision.[36]

Yet these same women finally admitted that they were powerless and felt that they were powerless to change situations which they admitted were unsatisfactory.[37] Thus, while certain formal vehicles have been provided, such as local councils and SWU units, these are basically not being utilized by women. Having been imposed from above their conceptions of problems are very often at variance with those of women. Furthermore many women who do not agree with current policies (especially educated women) take no part in their activities. These women are at present suffering from the lack of alternative, independent organizations which can struggle to change their positions.

Lastly, despite the existence of various venues for participation, women's lives are still being adversely affected by the pursuit of certain economic policies which are radically altering women's traditional roles without offering them viable alternatives. These economic policies are resulting in the continued expansion of the capitalist mode of production and the concomitant dissolution of the non-capitalist mode of life. These processes, as indicated, are not proceeding at the same pace in the different regions which is the main factor underlying the different situations of women in Sudan.

ENDNOTES

1. Cynthia Nelson, "Public and Private Politics: Women in the Middle Eastern World", in Saad el-Din Ibrahim and N. Hopkins (eds.), *Arab Society in Transition: A Reader*, p. 131, 1977.

2. *Ibid.*, p. 132.

3. *Ibid.*, pp. 133–4.

4. John Jaquette, "Female Political Participation in Latin America", in June Nash and Helen Safa (eds.), *Sex and Class in Latin America: Women Perspectives on Politics, Economics and the Family in the Third World*, p. 221, 1980.

5. *Ibid.*, p. 235.

6. Mona Hammam, "Labour Migration and the Sexual Division of Labour", *Middle East Research and Information Project*, No. 95, p. 5, 1981.

7. Rhoda Reddock, "National Liberation and Women's Liberation: A Discussion Paper", in R. Reddock (ed.), *National Liberation and Women's Liberation*, p. 11, 1982.

8. *Ibid.*, p. 20.

9. Margaret Stacey and M. Price, *Women, Power and Politics*, p. 10, 1981.

10. Reddock, *op. cit.*, p. 13.

11. John W. Burton, "Independence and the Status of Nilotic Women", *Africa Today*, Vol. 12, 1981, p. 56.

12. Ibid.

13. Sharon Hutchinsun. "Relations Between the Sexes among the Nuer", 1930 (unpublished paper).

14. Ian Cunnison, "The Position of Women among the Humr", *Sudan Society Journal*. No. 2. 1963, pp. 24–34.

15. Suad Ibrahim Ahmed, 1983 (unpublished thesis).

16. *Ibid.*

17. Mahasin Khidir El-Sayyid, "Women's Role in Agriculrure in Rural Khartoum Province", pp. 5–6, Khartoum, 1981, (Ph. D. thesis).

18. Fatima Abdel Mahmoud, *Dawr al-Mar'a al-Sudaniyya fi al-Tanmiyya al-Iqtisadiyya wal-Igtim' iyya*, pp. 12–13, 1973.

19. Margaret Snyder, "Women and Development", in Ali Mohamed El Hassan (ed.), *Growth, Employment and Equity*, p.232, 1976.

20. Ellen Gruenbaum, "Women's Labour in Subsistence Sector: The Case of the Central Nuer Area of Jonglei Province", p.3, 1978 (unpublished paper).

21. *Ibid.*, p. 9.

22. *Ibid.*, pp. 9–10.

23. Annemarie Russel, *Report on the Situation of Women in the Target Villages on the UNICEF Domestic Water Supply Project in Bahr El Ghazal Province, Sudan*, p.12, 1979.

24. Gruenbaum, *op. cit.*, p. 11.

25. *Ibid.*, p. 13.

26. El-Sayyid, *op. cit.*, p. 135.

27. Gruenbaum, *op. cit.*, pp. 13–14.

28. *Ibid.*, pp. 14–15.

29. *Ibid.*, pp. 4–5.

30. *Ibid.*, pp. 5–6.

31. Mahasin Khidir El-Sayyid, "Women's Role in Agriculture in Rural Khartoum Province", in D. Baxter (ed.), *Women and the Environment*, p. 118, 1981.

32. Mohamed Ahmed El Mahadi was the leader of

the Mahadist movement in Sudan. It was able to rid the country of Turco-Egyptian rule, establishing an independent state which lasted for thirteen years. He was defeated by the British in 1898. After the British conquest they tried to co-opt his family by offering them land and limited political power.

33. See Fatima Ahmed Ibrahim, *Tariqnu ila al-Tuhasur*, for details on Sudanese women's organizations.

34. Zeinab B. El Bakri, "The Politics of Local Government Councils in a Sudanese Urban Community", Hull, 1981 (Ph. D. thesis).

35. Judy El Bushra, Abebech Bekele and Fawzia Hammour, "Socio-Economic Development and Women Changing Status", p.15. Paper presented to conference on Women and the Environment, Khartoum.

36. Russel, *op. cit.*, p. 37.

37. *Ibid.*, pp. 38–39.

Womens' Work and their Struggle to Organize

ZUBEIDA M. AHMAD

The situation of women and policies to improve their employment and standards of living need to be viewed in the over-all context of deteriorating conditions of rural workers and in particular the conditions of the landless and near-landless rural households.

Traditional patterns of family life are becoming increasingly difficult to maintain in rural areas. Under the strains of extreme poverty, the household itself often begins to disintegrate, with male members of the family being forced to migrate in search of paid employment, whilst females remain behind and head the households, which consist mainly of old people and children.[1] In more and more situations women are forced by economic circumstances to seek wage employment outside the home and/or to undertake home-based income-generating activities, either because the male members of the family have migrated in search of cash employment (without necessarily sending back remittances) or because men have lost their jobs due to the adoption of capital-intensive techniques of farming also. In many areas, non-farm artisanal rural crafts have declined because of competition from factory-made products, which has also affected male employment. Chronic distress is a powerful inducement to women even to the point of defying cultural norms against seeking work outside the home, in their efforts to ensure family survival.

The general availability of a vast pool of female labour, which has been augmented by women from pauperised artisanal classes, leads to low wages and exploitative working conditions. Low female wages have lead in certain cases to decision by land owners not to mechanize tasks performed by women. In many parts of the world agriculture is reported to becoming increasingly dependent on low paid female labour.

There is ample evidence that women engage in a wide range of income-generating activities. The question to be considered is on what terms and conditions; what are the kinds of employment available to women? What payment can they expect? The extent to which women suffer from over-work and under-remuneration? In order to answer these questions, we must consider some others, particularly those concerning constraints under which women enter the labour market: what are these constraints and how are they different from those faced by the men? How do women manage to fulfill both their productive and reproductive roles and what kind of a strain does this impose on their physical and mental health? What are the implications for production and development?

Female Workers in the Rural Sector

In their world of work, rural women are handicapped in different ways, amongst others by limited access to land and related resources; by lack of control over their own labour and the fruits of their labour; and lack of mobility due to social and cultural restrictions as well as the responsibility women bear for family survival and subsistence. While it is recognized that many men also face the two first constraints, women's work situation is made worse

Ahmad, Zubeida M. Permission to reprint this article was received from *Development: Seeds of Change*. It appeared in Volume 4 in 1987 on pages 36–40.

because of cultural and other constraints to their mobility and choice of work.[2]

Although statistics are not readily available on the percentage of women either among the total agricultural labour force or under each category of worker, there is evidence from case studies that in many countries women constitute an important element of the agricultural workforce. Studies from several countries equally confirm that rural women participate extensively in agricultural work, either in the fields or within the confines of the compound, depending on the degree of their seclusion. Their share in agricultural operations is substantial in respect not only of food crops, but also of those non-food commercial crops that are labour-intensive and do not necessarily involve the use of mechanical implements.

Aside from women's extensive participation in the subsistence sector, they also work for wages in agriculture, being compensated often in kind, but sometimes also in cash. The trend for women to work outside the family farm is rising with the increase in landlessness. As more rural families find themselves without any ownership or tenancy rights in land, both men and women are forced to contract themselves out as seasonal and casual labour. Women are generally paid 40 to 60 percent of the male wage and given the more labour-intensive tasks like weeding, transplanting and harvesting. In parts of India, for example, the work of transplanting rice is done almost entirely by women, who are reported to work non-stop from 10.30 a.m. to 6 p.m. for a statutory minimum wage of 3 rupees a day (compared with 5 rupees for men).

In addition to working as seasonal and casual labourers in agriculture generally, women also work on plantations, either as members of a plantation worker's family or as labourers in their own right. On plantations in India, Malaysia and Sri Lanka, for example, contracts are often signed with the male head of the family, who is frequently required also to provide the labour of his wife and children. A recent study of plantation labour in Malaysia reports that women provide 50 percent or more of the labour force on rubber estates[3]. They work mainly as tappers and weeders, with the help of their children. Their wages, which are calculated as part of a "family" wage, fluctuate with the weather (rubber tapping is impossible on rainy days, which are frequent during the wet monsoons). Their employment is being adversely affected by the declining international demand for rubber and the resulting trend towards the conversion of rubber estates into oil-palm holdings, where labour requirements are much lower. Indeed, it is reported that women plantation workers all over the world are facing serious employment problems as a consequence of falling over-all demand for labour. Technological advances in field operations are increasingly enabling plantations to maintain or even to expand their output with fewer permanent workers. Part of the field work is becoming semi-skilled, requiring training in machine operation, normally provided only to males. On some of the plantations there appears to be a classification of jobs by sex, women being assigned to jobs with lower pay and poorer conditions of work.

In most developing countries women are active, along with men, in rural home-based industrial production: the biri-making industry in Northern India, which mainly employs secluded Moslem women (biri — also written bidi and beedi — is a cheap substitute for cigarettes), and the lace-making industry of Narsapur in Southern India may serve as illustrations. Work on biri production is mainly done at home by women who are paid at piece rates under a contract system. The contractor, who provides the raw material and collects the finished products, is frequently a powerful landowner, while the women are poor, illiterate and tradition-bound. The relationship thus becomes highly exploitative, the effective piece rate paid to women being less than the minimum wage pre-scribed by the Department of Labour.[4]

Women's Networks

Clearly, the fact that women often occupy a dependency status vis-a-vis men and the community generally, makes it more diffi-cult for them to organize to defend their interests. Whilst being badly in need of group solidarity, (because of the discrimina-tion they face in their world of work, i.e. lower wages, job insecurity, home-based production at piece rates dictated by private contractors) women face serious obstacles to organisation.

A rural women's organisation, for the purpose of this paper, will be defined as a workers organisation, formed by the com-ing together of a number of men and women (either together or separately) in an association established on a continuing and democratic basis, dependent principally on its own resources and independent of patronage, the purpose of which is to fur-ther and defend the interests of the mem-bers.[5] Before speaking of well set-up organ-isations, however, it is important to recognise that women's solidarity and mutual aid networks normally do exist in most traditional rural societies and that these could constitute the basis for the emergence of more formal organisations, with clearly defined aims and objectives. In Asia there are numerous examples of traditional saving societies or "chit fund" which enable women to accumulate small amounts of money for initiating income-generating projects, meeting social needs or merely purchasing consumer goods, otherwise out of the reach of the poor. Similarly, there are "burying societies", where the women get together to help each other when death or other calamity hits the family.

In many parts of Asia, there exist loose associations or informal support groups of women who continually work together in transplanting rice or harvesting crops. Maria Mies, in a still unpublished study on rural women in Andra Pradesh, India, describes the collective nature of certain types of women's work in the fields, especially transplanting and harvesting.[6] The women are reported to form themselves into groups of 10–30 women made up of small teams of neighbours, relatives and friends, develop-ing in the process a spirit of solidarity and mutual help which transcends the confines of the more limited family circle. This col-lective spirit among the women has been strengthened by the fact that the landlords are traditionally required to bargain wages and conditions of work with the women's groups collectively. They cannot recruit these women individually, but are forced by custom to negotiate with the spokes-woman who, in turn is held responsible by the other women labourers. The necessity to recruit large numbers of women during certain periods of the year, constitutes the basis for the development of women's col-lective spirit and organisational skill. The agricultural work process itself, e.g., rice transplanting and weeding, its regular rhythm of body movement, strengthens the workers' feeling of togetherness. The songs sung by the women as they work together relate to their problems, including man-woman relations and feudal oppression. The songs generate a feeling of collectivity, preventing atomisation of individuals, giv-ing the women a sense of human personal identity and dignity.

Women's Organisations

Beginning from such informal networks, more formal women's organisations have emerged in Asia which concern themselves both with immediate economic issues, such as higher wages and better conditions of work, as well as acting as pressure groups to protect the over-all interests of the mem-bers. One such organisation, although functioning on a very small scale, is the Women's Transplanting Organisation, Makulamada, in the Matale District of Sri Lanka. It was started in Sri Lanka in 1950 by 15 women who formed a voluntary organisation to jointly engage in transplanting. Although the organisation has no written constitution, it has a tradition of joint action, developed over a number of years. The women as a group enter into contracts with landowners who are required to provide minimum facilities, including transport, medical services and some advance payment, when the women enter into a contract of work. The members, in turn, work as a disciplined team and thereby achieve a higher level of productivity. Aside from obtaining specific improvements in working conditions, the organisation has resulted in increased consciousness amongst the members who are generally motivated and active in village socio-economic affairs.[7]

In Bangladesh, two grass-roots organisations, Nijeria Kori (Do it Yourself) and BRAC (Bangladesh Rural Advancement Committee) have concentrated exclusively on poor women, whilst emphasising self-help and collective investment activities. In fact, Nijeria Kori only allows the accumulation of group rather than individual profits from members' activities, which in turn strengthens group rather than individual action. By emphasizing self-help, particularly in the form of active labour inputs by the members themselves, a self-selection mechanism comes into operation, to automatically eliminate participation by the richer households who refuse to be involved in the organisation for reasons of prestige.[8]

Another instance of a spontaneous increase in consciousness amongst women has emerged as part of the Bhoomi Sena (Land Army) Movement in the Palghar District of Maharashtra State, India, the tribal women having been greatly "influenced" by the main Bhoomi Sena movement and reported to have gained a sense of self-importance and self-possession.[9]

Organizing home-based workers in rural areas needs special consideration, in view of

their atomisation and higher levels of exploitation (earnings per hour or per day are much lower in the case of women who work at home). The very fact that these women lack contact and mutual support amongst themselves makes organisation more urgent and also more difficult to achieve. There is a clear need to organise production and marketing so as to release the women from the uncertainties and exploitative practices of middle men and traders. In spite of the difficulties encountered, organisation among home-based workers is developing. For example, a branch of the Working Women's Union in the West Godavari District in India has succeeded in forming 300 groups of lace makers with 10 members in each group. Through these groups, lacemakers have been able to obtain credit from the State Bank of India. To the astonishment of the Bank the recovery rate has been 100 per cent. The entry point used by this organisation is credit, the strategy being to increase workers' access to credit and production inputs, with a view to strengthening their negotiating skills and collective power. Group meetings are utilised as a vehicle of communication between the organisation and members, to resolve areas of conflict in the locality, and to generate awareness/consciousness on a variety of issues. The smallest organisational unit of the Working Women's Unions is the loan group, consisting of 20/30 members. Each loan group is required to elect a group leader, according to the pre-requisites of the area-members. The group leader is responsible to the group for communicating organisational matters, organising group meetings, processing loans of members. The group members also depend on their leaders for a wide variety of services, such as health care, night schools, technological inputs, besides credit facilities at low cost. Group leaders are supervised by area leaders who have themselves risen from the ranks.[10]

Similar examples of spontaneously started

organisations of poor rural women no doubt exist in other countries and regions. However their experiences have not been written up, possibly because the organisations operate on a small scale and have not as yet been documented by outside researchers. In fact, the role played by women in starting and participating in joint (men/women) organisations has been considerably under-reported. Although peasant movements and workers struggles have been studied, the women of these classes and their role and contribution in such struggles are hardly ever mentioned. There has been little attempt made to locate and understand the role of women. The consciousness of oppression and the need to join together to fight this oppression (whether it consists of high costs of living, low level of wages, the struggle against forest denudation) appears to be even stronger amongst women than men, because of their basic concern with family survival. Written evidence, however, is lacking, and more attention needs to be given to such research.

Outsiders

Aside from spontaneously formed women's organisations, examples exist of *animateurs* or catalysts (outsiders) who have deliberately set out to work and live with poor rural women, in an attempt to deepen peoples' own participation in the development process. Such initiatives represent mostly non-government involvement in the development process.

One such illustration is from the Philippines and concerns the work of a community organiser (Anna, a graduate student from Metro Manila) who conducted a training/exposure/programme in a resettlement community village at a distance of around two hours' drive from the heart of Manila city. She, with the other trainees, worked closely with the Parish priest and through Church programmes. The trainees viewed their task as not to organise the women but to help them and the community to organise themselves and to discover for themselves how they would like to respond to their problems. The most significant turn in the women's organising efforts came with their decision to study deeply the social conditions in their community and their relation to national economic and political concerns. As part of this programme of action, the group organised a project to develop skills in the use of acupuncture, acupressure, fireglass and moxibustian, as people's medicine. After 30 months of community work, there were 13 full-time health workers for 34 blocks of the community, with the continuing process of conscientisation, mobilisation and organisation working out a dialectical relationship. After six months' training, all the community organising trainees left the area except Anna who came to be viewed by the community as a "reliable partner and friend" and who was provided with free board and lodging by the community.[11]

In west Bengal, Bankura District, as a direct consequence of a three-day camp/workshop organised by the government (Land Reform Commissioner) in 1980, as part of the programme for land distribution, the tribal women decided to organise themselves into a Women's Development Samiti. The organisation started with 64 members and received the full backing and support of the government. The Centre for Women's Development Studies (CWDS), with some ILO funding, was coopted to assist the Samiti. The initial success of this organisation helped to create a demand from women in other villages for assistance in organising themselves and developing employment opportunities. There are now three women's Samitis in Bankura district covering 22 villages with more than 600 women as members. Although women in this area have traditionally worked in teams, both in agricultural work as well as in the collection of minor forest products, it was found that the concept of team work differed substantially from the concept of collective organisation. Gradually, however, the women are coming up with collective proposals and are beginning to gain access to government funds previously unutilised. Government support at the top has not prevented growing opposition from the established local power structure, the dilemma before the CWDS is to prepare field workers as well as the women themselves to successfully confront and deal with such deep-rooted opposition.[12]

Government Initiatives

Aside from concerned individual social scientists working at the grass-roots level, certain governments, like that of Nepal, are actively encouraging, under the Small Farmers' Development Programme, the formation of poor women's (and men's) groups for collective action. The main aim of the small farmers development project is to increase the standard of living and economic status of small farmers, landless labourers and tenants by forming them into groups for purposes of undertaking common economic activities. It is also to strengthen the receiving and utilizing mechanisms of the group so as to harmonize it with service delivery mechanisms. Groups of women are gradually being involved in income-generating activities, which include livestock raising, paddy processing, the production and sale of cottage industry products and handicrafts, management of cooperative stores, health and nutrition education, etc. 192 women's groups have been formed, with a membership of 2300. Group organisers have been stationed in each district to play catalytic and monitoring role in the formation of "homogeneous, multifunction groups around a common-nucleus income-raising activity based on group work plans and group action, supported by an integrated programme of supervised credit, extension and technical backstopping".[13]

Government sponsored programmes,

like the one in Nepal raises the fundamental issue of independence of rural women workers organizations. In Nepal, for example, the aim was for the withdrawal of the Government paid Group-Organiser after two to three years, but in fact this has been only marginally achieved. Obviously, the contribution of "outsiders", whether government or others, is to further the initiative and autonomy of the rural women themselves and help to put the organisation on its own feet. This does not always happen. The question to be considered is how it can be advanced.

Limited Role of Trade Unions

Trade unions with the experiences gained in striving to improve wages and conditions of work in the organised sector, can play an important role in the development of rural workers' organisations, including women and men workers. They can act as valuable partners not only by helping to set up organisations and assisting them in the establishment of suitable work programmes, but also by giving more status and support to these organisation, whilst providing valuable horizontal linkages. It is in fact in the interest of the trade union movement to help rural workers to organise, and trade unions in developing countries are becoming increasingly conscious of the need to work in rural areas. If the trade union movement is really to become a mass movement in developing countries, representing working people in all walks of life, it will need to cater to women as well as male workers in rural areas.

In spite of this increased consciousness, however, trade unionism in most developing countries at the present time has hardly gone beyond the plantation sector, with its semi-industrial setting. From studies undertaken by the ILO on plantations in Malaysia and Sri Lanka, it is evident that even when women constitute a majority of trade union membership, they seldom participate in decision-making. For example, in Malaysia

40 per cent of the workers in the plantation sector are women, but only one per cent are active in trade union activities.[14] There are a number of reasons why women fail to climb up in the trade union hierarchy: because they are reluctant to speak up in mixed meetings, where men are present; because women, even more than men, are handicapped by lack of education and training (in Malaysia, for example, women said that their lack of knowledge of English handicapped them from actively participating in trade union action at the national and international levels); because working women with their double workload, at home and on the work site, generally have difficulty attending trade union meetings; and, because in most traditional societies there is male opposition to participation by women in public affairs (in fact in many parts of the world, women would have to seek the permission of husbands, fathers, mothers-in-law, etc. before they could attend trade union meetings).

Clearly, there is need for women to increase their participation in trade union activities in sectors, like the plantation sector, where trade unions exist and where women constitute a substantial percentage of the labour force. Whilst trade union federation are in fact sincerely committed to increasing women's participation at all levels, the progress is slow, both because traditional male attitudes towards women change only gradually and because there is lack of awareness even amongst women themselves of their need to participate more fully in trade union activities with a view to improving conditions of work and life.

Self-employed persons, men and women, find it even more difficult than wage earners to come together to form organisations. There is, however, one illustration of a self-employed women's union – the SEWA in Ahmedabad, India – which has set itself the task to organise the poor, self-employed women who constitute 94 per cent of all working women in India, with a view to

getting them a fair deal for their work and contribution to the economy. SEWA has been organising urban and rural self-employed women to help them become visible, to get better incomes and to have control over their own incomes. The work SEWA has been doing amongst poor women has led to a confrontation with big business, traders and middlemen. This confrontation and the difficulties put in the way of the women in obtaining required credit and marketing services, has led to SEWA's entry into development activities, including the setting up of a cooperative bank, providing trading information, technical inputs, legal aid, maternity benefits, health, social security, skill training, marketing services, etc. They have in effect organized more than 10,000 women – vegetable sellers, market porters, scrap merchants, old clothes sellers, etc. – into extremely effective organisations which combine the functions of a cooperative with those of a Trade Union. They are now in the process of identifying income-generating activities and other supportive measures for income enhancement for their rural members.

Autonomous or not?

Clearly, working on a one-to-one basis, women like men will continue to be exploited. They need to join together to take advantage of government programmes in particular those set up with the specific objective of assisting the rural poor. The purpose of organisation however is much more than economic, it is to constitute a platform (solidarity) against all forms of exploitation. Women need to come together to form organisations, either jointly with the men or separately for women, depending on specific socio-economic situations.

At the same time, women even more than men, face a variety of problems in their attempt to organise. To begin with, they are burdened with a double work load, at home and on the work site. They have therefore little time to attend meetings. This is reported to have been a problem, for example, for Chinese women in the immediate post-revolution period.[15] Moreover, in most traditional cultures women seldom speak up in meetings when men are present, so that their views are frequently not taken into account in arriving at organizational decisions. Also, very few women are represented in higher-level decision-making committees. In many cultures where seclusion is practiced, women have little freedom of choice in participating in organisational activities. They do not always control their own activities, even their decision on where to work being controlled by other household members – husband, mother-in-law, etc. – and this is equally true when it comes to making a decision on whether to join organisations, especially those which include male members. Finally, it needs to be recognised that part of the struggle in which women are engaged is in opposition to the male members of their family, e.g. when women are beaten by their husbands, when men use up women's hard-earned wages on drink; etc. In such circumstances, it needs to be considered whether separate organisations for women may not be the only answer, at least in the initial stage of organisation, before men's traditional attitudes to women undergo a change.

According to certain activists working at the grass-roots level, the strength of the class struggle is doubled when women have their own autonomous organizations. which it is believed provides women with a power base from which they can fight class exploitation, whilst at the same time struggling against sexual oppression. They are thus considered to have doubled the strength of the class and not weakened it.[16]

This need for separate women's organisations is contested by the workers' movement as a whole, where it is felt that women's special interests need to be addressed within the framework of joint organisations, in order not to divide the workers' solidarity. It is similarly rejected by political parties and national women's organisations allied to political parties.

The arguments for and against an autonomous women's organisation are complex. The chief criticism against an autonomous women's movement is that it diverts attention from the class struggle, allowing women's issues to become compartmentalised, cut off from a broader understanding of the social, economic and political conditions in a given country. On the other hand, it can be argued that provided it embodies such an understanding, and takes into account the duality of women's oppression on the basis of sex and class, autonomy might be considered a part of the strategy of double-militancy.[17] Moreover, experience has shown that at least some level of independent organisation is vital for the true achievement of women's demands. Women's struggle, while not breaking away from the class struggle, has to be conducted at two levels: in the larger context, against capitalist exploitation; as well as within the folds of the family and society, against the oppression of female workers by male workers. The class struggle must therefore be accompanied by a continuous fight against feudalistic and traditional attitudes towards women.

Development from Below

At the same time, it is crucial that grass-root organisations of women are affiliated with like-minded regional or national bodies, where possible jointly with men, so as to acquire the strength to defend broader issues and promote the poor women's interests at the national, regional and international levels.

Since 1970 there has been a general acceptance of the need for a "people-based" development "from below", which accepts "people's participation" not only as an end in itself, but also as a fundamental precondition for and a tool of any successful development strategy. The failure of past development strategies is directly linked to the absence of this missing ingredient – "participation".[18] At the same time there are wide differences in views as regards the definition of "participation". Whilst it is not intended here to enter into the controversy as to what exactly is meant by "participation", it should be argued that participation in the true sense can only be attained by the poor through their own authentic organisations. "Organisation means *strength* and strength is a prerequisite to taking action ... (action which) generates countervailing power to confront the already well-established power configuration within any particular context... This process is linked more tangibly to the creation of *assets,* ... building up of a minimal economic base for previously excluded groups...".[19] Broadly speaking, the purpose of organisation of rural workers is to provide a continuing mechanism for the pursuit of interests of its members as collectively perceived by them. The rationale for organisation of rural workers arises from the fact that it is the only way of their achieving effective participation in national life and economic development.

At the same time, grass-roots experience reveals serious structural difficulties in most countries in promoting participation. People's participation is the opposite of conventional top-down planning and project control, and risks being viewed by bureaucracies as a challenge to their sovereign right to deliver development. Field activities to encourage participation also risk grass-roots questioning or challenging of established structures and leaderships. In particular, since the poor need access to economic assets for their meaningful development, their organised voice has often pressed for redistribution of assets, particularly land. Resistance to organised people's initiatives from vested interests is, therefore, to be expected.[20]

Women's Organisations where they exist can and do play a crucial role in improving the situation of women workers. The scope of activities undertaken by them depends very much on the type and category of workers who are members. There are two principal tasks which rural workers' organisations including women's organisations, are called upon to perform: representation of rural workers' interests at different policy-making levels, including struggling for higher wages and better working conditions; and, providing services to the members, including training, credit and marketing facilities, advice on income-generating activities, childcare facilities, etc.

ENDNOTES

1. N. Youssef and C. Hetler: Rural households headed by women: Priority concern for development, forthcoming ILO publication.

2. More details provided in an article on "Rural Women's World of Work: Dependency and Alternatives for Change" International Labour Review, Jan-Feb. 1984.

3. Noeleen Heyzer: "From Rural Subsistence to an Industrial Peripheral Work Force: An examination of Female Malaysian Migrants and Capital Accumulation in Singapore", *Women and Development,* 1982.

4. Zarina Bhatty: "The Economic Role and Status of Women in the Beedi Industry in Allahabad", India, 1981 (ILO publication).

5. ILO, *Structure and Functions of Rural Workers' Organisations, A workers' education manual,* 1978.

6. M. Mies: *Poor peasant women between subsistence production and market economy,* forthcoming.

7. Written up in "Learning from rural women – village-level success cases of rural women's groups income-raising activities" .

8. Saleha Begum: IDS Study, "Women, Employment and Agriculture".

9. S. Mhatre: *Multiple transition for tribal women: A study of tribal women in Palghar Taluka, Maharashtra,* paper prepared for the ILO Tripartite Asian Regional Seminar on Rural Development and Women, 1981.

10. Nandini Azad and Research Team: "The Working Women's Forum: Dindigul Dairy Women's Project and Adiramapattinam Fisher-Women's Project". Documenation ILO Project on Successful Grass-Roots Initiatives. (Unpublished).

11. *The struggle towards self-reliance of organised, resettled women in the Phillippines* (Geneva, ILO, 1982, mimeographed World Employment Programme research working paper; restricted).

12. Draft Report on Proceedings of Consultation of National Consultants under the ILO Project, Employment Opportunities for Rural Women through Organization, Kathmandu, Nepal, 27–30 June 1983.

13. Dharam Ghai and Anisur Rahman: "The Small Farmers' Groups in Nepal" – A Pilot Programme Development: Seeds of Change, 1981 (ILO publication).

14. Report of IFPAAW Malaysia Workshop, 1983.

15. Elizabeth Croll: Women in Rural Development, The People's Republic of China, I.L.O., 1979.

16. M. Mies: Forthcoming Publication, 1983.

17. Miranda Davies: "Women in Struggle, An Overview" (TWQ 5(4) October 1983 p. 874–914).

18. P. Oakley and D. Marsden: *Approaches to participation in rural development*, preliminary paper for Inter-agency Panel on People's Participation, March 1983.

19. Oakley and Marsden, *op. cit.*

20. Anisur Rahman: Internal ILO paper on, "The ILO in Promoting People's Participation in Rural Development".

Tractors Against Women

GOVIND KELKAR

The theoretical framework of this paper takes into account the relationship between women's work in subsistence agriculture and the rural development strategies, both at the local and national levels[1]. In these strategies women are perceived as basically peripheral to agricultural and rural development programmes, and their multiple roles and work in the rural economy are generally ignored in the androcentric environment of planning and policy making.

The Green Revolution (supported by research interest in agriculture in Western countries with its package of high yielding varieties (HYV) machinery, a balanced dose of fertilizers and pesticides and carefully controlled irrigation) was introduced in Northern India in the 1960's. The direct results of the Green Revolution in the region have been sharply increased concentration of land ownership, massive dispossession of small holders, proliferation of landless workers and rural unemployment[2]. While there has been some mention in official documents of the slippage towards marginalization and pauperization in the development process, the dimensions of the Green Revolution inequality between women and men are still only partially beginning to be understood either by development planners, administrators or academics.

Less Employment, Less Wages

Green Revolution has brought in its wake the all-India trend of pauperization and

marginalization and the increased inequality between the sexes. On the one hand it denies women the employment opportunities otherwise available to them, and on the other hand stereotypes all those jobs which pay less and require less skill, forcing women to take up jobs which come to be regarded as purely female tasks. Whereas in the year 1901 and 1961 the proportion of women among cultivators had been between 289 to 498 per 1000 men; the ratio fell sharply between 1961 and 1971 to a figure of 135 women to 1000 men. Similarly, up to 1961 the female proportion among agricultural labourers had been relatively stable, but during 1961 and 1971 it dropped from 819 women per 1000 men to 498 women to 1000 men. Punjab, the heartland of the Green Revolution has the lowest rate of women's participation in the labour force i.e. 1.18 per cent[3]. The new agrarian technology in terms of pumpsets, tractors, threshers, etc. has caused a reduction of labour force to about one fifth of that involved in the traditional farming[4]. Haryana, has a 2.41 per cent over-all participation rate of women[5]. The sharp fall in the demand for female labour is also noticed in other high productivity areas of Tamil Nadu and Andhra Pradesh. In Thamjavur District of Tamil Nadu the number of male agricultural workers increased from 583.3 thousands in 1961 to 699.8 thousands in 1971, while the number of female agricultural labourers came down to 175.6 thousands from 321.2 thousands[6]. The removal of women from their means of production and from their productive functions by the introduction of new technologies in West Godovari district of

Kelkar, Govind. *Development: Seeds of Change* gave permission to reproduce this article, which appeared in its Volume 3, 1985 article on pages 18–21.

Andhra Pradesh has been pointed out by Maria Mies[7].

Increasing pauperization of the rural population is also evident from the fact that in Western Uttar Pradesh between the years 1961 and 1971 (a period of concentrated mechanization and technological penetration in agriculture), there was an increase of 138.9 per cent in the number of agricultural labourers[8]. In this trend of pauperization, women are exploited the most by labour-displacing technology for they are the foremost section to be ousted from economically productive activity. This is evident by the fact that in Uttar Pradesh per centage of rural female workers declined from 59.20 in 1961 to 9.54 in 1971[9]. This reflects that the competing power of the poor in general and women in particular is brought to a minimum, making them easier to control.

Women's withdrawal from the work force, however, is not an indicator of growing prosperity wherein women of the more affluent classes do not have to work in the fields. The kind of economic development that has taken place in this area does not alter the fact that for the majority of the households, agriculture is mainly a subsistence activity where most or all of the output is consumed by the family which produce it, either directly or indirectly by selling the produce to meet the minimum needs of the family and to repay consumption loans. Women generally share the heavy burden of the work in transplanting, weeding, threshing, carrying the produce home and processing of food grains[10].

The inequality between the sexes is even more evident in the wage-disparity between female and male wage earners. In India women are generally paid 40 to 60 per cent of the male wages and are given the more labour intensive tasks like weeding, transplanting and harvesting. It may be pointed out that in Hamirpur Ruru and the other villages of our study in Etawah District, women in agriculture generally get one third less than men agricultural workers. An all India disparity between the daily earnings of man and women belonging to labour house-holds in agricultural occupations has increased by approximately 50 per cent between 1964–1965 and 1974–1975. Although the wages in absolute amount are high in Uttar Pradesh, Haryana and Punjab, yet it is important to note that the rate of disparity between the wages of women and men nearly doubled in Uttar Pradesh and tripled in the case of Punjab and Haryana between 1965 and 1975[11].

It was evident in Hamirpur Ruru that women (and children) carry out the backbreaking task of transplanting paddy, while men concentrate mostly on the job of picking seedlings, which is considered skillful and demanding application of physical strength. Men receive more wages and their jobs are graded higher. Women toil as they do on the farm, alone with their responsibility of cooking for the family and attending the children. Women's jobs are absolutely essential to the existence of the family and yet tend to be very tedious and time consuming, do not provide them with much autonomy concerning decisions in the home or even with regard to the disposition of their earnings.

It must be noted that the grading of these tasks is neither based on volumes in terms of the tedium nor on the number of hours on their performance, nor valued in productive terms. The logic of superior and better paid work for men derives from the fact that they are assumed to be household heads and thus ultimately responsible for the family. Women's work is ignored as unpaid household work and their contribution to production is regarded as secondary, or supplementary to men's contribution. Therefore, more money is spent on a male child in terms of food, clothes and schooling, as he is seen as a potential earner for his natal family. This breeds in the males superior attitudes as they come to regard themselves as "the representatives of a new enlightenment". Women, therefore, tend to accept being treated as inferior, both at home and in the labour market[12]. This social reproduction of values, which devalues women's work, gets perpetuated and women get socialized into accepting their dependency on men.

Deteriorating Domestic Position

The neglect of women's work in reproduction and care of the labour force means that their contribution to production is consistently undervalued. Savings on the non-wage labour in domestic production and the unpaid labour of family helpers accelerates the accumulation of capital for investment in the development which aims at increasing production for an external market and not satisfaction of needs in a local economy[13]. This has led to erosion of the traditional ways in which agricultural and non-agricultural economic activities were organized. Traditional crafts, in the face of competition from urban industry, have been unable to survive. Earlier, women of the artisan castes had specialized roles to play in contributing equally towards the production of items of the village industry. Likewise, in traditional organization of agricultural activity, women participated in every activity except plowing. Women of artisan and peasant families played important roles in decision-making. With the cultivation of cash crops for the market women have no decision-making power regarding the requirement of grain at home, thereby losing their authority at home.

In this process, women lose their subsistence base, forcing them and their children to depend on the wages of their husbands, perpetuating in this way the dependency relations of women on their men.

In the traditional division of labour in the villages studies, women and men of the landowning caste Hindus and of rich Muslim households do not work in the fields. There is also a tendency of the smaller cultivators of various castes and communities to emulate the former, which creates a contradiction between theory (ideal) and practice (actual way of life)[14]. At first, during the course of the interviews, both women and man tended to deny that the women worked in the fields, but gradually they admitted it. Women carry out a major part of agricultural activity, especially at the time of transplanting paddy, weeding, threshing, harvesting and processing of food grains. Moreover, in the given structure of development in the country, more male labour is made available as wage labour both in urban and rural areas, throwing almost the entire responsibility of agricultural work on women. However, women's work is perceived as non-specialized by both men and women and this contributed to the formulation of a part of the 'house worker ideology' that views women's productive work as an extension of household work.

Thus in the stratified society in India, it is the landowning class of caste Hindus who define the dominant values. In the traditional society, caste Hindus did not allow their women to work in the fields or do other manual work outside the house. That the majority of women cling to their household role that 'women are supposed to work inside the house' indicates two trends, *First,* women have internalized the oppressive norms of their domestication and seclusion and uphold the inequality of their sex roles, justifying it as natural and sanctioned by religion and social norms. The poor women are inclined to share the prestige values of class and caste groups who do not allow their women to work outside the house. Therefore, the contradiction between theory (the diverse activities of women in agriculture and outside the sphere of the household) should be interpreted as class-related phenomena where only the life styles and social values of powerful castes matter. *Second,* there is a mystification caused in the process of the Green Revolution by the assumption that as women cannot work outside the house, so they cannot handle technology. In other words, the new agrarian technology has used the feudal practices of domestication and seclusion of women for increasing capitalist relations of production in the countryside.

Production is Masculine

The greatest importance in various agricultural and non-agricultural activities is given to the core productive activity, over which women have no control. Ploughing and operating the potter's wheel, for instance, are taboo for women. Women are prohibited from touching the grip of the plough, which is regarded as representative of the phallic symbol signifying fertility and creation. Pollution of this symbol by the touch of a woman would portend the wrath of the gods resulting in natural calamities. It is only in periods of drought that women plow the fields, totally in the nude at midnight, calling (symbolically) to the right landowners to bless their fields with water. Control of men over this vital productive tool and over the critical activity of ploughing in agriculture is in this way perpetuated. We find this to hold true in the case of artisans also. For instance, among potters, the women manage the collection, watering and beating of clay, which is both strenuous and tiring. Women would not, however, touch the potter's wheel, as it represents the phallic symbol. One finds a similar pattern in the case of other artisan groups. In grain-roasting, the activity of putting corn and other grains for roasting in the *Bhad* (earthen multi-mouthed oven), and in carpentry the operation of the *Aara* (saw) are socially defined male jobs. The attempts at keeping women out of the core productive activity results in the greater control of men in the social, political and economic spheres and in a total disregard for women's work and their role in social production

The second major activity for the preparation of land is irrigation. In earlier days, when fields had no direct access to water and water had to be collected in little ditches from where it would be thrown out via a bucket system (*lehendi*), women were very active in irrigating the fields. However, now the better-off landowners have acquired diesel pumpsets and manual labour is not required for this activity. Where the traditional system of irrigation still persists, women are active. Women, however, have no access to modern irrigation techniques. Most of the women, save those belonging to the landowning Brahmin and Thakur caste groups, help in weeding. This activity is not considered important by the men or the women and is given no more significance than house work. Weeding is mostly done in the afternoon after women finish most of their work for the day except cooking for the evening.

Participation of women in harvesting varies with the crop. It is intensive at the time of paddy harvest and less intensive at the time of wheat. However, women who work as wage labourers are equally active at the harvesting of wheat. Processing grain both for the family's consumption and for the market is a major activity which is carried out by women. They also use insecticides and pesticides to preserve grain and pack it in gunny/jute bags for the market. Women make large earthen containers (grain silos) reaching up to a height of ten feet, made damp proof by several layers of cloth and clay, for the storage and preservation of grain for home consumption. The task of cleaning, drying and storing of grain is performed entirely by women.

Like the core productive activities which are controlled by men, marketing too remains almost entirely the men's domain. In our study of the village Hamerpur Huru in Etawah, we interviewed women from 58 households. Out of the 58 households, interviewed only in 11 families women participate in decision-making and exercise some kind of control in marketing. Most of the women in these 11 families negotiate with the grain dealers at home. With the exception of two women, the remaining nine women in this category are either widows or own land in their names or otherwise provide for the family. Some of the women sell grain to the local dealers without their husband's knowledge, for they find it impossible to manage with the amount their husbands give them. These women also confessed that whenever their husbands find out about these grain transactions, they are beaten up. In almost all the cases, money is kept with the women, but they have no control over it. The women wage-workers, however, have considerable power and authority in their homes.

Among the major household activities performed by women are grinding of flour (in the early hours of the morning with each women grinding 5 to 10 kgs. of flour daily), pounding of rice and processing of lentil, sweeping and cleaning of house and utensils, plastering of walls and floor with mud and dung, feeding and taking care of the children, milking and providing fodder and cleaning up of the cattle, processing of milk and its produce, provision of fuel, making cow dung cakes, cooking, carrying of meals to the fields.

The household is regarded entirely as women's area of work and however active a woman may be economically, she is expected to do all of it, all by herself and with her children. In two or three such cases, women are active selling cloth, teaching in a school and labouring in the fields, in addition to their entire burden of housework. They find their husbands unreasonable, demanding and not extending any help at all. Men with full adult status do not care for children, especially for infants[15]. Women care entirely for infants and children and when they receive help, it is from children or old people.

Re-Feminize Technology

Our study, as well as many other village studies have demonstrated that marginality and low wages are prevalent among rural women throughout the region of the Green Revolution in India. Most of the manual and non-technological work is done by women, while men operate the new agricultural machines and control the inputs as well as the produce. Women are not recognized for their productive role in the economy. Their reproductive role is considered a natural one and taken for granted. Both men and women are socialized in a manner which prescribes public and economic sphere as the male sphere and regards the domestic as the non-productive, non-economic female sphere. The technological development has maintained and perpetuated this distinction through the process of social reproduction, i.e. reproduction of the conditions sustaining a social system. For the women in subsistence agriculture it implies the reproduction of exploitative relations of production, gender related differentiation in access to the new agrarian technology, the relationships of domination and subordination between the sexes and women's low position in the family and society.

The politics of agrarian technology often turns out to reinforce the androcentric development status quo, and the question remains, how do we check the process of underdevelopment of women? How do we analyze and respond to many conflicts between the potential value of technology and its actual effects on women in and subsistence agriculture? The ideology of planning encourages an image of agricultural women in which the technological and scientific solutions of the problems of development are constantly generated by an expert group of planners and policy-makers but are not accepted by the 'backward' peasant women. It is assumed that the reasons of acceptability and non-acceptability of development programs are to be found in the ignorance and conservatism of the rural women.

Indeed, the most realistic assumption on

which to base planning for development is that all women pursue a livelihood and their decisions about the rural development programmes are rational and call for immediate action of building up a participatory development system wherein women and man fully participate in the decision making process. The task of agrarian technology and the rural development programme is to integrate women within the mainstream of economic activity and not to segregate them into a mass, perpetually dependent on the benevolence of their male masters. There is urgent need to recognize women as the technology makers and as technology users, as they have always been, and to provide training opportunities and assistance that will enable them to handle and make use of modern technology. However, the strategy should not be to further the process of atomization, i.e. isolating these women from others through the very limited income-generating activities like breeding of silkworms, Bidi-rolling, masala-grinding etc. within the household. The problem of rural women is to be seen as a problem of mobilizing women through their organized efforts to understand their present situation in order to solve the problems of the past and to acquire ability to participate in decision-making and thus halt unequal distribution of economic power and technology between women and men. Our technological strategies have to be geared to provide collectivization of scientific knowledge and judicious distribution of development benefits among powerless, dependent and dispossessed groups of women and men.

ENDNOTES

1. This paper is based on my study: The Impact of Green Revolution and Women's Work Participation and Sex Roles (Prepared for ILO, Geneva, 1981.).

2. Frankel, Francine R. *India's Green Revolution, Economic Gains and Political Costs,* New Jersey Princeton University Press, 1971: Dasgupta, B. *The New Agrarian Technology and India,* Macmillan, 1980.

3. Based on the 1971 Census, Statewide Participation rates are given in Kumaresh Chakravarty and G.C. Tiwari "Regional Variation in Women's Employment: A Case Study of Five Villages in Three Indian States", ICSSR, 1979.

4. Billings, M. and Singh Arjan, "Mechanization and the Wheat Revolution: Effect on Female Labour in Punjab: *Economic and Political Weekly,* Dec. 1970, pp 169–192.

5. Charkavarti and Tiwari: "Regional Variation in Women's Employment", *op. cit.*

6. *Ibid.*

7. Mies "Capitalist Development and Subsistence Reproduction, Rural Women in India", *Bulletin of Concerned Asian Scholars,* Vol. 12, No. 1, 1980.

8. R. Nayyar "Wages, Employment and Standard of Living of Agricultural Labourers in Uttar Pradesh", in *Poverty and Landlessness in Rural Asia,* ILO Geneva, 1977, p. 78. The corresponding rise in agricultural labourers in eastern and central Uttar Pradesh was only 45% and 75% respectively. Population rise in Western, Eastern and Central Uttar Pradesh were 22.3%, 20.6%, and 16.9%.

9. *Towards Equality, Report of the Committee on the Status of Women in India,* Government of India, 1974, p. 156.

10. Ahmad, Iftikar "Technological Change and the Conditions of Rural Women" (Working Paper, ILO, Geneva, 1978) Ester Boserup and Christine Liljencrantz, *Integration of Women in Development, Why, When, How?* UNDP, 1975, Bhaduri, A. Technological Change and Rural Women: A conceptual Analysis, (Working Paper, ILO, Geneva, 1979).

11. *Rural Labour Enquiry,* Government of India, Ministry of Labour 1974–1975, p. 102–103.

12. Chinnery Hesse M. "Women and Decision Making ... *"The Traditional Division of Work, Between the Sexes" A Source of Inequality.* International Institute of Labour Studies, Research Series, 21, Geneva, 1976.

13. Mies, Maria. *The Lace Makers of Narspur,* Zod Press, 1982; also Loutfi Martha, *Rural Women, Unequal Partners in Development,* ILO, Geneva, 1980.

14. Mies, Maria in her *Indian Women and Patriarchy,* New Delhi, Concept, 1980 argues that in the case of Caste Hindus economic necessity forces women to work outside the house to secure family's subsistence which they consider as deviation. These women may deviate widely from the accepted social norms in practice but they never attack the norms directly.

15. N. Chodorow: "Mothering, Male Dominance and Capitalism", in Z. Eisenstein (ed.) *Capitalist Patriarchy and the Case for Socialist Feminism,* Monthly Review Press, 1979, p. 87, argues "That women perform primary parenting functions, then, is a universal organizational feature of the family and the social organization of gender".

State Policy on Women's Education in the Third World: Perspectives from Comparative Research

GAIL P. KELLY

In Third World countries of Africa, Asia and Latin America women's enrollment in schools lags behind that of men[1]... While there are major gaps in enrollment statistics (many countries simply leave unrecorded the number of females in school), there is little question that, in countries where education is yet to be universal, fewer girls go to school than boys; with few exceptions, where primary school is universal, girls remain in schools for a shorter time than boys; girls rarely receive the same education as their male counterparts; and usually enter fields of study, when and if they go on to higher education, that are predominantly female.[2]

Not surprisingly, the societal outcomes of education for women differ from males' in terms of income, occupation, and status.[3] The under-education of women is an established fact; so also is the fact that few governments, as Isabelle Deble found in her study of female educational wastage worldwide, are concerned about women's education. Fewer governments still have policies that focus on enhancing directly women's educational provision despite efforts of the United Nations in the International Decade for Women that has just ended.[4]

My intent in this paper is not to recount the deficiencies of state policy toward women's education in the Third World; rather, it is to argue as follows. First, governments ought to be concerned about educating women – women's under-edu-

Kelly, Gail P. The author and Carfax Publishing Company granted permission to reprint her article. It appeared in *Contemporary Education*, 23(1), 1987, pp. 95–102.

cation is not only bad for women, it is bad for Third World countries for a number of reasons which are detailed in this paper. Second, specific policies are needed to deal with women's under-education. Currently many national governments maintain that policies designed to extend education to women are unnecessary – they believe that women's under-education relative to men will be remedied in the same way that under-education caused by poverty, urban/rural residence, and ethnicity has been addressed. Research on educational access for women indicates, as I will show, that such assumptions are unwarranted. Women's access to education depends on strategies quite different in many instances from those which have been successful with male populations. Finally, I will suggest specific policies that are implied by the fragmentary scholarship to date on how women's under-education might best be rectified.

Why Be Concerned About Women's Education?

Would that it were possible to convince governments that women ought to be educated because it is their right to be educated, just as it is a man's right or because education will make women's lives better. Most governments hardly pay attention to such arguments in a time of fiscal exigency. Today, many governments as well as international agencies feel they need to increase educational efficiency and deal less with social justice issues than with issues of productivity and what is considered the most effective use of resources.[5] Many governments have begun to think of women's education as less important than males' and have justified their stance by pointing to research showing that women's educational outcomes are not the same as men's. Women who are educated do not participate in the work-force at the same rate as do similarly educated men and the rates of return to investment in education (as measured by life-long earnings, presumed a measure of productivity) seem to be lower for women than for men.[6]

While this research literature cannot be refuted, it is not a basis for denying women education. Women's education may not have the same outcomes as men's because of discriminatory practices in the work-force which set lower wages for women and serve to bar women from occupations commensurate with their education.[7] While research tells us that the outcomes of women's education are not the same as men's, it also shows us that women's education does have something to do with economic development. Soviet modernization, for example, was made possible by the unprecedented rise in women's educational levels and their entry in large numbers into the paid workforce.[8] Studies of women's education in the Third World today, fragmentary though they may be, suggest that education enhances women's workforce participation: women who are educated enter and remain in the workforce in greater numbers than their less educated sisters.[9]

Other studies have shown that lack of a policy aimed at educating women has meant that women, productive in traditional economies as farmers and petty traders, have become less productive as modernization proceeds. They are driven from the workforce as the agricultural sector of the economy mechanizes and trade becomes further concentrated.[10] Lack of education has robbed women of what Elsa Schmink calls 'access to tools'. Withdrawal from productive labour has been one real result of women's lack of education as poli-

cies aimed at industrialization have displaced women's labour without providing them alternative paths to employment and productive labour. Such evidence implies that, even if women's educational outcomes are not the same as men's, lack of a policy that seeks to educate women undermines government rationales for providing education on economic grounds to anyone. It may be, in short, disastrous not to educate women.

There are reasons other than economic ones why governments ought to be concerned about women's education. Women's education has some relation to fertility and population control, although this relation is not consistent across nations.[11] Women's education, however, may have a stronger relation to population control than men's education: countries with higher levels of women's education tend to have lower birth rates than countries with lower levels of women's education. Research also suggests that women's education relates to depressed infant mortality rates, to child nutrition and to children's success in schools.[12] Women's education in many instances, may have a stronger relation to children's educational futures than does men's.

Research on women's education, fertility, childhood nutrition, children's educational achievement, and the like is far from comprehensive. However, the research that is available does suggest that governments ought to be concerned about women's education if only because women's education relates to other policy objectives. Government goals – among which are development, population control and childhood nutrition – are likely to remain elusive if women are not schooled.

Why Specific Policies Are Needed To Promote Women's Education

In order for women to become educated at a level and rate equal to men's, special policies are needed. The very real expansion of education world-wide in the 1960s and 1970s has not brought equality in education. In 1980 world-wide 79.5% of all males 6 to 11 years of age went to primary school as against 68.1% of females in that age group; 54.8% of all males as against 46.4% of all females 12 to 17 years old attended secondary school; while 20.2% of all 18 to 23 year old men and 15.2% of all 18 to 23 year old women attended some kind of higher education.

There are major regional differences in educational enrollment ratios. In Africa 69% of 6 to 11 year old boys versus 56.5% of girls of that age went to primary school; in Asia 77.4% of boys of that cohort versus 59.3% of girls went to school. In Latin America, North America, and Western Europe, where primary education is compulsory and universal, there are few differences in male and female enrollments on the primary level. On the secondary level, educational disparities deepen: in Africa 44.1% of all males and 30% of all females aged 12 to 17 attend school; in Asia, 43% of the males and 29.7% of the females' age cohort attend secondary school. In Latin America, where close to equality has been achieved in primary school enrollments, on the secondary level 65.4% of all 12 to 17 year old males compared with 62.7% of all females of that age group go to school. In higher education the disparities between males and females widen even more.[13]

The disparities that persist between male and female enrollments world-wide can be bridged by state policies that focus on promoting women's education. The existence of disparities is not a function of 'culture,' religion or level of a nation's development; rather disparities can be and have been changed as a result of government policy. The disparities have their origins in class, ethnic and regionally based inequalities as well as inequalities that are specifically related to gender. Government policies in the past that have sought to bring males into school have helped to bring girls into the school system as well, but not at the rate they have brought males.

Since 1960 the disparities between male and female enrollments have lessened somewhat.[14] However, providing full educational parity for women is unlikely to be achieved unless governments address those factors that specifically keep women from going to and staying in school. Those factors, which I will briefly discuss below, relate to (1) the nature of schooling provided for women, (2) the sex-role division of labour in the family and in production, and (3) wage structures and the structure of the job market. The way these factors affect women's education seem to vary considerably from country to country – certainly more research is needed to understand these factors in specific national settings. Despite the uneven nature of knowledge, current research suggests that setting state policy to provide women with education has much to do with identifying these factors and addressing them to ensure that women go to school.

Providing Schools for Girls

It goes without saying that the greatest single predictor of whether girls or boys go to school or not is whether schools are made available and accessible. Opening schools not surprisingly opens up educational opportunity regardless of gender, and the decision whether to open a school or not is a question of state policy. When governments provide free education in abundant supply, girls tend to go to school more than when schools are scarce and charge fees.[15] The clearest example of this is in Tunisia, where the government consciously attempted to provide universal education and made equal educational opportunity for both sexes a government priority. Once schools were made available, girls went to them.[16]

Just opening schools does not solve the problem of female under-enrollment entirely, since women's school attendance is based also on what types of schools are made available to women. Many Muslim societies, for example, practice sex segregation and women's access to schools depends in large part on the provision of single-sex schools. In Pakistan, for example, the government when faced with decisions about whether to build a school for boys versus a school for girls, has tended to build schools for boys.[17] Coeducation is not necessarily the solution to women's under-education. In some countries, the provision of single-sex schools – in Kuwait, for example – has not meant that women's educational opportunity is constrained.[18] The issue, it seems, is that of providing the kind of education that is acceptable to parents and to girls in sufficient amounts to accommodate all girls.

Girls' educational enrollments depend, more than those of boys, not only on decisions about opening schools and coeducation versus sex segregation in school provision; they also seem to depend on the quality and content of the education offered to girls. Jones's study of Tunisia suggests that girls' educational enrollments slackened when girls were provided with schools inferior in quality to those offered to boys.[19] In addition, parental demand for girls' education depended on whether the education the government provided for girls articulated with the needs of the workforce; girls' attendance was related to whether high-quality vocational education was made available to them.

Provision for girls' education more than that for boys relates also to where schools are placed. Distance from school, for example, tends to affect girls' attendance more than it does boys' – parents are less likely to send their daughters to school if schooling entails daily travel where girls are vulnerable to harassment. The location of schools, as Naik's action-research project in Pune, India, has shown, becomes a real issue affecting female access to schooling.[20]

Our knowledge of school factors that specifically affect women's school attendance is less than complete. However, the research that we currently have available suggests that educational policy-makers need to be concerned about what kind of schools are made available to girls and what factors make them accessible. Research also suggests that the nature of what schools teach, how they teach, and sex role socialization implicit in texts and curricular materials affect the question of whether girls go to school and how long they remain in school.[21] This research, however fragmentary it currently is, points to the fact that equalizing educational opportunity for women is a question of specific sets of policies that will address the full gamut of issues relating to factors that bring women into the school system and sustain them there, in view of the reasons why parents decide to send their daughters to school in the first place and the very real issues relating to girls' personal safety.

Sex-Role Divisions of Labour and Access to Schools

Sex-role division of labour in the family and in production have much to do with whether women go to school. Government policy makers, in attempting to provide education for women, need to understand how the sex-role division of labour in the household and in the family economy affects not only whether women can go to school, but also what kind of school provision is most appropriate for them.

In many Third World countries, girls constitute an important labour force both in the family and in production. Studies from India and from several African nations show us that girls are 'workers' – in the household they draw water, help to prepare food, tend younger children; in the workforce they help with weeding and hoeing, with handicrafts production and with trade.[22] Girls in parts of Tanzania, Burkina Faso, Ghana, and India, for example, engage in these activities from an early age

– sometimes as young as six. Their brothers do not participate in household economies until after puberty. In these countries, just opening a school solves in large part the problem of male access to schooling; it does not solve the problem of female access. To send a girl to school constitutes a real economic sacrifice, especially if school time competes with girls' time spend in generating income.

While, for the most part, sex-role divisions of labour in the household and in production in the Third World tend to militate against female education, in a few places this is not the case. In Northeast Brazil and parts of Mexico, men tend to be productive at an earlier age than women.[23] In these regions, women's school enrollments outstrip males' at the primary level, since household tasks can be more readily combined with the school day than work in trade or farming can be. The issue of the 'working' girl is not as strong in nations with stringent child labour laws. However, the research that we have available suggests that, given sex-role divisions of labour, school provision needs to take a different pattern from what is currently the case. In most countries schools are set up with the presumption that a child's only job is to go to school. Such a presumption tends to keep girls out of school.

The sex-role division of labour in the family and in production not only means that policy-makers need to be concerned about whether girls can combine school and work, it also means that policy-makers need to address conditions enabling girls' entry into school. McSweeney & Freedman's time-budget studies conducted in Burkina Faso suggest that girls and women have no time to go to school, regardless of how school time is scheduled. Water purification, water hauling, wood gathering and food preparation absorbed all girls' and women's waking time.[24] Boys and men, however, given their roles as farmers or wage labourers, had spare time so that they

could take advantage of literacy classes and schools. Getting women to school becomes, in this case, not only a question of opening schools, or making classes accessible and available to women: it is also a question of how women's work in the household can be alleviated. Digging wells, in this instance, is as important for promoting female school attendance as opening a school.

While there is much variance in sex-role divisions of labour in the family and in production, and in how they affect women's schooling, research shows us that providing women's access to education involves more than simply opening schools – which has often worked well with male populations. It involves special policies that deal with making schools accessible, given women's work day, and with alleviating women's work burdens in the household and in family economies so that women have time to go to school both as children and as adults.

Income and Job Opportunities

While women's access to education is affected greatly by the nature of educational provision for women and by the sex-role division of labour in the family and in production, it is also affected by the opportunities for women to obtain gainful employment once they have been schooled that they would not have had if they had remained uneducated. McSweeney & Freedman's study of women in Upper Volta showed, for example, that women, once their time was freed from the drudgery of household tasks by well-digging and other small scale technologies, did not attend literacy classes or send their daughters to school because they saw education as unrelated to income generation.[25]

The decision to go to school is often an economic one, based on the question whether girls can find jobs once they are educated. When employment is not open to women, girls' education tends to be depressed; when, however, employment opens up, the demand for women's education is much greater on the part of parents as well as of girls. Malaysia is an example of how opportunity structures in the workplace affect women's school enrollments. Malay girls attended schools in greater numbers once the Malay government announced an affirmative action scheme that favoured the employment of Malays, both female and male.[26] In Tunisia, women's enrollments in school leveled off when employment opportunities for women had closed.[27] In short, when remunerative employment is open to women, women go to school. In Chile women stay in school longer than do men precisely because education is a credential they can use on the job market to gain a reasonable wage.[28]

Evidence from industrialized nations such as the U.S.A. and U.S.S.R. clearly indicates that women remained in school longer as a result of government policies that promoted women's employment via affirmative action programs and sought to develop non-discriminatory wages for female labour.[29] All this is to say that developing a policy to promote women's education is a question of addressing discrimination in employment and wages, so that women have incentives to go to school and remain there.

ENDNOTES

1. The strongest statement on this can be found in Isabelle Deble (1980) *The School Education of Girls* (Paris, UNESCO).

2. *Ibid*. See also M. J. Bowman & C. A. Anderson (1982) The participation of women in education in the Third World, in: G. Kelly & C. Elliott (Eds) *Women's Education in the Third World: Comparative Perspectives*, pp. 11–30 (Albany, SUNY Press).

3. See Aisla Thomson (1986) *The Decade for Women: Special Report* (Toronto, Canadian Congress for Learning Opportunities for Women); G. Kelly Factors affecting women's access to education in the Third World: myths and realities, in: Sandra Acker (Ed.) *World Yearbook of Education, 1983–84*, pp. 81–90.

4. Deble, *op. cit.*

5. See Philip Coombs (1985) *The World Education*

Crisis: The View from the Eighties (New York, Oxford University Press) Barbara Rogers (1982) *The Domestication of Women* (London, Tavistock); Nelly Stromquist, *Empowering Women Through Knowledge: Politics and Practices in International Cooperation in Basic Education* (Stanford University, SIDEC, March 24, 1985).

6. See, for example, Rati Ram, (1982) Sex differences in the labour market outcomes of education, in: Kelly & Elliott (Eds) *op. cit.*, p. 203–227; Audrey Smock (1980) *Women's Education in Developing Countries: Opportunities and Outcomes* (New York, Praeger).

7. Smock, *op. cit.*

8. Gail W. Lapidus (1979) *Women in Soviet Society* (Berkeley, University of California Press).

9. Catalina Wainerman (1982) The impact of education on the female labour force in Argentina and Paraguay, in: Kelly & Elliott (Eds) *op. cit.*, pp. 264–82.

10. See Judith van Ellen (May/June 1974), Modernization means more dependency, *The Center Magazine* pp. 60–57; Norma Chinchilla (1977) Industrialization, monopoly capitalism and women's work in Guatemala, *Signs*, 3, pp. 38–56; Glaura Vasques de Miranda (1977) Women's labour force participation in a developing society, *Signs*, 3, pp. 261–74.

11. The classic work here is S. H. Cochrane (1979) *Education and Fertility: What Do We Know?* (Baltimore, Johns Hopkins University Press).

12. Robert LeVine (1982) Influences of women's schooling on maternal behavior in the Third World, in: Kelly & Elliott (Eds) *op. cit.*, pp. 283–310.

13. *UNESCO Statistical Yearbook*, (1983).

14. Susan McCrae Vander Voet, The United Nations decade for women: the search for women's equality in education and employment, in: Aisla Thomson (1986) *op. cit.*, pp. 75–88.

15. Deble, *op. cit.*; M. T. Jones (1982) Educating girls in Tunisia: issues generated by the drive for universal enrollment, in: Kelly & Elliott (Eds) *op. cit.*, pp. 31–50; see also, G.P. Kelly Factors affecting women's access to education in the Third World, *op. cit.*

16. Jones, *op. cit.*

17. Smock, *op. cit.*

18. A. I. Meleis, N. El-Sanabary & D. Beeson, (1979) Women, modernization and education in Kuwait, *Comparative Education Review*, 23, pp. 115–124.

19. Jones, *op. cit.*

20. Chitra Naik (1982) An action research project on universal primary education: the plan and the process, in: Kelly & Elliott (Eds) *op. cit.*, pp. 152–72.

21. J.D. Finn, J. Dulberg & J. Reis (1979) Sex differences in educational attainment a cross-national perspective, *Harvard Educational Review*, 49, pp. 477–503.

22. See Naik, *op. cit.*; M. Mblinyi (1969) *The Education of Girls in Tanzania* (Dar Es Salaam); B.G. McSweeney & M. Freedman (1982) Lack of time as an obstacle to women's education: the case of Upper

Volta, in: Kelly & Elliott (Eds) *op. cit.,* pp. 88–106.

Claire C. Robertson (1984) Formal or non-formal education? Entrepreneurial women in Ghana, *Comparative Education Review*, 28, pp. 639–58.

23. See, for example, D. Plank, Regional and Age Difference in Brazilian Enrollment Rates, paper presented at the Annual Meeting of the Comparative and International Education Society, Atlanta, Georgia, March 1983; P. Goldblatt, Progress in Schooling in Mexican Municipios, paper presented at the Annual Meeting of the Comparative and International Education Society, Atlanta Georgia, March 1983.

24. McSweeney & Freedman, *op. cit.*

25. *Ibid*. A similar point is made by Robertson, *op. cit.*

26. B.C. Wang (1982) Sex and ethnic differences in educational opportunities and labour force participation in six countries, in: Kelly & Elliott (Eds) *op. cit.,* pp. 68-87.

27. Jones, *op.cit.*

28. E. Schiefelbein & J.P. Farrell. (1982) Women, schooling and work in Chile: evidence from a longitudinal study, in: Kelly & Elliott (Eds) *op. cit.*, pp. 228–49.

29. Lapidus, *op. cit.*

About the Authors in Chapter 6

Dr. Zaneb B. El-Bakri is Coordinator of Women and Development Studies and Research Centre at the University of Khartoum. Her 1981 Ph.D. dissertation was titled "The Politics of Local Government Councils in a Sudanese Urban Community," Hull.

E. M. Kameir was in the Department of Sociology of the Faculty of Economics and Science at the University of Khartoum when this article was published.

Dr. Zubeida M. Ahmad is Director of the Rural Employment Policies Board of the International Labour Organization in Geneva.

Govind Kelkar is a Research Associate at the Center for Women's Development in New Delhi, India. Her paper is based on her study, "The Impact of Green Revolution and Women's Work Preparation and Sex Roles (prepared for the International Labor Organization, Geneva, 1981).

Gail P. Kelly is Professor and Chair of the Department of Educational Organization, Administration and Policy in the Graduate School of Education at the University of Buffalo. Her edited volume, *International Handbook of Women's Education* (New York: Greenwood Press), appeared in 1989.

CHAPTER 7

Education and Development

Introduction

Education is a profound agent of change. It prepares a society for fundamental change in social and economic institutions and alternative lifestyles. The positive effect of education on development, including poverty and income distribution, has been well-established in the empirical development literature, quite recently with new evidence by Tilak (1989).

The socioeconomic returns from investment in higher education have been demonstrated by numerous researchers over the years. Among those most prolific on this subject has been Psacharopoulos (1981, 1982, 1985, and 1986). This is not to say that mass education and vocational education do not have a place in overall development strategy, but a case can be made for proportionately greater emphasis on higher education in the developing countries.

On the other hand, Hyneman's (1980) research on investment in Indian education concludes that India's success in building a solid infrastructure of universities and technical institutes has not been without its problems. This success has unfortunately resulted in the creation of a large pool of educated unemployed threatening political stability if unemployment persists for long.

Sir Arthur Lewis (1962) long ago stated that: "Education was not invented in order to enable men to produce more goods and services. The purpose of education is to enable men to understand better the world in which they live, so that they may more fully experience their potential capacities...". In discussing investment strategy in education Lewis would also produce more educated people than can be absorbed as a part of the process of economic development.

Whatever we and leaders in developing countries think about the broader functions of education, current debates in planning educational programs in developing countries are related to the scope and nature of the educational strategies that are suitable for economic development. The gap between the rhetoric of educational reform since the colonial period and policy as well as the role of the elite has been detailed in Lungu (1985). Few understand the complexity of the problem and the importance of the process of interfacing education and the world of work as well as it was presented to a Conference of the Ministers of Education of African States in Lagos, Nigeria by Adebayo Adedeji in 1976 or in his public lecture on the Role of Higher Education in Development at Addis Ababa University in 1981 (Adedeji, 1989).

That strategy that focuses on the role of vocational skills necessary for self-employment has met with limited success in most developing countries. Whether it should have been successful is debatable. As you will read in her article, Jennings-Wray argued that one major reason for this is the lack of planning and a piecemeal approach toward overall educational reforms. Fortunately, few countries, such as India, favor mass literacy campaigns at the neglect of higher education. Although the impact of education on development has shifted from primary to secondary school, university training is becoming of increasing importance.

In the long run, the many contributions of higher education are readily apparent. Ram and Schultz (1979) have found that in India, 1950–1970, investment in education (human capital) produced large increases in life expectancy and little change in fertility, population growth, or productivity. Even today, the returns to higher education in India remains high enough to justify the investment. The rewards of education are positive and the educated do eventually find suitable economic roles. The role of higher education cannot be neglected if India is to maintain her competitiveness in international trade of manufactured goods and commodities.

In implementing various educational programs, regardless of the strategy pursued, developing countries face several barriers. Many countries do not have the financial resources to build schools and train teachers. Countries like Tanzania have failed to successfully manage the school system even as governments remain committed to the cause of universal education. Today a large proportion of children of school-going age are excluded from the educational system. As access to the public schools becomes limited, the upper class maintains its comparative advantage by securing and building well-staffed private schools. The problem of mass illiteracy has continued unresolved through the 1950s into the present decade. Even very small countries such as Nicaragua may be faced with the problem of bilingual and bicultural education (Docherty, 1988). Traditional attitudes, such as son preference, in many developing countries bring about large gaps in the educational attainment of male and female children.

Some of the political problems confronting developing nations around the world along with the rapid growth of higher education were examined over thirty-five years ago by Lipset (1964). It is, of course, debatable whether or not the consequences of almost free admittance to higher education has been as dire as suggested but at the very least youth have been given a role in their society at a higher level than would otherwise have been the case.

The Articles in Chapter 7

Baker's article addresses the problems of rural schools in developing countries. A combination of poverty, traditional negative attitudes, and soft educational bureaucracies inhibit the functioning of the village schools. These factors originate at different levels of the educational institution. Rigid centralization of educational programs at the national level allow for very little, if any, flexibility for adaptation of curriculum and resources suitable to the local level. At the classroom or school level, education is characterized by such problems as lack of materials, poorly trained teachers, and limitations placed on children's educational activities by familial demands for their participation in the production of household goods and services. For example, in many developing countries children perform such time-consuming chores as gathering firewood and taking care of the younger siblings at home.

Kaluba commences by reiterating many of the same concerns about education in developing countries as were detailed in *Baker's* article. He continues by pointing out the socio-demographic consequences of the lack of success in primary and secondary schools in Zambia. Large-scale urbanization and population growth have increased the demand for schools, which has created a huge backlog of over-age children who are awaiting entry. A large proportion of those who manage admission into Grade 1 will not pass the Grade 7 selection examinations. This creates the problem of huge numbers of school dropouts. Numerous private schools have sprung up to profit from this unmet demand for school admissions. A large proportion of them are poorly equipped and are run by unqualified individuals. A group of elite, well-equipped and well-staffed schools have also emerged. Admission to these schools is strictly controlled by school management and only the very rich can afford to send their children to them. As the overall quality of education in Zambia declines over time, the gap between the educational opportunities for children from the poor and the rich increases.

Jennings-Wray discusses in considerable detail the problems facing the agricultural education and work experience programs in schools in Jamaica. Jamaican agricultural education programs were the product of a political ideology espoused by the government and envisioned as a part of an overall strategy to increase food production and export. These programs, however, did not enjoy popular support, neither students nor their parents seeing agriculture as a subject to be studied for a secure job in the future. The government's unwillingness to address the socioeconomic aspirations and educational goals of the people, lack of effective communication, and mismanagement led to wastage and failure of the program. New and innovative programs may succeed only when they are linked to necessary socioeconomic reforms.

In conclusion, it should be noted that the educational transition time of three or four decades, that is, the time required for developing nations to catch up with the developed nations suggested by *Patel* (1965), has gone by with considerable educational distance remaining – as well as economic distance.

REFERENCES

Adedeji, Adebayo, *Towards a Dynamic African Economy: Selected Speeches and Lectures, 1975–1986*, compiled and arranged by Jeggan C. Sanghor (London and Totowa, NJ: F. Case), 1989.

Docherty, F.J., "Educational Provision for Ethnic Minority Groups in Nicaragua," *Comparative Education*, 24(2), 1988, pp. 193–201.

Hyneman, Stephen P., "Investment in Indian Education," *World Development*, 8(2), 1980, pp. 145–163.

Lewis, W. Arthur, "Education and Economic Development," *International Social Science Journal*, 14(4), 1962, pp. 685–699.

Lipset, Seymour Martin, "University Students and Politics in Underdeveloped Countries," *Minerva*, 3(1), Autumn 1964, pp. 15–56.

Lungu, Gatian F., "Elites, Incrementalism and Educational Policy-Making in Post-Independence Zambia," *Comparative Education*, 21(3), 1985, pp. 287–296.

Patel, Surendra J., "Educational Distance Between Nations: Its Origin and Prospects," *The Indian Economic Journal*, 13(1), July–September 1965, pp. 13–28.

Psacharopoulos, George, "Education, Employment and Inequality in LDCs," *World Development*, Vol. 9, 1981, pp. 37–54.

_____, "The Economics of Higher Education in Developing Countries," *Comparative Education Review*, 26(2), June 1982, pp. 139–159.

_____, Jee-Peng Tan and Emmanuel Jimenez, *Financing Education in Developing Countries: An Explanation of Policy Options* (Washington: The World Bank), 1986.

_____ and Maureen Woodhall, *Education for Development: An Analysis of International Choices*, published for the World Bank by Oxford University Press, 1985.

Ram, Rati and Theodore W. Schultz, "Life Span, Health, Savings, and Productivity," *Economic Development and Cultural Change*, Vol. 27, 1979, pp. 399–421.

Tilak, Jandhyala B.G., *Education and Its Relation to Economic Growth, Poverty, and Income Distribution* (Washington: The World Bank), 1989.

Schooling and Disadvantage in Sri Lankan and Other Rural Situations

VICTORIA J. BAKER

When I contemplate the primary school ... the first thing that strikes me is *not* that it is rote learning institution rather than a problem-solving, activity-oriented one. No, the most obvious shortcomings are: (a) the building is falling down and the roof leaks; (b) the teacher is an untrained teacher and in any case has gone to market and his class is unattended; (c) last time a supervisor visited the school on a professional visit was nine and a half months ago; (d) there are three English books among 35 children and no arithmetic books; (e) the teacher does not have a copy of the syllabus for the course... (Method, quoting a West African consultant, 1974: 133–134)

In 1984, as an idealistic teacher and anthropologist, I took up residence in a remote squatter settlement in a little-developed, Dry Zone district of Sri Lanka. There I intended to investigate the potential role of the village school in fostering rural development, while I made my contribution – as a participant observer – by teaching English in the wattle-and-daub schoolhouse.

Among developing countries, Sri Lanka has a long tradition in schooling and a history full of reformatory steps which have ultimately made it the pride of the Third World for the field of education. It has a literacy rate of 86.5%. It has allocated a consistently high percentage of the GNP to educational expenditure. It offers a free education from kindergarten through the university, providing free textbooks for the first ten grades. Its almost 10,000 schools are scattered through all corners of the island, never farther than about two miles

Victoria J. Baker. The Carfax Publishing Company of Oxfordshire, U.K., and the author granted permission to reprint this article. It was published in 1983 in *Comparative Education*, 24(3), pp. 377–388.

for the primary school child. There are progressive teacher training programmes and a Curriculum Development Centre. The ratio of pupils per teacher is only 31.3:1 in primary schools (grades kindergarten upwards) and even more favourable in schools with ten or twelve grades, the figure being 25.9:1 for all schools. The educational attainment figures have improved immensely in the last decade, and the number of children between the ages of 5–14 years attending school is 84% of that age group. A unified, centralised state system of education theoretically offers equal educational opportunities for all. One might surmise that in such a setting the school could be expected to play an especially progressive role in helping develop the community it serves.

Unfortunately, however, the national averages overshadow glaring imbalances between urban and rural education and the immense gap in educational opportunities between the rich and the poor. The schools in disadvantaged areas have very little in common with the prestigious schools. Sri Lanka remains one of the poorest countries in the world, and was so even before the recent ethnic strife played its part in ruining the economy. Viewing the actual reality, the positive aspects of the educational system seem to fade in light of the myriad of problems and constraints inhibiting the effective functioning of the schools. Structural barriers – social, political and economic – hinder the potential of the school to foster rural development in their communities.

••••

This article first presents an overview of the major problems of rural village schools signalled during the field research in Sri

Lanka. The succeeding section then gives the results of an extensive literature research (using the Library of the centre for the Study of Education in Changing Societies, CESO, in The Hague as well as the documentation centres at UNESCO and the International Institute for Educational Planning, IIEP, in Paris), in which empirical studies of schooling in disadvantaged areas were juxtaposed. Seeking a wider validity, I have compared the Sri Lankan findings with those from numerous other developing countries. The final section provides conclusions regarding the gap between theory and praxis. The high expectations with respect to the schools' potential role in development are seen in light of the dire reality present in disadvantaged rural villages.

Problems Facing the Rural Schools in Sri Lanka

On the basis of voluminous data from the three stages of field research in Sri Lanka, it can be stated that there are three broad categories of inhibiting forces for the effective functioning of village schools (i.e. effective functioning within the framework of the Sri Lankan socio-economic system and the Sri Lankan system of formal education): poverty, traditional and/or negative attitudes, and weaknesses in the system. These three categories penetrate every level of the educational network – from the national and ministerial level, through the district and circuit level, to the school level and the individual level. Some areas overlap one another and work together to intensify or frustrate the situation.

Poverty

Poverty is an obvious situation in the rural areas. Its effects are felt from the highest level downward to the poorest subsistence village. There is a shortage of funds for the training of teachers and the payment of salaries to attract capable people; for curriculum development, provision of school buildings, teachers' quarters, furniture and even the most basic equipment; for the writing and printing of textbooks, providing libraries, laboratories, visual aids, equipment for music or sport programmes; and for a host of other desirable elements which depend to a greater and lesser degree on capital. It appears to be inevitably the rural schools that are suffering from the most glaring shortage of funds, as opposed to the urban schools where more ample funds are allocated. Of course this discrepancy can also be placed in the categories of 'negative attitudes' and 'weaknesses in the system,' where checks should be built in to ensure equitable funding.

The district and circuit levels likewise suffer from a perennial shortage of money. A direct example is the small travel allowance which can be provided to the Circuit Education Officers who are to visit all the schools for supervision. The monetary limitations mean that many schools will not be visited for control; even the Annual Returns will not be regularly collected. An unvisited, 'forgotten' school is likely to slump into apathy and stagnation. The study showed that most of the promising village schools received frequent visits from the Department officials.

At the school level the poverty is self-evident: the barest of equipment, a paucity of learning aids, a frequent lack of space and poor building maintenance, including latrines and wells that are unusable. Teachers and principals boarding under primitive circumstances or living in the school office room or in a temporary mud building are commonplace situations. Such sombre surroundings and lack of supplies for creative or innovative activities may lead to lethargy and a minimum performance by principals and teachers, and thus by pupils.

On the individual level poverty also serves as a major constraint. In a poor rural village the children often have to be kept at home to work in the fields or to look after their younger siblings, particularly during certain cultivating seasons (when school attendance registers show a visible drop). Parents may have difficulty in providing their children with exercise books, pens and pencils; and buying uniforms for those beyond primary school can be problematic. Some parents simply cannot afford to keep their children in school after – or even during – the primary level. Another side of poverty is the fact that children may be undernourished, a situation which affects their general health and their performance in school. It is no coincidence that attendance rises on the days that snacks are served at school.

Traditional and/or Negative Attitudes

This broad category of constraints to effective education is likewise felt from the top level down. Attitudes on the national or ministerial level necessarily influence policy-making and the allocation of available funds. Examples of such attitudes might be that investment for equal education in backward rural areas is a losing battle, and not worth the poor prospects of returns even in the long run. The attitude that investment in educational areas relevant to science and technological advancement furthers the interests of national development leaves the schools of deprived areas as the lowest on the priority lists.

Negative attitudes towards the farmers of disadvantaged areas and the necessity for them to have good schooling have effects on the ministerial level as well as on the district and circuit level. An Education Officer or Circuit Education Officer who has the interests of the children's education at heart appears – according to the information gathered in numerous interviews – to be the exception rather than the rule. Key informants gave examples of officers who are more interested in the free firewood, the toddy and locally prepared drinks, the meal and fresh farm produce which may be given to them on their visiting rounds, rather than in supervising the proper functioning of the schools. Accepting such favors from principals or teachers usually means that abuses and shortcomings on the school level will be overlooked. The fact that negative attitudes which maintain and reinforce a cycle of patronage and minor corruption can be perpetuated is of course also due to the countless weaknesses in the school system. But the attitude often prevalent on higher levels, that the poor are unworthy of good quality education and are uninterested in their children's schooling, may help keep village schools in the position of marginal educational institutions.

The same negative attitudes tend to prevail among some teachers and principals on the school level. A number are convinced (and perhaps justly) that they are on a 'punishment transfer' assignment, a kind of exile in their own land, when they are sent to a school in a deprived rural area. They may have the attitude of passing the time in one way or another, often by taking excessive leave and putting forth a minimum of effort in the classroom. Many principals who have served for years in remote areas have a downtrodden perspective and may intend to get as much out of the system as they can with the least investment of work; they alienate themselves from the community in a deficient school.

Individual attitudes in the community can also undermine the quality of education. Examples are: the ease with which parents keep their children at home from school to do work; or do not even enrol them; or allow them to drop out of school after a few grades. Such behavior, however, may often be related to the fact that they are not convinced that a worthwhile education is being offered.

Weaknesses in the System

That there are weaknesses in the educational system could be said to be an understatement. From top to bottom, as numerous interviews revealed, there are structural drawbacks and loopholes which make possible corruption, bribes, back-scratching, favoritism, and a host of smaller weaknesses and abuses which have become so commonplace that one hardly bothers to try to cover them up. It is too often the politicians and not the educationists who are making many of the important decisions. The very nature of the strongly centralized system is fertile ground on which abuses can grow with fewer checks and balances. The 'systems' of appointments, transfer and promotion have become characterized by being 'unsystematic;' and they have become pressure levers and weapons of manipulation.

At the school level the weaknesses in the system are equally prevalent; and it especially the remote schools which lack proper supervision from the next higher level, where many abuses can take place – breaking rules of the system which itself may not be strong enough to provide a sound base for operation. The large amount of leave taken – some recorded, some unrecorded – inhibits continuity in an educational programme. Closing of the school too frequently, disrespect for school property by staff members (e.g. equipment being misused or taken to a principal's or teacher's home), multi-graded teaching for which many teachers are inexperienced and untrained, compounded with the problem of high absenteeism among teachers – are only a few of the constraints which can be listed under weaknesses in the system at school level.

The individuals in the community also play an important role in upholding the system. As interviews with parents made clear, a large percentage of them hope their children will become a teacher or other kind of government employee, an ambition which supports the maintenance of an educational programme not specifically relevant to the needs of rural children. Rather, when well implemented – which is frequently not the case – the present system prepares children for one of the very scarce office jobs or for passage to the university, after which the competition for jobs may be even more fierce.

Comparisons with Other Developing Countries

Sri Lanka is not unique, as writers with many years of experience in the field of education all over the developing world (e.g. Beeby, 1966; Griffiths, 1968; Coombs, 1968, 1985) testify in their generalizations.... A concerted effort was made to glean examples on certain issues from many different countries, particularly with a view to village or district studies in disadvantaged areas. For convenience the problems discussed are divided into the four levels noted in the previous section.

Constraints on the National and Ministerial Level

Most of the micro-scale studies encountered in the literature deal only summarily with this highest, decision-making level. What is apparent in all instances is a lack of sufficient resources despite relatively large proportions of the national budgets being directed toward educational expenditure (see World Bank Appendix Tables, 1986: 46–50, 54).

••••

This problem is endemic in disadvantaged areas. It is often further aggravated by the rapidly increasing population, and by a bias in the allocation of higher proportions of scarce resources to urban areas and more developed districts. A number of pointed cases are given in Carron and Chau's book on regional disparities (1980). In Thailand, for example, it is shown that there is an unequal distribution of resources (both human and financial) between the provinces, and within each province in terms of urban and rural areas (Sudaprasert et al., 1980:243).

Rigid centralization of education to the extent that local adaptations are not permitted is another upper-level constraint frequently cited in the literature. A study of the Philippines notes that approval from the

Central Office of the Ministry stunts creativity in administrators who may feel the need to come up with innovative organizational structures (Guerrero, 1982:80). A later study in the same country again emphasized a "centralized and inflexible system of educational delivery" (APEID, 1986:27). In her report of two village case-studies in Peru, Gianotten (1980:38–39) concludes that in spite of reforms specifically aimed at decentralizing the system and providing an 'authentic' educational model with roots in the culture of the people, the curriculum, books and methods are in fact determined by the Ministry, thus keeping policy planning and implementation in the centres of political power.

••••

Regarding teacher training, many developing countries in the throes of rapid expansion of education have had to make serious concessions in the length and quality. Tanzania is perhaps an extreme example: there 35,000 teachers were produced in three years during the thrust of Universal Primary Education in the mid-1970s (Omari et al., 1983:44). By necessity these teachers were recruited from all sources – from among retired personnel and those with little more than an elementary education themselves. Because training was to cover the teacher's role not only in the class but as a community leader, there was little room in the accelerated training program for learning pedagogical skills for teaching reading, writing and arithmetic.

••••

Another matter is that of rapid transfer of teachers, particularly in remote areas, resulting in an instability of the teaching force. Lyons (1981:124–125) cites this as a problem in the remote district he studied in Nepal. A grass-roots study of four Mexican rural primary schools also indicated rapid teacher-turnover rates and considerable instability in the teaching staff.... The authors (Brooke & Oxenham, 1980:28) note that the high turnover is accompanied by noticeable absenteeism and unpunctuality among the teachers. The most remote of the four schools received the teachers with the least experience, which reflects (according to Brooke & Oxenham, 1980:29), the policy of sending new young teachers to more remote rural schools. An inequitable or unsystematic transfer or assignment policy may very likely foster discontent, and using transfer as a punishment or a reward may well undermine the continuity and quality of the educational programme.

A study by Runawery & Weeks in the remote Enga province of Papua New Guinea stresses the extreme difficulty in attracting and holding teachers. Proposals were discussed for a tax-free inducement allowance for teachers in isolated schools, as many had quit their posts due to the difficult terrain, the high costs of imported food, and fears of aggressive natives (Runawery & Weeks, 1980:13). Ronde (1980:20), who researched the Dawahla tribe in the Sudan, also mentions the reluctance of teachers to go to hardships areas. The result was that hardly any school in his sample had the required number of teachers, and there was a strong tendency for teachers to stay away an additional few weeks at the end of vacation periods.

••••

A recent APEID (Asian Programme for Education Innovation for Development) regional workshop involving Bangladesh, the People's Republic of China, India, Malaysia, Nepal, Pakistan, Philippines and Thailand, listed the low quality of teaching as one of the common problems of educational underdevelopment in rural areas of these countries, because of: (a) low professional competence, inexperience, the absence of incentives and motivation for teachers; and (b) under-qualified and/or unmotivated teachers, and a lack of teacher support services and materials (APEID, 1986:3).

Other national-level policies, as in curriculum development, may additionally created constraints for rural education when local languages or cultures and local adaptations are not allowed for (see e.g. Srivastava 1982). Policies concerning the language in which the lessons are to be taught are important in numerous plural developing countries, although this was not an issue in the Sri Lankan study.

Constraints on the District and Circuit Level

One of the major problems to be found at this level is a lack of experienced, dedicated, or even sufficient numbers of administrative officers and supervisors or inspectors. A remote district in the Sudan and one in Nepal are given detailed attention on this issue in studies made by Lyons.... Considering transport difficulties and the numerous other duties of the Sudanese inspectors, it is little wonder that they could only visit 32 of the 67 schools in the district, making one visit in 1977 rather than two and leaving the remaining schools unvisited (Lyons, 1981:258).

••••

Lyons' case study of a remote Nepalese district provided similar information on supervision. Here inspection is only possible in the dry season, and then the inspector can reach the schools only by pulling himself across a deep gorge using a shaky metal cable and a bamboo basket. Because of time constraints a proportion of the schools are never visited. The inspectors' duties of pedagogical supervision, auditing work, inspection of facilities, fund-raising, administrative work concerning teachers and pupils, etc., must be shirked (Lyons, 1981:146).

••••

Transport problems were also a large constraint for supervisors who had to cover scattered one-classroom schools in Egypt. Although the criteria for judgment were omitted, the national report on these schools (1981) noted that the supervisor for the El Haddadin School has a motor-cycle, enabling him to pay frequent visits to the school, "which has actually led to raising the standard of the pupils" (National Centre for Education Research, Egypt, 1981:275).

••••

A comprehensive study made by Apelis specifically on the role of community school inspectors in the Enga Province of Papua New Guinea provided some interesting material which is very comparable to data from the Sri Lankan study. It was found that some very remote schools did not get a single visit from the inspector in a whole year (Apelis, 1979:16), as travelling was too time-consuming and considered to be a waste in such cases.

••••

The research additionally showed that special favors were given by inspectors to their friends and family members in their province. Apelis notes that politics often interfered with their official duties (1979:32–33). It should be mentioned that this study (1979:31) and also that of Runawery & Weeks (1980:74), concluded that proper inspection and advice are the key to improving the quality of schooling in the Enga province, and that constant transfers are detrimental to educational development. Apelis adds that "the degree of dedication given by teachers who are visited is different from those teachers who have never been visited".

••••

An emphatic denunciation of poor supervision was made in the last chapter of Brooke & Oxenham's study of four Mexican rural villages.... They make a plea to improve the ethics of the whole educational profession, stressing the need for teachers to be supervised and supported (1980:76)....

> The symptoms of disaffection from their jobs and postings are not only common ... they could not appear so blatantly without the condonation of authority. Unpunctuality, absenteeism, curtailing school time, unofficial holidays, dereliction of large parts of the syllabus, idiosyncratic allocations of time across what parts of the syllabus are taught, all

occur without apparent check from the (district, VB) directors of the schools. The directors themselves can permit these delinquencies only because the school authorities ignore them, because other authorities do not make it their business to intervene... (Brooke & Oxenham, 1980:75).

Constraints on the School Level

It would appear that the largest number of constraints is concentrated at the school level, but many of these problems originate at higher levels or are due to structural situations beyond the scope of the educational system.

The most obvious deficiencies are material ones: inadequate buildings, latrines, teachers' quarters, learning materials, books, sports equipment, etc.... There is hardly a case study to be found where material drawbacks are not brought out as a factor inhibiting the educational process. A 1974 statistical research of primary schools and their teachers in West Bengal (Bose *et al.*, 1974) revealed – among voluminous other material – that many schools were in improvised buildings with only one room and with pupils sitting on the floor, ... and that sanitary arrangements did not exist in most primary schools (1974:17). Moreover, teaching materials and books were lacking in most schools, and some did not even have blackboards (1974:18–20). Things had not much changed 11 years later in the Indian village where Rao made her case study. Here the majority of the children also simply squatted on the floor, there were no toilets or facilities for drinking water, and only half the pupils had the necessary books, slates and writing materials (Rao, 1985:182).

••••

School problems relating to teachers form a large category. Throughout the literature it was clear that many teachers and principals are discontent with their post in a disadvantaged area. The situation in a Burmese village school is described by Nash (1970:311).

The school is scheduled to have three teachers. In fact there is only one. There is a teacher shortage at the village level, and it is easy to understand why... For the young graduate from a teacher-training school, life in a poor village is repellent. Being assigned to a village is almost a sentence to isolation, boredom, and frustration for a young graduate. And the salaries of beginning teachers do not compensate for these evils. It takes great devotion and idealism for a rural teacher to stick out his job.

Another problem which was prevalent in Sri Lanka and is often signalled in the literature is the high incidence of teacher or headmaster absenteeism. Of the village school in southern India it is written that the headmaster frequently absents himself from school or comes late, leaving the other teacher in charge of four standards. On these occasions the other teacher must devote the whole day to enforcing discipline with little time left for teaching. She is also under pressure from the headmaster to teach solely what is required in the syllabus, as the latter must submit a monthly report to the authorities on lessons completed (Rao, 1985:187–188). For a rural school in the New Guinea Enga Province, Apelis mentions that some junior staff-members would just take off any time during school hours to attend to their personal business without the headmaster's knowledge (Apelis, 1979:45).

••••

In a lengthy research on the cause of teacher strikes in Colombia, some of the grievances were highlighted. These include: sentiments of futility by the teachers when education is of so little use; the maladaptation of the curriculum; schools lacking materials to the extent that the teacher must "buy the piece of chalk from his/her own pocket;" and the "triple inconsistency of status, functions and expectations". The teachers feel a sharp contrast between their own education and the financial remuneration for their work, placing them in an "ambiguous situation" (Gomez-Buendia & Losada-Lora, 1984:187–188).

The location (accessibility) of the school is an important factor. It is easy to sympathize with teachers who shun extremely isolated posts, when even including such schools in a research project is often problematical. For example, in the West Bengal research already mentioned in this section, out of the chosen sample of 1742 schools 207 could not be visited because they were either located in almost inaccessible regions, or could not be traced at the addresses given, or were cut off because of floods, landslides or political disturbances (Bose *et al.*, 1974:3). Likewise for Tanzania, in a survey of 170 schools across the country carried out by the Ministry's Primary School Sub-Sector Review (1981), it is reported that the original sampling plan proved unworkable and the researchers were forced to "reject remote and distant schools" (cit. in Carr-Hill, 1984:34). Another problem brought out in the Tanzanian study is the difficulty in distributing materials in the remote schools. Additionally, isolation limits many kinds of informal education (e.g. television, newspapers, movies, clubs, etc.) which could otherwise supplement the formal schooling.

Constraints on the Individual Level

Many instances plucked from the literature reveal that there are problems and constraints on the individual level. In India, for example, Srivastava (1982:31) points out the parents are reluctant to deprive the family of many years of labor assistance by sending their children to school. The Kawahla nomads of the Sudan include their children as soon as possible in the division of labor, and this is the primary reason for lack of attendance (Ronde, 1980:25). The same kind of situation holds for Botswana, where the boys are expected to put cattle-herding before school (Allison, 1983:14).

Poverty in remote, deprived areas can

mean that the children suffer from malnutrition (see e.g. National Centre for Education Research, Egypt, 1981:276; Ewalts, 1986:66; APEID, 1986:2) which may put them in a disadvantaged learning position. Frequently parents are unable to buy the required uniforms, exercise books, pencils, etc., thus placing a stigma or handicap on their children. Unfavourable learning conditions at home – from the lack of an appropriate place to study to the necessity of having to spend free time on chores – were also brought out in numerous studies.

A research in Bangladesh which interviewed 143 heads of households and other adult household members in four villages reports that there is a remarkable lack of awareness about the educational system. When asked about their 'views' of the existing system, 61% of the household heads and 77% of the other members remained silent. The researchers conclude that the respondents know little about what is going on in the schools; and many cannot spare their children from work that contributes to the family's livelihood (Qadir & Balaghatullah, 1985:212–213).

In the study of the village school in upper Burma, it is concluded that, in spite of all the parents and pupils desiring education, the school is not in a position to effect progressive steps because the necessary changes in the traditional local attitudes have not yet taken place (Nash, 1970:301, 306). In Zambia Hoppers ran into a similar situation of the school being stymied in its role as a change agent because of the influence of the home on the pupils' behavior, values and outlook on life.... The more sensitive issues, well rooted in tradition, such as treatment and prevention of disease or the use of various rituals, were held on to by the parents in spite of children trying to take new knowledge home. For example, one pupil said, regarding hunting traditions:

> When hunting they sacrifice meat to the spirits. I tell them not to spoil the meat. But they

won't accept when we say certain customs are bad. They say 'you are a small boy, we know more than you, you can't change our customs.' Then we give up (Zambian pupil cited by Hoppers, 1980: 89).

Later in Hoppers' conclusions (1980: 135) he states that the major influences of the pupils' learning – with regard to life- orientations, norms and values – seem to come from the home environment. The school has only a minor impact, which is sometimes complementary and endorsing.

Conclusions

A teacher with 50–80 children in a small bare room, with no equipment but a blackboard, a piece of chalk, and a few miserable dog-eared pieces of paper to go around, and another class within a yard of his, can scarcely be expected to encourage the unfolding of personalities and the emergence of creative minds... While watching teachers at work under these conditions, I have often been filled with admiration that they produce any results at all, however humble, and that some youngsters struggle through this barren wilderness to real education (Beeby, 1966:76).

The above quotation by Beeby, and the one at the beginning of this article cited by Method, both point out that practical constraints and existing problems on various levels greatly impede the processes of teaching and learning, i.e. the effectiveness of schools, in disadvantaged areas. In his writing of 1966 (pp. 48-76), which was recently revived and presented again in a World Bank publication (1986:37–44), Beeby presents the hypothesis that schools pass through evolutionary stages of growth in a primary school system: from the 'dame school' with an untrained staff and narrow subject content; through the rigid and ordered 'stage of formalism', with ill-educated but trained teachers; followed by the 'stage of transition', with better-trained teachers and more degrees of freedom; and

finally the most desirable stage, the stage of meaning, with activity methods, problem-solving and creativity, while individual differences are catered for. Beeby contends that school systems may speed the evolutionary process but cannot 'leapfrog' a stage because of the cumbersome linkage with teacher training (1966:69). He admits that teachers in many emergent countries work in conditions that make the highest stage virtually impossible (1966:77). It is well to take heed of such theses when idealizing education in the open air beneath a tree, or when having too-high expectations of the commitment of supervisors, headmasters and teachers.

The author's study in an under-developed Sri Lankan district, as well as empirical studies from a wide range of other developing countries, showed that innumerable constraints on all levels confront village schools in disadvantaged rural areas.... Many problems are rooted in the political, economic or social structure of the respective countries and as such have no short-term solution (e.g. corruption, financial shortages and culture-entrenched attitudes that may inhibit change). Others can be tackled with incremental improvements and reforms, for example; making the curriculum more flexible; making the transfer and promotion systems for educational personnel more equitable; good training for inspectors along with a feasible program for regular inspection and realistic remuneration; specific training for teachers and principals in remote or disadvantaged areas, together with possible compensation for hardship assignments. The lessons learned in Sri Lanka and elsewhere are that good teachers and headmasters can overcome or compensate for many barriers to effective schooling; but these people are only human beings and not miracle-workers. The problems and constraints facing rural village schools in poor areas should be more realistically assessed and followed by feasible strategies for improvement.

REFERENCES

Allison, C. (1983) *Constraints to UPE: more than a question of supply?* in: EDC Occasional Papers No. 4. (London, Department of Education in Developing Countries, University of London Institute of Education).

APEID (Asian Programme for Education Innovation for Development) (1986) *Relevance of Education to Rural Development.* Regional study group meeting on identification of causes of educational underdevelopment in rural areas and on relevance education to the rural environment, Bangkok, 22 Oct.–8 Nov. 1985 (Bangkok, Unesco Regional Office for Education in Asia and Oceania).

Apelis, E. (1979) *The Role of Community School Inspectors.* ERU Research Report No. 30 (Papua New Guinea, University Educational Research Unit).

Baker, V. J. (1988) *The Blackboard in the Jungle: formal education in disadvantaged rural areas. A Sri Lankan case* (Delft, Eburon).

Beeby, C.E. (1966) *The Quality of Education in Developing Countries* (Cambridge, Mass., Harvard University Press).

Bose, P.K., Bannerjee, P.K. & Mukherjee, S.P. (1974) *Primary Schools and their Teachers in West Bengal* (University of Calcutta, Department of Statistics).

Brooke, N. & Oxenham, J. (1980) *The Quality of Education in Mexican Rural Primary Schools* (Brighton, Institute of Development Studies, University of Sussex), IDS research report, Education report 5.

Carr-Hill, R. (1984) *Primary Education in Tanzania: a review of the research*, Education Division documents, No. 16 (Stockholm, SIDA).

Carron, G. & Chau, T.N. (Eds.) (1980) *Regional Disparities in Educational Development: diagnosis and policies for reduction* (Paris, Unesco – IIEP).

Coombs, P.H. (1968) *The World Education Crisis: a system analysis* (New York, Oxford University Press).

Coombs, P.H. (1985) *The World Crisis in Education: the view from the eighties* (New York, Oxford University Press).

Ewalts, M. (1986) *Lege schoolbanken in Santa Rosa De Cabal: een studie over het lager onderwijs in de koffiezone van Colombia* (Empty school benches in Santa Rosa de Cabal: a study of primary education in the coffee zone of Colombia) (The Hague, CESO).

Gianotten, V. (1980) *Onderwijshervormingen in een boerensamenleving in Peru* (Education reforms in an agrarian community in Peru) Verhandeling nr. 22 (The Hague, CESO).

Gomez-Buendia & Losada-Lora, R. (1984) *Organización y Conflicto: La Educación Primaria Oficial en Colombia* (Organization and Conflict: Formal Primary Education in Colombia) (Ottawa, International Development Research Centre).

Griffiths, V.L. (1968) *The Problems of Rural Education* (Paris, UNESCO).

Guerrero, J.S. (1982) National Case study – Philippines, in: *Multiple Class Teaching and Education of Disadvantaged Groups* (Bangkok, Unesco Regional Office for Education in Asia and Pacific).

Hoppers, W.H.M.L. (1980) *Education in a Rural Society: primary pupils and school leavers in Mwinilunga, Zambia* (The Hague, CESO).

Lyons, R.F. (1981) *The Organisation of Education in Remote Rural Areas* (Paris, International Institute for Educational Planning).

Method, F.J. (1974) National research and development capabilities in education, in: F.C. Ward (Ed.) *Education and Development Reconsidered* (New York, Praeger).

Nash, M. (1970) Education in a new nation: the village school in upper Burma, in: J. Middleton, (Ed.) *From Child to Adult: studies in anthropology of education* (Garden City, NY, The Natural History Press).

National Centre for Educational Research, Egypt (1981) The one classroom school in Egypt: an evaluative study. Final report. In collaboration with The International Development Research Centre (Canada).

Omari, I.M. et al. (1983) *Universal Primary Education in Tanzania* (Dar es Salaam, University of Dar es Salaam, Department of Education).

Qadir, S.A. & Balaghatullah, M. (1985) The role of education in integrated rural development in Bangladesh, in: D. Berstecher (Ed.) *Education and Rural Development: Issues for Planning and Research* (Paris, Unesco – IIEP).

Rao, S. V. (1985) *Education and Rural Development* (New Dehli, Sage).

Ronde, S. (1980) *De Kawahla en hun onderwijs* (The Kawahla and their education) Paper for CESO lecture series on Educational Problems in Developing Countries (The Hague, CESO).

Runawery, C. & Weeks, S. (1980) *Towards an Enga Education Strategy: education and rural development in Enga*. Working Paper No. 3 (Papua New Guinea, University Educational Research Unit).

Srivastava, L.R.N. (1982) National case study – India, in: *Multiple Class Teaching and Education of Disadvantaged Groups*. APEID (Bangkok, Unesco Regional Office for Education in Asia and Pacific).

World Bank (1986) *Financing Education in Developing Countries: an exploration of policy options*. Prepared by G. Psacharopoulos *et al.* (Washington, DC, The World Bank).

Education in Zambia: The Problem of Access to Schooling and the Paradox of the Private School Solution

L. H. KALUBA

Introduction

Zambia, like many other developing countries, is making serious attempts to address itself to the challenges of old and new problems of educational development. Some of these problems have increased and grown worse over time since the country's attainment of independence in 1964. Measures taken to reduce the magnitude of some of these problems have been successful. For example, the expansion of the secondary school sector in the mid-1960s enabled the country to meet the economic demand for educated middle-level manpower in various sectors of the national economy during the period of greatest need. The training of Zambian junior secondary school teachers made it possible to reinforce and later replace expatriate teachers in schools. However, despite these impressive achievements made so far, there is still a backlog of educational problems.

The following are some of the problems that have yet to be adequately solved: shortage of trained teachers especially in science subjects, lack of suitable and adequate teaching and learning materials such as text-books, inefficiency in utilization and management of existing educational facilities and the problem of access to schooling. The latter is now an acute problem which poses the biggest challenge to the government. These problems found also in other developing countries have led educational

L.H. Kaluba. The author and Carfax Publishing Company, publisher of *Comparative Education*, granted permission to reprint his article. It appeared on pages 159–169 of that journal's Vol 22, No. 2, in 1986.

development to be described as a crisis of growing maladjustment (Coombs, 1981). This paper intends to discuss the problem of access to schooling in primary and secondary schools and to assess the impact of other alternative school opportunities, especially the private schools, on reducing the problem of access to schooling. Access to schooling in this paper is discussed in relation to both entry into the school system and progression of individuals from one school level to another (e.g. from the primary into the secondary school sector).

Background to the Problem

Following the attainment of independence Zambia made policy decisions that were aimed at widening access to schooling. First, school fees were phased out. This meant that non-white children could attend former white fee-paying schools in urban areas. In 1966 the government introduced automatic promotion between grade 1 and 5 in urban areas (Mwanakatwe, 1974, 51). During the Emergency and Transitional Development Plan period (1965–1966) the government built 18 new co-educational secondary schools in rural areas and six day secondary schools in the Copperbelt province. In addition some extensions were made to some existing schools. This expansion allowed an unprecedentedly great intake to proceed from primary to secondary schools. The actual increase in the secondary schools' enrollments between 1964 and 1966 was 57.2%. Thereafter the progression rate began to decline. In the primary school sector self-help school projects which began enthusiastically were soon abandoned because of lack of sustained reciprocal support from the government. But in the main the factors that have seriously affected children's access to schooling are population growth, population movements which have resulted in greater urbanization, and the decline in financial resources especially after the fall of copper prices in 1974. It is against this background that the government is failing to cope with the rising demand for access to schooling at various levels in the school system.

Access to Primary Schools

Although the problem of access to schooling at grade 1 of primary school does not raise as much public concern as that of grade 7 primary pupils who cannot proceed to first (grade 8) level of secondary education, the problem exists, especially for statutory age-group access to schooling. At the individual level this problem often looks manageable as there is always another chance to enroll an over-age child in a school. A few parents of the high-income group nowadays bypass the primary school grade 1 registration bottleneck by enrolling their children initially in fee-paying private schools. Low-income parents cannot afford to take this expensive route; they must therefore be contented with trying a second time the following year. This is always possible because the official age entry-requirement of seven years is difficult to enforce very strictly in present circumstances. In the absence of official birth certificates the affidavits of birth which many parents present to headmasters have proved to be a very unreliable measure of children's ages. This is the major causal factor of irregularities in age-group access to schooling at the primary level. Because of limited places available, especially in urban schools, irregularities in admissions have always been suspected. The fact that the Anti-Corruption Commission was in 1984 detailed to monitor the

primary school grade 1 registration exercise is enough official evidence that the problem has taken on new dimensions. But generally the other reason for lack of sustained public concern is that at grade 1 level the private economic benefits of having a child in school are still very distant, whereas at grade 7 level of primary school that is of immediate concern to most pupils and parents. The consequence of pressure for school places is now reflected in over-enrollment of classes, a characteristic common to most urban schools.

However, at the national level the problem of age-group access to schooling has created enormous difficulties for educational planning. For example, as a result of the uneven age-group access to schooling a huge backlog of over-age children who cannot get into school has emerged. The problem facing planners is one of finding a suitable solution to this problem. Should separate schools be established for over-age children? In the country's present economic circumstances this would be very uneconomic, and socially and politically unacceptable to parents and the government. Should some existing schools be designated as special centers with over-age classes? This seems possible and less likely to bring about strong objection from parents. All the same, such schools may have to resolve the problem of providing additional classroom space where this is required and deciding who would pay for it. Should provision of such facilities be a responsibility of parents of over-age children only, or be a collective responsibility of the community in the schools' catchment area? These are some of the questions planners and policy-makers have yet to provide answers to.

The extent of the imbalance in age-group access to primary school grade 1 level is indicated by the fact that a large number of grade 1 places are occupied by 8- to 10-year-old children; this pattern is identical for all nine regions in the country. In fact the eight to ten-year-old cluster shared

62.21% of the total grade 1 school places across the country in 1980. This situation is unlikely to have significantly changed for the better in the last few years. The number of under-age children (five to six-year-olds) is however likely to go up as more children begin school at nursery and pre-schools. Another important feature to examine in relation to grade 1 enrollments is the over-all age-group populations. There were for example 25,457 seven-year-old children enrolled in grade 1 against a total popula-tion of 191,171 seven-year-olds in 1980. Because the problem of access to schooling at grade 1 level is as severe as ever in urban areas (Coombe & Lauvas, 1984) the nation-al objective to enroll all seven-year-olds in schools is far from being achieved. This is also reflected in the government's present efforts to draw up a new plan which could help implement a nine-year basic educa-tion.

Access to Secondary Schools

Above the problem of getting into primary schools at grade 1 level it is access to sec-ondary school level which has generated country-wide public and official concern. The number of pupils who pass the highly competitive grade 7 selection examinations are very few in relation to primary school pupils leaving that sector each year in each region. This is considered the most dreadful bottleneck by every parent. This apprehen-sion is genuine and stems from both social and economic considerations. Social mobil-ity, for instance, is still very much depen-dent initially on the level of schooling attained, especially secondary education. Despite the present declining labor market strength of certificates obtained at secondary schools, there is still tremendous economic importance attached to access to secondary schools and obtaining a certificate thereafter. This is because school certificates are still important screening and recruitment mech-anisms for both direct employment and post-secondary education. 'Good' certifi-cates can enable one to compete for a few training places in the tertiary sector.

The social consequences of having a large number of primary school leavers who are not at secondary school nor in gainful employment begin to be felt at this stage, both at individual and national level. While parents suffer anxieties, the children experience severe frustrations and feelings of despair at carrying the tag 'failure' or 'drop-out'. The government too is equally worried over this problem, particularly over its social and economic manifestations in most urban areas. Correspondingly the pressure for access to schooling at this level has had far-reaching consequences in the school system. Recent among these has been the widespread unethical practice of tampering with public examination papers (mainly grade 7 examination papers) at var-ious points (*The Sunday Times*, 18.11.84). In other cases parents have sent their brighter children to sit for examinations on behalf of their less clever children. In extreme cases a few parents have been found to have hired boys and girls outside the family to sit for their childrens' exami-nations.

••••

Push-outs and Alternative School Opportunities

There have always been alternative educa-tional programmes which are designed to benefit push-outs. Some are old pro-grammes, such as night schools, while oth-ers such as the supervised study groups (SSG) are relatively new additions. Within the formal school system repeating a grade is a possibility that is usually available in most schools though on a limited scale. Officially this practice is not encouraged. However, the incidence of repeating at grade 7 level is very high. But in general push-outs who are determined to pursue formal schooling can enrol at night schools or evening classes offering secondary education. Others enrol with the Luanshya Correspondence Unit, while others enrol in supervised study groups. This is a subschool system network run by the Ministry of General Education and Culture.

In this provision the Ministry makes every effort to offer tuition of comparable standard and quality. For example, the junior secondary school syllabus is identical in both sectors and only trained teachers are permitted to teach these classes. Nevertheless the environment in which teaching and learning takes place in most cases is less supportive. Cohorts usually comprise both adult and recent young school-leavers, and the availability and adequacy of facilities required in such classes depends on the generosity of the host school because there is little material provision made for them. In 1978 there were 12,629 pupils enrolled in supervised study groups throughout the country; in 1979 33,208 pupils were in night schools in the country, while a further 33,000 were reading junior secondary subjects by correspondence. These figures portray the existence of impressive and effective alternative school opportunities for push-outs. However, these figures have to be treated with caution because they do not tell everything. For example, the total form 1 (grade 8) enrollment in night schools is always a mixture of pupils from different grade-7 cohorts and includes large numbers of adult learners. Consequently, the figure has no significant relationship to the grade-7 push-outs just leaving schooling.

Private Schools

In the catalog of alternative options to access to schooling, the private school solution has been the most interesting and paradoxical attempt. It is also the most recent. It is a measure which has raised several questions on Zambia's educational policy. These questions will be raised and discussed in subsequent paragraphs.

A small missionary private-school sector had always existed since Zambia's attainment of independence in 1964. This sector operated according to the principles of government policy. The schools recruited children from all social and economic backgrounds, and – most important – they also followed a policy of free education like government schools. Their schools have always been the envy of others in the government sector and attract many children. This sector is different from the new private-school sector which has emerged in the post-school reform period. It was not until 1976 during the national debate on educational reforms that the Party and the general public seriously addressed themselves to the demand for a commercialised private education sector, which could complement government efforts in education provision.

The Party's (UNIP) socialist reaction to this demand was initially negative. Its view of private education in a Zambian Humanist society was not favourable:

> It is a fundamental principle of Humanist socialism that the state is responsible for the provision of education for its citizens. In discharging this responsibility, the state accepts many co-workers in the educational field under our participatory democracy. However, this is not a licence for any individual or group to engage in educational activities as a profit making business, since to make a business out of education, which is a right of all Zambians and necessity for national development, is a form of exploitation which cannot be allowed. (*Educational Reform Draft Proposals*, 1976, 28)

From the extensive national debate on educational reform proposals there emerged a complete reversal of almost all the socialist-oriented educational proposals (Clarke, 1979; Lulat, 1982). The proposal on non-commercial private education did not escape the wrath of middle-class interests. That proposal was dropped and consequently the government came up with a compromise recommendation.

> Private education institutions are permitted if they satisfy the requirements for registration and are run or operated in accordance of the relevant act. The main purpose of the legal

requirements is to protect the students concerned and the general public against exploitation, by ensuring that fees charged by proprietors of the institutions are reasonable in relation to the services rendered and that satisfactory standards of education provision are maintained (*Educational Reforms – proposals and recommendations*, 1977, 77)

With this came into being officially the new private secondary school sector, but unofficially a few illegal private secondary schools had been operating since 1975 in some big urban centres such as Lusaka and the Copperbelt province.

Why did the party and its government concede to a demand for an educational structure that fell outside Zambia's humanist-socialist framework? There could be several answers to this question. Among them are the following: the party was moved to accept the new private sector because of the magnitude of the problem of access to schooling between primary and secondary school sector in government and grant aided institutions. The objective was to find a solution which could help reduce the problem. It was also erroneously thought that through the new private secondary school sector the party could effect community participation in educational provision. But also in accepting the new sector the party successfully avoided being drawn into re-introducing school fees in government schools. This was in some measure a triumphant show of strong commitment to a long-standing party policy and principle on the provision of free education in Zambia. The private school solution was also seen from a different perspective as a way to accommodate minority class interests.

However, the emergence and developmental direction of the new sector has brought into sharp focus several issues that had hitherto not been considered or anticipated. First, its performance in the last few years has shown that the party and its government had overestimated the contribution in educational provision which could be derived from that sector. This has largely been a result of poor planning of policy implementation.

There are now 74 officially registered and approved private schools in both the primary and secondary school sectors. There are also still some schools which operate in the secondary school sector which are not officially recognised because they do not fulfil the registration requirements. The size of this sector is difficult to estimate because there are no records on their existence. However, a preliminary study of this sector on the Copperbelt region in 1980 (Kaluba, 1983) indicated that there were many such schools. In fact this study showed that there were only four approved private secondary schools, against 19 secondary schools whose status and existence were not known to the Ministry of Education. A study of the same sector in Lusaka (Sinkala, 1980) observed similar features again only four schools were registered and approved against 11 schools whose status was not yet clear. This has come about because of the rush to open schools by less competent and less qualified individuals, and the rush to make quick profits from school business.

In the approved sector it is secondary schools that are in greater numbers than primary schools; the reason is obvious, as already indicated in the preceding paragraphs. Primary schools which are in this category are old well-established schools in mining towns which were set up to serve the expatriate community. New additional private schools run by individuals are fewer and generally smaller, but they are of a comparatively superior quality like Mine Trust schools. This therefore suggests that the majority of schools in the new private secondary school sector are far from being the elite schools we are ordinarily accustomed to; if anything, these schools are condescendingly regarded as 'second chance' schools. And generally education offered in such schools is of doubtful quality (Schiefelbein, 1983). A greater disappointment has been the sector's failure to create enough school places to meet the present social demand created by the push-outs.

The private secondary school sector cannot absorb large numbers of push-outs, especially at grade 8 level. The reasons are mainly two: because of financial and other resource constraints most of the proprietors have not been able to establish larger schools. Land and finance capital have been the other major obstacles. This is especially noticeable in schools run by individuals. In the few good schools the fee levels have been very prohibitive for most average-income families. Actual school enrollment figures are difficult to get, or inaccurate because some schools do not keep reliable records. Some schools enrol pupils throughout the year to fill up places left by those who are unable to continue paying fees. The 1980 study on the Copperbelt found that the private secondary schools had only 1350 grade 8 places against 30,392 grade 7 pupils in need of secondary school places. The Lusaka study recorded a similar small capacity of six grade 8 classes with a total enrollment of 247 pupils. Granted that some pupils do enter the alternative forms of school mentioned earlier, it still shows that the new private secondary school sector has not made any impact on reducing the problem of access to schooling.

What is emerging now, in fact, is a group of elite private schools (both primary and secondary) which are aimed at serving high-income or middle-class expatriate and Zambian families. Evidence of class structure is beginning to appear everywhere; for instance, entry into some of these schools is very restricted. Applications for admission usually take a long time to process, during which period schools employ subtle methods to find out families' socio-economic backgrounds. In primary schools selection tests are administered as part of the screening process before admission. All these are networks of tight checks built into admission procedures to select only those considered acceptable. However, most average schools in the secondary school sector are generally unattractive because they operate in unsuitable premises such as noisy and busy shopping centres. Furthermore most of them lack adequate basic facilities, including staffing. This is still characteristic of most of the unapproved or illegal schools.

Fees

Consideration of fee levels in private secondary schools is crucial in any attempt to ascertain who obtains access to these schools. Although generally school fees vary considerably from one school to another, a few elitist schools charge very high fees, about K300 per term on average in primary schools and about K450 per term in secondary schools. This ensures that only children from high-income families can attend these schools. What is most puzzling about the fees structure is that they are fixed independently by school proprietors without the involvement of the Ministry of General Education and Culture. Although some parents have now started protesting at ever-increasing school fees, the Ministry has found it difficult to intervene. Another important aspect of the fees issue is that now there is a section of Zambian society which is paying school fees for the education of its children. This is significant, especially now that the current trend in educational financing is towards cost-sharing or outright cost-transfer to the consumers of educational services (Thobani, 1984; Psacharopolous, 1983, 3).

For the moment, attention is being drawn to the government's failure to arrest the escalation of school fees. Because the government does not have criteria for fixing fees levels and does not subsidise these schools it is difficult for the Ministry of General Education to intervene in this matter. So far any attempt to question fee levels in the private sector by government has met strong resistance from school proprietors. If school proprietors are pressed to lower their fees as a measure of widening access to these schools there is a real possibility that some would threaten to withdraw their services. But, given the schools' present high-income clientele, the schools do not feel threatened in any way because they enjoy indirect support from this socially influential group. Consequently we now have a few private primary and secondary schools which are well organised and better staffed but nevertheless highly inaccesible and others which are inadequately equipped and have a high staff turnover because teachers are constantly changing schools in search of higher pay. It is these latter schools that have moderate fees and an open-admission policy, but they are daily criticized by parents for various shortcomings such as hiring ill-qualified staff.

Conclusions

This paper has drawn attention to the existing problem of access to schooling, especially at primary and secondary school level.

It has identified and discussed existing types of alternative school provision which are aimed at reducing the problems of access to schooling. Finally, the paper had attempted to show that recent private-school initiatives are not in fact achieving the objectives desired. There is no community participation in the setting up and running of these schools, because they are first and foremost individual or group businesses. Furthermore, they have failed to create enough additional school places for push-outs from the primary sector. Most of them cannot provide satisfactory educational services, because of poor policy implementation on the part of the Ministry of General Education and severe resource constraints among some individual school operators. The present initiative is also largely an urban solution because that is where the private schools are, to benefit a few families who can afford high fees. Migration of youths from rural areas to urban centres is now likely to increase as youths move to towns, seeking initially extra school opportunities and later chances of employment. Therefore the biggest lesson to be learnt from the present experience of Zambia is

that, once a political policy decision has been made, it must be followed by working out a careful and comprehensive policy-implementation plan.

REFERENCES

Coombe, Trevor A. & Lauvas, Per (1984) *Facilitating Self-renewal in Zambian Education*, NORAD, Educational Report No. 1 (Oslo, NORAD).
Coombs, Phillip H. (1981) *Future World Critical Issues in Education Development: a report of preliminary findings* ICED (Princeton, New Jersey, ICED).
Clarke, Roy (1979) The rise and fall of the educational reform movement in Zambia, *Zambia Educational Review*, 1, pp. 4–8.
Fagerlind, Ingemar et al. (1983) *Education in Zambia: past achievements and future trends*, SIDA, Report No. 12 (Stockholm, SIDA).
Kaluba, Henry (1983) Private schools on the Copperbelt: some preliminary findings, *Zambia Educational Review*, 4, pp. 40-48.
Lulat, Younus G. (1982) Political constraints on educational reform for development: lessons from an African experience, *Comparative Education Review*, 26, pp. 235–253.
Mwanakatwe, John (1974) *The Growth of Education in Zambia* (London, Oxford University Press).
Psacharopolous, George (1983) *Educational Research at the World Bank, Research News*, 4, pp. 3–14.
Sinkala, Julius C.M. (1980) initial problems of private schools: a study of (take-off) problems, unpublished paper, Lusaka.
Schiefelbein, Ernesto (1983) *Educational Financing in Developing Countries: research findings and contemporary issues* (Ottawa, IDRC).
Thobani, Martin (1983) *Charging User Fees for Social Services: the case for Malawi* (Washington, World Bank).
Ministry of Education (1976) *Educational Reform Draft Statement*, p. 28 (Lusaka, M. of Ed.).
Ministry of Education (1977) *Educational Reforms – proposals and Recommendations*, p. 77 (Lusaka, M. of Ed.).
News Item in *The Times of Zambia*, 9 October 1984, p. 5; op cit., 8 January 1985, p. 5.
News Item in *Zambia Daily Mail*, 27 October 1984, p. 4.

Agricultural Education and Work Experience Programmes in Schools in a Third World Country: What Prospects for Human Resources Development?

ZELLYNNE JENNINGS-WRAY

Rejection of the Western concept of an educated man and in its place the vocationalization or diversification of education in order to produce people with the knowledge and skills relevant to their societies, has been seen as a key solution to educational problems in Third World countries. Educational innovations built around these ideas, however, invariably have met with limited success, not least because of the attitudes and values of the people for whom they are designed. Studies on acceptance of innovations have shown that people are not likely to accept an innovation that is perceived as not being relevant to their needs and interests, incompatible with their values or too complex for them to manage (Rogers and Shoemaker, 1971). Bacchus (1975) for example, has shown how conflicts of interest arose when attempts were made to introduce into the secondary level of the Guyanese educational system curricular reforms aimed at influencing occupational choices in the technical and agricultural fields. It was clear that these students and their parents did not see such programs as providing them access to better paid and more prestigious jobs. They wanted the 'irrelevant' Western – type academic curriculum which, in their view, afforded them the route to economic mobility and security.

To combat such conflicts in interest and

Zellynne Jennings-Wray. This is a revised and updated version of an article published in *Comparative Education*, Vol. 18, No. 3, in 1983 on pages 281–292. Permission to reprint was received from the journal's publisher, Carfax.

stem the failure of curricular reforms, Bacchus (1981) sees the need for "more profound social and economic changes", and a "radical rethinking and reform of the existing educational policies and priorities" in Third World countries. By examining some fairly recent developments in relation to agricultural education and Work Experience Programs in Secondary Schools in Jamaica, this paper both questions whether such 'radical rethinking' is needed in existing Jamaican educational policies and priorities and challenges whether the view that the whole future of developing countries like Jamaica is heavily dependent on effective agricultural programmes in schools can any longer be supported. Finally, based on the Jamaican experience I will suggest certain actions that Third World governments could take to facilitate more meaningful educational reform in the short term.

Curricular Reforms

Radical rethinking and reform in educational policies and priorities have taken place in Jamaica in recent years at all levels of the educational system. The Five Year Education Plan (1978–83) reflects the 'radical thinking' implicit in Bacchus' paper in its policy statement that educational programmes should include productive work as an integral activity of the school system both to maintain a balance between the academic and the practical and to "prepare students for entry to the world of work; impart to students the value of their involvement in economic productivity at the personal, school, community and national levels" (The Five Year Education Plan, 1977).

The José Marti New Secondary School, a gift from the Cuban government in 1976, is one example of attempts to achieve these ideals. It is the only school of its kind in the island, being the first all-boarding institution in which the entire school population is involved in a work-study programme which combines academic and vocational activities, the greater emphasis being on the latter. Agriculture is the only compulsory subject in the school and during the school day – which extends from 5:30 am to 10:00 pm – both students and teachers take it in turn to tend to the Piggery, Dairy, Poultry and Agronomy units. The sale of the products from these units enables the school to become self-sufficient (Earle, 1977).

No systematic evaluation has yet been done to attest to the efficacy (or lack of it) of the José Marti curriculum. But then educational innovations are rarely evaluated systematically, thus resulting in many promising ones being abandoned even before they have had a chance to lay roots (Dunbar, Humphreys, Webber, and Williams, 1979). The innovation strategy typical in the Jamaican educational system has been one characterized by poor planning, an inordinate haste to bring about change, lack of consultation of the relevant parties, impulsive action resulting from somebody's 'bright idea' with little or no thought for the implications either in terms of the values cherished by those for whom the innovation is intended or whether the necessary infrastructural requirements are in place. Two innovations will suffice to demonstrate this.

Agricultural Education

Bacchus (1981) points out that nearly every British educational commission to the colonies since the 1850s has recommended that agricultural education should be given a central role in the curriculum of schools.

In Jamaica, agricultural education in schools has been linked with achieving important "national goals for food production and to increase export commodities both of which are critical to the foreign exchange, unemployment and under-employment, and improve income distribution" (Dunbar, Humphreys, Webber, and Williams). How have these lofty goals been implemented? Two hundred and twelve schools are engaged in agricultural education, mostly of the school garden type, but some have tutorial farms and five have commercial farms. This, however, represents only 33% of the island's schools at the first and second levels of the educational system. Presently there are four special schools offering agricultural education, one of which was opened as recently as 1980. At the time of writing this article, there is no tertiary level institution in the island offering agricultural education. Up until September 1981, there had been one which began in 1910 as The Government Farm School and was renamed the Jamaica School of Agriculture (JSA) in 1939. Reasons that have been given for the closure of the JSA have ranged from a neglect of its feeder institutions over the past fifteen years to its removal from its location in Kingston where it had close links with the Ministry of Agriculture to an isolated site some ten miles outside Kingston where a creeping urbanization of surrounding areas gradually ate up its land. In addition, the cutting of the training period from three to two years, the lack of qualified staff, a rapid turnover of administrators who seemed incapable of handling the unionized power of the workers, the neglect of the Institution's buildings and facilities, together with the loss of its commercial farm to the José Marti School – which meant that the JSA lost its means to self-sufficiency – appear to have collectively led to the institution becoming inoperable. In a debate in Parliament a member of the Opposition posited that the Minister of Education had no authority under the JSA

Act to close the school as the Act gave the School Board responsibility for the running of the institution. Within less than three months, this Act was repealed and a short time after what used to be the JSA became the new home of the Police Training School which had long outgrown its original site at Port Royal.

Whatever the real reasons for its closure, it is the treatment of some 115 of its students that has been the centre of the furor over the school. With very little warning these students were sent to a recently opened Secondary School specializing in agriculture to complete their training. It is outside the scope of this paper to discuss the details of what happened there, although the public is much in the dark about this since the students were never allowed to tell their side of the story. Suffice it to say that these students were eventually expelled and their agricultural education came to an untimely end. Their expulsion has raised outcries against oppression, infringements of human rights and freedoms, particularly in light of the fact that these students were 'children of the poor' (*The Daily Gleaner,* 1982). The plight of the JSA not only shows how vulnerable education is at the hands of politicians, but it also has serious implications for agricultural education in Jamaica.

Which student at present is seriously going to want to contemplate a career in agriculture when he has no immediate prospects of a post-secondary training? The axing practically overnight of an institution in existence for over forty years is indicative of the low esteem in which agricultural education is held in Jamaica. Research has shown that agriculture is viewed by secondary level students and teachers as a course for low achievers, yet most agriculture students seek 'white collar jobs' in agriculture or choose careers unrelated to agriculture (Lowe and Mahy, 1978). An investigation conducted by the writer into the choice of occupations by ninth grade agriculture students after leaving school revealed that most of the girls wanted to be dressmakers/designers, nurses, teachers, secretaries and doctors: only one out of 30 selected agriculture as a career. 'It is a good subject for men', written by one girl, sums up the general attitude of the girls towards agriculture as a career. More boys contemplated careers in agriculture but mostly in farm management. A male student writing on 'Why I would choose agriculture as a career' spent most of the essay extolling the value of agriculture as a route to becoming a veterinary surgeon. He wrote: "one of the best advantages is the salary and in our Jamaican society a medical doctor is always well looked upon ... is classed as one of those who have made it to the top". Another student wrote: "it [i.e. agriculture] can help you to go to different countries on farm work", while yet another said: "individuals who have skills in agriculture could migrate and make their living in another country". So much for agricultural education and the achievement of national goals!

Negative attitudes towards agriculture have been blamed in measure on the quality of teaching in the schools. In 1978 there were only 130 qualified teachers of agriculture in the school system and many of the schools offering agriculture had no teachers with qualifications in agriculture (Dunbar, Humphreys, Webber, and Williams, 1979). The source for such teachers has dried up with the closure of the JSA. Admittedly, as External Examiner of the Agricultural Education course at the JSA for three years prior to its closure, I discovered that many of the graduates never reached the schoolroom. The very best either joined the Agricultural Extension Services, went into private enterprise or found ways of going abroad to study engineering. But the drift away from the classroom is not peculiar to agriculture teachers. It is a disease eating away at the entire Jamaican educational system. Principals of secondary schools often communicated to me their dissatisfaction with agriculture teachers who seemed inadequately equipped to deal with the practice of agriculture in schools: their courses, they said, were far too theoretical. However, these teachers without doubt encounter a number of circumstances in the schools which force them to make their programmes more theoretical that they would have liked. Not least, one would say, is the attempt to gain academic respectability not only for themselves in the school but also for the subject. In addition, their efforts are often thwarted by heads of schools who feel that the agriculture department is lowest in the order of priority for resources. Hence many schools suffer from a lack of agricultural tools, farm equipment, fertilizers, and even classroom space for the students of agriculture to do their theoretical work. Inadequate water supply, poor quality of the land, and absence of changing room facilities – which means that students have to do agriculture in their school uniforms – plague the effective operation of agricultural programs in schools. Perhaps the most serious problem faced by the schools, however, is that of praedial larceny. There have in fact been incidents where night watchmen have either been seriously injured or shot and killed by larcenists bent on rifling schools' farm products.

From what has been said, it must be evident that agricultural education programmes in schools are operating under very serious constraints. Not least of these is the fact that the programmes are being encouraged in certain types of schools only – namely, Technical and New Secondary schools. Many traditional high schools even in rural areas where there is ample land space do not have agricultural programmes. There is no escaping the fact that New Secondary schools are viewed as inferior institutions by the society generally, their curricula being more practical than academic. These schools have a low social class intake where previous educational experiences have been in basic or infant schools and government primary schools in which, for the most part, they have been taught under conditions of overcrowding, and inadequate physical, material and human resources (Jennings-Wray, 1980). Children from the upper and middle classes who have attended private preparatory schools and those from the government primary schools who have passed the CEE attend the traditional high schools. Since those who attend the New Secondary schools did not pass the CEE a sense of failure, exacerbated by inferior curricular offerings, pervades the life of these students. Different types of certification further segregate the secondary level students[1] with the high school student gaining qualifications which are not only valued by employers but also equip them for university matriculation.

Inspite of all the rhetoric about the value of agricultural education programmes for the development of the economies of Third World countries, the reality is that the students and their parents do not see agriculture as a subject to be studied by anyone with ambition. The 'in thing' now is Business Education. Most, if not all, of the 140 secondary level institutions in Jamaica are offering courses in Business Education and considerable curriculum development activity is going on presently in that field in the Commonwealth Caribbean, including the initiation of Caribbean Examinations Council (CXC) examinations in Principles of Business and Typewriting. Research has also shown that Business Education is presently the most satisfactory vocational course both from the point of view of meeting students' needs and interests and meeting labour requirements of the nation. Needless to say, most schools place their best students in Business Education courses (Lowe and Mahy, 1978). Is the "whole future of the UDCs ... heavily dependent on an effective agricultural education program in their schools" (Lowe and Mahy, 1978)? Certainly the people who have to do such programmes do not perceive it so.

And that is what really matters, given that innovation adoption behavior is dependent on how the receivers perceive the innovation, regardless of the intrinsic merit of the innovation itself (Rogers and Shoemaker, 1971). Agricultural education in most schools in Jamaica is breathing its last. It will take a miracle to make the phoenix rise from its ashes.

Work Experience Program

One of Bacchus's suggestions for educational reform is the elimination of the full-time secondary education course as it is now offered in most UDCs, and the establishment of a type of education which forges stronger links between education and productive work. The work experience orientation would involve students doing on-the-job training alongside master craftsmen in their chosen fields. Whether this strategy is the solution to the problems of a country that has one on the highest illiteracy rates in the Caribbean, as well as one of the highest unemployment figures, will not be debated here. There is no doubt, however, that some efforts have been made to link education and productive work more closely.

In 1974 the Jamaican government extended the life of the New Secondary Schools by two years with the introduction of the grade 10–11 programme.[2] An integral part of this further training is the Work Experience Program (WEP) which takes the form of grade 11 students being released for 21 days to get experience in the world of work. These students are placed in work stations or agencies in both the private and public sectors to sample at first hand a realistic employment situation tied closely to their vocational area of study. The students are not paid but are covered by insurance arranged by the government. Recent research (Teape, 1980) suggests that the WEP has met with a fair measure of success: some students perform so well at the work stations that they are employed immediately. However, the WEP labours under a number of constraints which make the objectives of the programme as viewed by the planners appear overly ambitious.

The WEP is envisaged by planners as having benefits not only for the students but also for the school and community. Students are seen as being helped to develop healthy self-concepts, good work ethic, positive relationships with fellow-workers as well as to discover whether their vocational choices were the correct ones. Benefits to the school include not only the use of the skills and knowledge of qualified members of the community to supplement and enrich vocational instruction, but also the possibility for students to receive training and exposure with equipment and facilities that the schools could not afford. Moreover the program is seen as enabling employers to participate in curriculum decision-making in schools, thus facilitating curricular responses to their specified needs. Benefits to the community include enabling students to gain the knowledge and skills needed for employment in their own communities, thus bringing school and community closer together (*Work Experience Handbook*).

A sample of grade X1 students who had done the WEP reported that whereas they found that the programme gave them some experience of the world of work, they did not find that it helped them to develop a healthy self-concept. They were only marginally convinced that the WEP enabled them to find out whether their vocational choices were correct. This was not surprising since some 55% of them were unable to find work stations where they could gain experience in their vocational subjects (Teape, 1980). The fact that only 5% of the managers were aware that students were not gaining work experience in the vocational areas in which they had specialized in school is an indication of the lack of communication between school and potential employers. What is more alarming is the apparent lack of communication within the schools themselves because none of the principals or Work Experience teachers felt that an inability to work in areas related to their vocational choices posed any problems to the students. Teape's study further revealed that whereas the students (and their teachers) felt that employers expected too much of them, none of the employers were aware of this shortcoming. Moreover, whereas most of the students (and 40% of their teachers) felt that they were not given sufficient supervision at work stations, only 5% of the managers admitted to this. Students living in the rural areas are clearly the most disadvantaged not only on account of there being insufficient work stations in rural areas but also because these students have to travel long distances to these work stations, often on foot because transportation poses serious problems. Financial embarrassment also proved a grave difficulty for both urban and rural students. Perhaps this could be attributed to the fact that although most of the managers gave students pocket or lunch money they did not feel obliged to do. How positive were the relationships developed between students and their fellow-workers is questionable since many students complained of having to do menial tasks – such as the cleaning and sweeping of factories and offices – which their co-workers did not want to do.

A random sampling of grade X1 students who had graduated in 1979 to ascertain how the WEP had benefitted their working lives revealed that of 20 students who responded, only two had obtained jobs both at the same place where they had done WEP (Teape, 1980). Six students, unable to find employment, were doing further training courses at Technical High Schools and Colleges. The remaining twelve graduates were unemployed, even though amongst them were a number of students who had been rated very highly by both teachers and work station managers. This is perhaps not surprising since in October 1979 the unemployed labour force stood at 299,100 which represented an unemployment rate of 31.1% which was most acute amongst the 14–19 age-range (*The Labour Force*, 1979). The Jamaican school leaver who has been prepared for the world of work faces months of job-seeking which in recent years has been well in excess of twelve months.

Implications of the Jamaican Experience for Development in Third World Countries

While one would agree with Bacchus (1981) that the key solution to the kinds of problems highlighted in this paper rests fundamentally in "more profound social and economic changes", this realisation is not particularly helpful to the educational planner who has to deal with the here and now. Social and economic changes do not come overnight. While we are waiting for such changes, what are we – who are helping to shape the lives of those on whom the future of our nation will depend – supposed to do?

Democratic Socialism was an ideology that championed profound social and economic changes in Jamaica. Manley saw it as creating a classless society in which individual social advancement was based on merit rather than inherited wealth (Manley, 1974). The development of greater self-sufficiency through self-help, the full utilization of available local resources which were geared more directly towards meeting the needs of the less affluent groups in the society, the provision of a basic level of education for the total population – an objective given prominence in the priority attached to the JAMAL[3] programme – all of which Bacchus (1981) sees as key factors in his new development strategy, were major goals of that ideology (Manley, p. 152).

The fate of Democratic socialism in Jamaica since it took a nose-dive in the General Elections of 1980 need not detain us. Suffice it to say that the Jamaican people are not hearing so much now about the need for a New Economic Order and even seemingly minor yet profound changes that were brought about in that era – changes that reflected the dignity of the Jamaican as a person, a free agent with the power to shape the course of his life – appear to have been trampled underfoot by a regression to a 'new era' of dependency and conservatism. For example, there has clearly been a backlash against the more casual form of dress, which is more closely identified with the working classes, that was promoted by the way in which Ministers of Government dressed. Now the sight of these Ministers addressing farmers and other workers in the hot sun in their immaculate three-piece suits and ties, is a subtle message to the working and lower class man not only to keep in his place but also to aspire towards those very ideals that educators and economists in the developed world are insisting he should reject.

The fact that Jamaica has to solicit funds from the World Bank and other external funding agencies in order to finance innovations in her educational systems raises the question of how far she is free to determine the educational destinies of her own people. Aid never comes without strings – a fact which makes the prospects for local initiatives at educational reform highly questionable.

Need for Employment-Generating Strategies

Clearly the major solutions to problems in Jamaica's educational system lies outside the education system itself. Oxtoby (1977) has argued rightly that provision of vocationally oriented curricula rooted in the practicalities of the world of work is not the panacea for educational problems in Third World countries. These need to be accompanied by structural changes and reforms in labor market practices, modification in the pattern of wage rates and the introduction of specific employment-generating strategies.

The latter are particularly important for the 14–19 age group which has the highest percentage of unemployed. In April 1981, for example, while for the total population there was a 26.2% unemployment rate, for the 14–19 age group, the rate was 57.1% (*Statistical Review:* November 1981, Department of Statistics, Jamaica 1982).

Need for Government Subsidy and Centralisation of Programmes

It is a misconception for governments of Third World countries to believe that schools can change 'almost overnight' from a state of dependency to one of self-reliance. Caught up in a general economic squeeze, many school in Jamaica are experiencing severe financial crises. In the face of the escalating cost of education in a country where the slogan, 'free education', did much to sway the populace in a past general election, the frequent complaint from principals of schools is that they have not received their annual subsidy for months and sometimes even years. Schools are, however, made to feel that they should bear with the 'struggle' for self-reliance and find ways of becoming economically self-sufficient. Admittedly, some schools succeed, especially those with supportive Parent-Teachers' Associations. But those are amongst the privileged. This call for self-reliance is often taken as an opportunity for the Ministry of Education to 'stay aloof', while individual schools struggle to implement programmes that have been thrust upon them – programmes which are costly both in terms of human and material resources yet ones which are seen as having significance for the economic productivity of the nation.

Agricultural programmes in schools are costly. Tools, farm equipment, fertilizers, seeds have to be bought. But money is not all that is needed. One principal summed up the general opinion of principals of schools with agricultural programmes thus: "much more 'support' is needed from the

Ministry of Education in the form of supervision of Agricultural Science teachers, feasibility studies for new crops, funding etc., if agriculture is ever to get off the ground – or rather onto the land!"

The WEP is also very costly to the work stations. In her interview of work station managers, Teape (Teape, 1980) found that they felt that the Ministry of Education should subsidize the WEP in order to ease the financial burden on the work stations. All the principals, moreover, expressed dissatisfaction at the seeming lack of concern with the WEP on the part of the Ministry. Work station managers also complained about the students' lack of in-depth knowledge of the practical skills in which they were gaining work experience. This is an outgrowth of the problems facing the vocational education programmes in the schools. These programmes are being crippled by lack of machinery and general equipment. Although many of these schools were originally equipped by World Bank Funds, machinery and equipment have either been vandalized or have fallen into disrepair due to lack of spare parts which have not been obtained on account of the island's foreign exchange problems in recent years. Furthermore, the small cadre of teachers skilled in vocational areas in Jamaica is spread very thinly throughout the system. Hence in any one school one is likely to find students being taught a vocational skill by a teacher who lacks adequate qualifications. Centralization of vocational programmes could ease this problem. This would involve equipping particular schools with the necessary equipment, staff and other resources for providing specialized training in one or two vocational subjects. Thus students wishing to study Electrical Installation, for example, would go to the school which has that programme fully operative.

Need for Effective Communication

In relation to the WEP, the fact that none of the managers felt that too much was

expected of the students at the work stations whereas a large number of both teachers and students did, coupled with the fact that the managers did not seem to realize that they were not providing the necessary supervision suggests a lack of adequate communication between the schools and potential employers. This is in fact the responsibility of the Work Experience teachers, namely, to coordinate the total operation and functioning of the WEP and act as the vital link between the school and the work community. Such a heavy responsibility suggests the need for Teacher Education Colleges to institute specialised programmes to equip these teachers with the necessary skills and expertise.

There is, furthermore, a need for public education with regard to the worth and working of the WEP and agricultural education programmes in schools. Media could be more effectively used not only to combat negative attitudes towards practical and manual work in schools (and in the society at large) but also to get employers to accept new types of certification. The average graduate of the New Secondary School obtains a Secondary School Certificate which employers consider inferior to the General Certificate of Education (CGE) and would give employment to the holder of the latter in preference to the former.

Rationalising Secondary School Curricula: Counteracting the 'Slave Mentality'

A lesson that Third World countries can learn from the Jamaican experience is that any educational programme – especially when it emanates directly from the political ideology of a government in power – needs to be carefully planned before implementation and integrated meaningfully into the schools' curriculum instead of being 'tacked on' to it at the end. The WEP is part of a curriculum package – the grade 10–11 programme, the motivating force behind which was the ideology of Democratic

Socialism which saw the necessity of tightly interweaving national policies for education and work in order that the economic production of the country and its social development could be fully realized (*Work Experience Handbook*). But it is one thing to have a political commitment and quite another to transform that commitment into curriculum reality in the schools. The grade 10–11 programme was altogether hurriedly put together. Self-instructional modules were developed by lecturers in Teacher Education Colleges and the University of the West Indies, and without trials in pilot schools and systematic evaluation were implemented in all New Secondary schools with the minimum of training on the part of the teachers who were to implement the programme. Plans to remedy weaknesses detected in these modules have been afoot for at least the past six years, but to date none have materialised with the result that very negative attitudes towards certain components have developed. Most notably the Life Skills component has suffered from a lack of teachers with the knowledge and skills to teach the subject and from a lack of content relatedness to the life experience of New Secondary school students. In many schools this component has been discontinued and in several others it is dying a slow death, being dubbed "Dead Skills". There was no attempt made to articulate the grade 10–11 programme with the rest of the New Secondary School curriculum so as to form a continuing whole from grade 7. Had this been done, the WEP might well have met with greater success.

A programme of three weeks' duration at a work station can hardly be taken as a serious attempt to interweave education and work and to combat the negative attitudes towards practical/manual work that prevail in the society. Such attitudes, Manley argues, reflect the misery of the historical experience of the Jamaican people whereby "instead of work being seen as a means by which a man expresses the creativity in himself while he earns his daily bread … work is seen as a condition imposed by a master upon a servant as the price of the servant's survival" (Manley, 1974). Agricultural education and Work Experience Programmes cannot be expected to have any major impact on stigmas against practical/manual work when such programmes are being encouraged in certain types of schools and not others. Admittedly, the plan is that "in future, the Work Experience Programme may be expanded to include the high schools and comprehensive schools" (*Work Experience Handbook*) but the programme has now been operative for some seven years and no change is evident in that direction, except on the initiative of one or two individual schools. But even in such instances it is Work Experience in Business Education (or perhaps Technical Education) that is being pioneered – certainly not in Agriculture.

Conclusion: The Importance of People in the Development Effort

This paper has sought to highlight Agricultural Education and Work Experience Programmes in a Third World country, pinpointing such factors as militate against the achievement of their desired objectives. Among such factors are problems associated with curriculum organisation at the Secondary level, and the negative attitudes which the society generally has towards a practical curriculum. Inadequate funding largely due to government's aloofness against the background of pressure on schools to become self-reliant, wastage of human resources in relation to programme organisation, and lack of effective communication both within the school system and between the school and community generally, are also proving to be constraints on achievement of objectives. The discussion in this paper has lent support to the observation of economists and educators who contend that any proposal for educational reform in Third World countries must begin fundamentally with "radical changes in the existing social and economic system aimed at reducing the relative massive income gaps which exist in these countries, especially those in the modern and those in the traditional sectors of the society" (Bacchus, 1981, p. 226). Before curricular innovations like the Agricultural Education programme and the WEP can have desired effects, Third World countries will not only have to deal constructively with negative attitudes and values in relation to practical and manual labor, but they will also have to find ways of initiating employment-generating strategies so that students who have been prepared for the world of work will be able to enjoy the right to work.

"Development does not start with goods: it starts with people and their education…" (Schumacher, 1974). But the people who have the greatest amount of responsibility for translating educational theory and political rhetoric into curriculum reality in the schools are the teachers and therefore it is with the teachers that change has to start.

This cannot be emphasized too highly especially in a Third World country like Jamaica where the status of the teacher has long been downgraded. The 'profession' has become a dumping ground for many who cannot find any thing better to do. Thus teaching has become a temporary repository for many seeking inroads into the insurance business or other private sector organisations or for some others who just want 'a little sideline'. But to have their fingers in many pies is a matter of survival for most teachers in Jamaica, whose earnings have been compared to that of the lowest categories of organised manual workers in large private sector establishments. Can we honestly expect to get engineers of human resources development for the price of factory floor sweepers?

The teaching profession needs a complete metamorphosis in order to function meaningfully in any development effort. And it is not just a matter of higher salaries.

It is a matter fundamentally of respect for persons: treating teachers as persons. It is a matter of requesting, consulting, asking instead of telling, ordering, treating with contempt.

"Why care for people? Because people are the primary and ultimate source of any wealth whatsoever. If they are left out, if they are pushed around by self-styled experts and high-handed planners, then nothing can ever yield real fruit" (Schumacher, p. 141).

ENDNOTES

1. The New Secondary student takes the Secondary School Certificate in grade 11 – which employers do not value – and is more likely to take the Basic Proficiency level of the Caribbean Examinations Council (CXC) while the High School student takes the General Certificate of Education (GCE) or most likely the General Proficiency level of the CXC. It is the top grades of the latter that are considered comparable to GCE certification.

2. This programme is practically and vocationally oriented and geared to equipping students with the knowledge and skills necessary for coping with the realities of everyday living. For example, there is a 'Life Skills' component which seeks to prepare students for the world of living by making sure they have knowledge and experience of, e.g. Child and Health Care, Nutrition, Household budgetting, how to do simple electrical repairs etc., which it is felt students might not have gained from other curriculum areas. The WEP forms the experiential component in preparing the students for the world of work.

3. The Jamaica Movement for the Advancement of Literacy Foundation which was established in 1974 to operate a basic adult education programme primarily to eradicate illiteracy by 1978. However, because so many students were still leaving school functionally illiterate the deadline was extended to 1982.

REFERENCES

Bacchus, M.K. (1975) Secondary school curriculum and social change in an emergent nation. *Journal of Curriculum Studies*, Vol. 7, No. 2.

Bacchus, M.K. (1981) Education for development in under-developed countries. *Comparative Education*, 17, p. 217.

The Daily Gleaner, Tuesday, January 26th 1982.

Dunbar, A., Humphreys, M., Webber, E., & Williams, L. (1979) *Agricultural Education as a Component of the National Agricultural Programme*, p. 11 (The Planning and Development Unit, Ministry of Education, Jamaica).

Earle, J.A. (1977) José Marti Secondary School: an experiment in the work-study concept, *CARSEA*, Vol. 2, No. 2.

The Five Year Education Plan (1978–1983), draft 2, pp. 7–8 (Ministry of Education, Jamaica, 1977).

Jennings-Wray, Z.D. (1980) A comparative study of influences and constraints on decision-making in the primary school curriculum: some implications for the teacher as an agent of change in Third World countries, *Journal of Curriculum Studies*, Vol. 12, No. 3.

The Labour Force 1979 (Department of Statistics, Jamaica, May 1980).

Lowe, K. & Mahy, Y. (1978) *The New Secondary Graduates of 1976 and 1977. Job expectations on leaving school.*

Manley, M. (1974) *The Politics of Change: a Jamaican testament*, p. 160 (London, Deutsch).

Oxtoby, R. (1977) Vocational education and development planning: emerging issues in the Commonwealth Caribbean, ibid.

Rogers, E.M., Shoemaker, F.L. (1971) *Communication of Innovations: a cross-cultural approach* (The Free Press).

Schumacher, E.F. (1974) *Small is Beautiful: a study of economics as if people mattered*, p. 140 (London, Abacus).

Statistical Review: November 1981, Department of Statistics, Jamaica 1982.

Teape, V.E. (1980) A study of the work experience programme in Jamaican New Secondary schools: an examination of its usefulness, *unpublished B Ed study*, UWI.

Work Experience Handbook: technical and vocational education (Ministry of Education, Jamaica, 1978).

About the Authors in Chapter 7

Victoria J. Baker is an Assistant Professor of Anthropology at Eckerd College in St. Petersburg, Florida. Her book, *The Blackboard in the Jungle: Formal Education in Disadvantaged Rural Areas. A Sri Lankan Case* (Delft: Eburon), was published in 1988.

Dr. L. Henry Kaluba is with the School of Education at the University of Zambia in Lusaka. His article, "Private Schools in the Copperbelt: Some Preliminary Findings," was published in Volume 4 of the *Zambia Educational Review*, pp. 40–48, in 1983.

Zellynne Jennings-Wray is Head of the Department of Foundations and Administration, Faculty of Education, at the University of Guyana in Georgetown, Guyana.

CHAPTER 8

Economic Development and Finance Problems in Developing Areas

Introduction

THE DEBT CRISIS IN DEVELOPING COUNTRIES during the last two decades presents one of the most important dangers to the stability of international economic order. With the "Third World debt" at $1.3 trillion as of 1991 and the demand for international capital increasing, agencies such as the International Monetary Fund have required debtor nations to comply with a set of economic austerity programs for loans. These measures have encouraged developing countries to specialize in the export of raw materials such as cash crops. As would be expected, an increase in the supply of raw materials precipitated a decline in the price of agricultural commodities. Thus, the developing nations continue to produce cheap raw materials for consumption by wealthier developed nations. Sometimes, as in the case of Haiti, they must even compete with industrial nations like the United States in the production of foodstuffs for domestic consumption. The debt cycle, like poverty, is a vicious one. For a detailed exposition of the situation in Africa and suggestions for correction, see Adedeji (1985).

Although the impression has sometimes been given that the developing countries with the highest external debt are in this position because of over-consumption, this has not been the case; non-oil-developing countries have borrowed to invest rather than consume (Zaidi, 1985). Sell and Kunitz (1986–87) have also shown, based on their analysis of foreign indebtedness and mortality rates, that international market participation does not evenly benefit the population of developing countries. The medicine suggested by international bankers is bitter, even when the importance of long-term economic growth is simultaneously considered (Orlando and Teitel, 1986).

Inflow of foreign resources into developing countries is not the only reason for the debt crisis. Many other factors such as trade balance and exchange rates play a role and must be appreciated in our search for a solution to the debt crisis.

In an excellent essay not included in this volume but valuable for its analysis of the international debt situation for developing countries, "Developing Countries in the World Economy," Paul R. Krugman (1989) has presented the various choices creditors and borrowers have for resolving the debt crisis. When countries in debt cannot make payments, the creditors have three options: to take the assets of the country; to allow for postponing payments; or to forgive their debts altogether. The strategy adopted by most banks in the past has been one of refinancing and postponing the debt payment. Although this may produce greater returns to creditor countries, it may become expensive for creditors if debtor nations fail to register adequate economic growth in the long run.

Although a confrontation between creditors and debtor nations appears more and more likely, the solution will be some refinancing strategy that stalls for time, both creditors and debtor nations being mutually dependent for maintaining world economic stability. Under some conditions at least partial debt forgiveness may be to the advantage of creditors. More recently Krugman has argued that both creditors and debtor nations would be better off if half the debt of the most debt-ridden countries were written off. Initiatives by the World Bank that would reduce foreign debt have made little headway.

The Articles in Chapter 8

As *Aliber* has pointed out, the developing countries borrowed billions of dollars to bridge the gap between export incomes and import costs. This was not difficult because a large number of developed nations were eager to lend money as petrodollars poured into the international banks following the oil price hikes in the 1970s. The dramatic increases in oil prices during this period led developing countries to double and treble their borrowing rates to guard against erosion of living standards. A cycle of spending and borrowing emerged. As borrowing increased, the interest rates increased and in a few years this trend found many nations unable to even pay the interest on their debts.

Papanek discusses the impact of foreign resources on the economic growth of developing countries. Many studies have suggested a negative relationship between foreign capital inflows and saving. Foreign inflows have stimulated saving in some countries while they have discouraged saving in others. In order to test the hypothesis of a negative relationship between foreign resource inflows and saving, a number of control variables such as exchange rates and tariffs on imports have to be explicitly taken into consideration.

The complexity of testing macro-hypotheses with national data becomes apparent as *Papanek* takes us through a labyrinth of economic data and historical events that sometimes produce associations but are far from supporting propositions about growth causality. It is this kind of contribution that makes us reflect on rather than make pronouncements about the impact of economic aid.

Shehab's 1964 article on Kuwait is unlike the other contributions in this chapter because it ends with what was almost a forecast: "Whether or not her extravagance will be excused because of her generosity, only time will tell." This is not the place to further judge such an unbelievably wealthy creditor nation or its debt-ridden former adversary but the world has seen *Shehab's* concern materialize. The aftermath of this chain of events has provided the Middle East with the need for an even greater infusion of foreign aid, aid that, rather than economic, is more likely to be military.

REFERENCES

Adedeji, Adebayo, "Foreign Debt and Prospects for Growth in Africa During the 1980s," *The Journal of Modern African Studies*, 23(1), 1985, pp. 53–74.

Krugman, Paul R., "Developing Countries in the World Economy," *Daedalus*, 1989, pp. 35–47.

Orlando, Frank and Simon Teitel, "Latin America's External Debt Problem: Debt-Servicing Strategies Compatible with Long-Term Economic Growth," *Economic Development and Cultural Change*, Vol. 36, 1986, pp. 641–671.

Sell, Ralph R. and Stephen J. Kunitz, "The Debt Crisis and the End of an Era in Mortality Decline," *Comparative International Development*, 21(4), pp. 3–30.

Zaidi, Igbal Mehdi, "Saving, Investment, Fiscal Deficits, and the External Indebtedness of Developing Countries," *World Development*, 13(5), 1985, pp. 573–588.

The Debt Cycle in Latin America

ROBERT Z. ALIBER

The Debt Cycle in Latin America

Changes in the volume of new loans issued by the developing countries in Latin America have had a significant impact on the foreign exchange value of their currencies, and on most of their domestic macroeconomic variables. During the 1972–82 decade, the annual increase in external debt of many of these countries exceeded the interest payments on this debt. The result was a net cash inflow derived from the sale of new loans abroad. Consequently, at the time, no real economic cost was associated with this increase in external debt. After 1982 this situation changed. The annual increase in external debt diminished to the point where it was less than the scheduled interest payments. At that point Latin American borrowers began to experience a net cash outflow on their debt account. Thus, in order to generate the foreign exchange needed to pay even part of these scheduled interest charges, the economy had to undergo a costly adjustment process.

The *first section* of this paper will discuss (a) the impact these changes in volume of net external loans had on the exchange rate, and (b) the impact exerted by domestic economic variables on borrower economies during the 1972–82 decade. The *second section* will evaluate some of the different explanations that have been given regarding the cause of the debt crisis. The *third section* will explore ramifications of the adjustment process that took place as a result of this change from a net cash inflow to a net cash

Robert Aliber. Permission to use this article was granted by the Institute of Interamerican Studies, which publishes the *Journal of Interamerican Studies* in which it appeared in Vol. 27, No. 4, pp. 117–125.

outflow on the debt account, and the impact these exerted on the borrowing countries.

The assumption of this article is that the financial markets in the industrial countries are partially integrated with those in the Latin American countries. These countries borrow abroad as an alternative to borrowing at home. The volume of external loans changes according to the willingness of foreign lenders to buy the loans; in this sense, the number of loans being made at any time are a function of lender decisions to grant or ration credit. Borrowers seek to sell more loans abroad when they anticipate that the low interest costs more than compensate for any loss incurred, either due to an increase in the domestic price of foreign exchange or as a reasonable recompense for assuming the exchange risk. Whether they can then sell more loans abroad depends entirely upon the demand.

External debt of developing countries frequently is tied to increases in the price of energy, as set by the Organization of Petroleum Exporting Countries (OPEC) beginning in 1973–74. From that time the surpluses generated by the OPEC countries became linked to the deficits of the (energy-importing) developing countries in a recycling process initiated and supervised by the major international banks. Two relationships evolved. On the demand side, oil-importing countries paid higher prices for their petroleum imports, for which some preferred to borrow the additional foreign exchange needed rather than to make economic adjustments at home, either by reducing imports or by increasing exports. On the supply side, OPEC members decided to deposit a substantial portion of their newly-acquired cash surpluses with the major international banks. In turn, the latter used these deposits as loans to developing countries. Two observations confirm the accuracy of this thesis. On an annual basis, external loans of oil-importing developing countries increased at a greater rate than their oil-import bills. This does not apply to oil-exporting countries (such as Mexico, Venezuela, Ecuador, Peru, and others), whose oil-export earnings increased along with their external indebtedness. Obviously the oil-import bills of these countries did not increase. The common factor explaining the increase in external loans of both oil-importing and oil-exporting countries is that international lenders were relaxing their credit-rationing standards.

I. A Model of Domestic Adjustments to External Debt Flows

Changes in the size and direction of net cash flows on the debt account, like changes in the volume of commodity exports, affect the foreign exchange value of a country's currency. During a period in which cash inflow from new loans exceeds both interest payments plus principal repayments on its outstanding loans, a country's currency should appreciate in real terms. (An analogous situation would be the sharp increase in foreign demand for US securities due to their high interest rates, which resulted in an increase in the foreign exchange value of the US dollar.)

The change in the value of a country's foreign exchange is a function of the change in the difference between the net foreign exchange obtained from sale of new loans and the cash payments for interest-and-principal on outstanding loans. If the cash inflow from the sale of new loans is *increasing*, relative to the cash outflow on outstanding loans, the borrowing country's currency should appreciate in real, price-level adjusted, terms. Conversely, if the cash inflow from the sale of new loans is *decreasing*, relative to cash payments on out-

standing loans, the borrowing country's currency should depreciate. If cash inflow from the sale of new loans is the same as the cash payments on outstanding loans, then the value of the borrowers' foreign exchange should remain unchanged, for the scheduled interest payments are fully capitalized, and the rate of growth of the external debt is equal to the rate of interest.

Net cash flows associated with a given volume of new loans may change either because the interest rate on the outstanding loans changes, or, perhaps, because the amount of principal repayment changes. Changes of this nature may be offset by other changes in the volume of new loan sales, so that the net cash inflow associated with new loan sales remains the same. The assumption made in the following paragraphs is that volume of new loans is independent of other factors, including autonomous changes in the trade balance, such as those associated with changes in the price of oil.

Corresponding to changes in the net cash inflow on the debt account may be that the country's trade balance will change in an offsetting way, on the assumption that proceeds from the sale of loans do not lead either to equivalent or greater changes in foreign exchange reserves, or to capital flight. Real appreciation of its currency can occur, changing the trade balance of the borrowing country when issuers of new loans take their loan proceeds to the foreign exchange market to acquire the domestic currency. Thus, an increase in net new loans means that both the country's trade deficit and its current account deficit should increase. An increase in the net export of loans displaces the net export of commodities. Commodity imports increase at the same time that commodity exports decline.

Real appreciation of the currency of the developing country borrower, and the increase in its trade and current account deficit, should work to reduce its rate of inflation. Two factors explain the decrease in inflation. For any given money supply, or any given rate of growth of the money supply, domestic price levels fall (or at least increase more slowly), as the supply of available goods increases in response to the increased trade deficit. Moreover, the decline in the domestic-currency-price of imports may lead to a decline in the rate of inflation since domestic producers will face increased competition from imports.

Interest rates within the borrowing country will also go down as a result of the increase in net cash inflow; the larger trade deficit means that the amount of foreign savings available to borrowers in the developing country increases. One explanation for the decline in domestic interest rates is that external borrowing becomes a substitute for domestic borrowing. A second explanation is that domestic saving increases as income increases (see following paragraph); and a third is that a reduced rate of inflation should be associated with a reduced premium on inflation in terms of nominal interest rates.

Increased net debt sales are often associated with an increase in the role of the government sector because the ability of the government, and of government agencies, to borrow abroad is greater than that of private firms, since lenders consider government to be more creditworthy. For one thing, government and its agencies are less likely to go bankrupt than are private firms because government can obtain any domestic currency needed through its access to the central bank. For another, the size of the government sector is apt to increase along with the volume of new debt sales.

Increased net debt sales abroad are also associated with an increase in the national income of the borrowing country, partly because a decrease in the nominal interest rates is associated with an increase in investment spending by private firms at home. In addition, increased government borrowing abroad is likely to be associated with increased government spending, hence

domestic income and employment are also likely to go up. As an increased supply of foreign goods becomes available, spending on domestic goods is likely to increase too. Domestic spending and foreign spending complement each other. The implicit assumption is that sufficient domestic unemployed and underemployed resources are available to satisfy the increased demand for domestic goods. Thus an increased inflow of cash, from the sale of loans abroad, is likely to be associated with an increase in the rate of growth of national income whenever unemployed and underemployed resources exist in the borrowing country. Equity values (or stock prices) go up in tandem with the net cash inflow into the borrowing country. One reason for this is the decline in interest rates. A second is that an increase in spending and income will lead to an increase in corporate profits. These two factors dominate the impact on corporate profits of the real appreciation of the domestic currency, reflecting the fact that corporate profits go down as domestic costs go up, relative to the level of world prices. The explanation is that most sales of firms in developing countries are made to the domestic market, which is protected from import competition. However, to the extent that some firms do export or are in substantial competition with imports, the effective real appreciation will lead to a lower level of corporate profit. The impact on the firm's equity value depends on the extent to which the lower interest rate exerts its influence on their profits.

The increase in long-term external debt of Latin American countries amounted to $197 billion between 1972 and 1982, going from $37 billion in 1972 to $234 billion in 1982; the growth rate exceeded 18% a year. In addition, the short-term external debt of these countries increased, probably at an even more rapid rate. One large component of the funds realized from the sale of loans consisted of paying the interest on these outstanding loans: $37 billion, compounded at the prevailing interest rate, amounted to $108 billion. Front-end fees connected with the issue of new loans also absorbed some of the foreign exchange. Latin America's foreign reserves increased by $30 billion. In the 1972–82 decade, payments abroad for imports of goods and services surpassed earnings from exports of goods and services by $15–20 billion, when compared to the previous 1962–72 decade, or by $1.5–2 billion a year. Most of this represented an increase in payments for imports of commodities relative to exports of same. The big difference between the increase in the external debt (in 1972–82) and the change in the balance of trade (from 1962–72 to 1972–82) provides a first guess as to the level of capital outflow, variously estimated to have been from $100–150 billion.

II. The Source of the External Debt Crisis

Once the developing country external debt had increased at rates from 20–30% for a decade, and the levels of external debt had begun to approach 40–50% (or more) of the national income, an external debt crisis became inevitable. The external debt of the borrowers could not continue to increase at rates substantially above the rate of growth of their national income indefinitely. As long as the debt increased more rapidly than income, the ratio of debt to income rose. As long as the debt's rate of growth was greater than its interest rate, the borrowers incurred no current cost by issuing more new debt abroad, since the foreign exchange obtained from the sale of new debt was more than sufficient to pay the interest on the outstanding debt.

When lenders became convinced that the ratio of debt to income could not continue to increase at this rate, their credit rationing would become more severe, the rate at which the debt grew would slow down, and the borrowers would find themselves increasingly less able to promote new

loans with which to pay the interest on the loans outstanding. At some stage, it was inevitable that the borrowers would need to make the adjustment from a position of net cash inflow on the debt account to one of net cash outflow. The degree of adjustment would vary according to borrower willingness to pay interest on a scheduled basis, and according to lender willingness to buy new loans from the borrowers, albeit at a reduced rate. Paradoxically, the greater the demonstrated willingness to pay all of the interest on a scheduled basis, the less likely the borrower might be obliged to do so because the mere act of demonstration might persuade the lenders to buy new loans – in this way the scheduled interest payments could be capitalized into an ever-growing amount of external debt.

Both the timing of the external debt crisis and its severity were affected by (a) the increase in nominal interest rates on securities denominated in the US dollar and (b) by the world recession. Higher nominal interest rates meant larger interest payments by the borrowers on the floating interest rate component of their external debt, while the recession meant their export earnings declined. The external debt crisis is particularly associated with the surge in interest rates on this debt, which reduced the net cash inflow associated with a given volume of debt sales. The greatest impact came from reduced net cash inflows produced by the diminished ability to sell new loans. Lenders rationed credit more severely. Lender willingness to buy new loans from Mexico deteriorated as the world recession became more severe and oil prices declined which led, in turn, to lender pessimism regarding Mexico's ability to service its debt. In the absence of cash coming in from the sale of new loans, Mexico could not pay the interest on its outstanding loans. Lenders reacted to the Mexican cash crisis by displaying increased reluctance to buy any new loans from other developing countries as well.

Traditionally borrowing has two purposes. One is to facilitate higher levels of growth by enabling the borrowers to acquire assets whose anticipated returns are greater than the interest rate on the borrowed funds. The second is to facilitate adjustment to external shocks, and especially to cyclical declines in income. The irony is that the borrowers used so much of their available credit lines in the effort to enhance income that their credit lines were exhausted soon after the combination of tight money and world recession had reduced their net export earnings.

III. Domestic Adjustments to the External Debt Crisis

As the cash inflows associated with new debt declined, many relationships noted in the first section became reversed. As a result, the currencies of these countries depreciated in real terms, or much more rapidly than might be inferred from the differentials in national inflation rates. Because the borrowers needed to generate trade surpluses in order to obtain the foreign exchange required to pay at least part of the interest on outstanding loans, real depreciation was extensive, due to both the inelastic demand for exports within the developing countries, and to the inelastic supply of goods for export.

One consequence of the very sharp, real depreciation of borrower currencies was to produce significant upward cost-push pressures on price levels from the higher local-currency price of imports. Moreover, the reduced availability of goods also forced up domestic price levels, so that the price level increase, for the same rate of growth of the domestic money supplies, went up so long as trade deficits were declining. In some countries, the combination of reduction in the trade deficit with increased domestic borrowing led to a surge in the inflation rate, as a result of rapid domestic monetary expansion.

These sharp, real depreciations squeezed both the public and private borrowers, since the domestic-currency equivalents of the scheduled payments of interest and principal on the outstanding loans were significantly higher. In some cases, the domestic-currency equivalent may have increased by a factor of 5 or 6. Both public and private borrowers needed to raise domestic receipts relative to payments to obtain the increased local-currency equivalent of their debt service payments abroad. The surge in the domestic-currency equivalent of interest and principal payments meant that the borrowers were bankrupt in many cases, or that they would have gone bankrupt if the external debt had not been effectively nationalized.

The inability to sell new loans abroad squeezed many borrowers who formerly had relied extensively on such sales for debt finance. Many of these borrowers sought to raise more funds at home as a substitute for funds they could not raise abroad. The result was that domestic interest rates increased sharply in many countries. Governments, especially, were able to use domestic finance as a substitute for external finance, because payments of interest and principal were partially, or fully, indexed to inflation rates. Thus, governments could raise the real returns on these domestic debt issues to the levels needed to sell the debt.

Increase in the real interest rate resulted in private borrowers being squeezed because the interest cost of funds was greater than any return on investment that companies might earn. Nevertheless, many such borrowers were still able to secure additional funds because lenders were reluctant to force private firms out of business. However, many private firms shrunk in size.

The squeeze on public and private borrowers meant that both income and employment declined in the developing countries. Foreign exchange earnings were needed to service debt.

All these adjustments became inevitable

once the ability of the borrowers to sell new loans declined, and once lenders lost confidence in borrower willingness to make the adjustments necessary to pay interest on a scheduled basis. The increase in the price levels, and the real depreciation in borrower currencies, were unavoidable, even in the absence of the IMF (International Monetary Fund) programs. The decline in income, and the squeeze on both public and private borrowers, were un-avoidable once the ability to sell new loans had declined because credit rationing became more severe as well. IMF programs may have exacerbated the decline in income and employment owing to the Fund's insistence on reducing the inflation rate. At the same time, IMF programs may have lessened the squeeze on the private sector because of the Fund's efforts to reduce fiscal deficits as a share of national income.

The Effect of Aid and Other Resource Transfers on Savings and Growth in Less Developed Countries

GUSTAV F. PAPANEK

The early literature discussing the impact of foreign resources on the economic growth of less developed countries was curiously naive, yet it remained essentially unchallenged until recently. Its basic assumption was that each dollar of foreign resources would result in an increase of one dollar in imports and investment. Given this assumption and a reasonably stable incremental capital-output ratio it was possible to calculate the effect of any given inflow of foreign resources on growth. Or to reverse the procedure, it was possible to calculate the inflow required to achieve a target rate of growth. Usually it was simply assumed that the significant component of such inflows was foreign aid. "Aid" and "total resource inflows" were often treated as though they were synonymous.[1]

••••

The Recent Challenge to Past Assumptions

Within the last year or two there has been a drastic change: numerous essays have concluded that only a fraction of foreign resource inflows has been additive to domestic savings, while a large share was used to increase consumption. Many of the articles focus on and are especially critical of aid. The statistical basis for their conclusions, however, is the deficit on current account, usually taken as measuring foreign

Gustav Papanek. With the author's consent, Basil Blackwell, publisher of *The Economic Journal*, granted permission to reprint this article which appeared in Vol. 82, 1973, pp. 934–950.

resource inflows. The deficit is, of course, financed in a variety of ways: by aid (whether in the form of grants or loans), foreign private investment, short-term commercial borrowing, changes in foreign exchange reserves and even "errors and omissions" and the liquidation of private assets abroad.

Some of the essays are "revisionist" in the true sense of the term. They argue that foreign inflows, and especially aid, make little contribution to economic growth, once account is taken of their effect in reducing savings, of the poor rate of return on aid-financed investment and of debt service charges. Aid may ease the lot of the recipient country's citizens by permitting higher consumption, which is considered desirable if the analyst's humanitarian instincts outweigh his Calvinist conviction that people should struggle for their economic salvation, but it does little for growth.[2] Furthermore, some critics have argued that aid and foreign private investment have undesirable social and political consequences, strengthening oppressive governments and institutions – consequences which need to be weighed against its short-term palliative effect in permitting greater consumption. In short, some recent articles[3] have reached almost the opposite extreme from the earlier analysis: these revisionists see almost no increase in investment, and no increase in growth from foreign resources. Most analysts did not go so far. They agree, however, that aid and other foreign inflows reduce domestic savings and are used in part to increase consumption.

These critics[4] made a very useful and significant contribution in challenging the naive view of the benefit of foreign inflows. It is certainly plausible that some share of foreign inflows increases consumption. Given the assumption which underlies all this work, that saving equals investment minus foreign inflows, as long as the effect of an additional unit of foreign resources on investments is less than one, its effect on savings will appear to be negative. The weaknesses in this procedure are discussed below. Much of the critical literature, however, goes beyond the argument that some part of foreign resources is used to increase consumption to suggest that there is statistical evidence that inflows *cause* a reduction in domestic savings, and that the magnitude of the reduction is measurable.

••••

Implicit Savings Functions

While the critics suggest that there is a negative causal relationship between foreign inflows and domestic savings they are generally not specific about the savings function which underlies their assumed relationship. Nor do they compare their implicit function with the functions derived from the rather limited work on savings in less developed countries.

There are at least two plausible savings functions[5] which alone or in combination would result in a fall in domestic savings, and a small or zero increase in investment, as a result of foreign inflows:

(i) Rahman, Griffin and Weisskopf imply that savings are substantially determined by government policy and that a government's saving effort will be less vigorous if greater foreign resources are available. Specifically, if one assumes that savings are a function of government effort or policies, that governments have a fixed growth rate as their objective, that achievement of this growth rate requires a given investment, then, if any resources for investment come from abroad, a government will change its policies and programmes to reduce domestic savings by an equivalent amount.

(ii) If savings are in part a function of investment opportunities, as suggested by Houthakker[6] and Griffin, and some opportunities are pre-empted by foreign capital, then again capital inflows will be offset in part by a compensating decline of domestic savings.

However, another set of plausible savings functions would produce a rise in savings, and a substantial increase in investment, as a result of foreign inflows:

(a) If investment is substantially a function of the foreign exchange available to import capital goods and inputs to keep installed capacity functioning, then it would increase with foreign inflows, and so raise both income and savings. The importance of the foreign exchange constraint is confirmed by some of Chenery's recent work. Foreign inflows are shown to contribute to growth in addition to their contribution to investment. Similarly, in Weisskopf's analysis, investment in eight out of thirty-one countries was foreign exchange constrained, and another six countries had both a savings and foreign exchange constraint.[7]

(b) If savings are a function of the level and rate of growth of the income of particular groups, such as industrialists or exporters (cf. Houthakker), capital inflows may rapidly raise savings by increasing the income of these groups, even if average income changes little.

(c) If savings are a function of income and the Government has no effective mechanism for achieving a reduction in the savings function (in the way postulated under (i)) to compensate for any increase in investment directly financed by foreign capital, the net effect of foreign inflows on investment will depend on the proportion of inflows allocated to investment. When foreign resources first flow into a country, a large share is directly invested – almost all of aid and of foreign private investment – and aid donors exert pressure for increases in domestically financed investment: the resulting extra income will lead to an initial increase in saving. The question then is whether in a second round the Government can and will make compensatory adjustments in domestic savings and consumption in order to meet its specified objective function (if it has one of the kind postulated).

In short, there are plausible savings functions which could result in one dollar of foreign inflows producing either a positive or a negative effect on savings and anything from no increase in investment to more than one dollar of additional investment. But all of the critical analyses agree that the average impact has been to increase investment by only $0.11 to $0.77 for every dollar of inflow. While other results might be plausible, are there any reasons to question these quantitative results? In fact, their usefulness and reliability can be doubted because the measures of savings reflect an accounting convention rather than a behavioural relationship, because of statistical problems and, most important, because in many cases the measures involve only correlation, not demonstrated causality.

Accounting Convention vs. Behavioral Effects

The negative statistical relationship between savings and foreign inflows found in recent analyses can be in part the result of an accounting convention, not of a behavioural relationship. Confusion arises because domestic savings are calculated, following conventional economic practice, by subtracting foreign inflows (estimated in the way described above) from gross investment. This is quite appropriate to the extent that foreign resources are either (i) used for investment or (ii) are a claim on past or future savings. If foreign resources

are used directly or indirectly to increase investment then one needs to subtract the inflow of such resources from total investment to estimate the contribution of domestic savings to capital formation. On the other hand, even if foreign resources are used to increase consumption, not investment, but have to be repaid, they represent a claim against future savings. Similarly, if the foreign resources are derived by drawing down foreign exchange reserves, they represent a use of past savings. In either case it would be both standard practice and quite appropriate to subtract them from investment to obtain current real savings.

However, to the extent that foreign resources are used for consumption *and* have a grant element one obtains misleading results by following conventional procedure. An extreme example would be a gift of foreign food directly to a starving group. Even if the magnitude of neither investment nor domestic savings (in the normal sense) is affected by the gift, the conventional method will show a decline in savings: the starving group has consumed in excess of its income. Or take the case of government using a foreign grant to expand government services (*e.g.*, education or health) or even receiving military aid in the form of tanks: in all these cases investment remains unchanged and there is no effect on current savings, no use of past savings and no claim on future savings.

It remains appropriate in these cases to conclude that foreign resources were used to increase consumption, not investment. It is, however, misleading to reduce domestic savings by the amount of foreign resources received as a grant for consumption purposes. Nevertheless, analyses have ignored the differences in uses and sources and have subtracted all foreign resources from investment in calculating domestic savings.

Data are admittedly defective for more sophisticated calculations and the estimates given below also use the conventional approach. It is, however, quite likely that any resultant error will not be random. Precisely the poorer, more slowly growing countries are likely to receive a higher proportion of grant aid and to use it to increase consumption. They are also likely to be countries with low savings rates. The use of the accounting convention may therefore by itself produce a correlation between low (apparent) savings and high aid inflows.

Inappropriate Aggregation, Conflicting Results and Other Statistical Problems

The critics' analyses suffer from some serious statistical problems. First, they aggregate all foreign inflows and deal with the net total flows only. Yet one would not expect aid to have the same impact on growth and savings as foreign private investment. Both are likely to differ in effect from changes in reserves, capital flight, short-term speculative movements or commercial borrowing. To draw any conclusions about the effect of one component, such as aid, one needs to analyze it separately from other flows.

Second, some of the data used inevitably have an unusual margin of error, which may introduce systematic bias.[8] Non-monetary investment is widely underestimated and is especially important in the least developed countries. The same countries also tend to underestimate monetary investment, since their calculations are often based on capital goods imports and production, with inadequate allowance for domestic value added. On the other hand, some of the more developed of the less-developed countries tend to overestimate investment, since their capital goods are more highly protected than other commodities. Argentina is an example. Savings estimates, when calculated as a residual by subtracting inflows from investment, are subject to greater error than investment estimates. Then if the least-developed countries, that is the poorest ones, receive more aid, there would tend to

be a specious correlation in cross-country analysis between aid and low savings rates.

Third, most of the analyses compound possible error by incorrect calculation of the magnitude of foreign resource inflows. With the exception of some of Chenery's work all ignore net factor payments to abroad. They calculate foreign resource inflows as the difference between current imports and exports of goods and services, but actual foreign inflows are larger by the net factor payments made to foreigners. Such payments are of considerable importance. With a mean of 2% of G.D.P., they almost equal foreign inflows as usually measure. Their range is considerable and closely correlated with export earnings: e.g., − 8% of G.D.P. for Jordan and − 4% for Morocco; +15% for Iraq, 10% for Venezuela, Trinidad-Tobago and Zambia, and 7% for Iran.[9] To ignore flows of such magnitude creates the possibility of serious random error and bias. For instance, if current foreign inflows just offset net factor payments to abroad arising from past investments, the country may have a low growth rate despite substantial foreign inflows. But in the absence of such inflows, and with continued factor payments, growth would have been even less. This description applies to some mineral- and oil-rich countries.

Weisskopf also ignores service payments, and deals only with commodity flows, reducing his average estimate of foreign resource inflows. Most analyses, except Weisskopf's, include a few countries that have a net outflow of resources. In effect, they suggest that since countries with capital exports have high savings and growth rates, capital imports *cause* low savings and growth rates.

Finally, it is clear that different analysts obtain strikingly different results, which casts some doubt on their reliability. The variations between 11% and 77% in average impact of foreign inflows on investment and the general dispersion might be explained in part by differences in sample, time period and method of analysis. However, comparing time series results for the same countries still produced widely different estimates (*e.g.*, for roughly the same time period for Brazil, Chenery calculates the impact of inflows on savings as +0.07, Areskoug at −1.02). Of course, the specifications of the models differ among analysts, but the very large variations should give one pause, especially since the differences are not systematic as one might expect if they were due to differences in specification.

Correlation vs. Causality

The most serious question on recent claims about a negative causal relationship between foreign inflows and savings is with respect to the existence of any causality. There are clearly many cases where high foreign inflows are *associated*, among countries or over time, with low savings and, in some cases, low growth rates. However, quite frequently a look at the specific circumstances will lead to doubts that low savings and growth are *caused* by high inflows. Rather, both are more likely to have been caused by a poor or deteriorating economic and/or political situation.

Poor countries, and countries passing through a temporary crisis often have low savings rates and (*ceteris paribus*) low growth rates. If, at the same time, such countries frequently have greater inflows because of greater need, then savings and growth will be negatively associated with inflows for many countries without any causal relationship between them. Aid is a major part of foreign inflows which goes primarily to the needy: poor or crisis-ridden countries. This is not the same as arguing that aid is allocated to all needy countries and in aid proportion to need. Clearly, most aid is allocated in large part on the basis of political considerations. But among countries who have a claim for political reasons it tends to go disproportionately to those who need foreign

resources more, and any one country is likely to receive more than its average allocation during its periods of greatest need. For instance, Mexico is undoubtedly more important politically to the United States than is Pakistan, and Poland is more crucial to the U.S.S.R. than is Cuba. Yet Pakistan and Cuba are major aid recipients because they need foreign resources if their economies are to function and their governments to survive, while neither Mexico nor Poland is as dependent on aid. Both of the former countries also received more aid in periods of bad harvest than when the weather had been good. At least one study supports the contention that the amount of aid is clearly related to need.[10]

Some foreign inflows other than aid also increase in times of crisis. This is obviously true of the use of exchange reserves and IMF credits, but it applies in more sophisticated ways also. When foreign exchange is scarce, for instance, businessmen in that country are likely to look more assiduously for foreign private investors and foreign commercial loans, and governments are likely to draw more on suppliers' credit and commercial loans.

There are several categories of exogenous factors which simultaneously make for higher foreign resource flows, and lower savings and growth rates, or vice versa:

(i) *War, civil war or major political disturbances.* Most recent analyses include South Korea, Taiwan, Philippines and Israel. All of these countries had high inflows of aid and relatively low savings rates in the early 1950s when they were recovering from war or civil war (plus absorption of immigrants in the Israeli case). Some also had lower growth rates until recovery was well under way. By the 1960s savings were up and inflows were lower. It is at least as plausible to conclude that higher savings and lower inflows were both the result of recovery as to believe the alternative hypothesis that lower inflows caused higher savings. As a matter of fact, aid advocates have cited the same data as the aid critics for their contention that aid has been highly successful; that substantial aid in the 1950s resulted in a high growth rate, which produced higher savings subsequently and thus reduced the need for aid. The Dominican Republic, also included in many analyses, had quite respectable savings and growth rates in the 1950s. After its civil war and United States intervention, both plummeted and aid increased. Nigeria's savings rates were low in the 1960s during its civil war, when aid and foreign private investment in newly discovered oil were both high. For all of these countries, a negative correlation between savings (and sometimes growth) and foreign inflows (especially aid) will show up in both cross-section and time series analyses, but it is unlikely that there is a causal relationship.

(ii) *Terms of trade.* A very substantial change in the terms of trade, especially for countries heavily dependent on exports, generally has a substantial impact both on inflows (especially movements in reserves) and on savings rates. Export earnings from minerals or plantation crops often produce more concentrated incomes than production for the domestic market and savings are therefore derived disproportionately from the export sector.

Colombia, for instance, experienced a drop of 47% in the price of its coffee between 1954 and 1963. Coffee provided 70–80% of export earnings. During the period of high coffee prices in the early 1950s Colombia substantially increased its foreign exchange reserves (it had negative inflows) and growth exceeded 5% *per annum.* Following the coffee price crisis, foreign inflows reached 2% of G.D.P. but the growth rate fell to 3%, while domestic savings declined somewhat.[11]

Ghana, as dependent on cocoa as Colombia is on coffee, experienced a drop in its terms of trade index from 112 to 57 between 1959 and 1965. As a result, savings fell from the rather high rate of 16.5% of

G.N.P. which had been reached in 1960. In an attempt to maintain imports and investment, foreign exchange reserves were drawn down and resort to suppliers' credits was expanded, both steps increasing foreign inflows.

Over time, foreign inflows were negatively correlated with both growth and savings for these two countries. In cross-country analysis, Ghana in the 1960s was an example of a country with relatively low savings and high inflows. This was partly the result of the deterioration in the terms of trade.

(iii) *Weather and other exogenous variables.* Several years of good or of unfavourable weather sometimes occur in sequence, especially in monsoon agriculture. In countries where agriculture directly provides around 50% of G.D.P. and of exports, and affects the income generated in agriculture-based industry, trade and government revenues, two years of bad harvests can substantially reduce savings and growth rates for three or four years. During the same years, foreign exchange reserves are likely to be drawn down, while foreign borrowing and foreign aid are likely to be increased, especially since the United States has made surplus agricultural commodities available. For instance, in India the good harvest of 1964 produced high savings, growth and export rates, accompanied by low inflows of surplus agricultural commodities. The poor harvests of 1965 and 1966 resulted in a reversal. 40% of the borrowing examined by Areskoug was for the import of United States surplus agricultural commodities. The vagaries of weather obviously have a substantial influence on this important category of foreign inflows.

There are other exogenous shocks to an economy which simultaneously reduce economic performance and savings and lead to increased inflows. With the phasing out of its Malta naval base, Britain substituted a subsidy ("aid") for payments ("exports") which had made higher savings possible.

With the nationalization of foreign enterprises and some other steps, savings dropped sharply in several countries, but increased aid from the Soviet Union became available. Earthquakes in Morocco, floods in Tunisia and similar catastrophes meant that lower savings and higher aid were correlated over time. The opposite case is the initial output of oil or other natural resources, with further development paid for by revenues from their export, not by the same foreign resources coming as investment. Savings, growth and exports all rise, while foreign aid drops, foreign investment can remain negligible and "other" foreign inflows can turn negative, as Swiss bank accounts are fattened. Again a negative correlation between savings and inflows would be shown, without direct causality.

The above three sets of factors generally make for a negative correlation of foreign inflows with savings and often growth, in time series and in most cross-country analyses. The length and severity of some swings accounts for the fact that cross-country analyses are also affected, although the correlation is temporal. Cross-country analysis is affected not only by these exogenous temporal factors, but also by long-term differences in societies.

(iv) *Low or high savings societies.* Some countries are low savers and, *ceteris paribus*, have low growth rates, while others are high savers and have high growth rates for a number of social, economic and historical reasons. Religious, ideological or cultural factors can result in thrifty or extravagant societies. A history of inflation and political upheavals may discourage savings. Concentrated non-entrepreneurial income, for instance from mineral wealth, combined with further opportunities to invest in mineral development may produce high savings rates. Where aid is the principal component of foreign inflows and low savers receive more aid because of greater need, low savings and high inflows would again be correlated in cross-country analysis. If then the inflows are inadequate to compensate for low domestic savings in providing the resources for growth, high inflows will also be associated with low growth rates.

Savings, Inflows and Exports

An examination of countries with high and low savings rates confirms the significance of exogenous factors – political and military disturbances, terms of trade, weather and other shocks, and historically low or high savings propensities – in explaining the negative correlation, on a cross-section basis, between savings and foreign inflows. Table I includes all less developed countries with especially high or low savings rates from a universe of 34 countries for the 1950s and 51 countries for the 1960s.

Most of the high savers are rich in oil, metals or other natural resources. Their primary exports average more than twice those of the low savers. As one might expect they receive little aid. Curiously, on the average this resource-rich group also received little foreign private investment. For many of these countries considerable foreign private investment took place before the mid-1950s. Thereafter they either discouraged foreign investment or it declined because the mines or oil fields were largely developed. Therefore analyses which begin about 1953 would not show high foreign private investment in these resource-rich, high savings countries. In some cases, capital flight,[12] or servicing of foreign investment and loans, produced an outflow in the "other" category, balancing actual foreign private investment in analyses using only total net flow figures. The only high savings/low inflows society which is not resource-rich is Japan,[13] where high savings rates were not due to natural resource wealth, but historically high savings propensities.

The low savers include the war or civil-war devastated countries, and those like Jordan with a very underdeveloped econo-

Table I: Countries with Exceptionally High or Low Savings Rates
(All figures as percentage of G.D.P.)

	GROWTH	GROSS SAVINGS	NET AID	NET FOREIGN PRIVATE INVESTMENT	PRIMARY EXPORTS	OTHER EXPORTS
LOW SAVERS – 9% OF G.D.P. OR LESS						
1950s						
Indonesia	3.6	7.4	0.4	0.6	11.5	0.4
Pakistan	2.6	6.9	1.0	0.0	4.1	0.6
Panama	4.4	5.8	1.3	3.1	10.9	0.2
Philippines	6.6	5.3	4.3	3.3	9.5	0.3
S. Korea	7.3	4.8	8.0	0.0	1.5	0.3
1960s						
Bolivia	5.6	8.2	7.0	1.6	17.4	0.0
Guatemala	5.0	8.3	2.4	1.8	13.4	0.5
Jordan	9.3	-2.5	18.6	1.0	14.5	0.9
Liberia	6.0	-1.9	10.8	15.0	45.6	0.0
Nigeria	5.1	8.0	1.2	3.0	14.5	0.4
S. Korea	7.6	5.4	7.0	0.9	4.4	1.2
Average	5.7	5.1	5.6	2.8	14.3	0.4
HIGH SAVERS – 18% OF G.D.P. OR GREATER						
1950s						
Burma	5.6	19.1	2.3	0.2	19.8	0.7
Iraq	5.8	27.2	1.7	-4.5	56.2	0.2
Peru	4.6	19.4	0.7	2.7	18.3	0.8
Venezuela	7.8	28.0	0.2	3.1	32.1	0.3
Japan	10.5	28.4	-0.1	0.1	1.4	9.8
1960s						
Argentina	2.9	19.6	0.1	0.5	9.4	0.4
Iraq	4.7	18.8	0.8	0.9	33.3	0.3
Ivory Coast	8.1	18.5	3.3	2.2	31.2	0.4
Malaysia	5.0	20.4	0.7	1.3	39.0	1.9
Peru	5.5	19.8	0.6	1.3	20.2	1.5
Thailand	7.7	18.7	1.2	1.3	17.1	0.4
Trinidad-Tobago	5.2	20.0	1.4	6.8	50.8	1.3
Venezuela	4.5	27.7	0.0	-0.2	31.0	0.4
Zambia	8.2	32.0	-4.4	1.6	66.7	0.5
Japan	9.4	36.0	-0.1	0.1	1.0	9.0
Average	6.3	24.0	0.4	1.2	31.7	2.2

NOTE: Sources, methods of calculation, definitions, and data for all countries are given in a Statistical Appendix available from the author. The basic source is the I.B.R.D. *World Tables* and in general its definitions have been accepted. "Aid" includes only funds supplied by governments or international organisations (*e.g.*, I.B.R.D.) after subtracting debt amortisation. Foreign private investment is net of repatriation of capital. For many countries (*see* Statistical Appendix) a careful examination of detailed I.M.F. statistics was undertaken because the *World Tables* provided inadequate information.

my, that received a high level of aid. They also include some countries with high private foreign investment: the Philippines where savings were affected by recovery from war, while private investment reflected a return by United States capital after the

Japanese occupation; Nigeria in the 1960s, where the civil war reduced savings and high foreign investment followed the discovery of oil; and Liberia, essentially a subsistence economy with an expected low savings rate, but with an enclave of foreign investment attracted by her iron ore and other natural resources.

There is some evidence that many less developed countries fall into three groups with respect to savings, foreign inflows and growth. Since the evidence suffers from many of the problems and biases discussed earlier, it is at best suggestive of relationships that might be explored further:[14]

(a) Countries which are well endowed with natural resources: often these were developed by foreign investors during an earlier period, in which case later foreign private investment is low or negative (Iraq, Ceylon, Venezuela in the 1960s). In other cases, heavy foreign private investment in mining, oil, or plantations was still taking place during the period under review (Liberia, Trinidad, Venezuela in the 1950s). These countries have a high level of primary exports, and consequently high savings rates and no severe balance of payments constraint. They have little need for foreign aid and receive little. In terms of total population none of these countries is large.

(b) Countries that are rather poor in known natural resources and that have not yet developed much of an industrial sector: they often suffer from other economic, as well as political, difficulties. Both primary and other exports are naturally low. Low exports and other problems mean low savings rates and little foreign private investment. Many of these countries are major aid receivers and the growth rate of individual countries depends very much on their level of aid. On the average, aid levels are inadequate to loosen the constraints imposed by low savings and low exports and growth is only average.

(c) Countries which have become semi-industrialized (or industrialized in the case of Japan) and which export manufactures. However, only in the case of Japan is the level of manufactured exports comparable to the level of primary exports for countries rich in natural resources. The rate of savings of these countries then depends in part on their primary exports. Some are major aid recipients because they are politically impor-

Table II: Summary of Patterns of Exports, Savings and Foreign Inflows
(All figures are percentages of G.D.P. or G.N.P.)

	GROWTH	SAVINGS	AID	FOREIGN INVESTMENT	PRIMARY EXPORTS	OTHER EXPORTS
Average for 34 countries in 50s	5.0	13.4	1.7	0.9	15.9	1.0
Average for 51 countries in 60s	5.6	14.1	2.6	1.9	19.7	1.5
Average for 85 observations	5.3	13.8	2.3	1.3	18.1	1.3
(a) High primary exports,* low aid pattern	5.7	19.2	1.5	2.2	39.0	0.8
(b) Low primary exports,† high aid pattern	5.3	10.2	2.8	1.2	7.3	0.5
(c) High manufactured exports,‡ variable aid pattern	6.6	15.7	3.6	0.8	12.5	4.7

* Primary exports of 29% or more of G.D.P. ($n = 14$)

† Primary exports below 10% and manufactured (other) exports below 1.5% of G.D.P. ($n = 13$)

‡ Manufactured (or "other") exports 1.7% of G.D.P. or higher. ($n = 14$)

tant, and because they suffer from more serious savings and balance of payments constraints than the resource-rich. Since they already have a substantial industrial base they are countries which grow rapidly if they receive substantial foreign inflows.

Table II shows the figures for these three groupings, which accounted for 41 or the 85 observations.

Conclusions Concerning the Negative Impact of Inflows on Savings

In short, the critics' case for a negative causal relationship between foreign inflows and savings is not proved by their quantitative analyses. In many instances causality is more complex than they assume. For a number of countries it is plausible to conclude that exogenous factors caused both high inflows and low savings rates and generally low growth rates as well. For time series analyses, if one takes account of the six countries where wars or similar disturbances affected the economy, the two countries where terms of trade changed sharply and the two or more countries where weather and other exogenous shocks played a role, very little is left of the critics' evidence. For cross-country analyses another dozen countries were added, most of them with historically high savings propensities and with low inflows, without any necessary causal relationship between them.

In effect, any statistical attempt to assess the causal influence of foreign inflows on savings would need to consider whether high (or low) inflows were associated with savings which were lower (or higher) *than one would otherwise have expected*. This is true whether one uses a cross-country approach or a time series for an individual country, but the reasoning is simpler to follow for the latter. The critics' method effectively judges whether saving is higher or lower than "expected" simply by expressing the figure for each year as a percentage of G.N.P., and comparing this with the aver-

age percentage for the available years. It is, however, fairly obvious that (for example) a bad harvest, or a sudden fall in export prices, is likely to affect savings proportionately more than it affects income: consequently, this *simpliste* approach produces entirely spurious "short-falls" in savings in those years, which would not appear if one had a more sophisticated savings function to judge what is to be "expected." There will also be corresponding spurious "excesses" in the years when the harvest or export prices are unusually favourable.

These statistical deficiencies on the savings side might not matter very much if they could be regarded as random in relation to the level of the foreign inflow for the year in question: they might then do no more than partially conceal a true relationship, in the way that is normal when there are random errors. In general, however, factors which produce below-average savings rates will produce above-average foreign inflows (including run-down of exchange reserves), and conversely for factors which produce above-average savings rates. There is a real risk, therefore, that the implicit use of a *simpliste* savings function will serve to *create* the appearance of a causal relationship, when none really exists.

But while a negative causal relationship between inflows and savings is not supported by the quantitative evidence it would be surprising if there were not some countries where the availability of foreign resources resulted in savings lower than they would have been in their absence. A careful study of Korea, for instance, concludes that in the mid-1950s the Government followed policies "for maximizing the inflow of foreign aid," by "an overvalued exchange rate, relatively low tariffs on imports, no efforts to encourage exports, a deficit budget ... and low interest rates."[15] The after-effects of the war plus conscious policy seem to have combined to produce low savings and high aid flows. Other analysts have suggested that India and Pakistan neglected agricultural development, and therefore the savings which a rapidly growing agriculture could have provided, because they knew that shortfalls would be made good by United States surplus commodities; that opportunities for Cuban, Mexican and Central American investors were preempted by United States capital; and that negative savings rates in Liberia and extravagant expenditures leading to lower savings in Ghana were due to the ready availability of suppliers' credits.

But only careful analysis of individual countries can really shed any light on the impact of foreign inflows on savings, exports or growth, and even such analyses are invariably subject to disagreement and dispute. For instance, what if Korea had received less aid? Would it have devalued, raised tariffs, encouraged exports, raised taxes and interest rates, or would it have imposed stricter quantitative restrictions on imports, nationalized the export industry and banks, and further depressed agricultural income, and what consequence would either set of policies have had on savings just after the civil war? In the Pakistan case, the argument that surplus commodities weakened the agricultural development effort has been countered by the contention that their availability made possible a policy of price stabilization and the termination of the allocation system, both crucial to increased agricultural output.

There are no good answers to the question "what would have happened with less or more foreign resource inflows?" In some circumstances, foreign inflows undoubtedly stimulated savings, so that each dollar of inflows led to more than a dollar of investment, while in other cases they discouraged savings and a dollar of inflows may have led to much less than a dollar of investment. However, as long as both savings and inflows are substantially affected by third factors, the negative correlation between the two found in many studies sheds little or no light on their causal relationship.

ENDNOTES

1. The names most prominently associated with this approach are Rosenstein-Rodan (e.g., "International Aid for Underdeveloped Countries," Review of Economics and Statistics, May, 1961); Millikan and Rostow (e.g., A Proposal: Key to an Effective Foreign Policy, New York: Harper 1957); and H. B. Chenery (e.g., "Foreign Assistance and Economic Development," American Economic Review, September, 1966, with A. Strout; "Development Alternatives in an Open Economy: The Case of Israel," Economic Journal, March 1962, with M. Bruno; and "Foreign Aid and Economic Development: The Case Of Greece," Review of Economics and Statistics, February 1966, with I. Adelman).

2. Anisur Rahman (in "The Welfare Economics of Foreign Aid," Pakistan Development Review, Summer 1967) suggests, however, that it may actually be considered desirable, in the interests of intertemporal equity, to use foreign resources to increase consumption rather than investment.

3. Most notably Griffin and Enos; cf. footnote following.

4. They include: (a) K.B. Griffin and J.L. Enos, "Foreign Assistance: Objectives and Consequences," Economic Development and Cultural Change, April 1970; and K.B. Griffin, "Foreign Capital, Domestic Savings and Economic Development," Bulletin, Oxford University, Institute of Economics and Statistics, May 1970; (b) Anisur Rahman, "Foreign Capital and Domestic Savings: A Test of Haavelmo's Hypothesis with Cross-Country Data," Review of Economics and Statistics, February 1968; (c) Kaj Areskoug, External Borrowing: Its Role in Economic Development (Praeger, 1969); (d) Thomas Weisskopf, "The Impact of Foreign Capital Inflow on Domestic Savings in Underdeveloped Countries," Journal of International Economics, Vol. 2, No. 1, February 1972; (e) H.B. Chenery, "Development Alternatives for Latin America" (with P. Eckstein), Journal of Political Economy, July/August 1970; "A Uniform Analysis of Development Patterns" (with H. Elkington and C. Sims), Economic Development Reports, Nos. 148 and 158, Center for International Affairs, Harvard University; and "Targets for Development," Economic Development Report, 153.

5. Griffin suggests, in addition, that the availability of foreign capital reduces the incentive to save of domestic investors and that the availability of imported consumer goods, financed by foreign capital, also reduces savings incentives. It is questionable whether these would be major factors in the overall rate of savings.

6. H.S. Houthakker, "On Some Determinants of Savings in Developed and Underdeveloped Countries," in E.A.G. Robinson (ed.) Problems in Economic Development, London, 1965.

7. Robin Marris ("Can We Measure the Need for Development Assistance?" Economic Journal, September

1970) concludes that an equal number of countries had a dominant savings and foreign exchange constraint.

8. For the United States, Paul Taubman found that different savings series gave quite different marginal propensities to save out of normal income, ranging from 0.07 to 0.20 for the same model. ("Personal Savings: A Time Series of Three Measures of the Same Conceptual Series," *Review of Economics and Statistics*, February 1968.)

9. All figures rounded decade averages. Source: I.B.R.D. "World Tables." A Statistical Appendix is available from the author, giving basic data by country, sources and definitions.

10. A. Strout and P. Clark in an extensive study of aid (*Aid, Performance, Self-Help and Need*, A.I.D. Discussion Paper No. 20, Agency for International Development, July 1969) found a significant correlation of aid with *per capita* income (negative) and a calculated foreign exchange gap.

11. Papanek, Schydlowsky and Stern, *Decision-Making for Economic Development*, Houghton Mifflin, 1971.

12. As pointed out by Raymond Vernon, capital flight by citizens of a country, like other transactions of theirs, represents (negative) "foreign resources" only in a definitional sense. Usually subtracted from foreign private investment, capital flight by citizens can lead to an understatement of actual foreign private investment, calculated on a net basis.

13. In the 1960s Argentina also falls into this category in Table I. However, for peculiar structural reasons, the high savings rates of Argentina are almost certainly spurious. If both capital goods and agricultural exports were valued at world market prices in the national accounts, Argentina would not appear among the high savers.

14. Some additional work involving cross-country regression analyses of the relationship of growth with savings, aid, foreign private investment and other resource inflows and of savings with exports, inflows and other factors is reported in my "Aid, Foreign Private Investment, Savings and Growth in Less Developed Countries," *Journal of Political Economy*, January/February 1973.

15. D.C. Cole and P. Lyman, *Korean Development – The Interplay of Politics and Economics*, Cambridge: Harvard University Press, 1970, p. 170.

Kuwait: A Super-Affluent Society

FAKHRI SHEHAB

Stretching over some 6,000 square miles of the hard, gravelly and waterless northeast corner of the Persian Gulf, Kuwait has been thrust from oblivion into sudden prominence by her hidden wealth and the creative genius of Western enterprise and technology. In less than two decades, since the first shipment of oil left her shores, material riches have changed the face of her barren territory, and Kuwait is now experiencing a host of complex social, political and economic problems which are shaking her essentially tribal and primitive structure. The purpose of this essay is to discuss the nature of the challenge presented by this transitional phase and to examine Kuwait's response to it. But in order to appreciate the magnitude of the task that confronts this city–state, the reader must first know something of the static society that used to exist and of the main events that have so radically transformed it into what it is now.

Present-day Kuwait was reportedly founded in the early eighteenth century by tribesmen driven from their home in inner Arabia by warring kinsmen. The tiny fishing village they founded offered few and meagre resources; but its very austerity was perhaps its main asset. For the rigorous physical environment rendered the individual tough, imaginative, enterprising and excellent in team-work. These qualities have, for over two centuries, distinguished the Kuwaitis as the Gulf's most successful businessmen, sailors and sea-farers.

Broadly speaking, Kuwait was comprised of three main groups: a ruling family, an oligarchy of merchants and a working class

Fakhri Shehab. This article is reprinted with permission of *Foreign Affairs* (April 1964), Copyright 1964 by the Council on Foreign Affairs.

– mostly fishermen, pearl-divers and ship-builders. Of these groups, the second has been by far the most powerful and dynamic social force. It was the merchants' enterprising spirit that provided the ruling family with their meagre income in the shape of customs duties and provided employment for the rest of the community. A triple social structure still exists in Kuwait, although, as we shall see, new circumstances are altering it.

This small community needed peace first and foremost to enable it to eke out a living, and, in the two and a half centuries since they settled on the Gulf, the Kuwaitis have had no more than two internal crises involving serious violence, and only a few skirmishes with neighboring tribes. Crimes of violence are almost unknown and even litigation is a rare indulgence. As with individuals, so with the state: the desire for peace eminently characterizes Kuwait's relations with her neighbors – a monumental diplomatic feat considering the struggle for power that divides the Arab states.

Of governmental organization Kuwait possessed little more than the traditional tribal type in which power was vested in an autocratic ruler, who, in conformity with tradition, was chosen from among members of the Subah family for his superior personal qualities. The choice of a new ruler was usually regarded as a family affair; and while clearly it was no democracy, this primitive political system allowed the Kuwaiti wide freedoms of action and expression. Regard for tradition made public opinion an important political force. Hence, it was the general practice for the ruler to consult the elders of the community on matters involving serious decisions. Law and order were maintained in a simple and unceremonious way in accordance with Islamic law as modified by tribal usage and local custom. Internal security was preserved by a small bodyguard, and in times of emergency external security was the responsibility of all able-bodied men (and sometimes women). Education was confined to a few primitive and privately run semi-religious institutions and not until 1912 did the town notables organize the first elementary school. As for health services, Kuwait's first hospital was not opened until well after her oil had begun to flow, in 1949.

This tribal structure held sway until 1937 when popular endeavors to modernize it finally led to the election of the short-lived Legislative Assembly whose only legacy was the creation of certain government departments with broadly defined functions. These departments formed Kuwait's basic administrative framework until 1962, when constitutional government was introduced.

Import duties, varying between 4 and 6 percent, constituted the main source of public revenue. The scope of the government operations may be seen from the fact that in 1938–39 public revenue totaled some £60,000 (approximately $290,000), of which nearly two-thirds came from import duties and the rest from miscellaneous dues and fees, plus a small royalty paid by the Kuwait Oil Company following the discovery, though not the actual extraction, of oil. This primitive financial system drew no distinction between public domain or revenue, on the one hand, and the ruler's personal estate and income on the other. At this stage, the city-state had hardly emerged as an independent and recognizable entity and the ruler, still resembling a tribal chieftain, combined with his basic responsibilities of maintaining law and order the traditional and costly functions of tribal hospitality.

As for the private sector, pearling and seafaring together absorbed the majority of Kuwait's labor force (estimated at some 8,000 to 10,000 men). It is said that average earnings in pearling hardly exceeded 100 rupees (just over $35 at the prewar rate) for a season of three to four months. This was often supplemented by seafaring, which brought in an additional 150 or 200 rupees for an expedition of some six months. Exceptionally, an enterprising man could add to these two sources of income by trading, and might make a profit of some 100 or 200 rupees. Thus, at best, average family earnings from various sources barely touched 500 rupees (rather less than $180) a year. Assuming an average family of five, these calculations would suggest an average personal annual income of some 100 rupees (roughly about $35). As for an unskilled laborer, he barely managed to reach subsistence level. His daily wage was not more than a half rupee, and employment was rarely available throughout the year. These conditions were far worse than those then obtaining in the agrarian communities of Iran or Iraq.

II

Today such conditions exist only in memory, for Kuwait now is a land of superlatives. It is the largest oil producer in the Middle East and the fourth largest in the world; it boasts the world's largest oil port where the world's largest tankers are loaded in record time; at 62 million barrels, its proved oil reserves are the largest in the world; and the magnitude of its oil receipts in relation to the size of the native population is such that even if all other sources of income in both the private and public sectors are disregarded, the annual revenue per citizen amounts to K.D. 1,200 (Kuwait Dinar = U.S. $2.8).

In sharp and dramatic contrast with the austerity of former times, Kuwait's current foreign trade statistics list an extraordinarily wide range of luxury goods transported by sea, land and air from some 60-odd countries, at an annual expenditure averaging in recent years nearly $300,000,000, or about $825 per inhabitant. More impressive still is the present-day expenditure on fresh water distillation and power supply which costs the state not less than $140 per inhabitant, while every tree and shrub that decorates her thoroughfares and public squares costs an average of some $250 a year. As for social services, a welfare state of unsurpassed munificence has suddenly emerged. Expenditure on health and education and other benefits (mostly in pecuniary forms) has placed this tiny state on a higher level than some of the most sophisticated societies in the world; for in the fiscal year 1961-62 it reached some $240 per inhabitant as compared with $210 in the U.K. and slightly less in Sweden. [1]

What has been the impact of the sudden explosion of wealth upon this primitive society? In less that two decades the whole face of Kuwait has changed beyond recognition. But behind the spectacular physical change lie fundamental problems which have rarely, if ever, been faced by an affluent community before.

One basic question has always been asked: how long is it going to last? The Kuwaitis are quite alive to the precariousness of their riches. Anxiety over the future dominates their thoughts and many of their actions. It is evident in the attempt to build up their social capital, to set up an organized public service and to foster rapid industrial development; it is evident in the determined effort to accumulate foreign reserves; and, above all, it is evident in the desire to achieve all this in a desperately short time. Haste is, indeed, the order of the day.

But growth is a function of time and the hurried transformation of Kuwait from the poor, obscure and stagnant society it used to be into one of uncommon complexity and sophistication has proved challenging and, at times, even dangerous.

Oil receipts began to accrue in 1946. In the early stages no more than rudimentary physical planning of the town was needed. The sharp increase in revenue in 1951

made clear that planning required expert advice, and foreign consultants were engaged for this purpose. Subsequently, a group of five engineering firms was engaged to carry out the work on a cost-plus basis. It was soon discovered, however, that this procedure pushed up costs unduly and left much room for abuse, and it was abandoned. It was realized that the task of building could not be simply farmed out to foreign contractors. Responsibility for planning and executing a development program was then entrusted to the Public Works Department. This was a tribute to the courage of the government, considering Kuwait's small population and the acute shortage of trained personnel.

Paucity of population is not necessarily associated with economic backwardness; the shortage of trained people is. The presence of both in a setting of extreme wealth makes the story of Kuwait unique. The earliest population figures available for those years are from the first census of 1957. They give Kuwait's total indigenous labor force as being 23,977, all between 15 and 60 years of age. By far the largest group (over 19,000) was composed of those with either no training at all or with only minimal professional qualifications. Another group, designated "professionals and technologists" and totaling some 4,000, includes only one chemist, one geologist, two physicians, two author-journalists, eight accountants and 156 clergymen.

The government's difficulties thus can hardly be exaggerated. To ensure control of its own affairs, it gave preference to its own citizens; and if suitable Kuwaitis were not available preference went to other Arab citizens and only in the last resort to non-Arabs. With abundant financial resources and in the absence of a strong civil service tradition, there soon evolved an administrative machine which was vast, complicated, cumbersome and not always guided by the highest ethical standards.

This created more problems for the state

than it solved. Since all top administrative and executive jobs were reserved for citizens, the responsibility for final decisions invariably lay with them; the presence of the foreign technician or adviser did not help much. The Kuwaiti policy-maker was still called upon daily to evaluate highly technical, and not infrequently conflicting, proposals which ranged from the choice of some complex electronic equipment for an ultra-modern telephone system to the assessment of the chemical components of local soils as factors affecting the choice of road-construction techniques. As the great majority of Kuwaiti executives came to their new responsibilities unprepared, vital decisions were often deferred, and when they were made, showed the pressure of vested interests.

There was also the problem of the mere volume of the new business. At the start, far too many projects were undertaken and as time went on the number increased. The demands on the limited time of the Kuwaiti executives and policy-makers grew correspondingly, resulting in insufficient guidance from the top. This shortage of leadership in Kuwait was alarming, since it involved the one thing that could not be imported from abroad.

Meanwhile, business was offering unlimited scope for success and, to the qualified few, its attraction was too powerful to be resisted. Some sort of a compromise had therefore to be devised to eliminate this competition, and it was found by permitting civil servants to run their own businesses side-by-side with their public offices. This concession caused immense harm. It overtaxed the limited time and energy of those in key positions, strained their allegiance to the state, exposed them to grave temptations and meant that the public service ceased to be considered a career. Senior appointments were generally accepted for prestige reasons, mostly by those who lacked distinction; and employment in the lower echelons was regarded

more or less as a sinecure, or as a means of channeling a certain amount of the wealth to the average citizen.

These factors have led to such overcrowding in the public service that salaries and wages now create a very serious drain on the treasury. The city-state at present has on its payroll no less than 53,000 men and women, both indigenous and aliens, excluding those in the armed forces, at an annual cost of nearly $168,000,000. This means that every three citizens are being served by one public servant at an average cost of about $1,120 per citizen.

This, then, was one of the results of the second phase of the experiment. It raised public expenditures for administration to an incredible level. It placed in positions of great responsibility either men of an older generation, whose views and standards were hopelessly outdated, or very young persons, who lacked the required experience; and it put a heavy strain on their loyalties. Further, it eliminated competitive selection for the public service and thus encouraged complacency in the new generation and a tendency to judge performance by local standards alone.

III

It was only natural that the new wealth should create a demand for services hitherto unknown in the country. The resulting problem was made especially acute by the ambitious projects planned by the government, and its determination to carry them out all at once. Inevitably, a uniquely attractive market for labor was created and a flood of skilled and unskilled workers flocked from the four corners of the globe, but mostly from neighboring countries. This influx created new problems. The ethnic and political composition of this immigrant labor was heterogeneous, though the largest proportion (about 70 percent) were Arabs. Their social habits, cultures, creeds and, above all, political leanings were numerous and widely divergent.

Moreover, by far the largest group of these aliens (73 percent) were males mostly between 15 and 50 years of age, which meant that they were transient immigrants. [2] It is this transient population that provides the bulk of Kuwait's skilled labor and 78 percent of her unskilled workers. It is they who supply the city-state with her teachers, doctors, architects, engineers and administrative and managerial personnel. They are the makers of her laws, the builders of her industry and the founders of her financial institutions. So pervasive has been their influence that there is hardly an aspect of national life which does not bear their mark. It affects the Kuwaitis choice of fashion, architecture and interior decoration; their cultural and artistic interest; their entertainments and dietetic habits; and even their colloquial Arabic, which has considerably changed under the influence of the newcomers.

Yet this all-powerful community of aliens has no permanent ties with the host country. Their services will apparently continue to be in demand indefinitely; yet the individuals themselves are constantly changing and are regarded by their hosts as changeable. This situation has inevitably led to a lack of continuity in planning and performance as well as to a sense of instability among the resident aliens, discernible in their behavior and their attitudes to the state.

The ephemeral status of the members of this community is especially marked among manual and menial workers. Grim unemployment in neighboring countries has driven tens of thousands of these men to search for a living in this rich oasis. But in turn the unlimited supply of labor has inevitably depressed wages to the point where the now derelict and nearly forgotten "iron law" may be seen in full swing. At present an unskilled laborer in Kuwait makes between nine and twelve shillings a day (about $1.25 to $1.65). This is generally higher than average earnings in the region; but the advantage is lost in a country where most goods are imported, where major imports are controlled by oligopolies and where rents and utilities are inordinately high. The result is that families are often left at home, and the wage-earner's remittances to his dependents reduce him to hardly more than subsistence. Thus the fate of thousands of aliens is to live in squalid hovels, indefinitely separated from their homes and families, desperate for employment; they have exchanged the best of their working years for wages that can just keep them and their dependents alive. Against the background of superabundance and prodigality existing in Kuwait, the wide gulf between the two segments of the population is not only indefensible but is bound to engender social resentment and instability.

Nor is this all. The remittances of the resident aliens are a permanent drain on the national income. The extent of it cannot be ascertained, but is conservatively estimated at some $120,000,000 a year. If this labor force could be persuaded to strike roots in Kuwait, this drain on national wealth would be minimized and the base of the economy would be broadened. This viewpoint is gaining recognition, but not fast enough.

Finally, the growing size of this foreign labor force has suddenly awakened the Kuwaitis to the fact that they are about to become a minority in their own country. According to the 1961 population census, they barely exceed half the total. This would be serious enough in any country, let alone in one so small, under-populated and rich, and where the indigenous community lacks all the vital technical skills.

IV

The discovery that it was being swamped by aliens alarmed Kuwait and prompted defensive measures. Foremost among these was the naturalization decree of 1959 and its amendment in 1960. This legislation, a landmark in Kuwait's history, confined

Kuwaiti citizenship to residents in Kuwait prior to 1920, to their descendants in the male line and to foreign women upon marriage to Kuwaitis. For Arabs, naturalization is now possible only after 10 years of residence, and for non-Arabs after 15 years, commencing, in both cases, from the date of the amending decree. Moreover, only 50 persons are to be granted citizenship in any one year. Exceptions to this general rule are that Arabs in residence before 1945, and foreigners before 1930, as well as other Arab nationals who have performed outstanding services to the state, may be granted citizenship without waiting.

The legislation also confined certain basic rights and privileges to the citizen class. All imports and retail trades and all contractual business are either limited to Kuwaiti nationals or have to be transacted through Kuwaiti agents. In the civil service, pension rights, permanent tenure and certain key executive positions are the exclusive privileges of citizens. The entry of aliens into some professions such as medicine and law, where not many citizens could compete for a long time to come, is restricted to a stringent licensing system.

A unique feature of this transformation is the ingenious device evolved to diffuse the new wealth among the citizen class through public expenditure. As we have seen earlier, the distinction between public income and property and the ruler's income or property was unknown in Kuwait. Gradually, as budgetary practices and controls were introduced, all public receipts were paid into the Exchequer.[3] Since the process was confined at first to annual disbursements and receipts of money, control of the public land was overlooked; and so long as realty was not of great economic significance the oversight was not serious. But then real estate prices rocketed. Meanwhile, large tracts of worthless desert had been seized and fenced in by those who had either the foresight or foreknowledge to anticipate the coming public projects; and

they subsequently were compensated handsomely by the state. With a rapid turnover of land and in the absence of legislation covering the acquisition of land for public uses, the cost to the Treasury was fantastic.

The process within the city itself differed somewhat from that outside the old city wall. Land was purchased in excess of what was actually required for public projects, and the surplus was later sold back to the public, often at a fraction (estimated at 4 percent) of its cost to the Treasury. Enormous private fortunes were amassed by both selling to, and buying from, the state. It has been estimated that between 1957 and 1962 close to $840,000,000 of public money was spent on land.

This huge expenditure would have been justified on the grounds that it engendered economic activity and diffused a large portion of the new wealth, were it not that in fact only a limited amount was piped into the local economy. By far the larger part was remitted abroad either directly, or indirectly through the banking system. Further, the wealth was not spread evenly, the greater part going to those at the top of the social pyramid, even though, because of the small size of the indigenous community, a fair amount did go also to the masses. It now is argued that unless the process is continued, large-scale bankruptcies will wreck the economy, since substantial bank advances have been made to merchants who are said to have invested them in land. It is difficult to ascertain whether this is true; but banking statistics show that advances to Kuwaiti residents (about $110,600,000 toward the end of 1963) represent just over 40 percent of total visible imports – a fact that hardly bears out the argument. Yet the practice continues unabated despite serious warning by government advisers and the recommendation of the World Bank.

The process of diffusing the new wealth was not confined, however, to land purchases. Social security benefits and state aid in most generous and varied forms, free medical treatment and scholarships for training abroad, the granting of free building sites and loans at very low interest – all were made available to the citizen as his birthright.

V

The effects of these measures on Kuwait must be evaluated from two standpoints: the response they evoked from the aliens and the impact they had on the citizen class.

That they have been effective in achieving their aim is obvious enough. They have introduced a sharp distinction between the two classes of society; and they have reserved to the citizens all the fruits of the windfall of riches (with the lion's share going to a relatively small group within this class). Little else can be said in favor of these measures. They have permanently estranged and embittered the most efficient and indispensable element in the community – the resident alien. Uprooted, often separated from his family, insecure and unsettled, he has now become envious and resentful. With little or no hope of being permanently integrated into the community, he is left without any sense of allegiance to Kuwait.

Let us look now at the impact of these protective and restrictive measures on the citizens for whom they were devised. An immediate consequence was the reversal of the old order that made the state and members of the ruling family dependent on the merchants, for now it was the latter who sought favors from the state. They wanted not only compensation for land but also the preservation of their commercial interests. While the state has been strengthened by its financial independence and has become less susceptible to pressures from this group, the change was not an unmixed blessing, considering that the government is not dependent upon popular consent for its annual income.

Further, the ease with which wealth has been acquired has impaired the enterprise of the mercantile class and made them dependent on the state. Hardly any worthwhile financial or industrial venture which deviates from the established pattern is ever attempted by Kuwaiti entrepreneurs (of whom there are, in any case, very few) unless it is assured of state financing, protection or guarantee. Conversely, private capital can be forthcoming to excess when an expatriate entrepreneur, acting with state cooperation, comes forward with new ideas for investment.

Developments are disturbing, too, at the other end of the social scale. Here the state's compensatory payments were naturally less extensive, since the property involved was mainly private dwelling houses. The money received was promptly spent, usually on prestige items or travel abroad. When this spurt was over, the common citizen was assured a modest income from a minor government sinecure, and various state benefits, plus a small private income from, say, a taxi or a tiny retail store – the whole accepted in much the same spirit as that of a pensioner receiving his dole.

Originally intended to preserve the identity of the old community, reserve the bulk of the new wealth for its citizens and protect them against the intruding aliens, these measures have inadvertently forced competition out of national life and made Kuwait an insular society. The elimination of competition now probably presents the most serious social danger facing Kuwait. Young people have lost their perspective, their urge to acquire knowledge, their acceptance of discipline. As a result, the drive, diligence and risk-taking that characterized the old Kuwaiti are no more. At both ends of the social scale the new citizen is content to enjoy a life of leisure and inertia, and is unwilling that this happy state of affairs should be disturbed. Protected, pampered, lavishly provided for and accountable to no one, he lives in a world of make-believe.

Another serious threat is posed to Kuwaiti society by the social vacuum which these measures have created. By relegating the traditionally dynamic classes to a position of only titular authority at the apex of the social pyramid or else to one of passive contentment, they have placed a premium on inertia and prevented the rise of an indigenous and dynamic middle class. The vacuum thus created is naturally filled by watchful and enterprising aliens.

The people attracted to Kuwait by its new wealth were of varied backgrounds, experiences and standards of conduct. The avarice and intrigues of many of them have brought bitter disillusionment to the Kuwaiti. Consequently, traditional Kuwaiti behavior is changing and men for whom the spoken word used to have the sanctity of a written contract have become instinctively suspicious of strangers and new ideas.

Further, the magnitude of the new wealth has given money and material possessions an importance and their owners a sense of power hitherto unknown. Naturally this has resulted in false perspectives. Ostentatious consumption, prodigal expenditure, idleness and pleasure-seeking are common; frugality, moderation and enterprise have become the antiquated virtues of a bygone age.

Finally, and most important of all, the new wealth has assumed such proportions that it is beginning to threaten the very concept of the state. This is because the lavish welfare benefits and privileges have entailed no effort or sacrifice on the part of the public, which sees no need to contribute to a state whose chief problem is what to do with its income. A fundamental principle in the relationship between state and citizen has therefore been jeopardized – namely, that in exchange for protection and benefits, the citizen has a duty to serve it and to make necessary sacrifices for it. The idea of the state as a communal institution demanding service, sacrifice and devotion, and as an embodiment of political and social ideas, exists today in the minds and hearts of very few and exceptional Kuwaitis.

VI

This tiny city-state: prodigal, complacent, short of technical skills, unperturbed by the acquisitiveness of its upper classes, the torpor of its common citizens and the savage rivalry among its resident aliens – what chance has it of survival in a poor, covetous and unstable region?

First it must be noted that most major events in the Middle East are influenced by external and regional forces; the survival of political regimes does not solely depend on their own economic or social merits. However, the record of Kuwait's achievements is such that (barring the unexpected) one may suppose that disruptive forces from outside will encounter there an exceptional degree of viability and resilience.

Kuwait entered the modern era of welfare and technology with very few handicaps from her past. Unfettered by rigid traditions or conventions, she was free to experiment and adopt institutions and practices best suited to her own circumstances. Naturally anyone willing to follow the rough path of trial and error must be prepared to pay the price; Kuwait was willing and has done so. This willingness to experiment with new ideas gives the state both dynamism and flexibility not often found in old societies. Kuwait is not stagnant, nor has her social fabric as yet assumed final form. Her social and economic legislation is constantly revised and improved; her public services are being reorganized and streamlined; her city planning is being reviewed.

There is, further, a feeling on the part of the indigenous community that its present privileged position can be preserved only by total and unqualified domestic solidarity. Solidarity among the Kuwaitis is a time-honored tradition, and the recent waves of immigration have so strengthened the need for it that any deviation is now simply inconceivable. This was plainly demonstrated in 1961 when the entire community rallied around the Emir in the face of Kassem's threats; all past rancor was forgotten as autocratic rule was wisely replaced by constitutional government.

Despite the shortcomings and dangers attending the rapid transformation of a primitive society into one of great sophistication, certain fundamental traits in the character of the individual Kuwaiti remain unimpaired. He still remains tolerant, placid, and, above all, devoted to and proud of his freedom. These qualities explain why differences of opinion continue to be settled by debate and not violence; why the fundamental freedoms of speech and the press are respected; why censorship and the secret police – two monumental features in every Arab state – do not figure in Kuwait's political life, and have no impact on the thoughts or actions of her people. It is fortunate that the drafting of the constitution should have been completed during this period of Kuwait's history when these qualities are still a salient feature of the Kuwaiti personality.

There remains one more item on this balance sheet which calls for special mention, namely Kuwait's attitude toward the massive, woeful and demoralizing poverty outside her boundaries.

Here again, Kuwait's perspicacity and high-mindedness have been extraordinary. Transcending all the animosities and feuds of contemporary Arab politics, she has single-handedly set up the most enduring and constructive institution ever attempted by a small state. This is the Kuwait Fund for the Economic Development of the Arab Countries, with capital resources totaling altogether K.D. 300,000,000 ($840,000,000). This institution has been established to make loans to other Arab states to enable them to carry out projects directly useful in developing their economies. It is a permanent, well-administered organization with clearly defined objectives and intelligent criteria for evaluating projects. It stands out

as a monument to Kuwait's foresight and generosity. It also marks a turning point in her development as a state, for it demonstrates that she recognizes her responsibilities and is willing and able to live up to them. Within less than two years of its inception, the Fund has already lent $19,600,000 to the Sudan for the modernization of its railways; $21,000,000 to Jordan for agricultural and industrial projects; and $18,200,000 to Tunisia; besides substantial sums pledged to Algeria, the Yemen and the U.A.R.

Naturally, Kuwait is very proud of her achievement; but in determining her fate her own assessment of her performance is far less important than the opinion of her neighbors. Whether or not her extravagance will be excused because of her generosity, only time will tell. What is certain is that she can justify her survival as a political entity in this age of regional internationalism only by serving effectively and impartially as a distributor of substantial economic aid to her neighbors. Herein lies Kuwait's present *raison d'etre*. In order to maintain her independent identity she will have to pursue her plans for economic aid with a zeal induced by the knowledge that it is an essential part of her struggle for survival.

ENDNOTES

1. Both the British and the Swedish figures include payments by the private sector in the form of employers' and employees' contributions.

2. This fact is reflected in the number of air travelers, which in recent years has reached some 230,000 annually, or more than 70 percent of the total population.

3. However, this new practice does not include Kuwait's substantial reserves which still remain with the Bank of England in the name of His Highness the Emir.

About the Authors in Chapter 8

Robert Z. Aliber teaches international finance at the University of Chicago. He is author of *The International Money Game*, 5th ed., rev. (New York: Basic Books), 1987. His edited volume, *The Handbook of International Financial Management* (Homewood, Ill.: Dow Jones-Irwin), was published in 1989.

Gustav Papanek is Professor of Economics and Director of the Asian Program in the Institute for Economic Development of Boston University. This article was written at the time that he was Director of the Development Advisory Service and on the faculty of Economics at Harvard University. "Aid, Growth and Equity in Southern Asia," a related article, was published in *Poverty and Aid*, J.R. Parkinson (ed.) (Basil Blackwell), 1983.

Fakhri Shehab was on the Faculty of Social Studies in Oxford University at the time that this article was written in 1964.

CHAPTER 9

Participation in the Process of Development

Introduction

IN MORE RECENT YEARS it has been recognized that western models of development have been presented to developing areas rather than a mixture of western and indigenous approaches. Wiarda (1987) has addressed the problem of ethnocentrism in relation to the politics of agrarian reform, community development, law and development, and family planning, concluding that it will be many years before newer models of development generate more appropriate programs.

On the other hand, there is already some realization of this. The participatory model of development assumes that the goal of development is to meet the needs and aspirations of the people. It stresses that development should start from where people are in terms of desires and beliefs. Individuals, administrative bodies, external agencies, and national government become involved in a dialogue. The dialogue and interaction between people and external agencies may become fruitful only if people's goals and desires are placed above the objectives of the external agencies participating in plans for development. This is a difficult and time-consuming process. Even if the results are not always what are anticipated, the involvement of people in development planning adds to the community's understanding of the process of development.

Mass communication has a role to play in development and may be used to improve productivity, equality, and the standard of living in developing countries. These ends are achieved by improving the access to information and by effecting structural changes necessary to achieve development. Communication for development, development communication, can be effective only if there is a political will for necessary socioeconomic changes. Boafo (1985), after discussing various definitions of development communication, states that he conceptualizes it as "the planned, conscious and systematized use of communication strategies and processes to bridge informational and attitudinal gaps and to establish or sustain a climate that favors the process of change and development." Since three-quarters of the African population lives in areas served only by the traditional media, this is difficult. This is particularly true when the ruling elite have other goals, such as building personality cults around themselves. When there is no question of the desirability of bringing modern world development to rural areas by radio and television, there are equipment problems that reduce program effectiveness even in a country as determined and experienced as India (Sinha, 1986). If all else is surmounted, there is still the problem of news being predominantly produced and processed by developed nations (Haule, 1984). This has become a topic of international controversy but it remains to be seen if such an organization as the Pan African News Agency can be more effective in producing objective accounts of events relevant to the complex problems of social and economic development.

The Articles in Chapter 9

Participation in development is defined as an organized effort to empower groups that have previously been excluded from controlling resources vital to their welfare. *Goulet* suggests that modes of participation may vary across types of development. For example, in a people-centered development program the focus is on fulfilling basic human needs and participation must occur at the grassroots level. Participation is both an end and a means, which implies that the process of participation involves making compromises between the requirements of efficiency and equality.

Perlman describes differences in perception between public officials who try to control developmental activities from the top and the urban poor at the bottom who are engaged in development activities. These differences give rise to misconceptions about the nature of people who reside in urban favelas and the developmental activities in which they are engaging along with the construction of housing. Those who are not familiar with these slum dwellers believe that they are, among other things, morally inferior and socially disorganized. These are myths. Socially, squatters are well organized and cohesive. Housing for the poor takes a variety of forms that must be understood by authorities who wish to help the poor with their housing needs. Since housing has a variety of goals, these must also be taken into consideration by authorities who are planning programs for development.

Siamwiza examines the administrative and organizational factors that constrain effective implementation of a participatory model (self-help) of development in Zambia. Although government units, non–governmental organizations, and external donors have played roles in assisting self-help projects, people and material shortcomings have resulted in disappointing results in both urban and rural Zambia. Furthermore, the components necessary to generate community participation, i.e., projects based on local needs and desires and democratic ways of participation, have often been lacking.

Leslie provides critical evaluation of the positive and negative effects of mass communication in developing societies. He argues that the mass media in developing countries are oriented toward promoting consumption of goods and services. The mass media disseminate western values, ideals, and stereotypes for which the technology is often very expensive. Thus, many developing nations have acquired expensive mass communication technologies while their educational and health services are deteriorating. Some have suggested that journalists should provide leadership in directing mass media toward development by examining and defining the link between underdevelopment and the foreign aid development community.

REFERENCES

Boafo, S.T. Kwame, "Utilizing Development Communication Strategies in African Societies: A Critical Perspective (Development Communication in Africa)," *Gazette*, Vol. 35, 1985, pp. 83–92.

Haule, John James, "Old Paradigm and New Order in the African Context: Toward an Appropriate Model of Communication and National Development," *Gazette*, Vol. 33, 1984, pp. 3–15.

Sinha, Arbind K., "Communication in Rural Development: The Indian Scene," *Gazette*, Vol. 39, 1986, pp. 59–70.

Wiarda, N.J., "Ethnocentrism and the Third World Development," *Society*, 24(6), 1987, pp. 55–64.

Participation in Development: New Avenues

DENIS GOULET

1. Introduction

The political redemocratization now under way in numerous countries of Asia and Latin America radically challenges the development strategies pursued during periods of dictatorial rule. The cry for greater political freedom is paralleled by demands for more equitable development policies. This linkage needs no explanation, since dictatorships employ high degrees of coercion to impose development policies conceived at the summit, and distribute the fruits of those policies to only a small circle of privileged clients and allies. On both counts, the majority of a nation's populace is excluded. Not surprisingly, therefore, that majority, actively or passively, seeks to change both its political rulers and their development strategies. The present essay argues the need for new forms of non-elite participation in the transition to equitable development strategies.

Before proceeding, however, a definition of participation is in order. Development theorists and practitioners readily associate participation with the writings of Ivan D. Illich (1983, 1976, 1978), who urges deprofessionalization in all domains of life – schooling, health care, transportation, planning – in order to make "ordinary people" responsible for their own well-being. A similar message was preached by the late Indian educator J.P. Naik (1975, 1977a, 1977b). The strongest affirmation of the

Denis Goulet. *World Development*, published by Pergamon Journals Ltd., Oxford, United Kingdom and the author, gave permission to reprint this article from Vol. 17, No. 2 (February 1989) in which it appeared on pages 165–178.

superior value of participation over elite decision making, however, comes from the pen of the Brazilian pedagogue Paulo Freire. For Freire (1970a, 1973, 1970b), the supreme touchstone of development is whether people who were previously treated as mere objects, known and acted upon, can now actively know and act upon, thereby becoming subjects of their own social destiny. When people are oppressed or reduced to the culture of silence, they do not participate in their own humanization. Conversely, when they participate, thereby becoming active subjects of knowledge and action, they begin to construct their properly human history and engage in processes of authentic development.

Although the general images related to participation are clear, to give the term a precise operational definition is most difficult. Most definitions are either too narrow or too broad, too strict or too loose. Nevertheless, the working definition adopted by Marshall Wolfe and the United Nations Research Institute for Social Development (UNRISD) is highly useful in development circles. According to Wolfe, participation designates "the organized efforts to increase control over resources and regulative institutions in given social situations, on the part of groups and movements hitherto excluded from such control" (Wolfe, 1983, p. 2).

This definition has the advantage of being simple and practical and can serve as a springboard from which to assess the merits and limits of participation in development. These merits and limits are perhaps best analyzed by classifying the diverse forms of participation along several axes.

2. Participation: A Typology

How many kinds of participation are there?

(a) *An important difference must initially be posited between participation taken as a goal or as a means*

In practice, participation is never prized exclusively as a goal; over time the goal necessarily ceases to be valuable unless it also manifests some instrumental merit as a means. Nevertheless, depending on whether one places dominant emphasis on the teleological or instrumental quality of participation, diverse criteria of measurement and assessment emerge. Hence instrumentalists judge participation favorably to the degree that it leads to "better" decisions or actions, whereas teleologists grant only secondary importance to efficiency. Political militants committed to egalitarian participation on ideological grounds accept "wasting time" in order to engage in full consultation, whether or not the practice proves effective. For them, participation is primarily a goal. On the other hand, some problem solvers defend popular consultation on the grounds that it is the best way of getting the job done or achieving lasting results. Here, evidently, problem solvers are treating participation primarily as a means. One may also view participation, however, as a hybrid reality which has the characteristics of both ends and means. Paulo Freire does this when discussing agricultural extension in "Extension or Communication" (1973, pp. 91–164). The ideal to be sought in agricultural extension, he explains, is true communication or reciprocal dialogue, not the mere issuance of "communiques" by expert agronomists to peasants or farmers. Therefore, extension agents must accept that "time be wasted" in order to engage in active dialogue with the final utilizers of the knowledge which is being "extended" or disseminated. Here participation clearly displays value both as a means and as an end.

This dual character of participation is evident in most development settings. Even instrumentalist champions of participation have come to discover that nonexpert populations, once consulted, insist on expressing their views even when immediate expert intervention might, in a purely technical sense, prove more efficient. Conversely, those who engage in participation primarily because they view it as a value for its own sake will also, over time, come to relativize its value as a goal and demand that it demonstrate some instrumental efficiency as well.

(b) *Participation may also be classified according to the scope of the arena in which it operates*

Participation sometimes exists within small arenas, the domestic affairs of a family, let us say, when children and spouses all have some voice in decisions. The arena of participation may be confined sectorally, as when school teachers are given freedom to shape the curriculum in collegial fashion, but not the budgets of their respective departments. Under Mao Ze Dong, the Chinese government resorted to mass participation covering numerous aspects of life in society at large: political campaigns, health programs, education, collective labor, and ideological education.

Depending on the scope of the arena or field in which participation occurs, its impact on development will vary accordingly.

(c) *A third criterion of classification is participation's originating agent*

Participation starts from three distinct sources: it can be induced from above by some authority or expert, generated from below by the non-expert populace itself, or catalytically promoted by some external third agent. Diverse social actors pursue quite different objectives when they initiate participation. Elite groups, governmental or other, usually seek some measure of social control over the process and the agents of participation. One classic example of such control was the Sistema Nacional de Movilizacion Social (SINAMOS) in Peru under the Velasco regime (Palmer, 1980, pp. 113–114 and Collier, 1975, p. 155ff).

Moreover, as Wolfe notes (Wolfe, 1983, p. 13 aff), state promoted participation usually aims at getting people to produce more or more efficiently; it focuses on inputs from those who participate. Basically, authorities view participation as a way of getting subordinates to help them achieve their own purposes.

Matters are different when participation is spontaneously generated from below. Usually, participation springs from below during a crisis and in response to some threat to a community's identity, survival, or values. With no prior plan, perhaps even with no precedent (although research into oral histories suggests that many allegedly "passive" communities of exploited people have been, in the past, active "communities of struggle") (Borda, 1979, 1975), some hitherto passive group mobilizes itself to protest, to resist, to say NO.

Paradoxically, as Camus argues in *The Rebel,* (Camus, 1956, pp. 13–14). any oppressed group's refusal to accept its condition is always the latent bearer of all affirmations of possible new orders. To say NO is to open up possibilities for saying YES in a multitude of ways. Those who begin by saying NO to their oppressors soon feel the need to utter some YES of their own. Thus, even the spontaneous mobilization of a powerless group to defend itself against destruction bears within it latent seeds of organization for multiple new developmental actions. Unplanned or spontaneous mobilization does not, however, exhaust the gamut of possibilities covered by the term "participation from below." Bottom-up participation may also result from deliberate initiatives taken by members of a "community of need" to obtain, or pressure others to obtain, some benfit from society at large or some particular group

therein. Unlike state initiated participation, which usually seeks to increase production on elicit new inputs, the type generated from below seeks consuumer benfits or a greater share of the pie, that is, some greater output.

A third originating source of participation is the catalytic action of third party change agents – technicians, community organizers, missionaries, or militants of some movement. Many such change agents adhere to ideologies which view self-reliance in poor people as a desirable goal. Accordingly, they see their own activation of the masses as "facilitation" or "pump priming," destined to disappear after the people awaken to their dormant capacities to decide and act for themselves. Although both types of participation originate *outside* the populace in question, intervention by third party change agents differs in important respects from top-down participation induced by the state or other elite groups. Like the form initiated from below, third party participation usually aims at empowering hitherto powerless people to make demands for goods, not to contribute their resources to someone else's purposes. In most cases, moreover, external facilitators are not content to help a populace mobilize; they also want it to organize. Mobilizing leads to joint action around some discrete, limited objective seen as urgent or important, whereas organizing is a longer-term pattern of collective action which postulates the need to meet and build solidarity even in the absence of specific tasks to conduct. The broader purpose of organization is to make people conscious of their strength – actual or potential – precisely *qua* group. That strength is to be utilized not only to resist injustices, but also to gain a deeper understanding of one's situation and consider alternative plans of action, including future or contingent action. Mobilization does not always lead to organization although, conversely, organization usually requires prior mobilization.

(d) *Participation can also be classified according to the moment at which it is introduced*

Different types of participation exist according to the time when they first occur: at the moment of diagnosing a problem, of selecting one possible course of action, of implementing a selected action, and so on. A patterned sequence culminating in final action is discernible. At any point in the sequence, a nonexpert populace may "enter in" and begin to share in its dynamics. These sequential moments are:
— initial diagnosis of the problem or condition;
— a listing of possible responses to be taken;
— selecting one possibility to enact;
— organizing, or otherwise preparing oneself, to implement the course of action chosen;
— the several specific steps entailed in implementing the chosen course;
— self-correction or evaluation in the course of implementation; and
— debating the merits of further mobilization or organization.

The quality of participation depends on its initial point of entry. Therefore, if one wishes to judge whether participation is authentic empowerment of the masses or merely a manipulation of them, it matters greatly when, in the overall sequence of steps, the participation begins.

Is participation necessary for development? From the typological analysis just presented, it follows that different kinds of development require different forms of participation. A "people-centered" development, which assigns priority to the satisfaction of basic human needs in the poor masses, to job creation, self-reliance, and the active preservation of cultural diversity, obviously requires a form of participation in which non-elites play an active role in the diagnosis of their own problems.

If, on the other hand, top-down, growth-oriented approaches to development are adopted by a particular country, it is most likely that whatever participation does occur will not be generated by the people themselves from below. Rather, participation will be imposed by the government for the purpose of rallying the populace to implement activities planned for it. In this case, bottom-up participation will generally be confined either to resistance, or to micro "do-it-yourself" activities. One notable exception is Korea's *Saemaul Undong* (New Community Movement), which allies governmental overtures with vital initiatives from the populace in exceptional fashion.[1] As for participation launched by outside change agents, the two decisive variables are the realm in which it operates – diagnosis, the selection of options, implementation of activities chosen, subsequent evaluation – and how quickly it phases out.

Most national development strategies can tolerate considerable participation in micro arenas, provided it poses no threat to the rules of the game operative in macro arenas. Thus a highly dictatorial and technocratic development pattern may allow considerable participation at local, problem solving levels. The Brazilian sociologist Fernando Henrique Cardoso (1983, p. 4) pointedly warns that a one-sided interest in promoting local self-reliance and participation may easily leave the way clear for oppressive central governments, or other elite institutions of society, to impose their will in those arenas which decisively shape the social forces at work in a nation at large. Cardoso concludes that participation ought to be linked to political activity in broader arenas, and not confined to small-scale, problem solving efforts.

The best indicator of whether participation is purely ornamental or a vital element of strategy is the relative weight assigned to it in the overall development practice of a given society. The mere existence of participation does not, by itself, reveal the quality of a nation's developmental style. This is one of several important lessons learned from three decades of efforts at participation in highly varied development settings.

3. Lessons of Experience

Experience suggests that it is *relatively* easy to achieve participation at micro levels of activity where homogeneous values and interest are not difficult to find and mobilize.

The very exiguity of scale facilitates the active involvement of all those concerned. Hundreds, if not thousands, of cooperatives, associations, and special interest groups have prospered in Third World countries. The annals of community development and self-reliance are replete with instances of such limited success (Du Sautoy, 1958; Galtung, O'Brien, and Preiswerk, 1980; Gran, 1983; Wasserstrom, 1985; Hirschman, 1984).

It is also relatively easy for participation to remain authentic, i.e., not to degenerate into manipulation by leaders, if it confines its operations to the modest arenas in which it began. Such participation creates, in effect, islets of social organization, which obey their own rules of problem solving irrespective of dominant rules governing society at large.

Participation of some sort is likewise quite easy to obtain when it is induced by power wielders at the macro level. Strong governments easily "mobilize" large masses to lend the appearance of support to their policies or leaders. Elements of coercion, threat, and fear are clearly at play here. Although such "participation" is easy to promote, only with great difficulty can it achieve authenticity. Authenticity means locating true decisional power in non-elite people, and freeing them from manipulation and co-optation. Moreover, in cases of "pseudo-participation" it is almost impossible to move from mobilization to organization which can truly empower people and transfer voice to them.

To illustrate, during the experiment in participatory municipal governance in Lages, Brazil (1976–82) (Alves, 1982) a progressive mayor mobilized the populace around spectacular achievements for a few years. After the mayor failed to win re-election for his designated successor, however, the former patterns of passivity took hold of the populace once again. The reason is that the people had not gained true empowermnt to organize themselves on their own terms. Similar experiences have been repeated elsewhere. Given the monumental changes now occurring in China's policy, one suspects that the much heralded Cultural Revolution may have had greater success in mobilizing than in organizing the masses (Wang 1985, Chapt. 7). In order to survive, induced or enforced participation requires continued coercion or pressure.

Not surprisingly, the most difficult form of participation to elicit and sustain is also the most indispensable to genuine development. This is the type of participation which starts at the bottom and reaches progressively upward into ever widening arenas of decision making. It is that form of participation which is initiated, or at least ratified, by the interested non-elite populace at an early point in the sequence of decisions. It matures into a social force wielding a critical mass of participating communities now enabled to enter into spheres of decision or action beyond their immediate problem solving. From micro to macro arenas the itinerary is followed. Experience shows that numerous successful micro operations never expand beyond their initial small scale. Many others, although they may grow to achieve "critical mass," do not successfully resist being repressed, co-opted, or marginalized. The supremely difficult transition is, precisely, that which takes a movement from the micro arena to the macro without dilution or destruction. One rare example of making that passage with a high degree of success is offered by the Sri Lankan Sarvodaya Shramadana movement (Goulet, 1981; Kantowsky, 1980; Macy, 1983; Ariyaratne, 1980).

Accordingly, a brief review of the philosophy and practice of Sarvodaya yields suggestive lessons regarding the possibilities, obstacles, and limits of participation.

4. Sarvodaya

(a) Development philosophy

A.T. Ariyaratne, founder of Sarvodaya, state that "a poor country like Sri Lanka would have gone 99% on the road to development if development goals were properly defined and understood by the people" (Ariyaratne, 1979, p. 2).

In its first decade (1958–68) Sarvodaya concentrated its efforts on the personality awakening of participants in Shramadana camps ("Shramadana" is the voluntary donation of labor to accomplish some task useful to one's community) (Ratnapala, 1979; Cf. Macy, 1980, pp. 316–317).

Sarvodaya's emphasis on "awakening" is incomprehensible without reference to classical doctrines of Theravada Buddhism, which counsels a middle way between all extremes: indulgence and abnegation, absorption in the world and total flight, atomistic salvation and collective deliverance. Theravada Buddhism summons each person to awaken fully to a reality replete with evils – suffering, death, old age, and corruption. All human ills have a deep underlying cause, namely, the stubborn persistence in individuals of *tanha*, that immoderate craving which makes them acquisitive, competitive, manipulative, exploitative and violent. All satisfactions of desire are ephemeral and addict one to further desires, themselves condemned to futile repetition in a Karmic cycle of birth, death, rebirth, and new death. The key to deliverance is to break out of this vicious circle by putting an end to the radical cause of human suffering. That the Buddha, 25 centuries ago, should have achieved enlightenment and deliverance, is the basis for hope. For Buddha, after reaching full understanding, did not withdraw to blissful *Nibbana*, the serene and total absence of suffering and craving, but remained in this perishable flesh to teach others the eightfold path to deliverance. Moral efforts to achieve enlightenment center on the prac-

tice of four virtues or basic principles of personality development: *metta*, loving-kindness and nonviolent respect for all life; *karuna*, compassionate action to remove the causes of evil; *mudita*, altruistic joy which is the short-term reward of service to others; and *upekka*, equanimity in the face of success or failure.

For Theravada Buddhism, which is the value base of Sarvodaya's village action, the goal of true development is that all individuals progress toward full enlightenment. The task of social policy, therefore, is to create conditions that favor such progress. Progress requires that the basic needs of all people be satisfied and that society at large obey the rules of *Dharma*, or righteousness. Sarvodaya draws its definition of development from dialogue with villagers who identify six intertwined elements in what modern thinkers call "development" (Ariyaratne, n.d. p. 4): a moral element (right action and righteous livelihood), a cultural one (accumulated beneficial experiences along with customs, beliefs, art, music, song, dance and drama, which help to keep a community of people together as a cohesive whole), a spiritual one (awakening of one's mind, through concentration to wisdom and unconditioned happiness), a social one (access of all to physical and mental health, knowledge, culture, etc.), a political one (the enjoyment of fundamental rights by all and freedom to shape one's political environment), and an economic one (meeting human needs). Over five hundred families surveyed identified ten basic needs: a clean and beautiful environment, an adequate supply of safe water, minimum clothing, a balanced diet, simple housing, health (optimum spiritual and social as well as physical well-being of the individual), communication, fuel, education, and cultural and educational development (Sarvodaya Development Education Institute 1978, p. 54).

Sarvodaya relativizes all the goods held out by standard capitalist and socialist models of development; it also refuses to consider as absolute the manner in which these goods are to be sought. Benefits are not to be pursued in violent ways, in a mode which confirms men and women in craving after illusory satisfactions, or in a manner which substitutes the political participation of the masses for decisions made by any despot – royal, presidential, bureaucratic or a collective party.

A wall chart displayed at national headquarters contrasts the present social order and Sarvodaya's preferred social order. It is reproduced as Table 1.

••••

Such is Sarvodaya's vision of development; but what form do its practical activities take in villages?

(b) *Action in the village*

After experimenting with Shramadana camps for ten years, Sarvodaya undertook more comprehensive programs in 100 villages. The scheme rapidly expanded to cover 1,000, 2,000, and later 3,000 villages, although, obviously, not all activities were launched in each village. Usually a preschool is opened, with young village women recruited to serve as teachers. The curriculum emphasizes moral values, work in a common garden, and initiation to basic health and hygiene. Where possible, specific groups in villages are organized around their work interests: there are farmers' groups, others for young adults, mothers, children, and so on. Other programs center on creating new opportunities for a "right livelihood": batik and sewing shops, mechanical repair and carpentry, farming on new plots, technology innovation units, and printing presses. Social and community service activities, in turn, range from health care centers, to community kitchens, trust funds for local credit, and libraries.

The key activity, however, is training of village leaders in development education institutes, some local, others regional or national in scope. Sarvodaya favors a model of the learning society – a lifelong process of awakening ever more deeply to reality, to one's place in shaping that reality, and to the meaning of one's action in any arena of work. Education reserves a large place for artistic expression. In daily meetings, called "Family Gatherings," participants take turns singing, dancing, playing musical instruments, performing plays and skits, reciting poetry and otherwise sharing individual talents with the wider community. At these gatherings, moments are reserved for prayer and meditation, for group discussion of practical problems encountered daily, and for talks by leaders or outside visitors. Young trainees are themselves responsible for scheduling the meetings, preparing them, properly setting agendas, and evaluating their peers. Trainees take turns planning the meetings and speaking or singing – all with a view to helping them overcome stage fright in public and acquire leadership qualities.

Considerable energies are spent coordinating local activities with Sarvodaya groups in neighboring villages and districts. The goal is to link villages one to another, to the nation, and eventually to the world itself. Not only has Sarvodaya encouraged international student exchange, it has also begun to promote International Sarvodaya Seminars.

The World Bank praises Sarvodaya's success in promoting village activities inexpensively. To the question "how much has all this cost?" the Bank replies:

> The Sarvodaya budget for 1979–80 was $2.3 million, an average of less that $1,000 per village assisted. Voluntary labor and other payments in kind contributed many times that amount. Of the cash budget, some 80% came from international assistance (both private and official), 10% from Sri Lankan donations and 10% from the sale of commodities produced in Sarvodaya's training farms and schools (World Bank, 1980, p. 75).

What impresses the Bank most favorably,

Table 1

Present social order Nature and Results	Sarvodaya social order Nature and Results
1) Absence of self-knowledge and self-reliance.	1) Striving for self-knowledge and self reliance.
2) Blind imitation of materialistic values.	2) Motivation based on spiritual values rooted in national culture.
3) Worship of wealth, power, position, untruth, violence, and selfishness dominate.	3) Respect for virtue, wisdom, capability, truth, non-violence, self-denial dominate.
4) Organizations based on possessive and competitive instincts become powerful, capitalist economy, bureaucracy, and power and party politics become major social forces.	4) Organizations based on sharing and cooperation become powerful, social trusteeship economy, people's participation in administration, and party-less people's politics become social realities.
5) Evil in man is harnessed, society is fragmented through considerations of race, caste, class, religion, party, etc.	5) Good in man is harnessed, society integrated as one human family.
6) Economic resources improperly combined, production suffers, unemployment.	6) Economic resources properly combined, production increases, employment.
7) Import-export economy based on production of commodities inherited from colonial times, foreign debts, subjugation to neocolonialism.	7) Self-sufficient economy based on the primary needs of the people, national solvency, national self-respect and economic freedom.
8) Dependence on large-scale organizations, capital intensive, wastage of human labor, corruption increases, environmental pollution.	8) Dependence on small-scale organizations, labor-intensive utilization of human labor, corruption decreases, protection of environment both physical and psychological.
9) Village subserves the city, rural exodus, moral degeneraton, social unrest and stagnation.	9) Balanced rural and urban awakening, moral regeneration.
10) Laws of punishment, instruments of law enforcement and state power increase, laws of *Dharma*, strength of *Dharma* and power of people diminish. Rulers become all powerful and people powerless.	10) Laws of righteousness, strength of *Dharma* and power of the people prevail. No ruling class, people all powerful. Sarvodaya realized.

however, is the way Sarvodaya "has involved the people in development."

In recent years, while continuing and even expanding its village activities, Sarvodaya has devoted its greatest energies and resources to peace-keeping activities between the Sinhalese and Tamil populations in Sri Lanka. The movement's efforts have ranged from staging peace marches to reconcile contending ethnic communities, to rehabilitation and relief work in areas affected by communal violence, to an ambitious People's Peace Offensive.

••••

5. Participation: A New Concept

Participation, viewed both as an instrument of development and as a special mode thereof, has not yet been adequately conceptualized. Although it is analyzed in numerous ways, none of these link it centrally to core decision making processes which shape national development strategies. Consequently, participation is considered either as lying outside these processes or as subordinated to them by those who control the "real" and vital dynamics of such social processes. Certain new experiences in participation, however, reveal it to be capable of entering into the very inner sanctum of developmental decision making, by conferring a new voice in macro arenas of decision making to previously powerless communities of need. These new avenues suggest how participation as a strategy may be conceptualized in a novel fashion.

Specifically, participation can fruitfully be understood as a *moral incentive* enabling hitherto excluded non-elites to negotiate new packages of material incentives. The term "incentives" refers to the full array of rewards and deterrents held out to induce or dissuade some behavior judged desirable or reprehensible by those holding out the rewards. Incentives are material when the objective inducements or penalties proffered are material goods or benefits: cash bonuses, free housing, or the threat of prison. Incentives are moral, on the other hand, when the inducements – positive and negative – are nonmaterial or nontangible in character. To appeal to the patriotism of the populace and exhort it to donate an unpaid weekend's labor to harvest a crop is to make use of a positive moral incentive, while to threaten loss of prestige or status to those who fail to do so is to hold out a negative moral incentive. All societies resort to arrays of incentives to stimulate their members to perform certain actions and to avoid certain others. These arrays of incentives make up a society's "incentive systems". [2] In the pursuit of their development goals, governments hold out various moral incentives ranging from threats to exhortations, promises of praise or designation as hero or model worker to denunciation as an enemy of the nation, ostracism, and deprivation of honorific titles. The point being argued here is that participation can be fruitfully regarded as a moral incentive within the particular context of a mixed system of social incentives.

A "mixed system" combines material and moral incentives. The new element in the mix proposed here is participation, which takes the specific form of expenditures in time, interest, energy and resources by non-elite people, as their means of gaining power to negotiate a new package of material incentives for themselves.

Incentive systems are nearly always designed by elites and held out as enticements to different categories of citizens. But in new patterns of participation now discernible in several Third World countries, the elites' previous monopoly of the design function is being challenged by the hitherto powerless people most directly affected by the incentive packages in question. "Communities of need," which have struggled to mobilize and organize themselves at some micro level of problem solving close to their own concerns, are now gaining entry into larger macro arenas of decision making and beginning to play new roles as decisive actors in these arenas. More specifically, their leaders' appeals to invest time, attention, energy, and resources in participation are now portrayed to the people as their passport to influence higher, macro realms, where decisions of crucial importance to their welfare are made. The dynamics of this new practice are best elucidated, however, not through abstract analysis, but by illustration. One example of participation in this new mode – i.e., as a springboard for negotiating a new package of material incentives – will now be given. It is drawn from Brazil, at a time when the nation is struggling to make the transition to full political democracy.

6. The Itaparica Dam[3]

(a) Background

Most development planners view large dams as a suitable means of providing abundant and cheap electrical power, water for irrigation, and flood control. Of late, however, the harmful effects of such projects have received much critical attention (Cohen, Franco, and Suarez, 1984). Damaging effects include the economic and geographical dislocation of large numbers of poor people, siltation of dams leading to economic inefficiency, salination and waterlogging accompanying large-scale irrigation activities, and health risks from the creation of new breeding grounds for malaria, river blindness, bilharzia, and other tropical diseases (Goldsmith and Hildyard,

1984; Eckholm, 1986, pp. 1, 9). The case study outlined below focuses on social problems surrounding the resettlement of displaced populations.

The Brazilian government pursues a general policy of building many large hydroelectric dams to generate electricity on a vast scale. Recently constructed dams include Itaipu, the world's largest facility with a capacity of 12.6 million kilowatts, and Tucurui with over 7 million kilowatts. In addition to such spectacular works, a network of medium-sized dams is under construction along the Sao Francisco River, which courses through much of the dry and impoverished northeastern states of Bahia and Pernambuco. Dams have been completed at Paulo Afonso, Sobradinho, and Moxoto, with several others projected for the near future. The Itaparica dam (installed capacity will be 2.5 million kilowatts) is the site of new patterns of participation by non-elite actors in arenas of macro decision making.

At Itaparica, some 37,000 people (c. 20% of the total population in the eight "municipios" or counties affected by construction) had to be resettled to make room for a reservoir 100 miles long and 22 miles wide to be formed in October 1987. In previous dam resettlement schemes, poor residents along the Sao Francisco River exercised no voice in negotiating the site and terms of their relocation or the criteria of indemnification for their goods and property. Grave popular disaffection on these two counts, at times leading to violence, especially at Moxoto in 1975 and Sobradinho in 1979, led agricultural workers' unions to organize the populace of Itaparica. The main objective of these unions was to make the technical organzations and political agencies which formerly monopolized decision making accept the poor agricultural workers living on the banks of the river as negotiating partners. In earlier instances, residents were not informed of flooding schedules and had no say either in setting levels of monetary compensation or in choosing relocation sites. In contrast, the population to be resettled at Itaparica actively negotiated with government and technical agencies specific details of these issues.

Itaparica became a decision making arena, where the micro participation of poor residents at the local level escalated into a partnership with political and technical elites at a sectoral macro level of decision making.

(b) *From micro to macro arenas*

Initial efforts to organize Itaparica's poor rural inhabitants centered on modest objectives:

(1) to inform the local populace of past abuses of their rights by technical and political authorities, and of the calendar of events affecting their resettlement. The organized residents had to resort to mass protest marches to extract from authorities needed information, such as detailed maps of the projected areas to be flooded;

(2) to form lobbying groups to make specific demands of local authorities, such as: stopping the practice of forcibly summoning squatters to the police station for purposes of intimidating them into accepting pittance payments as compensation for their goods; preventing the dam building agency from harassing them by opening truck and tractor work lanes across their croplands; tearing down barbed wire fences erected to facilitate the "zoning" operations of land speculators; assuring a supply of water to their homes and farms (officials had begun cutting off water deliveries for all but two hours daily); and similar harassing moves.

After the peasant unions entered macro arenas of decision making, their agenda changed. The central issues now became:

— to extract from government officials the guarantee that displaced workers would receive clear title to the new lands on which they would be resettled;

— to award residents a primary voice in deciding where they would be relocat-

ed and under what regime (i.e., on individual lots, in residential nuclei, or in large settlement colonies);
- to fix a just price for compensating displaced persons for their improvements on lands they worked; and
- to agree on working conditions for rural workers in new, irrigated lands to which some of them would be moved.

In order to understand the interests and constraints faced by the negotiating actors, a more detailed descriptive profile of each may be useful.

(c) The actors

Companhia Hidro-Eletrica do Sao Francisco (CHESF), a subsidiary of Eletrobras, is a government utility company. At Itaparica, CHESF is the main agent of technical rationality,[4] whereas a Mayors' Association comprising the eight mayors of the affected municipalities represents political logic, and the Syndicate of Agricultural Workers ethical or humane rationality.

CHESF, whose primary objective is to build a dam on schedule and get electricity flowing, was impatient with having to engage in complex negotiations with a multiplicity of social actors. Its technicians contended that the populace should not be relocated near the borders of the future reservoir where, they claimed, the soil is infertile and could only yield acceptable crops if irrigation were adopted. (Of the 37,000 people to be resettled, some 21,000 were poor rural dwellers living near the river's edge.) The Workers' Syndicate, on the other hand, asserted, during the initial phases of negotiations, that its people wished to relocate by the lake's edge. CHESF retorted that, were they to do so, economic costs would become prohibitive, because irrigation and costly new technological inputs would be required. Culturally speaking, however, the populace considers itself to be amphibious, living with one foot in water, as it were, and another on land. Its cultural and psychological prefer-

ences conflict with CHESF's cost-benefit calculations, conceived in purely technical terms. The agency argued that it was seeking the least expensive and most "rational" solution, which consisted of relocating people where their traditional agricultural practices might still be employed. Clearly, CHESF's notion of cost effectiveness treats the site preference of residents as an externality in its rational calculus, not as an internality to be weighed in assessing total costs and benefits.

For its part, the Mayors' Association was mainly interested in not losing voters or taxpayers once the resettlement occurred. The mayors, obeying a conventional political calculus, favored relocation schemes which would keep residents within their municipal boundaries. The mayors also tried to get residents to allow them to represent their interests on compensation levels in discussions with CHESF. This overture was rejected by the Workers' Syndicate. The participation of a political actor, the Mayors' Association, allied to the new role conquered by the Workers' Syndicate, vastly complicated negotiations. Notwithstanding its own procedural preferences, CHESF was reluctantly obliged to bargain with both the Municipal Association and the Syndicate. At times, CHESF accused both entities of introducing too many "extraneous" considerations into the bargaining process. Indeed, if it were allowed to do so, CHESF would prefer to treat everything as a technical issue, not as a political one or as a contentious ethical question of justice.

Some progress toward achieving a mutually acceptable formula was made, however. In 1984, the Workers' Syndicate engaged the services of an agronomist and an economist and, armed with their expert advice, found new grounds for possible agreement with CHESF. That technical agency, in turn, accepted a text drafted by the Syndicate as the basis for negotiating the criteria of relocation and compensation.

Significantly, CHESF will now meet Syndicate representatives in the latter's office, an important symbolic concession, which legitimizes a new "turf" and confers decisional status on those previously lacking it. Emerging patterns of mutuality serve as a counterweight to the initial disparities of bargaining power among the actors. Thanks to its technical expertise, material resources, and support from the highest reaches of government, CHESF wields a degree of power clearly disproportionate to that exercised by the Mayors' group and Syndicate. Nevertheless, the Mayors' group counters its relative inferiority through alliances with nationally influential political parties and bureaucratic supporters in upper echelons of federal agencies, including CHESF's own parent Ministry of Mines and Energy. For their part, the poor rural residents who were totally powerless in earlier negotiations at Moxoto and Sobradinho, have gained new strength through the collective Syndicate. Only after mobilizing agricultural workers successfully at the horizontal level of micro activity, however, did the Syndicate achieve their entry into the macro arena of decisions governing the terms of relocation and criteria of compensation, two domains previously reserved to technical and political decision makers. As of October 1987, the scheduled date for filling the reservoir, arduous negotiations still continued. After a public protest staged by the union syndicate in December 1986, CHESF agreed to a timetable and to a set of directives for resettlement. The main points of attrition dealt with guarantees that resettlement sites would be chosen, marked out in lots, and houses built on them before the reservoir was to be filled, as well as financial conditions for providing cash to displaced families. The union threatened to obstruct the reservoir filling operation if its demands were not met. Its appeal went over the heads of CHESF and local political leaders to the Minister of Mines and Energy. At the same time, it obtained from President Sarney a signed decree declaring CHESF's right – on grounds of public utility and social interest – to appropriate lands in the states of Pernambuco and Bahia for purposes of establishing irrigation projects for the resettled population. The manifesto issued by the unions on this occasion evoked earlier resettlement conflicts at Sobradinho, where "more than 70,000 persons, in their great majority rural workers and our companions, still until today suffer the consequences of a project constructed by CHESF in the name of progress."[5] It is clear that new rules of the game are now in operation at Itaparica. Popular organizations have brought ethical rationality to the bargaining table, joining their voice to those representing the technical and political rationality of elite decision makers.

Itaparica yields three lessons:
– the non-elite populace affected by technical and political decisions can engage in joint policy negotiations on issues of vital importance to it;
– the ability to participate in a sectoral macro arena must be achieved by prior mobilization and participation in lower micro arenas; and
– participation in larger arenas is most fruitfully presented as a moral incentive, that is, as a promise of future negotiating power, inducing people to expend effort, time, talent, and risks, in order to negotiate a new package of material incentives.

7. Conclusion

Participation, or some active role playing by intended beneficiaries, is an indispensable feature of all forms of development. Even technocratic or dictatorial regimes which monopolize decisions as to what and how much people will consume must obtain some minimal acceptance of their decisions. At the very least, the populace must avoid boycotting the consumer goods in question, or actively resisting decisions reached via strikes or civil disobedience.

Therefore, it is the nature and quality of participation, as gauged by the criteria analyzed above, which largely determine the quality of a nation's development pattern. Where the populace has a voice in defining, or diagnosing, its problems – where, in other words, it enters into the sequence of development decisions and actions early – development has a solid chance of centering on basic human needs, of attending to job creation, of offering opportunities for the consolidation of local and regional autonomy, of promoting patterns of interdependence of a horizontal type, and of respecting cultural integrity and diversity.

Conversely, where participation makes its appearance late in the sequence of decisions and actions, it is likely to be inauthentic, marked by manipulation or overt coercion, and to elicit patterns of development not chosen by the affected populace.

When it is self-initiated by grassroots groups, participation aims primarily at improving the groups' own positions. On the other hand, when it is imposed or induced from the top down, it usually aims at extracting some resource input from the populace. Consequently, if equity, respect for human rights, and the empowerment of local populations in ways consonant with their values, together with increasing output, raising productivity, and achieving institutional and technical modernization, are taken as development objectives, then a policy bias in favor of authentic participation correlates highly with genuine development. Ultimately, a vital connection exists between democracy and development, although as social historian Barrington Moore warns, there are limits to participatory democracy, political or economic (Moore, 1972, pp. 66–67). Moreover, there is no way of fully suppressing the three-way tensions which pit the state's effort to control participation against attempts by grassroots movements to shape governmental decisions, and attempts by powerless non-elite populations to gain

some measure of control over their own destiny (UNRISD, 1985, p. 39). Participation, in short, is no panacea for development: its dual nature as both goal and means implies unending compromises between the antagonistic requirements of efficiency and equity.

Further ambiguities appear when participation initiated by one actor – the state – is "taken over" by another – the affected populace – or some mobilizing third party. The usual pattern in such cases is that the language of participation, which both parties want to preserve, may mask unavowed mutual manipulation around conflicting priority goals. To illustrate, the government may seek increased production or diversified agricultural production, whereas the rural cooperative it "aids" may take as its goal the conquest of some measure of local, countervailing power against the government and of the freedom to pursue its own traditional forms of agriculture.[6]

Limits exist as to how much participation can occur, and as to what goals it can achieve. Even generalized participation within a society cannot dispense a government from having recourse to nonparticipatory decisions and actions aimed at endowing a nation with infrastructure of various kinds, or at producing on competitive terms with an international export market. When taken as a vital component of development strategy, participation has three positive functions to play:

(1) it guarantees government's noninstrumental treatment of powerless people by bringing them dignity as beings of worth, independent of their productivity, utility, or importance to the state's goals;

(2) it serves as a valuable instrument for mobilizing, organizing, and promoting action by people themselves as the major problem solvers in their social environments. Poor people need not wait for some political patron, state agency, or beneficent philanthropist to bring them salvation, in the form of a new road, electricity, a

school, or a supply of fertilizer. At the local level, participation enables people to do things for themselves;

(3) it functions as a channel through which local communities or movements gain access to larger, macro arenas of decision making. The strength and solidarity won at local levels of problem analysis and solving serve as springboards of credibility for hoping that some voice in larger decisions affecting material incentives – sectorally, regionally, or nationally – is possible. Consequently, the contributions in time, effort, energy and resources made by local populations are viewed as moral incentives for them to improve the material rewards they will receive in the future.

That moral incentives work best when joined to a parallel package of material incentives is the main lesson learned from the experience of developing countries pursuing a dominantly material incentives policy, on the one hand, or one emphasizing moral incentives, on the other. Moral incentives, in the form of exhortations or appeals to donate time or resources for others, are widely perceived by the target population as potentially coercive. This is why moral incentives alone probably do not produce good results. Conversely, the one-sided reliance on material incentives may be efficient, but does not produce much equity. A more fruitful approach consists in discovering, or creating, new mixes of the two types of incentives.

Special problems confront governments or other elite agencies which seek to promote, induce, or foster participation. Past efforts, whether it be the Cultural Revolution in China or the SINAMOS program in Peru after the populist revolution of 1968 do not leave analysts optimistic. Nonetheless, it remains true that in growing numbers of Third World nations, especially in Latin America, newly democratic governments are searching for ways to enter into participatory alliances with grassroots groups already initiated to the practices of participation. Such cooperation is difficult for many reasons, not least of which is the distrust of government embedded in participatory movements or organizations which have had to resist repression and co-optation. Moreover, even well-intentioned governmental agencies suffer from the occupational hazards of bureaucracies; they define success by their capacity to survive, or to process a problem without troubles, or to achieve results within a specified period of time discernible to evaluators. Another lesson gleaned from the experience of participating communities is that gestation times for success are long and unpredictable. Yet bureaucracies are not designed to relate to the administered populace in a mode which respects these periods (Goulet, 1974, pp. 27–58). Consequently, the stance of governmental agencies seeking participation should be more passive than active. Negatively, this stance consists of not impeding the entry into macro arenas of participating groups which have previously operated in micro arenas. More positively, however, such agencies ought to create a free space, as it were, for neophyte participants to win legitimacy and voice in negotiation processes. Legitimacy and freedom do not suffice, however; participating groups also need information, documentation, expertise, and funds to conduct the discussions and studies needed to serve as effective negotiating partners in arenas where incentive packages are designed. Technical and political elites – partners – enjoy such resources, and parity requires that their poorer partners likewise have access to them. Successful experiments in empowerment of local communities to shape larger decisions affecting them have always had some component of training of local people to master larger issues transcending the boundaries of their immediate problems.

Participation began largely as a defense mechanism against the destruction wrought by elite problem solvers in the name of progress or development. From there it has evolved into a preferred form of "do-it-yourself" problem solving in small-scale operations. Now, however, many parties to participation seek entry into larger, more macro, arenas of decision making. Alternative development strategies centering on goals of equity, job creation, the multiplication of autonomous capacities, and respect for cultural diversity – all these require significant participation in macro arenas. Without it, development strategies will be simultaneously undemocratic and ineffectual. Without the developmental participation of non-elites, even political democracy will be largely a sham.

ENDNOTES

1. On *Saemaul Undong*, see Korean Overseas Information Service (1978), pp. 583–617. For an analysis of the broader issues posed by linking governmental efforts on behalf of equity with participation by the intended beneficiaries of these efforts see Lamb and Schaffer (1981), p. 104.

2. For a discussion of this issue, see Goulet (1984), pp. 95–106.

3. Sources for this account are interviews conducted by the author in June–August of 1983 and 1984 with representatives of CHESF, the Polo Sindical, church groups, residents to be resettled, and government officials. I have also relied on newsletters, internal memoranda, and working documents prepared by the interested parties. For an introduction to problems discussed here see *Projeto Sobradinho* (1983) and Barros (1984).

4. For a detailed analysis of conflicts among three types of rationality (technical, political, and ethical) in decision making, see Goulet (1986).

5. "Manifesto dos trabalhadores rurais atingidos pela barragem de Itaparica a onze meses da inundação" (1986), p. 2.

6. For detailed analysis of such conflicts, see Hyden (1980).

REFERENCES

Alves, Marcio Moreira, *A Força do Povo* (São Paulo, Brazil: Editoria Brasiliense, 1982).

Ariyaratne, A.T., "Integrating national development with the rural sector," address to the Society for International Development, Sri Lanka chapter (Colombo, Sri Lanka: 1979).

Ariyaratne, A.T., *Collected Works, Volumes I and II*, collated by the Sarvodaya Research Institute (The Netherlands: December, 1980).

Ariyaratne, A.T., *A People's Peace Offensive, a Humane Approach Towards Solving the National Problem* (Ratmalana: Sarvodaya Publications, 1987).

Ariyaratne, A.T., *Sarvodaya and Development* (Moratuwa, Sri Lanka: Sarvodaya Press, n.d.).

Barros, Henrique Oswaldo Monteiro de, "A dimensão social dos impactos da construção do reservatorio do Sobradinho," *Trabalhos Para Discussão*, No. 15 (Recife, Brazil: Fundação Joaquim Nabuco, May 1984).

Borda, O. F., *Historia de la Cuestion Agraria en Colombia* (Bogotá, Colombia: Publicaciones de la Rosca, 1975).

Borda, O. F., *Historia Doble de la Costa* (Bogotá, Colombia: Carlos Valencia Editores, 1979).

Camus, Albert, *The Rebel, An Essay on Man in Revolt* (New York: Vintage Books, 1956).

Cardozo, Fernando H., *Las politicas sociales en la decada del 80: nuevas opciones?* (E/CEPAL/ILPES/SEM.1/R.r, 12 April 1982), cited in Marshall Wolfe *(Ed.), Participation: The View From Above* (Geneva, Switzerland: UNRISD, March 1983).

Collier, David, "Squatter settlements and policy innovation in Peru," in Abraham F. Lowenthal (Ed.), *The Peruvian Experiment* (Princeton, NJ: Princeton University Press, 1975).

Cohen, Ernesto, Rolando Franco, and Francisco M. Suarez, *Efectos Sociales de las Grandes Represas en America Latina* (Buenos Aires, Argentina: Centro Interamericano para el Desarrollo Social, 1984).

Du Sautoy, Peter, *Community Development in Ghana* (London: Oxford University Press, 1958).

Eckholm, Erik, "Giant dam planned by China seen as dream or nightmare," *The New York Times* (January 20, 1986).

Fantini, Flaminio, "Heranca de desafios," *ISTO E*, Vol. 9, No. 471 (January 8, 1986).

Freire, Paulo, *Cultural Action for Freedom* (Cambridge, MA: Harvard Educational Review, 1970a).

Freire, Paulo, *Pedagogy of the Oppressed* (New York: Herder and Herder, 1970b).

Freire, Paulo, *Education for Critical Consciousness* (New York: Seabury Press, 1973).

Fundação Joaquim Nabuco, *Projeto Sobradinho: Avaliação Socio-Económica da Relocalização Populacional* (Recife, Brazil: Fundação Joaquim Nabuco, 1983).

Galtung, Johan, Peter O'Brien, and Roy Preiswerk, (Eds.), *Self Reliance: A Strategy for Development* (London: Bogle-L'Ouverture Publicatons Ltd., 1980).

Goldsmith, E., and Hildyard, N., *The Social and Environmental Effects of Large Dams, Volume I: Overview* (Camelford, Cornwall, UK: Wadebridge Ecological Centre, 1984).

Goulet, Denis, "Structural vulnerability in adminsitration," in E. Philip Morgan (Ed.), *The Administration of Change in Africa* (New York: Dunellen Publishing Company, Inc., 1974).

Goulet, Denis, *Survival With Integrity: Sarvodaya at the Crossroads* (Colombo, Sri Lanka: Marga Institute, 1981).

Goulet, Denis, "Incentive systems as policy instruments for equitable development: A research agenda," *Comparative Rural and Regional Studies* (Guelph, Canada: University of Guelph, Fall 1984).

Goulet Denis, "Three rationalities in development decision-making," *World Development*, Vol. 14, No. 2 (February 1986).

Gran, Guy, *Development By People* (New York: Praeger Publishers, 1983).

Hirschman, Albert O., *Getting Ahead Collectively* (Elmsford, NY: Pergamon Press, 1984).

Hyden, Goran, *Beyond Ujamaa in Tanzania* (Berkeley, CA: University of California Press, 1980).

Illich, Ivan, *Medical Nemesis* (New York: Pantheon, 1976).

Illich, Ivan, *Toward A History of Needs* (New York: Pantheon, 1978).

Illich, Ivan, *Deschooling Society* (New York: Harper & Row, 1983).

Informativo Municipal (Diadema: Mayor's Office, published bimonthly).

Kantowsky, Detlef, *Sarvodaya: The Other Development* (New Dehli, India: Vikas Publishing House PVT Ltd., 1980).

Korean Overseas Information Service, *A Handbook of Korea* (Seoul: Ministry of Culture and Information, 1978).

Lamb, Geoff, and Bernard G. Schaffer, *Can Equity Be Organized?* (Paris: UNESCO, 1981).

Macy, Joanna Rogers, "Shramadana giving energy: A Sri Lanka invention good anywhere," in Steward Brand (Ed.), *The Next Whole Earth Catalog* (New York: Random House, 1980).

Macy, Joanna Rogers, *Dharma and Development* (West Hartford, CT: Kumarian Press, 1983).

"Manifesto dos trabalhadores rurais atingidos pela barragem de Itaparica a onze meses da inundacao" (Petrolandia, Pernambuco: December 1, 1986).

Moore, Barrington, Jr., *Reflections on the Causes of Human Misery* (Boston, MA: Beacon Press, 1972).

Naik, J. P., *Equality, Quality, and Quantity* (New Delhi, India: Allied Publishers Private Limited, 1975).

Naik, J. P., *An Alternative System of Health Care Service in India* (New Dehli, India: Allied Publishers Private Limited, 1977a).

Naik, J. P., *Some Perspectives on Non-Formal Education* (New Dehli, India: Allied Publishers Private Limited, 1977b).

Palmer, David Scott, *Peru, the Authoritarian Tradition* (New York: Praeger Publishers, Inc., 1980).

Partido dos Trabalhadores, *PT – Diadema, Pela Construcao do Partido dos Trabalhadores* (April 1984).

Projeto Sobradinho: Avaliacao Socio-Economica da Relocalizacao Populacional (Recife, Brazil: Fundacao Joaquim Nabuco, 1983).

Ratnapala, Nandasena, *Sarvodaya and the Rodiyas, Birth of Sarvodaya* (Dehiwala, Sri Lanka: Sarvodaya Research Institute, 1979).

Sarvodaya Development Education Institute, *Ten Basic Human Needs and Their Satisfaction*. Sarvodaya Community Education Series, # 26 (Moratuwa, Sri Lanka: Sarvodaya Press, 1978).

UNRISD, *UNRISD Research Notes, No. 7* (Geneva, Switzerland: UNRISD, 1985).

VAMOS Governar Juntos! Por Uma Cidade Mais Humana (Diadema, Brazil: April 16, 1983).

Wang, James C. F., "Mass participation and political action – Chinese-style," in *Contemporary Chinese Politics: An Introduction* (Englewood Cliffs, NJ: Prentice-Hall, Inc., 1985).

Wasserstrom, Robert, *Grassroots Development in Latin America and the Caribbean* (New York: Praeger Publishers, 1985).

Wolfe, Marshall, *Participation: The View From Above* (Geneva, Switzerland: UNRISD, March 1983).

World Bank, *World Development Report, 1980* (Washington, DC: The World Bank, August 1980).

Six Misconceptions about Squatter Settlements

JANICE PERLMAN

I have distinguished six major areas in which the perceptions of public officials are frequently at odds with the reality of the urban poor or the so-called "informal sector" in third world cities. These misperceptions are certainly understandable since the background of most elected or appointed officials is generally middle or upper class and does not provide many opportunities for firsthand contact with rural migrant, squatters, or their local breed of entrepreneurs. It is not uncommon to extrapolate from one's own experiences and standards in sizing up different situations. However is this case, the policies which flow from these misperceptions have had devastating consequences not only for the informal sector but for the cities and often countries as a whole. It is therefore of value to illuminate for each of these areas, the misconceptions that have come to light over the past two decades of evolving research and practical experience such that future policies can be well-grounded in reality and better positioned to achieve their stated goals.

1. What kind of people live in shanty towns?

The first area of misconception deals with the characteristics of the migrants and squatters. Unfavorable stereotypes about the poor which tend to "blame the victim" are not unique to polity-makers in developing countries or to the current context. A high school civics textbook from the

Janice Perlman. Permission to reprint this article was granted by *Development: Seeds of Change*. It appeared in that journal's Vol. 4, pages 40–44, in 1986.

1930s in the U.S. makes clear the assumptions about immigrants in its statement that one of their obligations was that "they should not crowd themselves into unsightly slums", and a more recent journal article (Monson, 1955) points to the "all too familiar vicious circle of poverty, bad housing, family breakdown and social disorganization" (Quoted in Peattie, 1969).

This refrain is echoed loud and clear in the following excerpt from an official 1968 document from the Fundacao Leao XIII, a major social welfare organization in Rio de Janeiro:

"Families arrive from the interior, pure and united – whether legally or not – in stable unions. The disintegration begins in the favela as a consequence of the promiscuity, the bad examples, and the financial difficulties there. Children witness the sexual act. Young girls are seduced and abandoned; they get pregnant but don't feel any shame... Liquor and drugs serve to dull the disappointments, humiliations, and food deficiencies of favela life. The nights belong to the criminals... In the quiet of night one can hear the screams for help but no one dares to interfere for fear they will be next... Policemen rarely penetrate the favela, and then only in groups".

To those who have lived or worked in squatter settlements this description is patently absurd. Yet it speaks to the darkest fear of city officials aroused by the massive urban explosion of the 1960s and 1970s. Migrants from the countryside were seen as "uprooted masses" *pushed* off the land, knowing no one in the city, having no place to go and circling aimlessly within the city unable to adapt to modern urban life.

Careful research over the past two decades has revealed quite the opposite. Rather than the "losers" of rural society, cityward migrants have tended to be "the cream of the crop". In many cases, the migrants are the more highly educated, highly motivated members of rural society: who have a vision of the greater opportunities afforded by the city ("pull factors"), some connection to a relative or friend already in the city, and the financial means to get there and start anew. Native-migrant comparisons have shown the same pattern for many cities – migrants tend to find jobs more quickly, have higher urban incomes and pursue education more avidly. (See, for example, Nelson, 1971; Yap, 1970; Balan, 1969, 1973; Perlman, 1976; Cornelius, 1971; Little, 1970).

But the issues of who the migrants are and how they adapt to city life is only the tip of the iceberg as far as misconceptions go. Since squatter settlements are seen as visual symbols of "cancerous growth" on the healthy body politics, the squatters themselves are invested with a wide variety of other stigmas. Aside from being accused of social breakdown, crime and prostitution, and of maladaptive rural behaviors, they are seen as parasites on the economy, draining it of its vital service resources and contributing nothing in return. And finally, they were presumed, by leftists and rightists alike, to pose a threat of violence and radicalism as their frustration and invidious comparisons with the wealth around them turned to anger and was channeled against the political systems, if not in the first generation than in the second.

It is this "conventional wisdom", this set of perceptions which I have called "the myth of marginality". Again, systematic research over many years has revealed quite the opposite. *Socially*, the squatters of the informal sector are generally quite well organized and cohesive and make wide use of the urban milieu and its institutions. *Culturally*, they are highly optimistic and aspire to better education for their children and to improving the condition of their houses. The small piles of bricks purchased one by one and stored in backyards for the day they can be used is eloquent testimony to how favelados strive to fulfill their goals. *Economically*, they work hard, they consume their share of the products of others (often paying more since they have to buy where they can get credit), and they build – not only their own houses, but also much of the overall community and urban infrastructure. They also place a high value on hard work, and take great pride in a job well done. *Politically*, they are neither apathetic nor radical. They are aware of and keenly involved in those aspects of politics that most directly affect their lives, both within and outside the favela. They are responsive to the changing parameters in which they operate (bargaining with candidates astutely in the populist period and keeping wisely apolitical in the authoritarian period), and they are generally aware of their vulnerable position. As for any signs of radical ideology, or propensity for revolutionary action, these are completely absent. Squatters are often system-supportive and see the government not as evil, but as doing its best to understand and help people like themselves. Though this benign attitude may have changed with forced relocation to public housing, they remain, generally unwilling to take political risks.

In short, *they have the aspirations of the bourgeoisie, the perseverance of pioneers, and the values of patriots.* What they do *not* have is an opportunity to fulfill their aspirations.

2. Why do they move there?

The second set of misunderstandings concern the motives of people who are moving into non-regular housing. Those people who live in squatter settlements just as those who work in the informal economy may be doing so by default, i.e., because by income or skills respectively they are excluded from the formal housing or job market. However, all the research of the past 15 years has shown us that, indeed, in both cases, they are often there by *choice*. In the case of squatter settlements, there are numerous families and individuals whose incomes derive from wage earnings, self-employment or a combination of both, or who have *other housing options* including renting or even buying in the periphery. They have instead chosen to minimize resource expenditure for shelter in order to maximize other values including life style, proximity to job markets, education or other capital investments. I would estimate that 20–30% of squatter residents, depending on the location, would be able to afford "formal sector" accommodations if they so chose.

Likewise with the informal economy. It was originally thought that these activities were stopgap measures until wage employment could be found, but further examination has revealed that many men and women *choose* informal sector work because of flexibility, freedom, life style and a host of other reasons, including higher earnings. In Montevideo for example, individuals and household heads, on an average, earned approximately the same in the formal and informal sectors, while in the informal sector, small employers earned twice as much as that average. Studies in Colombia (Lopez Castano, 1982), Brazil (Souza, 1984), Nicaragua (Redondo, 1985) and Chile (Uthoff, 1984) reveal the same pattern. This also helps explain why a large percentage of formal workers abandon their protected jobs to become informal artisans and entrepreneurs. Peattie (1981) found in Bogota that in the footwear industry, most informal entrepreneurs were former workers of the large factories who had learned the necessary skills on the job and used their severance pay as working capital to set up their own businesses.

While living in a squatter settlement confers certain advantages in terms of utiliz-ing the dwelling as a warehouse, factory or shop (as discussed below) and in terms of access to certain sub-markets, clearly not *all* informal sector workers live in squatter settlements nor do all squatters earn their livelihood in the informal sector.

3. The nature of informal settlements

The third set of misleading stereotypes relates to the nature of the "informal" settlements themselves.

First is the now-classic distinction between "slums of hope" and "slums of despair" (Stokes, 1962). The shantytowns of Central and South America are clearly in the former camp. They are vehicles of upward social mobility.

Rosser's work in Calcutta shantytowns is quite applicable to those of Latin American in regard to their functions of (*a*) free housing; (*b*) reception centers for immigrants; (*c*) employment in family and cottage industries; (*d*) mobility within the city so people can locate closer to their jobs; (*e*) sense of community and social support during times of difficulties; and (*f*) encouragement and reward of small-scale entrepreneurs who invest in shanties and rent them to other poor people.

I have written elsewhere at length about the positive functions of the favela for the families and individuals who live there and for the society as a whole (Perlman, 1976). Suffice it to say here that as land values rise and vacant lands become more scarce within cities and around them and as new technologies make it increasingly attractive to build on steep hillsides or swampy marshes which were once the exclusive domain of the poor, incoming migrants of the 80s will face even greater challenges than their counterparts of the 60s and 70s.

Despite their visual disarray and clear spatial distinction from the rest of the urban grid, squatter settlements are both highly organized within themselves and highly integrated into the rest of the housing system. Officials would surely achieve greater success with housing programs in the informal sector if they understood these factors more fully. Knowing, for example, that there is enormous heterogeneity within the settlements in terms of income, education, occupation, size and material of the dwelling units and reason for being there is a prerequisite to designing flexible housing programs in upgrading schemes. Likewise, the degree to which renting, subletting and leasing are prevalent within these areas has been little recognized. Whereas the image is generally of almost all owner/occupancy, frequently as many as half or more of the shacks have rental units within them and this proportion is growing in the 1980s as both inner city and peripheral lands become more fully saturated.

Furthermore, whether serving as housing for renters or owners, squatter settlements are closely interconnected to formal housing markets. Fluctuations in the price of land, capital, energy, labor or building materials in the formal sector have tremendous trickle-down (or "pour-down") effects on the price and availability of shelter at the bottom. For example, as the price of steel, cement and electrical energy has risen faster than Gross Domestic Product over the past decades throughout Latin America, more pressure is placed on the coping mechanisms and ingenuity of the poor to improvise self-help solutions for materials and energy. Since much of the self-help involves discards from construction sites or irregular hookups, even these sources tend to dry up when the formal markets are pressed (Mourad, 1983).

Finally, it is a misconception in itself to associate informal housing with squatting, since, depending on the city in question, a significant portion of the urban poor live otherwise. As part of a realistic housing policy, officials need both facts and insights into the workings of theses other systems, including:

– *corticos* or *vecinidades* (Turner's "bridge-head settlement"): built as kind of workers' or family barracks for single room occupancy with jointly shared courtyard;

– *cabeca de porco*: deteriorated single family homes and mansions subdivided into single room dwelling units for multiple families;

– *pirate settlements* or clandestine subdivision which illegally develop and sell off land which is not zoned for such and not serviced;

– *residential hotels* and flophouses often in the old central city areas;

– *rural housing* for which workers commute into the city at vast distances;

– *workers' housing* or union housing linked to a job;

– *public housing* including high rise walk-ups (*conjuntos*), row houses, detached houses and *casa de triagem* (triage houses for the destitute);

– *construction-site dwelling* – moving from job to job and sleeping on location;

– *shelter for the homeless* (*albergues*), orphanages, etc.; and

– *homelessness* itself – sleeping under bridges, in bus or railway stations, or by river or road beds.

Laquian (1983, p. 149) quotes one housing official in a developing country as saying:

"I am told that our housing deficit amounts to some 10,000 units per year and that we will have to build about 4,000 houses just to keep up with the housing backlog. However, each day, as the sun sets in my country, every person has a home to go home to. So where is the housing shortage?"

Indeed, there are many systems which together deliver housing solutions daily to satisfy the needs of low-income people, but the information about the magnitude of housing provision by each sub-system is still unknown (see Angel, 1977). Much work remains to be done in this regard.

4. The image of "standard housing"

The above discussion leads directly into the fourth point – officials' views of shelter as

(a) a "standard" home with a roof and four walls and (b) a nonproductive consumer commodity. As we come to better understand the workings of the informal sector, it becomes increasingly clear that neither of these notions reflects the reality and that being widespread and deeply held, they have led to misguided investments in "finished product" homes and self-defeating codes, standards and zoning regulations.

Although no one would argue that all things equal, the favelados would prefer a finished well-equipped home to a shack on a hillside, all other things are *not* equal. Direct observation, structured research and housing policy outcomes have all shown conclusively, however, that for individuals and families in different stages of their life cycle, other aspects of shelter can be much more important. John Turner's early work in Peru, for example, (Turner, 1966) showed that proximity was most critical in the initial stages, trying to get established. Later, other factors such as security became more important. But in any case, urban services such as running water, electricity and sewerage consistently took priority over the physical completion of "shelter" in terms of "user-needs". Follow-up research over the past 20 years has confirmed this for a wide variety of cities and situations and shown that *shelter is an ongoing process of incremental improvement* for this population, *rather than a finished product*. This is the key to the concept of "housing as a verb" rather than a noun (Turner, 1972). The policy implications are striking insofar as the very procedures by which both housing deficits and housing progress are accounted for, do not yet reflect this fact. Most government agencies count only new units as progress whereas the vast majority of informal sector housing investment is channeled into upgrading or expansion of existing units.

But there is even a broader misconception in this regard, and that has to do with the way governments view investment in housing (as a consumer good or welfare measure) as opposed to investment in industry which they see as generative of economic development. Urban economists and anthropologists have shown conclusively that this distinction is not functional. As Peattie puts it:

"A house is a machine for living – a place for eating and sleeping and talking to friends and making love and sewing clothes and helping children with their homework – but it is also an aggregation of resources. People's resources are limited. At any given time they must deploy them as well as they can to solve the problems which are for them at that point most pressing".

Therefore, the dwelling is more often than not used as the base for income-producing activities other than rental income. Simon Fass's work in a Port-au-Prince squatter settlement found the making, storing, and selling of goods so universal that he treated it as a piece of productive infrastructure rather than consumption in his book for USAID (Fass, 1977).

Another USAID-sponsored study in San Salvador (Farbman, 1981) showed that 85% of households in the poor neighborhoods are engaged in small businesses which provide up to 50% of a family unit's income. He documented, for example, carpenters, furniture-makers, food sellers, candy makers, street vendors, bottle re-sellers, shoemakers, and laundry, tailoring, and retail shops. Thus a recent article on "Low Income Urban Housing in the Third World" (McCallum and Benjamin, 1985) includes five new functions of housing to the five classic ones as follows:

Classic functions of housing

1. housing as (social) consumption;

2. housing as improver of health and well-being;

3. housing as (macro) economic sector;

4. housing as stimulus to savings and investment; and

5. housing as indirect contributor to income and production.

New functions of housing

1. housing as shop;
2. housing as factory;
3. housing as rental income;
4. housing as financial asset; and
5. housing as entry point in the urban economy.

From my observations, I would add, housing as storage space or warehouses, a function much harder to achieve in high rise situations than shantytowns, despite the Hong Kong and Singapore examples to the contrary.

5. The meaning of "self-help"

The fifth major misconception among officials developed at a slightly later point in the evolution of housing policy – in response to clarification regarding the first four areas – as self-help and user-participation became the new panacea. The problem was that the officials and the "self-helpers" had quite different ideas about what was involved. For officials, the notion that squatter settlements were to be seen as the "solution" rather than the "problem" meant that they could lower their costs of housing production by counting on contributed labor, or "sweat-equity" to construct new housing projects. This had both an economic and romantic appeal. They were thus perturbed and even vindictive when – in the course of these projects – they discovered that some of the would-be self-helpers were subcontracting out for the manual labor; and that they sometimes leased or sold their units.

From the viewpoint of the squatter, "self-help" is neither romantic nor a way to relieve government of the burden of housing. It is a survival strategy based on the widest possible freedom of choice to allocate scarce time and resources. Flexibility is the critical element in achieving the "highest and best use" for the squatter. Living in the informal sector is precarious and unpredictable. Favelas do not require monthly rents, bulk purchase of materials, or predictable free time for home upgrading. As

income opportunities expand and diminish, housing work can stop and start and materials can be acquired piecemeal over months, even years. When time is precious and cash is more available, progress is made by acting as a general contractor on one's home and paying the subcontractors. Since unskilled construction labor within a squatter settlement receives quite low compensation compared to outside jobs it is often too high an opportunity cost to forego an income-producing activity to work on one's home. And, as now fully documented, many squatters and their families juggle 2–3 jobs, each in order to make ends meet. The concept of the "idle poor" has no place here.

Thus self-help is not necessarily self-built, and participation is not necessarily physical. To the users, participation in housing relates to *choice* over the decisions that affect them, i.e., when, where, how and over what time period to expend energy on shelter. Furthermore, it can be individual or collective self-help (mutirao) and fluctuate between these. Once this is controlled and organized from above as part of a "housing project", the point is defeated.

Furthermore, to prevent resale and speculation with the upgraded unit, is to remove one of the fundamental motivations for the upgrading – the acquisition of capital. If the self-help family decides to "capitalize" on its sweat-equity upgrading investment by selling and using the cash to invest in another dwelling or enterprise, why should this be prohibited any more than it is for any other player in society's mobility game?

6. The definition of "success" in housing projects

While the new strategies for housing and income generation are a giant step closer to responding to the realistic needs, resources and capabilities of the informal sector, they are no cure-all for the problems of urban development and social inequity.

Table 1: Interpretations of Success

	PRIORITY	
INDICATORS OF SUCCESS	SPONSOR INSTITUTION	SELF-HELP HOUSEHOLD
Value created by self-help	High	High
Cost recovery	High	Low
Construction speed	High	Low
Physical appearance in early stages	High	Low
Adherence to building codes and standards	High	Low
Adequate shelter and safety	High	High
Security of tenure	Low	High
Proximity of central city	Low	High
Proximity of friends and family, and so on	Low	High

First of all, even though upgrading and serviced lots have become, in many circles, the current conventional wisdom, the vast majority of housing institutions – at both national and city levels – are ill equipped to implement them. These institutions were established to deal with large-scale standardized construction, to finance conventional loans, to facilitate purchase of bulk supplies and materials and to make decisions through a top-down hierarchical structure – all of which are totally antithetical to the implementation of the new policies. Asking these large bureaucracies to deal with the individualized needs of self-help builders, small-suppliers, precarious borrowers, and protracted time frames is akin to expecting an elephant to thread a needle. And, after all of that time and effort, the results are no "photo opportunity" for a politician.

Thus, the sixth misconception concerns the question of whether sponsored self-help is successful, and the logical query is from whose point of view? While sponsors and clients may agree on certain overall objectives, they tend to assign very different priorities to the various indicators of success as I have shown schematically in Table 1.

The issue of construction speed is illustrative. To many households, their home is

never complete *per se* and represents a continuing process over the course of generations. To them, speed or time of completion may be rather irrelevant, except for seeking to pace the construction rate by available cash in hand to avoid usurious interest charges (which can range on the order of 10 percent per month for building materials or services bought on credit). To the project sponsor or official, on the other hand, it may be the most important thing so that files may be closed and credit given. While the self-helper may focus on the speed of attaining simply a minimum, secure, and weather-proof space, project officials may speak of project "failings" due to the incomplete state of the homes or their uneven or slow-paced improvement.

Likewise, early project appearance may be viewed differently by officials and by self-helpers themselves. Policy makers have often voiced objections to self-help on the basis of the apparently untidy and uncontrolled appearance of self-built houses and community environments. The ambiguity of doing nothing has often been preferred by such policy makers to decisions to make public investments in what looks like ugly or blighted slums. Certainly few site-and-service projects or schemes for squatter legalization and upgrading can compare visually with the image of a flag-bedecked, new, high-rise apartment on ribbon-cutting day.

Capital cost comparisons and numbers of people reached by such projects notwithstanding, the relevant visual comparison is perhaps better made several years into project life. It has been widely observed that 60 to 90 percent of the self-help houses will have improved within five to fifteen years if allowed by the authorities. Exceptions are due to such exigencies as family crises, disability, or loss of income. The dwellings will become more fireproof, with temporary and scavenged materials yielding to permanent masonry and tile construction; additions and multiple stories may have been added; and the houses may even exhibit a rich array of decorative elements. Ironically, the most striking negative perception of such matured self-help settlements is often not associated with the self-built homes, but with the lack of utilities and public services, dependent on public investment well beyond the capabilities of the self-helpers themselves. Self-helpers often provide outdoor stairways, storm drainage, retaining walls, and other infrastructural works. These contributions are sometimes obscured by open sewers, acute erosion, and makeshift electric lines, which stand in sharp contrast to the stable and decorated homes.

Despite some degree of unevenness in community upgrading (which varies with the vicissitudes of individual households) experience in self-help communities has shown that when the values of the settlement itself are taken into account, self-built communities are often perceived as adequate, while outside sponsors or institutions may view the same community as a visually unacceptable failure; and that after the passage of time (5–15 years), both community residents and institutions may view upgraded self-help settlements as more satisfactory than comparable government housing projects, which typically deteriorate over time

due to cost-cutting during the original construction, chronic non-maintenance, and vandalism. Thus, our definition of success must also anticipate differences over time, as well as differences arising from diverse actors and viewpoints.

REFERENCES

Balan, Jorge. 1969. "Migrant-Native Socioeconomic Differences in Latin American Cities: A Structural Analysis". *Latin American Research Review 4*, no. 1.

Balan, Jorge. 1973. "Un Siglo de Corrientes Migratorias en el Brasil: Ensayo de Interpretacion Historico-Comparativa". Department of Political Science, Universidade Federal de Minas Gerais. Mimeographed.

Cornelius, Wayne A., Jr. 1971. "Local-Level Political Leadership in Latin American Urban Environments: A Structural Analysis of Urban *Caciquismo* in Mexico". Paper presented at the American Political Science Association Meeting, Chicago, September.

Farbman, M. (ed.), 1981. *The Pisces Studies. Assisting the Smallest Eco-activities and the Urban Poor*, Washington, D.C.

Fass, Simon. 1977. "Families in Port-au-Prince: A Study on the Economics of Survival". USAID.

Laquian, Aprodicio. 1983. *Basic housing: Policies for Urban Sites. Services, and Shelter in Developing Countries*. Ottawa, Canada: International Development Research Centre.

Little, Kenneth. 1970. *West African Urbanization*. Cambridge: Cambridge University Press.

Lopez Castano, Hugo, Marta L. Henao, and Oliva Sierra. 1982. "El Empleo en el Sector Informal: El Caso de Colombia". Working Paper, Center for Economic Research, University of Antioquia, Medellin.

McCallum and Benjamin. 1985. "Low Income Urban Housing in the Third World".

Monson, Astrid. 1955. "Slums, Semi-Slums and Super-Slums". *Marriage and Family Living*, Vol. 17:2, p. 118.

Mourad, Moustafa. 1983. "The Need for a New Approach to Analyses of Informal Settlements and Public Housing Policy in Egypt". M.I.T., Ph.D. thesis.

Nelson, Carlos. 1971. "The Bras de Pina Experience". Massachusetts Institute of Technology. Mimeographed.

Peattie, Lisa. 1969. "Social Issues in Housing". In *Shaping an Urban Future: Essays in Memory of Catherine Bauer Wurster*. Edited by Bernard J. Frieden and William W. Nash, Jr.

Peattie, Lisa, 1981. "What is to be done with the 'Informal Sector': A Case Study of Shoe Manufacturers in Columbia". Department of City and Regional Planning, M.I.T. Manuscript.

Perlman, Janice. 1976. *The Myth of Marginality: Urban Politics and Poverty in Rio de Janeiro*, Berkeley: University of California Press.

Perlman, Janice. 1981. "Strategies for Squatter Settlements: The State of the Art as of 1977", in *The Residential Circumstances of the Urban Poor in Developing Countries*, New York: Praeger Publishers for the United Nations Centre for Human Settlements (Habitat).

Redondo Lubo, Aida. 1985. "El Sector Informal: Controversias e Interrogantes". *Estudios CIEPLAN* 13.

Souza, Paulo R. 1984. "Elementos para un Modelo de Determinacion de Movilidad Ocupacional". PREALC Research Report, Santiago de Chile.

Stokes, Charles J. 1962. "A Theory of Slums". *Land Economics*, Vol. 38:3, pp. 187–197.

Turner, John. 1966. *Uncontrolled Urban Settlements: Problems and Policies*. Pittsburgh: University of Pittsburgh Press.

Uthoff, Andras. 1984. "Subempleo, Segmentacion, Movilidad Ocupacional y Distribucion del Ingreso del Trabajo: El Caso del Gran Santiago en 1969 y 1978". PREALC Research Report, Santiago de Chile.

Yap, Lorene. 1970. "Rural-Urban Migration and Economic Development in Brazil". Mimeographed.

Community Participation and Self-Help: The Zambian Case

ROBIE SIAMWIZA

Introduction

Community participation and self-help became popular development strategies during the 1980s. The economic crisis in Zambia coupled with a burgeoning increase in the population growth rate placed intolerable strains on national resources and presented a number of intractable problems for the centralized planning system. This state of affairs necessitated innovative thinking and renewed consideration of local-level possibilities. Community responsibility through local-level initiative (also referred to as self-help) was perceived as a viable alternative to the national government's shrinking ability to respond to service demands.

In spite of the attractiveness of community participation and self-help, they present a number of challenges to development planners. Major challenges concern organization and management of self-help endeavors. This paper looks at these issues, specifically exploring self-help dynamics and processes in Zambia and the possibilities and constraints to the operationalization of a participatory development model.

Zambia covers an area of 753,000 square kilometers and has a population of approximately 8 million people. Unlike most African countries South of the Sahara, Zambia has a large and relatively stable population. It is estimated that almost half of the population lives in urban areas, most of which are concentrated along the line-of-rail, i.e., the railroad that transverses the center of the country along a

Robie Siamwiza. This article was requested and written for this volume. It has not been previously published elsewhere.

North-South axis. It has been said that Zambia is, concurrently, both homogeneous and heterogeneous in its sociocultural make up (Kaplan, 1979). Whereas eighty distinct linguistic entities serve to divide the country along ethnic lines, sufficient cultural similarities exist to allow generalizations to be made on a number of issues, including community participation and self-help experiences.

Community Participation as a Development Strategy

Community participation is a strategy transcending practical consideration but imbued with moral precepts commanding acceptance and adherence. Arnstein (1969: 7) observes: "Participation of the governed in their government is, in theory, the cornerstone of democracy – a revered idea that is vigorously applauded by virtually everyone." This perception is not limited to Western countries but also obtains in Zambia where participatory democracy is the professed mainstay of all development strategies (Kandeke, 1977; Ollawa, 1979).

Declaration of philosophical orientations can be useful in guiding policy decisions but can also be quite troublesome operationally when policy must be interfaced with implementation strategies and evaluation processes. As a concept and practice, no universal meaning exists in Zambia to define community participation in terms of type, level, and amount of involvement. Operationally, it may mean more assent by community leaders to a project or plan of action or it may require more substantial involvement, such as the provision of cash, materials, and/or labor.

The multitude of definitions and interpretations is not in itself an unfavorable situation. To imply that popular participation is a single, undifferentiated, and overriding strategy is misleading (Burke, 1968). It is more accurate to speak of several strategies defined in terms of given objectives. Burke (1968) notes that the objectives will be limited by available resources as well as by the organizational character of community activities, particularly community planning. The problem arising in Zambia is the lack of consensual agreement on the kinds of objectives and situations amenable to various strategies of community participation. At any given time, government and nongovernment organizations (NGOs) tend to adopt unilateral approaches which are applied in the field universally, regardless of situation or circumstances.

During the colonial and immediate postcolonial period, governmental policy emphasized self-help on a situational basis, i.e., primarily in rural areas. Self-help became synonymous with rural community development, which stressed practical skills assumed to promote individual self-improvement and the uplifting of general living conditions. Complete autonomy or absolute self-reliance were never advocated. African communities were expected to cooperate with the implementation of colonial policy. Many colonial community development programs were actually pacification activities designed to gain the cooperation of the non-white population (Batten, 1957; Brokensha and Hodge, 1969; MacPherson, 1982).

The purpose of community development changed after independence. Emphasis was placed on community participation as a method for forging a mutually helping relationship with government providing most of the resources and the communities expected to make token contributions to symbolize involvement.

The concept of community participation, from the late 1970s onward, has been one of modified self-reliance. Communities are being informed that local and national government resources are limited and financial and material resources can no longer be provided at the level granted during the post-independence period when the country was economically affluent. Today, community participation is primarily an alternative strategy for meeting social needs. In addition, it is being enthusiastically supported in urban areas. Self-help and self-reliance are banner calls utilized to motivate communities to action.

The justification for shifting responsibility back to the people is explained in terms of Humanism, Zambia's national ideology. President Kenneth Kaunda, in an address to the United National Independence Party (UNIP) Council in 1970, coined the word "communocracy" to explain this aspect of development in which power over resources and public affairs is diffused, collectivized, and used on a communal basis by all the people.

Some people, however, perceive communocracy and its stress on community responsibility as an imposition rather than an acceptable policy strategy. They feel that government is failing to satisfy its obligation of providing basic services to the public. Rather than relying on local resources, many communities are turning to NGOs for assistance. A survey of sixty-three selected human service organizations in Zambia revealed the 55% began their activities after independence (ZCSD/FAO, 1981). Overwhelmingly, the majority of these organization are NGOs. Their proliferation suggests that they are assuming duties and activities formerly performed by government. Instead of becoming self-reliant, communities are increasingly turning to NGOs for social service provision.

Even among government officials the role of communities versus the role of the state in service provision is not clearly delineated. In 1986 the then Minister of Labour and Social Services, Honourable

Frederick Hapunda, said "Self-help projects should act as gap-fillers to the efforts by the government aimed at providing services to the less privileged people" (Hapunda, 1986). The implications of this statement are: the state has an obligation to provide basic services to its citizenry and, when it cannot, self-help projects are justifiable. Such projects should be conceived as stop-gap measures rather than as preferred alternatives.

The above serves to amplify the point that interpretations of the nature and purpose of community involvement are both universal and fuzzy. At the policy level there is widespread acceptance of community participation as a principle but, operationally, lack of clear and consistent guidelines promotes confusion. There is evidence that communities are responding to this uncertainty by transferring their expectations for assistance to NGOs.

The Self-Help Concept

Self-help as a development tactic has evolved over the years as a convenient adjunct to the community participation philosophy. In this regard, it is a concept that is as flexible as "community participation." There does not exist a coherent policy at either the national or local level to provide guidance to governmental institutions, NGOs and other utilizing this approach to development. Nevertheless, various operational interpretations prevail. This is desirable in terms of Burke's observations on the need to link operational definitions to desired objectives, resources, and situations. But, flexibility of this type can be troublesome in the field. Conflict and confusion often prevail because different agents of change – governmental departments, NGOs, and donors – have diverse expectations about a community's role and responsibilities. It is not unusual to find two or more change agents working in a particular community on similar projects but using different approaches to community involvement.

External agencies may intervene in a community solely on the basis that it has demonstrated a desire to improve itself. This demonstration may be verbal or through written communication. Other agents demand material proof of commitment to self-help. Communities are only assisted once they have embarked upon a project and are nearing completion, having demonstrated the ability to plan and execute a project on their own. A few NGOs pay community members for their labor in self-help projects, thereby paying people to help themselves. Although the motivation for this may be valid (i.e., to provide incomes in the community to stimulate the local economy), the end result undermines the spirit of self-reliance and raises expectations that this is the correct and most appropriate form of assistance that an external donor may provide.

Governmental departments such as Social Development in the Ministry of Labour, Social Development and Culture, and Community Development Departments have animators who stimulate and mobilize communities to undertake projects on a self-help basis. A few NGOs also use this approach. The emphasis is for communities to utilize local resources, expertise, and technologies as much as possible in the construction of public facilities and physical infrastructure.

While diversity prevails, none of the agents of change perceive the self-help as total self-reliance. The most popular interpretation is that communities should cooperate with the government for the purpose of service provision (Siamwiza, Chibaye and Mphaisha, 1983). Within this context, communities use local resources to achieve objectives identified in provincial and national development plans. Rarely are they assisted in pursuing objectives emanating from local-level initiatives that deviate from objectives identified by the provincial and national planning systems. National goals and inter-governmental coordination take precedence over idiosyncratic community desires.

The rapid spread on NGOs has led to other operational definitions of self-help and strategies for assisting communities to pursue their objectives. NGOs such as Save the Children Federation and World Vision International stress community empowerment. Communities are encouraged to form grassroots development committees whose functions are to identify local needs, determine development objectives, and embark upon programs of action. This approach is more flexible and versatile in the promotion of self-help activities. Communities can be assisted in numerous ways, depending upon their needs and desires; however, it is assumed that local-level desires will neatly interface with regional and national plans.

Governmental departments are bureaucratic, and thus considerably less pliable in decision-making options and procedures. They tend to deal with all communities in a uniform manner, trading off effectiveness for accountability (Titmuss, 1970; Gilbert and Sprecht, 1974). NGOs, in theory, appear to be more adaptable but, in practice, a number of constraints influence their operations. Most NGOs in Zambia rely on external donors for financial support. Consequently, the type of development activities as well as form of intervention very often reflect sensitivity to the donor's ideas of what needs to be done and how it should be accomplished.

Self-help as local autonomy and total community self-reliance is not widely accepted in Zambia. In fact, it is unlikely that the Party (UNIP) and its government would be supportive of this interpretation. The ramifications of local autonomy are many and uncertain, especially in a culturally pluralistic society like Zambia where ethnic loyalties are stronger than a national identity. Local autonomy has the potential for becoming secessionist, particularly if the people feel that they have been neglected by the government. Under circumstances of this nature, community empowerment has dangerous political overtones. A self-help project could become a rallying point for dissension and the expression of general dissatisfaction with the status quo.

It has been said that community self-help can only function where there is group solidarity and that it cannot be led from above (Winblad and Waern, 1987). Self-help must include a transfer of power to the local community. This conceptualization of self-help is not sufficiently cognizant of existing social and political realities. Group solidarity is presented but founded upon blood and ethnic ties as opposed to political consciousness. Winblad and Waern also do not adequately take into consideration Frank's (1969) observation about internal conflict being an inherent characteristic of most communities. The conflict emanates from dissimilar economic interests and, sometimes, can be so intense as to undermine most forms of communal cooperation other than that commanded by family obligations and mutual reciprocity.

Frank's analysis is quite important to community work in the African context. Many rural villages are culturally homogeneous with very subtle socioeconomic divisions. Moreover, they are populated by people who could claim blood ties or kinship allegiance with their neighbors. These characteristics often mislead agents of change, particularly outsiders, to assume the existence of cohesiveness and consensus. This state of affairs masks internal conflicts that are contraindicative to self-help endeavors. Yet, the group solidarity obtaining may not be that helpful. Some projects, like schools, clinics, or water points, require several villages to unite their efforts to achieve desired goals. Cooperation can be undermined by interpersonal disputes that have wider ramifications, i.e., working to destroy sociopolitical consciousness while magnifying family allegiances.

Self-help and self-reliance, operationally, are concepts that must be handled with care.

Centralized authorities are compelled to support activities that promote national unity in the context of a national identity while, yet, decentralizing decision-making for the purpose of promoting local development. This explains, to some extent, contradictions existent in government policy where certain national goals are stressed even in the face of local disinterest or opposition. These goals, from the planners' and politicians' perspective, promote social integration and national unity. On the other hand, government also wishes to exploit the form of group solidarity existent in most rural communities and to build upon it to promote local-level development.

Organization and Management of Self-Help Activities

It seems somewhat contradictory to talk about organization and management in regard to self-help activities, especially from the perspective of an external agent. Self-help activities are supposed to be organized and managed by the initiators (be they individuals or community-based groups) with outsiders having only a modicum of involvement. At least this is the theoretical assumption.

However, there is a tendency to overlook, if not ignore, many tangential but significant issues in the self-help process. Communities or community-based groups do not go about conducting their affairs in isolation or without forming supportive coalitions. Gilbert and Specht (1974) observed that the environment in which a program or project is to operate is crucial to its success. This section looks at some project management experiences in the organization and administration of external supports to local-level initiatives. Projects in the educational sector are used as examples.

Institutions that Assist Self-Help Projects

There are three types of organizational/institutional supports available for assisting communities and groups in their self-help endeavors. These are government (district councils and ministerial departments), non-governmental organizations (local voluntary associations and churches), and external donors (multi-lateral and bilateral aid organizations, international voluntary associations, and overseas religious bodies). Some of these organizations purposely coordinate their activities with others while others prefer to work independently, for instance, directly with community groups. All employ variants of the participatory management approach.

1. *Government Units.* The Department of Social Development (DSD) is responsible for community development programs including literacy and self-help projects. Most of DSD's activities are in the rural areas. DSD has staff in all fifty-one districts of the country and in the sub-centers located at the village and township levels. The department's work involves sensitizing, organizing, and assisting communities to embark on community development.

Organizationally, the DSD has responsibility for managing and supervising government-aided self-help projects, such as schools and health care facilities, to completion. Government-aided projects are, invariably, infrastructural in nature (i.e., classrooms, clinics, improved roads, etc.) and must be approved by the appropriate authorities before construction work begins. After completion, the facility is handed over to the appropriate ministry for operation and maintenance. For example, the Ministry of General Education, Youth and Sports is responsible for education structures such as classroom blocks, teachers' houses, etc., and the Ministry of Health is responsible for clinics and hospitals.

Project management under DSD consists of a social development assistant (SDA) or assistant social development officer (ASDO) being assigned to a project. The SDA is usually stationed at a sub-center located in the community that constitutes the worker's catchment area. When the self-help project involves a school, the SDA or ASDO works with the ward development committee (WDC) and the parent-teacher association (PTA). Once a project has been identified and a group organized to undertake it, the SDA's role is to monitor project progress and to identify other potential funding sources for project completion, if needed. The SDA and ASDO work under the supervision of the district social development officer (PSDO). Final decision-making lies with the Commissioner of Social Development, who is based at headquarters.

Some district councils have departments of community development that are separate and distinct from DSD. Councils in large cities like Lusaka, Kitwe, Livingstone, and Kabwe have such departments. They fall under the direct administrative responsibility of the Council's Social Secretary, although ultimate responsibility rests with the District Executive Secretary.

Presently, all community development departments are urban-based, having evolved from early township councils' responses to massive population influxes during the 1960s and 1970s. As a result of their early history, community development departments function in a manner that is biased toward urban concerns. Even the issues addressed reflect urban problems that are universal to cities, globally. Many of these issues do not lend themselves to community solutions as noted by Warren (1975) and, consequently, are not conducive to self-help approaches. In the educational sector, where self-help has been, quite successfully applied in rural settings, there are distinct limitations in the urban environment. Although residential patterns of settlement produce culturally heterogeneous neighborhoods, group solidarity and patterns of socialization continue to be based upon kinship and ethnic ties similar to what occurs in rural areas. These factors undermine community consciousness and social cohesion.

Community development departments have concentrated on programs that promote social integration and preparing low-income urban dwellers to adapt to an urban way of life. CDOs have shied away from innovative efforts that are outside the domain of the council but have focused upon traditional activities such as women's clubs, youth work, recreational activities, etc. These are activities funded by the Council with little community input.

When CDOs get involved in self-help projects like the construction of a classroom block for the local school, assistance is supervised by the office of the District Executive Secretary. The DES is administratively accountable for all development projects under the council's auspices.

2. *Non-Governmental Organizations.* There are a number of local voluntary organizations promoting community development through support to self-help schemes. The exact number of NGOs existing in Zambia is not known but the Zambia Council for Social Development (ZCSD), the umbrella body for voluntary associations, listed sixteen NGOs among its membership in 1984. This number may be a small fraction of the voluntary associations operational in the country. It is not obligatory for an NGO to become a member of ZCSD; therefore, it is quite possible for a large number of organizations of this nature to exist without the knowledge of the coordinating body.

A distinction is made between local NGOs and external organizations, although some local NGOs exist entirely on external funding and may be affiliated with an international organization. World Vision, Save the Children Federation, and Christian Children's Relief Fund are examples. These local organizations are situated in Zambia but tied to mother bodies.

NGOs have two ways of providing community support, directly and indirectly. Some organizations have their own field staff who work directly with grassroots groups and community development committees. In this case, managerial responsibility for a project falls completely under the NGO. It provides supervisory assistance to the community in the form of a project officer as well as financial and material supports. Other NGOs rely on DSD field staff to do the day-to-day project supervision. Under these circumstances the DSD is providing extension services for the NGO. Regional officers or personnel from the national office of the NGO visit the project periodically to check upon progress. When the DSD provides extension services, the ASDO or SDA is expected to provide periodic reports to the assisting NGO on project progress.

Many of the Zambian churches have programs at the community level to promote socioeconomic development. Church projects may be organized and managed by a particular congregation at the diocese or synod level or by an umbrella organization such as the Christian Council of Zambia, Zambia Episcopal Conference, or the Zambia Evangelical Fellowship. The larger church organizations such as the Catholic Church, Reformed Church of Zambia, and United Church of Zambia have their own development departments staffed by development officers.

Church-sponsored programs are designed to serve the entire community, regardless of religious creed or denominational affiliation. Non-Christians as well as Christians are target beneficiaries and are eligible for services. The church has had a significant impact on social development in Africa, most notably in the field of education. Although their responsibilities in education have been reduced and circumscribed through government policy over recent years, many churches have begun to initiate alternative schools for young people unable to be accommodated into mainstream programs of education.

3. *External Donors.* Bilateral agencies (such as the Norwegian Agency for International Development, Finnish Agency for International Development, etc.) and multilaterals (such as the World Bank, United Nations Development Program, etc.) direct their assistance through formalized government channels. The National Commission for Development Planning (NCDP) negotiates with the donors on behalf of the Government of the Republic of Zambia (GRZ) and identifies sectorial priorities. The process assumes that NCDP is aware of the community needs and priorities by virtue of its planning function and mandate to produce national development plans. NCDP also identifies appropriate structures for linking funds to specific projects besides assisting recipient ministries to monitor project implementation and operations.

Bilateral organizations have a limited amount of discretionary funds falling outside the official country program. Monies available under this category can be allocated to NGOs or directly to a grass roots group undertaking a self-help project. The management of funds or materials received under this scheme is the responsibility of the recipient.

International voluntary associations such as Bread for the World, Africare, and Norwegian Church Aid fund a number of development projects in Zambia. Funding is generally made to NGOs, churches, or grass roots groups, without channeling via government offices. However, some donors prefer to work through umbrella organizations like the Zambia Council for Social Development (ZCSD) or Christian Council of Zambia (CCZ). The umbrella or coordinating body allocates the funds to what they consider to be deserving projects and they assume responsibility for overseeing project operations.

International NGOs may fund a member of an umbrella organization individually by earmarking the funds. The money is received and administered by the umbrella organization but can only be used by a specific group. For example, churches operating schools get assistance directly from overseas partner churches. Some of the money comes through the Zambia Episcopal Conference or CCZ while other funds are sent directly to the church. In circumstances where the donor has a direct link to the recipient, accountability becomes the responsibility of the recipient. However, umbrella organizations sometimes provide services that enable community groups or churches to utilize the resources of the coordinating body for the purpose of documenting activities, completing reports, or giving evaluative feedback to donors.

Managing Self-Help Projects

This section examines two geographical areas to assess their experience in managing self-help projects. The districts considered are Lusaka and Mazabuka. These two areas reflect different social dynamics, infrastructure, and resource availability. Lusaka was chosen because of its national status and cosmopolitanism while Mazabuka was chosen because of its rural-urban mixture featuring characteristics common to line-of-rail communities as well as those on the periphery.

Lusaka Urban District

Lusaka Province contains the nation's capitol and, by virtue of this status, has special advantages and disadvantages. The city of Lusaka is the most populous city in the country and has been the focus of migration from smaller towns and rural areas.

The contrasts between the rich and poor Zambian and non-Zambian and African and non-African segments of the population are clearly visible. Lusaka is probably the most heterogeneous area in Zambia, socially and culturally. It is a cosmopolitan city with strong elements of traditionalism. Traditional African norms and values coexist, intermingle, and compete with values and forms of behavior associated with Westernization.

Lusaka's experience with community self-help projects has been primarily in the area of housing. Until the recent adverse economic changes began to occur, the district council and ministerial departments had managed to maintain minimum levels of service to meet social needs. During the late 1960s and early 1970s there existed a definite urban bias in the allocation of funds for maintenance and capital projects. The towns along the line-of-rail received up to two-thirds of the national budget (International Labor Organization, 1981; Lulat, 1980; Ramakrishna, 1985). With the rapid increase in population compounded by negative economic growth, urban services have been in decline. All of the communities, high income as well as low income, are being requested to meet their own needs through self-help activities.

School self-help projects have not been synonymous with community development or local area development. They have been confined to the perceived needs of parents/guardians having children in the school. Because of this circumscribed interest, involvement has been equally restricted on the part of community members. Lack of local community interest, social cohesiveness among the parents, and competing demands have led to PTAs relying on specific techniques for generating resources for self-help projects. PTAs can levy parents a sum agreed upon at the AGM. These fees are placed in a special fund, controlled by the PTA, and earmarked for specific projects such as classroom extensions, purchase of equipment, or a bus. This method of raising funds has been quite successful and seems to be preferred, albeit parents/guardians complain about the "excessive" sums demanded by PTAs, and most manage to contribute.

Another popular method of raising funds is to request donations from companies, embassies, and other aid organizations. It is relatively easy for Lusaka residents to contact potential donors and for the donors to verify that a project exists. Thus, some schools benefit by their proximity to sources of assistance. A PTA committee may be fortunate to have a notable person associated with the school, i.e., serving on the PTA or having a child attending the school. The notable can always be prevailed upon to use his/her contacts to secure assistance for the school. Since Lusaka is the main base for a number of companies, parastatals, and other organizations, it has more than its fair share of such personages.

Donation of time and labor to self-help projects is not very popular. Lusaka residents are very much integrated into the money economy and generally feel that they must be compensated for work. A carpenter or bricklayer would not like to donate his/her skills. Headmasters and the district education officer report that it is very difficult to get this type of support for a self-help project.

The future of some geographical areas is uncertain, i.e., in regard to whether they will be residential or industrial and whether they will be recognized as legal settlement areas. There are a number of squatter areas in Lusaka in which people do not have the security of tenancy. The district council and ministries will not provide basic services because of the uncertain legal status of such areas. This uncertainty discourages self-help besides undermining the formation of community cohesiveness.

In regard to management and administrative experiences, most self-help projects have a relative degree of autonomy compared to rural projects. This may be due to the way in which urban PTAs operate. They are less linked to WDC deliberations than rural schools. However, this may change as communities are forced to devise solutions to the other one's needs.

Presently schools are not localized, although in the high density areas primary school children are more likely to attend the schools situated in their immediate locality. Secondly, schools are few, hence their localization is not foreseen in the near future. When localization is achieved, it

will be easier to involve township WDCs in school projects.

Mazabuka District

Situated in the Southern Province, along the line-of-rail, Mazabuka District is a combination of rural and urban settlements. It typifies small towns along the old line-of-rail running north from the Copperbelt to Livingstone in the South.

Mazabuka is a relatively affluent district, although there are decided pockets of poverty. The main economic activities are farming and ranching at both commercial and peasant production levels. The Nakabala Sugar Estate is the largest industrial concern in the area, offering employment to nearby and migrant laborers. Kafue Gorge, a Zambia Electricity Supply Corporation (ZESCO) installation is also located in the district. Namalundu Village, a community made up primarily of ZESCO employees, provides a contrast to the general bucolic setting, for it is really a small township placed in the countryside. Namalundu has a relatively unusually high number of educated people concentrated in one area because the majority of the male residents are employed by ZESCO.

Chikankala Mission Station is also located in the district. This is one of the Salvation Army's largest mission stations in the world. The mission consists of a hospital, secondary school, and training college for nurses and laboratory technicians. As a result of the mission's activities, a large number of people have settled in the area, many of whom have become adherents in the Salvation Army Church.

Self-help projects have been generally successful in Mazabuka District. This has been attributed, partly, to the relative affluence of the area, for people can afford to donate large sums of money to projects. Mazabuka also has the advantage of having developed physical infrastructure (compared to other districts in the country), that is, in terms of roads and communication links within the district and to outside areas.

The presence of specialized communities such as Chikankata Mission, Nakambala Sugar Estate, and Namalundu Village also facilitates development. These areas serve as centers of development, providing services to the surrounding communities. Chikankata has a very progressive community-based health program that combines health education with preventive and curative services. Nakambala donates to community projects and thereby provides local support to grass roots initiatives. Namalundu expanded its primary school to a basic school on a self-help basis. Although the project was assisted by NORAD, community members were at the forefront in the planning and implementation of the project.

The district also has areas where it is difficult to mobilize people for self-help endeavors. Parts of Kafue Flats exemplify this problem. A number of fishing communities are situated in the Flats, an area on the banks of the Kafue River. Periodically, the Flats become inundated by floods, forcing people to be evacuated from the area. To assist the flood-stricken communities, various programs of rehabilitation were introduced, including the provision of materials to construct a school on a self-help basis. While accepting the donations, the communities have done nothing toward constructing facilities for their children.

The attitudes and behavior of the fishing folks of Kafue Flats are not unusual. In fact, they are prevalent among fishing communities throughout the country. In Luspula Province around Lake Mweru and Chilubi Island in the Northern Province, parents frequently remove their children from school in order to utilize their labor during peak production periods. Since these activities are prioritized, they do not augur well for self-help school projects.

Problems and Constraints to Self-Help

Problems and constraints to self-help projects have been mentioned in the preceding sections of this paper. Still, these issues are of sufficient importance to consider in more detail. This section examines some of the factors that constrain self-help and local-initiative strategies.

Geographical Setting

Areas located far from the main communication and transportation networks have more difficulty utilizing a community participation strategy than those located along the line-of-rail in big towns. Isolation contributes to a community's insensitivity to certain needs such as educational facilities for its children. Formal education is linked to formal employment in the minds of most people and is perceived as a causal relationship. When employment opportunities are remote, as is usually the case in isolated areas, it is difficult for parents to appreciate primary school education. Even in towns, programs of formal education are being perceived as expensive but not reliable investments because of declining job opportunities. If one's children are to become farmers or petty traders in the informal sector, extensive formal education is not needed.

Sources

1. *Finance.* Intangible as well as tangible resources play important roles in determining the success or failure of a project. Finance is obviously a resource that is crucial to project success. However, attitudes vary on how much money is needed and how it should be generated. In isolated or peripheral areas of the country, cash is difficult to obtain, as most people live a subsistence lifestyle and depend almost entirely on their own resources. Residents of such communities are reluctant to part with the little cash they may have, but prefer to make in-kind contributions such as a bag of maize or labor. Money is perceived as more valuable than the in-kind substitute.

In contrast, urban dwellers are more apt to contribute money than materials or labor. The latter is seen as more intrinsically valuable and, thus, must be preserved for more fortuitous circumstances. Self-help projects in town may have greater access to cash by virtue of being situated in the midst of a cash economy but they must also spend more on labor and material.

2. *Human Resources.* Invariably, human resources are in short supply in rural and urban community projects, though this fact is manifested in different ways. Rural communities generally lack a reservoir of educated people who have requisite managerial and/or leadership skills to adequately superintend a project. SDAs and ACDOs are not available in all subcenters; therefore, extension assistance is severely limited. NGOs supplement the government's efforts but, too, are equally constrained by finite resources in the face of seemingly infinite demands.

In urban communities, human resources are existent but not always available for self-help projects. People with special skills are either preoccupied with other matters and/or unwilling to donate their time on a gratuitous basis. Sometimes this problem can be overcome if the group initiating the project has instrumental social contacts. Certain people with the necessary skills may be prevailed upon to assist. This is likely in the highly urbanized areas like Lusaka or one of the Copperbelt towns where the population size is sufficiently large to have a pool of socially conscious people who are willing and able to volunteer their services.

3. *Materials.* Non-availability of materials can be a serious handicap for projects involving construction. For example, MGEYS has regulations that teachers' houses built on a self-help basis must be made of permanent materials. However, cement and steel door frames are difficult to obtain in rural areas or they may be obtainable only at great expense. Impermanent shelters made from pole, dagga, grass, and mud plaster are usually constructed of necessity, although they are seen as undesir-able and a negative factor in the recruitment of teachers. This is especially true for basic school teachers of grades 8 and 9 who, because of their educational qualifications, have other alternatives.

Materials are more readily available in towns, comparatively, but are also subject to periodic shortages. Some self-help projects suffer long delays because of such shortages and, even when the requisite materials become available, inflationary prices make them unaffordable.

4. *Back-up Services.* Many self-help projects succeed because the environment is supportive and conducive to project achievement. To some extent this is an area of intangibles in the sense that back-up services are not always material or identifiable. Encouragement by the relevant ministry may be a critical element to project success; for instance, linkage between the DEO's office and the school that is being built on a self-help basis. Frequent inspections are needed by the building's officer to ascertain construction standards and to advise. Nothing is more discouraging to a community group as having its project declared unacceptable because of construction flaws. Situations of this nature could be avoided through adequate back-up services.

5. *Absorptive Capacity.* National governments as well as donors have been criticized for "blaming the victim," in this case communities that fail to use aid in order to achieve development objectives (World Bank, 1984; Timberlake, 1985). A counter-argument is to blame the donors for pushing the wrong sort of aid, i.e., that which is conditional upon the recipient meeting specific objectives. There is more than a modicum of truth to these criticisms as grass roots groups are seldom consulted about their wishes and desires but end up having development objectives foisted upon them by national leaders under the guise of promoting socioeconomic development or by external donors who assume a "we know best" posture.

Notwithstanding the legitimacy of these criticisms, lack of absorptive capacity remains an intransigent problem, having many facets. Not all communities have the ability to utilize aid, even when it is designed to help them achieve locally derived aims. This is partly linked to the problem of human resources, i.e., lack of managerial skills. Other problems relate to the timing of the assistance. It may be too early or too late, lack supportive infrastructure to complement local initiatives, or be in a hostile political environment. Timberlake (1985) observed that governments often pay lip-service to community-initiated efforts while concurrently fearing the political implications of a truly self-reliant group.

6. *Attitudes and Perceptions About Aid.* There is a debate among NGOs on "when" to provide assistance to a community to help it with a self-help project. Increasingly, concern is being registered over the growing dependency on external assistance. It is commonly recognized that aid can kill initiative as well as it can motivate. Therefore, timing of aid and the establishment of some prerequisites for the recipient community to meet are very important in fomenting the type of action and results desired.

Very little has occurred in regard to studying recipient communities' attitudes about aid. ZCSD sponsored a survey to ascertain attitudes toward its Self-Help Assistance Fund (Siamwiza, Chibaye and Mphaisha, 1983). It was found that aid stimulates communities to embark upon more projects. However, they tend to look outward rather than inward for resources to support their projects. Also, such communities become more sophisticated and skillful in approaching potential donors for assistance. This is a form of dependency that should be avoided, i.e., inculcating skills that enable people to beg more effectively.

Communities have not been very suc-cessful in maintaining self-help projects once they have been completed. There are numerous reasons for this, not all attributable to the fault of the community. Quite often donors are approached a few years after having funded a community for additional funds to assist the same group to rehabilitate a poorly maintained facility. This can be linked to inappropriate attitudes about community responsibilities for a facility, i.e., responsibility ends with project completion.

Conclusion

Integrating community participation strategies into national development efforts is ideologically appreciated in Zambia yet, in practice, fraught with many ponderous problems. Chiefly, three dominant questions confront decision-makers; "Under what conditions should help be rendered to local-level initiatives?," "When?," and "How?"

Obviously responses to these questions will be influenced by the underlying purpose for promoting popular participation and self-help. It is quite clear that purpose is influenced by a combination of social, economic, political, and temporal factors. As noted by Conyers (1982), support for popular participation can be succinctly categorized into three general reasons: (1) to obtain information about local conditions regarding problems, needs, and desires, (2) to obtain the compliance of target groups, and (3) to promote democracy.

Explanations such as Conyers's provide general guidelines to decision-makers through articulating the "why" of using popular participation strategies. However, they do not adequately highlight issues of how and when. This paper has tried to illuminate these issues through practical examples. It has focused upon organizational and administrative issues germane to self-help projects in Zambia.

In the promotion of self-help projects attention should be focused upon a number of practical issues, including the availability of personnel to oversee or superintend project implementation. Local-level initiatives often need more than money and materials but a range of services including intangibles like encouragement and a supportive environment.

REFERENCES

Apthorpe, R. (ed.), 1970, *People Planning and Development Studies* (London: Frank Cass).

Arnstein, S., 1969, "A Ladder of Citizen Participation," *Journal of the American Institute of Planners*, 35(4).

Batten, T. R., 1957, *Communities and Their Development: An Introductory Study with Special Reference to the Tropics* (London: Oxford University Press).

Boissevan, J. and J. C. Mitchell, 1973, *Network Analysis: Studies in Human Integration* (The Hague: Mouton).

Brokensha, D. and P. Hodge, 1969, *Community Development: An Interpretation* (San Francisco: Chandler Publishing Co.).

Burke, E., 1968, "Citizen Participation Strategies," *Journal of the American Institute of Planners*, 34(5).

Chonya, I., 1987, *Baseline Study on Church Development Efforts in Zambia* (Lusaka: Christian Council of Zambia).

Conyers, D., 1982, *An Introduction to Social Planning in the New World* (Chichester, U. K.: John Wiley & Sons).

Frank, A. G., 1969, *Latin America: Underdevelopment or Revolution* (New York: Monthly Review Press).

Gilbert, N. and H. Specht, 1974, *Dimensions of Social Welfare Policy* (Englewood Cliffs, N. J.: Prentice-Hall).

Hapunda, F., 1986, "Resources: More Needed to Do More, Self-Help Projects Must Be Gap Fillers," in *The Anthill: A Community Action Magazine*, 1(1).

International Labor Organization, Jobs and Skills Programme for Africa 1981, *Zambia: Basic Needs in an Economy Under Pressure* (Addis Ababa).

Kandeke, T., 1977, *Fundamentals of Zambian Humanism* (Lusaka: National Educational

Company of Zambia, Ltd.).

Kaplan, I. (ed.), 1979, *Zambia: A Country Study,* Washington, D.C.: American University.

Lulat, Y. G. M., 1980, "Educational Planning: The Need for New Directions with Special Reference to Developing Countries," *Zango*, No. 1 (Lusaka: University of Zambia).

MacPherson, S., 1982, *Social Policy in the Third World* (Brighton: Wheatsheaf Books Ltd.).

Mitchell, J. C., 1954, *African Urbanism in Ndola and Lusaka* (Lusaka: Rhodes-Livingstone Institute).

Ollawa, P. E., 1979, *Participatory Democracy in India* (Devon: Arthur H. Stockwell, Ltd.).

Osei-Hwadie, K., 1981, "Voluntarism in Zambia: The Relevance of Indigenous Voluntary Concepts and Methods," a report commissioned by Zambia Red Cross Society.

Ramakrishna, S., 1985, "Budgeting and Financial Management in the Education Sector, Zambia," *Institutional Development in Education and Training in Sub-Saharan African Countries* (Washington, D. C.: World Bank).

Serpell, R., 1987, "Teachers, Pupils and Parents in Rural Areas: Experiences and Opinions of Some Primary School Teachers in Zambia's Eastern Province," a seminar paper presented at the Educational Research Bureau's Seminar.

Siamwiza, R., C. Chibaye, and C. J. Mphaisha, 1983, *An Evaluation of the Self-Help Assistance Fund* (Lusaka: Zambia Council for Social Development).

Timberlake, L., 1985, *Africa in Crisis* (Washington, D. C.: Earthcan).

Titmuss, R., 1970, *Commitment to Welfare* (New York: Pantheon Books).

Warren, R. L., 1975, "A Community Model," in Kramer, R. M. and H. Specht (eds.), *Readings in Community Organization Practice* (Englewood Cliffs, N. J.: Prentice-Hall).

Winblad, H. and K. Waern, 1987, *Community Self-Help in the Construction and Maintenance of Primary Schools: A Pre-Feasibility Report,* Swedish Agency for International Development.

World Bank, 1984, *Toward Sustained Development in Sub-Saharan Africa: A Joint Program of Action* (Washington, D. C.)

Zambia Council for Social Development/United Nations Food and Agriculture Organization, 1981, *Programs for Better Family Living* (Lusaka).

Mass Communication and Development – A Critical Review

MICHAEL LESLIE

Introduction

The use of mass communications as an aid in modernizing developing countries has been a popular idea in the West and among the leadership of many developing countries for over thirty years (Sinclair, 1990). These "modernizers" hoped that the mass media would provide people in the developing world with the necessary information to become more effective citizens, enabling them to participate in the process of political, economic, and social development (Schramm, 1964; Pye, 1963).

Frequently, however, the content of mass media has fallen far short of these lofty objectives. It has often been dominated by commercial and entertainment content, rather than educational programs, and much of the programming has been imported (Tunstall, 1977). As a consequence, users of mass communications in developing countries have often found precious little that can aid them in their daily struggle for survival.

This paper asks some critical questions about the contribution of mass communications to development, outlines some topics in need of further empirical study, and suggests some ways in which the new communications technologies can be made more useful in the service of development.

Mass Communications: For or Against Development?

Do mass communications in the hands of elites help solve the social, economic, and

Michael Leslie. This article was requested and written for this volume and has not been previously published elsewhere.

political problems of developing countries? Or is it an agency of social control that perpetuates elite advantage?

Without question, radio has made an important contribution to the development process. In health, education, information, and agriculture (Hornik, 1988), radio has served the rural masses in the developing world. However, despite the conventional view that the other mass media, i.e., books, newspapers, television, and film, are equally useful tools in the development process, their utilization has suffered from major limitations.

To begin with, much of the content of these media is either imported or modeled on imports from the developed countries (Herold, 1988; Traber, 1989). It is designed for populations with sensibilities, values, and drives quite different from those of most readers, listeners, and viewers in developing countries. Such content has little relevance for workers, peasants, artisans, and farmers living in developing countries. Instead, it appeals and is directed essentially to elites who have already been "westernized" by prior educational or life experiences.

Most of the information content of these new media is designed to build support for the status quo and to stimulate consumption of imported products and manufactured goods. Relatively little content could be described as development oriented, that is, seeking to empower people to improve the economic and social conditions of their existence. It fails to systematically explore the needs and aspirations of the common man and discuss situation-appropriate solutions (Traber, 1987).

Problems with Popularizing Mass Media in Rural Areas

One of the key problems that anyone seeking to popularize the mass media in rural areas must face is the high cost of mass communications. Newspapers, for example, are often difficult to obtain in rural areas because of scarcity of newsprint and also because of the poor infrastructure of roads and transportation to the rural areas (Kasoma and Leslie, 1990).

In addition, people in rural areas are often cash poor and cannot afford to purchase and maintain equally scarce radios and television sets. For example, in Nigeria the cost of a black-and-white television set is more than an average wage-earner's annual salary (Adesonaye, 1990).

Even when a rural dweller can afford them, modern mass communications are often not available. For example, because of a general paper shortage, local language (and other) newspapers are sometimes sold as wrapping paper (instead of reading material) in rural areas. Radio and television signals often do not reach many people living in remote destinations.

Furthermore, the content of the mass media is frequently irrelevant to the needs of the rural resident. More often than not, it is edited in the capitol with little or only token regard for the interests, concerns, and perspectives of rural dwellers – or any group other than the elite. If there is news from the village, it is often stale by the time it finds its way into print (Hachten, 1971). Sometimes political considerations keep village news from being reported. For example, in Zambia, news of crop failures or labor unrest is sometimes censored from the rural newspapers (Kasoma and Leslie, 1990).

Frequently, people in rural areas are suspicious of the content of the urban-based mass media, since mass communications that come from the capitol often omit or distort rural perspectives on economic and political issues. One effort that has been made to address this problem is the creation or rural-based newspapers, that is, newspapers that are edited and published in the rural areas rather than in the capitol. In some countries, such newspapers have enjoyed success, even though erratic funding makes it difficult to sustain their regular publication. Such newspapers have also been shown to be useful for promoting literacy among new readers (Kasoma, 1988). Thus, poor distribution, high cost, illiteracy, irrelevance, and suspicion of content are some of the barriers to popularizing the mass media in developing areas.

Mass Media and the Diffusion of Western Values

It is likely that the mass media have succeeded in diffusing the desire for the products of consumer society in underdeveloped countries. For example, even the most impoverished slum dwellers in the underdeveloped world now clamor for the artifacts of the industrialized world most frequently advertised in television, radio, and print: liquor, clothing, cars, household products, travel, distractions, etc. (Schiller, 1976).

The new media, especially television, seem to also be successfully cultivating in some Third World audiences the concept of individualism, that is, putting one's own desires and objectives before those of the group. The idea of working hard for a delayed reward and the pleasure orientation are apparently also being successfully diffused (Lerner, 1958; Rogers, 1969; Tsai, 1970; Inkeles and Smith, 1974; Beltran, 1978).

Continued measurement of the actual degree to which these new values, conveyed by the mass media, are displacing the old should be the object of ongoing empirical research in the developing countries.

Mass Communication Failures in the Developing World

Mass communication has failed to bring about the rapid educational, social, and

political changes that many of its proponents hoped for in the Third World
(Rogers, 1976). The reasons for this failure
are manifold but include the following:

a) indigenous resistance to many of the
   mass media messages produced in the
   west;

b) political resistance on the part of elites to
   the democratic ideologies (or mytholo-
   gies) often purveyed by the mass media;

c) the unavailability of the mass media to
   most inhabitants of the developing
   world;

d) the inappropriateness of many of the
   mass mediated messages directed towards rural dwellers, who make up 70%
   of Third World populations; and,

e) the relatively poor quality of many of
   the local and regionally produced media
   messages.

For example, a very ambitious television
education for literacy project in the Ivory
Coast has foundered because the government is unable to provide and maintain sufficient television sets for the rural population of the Ivory Coast (McAnany, 1980).
In Zambia, educational radio has reached
the limit of its effectiveness because the
government can no longer afford to pay
and provide transportation for educational
extension workers to remote villages. Many
villagers lack the money to buy or maintain
the radio receivers necessary to receive the
programs (Leslie, 1988).

Also, in some instances, the language
level of the mass media is far above the level
of comprehension of the average villager
who may be able to receive the message but
unable to interpret it, especially if it is prepared in a non-indigenous language such as
English or French.

Cost Effectiveness of Mass Communi-
cations: A Research Agenda

Some wonder whether the entertainment
and educational content of mass media really justify the tremendous cost of creating
and maintaining this apparatus, especially

when pressing economic problems face the
developing countries that use it.

The modern mass media consume an
enormous amount of the GNP of small
nations. For instance, the creation of the
Cameroonian national television system
(inaugurated in 1988) cost several hundred
million dollars and requires a yearly operating budget of several million more; still
more expenditures will be required before
the entire country is able to receive television signals from the national system.
Meanwhile, the national education system
remains woefully underfunded and the university budget was slashed by some 50% in
1989 (Leslie, 1989).

Unemployment and underemployment
are rampant in most Third World countries, yet resources that could be used in job
development are diverted to expensive
media projects that consume rather than
produce revenue. As mentioned before,
advertisements carried by the mass media
often stimulate people to consume rather
than to save, to seek immediate gratification
of artificially stimulated wants, rather than
to make the investments necessary in order
to achieve financial independence and sustained growth.

The assumption that mass-mediated
"education" is more cost-effective than
person-to-person education as delivered by
trained teachers must also be empirically
examined. One might ask: Are the literacy
levels obtained from the mass-mediated
approach appropriate to development aims?
Are the literacy skills so obtained long-last-
ing or temporary?

One might also explore empirically
whether the entertainment content of the
mass media actually serves rural audiences.
Entertainment provides relaxation, but it
simultaneously conveys values and culture.
Although the media's ability to disseminate
indigenously produced and sourced entertainment programs is laudable, many
imported entertainment programs are still
being widely disseminated. The latter con-

vey foreign values and culture that are often alien to rural audiences and may promote anti-social rather than pro-social behaviors. Accordingly, some countries have banned or severely limited the presentation of Kung-fu movies, claiming such films have inspired imitative acts of violence (UNESCO, 1980).

Traditional culture may also be negatively impacted by the attention increasingly paid to the mass media. For example, attendance may decline at public events, i.e., sports, festivals, and political rallies, because people find it more convenient to watch or listen at home. Time for interpersonal communication and community discussion may also be shrinking for similar reasons.

One could expect such a shift in audience attention and communication patterns to have significant effects on the ability of a society to transmit its values and culture from one generation to another. Since mass communication imposes its own codes and production structures on the content it conveys, often significantly altering the meaning of the original event in the editing, transmission, and representational process, the portrayal of traditional cultures might also be distorted in the process of being mass communicated (Morgan, 1986). Thus, mass communication's content may actually destabilize underdeveloped societies rather than lead to a greater sense of cultural coherence and unity.

Communication Dependency vs. Self-Reliance

One might also ask: Whose economic and political interests are served by continual adoption and reliance of the developing countries on modern forms of mass communication? Is the dependency of developing countries heightened or diminished by the incorporation of the modern mass media apparatus into their internal and external communication structures?

Modern means of mass communication allow elite groups to exercise central control over the content of these media. They also allow for an unparalleled flow of commercial messages, supplied by multinational corporations, to be transmitted to audiences in developing countries, creating new demand for imported products (Hamelink, 1977).

The heavy flow of commercial messages, foreign produced entertainment programs, and government-censored information programs has several results:

First, it often undermines local creativity in programming, which is often made to compete with and imitate slick, foreign formats in order to satisfy audiences pre-conditioned to prefer foreign styles.

Second, it forces local entrepreneurs to compete prematurely, both in presentation and in quality, with foreign imports. Infant local industries are asked to produce promotional messages to compete with the polished commercial advertising of international conglomerates. Given the astounding cost of commercial advertising time in the mass media, it is not surprising that local advertisers find it difficult to successfully meet this challenge (Schiller, 1973).

Third, because it is very expensive to produce content for the new media, especially news and entertainment programs, media in developing countries rely extensively on imported program material that must be purchased from foreign suppliers. the result is a net cash transfer to the foreign suppliers of the material (Mason, 1974). In addition, especially in the case of news, the foreign supplier can control the kind of information that the developing country will receive; most often this information conforms to the ideology and interests of the supplier country and not the interests of the purchasing country (Reyes Matta, 1976).

Fourth, since the technology of mass communications is continually being updated and improved, the developing countries find that they must also upgrade their transmission and reception technology on a regular basis. These upgrades and improvements result in additional capital expenditures and cash transfers to the sellers of the technology, further increasing the debt burden of the developing countries and further enriching the developed countries (Thebaud, 1977).

Finally, central control of the political content of mass communications allows the dominant political group to set the agenda for political discourse in the country and exclude the political opposition from that dialogue. This results in a deformation of the political culture of the developing nation, which is deprived of the vitality often found in diversity; it becomes single-faceted rather than multifaceted (Tehranian, 1979).

All of this is not to say that the developing countries receive no benefit from these mass communications technologies. Certainly, the technology has enable them to create stable one-party states, to diffuse prosocial messages, and to create some sense of nationhood (Ugboajah, 1985). It has also successfully promoted the use of a common language throughout these newly emerging states. However, in many ways, the new mass communications technology has also served to strengthen existing patterns of domination rather than to open up new channels for communication and profit for the developing countries.

Negative Effects of Commercial Programming

One could speculate on the negative consequences for the populations of developing countries from continued exposure to commercial television entertainment programs and advertising. For example, it is possible that people who are exposed to media messages may come to believe they are less worthy or able than those they see portrayed in the media living affluent material lives. It is not uncommon for the traveler to the Third World to meet people who believe that all people in Europe and American are rich and have plenty of money, that there is little government corruption in the industrialized countries, and that the West's criminal justice system punishes the rich and poor criminal equally. I have met many people in underdeveloped countries who believe that most Blacks in America are engaged in criminal activities and that most White Americans live in homes with swimming pools.

These kinds of stereotypes can lead people to become dissatisfied with the performance of their own governments, which cannot measure up to the fantasy of the developed world portrayed by the mass media. Also, some segments of the population in the developing countries may come to believe they are entitled to products and services that the incipient industries of their countries can neither produce nor sustain, i.e., a revolution of rising expectation – and frustration.

Mass Communications for the Poor

What can be done to increase access to the national mass communications network for the disenfranchised and the poor? This is a difficult question to answer because in some ways the national communication network was never intended for horizontal communication, but for top-down, administrative communication. But Traber (1987) says access for the disenfranchised requires a participatory communication system and their empowerment to use the modern communications technology for that purpose.

One way to achieve this participation is to establish local, rural-based newspapers, local radio stations, and a truly national telephone system so that people can discuss and share possible solutions to their problems in a direct way at the local level. The Chinese experience with technology demonstrates that all of this and more are feasible for most developing countries today (Renzhong, 1988; Xinbo, 1990).

Unfortunately, the central governments in many developing (and developed) countries fear decentralization, since it implies some sacrifice of their ability to directly control all of the content of mass communications. They fear that some citizens may opt for autonomy or even seek to contest the dominance of the center and that voices critical of the government may persuade others to opt for self-determination. Government leaders also feel that the national fabric of developing countries is too fragile to allow such liberty of expression, that their new nation-states could easily be destroyed by internal dissent.

Yet, it is clear that intolerance to alternative viewpoints has brought some developing countries to the brink of civil war and motivates dissenters to seek expression through the *coup d'etat* rather than through the process of communication and negotiation. If a government is serious about economic, social, and political development, it must allow and even promote the kind of discussion and dialogue that will allow the energies inherent in diversity to be harnesses for development.

In short, a bona fide commitment to increase the mass communication capability of the disenfranchised requires a willingness to allow non-elite views to be heard and published, acknowledging the risk to the existing social order that such access implies. It is the peoples of the developing nations who must find the will and create the means to meet this challenge (Traber, 1989).

Of equal, if not more, importance is the question of how to finance the technology that would make mass communications possible at the local level. Granted, the creation of rural presses requires a relatively small investment, but telephone, radio, and especially television require substantial financial investments in equipment, technology, and professional personnel.

Developing countries with limited financial resources must identify and obtain economically practical alternatives to high-cost, high technology communication equipment.

The Role of Journalists in Developing Countries

It has become clear that journalists in developing countries cannot afford the adversarial position that is advocated by the Anglo-Saxon school of journalism. Their countries have a more pressing need, which is to harness all energies towards improving the material conditions of the citizens of the nation.

So, although the Third World journalist is often asked to play the role of public relations specialist for the government, a more useful role for such journalists is that of *professional communicator*, in which all the tools of communication are harnessed for the development process (Moemeka, 1989). Such a journalist gives voice to the voiceless by examining the economics of seemingly unsolvable problems, suggests solutions, and provides a communication bridge between the various segments of the social order (James, 1990).

In short, the Third World journalist must redefine what it means to be a journalist. One suggestion along this line is offered by the developmental school of journalism, which maintains that Third World and other journalists must more critically examine the links between underdevelopment and the foreign aid development community, with special attention to the impact of development programs on Third World populations (Aggarwala, 1978).

Summary

Mass communications technology in the service of development is a double-edged sword, often serving to maintain and strengthen the elite's domination of political, social, and cultural life as it mobilizes, educates, informs, sells, and entertains.

New ways must be found to finance, create, and use the content of this powerful technology if it is to truly emancipate rather than further enslave the people of the developing world.

REFERENCES

Adesonye, Festus, 1990, "On Mass Communication and Mass Incommunication in Nigeria," *Africa Media Review*, 4(1), pp.60–73.

Aggarwala, Narinder K., 1978, "News with Third World Perspectives: A Practical Suggestion," in P. Norton (ed.), *The Third World and Free Press* (New York: Praeger).

Bagdikian, Ben, 1971, *The Information Machines* (New York: Harper and Row).

Beltran, Luis Ramiro, 1978, "TV Etchings in the Minds of Latin Americans: Conservatism, Materialism and Conformism," *Gazette*, 24 (1), pp. 16–85.

Cruise O'Brien, Rita, 1975, "Domination and Dependence in Mass Communications: Implications for the Use of Broadcasting in Developing Countries," *Institute of Development Studies Bulletin*, 6(4), pp. 85–99.

Fejas, Fred, 1980, "The Growth of Multinational Advertising Agencies in Latin America," *Journal of Communication*, Autumn, pp. 36–49.

Hachten, William A., 1971, *Muffled Drums: The News Media in Africa* (Ames: Iowa State University Press).

Hamelink, Cees, 1977, *The Corporate Village: The Role of Transnational Corporations in International Communication* (Rome: IDOC International).

Herold, Cacilda M., 1988, "The 'Brazilianization' of Brazilian Television: A Critical Review," *Studies in Latin American Population Culture*, Vol. 7, pp. 41–57.

Hornik, Robert C., 1988, *Development Communication: Information, Agriculture, and Nutrition in the Third World* (New York and London: Longman).

Inkeles, Alex and David R. Smith, 1974, *Becoming Modern: Individual Change in Six Developing Countries* (Cambridge, Mass.: Harvard University Press).

James, Sybil L., 1990, "Development of Indigenous Journalism and Broadcast Formats: Curricular Implications for Communication Studies in Africa," *Africa Media Review*, 4 (1), pp. 1–14.

Kang, Guen Kang and Michael Morgan, 1988, "Impact of U.S. Television in Korea," *Journalism Quarterly*, 65(2), pp. 431–438.

Kasoma, Francis P., 1988, *Publishing a Rural/Community Newspaper in Africa* (London: WACC).

_____ and Michael Leslie, 1990, "The Vernacular Press in Zambia: A Pilot Study of a Provincial Newspaper," *Africa Media Review*, 4(3), pp. 62–78.

Lerner, Daniel, 1958, *The Passing of Traditional Society* (Glencoe, Ill.: Free Press).

Leslie, Michael, 1989, Field Observations.

Mason, Hal R., *et al.*, 1974, "Balance of Payment Costs and Conditions of Technology Transfer to Latin America," *Journal of International Business Studies*, Vol. 1, pp. 5–77.

McAnany, Emile G., 1980, *Communications in the Rural World: The Role of Information in Development* (New York: Praeger).

Moemeka, Andrew A., 1989, "Perspectives on Development Communication," *Africa Media Review*, 3(3), pp. 1–24.

Morgan, Michael, 1986, "Television and the Erosion of Regional Diversity," *Journal of Broadcasting and the Electronic Media*, Vol. 30, pp. 123–129.

Nordenstreng, Kaarla and Herbert Schiller (eds.), 1979, *National Sovereignty and International Communication* (Norwood, N. J.: Ablex).

Pye, Lucian, 1963, *Communication and Development* (Princeton, N. J.: Princeton University Press).

Rachty, Gehan, 1980, *Importation of Films for Cinema and Television in Egypt* (New York, Paris, Geneva: UNESCO).

Rao, Laksmann, Y. V., 1966, *Communication and Development: A Study of Two Indian Villages* (Minneapolis: University of Minnesota Press).

Rogers, Everett M., 1983, *Diffusion of Innovations*, 3rd ed. (New York: Free Press).

_____, 1976, "Communication and Development: The Passing of the Dominant Paradigm," *Communication Research*, Vol. 3, pp. 213–240.

_____, 1969, *Modernization Among Peasants: The Impact of Communications* (New York: Holt, Rinehart and Winston).

Renzhong, Wang, 1988, "Major Developments in Chinese Telecommunications: An Overview," *International Communication Bulletin*, 23(3–4), pp. 4–9.

Reyes Matta, Fernando, 1976, "The Information Bedazzlement of Latin America: A Study of World News in the Region," *Development Dialogue*, Vol. 2, pp. 29–42.

Schiller, Herbert I., 1976, *Communication and Cultural Domination* (New York: International Arts and Sciences Press).

_____, 1973, *The Mind Managers* (Boston: Beacon Press).

_____, 1969, *Mass Communication and American Empire* (New York: Augustus Kelley).

Schramm, Wilbur, 1964, *Mass Media and National Development* (Stanford: Stanford University Press).

Sinclair, John, 1990, "From Modernization to Cultural Dependence: Mass Communication Studies and the Third World," in L. John Martin and Ray Eldon Hievert (eds.), *Current Issues in International Communication* (Boulder, Colo.: Westview Press).

Tan, Alexis S., Gerdean K. Tan and Alma Tan, 1987, "American Television in the Philippines: A Test of Cultural Impact," *Journalism Quarterly*, Vol. 64, pp. 65–72, 144.

Tehranian, Majid, 1979, "Iran – Communication, Alienation, Revolution," *Intermedia*, 7 (2), pp. 6–12.

Thebaud, Schiller, 1977, "An Evaluation of Technology Transfer in Underdeveloped Countries," in Marvin J. Cetron and Harold F. Davidson (eds.), *Industrial Technology Transfer* (Leiden: Noorhoof International Publishing).

Traber, Michael, 1987, "Towards the Democratization of Public Communication: A Critique of the Current Criteria of News," *Africa Media Review*, 2(1), pp. 66–75.

_____, 1989, "African Communication: Problems and Prospects," *Africa Media Review*, 3 (3), pp. 86–97.

Tsai, Michael R., 1970, "Some Effects of American Television Programs on Children in Formosa," *Journal of Broadcasting*, Vol. 14, pp. 229–238.

Tunstall, Jeremy, 1977, *The Media Are American: Anglo-American Media in the World* (London: Constable).

Ugboajah, Frank O., 1985, "Inspirational and Cultural Symbols in Nation Building," in Frank O. Ugboajah (ed.), *Mass Communication, Culture and Society in West Africa* (London: Saur).

Xinbo, Qian, 1990, "Recent Developments in Chinese Journalism," in L. John Martin and Ray Eldon Hiebert (eds.), *Current Issues in International Communication* (New York and London: Longman).

About the Authors in Chapter 9

Denis Goulet is a Professor in the Department of Economics of the University of Notre Dame where he holds the O'Neill Chair in the Education for Justice Faculty and is a Fellow in the Kellogg Institute for International Studies and the Institute for International Peace Studies. His volume, *Incentives for Development: The Key to Equity*, was published in 1989 by New Horizons Press of New York.

Janice Perlman was Director of Science and Public Policy Programs at the New York Academy of Sciences when her article was published. Her book, *The Myth of Marginality: Urban Poverty and Politics in Rio de Janeiro*, was published by the University of California Press in Berkeley in 1976.

Robie Siamwiza is a Lecturer in the Department of Social Development Studies of the University of Zambia in Lusaka. *An Evaluation of the Self-Help Assistance Fund*, by R. Siamwiza, C. Chibaye, and C. J. Mphaisha, was published in Lusaka by the Zambia Council for Social Development in 1983.

Dr. Michael Leslie is an Assistant Professor in the Department of Telecommunications in the College of Journalism and Communications of the University of Florida. His current research interests are media and development and media and socialization with a focus on comparative international studies of television content and effects.

CHAPTER 10

Technical Assistance to Developing Areas

Introduction

THE IDEA OF HASTENING TECHNOLOGICAL DEVELOPMENT in countries that have not completed the industrial and agricultural revolution goes back to the seventeenth century. As Fransman (1985) reminds us at the beginning of his superb interpretive survey and almost book-length article on the concept of technical change in developing areas in the 1980s and again in the conclusion, Adam Smith's first chapter in the Wealth of Nations dealt with the question of technical change and productivity improvement.

A quite different perspective comes through in the literature of those who, in addition to their economic backgrounds, have a sociological, culturological, anthropological, or social organization orientation (Hoselitz, 1954, as an early example). The contributions of each may ultimately be combined to generate more all-encompassing models with greater explanatory value.

As a national policy for the United States, technical assistance to developing areas was first advanced as Point Four by President Harry S. Truman in his inaugural address in 1945. Since then the United States and many other countries of the world have encouraged the transfer of technology to developing countries through public and private organizations.

Many nations such as Japan have adopted western technology in full scale. A few countries such as Tibet have resisted new technology. The adoption of western technology has created new social, economic, and political problems. Unfortunately, very little is known about the effectiveness of various approaches to the process of technology transfer.

Nevertheless, to technologically-oriented persons, the wholesale transfer of technology to developing countries is still seen as one of the most effective strategies for development. Technologies ranging from an improved hose and small tractors to advanced missiles have been transferred and agents including small scale entrepreneurs and multinational organizations have participated in the process for the last four decades. A large share of the technology transfer has occurred through multinational organizations (Marton, 1986) which have had enormous financial benefit from the transfer of military, industrial, and managerial technology. In some respects, the results have not been encouraging. Countries such as Zambia have acquired advanced aircraft for their national airways even though many villages are less accessible today than they were 10 years ago. The failure of western planning in Tanzania has been recounted for years (Armstrong, 1987).

Beyond arguments over specific needs and appropriate technology, the issue of unit size, the importance of large-scale operations as a part of industrial strategy has also received considerable attention. Aubrey (1951) has argued that small enterprises may be more efficient in some cases. As a matter of fact, some of the largest U.S. industrial concerns in the world (firms that continue to be highly profitable giants) made this discovery fifty years ago and, as a consequence, urged smaller enterprises to subcontract fabrication of parts for them.

While the emphasis in the literature seems to be on group or national developments there have also been important concerns at the individual level. For example, how are individuals prepared for urban vs. rural life? This may involve the preparation of children for urban-industrial careers while they are still in the village. In reviewing various strategies in Turkish villages, Lemel (1989) finds that, although there are complexities and locational variables, the wealthiest villagers have the easiest time preparing their offspring for urban careers.

The other side of the coin is that technological changes displace workers. Sathiendrakumar and Tisdell (1989) examine the capital-intensive tourist industry in the Maldive Islands and the extent to which it provides limited opportunities for local inhabitants as well as foreigners, aside from its earnings in foreign exchange, which may be markedly reduced by imports. In short, tourism in the Maldives has had little impact on poverty and disguised unemployment – as has been the case in many other developing nations.

The Articles in Chapter 10

Varas and *Bustamonte* discuss the impact of military technology on developing countries. The transfer of military technology and arms production systems occurs through a number of international channels including production under license, subcontracting, and joint ventures. Production under licensing and subcontracting make use of cheap labor and the research and development infrastructure available in developing countries. Joint ventures are attempted by those nations that are more highly developed among the developing countries. Perhaps the most undesirable consequence of military technology transfer is that such transfers tend to empower and benefit the military elite rather than the people. Argentina, for example, possesses highly sophisticated military technology but lacks the more modern technologies for producing goods and services for the civilian sector.

According to *Perrin* the problem of the transfer of industrial technology to developing countries presents yet another bottleneck in the process of development. The imported equipment may not function at the expected levels because it was designed for use in a different environment, climactic and social, for which adjustments have not been made. The imported technology requires well-developed maintenance service and technical assistance systems which may not be available.

Developing technical know-how is essential for absorbing imported technologies and is more important than is usually realized. More broadly, the process of gaining familiarity with the new industrial technology is more complex and time-consuming than was previously assumed, in part because working values and procedures of a different nature already exist, including informal information circuits among the workers. The organization of exhibitions, study panels, and technical journals will be helpful in promoting the exchange and storage of industrial experience and know-how in developing countries.

The next article in this chapter on technology, that by *Deihl*, is concerned with how technology transfer to developing countries is hampered by a gap in the managerial capacity that exists between the developed and developing countries. Even though management literature is readily available, most management techniques are seldom utilized without training and on-the-job experience.

The problem of communication is paramount. Few developing countries hold conferences or training programs where new managerial innovations are interpreted and exhibited. Instead, management tools and techniques are often exported to developing countries via aid institutions and voluntary organizations, which transfer management technology through time-bound examples. In addition, conflicting value systems of the donor and recipient countries hinder effective transfer of technology. Agents who are involved in the managerial technology transfer are often inappropriate and unqualified. Finally, unrealistic expectations may hinder the role and impact of management technologies that are transferred.

Fraser points out that mass communication via radio broadcasting, television programs, and video training could be effective tools given the high illiteracy level in rural areas. However, these technologies have not been effectively applied. For example, studies show that real time given to rural broadcasting is very small. A second barrier to the effective use of media is the unwillingness of governments to allow public access to mass media. Politicians are unwilling to be criticized.

REFERENCES

Armstrong, A., "Tanzania's Expert-led Planning: An Assessment," *Public Administration* 7(3), 1987, pp. 261–271.

Aubrey, Henry G., "Small Industry in Economic Development," *Social Research*, 18(3), 1951, pp. 270–312.

Fransman, Martin, "Conceptualizing Technical Change in the Third World in the 1980's: An Interpretive Survey," *Journal of Development Studies*, 21(4), 1985, pp. 572–652.

Hoselitz, Bert, "Problems of Adopting and Communicating Modern Techniques to Less Developed Areas," *Economic Development and Cultural Change*, 2(4), 1954, pp. 249–269.

Lemel, Harold, "Urban Skill Acquisition Strategies: The Case of Two Turkish Villages," *Human Organization*, 48(3), 1989, pp. 252–261.

Marton, Katherin, "Technology Transfer to Developing Countries via Multinationals," *World Economy*, 9(4), 1986, pp. 409–527.

Sathiendrakumar, Rajasundram and Clem Tisdell, "Tourism and the Economic Development of the Maldives," *Annals of Tourism Research*, Vol. 16, 1989, pp. 254–269.

The Effect of Research and Development on the Transfer of Military Technology to the Third World

AUGUSTO VARAS and FERNANDO BUSTAMANTE

••••

R&D and Arms Exportation

One of the main characteristics of R&D in the arms field in the developed countries has been its rapid transformation into a powerful and profitable national industry.[1]

This new factor, which is speeding up the world arms spiral, is having a great impact on the transfer of military technology from the industrialized centres to the underdeveloped periphery. The main effect of the industrialization of R&D in the developed countries is to stimulate the transfer of increasingly technologically sophisticated products to the peripheral countries. These products, in turn, generate a climate in the recipient countries whereby a quantitatively and qualitatively higher demand for military products is stimulated. Thus, arms imports are almost inevitably followed by the development of a local arms industry. This is brought about through the aid of subcontracts and production under licence which serve as the seeds of a fully-fledged local arms industry. Obviously, as will be seen below, this process occurs in those developing countries that have managed to establish a minimum industrial base from which this new industry can be developed. In some cases, it is established on the basis of a previously existing arms industry but which had been unable to develop to sufficiently high prof-

itability levels to be included in programmes for national development. Hence, licences, subcontracts and co-production agreements allow these local industries to attain the same levels of profitability and expansion as the developed countries' arms industries.

From this point of view, the arms industry at present is a highly profitable economic activity and, by strict business criteria, produces increasing returns. However, at the root of this economic military activity lies a complex system of technological research and development that enables ever higher levels of complexity of the military product to be attained. This, in turn, is supported by a scientific base which, through the development of certain fundamental sciences, enables scientific knowledge to be translated into technological terms. This combined scientific and technological research has enabled the developed countries to manufacture products of such high military sophistication that at present the majority of new armaments incorporate the last word in science and technology.

It was the policy of the first phase in the process of industrialization of R&D in the developed countries to transfer military technology to the Third World in the form of finished products without at the same time transferring the scientific and technological know-how that had inspired them. In these circumstances, the transfer of military technology to the underdeveloped periphery takes place mainly in the form of finished products. That means that the finished product is transferred, but never the scientific and technological capacity that

Varas and Bustamante. This article from the *International Social Science Journal*, 35(1), 1983, is reproduced with the permission of Unesco.

enabled the arms industry of the exporting country to develop and produce the weapon in question.

The monopolization of this scientific and technological basis which permits the development of new arms and weapons systems by the industrialized countries was one of the most important factors in the expansion of this powerful military industry, and characterized the first phase in the process of the transfer of military technology to the Third World.

The export of arms avoided transferring the capacity to generate the means of production of capital goods. This capacity to generate new, ultra-modern technology was maintained firmly in the hands of the producers in the industrialized countries. By transferring military technology in this way, the producing firms were creating a long- and medium-term captive market for their products and associated spare parts. At the same time they restricted the Third World countries' initiative to implement their own military technology development policies.

The existence of a scientific and technological R&D industry and its monopolization by the developed countries bred fierce competition among its principal producers. Simultaneously, in a few countries this took the form of a reaction to the loss of competitiveness on the world market of their industries producing non-military goods.

The weight of scientific and technological R&D and the amount of funds allocated by central governments in the technology of exporting countries is difficult for the Third World countries to match. To give an example, the United States and France allocate funds for military electronics equivalent to 24.5 and 29.5 per cent respectively of the total electronics markets of their economies.[2]

It may be observed that, as long as the United States, France and the United Kingdom maintained their dominance and control of the markets in their respective spheres of influence in the post-Second World War period, it was not necessary to resort to the sale of arms to make good trading deficits. Their overall trading situation was sufficiently strong for them to disregard any competition.

••••

However, in the 1960s the civil industries of the Federal Republic of Germany and Japan (countries that had emerged from the war without their own arms industries) began to erode the base of the commercial hegemony of the victors of the Second World War. One after another, different branches of the civil market began to be cornered by Japanese and German industries: such as shipbuilding, industrial equipment, chemicals, electronics and the motor industry. Products from the Federal Republic of Germany and particularly Japan began successfully to encroach on the domestic markets of the victorious powers. The growing competitiveness and technological efficiency of these countries considerably damaged their competitors' hitherto almost unlimited capacity to dispose of their products on the foreign market and also to control their own local markets.

As competition among the industrialized nations becomes greater, there is a tendency to view the military sector as an alternative whereby a still unexplored advantage might be exploited, so as to equalize the trading currents between the industrialized nations themselves and in the overall balance of trade with the Third World. This, for example, accounts for the recent pressures put on Japan (apart from purely military and strategic reasons) to increase its defence budget and its arms purchases in the United States.

In the same way, France is attempting to meet the Japanese challenge and offset its balance-of-trade deficit with Japan by exporting military equipment and nuclear technology.[3] The situation is somewhat similar with regard to the Federal Republic of Germany, a country which has been developing its own arms-producing capacity. As the exporting power of this country's economy has declined, the idea has gained ground of stepping up arms sales to the Third World, especially the Arab, countries. Although these sales have had a serious setback with the ill-fated German-Saudi Arabian agreement, the general tendency still holds good for the Federal Republic of Germany. Ample proof of this is provided by the increasing transfers of military material to the underdeveloped areas in the last year.

In short, for those countries with comparative advantages in this field, arms production and exports have come to represent an effective way of competing for world markets. This was possible thanks to the systematic industrialization of R&D. However, the transformation of R&D into an ever more profitable industry demanded larger markets than the mere arms exports could offer. For these reasons, the very growth of R&D was instrumental in bringing about a change in the pattern of military technology transfer to the Third World.

The Industrialization of R&D and its Effect on the Transfer of Military Technology to the Third World

As R&D activity has become transformed into a highly profitable industry, which in turn has stimulated dynamic arms production, the nature of the transfer of military technology from the developed countries to the Third World has changed considerably.

After the Second World War and well into the 1960s, the main form in which military technology was transferred to the underdeveloped periphery was by the export of arms or weapons systems. However, the inherent dynamics of the science and technology industry (R&D) and the competition among those countries possessing greater R&D installed capacity led to the export of finished products giving way to the transfer of production processes.

One of the characteristics of the R&D industry is it constant innovation with a

view to outdoing its competitors in the struggle for markets. For these reasons, it was not possible to limit the technology to be transferred permanently and exclusively to the traditional finished product, nor could it consist of the transfer of the expertise that would allow competitive scientific and technological capacity to be generated. For these reasons, the exporting of military technology to the Third World, in the competition stage between R&D industries, is characterized by the transfer of arms production systems which is carried out through a variety of mechanisms, including production under license, subcontracting and joint production of weapons.

This change in the structure of transfer from developed countries to the underdeveloped periphery can be observed from the diminishing proportion of military products transferred to the Third World.... While there is a greater increase in the transfer of civil technology than in the export of military products, this is due in part to a drop in the rate of exports of finished weapons during the 1970s. Thus, the United States, which had doubled its arms exports in the 1960s, increased this trade by only approximately 25 per cent between 1972 and 1976.

In this respect, the USSR maintained a more traditional policy, transferring a steady proportion of weapons and substantially increasing exports of products for civil use. However, in recent years, because of competition with the Western industrial powers on the politico-military plane, the USSR has also been obliged to transfer part of its production capacity to the Third World. Licences to produce the MiG-21 in the Democratic People's Republic of Korea and in India are indicative of this change.

Manufacture under licence is one of the most important forms of transfer of military technology to the Third World. It is by this method that a system for the manufacture of a specific type of armament previously developed by the arms industry of the industrialized countries is exported. This process derives essentially from the need of the science and technology industry itself to prolong the useful life of a particular military technology and maintain the profitability of equipment which is already obsolescent in the supplier countries. For firms producing military scientific and technological know-how, it adds to the profits if technologies that have already been fully developed and can no longer compete with new products are taken over and applied locally by Third World customers.

The American Northrop fighter F-5E/5, Tiger II, the Mirage 5, the French ERC-905 armoured car and the Swedish Saab Supporter aircraft are all good examples.[4] These are already outdated from the point of view of American, French and Swedish defense. Even though they are high-technology equipment, transferring their production to a country of the periphery enables them to continue as a profitable item after adaptation to a production scale compatible with a smaller market. It is disadvantageous for the respective industries to maintain this product with all the corresponding infrastructure in the United States, France and Sweden. If, on the other hand, the Republic of Korea or Taiwan set up as producers of such arms, not only for their own requirements but also for a regional or subregional area, the new plant that would be installed in those countries would be adapted to the type and level of output required by the new market.

Since agreements for the sale of technology to Third World countries involve the sale of patents, it is possible to continue to extract revenue from technologies already 'exhausted' in the industrialized countries.[5] It must be stressed that the most advanced technology is not sold, only its products. On the other hand, relatively less advanced technology is transferred to the Third World countries.

••••

This process of transfer of systems for manufacture under licence has enabled the countries receiving this technology to establish a military industry that tends to minister not only to its own needs in military equipment, but also those of other Third World countries. For example, the development of the military industry under licence in Brazil, Israel and South Africa has enabled those countries to export a large proportion of what they produce to other Third World countries.

••••

Brazil has used its local arms industry as a basic means of offsetting its vast balance-of-trade deficits caused by the increasing imports of oil needed for its dynamic civil industry. Israel and South Africa tend to get into Third World markets through the direct sale of arms to developing countries[6] and through association with other local Third World producers, which has been made easier recently by the lifting of the American embargo on exports of Israeli military products manufactured under American licences[7] and the ineffectiveness of the world embargo against South Africa.

In this way, armaments production under licence permits the export of military technology, overcoming the restrictions imposed on the mere transfer of finished products. Thus, the arms industry of the developed countries can attain higher levels of competitiveness in Third World markets without transferring all the scientific and technological know-how that enabled the arms to be developed. This prevents such transfers resulting in the creation of an equivalent competitive capacity.

Despite this temporary solution to the commercial problems facing the R&D industry, there is still pressure to obtain returns on the increasing investments. Subcontracting is one of the ways that have been tried to solve this problem.

This new procedure owes its origin to two sets of factors. First, the R&D industry is beginning to require increasing investments to maintain its level of productivity and competitiveness on a worldwide scale. Costs then go up as the marginal productivity of these investments tends to drop. Accordingly, new ways are sought of producing ultra-modern military material in regions offering advantages as regards natural resources and labour costs. For these reasons, the R&D industry is searching for areas of production and development which will enable it to cut costs. This is achieved by subcontracting in countries with relatively cheap labour.

Secondly, this same activity has of late been a characteristic *modus operandi* of transnational capital which is seeking to develop the capacity to distribute geographically the different phases of its production in areas where costs are lowest. This enables transnational activities to be developed in various parts of the globe with the support of international capital.

Inasmuch as the R&D industry is founded in part on this transnational capital, depends on it and nourishes it, subcontracts are a good way of solving both problems. Thus, a specific type of highly specialized, but at the same time fragmented, know-how is transferred, which enables ultra-modern technology to be reproduced in part – but never the whole product. This new procedure has been widely expanded in recent years as can be seen from the various subcontracts existing around the world.

R&D and Co-production Agreements

Co-production agreements are the most advanced form of transferring military technology from the developed countries to the Third World. Such agreements are generally concluded between industries with relatively complementary levels of scientific and technological development so that the input from the industrialized countries is harnessed to locally developed military technology. In this way, Third World arms industries receive an added stimulus for their own expansion. This phenomenon is

due to the dynamic quality of R&D in the developed countries, and, latterly, in those Third World countries which have either developed their own civil or military R&D or have been particularly favoured by armaments imports in their various forms.

As R&D requires more and more investment, in order to stay competitive and win markets, the pressures for appropriate returns on this sort of spending increase. Merely selling the finished product and transferring production systems are not enough to attain the necessary profit levels at a time when the importers' economic capacities are decreasing, even though their financial resources are increasing. Consequently, co-production agreements help to solve the problem of over-equipping Third World armed forces by establishing a dependent export industry operated, in part, on the basis of co-production agreements.

••••

Military R&D is thus becoming one of the major factors not only in the transfer of products, production systems (licences) and weapon parts (subcontracts), but also in the export of production capacity that can combine with another pre-existing capacity under co-production agreements. These agreements therefore represent the most advanced stage in the transfer of military technology, since the transfer is in this case based on a growth of scientific and technological know-how which further intensifies as a result of the agreements.

••••

The international monetary system has encouraged the accumulation in the hands of international financial interests of large floating foreign currency amounts. It is difficult for this money to find an outlet in industrial projects and in traditional economic activities in the developed countries. One way of adapting to the crisis of excessive liquidity has been to offer short- and medium-term credit to the countries of the Third World. For the first time these countries have enjoyed the availability to them of very flexible funds. Such new credit, in addition to being readily accessible, has been increasingly freed of the constraints and controls previously imposed by the developed countries' foreign-aid policies. The Third World countries have had therefore much more freedom of manoeuvre to implement their own policies of acquisition of military technology.

This tendency was reinforced by the situation created by oil prices from 1973 onwards. The balance-of-payments problems caused by the new prices made it necessary for the industrialized powers to compensate for their growing deficits. In order to solve this problem, one of the policies pursued was to encourage weapons sales to those countries that had become clients with considerable purchasing power because of the excessive liquidity. The great liquidity in the hands of the petroleum-producing countries was recycled, in part, through the transfer of military technology. Iran is an extreme example of this.

For the majority of the Third World countries, especially those without oil, this possibility of obtaining financial resources on the international capital market is accompanied, however, by the countervailing factor of an increase in their foreign debt and exacerbation of long- and medium-term balance-of-payments problems, as can be seen in the case of Latin America.

••••

Many countries possessing a basic industrial infrastructure have therefore attempted to use it in order to absorb the weight of their arms imports expenditure. The aim has been to transfer to the local arms industry part of the military procurement for the armed forces of these 'intermediate' countries.

In view of the existence of this great international financial liquidity and the growing external debt of the Third World countries, the solution adopted by these countries, in order to replace their imports of military equipment and at the same time solve their balance-of-payments problems, has been to develop a local arms industry which aims at exporting to and conquering the subregional markets of the Third World.

Effects of the Transfer of Military Technology on the Countries of the Third World

The effects on the Third World of the new forms of transfer of military technology are of two types – politico-social and economic.

Politico-social effects

One initial effect of these processes is the isolation or 'corporative wall' which the armed forces have built around themselves. They develop a consumption capacity and a level of professional expertise which make it difficult for them to find outlets in the ordinary local society. Consequently, they are continually forced to resort to a permanent link with the world of the transnational corporations and the hegemonic countries. The transfer of military technology is helping in this way to develop a social sector endowed with relative autonomy *vis-à-vis* the peripheral sector of society, and to introduce, as a foreign body, life-styles and technological nuclei which have no relevance to the problems of the majority. It is a mechanism that alienates social sectors which could otherwise contribute to local development. It also further distorts the distribution of income and educational opportunities in favour of intermediate sectors situated between the Third World countries and the suppliers of technology.

A second factor closely linked with the first concerns the integration of the armed forces in an international system of military relations. This system is composed of a local military complex which, from a technological standpoint, keeps it independent of the national environment, and a transnational industrial and military complex.

As the leading military groups see their

expansion as a social group, their prestige and their access to means of livelihood and employment conditioned by their link with the transnational military-industrial complexes, they develop a specific and corporative view of national needs. They acquire a particular notion of the type of development and type of state that will be compatible with maintenance of the military links that will ensure the flow of resources and the structure of internal political growth and power.

Being fundamentally dependent on the transnational groups, these strongly corporative military elites tend to share with the military ideology groups the same sphere of concerns, and to alienate themselves from the popular and civilian parts of their own societies. It even reaches the point where the military forces become internal political and social 'representatives' of multinational arms-producing interests.

It also leads the local armed forces to become advocates of development models that guarantee an expansion of resources for the import of means of creating a national defence structure based on massive imports of military technology.

The involvement of military elites in this international system of transfer of military technology leads to a distortion of national defence policies and tends towards its enforced standardization, notwithstanding differences in national needs and political objectives.

Any policy for the acquisition of military technology is in fact linked to and determined by a particular conception of the type of national defence which it is desired to promote and which is necessary, given the national conditions and politico-strategic objectives.

When the Third World countries import military technology created and suited to the particular needs of the arms-producing powers, they are importing the answer to a question they have not asked. In other words, the transfer of military technology implies

importation of needs for which that particular technology is appropriate. The national armed forces thus have to adjust themselves to a framework of national defence procedures and doctrines for which the purchased arms and technology are useful.

In the industrialized countries political and military policy determines the military technological structure, whereas in the Third World countries it is the structure that determines policy. In this way, national defence-policy options that are more consistent with the real needs of the people are supplanted. This has international policy implications, since it affects the way governments view the prevailing international situation. The logic that, in the central countries, gives rise to a policy of armament and of constant preparation for war is thus reproduced on a local scale.

A fourth effect that should be taken into account in analysing the impact of the transfer of military technology on the countries of the Third World is the increase in the levels of force on which local conflicts in this area are based.

The fact that these countries now possess a much higher level of modern military technology and local production capacity than they did in the past enables Third World political leaders to escalate conflict to higher levels than heretofore.

At the same time, these high levels of technology do not allow the total, overall mobilization of national resources which would be consistent with the military programme. The military effort remains relatively limited and excludes a large number of domestic protagonists who can do little more than witness the conflict.

Finally, the readier availability of military technological resources facilitates and stimulates regional and subregional arms competition, creating among governments the illusion that they can in this way increase their power and influence *vis-a-vis* their potentially hostile neighbours.[8]

The transfer of sophisticated military

technology not only quantitatively alters local conflicts and the relations between Third World countries; it also alters the quality of the conflicts. Armaments facilitate the involvement of the great powers in conflicts in which they normally would have no direct interest.

In view of the fact that the large arms-supplying countries regard military technology as a weapon of political influence and a factor of national prestige, they cannot be indifferent to the outcome whenever a client country is involved in local conflicts with other countries of the Third World.

The supplier–purchaser relationship and the dependence of one military system on the other causes these systems to be viewed as a political investment to be safeguarded. The outcome of these local conflicts thus becomes part of the logic of East–West confrontation. It is also affected by pressures exerted by the great powers, who do not wish to see any deterioration of what they consider to be their positions in the Third World. The transfer of military technology produced by the industrial countries thus tends to export the latter countries' conflicts and to transform the Third World countries into the battlefield – in the literal sense – of the conflict in which the great powers cannot engage directly because of the ever-present nuclear threat.

The converse and complementary aspect of this is that the traffic in arms tends to transform the great-power suppliers of military technology into hostages of local conflicts whose origins may have no direct bearing on the problems of the developed countries.

On becoming suppliers to the peripheral countries, the central countries find themselves obliged to support politico–military regimes and enterprises whose cost may prove excessively high and seriously distort the policy of the donor countries. These involvements, resulting from the need to maintain positions for fear of being sup-

planted within a competition for direct military influence, jeopardize the general climate of détente between the blocs.

It would be necessary to assess the role which this type of confrontation and the consequent local arms escalation have had in creating a climate unfavourable to disarmament and détente.

Economic Effects

The transfer of military technology also has economic effects. Although some countries that undertake the production of certain items may see their balance of payments favourably affected, there are two types of effects which clearly cause distortion of national economies. In the first place, an intensification of internal technological imbalances occurs which widens the gap between the advanced, modern high-productivity sector, and the large underdeveloped economic hinterland, which is neither drawn along nor stimulated by arms-related activities.

The technology introduced is generally of a high level and involves a complex of elements far above the local norm. The local economic base is not greatly affected by defense spending, which makes few demands on the local economy and provides no major spin-offs, neither does it make any significant demand for inputs. For example, it employs very specialized labour; the manufactured inputs are generally only partially produced locally, when they are not directly imported; the same applies to most of the raw materials, etc. The only requirement is cheap labour. Secondly, the products imported or produced locally by the defence sector do not contribute to the total supply of goods and services for the non-military economy as a whole. The military sector thus diverts substantial capital, removing it from the reproductive circuits of the economy and making no indirect contribution.

The growth of military technology thus takes place independently of technological

Table 1: Per Capita Public Spending on Defence, Education and Health of Arms-producing Third World Countries (in US$)

	(1) Defence	(2) Education	(3) Health	(2) : (1)	(3) : (1)
Argentina	37	37	15	1.00	0.40
Brazil	15	28	13	1.86	0.86
Egypt	152	21	8	0.13	0.05
India	5	4	2	0.80	0.40
Pakistan	11	4	1	0.36	0.09
Indonesia	8	4	1	0.50	0.12
Democratic People's Republic of Korea	59	11	1	0.18	0.01
Republic of Korea	37	19	1	0.51	0.02
Philippines	13	6	3	0.46	0.04
Taiwan	72	37	25	0.51	0.34

Source: Ruth Leger Sivard, *World Military and Social Expenditures: 1979*, Washington, D.C., July 1979.

development in the areas of civilian production and is unrelated to the average technical level of the peripheral society as a whole. A case in point is Argentina, which has a growing capacity in the area of military technology, including nuclear capacity, but whose civilian industries are experiencing a dangerous fall in productivity owing to a lack of technical innovation.

A second factor to be taken into consideration is the opportunity cost created by military production in Third World countries, through the absorption of resources which could otherwise help to improve the social infrastructure and to raise the living standards of the population. There is thus a loss of long-term social investment which it is very important to make good (see Table 1).

It could be argued, for example, that military spending could not find productive alternative channels, in view of the known structural problems of the peripheral economies. In other words, military expenditure might be said to constitute a form of defence against a relative over-capitalization of the peripheral economies. Since most of the population of the Third World do not constitute a market for basic commodities, entrepreneurs would not find it advantageous to make investments aimed at satisfying basic needs. The problem would thus appear to lie in the economic structure and not in the allocation of defence spending.

Here we may note an economic and ideological effect of military spending. By reducing relative over-abundance of capital, spending on military technology allows the deeply rooted political imbalances to be concealed and deactivates social struggle aimed at correcting them.

It is thus much simpler to conceal imbalances in the social allocation of resources by focusing on defence spending, which can easily be presented as meeting an urgent and natural need. This obviates the need to justify the paradox of available resources which cannot be used to meet basic needs because the economic and institutional structures allow this to be done only in the case of needs that constitute an effective demand, i.e., the needs of the high-revenue sectors.

In this way an economic function fulfills an ideological purpose of concealing existing inequalities.

[Translated from Spanish]

ENDNOTES

1. We are discussing here the profitability of the arms industry rather than military expenditure. Although the two are related, the arms industry, inasmuch as not all its production is necessarily consumed locally, is becoming an increasingly substantial source of profits. Even part of military spending seems to have positive effects: 'On the other hand, technological "spin-off" from military expenditure may have the opposite effect, stimulating growth; for example, higher productivity growth through R&D in military industries may increase growth rates for these countries.' Cf. Dan Smith and Ron Smith, *Military Expenditure, Resources and Development*, April 1980 (mimeo).

2. See Helena Tuomi and Raimo Vayrynen, *Transnational Corporations, Armaments and Development*, pp. 56–7, Tampere Peace Research Institute, Finland, 1980.

3. *Le Monde*, 22 April 1981.

4. *Strategic Week*, 12–18 January 1981. For sales of the Federal Republic of Germany, especially ships and submarines, see: *SIPRI Yearbook 1980*, p. 79, London, Taylor & Francis, 1980.

5. R. Vayrynen, 'International Patent System, Technological Dominance and Transnational Corporations', in Kirsten Worm (ed.), *Industrialization, Development and the Demands for a New International Economic Order*, Copenhagen, Samfundsvidenskabeligt Forlag, 1978.

6. Ignacio F. Klich, 'L'Amerique Latine, principal client de l'industrie d'armement israelienne', *Le Monde diplomatique*, September 1980.

7. See *Strategic Week*, 24–30 November 1980, and *Herald Wire Service*, 1 November 1980.

8. Augusto Varas, Carlos Portales and Felipe Aguero, 'National and International Dynamic of South American Armamentism', *Current Research on Peace and Violence*, Vol. 1, 1980.

The Production of Know-How and Obstacles to its Transfer

JACQUES PERRIN

The underdeveloped countries purchase technology from companies in industrialized countries in order to implement their industrial development policies. A variety of arrangements may be made: agreements may be reached on licensing, the transfer of know-how, project studies, assistance for technical organization, turnkey projects or the purchase of equipment. It must be acknowledged, however, that these technology-transfer operations often fail to live up to expectations and industrial investment ventures rarely prove as financially successful as preliminary studies seemed to indicate: start-up and trial production periods are long and costly, breakdowns and technical hitches are frequent and output is often much lower than planned.

Unsatisfactory technology transfer can be traced to a great variety of causes: poor preliminary assessment of investment and production costs or of markets and competition, mistakes in production unit planning studies or in the choice of equipment, irregularities in the supply of raw materials, intermediary goods and fluids (water, energy, etc.), unavailability of spare parts or workers' lack of familiarity with the production technology. All these situations can result in any number of breakdowns and assorted problems.

Difficulties in mastering the use of manufacturing technology, as well as unsatisfactory training procedures, the subjects dealt with in this study, are often due to an erroneous conception of technology, which is

Jacques Perrin. This article from *Prospects*, Vol. XIV, No. 4, 1984, is reproduced with the permission of Unesco.

understood in very general terms to be a mass of techniques moving freely from the industrialized to the developing countries and capable of being assimilated in time without undue difficulty. It was this kind of view that led Arrow[1] to introduce the concept of 'learning by doing'. He holds that techniques are effectively mastered through a gradual, automatic process of learning on the job. The effective productivity of technology in developing countries should therefore catch up with effective productivity in advanced countries after a certain learning period has elapsed. As Benachenou points out:

> This ideology of technology as a mass must be countered by the theory of technology as an ongoing process, as the continual transformation of the means of production of the work-force and of forms of organization that accompanies the use of the means of production and work-force.[2]

The introduction of new technology into an industrial production unit, even when nothing but the ability to imitate seems to be involved, does not depend solely on the gradual acquisition of knowledge and know-how; it calls for the production of new knowledge, and especially new know-how, by the work-force of the receiving company. For all technologies are the result of a social process of production, which comes into operation both in the designing of new technologies by researchers and in the process of selection (innovation), and at the stage of industrial implementation.

The essential characteristics of a production unit are not immutable. Productive capacity, production costs and overall productivity as well as the separate productivity of capital, labor and inputs change in time. These changes are particularly marked during the start-up stage but they continue to occur throughout the life of any industrial undertaking.

There are very few studies dealing specifically with the process of increasing efficiency during the start-up phase of the productive history of an industrial undertaking. However, some works have been written on this subject, and they show that: (a) the productivity may improve substantially during the start-up phase; (b) the duration of the start-up phase may vary considerably form one sector, company or country to another; and (c) the start-up period may merge almost imperceptibly into a phase of uninterrupted improvement leading to levels of productivity and efficiency higher than those initially foreseen.

Baloff's study[3] presents the results of an analysis of the start-up phase in twenty-eight plants in the United States. Although concentrated in the steel industry, the cases studied cover enterprises in different branches. The 'magnitude' of the start-up is defined as the ratio of productivity achieved at the end of the period to productivity during the first month of production. In about half of the cases, productivity tripled during the start-up phase and in over a third of cases the level of productivity at the end of the period was at least four times higher than at the outset. The start-up period varied from four months to two years.

Maxwell[4] studied the duration of the start-up phase in Latin American steel plants. His study dealt with the creation of new units of production and the expansion of older factories. The duration of the start-up phase varied from two to three years for some new factories to over six years in other cases.

There are very few in-depth studies of the process of productivity improvement in factories after the start-up phase. One of the most interesting is the study by Hollander,

who analysed the causes of increased efficiency in five American rayon plants. Hollander first shows that throughout the observed lifetimes of the plants (periods ranging from seven to about thirty years), unit costs dropped quite dramatically by 4 to 5 per cent per annum in most cases. He then considered the various types of change underlying these ongoing improvements: expansion of productive capacity by the introduction of new units of equipment, major technical changes (new manufacturing procedures) and minor technical changes (organizational changes, improvements in equipment). Hollander arrives at the following conclusion:

> Consideration by investment outlays at various plants suggests that relatively small investment expenditures incorporating modifications to *existing* plants are capable of generating large improvements in efficiency. Such improvements are sometimes sufficient to permit an older plant to produce at a unit cost which is not substantially higher ... than [that] at a *newly constructed* plant embodying the latest technology.[5]

Studies of workers' facility in using production techniques, both during the start-up phase and afterwards, have dwelt in particular on levels of technological knowledge, which affect the ability to assimilate imported production systems. For example, Baranson[6] has shown quite clearly the effect of technological knowledge on the speed of assimilation of imported technology in the case of diesel-engine production in India and Japan. The various kinds of practical knowledge (at the level of both production and management operations) required for rapid assimilation of systems of production may be acquired to some extent through training programmes. However, such practical knowledge also depends in large measure on accumulated experience, that is to say, it must be acquired in the learning process constituted by the actual execution of production operations. This is the explanation customarily given for the improvement in efficiency observed in industrial installations during the take-off phase: over and above the advantages accruing from formal training, additional efficiency gains would appear to result from a passive process of acquiring production experience.

Once a factory has been built and the workers trained, it might be assumed that all the technological requirements needed for the production unit to operate had been met. But this is far from being the case: the launching of new production units in both industrialized and developing countries is frequently lengthy and difficult to plan. During the start-up phase, the equipment frequently has to be adjusted, adapted in various respects and in some cases changed. Changes and improvements continue to be made to the equipment after the launching phase, to enable the plant to sustain, or if possible improve, its performance. The equipment of a production unit cannot, therefore, be managed like a stock of commodities; its productive capacity is not something fixed and immutable. The equipment must be constantly maintained and improved. In the absence of continuing technological inputs its productive capacity will decline very rapidly.

As Lall[7] notes, the need for changes to be made to equipment is even greater for industries in developing countries, as they frequently use equipment designed by the industrialized countries for use in a different environment. These environmental differences result from differences in relative prices, in the availability and quality of inputs, in the level of personnel training and in demand characteristics and climatic conditions. As Mytelka[8] points out in his study of the textile industry in Africa, the ability to assimilate imported production systems effectively will depend on the availability of technological resources capable of maintaining, adapting and improving equipment. To a large extent, these technological resources must be present within the production unit (research division,

maintenance services, technical assistance team), though some of them may also be provided by equipment manufacturers.

A similar approach must be adopted to the work-force. Learning cannot be considered as a passive process depending solely on workers' initial level of training and the amount of experience acquired. We would thus support Bell and Hoffman's observations:

> Almost all the studies of start-up improvement 'explain' the observed efficiency increases by either the passage of time or the growth of total accumulated output. The improvements simply 'happen' given these conditions, and the indices of improving efficiency are described as 'learning curves'. The observed effects (performance improvement) are thereby identified with their presumed source (learning); and both are 'explained' as the largely inevitable outcome of the passage of time or the growth of cumulated output ... To the extent that the notion of 'learning' implies a passive process whereby efficiency gains simply 'happen', it is likely to be a misleading idea.[9]

As they gradually come to terms with new machinery, the teams of workers have to produce new know-how, create new information networks among their members and encourage new reflections and new modes of behavior. Learning is the result of an active process of production and this is true not only during the start-up phase but throughout the life of a production unit.

In many cases, knowledge cannot be passed on through written or oral information alone: those receiving the information must also have access to know-how. 'Know-how is the result of an accumulation over the years of positive experience but also of difficulties and mistakes.[10] It is accumulated in the brains and hands of a limited number people.'[11] Know-how is therefore a form of technical knowledge that cannot be codified in a single (oral or written) medium for transmission to others. 'The paper-machine operator, the cement-maker or the smelter can only transmit their empirical knowledge to younger colleagues through collaboration on the job.'[12]

Know-how plays a more important role in industry than is generally supposed.[13] For example, procedures for adjusting equipment and conducting production operations depend more on technical know-how than on technological knowledge. This is also true of highly sophisticated branches of industry heavily dependent on technological knowledge and the latest scientific discoveries. In production service units, organizational and decision-making procedures also depend more on know-how than on fully formulated technological knowledge which is completely codifiable.

Technical know-how may be compared with the 'practical knowledge' as defined by Robert Linhart in his analysis of how workers master the technicalities of petrochemical installations. The practical knowledge acquired on the job by manufacturing workers, operators, assistant operators and especially overseers is handed down orally. Based first of all on practical familiarity with the physical plant, piping, valves, fittings, etc., it grows into a wider understanding of the process through repeated experience of how the installations work and what is likely to go wrong. This practical knowledge ultimately acquires a definite structure, taking the form of a collection of 'tips', and may also be contrasted with the 'theoretical knowledge', of which the engineers are the official depositories, and which consists of a set of official orders and operating instructions. Practical knowledge and theoretical knowledge, 'built up from different starting-points and maintained by entirely different means, do not coincide; hence there is a discrepancy between the official mode of operation of the production unit and its actual mode of operation'.[14]

The difficulties inherent in the transfer of workers' technical know-how are primarily due to the nature of this kind of knowledge, which can only be transmitted direct-

ly by workers in the 'owner' company to workers in the receiving company in the course of work carried out jointly in training sessions organized at one or other of the factories. Manual workers in companies that transfer their technology must therefore be involved in this kind of operation.

The main reason for the difficulties encountered in transferring technical know-how consists in the refusal to acknowledge the role played in learning techniques by the knowledge produced by the workers themselves. Many technology transfer operations deal only with the engineers' theoretical knowledge and the general instructions drawn up by the methods division, while the know-how acquired by the workers is disregarded or ignored. It should come as no surprise, therefore, when technology transfers that fail to take account of manual workers' know-how yield disappointing results or end in failure.

The second cause of unsuccessful transfers of know-how is the failure to reorganize the existence of purchasers' own technical structures. No transfer of technology and certainly no transfer of know-how can succeed unless it is integrated into the structured representation or memory of the recipient of technology. Contrary to the opinion or practice of many promoters, there is no such thing as a technical and cultural vacuum, even in what are considered the most traditional societies.[15] Some people attribute difficulties in learning modern techniques to the low level of general knowledge of the personnel concerned or to congenital or racial incompatibility with this type of learning process, whereas difficulties in learning Western techniques can actually be traced to the existence of technical habits that stand in the way of those to be acquired. 'Workers to be trained in Third World countries have already acquired working values and procedures; any useful analysis of training problems must concern itself with these conflicts.'[16] The causes of inefficiency in the learning of techniques may often be traced to a failure to recognize differences in value systems, and patterns and systems of knowledge.

A third source of difficulties in assimilating imported techniques lies in changes in the distinguishing features of know-how. This kind of knowledge is possessed by both individuals and groups of workers. With the advance of technology and changes in machinery, collective knowledge acquired at workshop level is constantly being discarded and reconstituted. The increasing complexity of the technical and social division of labor, stemming from the development of new technologies and especially from automation, tends to increase the role of collective know-how at workshop level but also and perhaps above all in activities ancillary to production.

Before the industrial revolution, when know-how was concentrated in the hands of craftsmen, technology transfer took place through apprenticeship. In our day, however, 'collective know-how' or technology – which extends far beyond purely technical aspects and includes commercial, legal and financial aspects and management itself – is (in some cases) no longer to be found in the workshop. Real technological know-how in now (also) to be found in design groups, control teams, after sales services, the commercial network – in short in the brains and hands of a pluridisciplinary team who, often enough, do not themselves know all the constituent details. Moreover, in every business this know-how is constantly changing. Outside information of a general character if it concerns methods or processes, or specific information from other firms in the same sector, can, when assimilated by the firm, change its own appreciation of a situation. Pressure from customers, or from the requirements and wishes of the management, leads constantly to the creation of new know-how. This individual or collective creative process may pass unnoticed just because it takes place at a very low level. It may also give rise to new information which may be disclosed or kept confidential. … It is however only with the emergence of 'collective know-how' that the problem of

transfer has become acute, for it has ceased to be an individual problem and thus a simple one, and become instead a group problem which has organizational dimensions.[17]

It is in the area of methods of organization that the transfer of systems of production encounters the greatest resistance and the largest number of obstacles. A UNIDO note on design services in India indicates that instrument companies are not lacking in basic mechanical training and manufacturing ability but rather in the modern engineering management techniques as practiced by the more industrialized countries.[18]

••••

Various surveys[19] carried out in France have shown that the organization of jobs and workshops is very frequently not that initially envisaged by management and engineering staff. No two groups of workers will reorganize a given system of production in the same way, and in a country like France it can vary in terms of workers' origins and past experience.[20]

As in the case of technical know-how, the reorganization of production and the informal information circuits established by workers are just as necessary for mastering production techniques as the organization systems designed by specialists or experts. This reorganization of production

is rendered all the more necessary by the fact that the official circuits responsible for transmitting instructions and norms are unable to pass on all the technical details needed. These informal circuits thus seem necessary for the attainment of official production norms.[21]

It may be accepted that reorganization by a team of workers of the sequence of production in which it operates is a general feature of production.

It is important to underline the implications, both social and individual, of this kind of practice, for example adapting the job to suit one's personality, structuring work time in such a way as to keep or tolerate the pace more easily, and in the process developing a whole series of 'knacks' and a practical work sense which encourages a better mental and biological adaptation to work in the individual while at the same time, although under supervision, creating areas of freedom and chipping away at time and space in order to fulfill social functions other than those of a mere productive instrument.[22]

It is a way, for both individuals and groups, of coping with the pressures and oppression of the world of work: of reconciling dominant production norms with forms of social and economic gratification.

••••

As the social component of collective know-how comes to play an increasingly important role (as compared with the technological component), working conditions will exert a growing influence on the way of life of individuals and social groups. Several research projects have shed light on this kind of relationship, either by analyzing the structuring of social zones in an urban area or by studying the impact of the development of a particular technology (automation for instance) on the evolution of life-styles.

The relationship between work situations and life-styles is not one-way: different life-styles lead to different behavior in the work environment. In France, this social reality has served as the basis for the relocation of certain production units so as to draw on a different pool of labour, thus changing the team of workers in such production units and reducing their bargaining power.[23] A study on the vocational retraining of former miners and fishermen in the Usinor-Dunkerque, steel plant has drawn attention to the difficulties that workers encounter in adjusting to new working methods and conditions when they differ substantially from those they were accustomed to previously. As Usinor-Dunkerque, former fishermen feel as though they are living in an enclosed space, a 'prison', and they regret the loss of independence in their working life. But the most interesting aspect of the study lies in its analysis of the dynamics of the interrelationship between working methods (modes of production) and life-styles. After showing that the main feature of the fisherman's life-style is its irregularity, due to the mode of production (an irregular family life with the men away at sea for long and variable periods, variability of resources calling for an extended form of family organization), the authors of the study note that this traditional life-style has been heavily undermined by the new constraints associated with industrial work:

> As soon as fishermen or sons of fishermen become workers at Usinor, they demand very strict regularity in their life-style in the family and away from work....The worker henceforth feels a need for ordered domestic arrangements and role of the extended family gradually declines, indeed comes to be felt as a constraint.[24]

Gramsci was the first to draw attention to this interdependence between new working methods and changes in lifestyles: 'One cannot be successful in one field without achieving tangible results in the other.'

••••

These observations by Gramsci referred to the first mass automobile plants in the United States, and at that time assembly-line work called for greater plant discipline than was to be found in the mass of unskilled workers. Nowadays, his ideas are primarily applicable to large automated production units needing a stable workforce to ensure the safety of the installations.

These considerations on the relations between modes of production and life-styles are particularly important in the case of technology transfer operations, especially when they involve the training in modern techniques of workers from a traditional agricultural background. The transfer of techniques from industrialized countries can on no account be reduced to the learning of techniques. It is also a social learning process involving the reconstruction of a system of work organization. This social training cannot be confined to the factory but must be extended to the environment outside work through a change in life-style.[25]

The transfer of techniques thus links up with problems of social change and, more generally, of development. It is because this essential aspect of the transfer process has been neglected that many production units in the developing countries function poorly. These failures are too hastily put down to a lack of motivation on the part of the workers of a 'congenital' intellectual or mental incompatibility.

The fact that workers in the developing countries lack the motivation to operate production units based on models and standards prevailing in industrialized countries implicitly reflects their attachment to cultural values that are negated by the transferred development model.[26]

The difference observed, in respect of the same type of industrial undertaking, in the duration of the start-up phase, productive innovations introduced throughout the life of the investment and workers' technical and social know-how confirm that there are no ready-made models of technical and social training. Differences in ways of learning are not eliminated when workers' basic training is identical; it is strongly influenced by their vocational and cultural background.

These observation also show that mastery of production techniques by a team of workers is achieved through an active process of technological production calling for the acquisition of knowledge and know-how, possibly to some extent through transfer operations. Such operations will prove all the more effective for the recipients if the workers in the company possessing the technology participate actively in the operations for transmission of know-how. But it must be stressed that

there can be no complete, mimetic transfer of know-how of one team of workers to another. An exclusively mimetic transfer will not result in complete mastery of the technology. Taking the received knowledge and know-how as their starting-point, the team of workers must produce new forms of technical and social know-how.

In order to produce these new forms of know-how, workers in the developing countries must commit to memory the industrial experience acquired mainly through transfer operations. As the transmission of technology is governed by the same principles as information, it stands to reason that new information cannot be produced in the absence of a memorizing process.

In the nineteenth century, when France set in motion its process of industrialization by importing technology from Great Britain, a number of 'learned societies' were established: the Academy of Science, the Society for the Encouragement of National Industry and the Mineral Industry Society. These societies took a more or less immediate interest in the progress of metallurgy and played 'the role of discussion and meeting-places as well as stimulating initiative by awarding prizes'.[27] Such associations were responsible for launching some of the scientific and technical periodicals that proliferated in the nineteenth century. For example, the Newsletter of the Society for the Encouragement of National Industry sought 'to draw attention to foreign discoveries that should be imported into France and to procedures for their successful transplantation.'[28]

In Japan, the government organized national technological exhibitions, known as *Kiyoshen-Kai*, from 1879 onwards to promote the development and dissemination of improved technologies, particularly in the traditional sector. The objective was to draw up an inventory of national technologies, to stimulate innovative activities by industrialists and to encourage the dissemi-

nation of improved techniques and practices. Exhibitions were generally based on a
particular product (exhibitions of tea and
silk cocoons in 1879, exhibitions of cotton
and sugar in 1880, etc.) selected by the government in the light of essentially commercial considerations, and lasted anything from
30 to 200 days. These events were very well
attended; in 1887, for example, 317 exhibitions involving 180,000 industrialists attracted over 2 million visitors. Each exhibition
was followed by a debate that might go on
for two weeks among participating industrialists, civil servants and other interested parties who engaged in a joint effort to discover practical ways of developing the industry
concerned. As this evaluation and examination of existing technology was conducted
with reference to the modern technology of
foreign countries, these exhibitions became
a nursery for hybrid technology.[29]

Developing countries seeking to assimilate technologies today must also create discussion and meeting-places for their industrialists, engineers and technicians involved
in technology selection and transfers.

It is therefore imperative that the developing countries organize exhibitions, technical journals and study panels at the national and regional levels in order to promote
the exchange and storage of their own
industrial experience and their own know-
how. Such initiatives would undoubtedly
enable purchasers of technology in the
developing countries to improve their
negotiating ability and to make better
choices when dealing with firms from the
industrialized countries for the purchase of
technology. More generally, they should
enable those countries to assimilate their
new techniques more rapidly.

ENDNOTES

1. K. Arrow, 'The Economic Implications of Learning by Doing', Review of Economic Studies (Princeton,
N.J.), Vol. 29, 1962, pp. 155–72.

2. A. Benachenou, 'Division internationale du tra-
vail et formes de consommation des techniques en
Afrique', Technologie et industrialisation en Afrique,
Dakar, Codesria, 1982.

3. N. Baloff, 'Startups in Machine-intensive Systems', The Journal of Industrial Engineering, Vol. 17, No.
1, 1966; cited in M. Bell and K. Hoffman, Industrial
Development with Imported Technology: A Strategic Perspective on Policy, Brighton, University of Sussex, Science Policy Reserach Unit, 1981. The case-studies
referred to below are taken from the Bell and Hoffman
publication.

4. P. Maxwell, 'Technical and Organization
Changes in Steel Plants: An Argentine and a Brazilian
case'; paper presented at a symposium on organizational analysis, Buenos Aires, 16–18 October 1980.

5. S. Hollander, The Sources of Increased Efficiency: A
Study of Dupont Royo Plants, p. 156, Cambridge, Mass.,
MIT Press, 1965.

6. J. Baranson, 'Diesel Engine Manufacturing: De-
automation in India and Japan', Automation in Developing Countries, Geneva, International Labour Office,
1972; cited in Bell and Hoffman, op. cit.

7. S. Lall, 'Developing Countries as Exporters of
Industrial Technology', Research Policy (Amsterdam),
Vol. 9, 1980.

8. L. Mytelka, 'Technology Transfer: The Case of
Textiles in Africa'; paper prepared for the Conference
on Technology transfer organized by the Social Sciences Research Council, New York, 2–3 June 1983.

9. Bell and Hoffman, op. cit., pp. 133, 134.

10. J. Perrin, Les transferts de technologie, Paris, Editions La Decouverte, 1983.

11. UNIDO, Workshop on Creation and Transfer of
Metallurgical Know-How, p. 5, Vienna, UNIDO. 1971
(ID.WB/110/3).

12. L'automatisation des processus de production. Impacts
techniques, economiques et sociaux, Paris, Association
Nationale de la Recherche Technique, 1978.

13. A. Rosanvallon, Formation continue et apprentis-
sage, Grenoble, Institut de Recherche Economique et
de Planification du Developpement, 1981.

14. J. J. Troussier, Travail individuel et collectif dans
quelques industries, Grenoble, Institut de Recherche
Economique et de Planification du Developpement,
1981.

15. In a study on the transfer of knowledge in a
Mexican yogurt factory built by a French company
and employing rural workers, the author notes that
'practical know-how was not provided by the French
firm but was developed on the job within the cohesive
cultural group'; J. Ruffier, Transfert de technologie et
transferts de qualifications, Lyons, Groupe Lyonnais de
Sociologie Industrielle (GLYSI), 1983.

16. M. C. Guillevic, 'Apport possible de la psy-
chologie du travail: quelques hypotheses sur les diffi-
cultes d'acquisition d'habilete professionnelle dans les
pays du tiers-monde', Formation et transfert de techniques,
Nancy, University of Nancy, Centre Universitaire de
Formation Economique et Sociale, 1980.

17. OECD, *North-South Technology Transfer — The Adjustments Ahead*, Paris, OECD, 1982.

18. UNIDO, *Development of Engineering Design Capability in Developing Countries*, p. 6, Vienna, UNIDO, 1971 (ID/67 ID/WG/56/28).

19. R. Linhart, *L'etabli*, Paris, Les Editions de Minuit, 1978; G. N. Fisher. *Espace industriel et liberte*, Paris, Presses Universitaires de France, 1980.

20. This difference may be observed, for example, in the same Merlin-Gerin plant established in two places, the Grenoble region and Normandy.

21. P. Pharo, 'Soumission ou detournement: l'efficacite pratique des savoirs sociaux', *Critique de l'economie politique* (Paris), No. 23/24, 1983, p. 90.

22. Ibid., p. 92.

23. B. Convert and M. Pinet, *Logiques industrielles de reconversion et politique de mobilisation*, Villeneuve d'Ascq, Laboratoire d'Amenagement Regional et Urbain, 1980.

24. E. Campagnac and F. Tabarly, *Transfert des modes de vie et habitat ouvrier*, p. 27, Paris, Centre de Recherche et de Rencontre d'Urbanisme, 1979.

25. R. Cornu reaches the same conclusions: 'We conclude from our previous studies that the process of learning know-how depends not only on knowledge but also on "savoir-vivre", that is to say on socialization and acculturation.' R. Cornu, 'De la boite a outils a la boite a idees: jalons pour une etude du savoir-faire et de la creativite ouvriere'; paper prepared for the Colloque National d'Ethnologie Francaise, Isle d'Abeau, May 1982.

26. See F. Perroux, *A New Concept of Development*, London/Paris, Croom Helm/Unesco, 1983.

27. F. Russo, 'La diffusion de l'information dans le domaine de la metallurgie en France au XIXe siecle', *L'acquisition des techniques par les pays non-initiateurs*, Paris, Centre National de la Recherche Scientifique, 1973.

28. *Histoire des sciences*, p. 260, Paris, Presses Universitaires de France, 1952.

29. UNCTAD, *Technology Transfer and Development Policy in Pre-War Japan (1868–1937)*, Geneva, UNCTAD, 1978 (TD/B/C.6/26).

The Transferability of Management Technology to Third World Countries

LINCOLN W. DEIHL

In this paper we examine the transfer of a particular technology – the technology of getting results through organization – that is, "management technology." The successful transfer of appropriate management technology can be important in improving the capacity of Third World managers to respond to the multitude of institutional demands that accompany the process of economic development.

The Growing Management Gap

In a great many instances, the inability of a Lesser Developed Country (LDC) to achieve expected goals is partly due to the fact that institutional demands have outpaced the capacity of civil servants and business managers to cope with them. The commodity in this case is "management capacity," the ability of managers to successfully mobilize scarce resources so as to achieve organizational goals. The result is a growing "management gap" between demands and their fulfillment.

Management, according to Jedlicka (1982), is the major variable that affects the technology transfer process, negatively or positively. In instance after instance, the failing dimension in technology transfer efforts has been the management of the process. That failure ranges from bad planning to improper training of middle-level people to a formal style of conduct between representatives and clients that too often result in rejection of any technology offered regardless of suitability.

Lincoln W. Deihl. The *Akron Business and Economic Review*, in which this article appeared in 18(3) in 1987, has given permission to reprint it.

Transfer studies over the past three decades, Jedlicka reports, indicate failure often occurred because clients were not effectively involved in the transfer process. The primary reason for this lack of involvement concerns the philosophy of the transfer agency. If the agency assumes that clients do not have decision-making skills or cannot be provided skills to plan and implement a specific transfer strategy, then the result will likely be a self-fulfilling prophecy.

One factor influencing the growing management gap is the phenomenal growth in the number, size and complexity of Third World institutions. In the public sector, growing institutional demands are caused not only by the fact that the population of many LDC's has been growing at rates exceeding those experienced by the Industrialized Nations during comparable periods of industrial expansion but also by the fact that the scope of public sector activities has been rapidly expanding. These phenomena are exacerbated by the high degree of urbanization in LDC's.

Larger Organizational Units

In an increasing number of Third World countries, the public sector is not only responsible for traditional public sector activities in a Western capitalist sense but for an expanding range of commercial, financial, and manufacturing activities as well. Historically, production processes in these and other activities have tended to progress toward larger organizational units due to economies of scale and available technologies (Bryce, 1960 and Pratten, 1971).

As a result of these factors, economic growth has been accompanied by organizations of increasing size and complexity and by an ever expanding need on the part of management for greater control and coordination. In the public sector, development goals and programs must be prioritized and the multitude of sectoral inputs and outputs effectively balanced. In the private sector, functional goals must be coordinated and monitored in a timely manner.

While the situation certainly varies from country to country and within country from sector to sector, it does appear that complex organizations of greater size and responsibility are proliferating in the Third World and that they will play an increasingly larger role in the process of economic development. As a result, the expanding demands placed on Third World managers are sufficient to strain the capacity of even the most effective managers in the Industrialized Nations.

Lagging Management Development

Rapidly expanding institutional requirements, however, only represent the demand side of the equation. The supply side is dictated by the lagging of Third World management development and innovation. The rapid growth of institutional needs simply has outpaced the capacity of many Third World managers to create, borrow, or adapt suitable organizational technology.

This lagging innovativeness in LDC management is no simple matter to analyze. Indeed, it appears to be the result of a confusing web of historical, economic, and cultural factors. For example, it has been argued that in many LDC's the administrative systems left behind by European colonial powers were not especially geared to fostering rapid organizational change (Weidner, 1964). In addition, many managers in LDC's are not adequately trained in the skills that might allow them to control and direct larger complex organizations. In many instances, these managers are appoint-

ed for their function skills (e.g., physicians, lawyers, and engineers) rather than for their management training or capabilities.

Similarly, where education for public and business administration is available, curricula tend to emphasize theory rather than techniques of problem solving. The problem is further compounded by bureaucratic methods that unduly emphasize formalistic approaches not responsive to organizational goals.

Finally, a myriad of cultural variables influences management innovativeness through the established set of civic values, methods of social interaction, and attitudes toward certain types of work (Phatak, 1983).

The end result of these influences is the maintenance of administrative systems that fail to emphasize the process of goal specification and attainment. As a result, the institutional rewards for innovation and problem solving are insufficient to warrant the required effort on the part of local managers. The management gap continues to grow, and critical needs go unmet.

Emphasis in the literature has been placed on the general notion that transfer of management techniques is necessary to bridge the "effectiveness gap" between industrialized and less developed countries. Ghymm and Evans (1979) concede that there may be some validity to such a generalization; however, as a practical matter, cross-cultural transferability from a developed country to an LDC should not necessarily be assumed.

Technology Accessibility

It can be reasonably argued that management techniques are capable of assisting Third World managers to utilize effectively scarce institutional resources, including themselves. The question is, how available and how accessible are these techniques? They are generally available but not always accessible.

Most process- and person-embodied techniques can be theoretically "acquired" simply by purchasing one or more management handbooks. The majority of such techniques are not governed by patents or royalty agreements. Ample literature is available regarding practical problems or implementation. In reality, however, their true accessibility is limited by the fact that they are difficult to implement without formal training and on-the-job experience.

Product-embodied technology, on the other hand, may be relatively more "accessible." The technology used to produce management-related devices is highly competitive and, where licensed for overseas manufacture, generally is governed by patents, royalties, and foreign supervision and control. However, the use of this technology in its "finished product" form is actively encouraged by equipment manufacturers. Accessibility is limited by financial resources (Garland and Farmer, 1986).

Inadequate Communication of Innovations

The problem of technology accessibility generally is not a matter of the existence of appropriate management tools. Rather, the problem is one of adequate communication. In Industrialized Nations, management innovations are communicated through a wide array of professional journals, conferences, commercial training programs, and promotional literature of one sort or another. Indeed, managers find themselves literally inundated by the constant flow of program announcements and publication lists.

This process of continually announced innovation does not exist, or exists only weakly, in most LDC's. The Third World manager generally has received little if any formal management training, and he does little if any "managerial" reading. His sense of professional identity is more likely to be tied to the agency or company in which he is employed than to the task he performs.

Where functional identity does exist, it is likely to be tied to the type of academic training received (e.g., agriculture, engineering, law, economics) rather than his current position. Membership in professional associations tends to be related to these disciplines rather than to specific business or public administration activities.

Where management-related associations do exist, their role in actively communicating management innovations is restricted by limited membership and even more limited financial resources.

Where university programs in business and public administration play an active part in training and publication, these channels tend to emphasize theoretical issues over innovative adaptation of available technology to day-to-day problems.

The one area where communication of management innovation appears strongest is in the area of product-embodied technology. In this instance, the desire to sell is the prime motivator. The degree of active promotion in this area depends in large part on the perceptions of potential markets by producers.

In a growing number of instances, promotion of management-related equipment in LDC's is being seen as an integral part of world markets by multinational firms. Japanese, European, and American computer salespeople are becoming a common sight in some Third World capitals. There is some recognition, however, that such "modernization" may result in the acquisition of inappropriate "gadgets" using scarce funds. Nevertheless, vendors of management-related equipment can play an important role in introducing new solutions to traditional problems.

It would appear that modern management technology certainly is available but not necessarily accessible to many Third World managers. Now, let us examine past and current attempts to improve this situation.

Transfer Agents and Programs

The process of transferring management technology can be considered as either "autonomous" or "induced" (Sequeira, 1979). "Autonomous" technology transfer refers to those activities that occur as a natural result of international trade and foreign investment. The transfer agents involved in this process during the 1950s through the mid-1960s were generally multinational companies. The most recent wave, which is still ongoing, consists of the attempt to transfer the technology of U.S. business management to specific Third World institutions.

Colonial Administrators

The transfer agents involved in the first wave were primarily colonial administrators. The transfer process they employed was less one of management development than that of bureaucratic transplantation. In spite of the darker side of colonial rule, the results of this first wave were rather remarkable. The major drawback was that the resulting systems primarily were designed to "administer" policies and programs created by the colonial authorities rather than to design and develop "management capacity" to respond to local needs. As a result, the colonial legacy generally was one of lagging management innovation.

Agencies and Institutions

The transfer agents involved in the second wave sought to overcome this legacy through formal education and training in modern public administration. Throughout the 1950s and 1960s, training in public administration was big business. During this period a number of agencies and institutions were involved in the effort.

The second wave of technology transfer began to fade in importance during the mid-1960s, and the transition was nearly complete by the early 1970s. By this time, the annual rate of public assistance provided by the U.S. Agency for International Development was less than half the average for the period 1955–1963. The reason for this decline was the growing conviction that the key to development was not so much the general improvement of public administration as the fostering of indigenous economic growth through effective domestic and international policies (Siffin, 1976).

Business Management Models

The third and present wave of technology transfer involves many of the same agents involved in the second wave. The most noticeable in terms of expenditure appear to be the USAID and the United Nations Development Program. In both these cases, the emphasis has swung from national training and civil service reform to the implementation of business management models within specifically targeted institutions. This is not to say that assistance is not provided to national training institutes or civil service organizations, especially by the UNDP, but merely that the emphasis appears to have moved in another direction.

Another group of transfer agents consists of the World Bank and the various regional development banks. In this group, the emphasis is placed on management and organization reviews intended to assess the institutional viability of prospective borrowers. These reviews generally are performed by private consultants as a "condition" for loan approval. The World Bank encourages the employment of consulting firms of the borrower's nationality and generally leaves to the borrower the responsibility for selection, administration, and supervision of the consultant. In certain cases, these reviews may lead to follow-up efforts aimed at organizational improvement.

From this review of past efforts at "induced" management technology transfer, it can be seen that management tools and techniques have been actively exported to the Third World via international lending agencies, voluntary organizations, aid institutions, and providers of management related services. Such technology transfers, however, are likely to be a poor substitute for the continuous flow of information regarding management innovation that takes place in Industrialized Nations via professional associations, conferences, and publications.

The "induced" export of management technology is primarily temporary, project-specific action rather than an intrinsic and continuous process. In addition, the adaptation of technologies principally designed to meet the needs of Industrialized Nations certainly is not as satisfactory as the creation of management innovation and communication capabilities within LDC's themselves. Nevertheless, until such indigenous capability reaches maturity, "induced" technology transfers are likely to provide valuable assistance.

Technology transfer activity, of course, is not synonymous with actual technology transfer. The potential transferability of management technology is a matter for dispute.

Problems of Transferability

Historically, it is clear that a great deal of transfer activity has taken place. It is less clear how much actual technology transfer has occurred. The results are mixed. In certain instances, success has been significant and of continuing impact. In others, the only constructive output appears to have been the provision of temporary employment (and a few interesting experiences) for a number of consultants, professors, and agency representatives.

Some of the more obvious problems of transferability can be grouped under the following headings: (a) conflicting value systems, (b) inappropriate transfer agents, (c) inappropriate use of transfer mechanisms, and (d) unrealistic expectations.

Conflicting Value Systems

Eager to spread their particular management philosophy, many technical assistance experts fail to be aware of the normative foundations of Western management technology. Even relatively value-free management techniques are not value-free altogether. Rather, many are biased toward

such implicit values as "rewarded achievement," "wage motivation," "individual accountability," and "productive efficiency." To an unknown degree, these values may be responsible for the past success of Western management methods. The problem is that these values are not universally shared (Adler, 1986 and Ronen, 1986).

Social prestige systems in LDC's often lean toward "ascriptive" rather than "achievement" related variables (Riggs, 1964). Where the former are predominant, managers are rewarded according to "who they are" rather than "what they accomplish." In these cases family position, education level, organizational rank, and personal contacts are more important than "results." Much of a manager's energy is expended in building systems of friends and supporters – often via the judicious distribution of organizational rewards. In certain instances, the manager may also be called upon to favor those with ascriptive characteristics similar to his own. These may be members of the manager's family, tribe, or religious affiliation. Employment and promotion based on ascriptive characteristics may not only be considered acceptable but also may be viewed as morally commendable (Deihl, 1981).

Similarly, the Western belief in "wage motivation" may run counter to local economic realities. The most obvious difficulty is the scarcity of available funds due to low productivity or to government attempts to hold the lid on wage-push inflation. In these cases, however, incremental wage and bonus schemes can still be effective. The more intractable cases occur when wages represent only part of the individual's income. Professional level positions in government and business are often seen as "respectable" occupations by members of the elite class whose main income flow is derived from elsewhere. In still other instances, public sector and private sector employees hold multiple jobs in an effort to increase earnings. Where the second job provides the main source of income, wage policies in the first location of employment tend to be less effective.

The American business model's preoccupation with "accountability" has also been found to run counter to certain values regarding appropriate modes of decision-making. An example is the consultation decision-making process of *ringi-sei* practiced in Japan. This decision-making process acts to diffuse rather than pinpoint responsibility (Robinson, 1984). By the time a decision is reached, "not one man, but all those who took part in the process have become responsible for the decision. Responsibility has been diffused and all are committed to success" (Stifel, Coleman, and Black, 1977). In this environment, strict accountability in the traditional MBO fashion is not considered desirable by business and public executives (Schnitzer, Liebrenz, and Kubin, 1985).

A final example of conflicting values concerns the Western ideal of "efficiency." This is generally construed to mean maximum output per unit of labor. It has been argued that this value is a direct descendant of the "Protestant work ethic" (Weber, 1958). In certain instances this work ethic may conflict with the local "leisure ethic." To some extent, the local preference for leisure may be influenced by poor wages, undesirable working conditions, and dietary and other health disorders. However, even controlling for these effects, it appears that the value of non-work time is more highly regarded in certain cultures than is generally assumed by Western models.

••••

Inappropriate Transfer Agents

In spite of the sincere efforts by international and domestic organizations in selecting transfer agents, the best are not always selected. Whenever much must be done in little time under great uncertainty, mistakes are inevitably made. Consulting firms and universities are asked to perform tasks that

are only marginally within their scope of expertise. Many find it difficult to decline. In addition, the choice of individual members of the technical assistance teams themselves has a major impact on the potential for the successful transfer of management technology. Finding qualified individuals is no easy matter. The exigencies of getting the job done do not always allow for getting it done with the right staff. A Latin American observer, for example, characterized the staff of one U.N. effort as "including about 20 percent who were successful, 40 percent 'so-so,' 20 percent poor, and 20 percent terrible" (Weidner, 1964).

••••

Inappropriate Use of Transfer Mechanisms

The successful transfer of management technology has also been hindered by the use of inappropriate transfer mechanisms. By these we mean the institutional arrangements designed to convey information and knowledge. Some of the more common problems encountered include inadequate executive support, inappropriate selection or use of counterparts (Globerson, 1978), overemphasis on formal training, and inadequate provision for follow-through.

What has often not been recognized is that the "real" work begins after the reports and recommendations have been completed. Successful implementation is the "acid test" of management technology transfer, not the existence of impressive feasibility studies or well designed recommendations no matter how detailed. The problem, however, is that studies and recommendations can be prepared within a reasonably short time-frame, usually one year or less. Implementation, on the other hand, is open-ended. Depending upon the type of activity involved, successful implementation may take one to five years and sometimes longer.

Unrealistic Expectations

A final factor that can be said to contribute to the poor performance of previous attempts at transferring management technology is the existence of unrealistic expectations. The first of these is excessive time optimism. This tends to place an undue burden on the task team and counterparts and reduce the potential for lasting change.

Secondly, there is an unrealistic tendency to view host-institution executives as enlightened and benevolent leaders of economic development. Merely because an executive is eager to receive technical assistance does not necessarily mean he is eager to introduce change.

Thirdly, technical assistance teams tend to believe what they are told by host-institution representatives. In many cases, however, what they are told does not reflect reality. This is not to imply that host-institution representatives are misrepresenting the facts. Rather, technical assistance teams are often unfamiliar with the degree of "formalism" found in Third World institutions (Riggs, 1964 and Thurber and Graham, 1973). This problem may be characterized as one in which formal goals, policies, and procedures are not put into practice. Although this problem occurs in Industrialized Nations as well, the extent of such formalism is not as material (Hardiman and Midgely, 1978).

The problem for technology transfer occurs when institutional formalism is overlooked. In such cases the technical assistance team may spend a good deal of time revising current procedures (which were never followed) and preparing detailed programs that (as their predecessors) will be reviewed by executive committees, issued over the signature of the top executive, and never implemented.

••••

Effect on Employment

It is Stewart's (1979) contention that advanced technologies are often detrimental to developing countries due to their inherent bias toward capital intensive methods of production. Stewart argues that modern technologies were designed in response to high-income demand and the relative factor endowment (land, labor, and capital) of the Industrialized Nations. Their transfer to LDC's that do not share these same relative endowments necessarily leads to distortions in local factor utilization. Among the results of these distortions is widespread unemployment.

The problem is that modern technologies are often "superior" to traditional methods insofar as they are able to generate a given level of output using less labor and less capital. Since these technologies are used to produce goods for a given level of demand, the degree of employment generated is less than would have occurred had simpler or more traditional methods been used. While "superior" technologies are necessarily the most appropriate given the shortage of capital resources in most LDC's, Stewart argues that the products produced by this technology may have superfluous characteristics that exceed the needs of LDC's. LDC's may be paying for these superfluous characteristics by unnecessarily high unemployment. The proposed solutions to these problems are the redesign of product characteristics so as to make them fit local needs and the reduction of scales or production so that more labor intensive techniques are once again advantageous.

When extended to management technology, this argument suggests that the methods of management that result from the adoption of modern management technology may exceed what local conditions require and that the capital (financial and human) invested in this technology might better be used to promote more widespread use of basic management tools (such as simple accounting manuals for cooperatives). In addition, there is a presumption that modern management technology is designed to complement organization and production systems that are themselves inappropriate to the needs of LDC's. These systems should be changed rather than propped up by modern management technology.

Finally, Stewart suggests that the adoption of inappropriate production processes and accompanying organizational structures many have unnecessarily created the existing "management gap." She implies that the use of more "appropriate" organizational structures would reduce the need for managerial and entrepreneurial talent and thereby reduce the need for imported managers and management technology.

"Labor Saving" versus "Resource Saving"

The critical question in this debate is whether or not modern management techniques are principally "labor-saving" or "resource-saving" in their impact. To the degree that they are "labor-saving," adoption of these techniques may contribute to the unemployment problem. On the other hand, to the degree that they are "resource-saving," i.e., capable of maximizing the productivity of land, capital, and perhaps even scarce management skills, they will improve overall factor utilization and increase national welfare.

Although there has been no empirical study of the labor impact of modern management technology in less developed countries, there is reason to believe that the "resource-saving" emphasis is likely to be greater than the "labor-saving" emphasis. In the majority of technology transfer engagements, it can be argued, increases in management productivity have allowed the existing number of managers to better control organizational resources. More importantly, this additional control could not have been obtained simply by increasing the number of managers or subordinates. The introduction of modern management technology, therefore, may not result in higher unemployment but rather in increased managerial effectiveness.

Relevance of Organization Size

There is an additional aspect of the Stewart argument that merits consideration. This is the accusation that modern management techniques are necessarily tied to large scale organizations that in themselves are inappropriate to Third World needs. This is an important point, for it must certainly be admitted that many management tools are designed to solve problems of large scale organizations. In response to this accusation, would one agree that in certain instances the size of public and private institutions is inappropriate and that a move toward "intermediate" size institutions is desirable (Berger, 1974)? This certainly appears to be the case in relation to agricultural credit and extension services (Johnson and Mellor, 1961).

However, not all Third World needs are best served by "intermediate" size institutions. It is difficult to conceive of efficient small scale telecommunication networks, hydroelectric programs, or public water and sanitation systems. Even where operational units might be of intermediate dimensions, the problems of central coordination and allocation will inevitably dictate the need for large scale approaches to comprehensive planning and budgeting. What must be acknowledged by adherents of the "small is beautiful" approach is that LDC's do not face the problems encountered by the Industrialized Nations at the turn of the century. The current size of Third World populations and the extent of public service and production are vast by comparison. Telephone companies do not serve hundreds but hundreds of thousands. Public utility customers do not number thousands but millions. If the needs of these organizations cannot be met through efficient "decomposition," then they are logical candidates for techniques designed to serve the needs of "bigness."

In general, the instances in which modern management technology is distorting appear to be the exceptions rather than the rule. However, this is based on the assumption that appropriate techniques will be applied to appropriate needs. There is always a danger when introducing modern technology that certain techniques will be adopted because of their "modernness" rather than their effective contribution. In these cases, the funds could best be applied elsewhere.

Conclusion

This paper has introduced the concept of management technology and examined several of the critical issues related to the transfer of this technology from more developed to less developed countries. It has been argued that there exists a serious management crisis in many, if not most, less developed countries. It has been suggested that this crisis is due to the "management gap" between rapidly expanding institutional requirements and lagging management capacity. We have also argues that a set of product-, process-, and person-embodied techniques have evolved in the Industrialized Nations in response to many of the same needs found in Third World institutions. These techniques constitute what may be termed available "management technology." We have suggested that this technology is readily available but not nearly as readily accessible or transferable. Nevertheless, we believe that with proper adaptation, this technology is capable of assisting Third World managers to effectively utilize scarce development resources. In this manner, the transfer of management technology is capable of accelerating the process of economic development.

In all of these areas, however, our discussion merely represents an initial attempt to address the major issues as we perceive them. Very little is empirically known about the transfer of management technology. By admitting what we do not know and attempting to explore the myriad of unanswered questions that exist in this area, we may be able to improve our track record.

REFERENCES

Adler, Nancy J. *International Dimensions of Organizational Behavior*. Boston: Kent Publishing Co., 1986.

Berger, Peter L. *Pyramids of Sacrifice: Political Ethics and Social Change*. New York: Basic Books, 1974.

Bryce, Murray D. *Industrial Development*. New York: McGraw-Hill Book Co., 1960.

Deihl, Lincoln W. "The Environmental Constraint on Certain Management Practices." *Akron Business and Economic Review*, 12, 4 (Winter, 1981), 12–16.

Garland, John, and Richard Farmer. *International Dimensions of Business Policy and Strategy*. Boston: Kent Publishing Co., 1986.

Ghymm, K., and G. S. Evans. "Cross-Cultural Transfer of Management Practices." *Asia Pacific Dimensions*, Proceedings of the Academy of International Business, 1979, pp. 123–29.

Globerson, Arye. "Interaction Between Foreign Assistance Personnel and Local Counterparts." *Kyklos*, 31, 2 (Winter, 1978), 48–62.

Hardiman, Margaret, and James Midgely. "Foreign Consultants and Development Projects: The Need for an Alternative Approach." *Journal of Administration Overseas*, 17, 4 (October, 1978) 32–41.

Jedlicka, Allen. "Technology Transfer in Latin America: The Managerial Imperative." *Change and Perspective in Latin America*, Proceedings of the Rocky Mountain Council on Latin American Studies, 1982, pp. 11–15

Johnson, Bruce, and John Mellor. "The Role of Agriculture in Economic Development." *American Economic Review*, 51, 2 (Spring, 61), 44–52.

Phatak, Arvind. *International Dimensions of Management*. Boston: Kent Publishing Co., 1983.

Pratten, C. F. *Economies of Scale in Manufacturing Industry*. New York: Columbia University Press, 1971.

Riggs, Fred. *Administration in Developing Countries: The Theory of Prismatic Societies*. Boston: Houghton Mifflin, 1964.

Robinson, Richard. *Internationalization of Business*. Chicago: Dryden Press, 1984.

Ronen, Simcha. *Comparative and Multinational Management*. New York: John Wiley and Sons, 1986.

Schnitzer, Martin, Marilyn Liebrenz, and Konrad Kubin. *International Business*. Cincinnati: Southwestern Publishing Co., 1985.

Sequeira, John H. "The Transfer of Management Technology to Less Developed Countries." Unpublished manuscript, Arthur Young and Co., 1979.

Siffin, William J. "Two Decades of Public Administration in Developing Countries." *Public Administration Review*, 36, 1 (January/February, 1976), 27–42.

Stewart, Frances. "International Technology Transfer: Issues and Policy Options." World Bank Staff Working Paper, 344, July, 1979.

Stifel, L. D., J. S. Coleman, and J. E. Black.

Education and Training for Public Sector Management in Developing Countries. New York: Rockefeller Foundation, 1977.

Thurber, Clarence, and Lawrence Graham. *Development Administration in Latin America*. Winston-Salem: Duke University Press, 1973.

Weber, Max. *The Protestant Ethic and the Spirit of Capitalism*. New York: Columbia University Press, 1958.

Weidner, Edward. *Technical Assistance in Public Administration Overseas: The Case for Development Administration*. Chicago: Public Administration Service, 1964.

Communication for Rural Development

COLIN FRASER

Introduction

Anniversaries are good occasions for looking back over past experience and for drawing conclusions for the future. Given the British Council's long involvement in communication for development, some reflections emerging from FAO's (the Food and Agriculture Organization) experience in this field over the last 15 years may be appropriate at this time.

We are in an epoch of startling progress in communication technology. Miniaturization and constantly lower costs of electronic devices can easily lead to highly imaginative plans for how this technology could be applied to help relieve the poverty and misery so common in the world's rural areas. Doubtless, these plans could in fact be realized, but whether they will be is a different matter. A look back over the years at the experiences of those of us who have been working in development communication does not give rise to much optimism.

Let us remind ourselves for a moment of the situation that prevails in most Third World rural areas and see how it relates to communication. A primary characteristic of many rural communities is physical isolation.

Lack of infrastructure

Roads are often poor, and sometimes impassable; telephone services are non-existent; postal services can be no better than the roads, and even if they were, the 65–95 per cent illiteracy levels typical of most Third World rural areas would remain

Colin Fraser. Tyler and Francis Ltd., publishers of *Media in Education and Development*, granted permission to reproduce this article. It appeared in Volume 12, No. 2, 1984, of that journal on pages 114–119.

a barrier to the flow of information via the written word. This lack of physical communication infrastructures and the resulting isolation, conditions the attitudes of rural people, which are of fundamental importance in development work.

Most isolated rural communities remain turned in on themselves, apathetic and fatalistic about their situation. Often locked into such a pattern of bare subsistence from year to year that they are afraid to take risks which could mean starvation, peasants can seem conservative. It is very easy for outsiders to be critical of their 'traditional methods', forgetting that these have, for generations of peasants, provided for survival, often in hostile environments. And until not so many years ago, most rural societies and the activities that supported them were in tune with their particular environment.

Recently, however, burgeoning populations of both humans and animals have thrown the balance out of kilter. Just one example is the desertification in many parts of Africa caused by overgrazing. Or the exhaustion of the land in many parts of the world caused by shifting cultivation.

With these changes in circumstances in recent decades, it is no longer possible to rely on traditional methods to improve rural life, or even to guarantee survival at the existing miserable levels; witness the decline in per capita food production in Africa over recent years. Only a worldwide and major effort to accelerate agricultural and rural development can prevent things from getting even worse.

Human dimension

In day-to-day terms, rural development means that people in rural areas have partly to change their working and living habits. Any assistance from the outside has to be geared toward helping them to change, both by informing and motivating them and by passing on know-how, as well as by making available the necessary inputs to which they would otherwise not have access.

This planned introduction of change, as development has been defined, must take into account the needs and aspirations of the people concerned and their ability to play their part in the process. Rural development programmes, if they are to succeed, must be co-operative ventures between rural people and the development agency or the authorities. There must be a full and constant exchange of information between both parties, from the day that the first plans are drawn up to the day when the development agency can phase itself out.

While all of this may appear obvious, the human dimension in rural development has often been overlooked completely. Many technicians felt that, for example, once an irrigation system had been built, the development job was done. Underutilized or ineffectively utilized irrigation schemes all over the world have proved otherwise.

There are numerous examples, too, of development programmes which, even though drawn up on a sound economic and technical basis, have made little if any impact owing to apathy among the so- called beneficiaries. Other projects have even run into outright hostility. These problems have arisen because the human dimension of the project was insufficiently researched during project formulation and insufficiently catered for during the operational phase.

More systematic media use

It was precisely the growing recognition of the need for better participation in development programmes by rural people, and for improved transfer of know-how to them, which led to the idea that communication media and techniques could be used to greater advantage than they had been.

Extension systems, relying primarily on inter-personal communication, were (and still are) afflicted by many problems. Shortage of trained extensionists, of transport and fuel, and the sheer size of the task facing them, made it necessary to redimension their efforts through the complementary use of mass media. And with illiteracy at such high levels, audiovisual training systems could be of prime importance. Creative use of communication media could also provide a two-way channel for information flow between rural communities, and between these communities and the authorities. In this way, the information exchange necessary between all concerned in co-operative efforts could be assured.

This thinking is just as valid today as it was when it began to be generally accepted about 10 to 15 years ago. Regrettably, systematic use of communication for rural development has not kept pace with acceptance of the theory.

Radio broadcasting

Let us look at radio broadcasting for rural audiences as an example. There were excellent examples of how radio programmes had been able to support agriculture in industrialized countries. The *Radio Farm Forums* of Canada in the 1930s was one; and *The Archers*, the farmers' BBC radio series, begun in 1951 and still going today, was another.

Both the Canadian *Farm Forum* experience and *The Archers* in Britain were launched at a time when there was a serious need to improve agriculture and raise food production in the respective countries, a condition applying to developing countries today. *The Archers* format, a dramatized serial about a farming family with 15 per cent instructional content and the rest entertainment had, and still has, an enormous following among town dwellers too. In fact, in 1953, one adult person in three of the whole population of Britain listened to it regularly, thus helping to keep the urban sector interested and informed about farmers and their problems and enhancing the prestige of agriculture. (This function of good rural broadcasting would be an extremely important factor in developing countries today where the urban–rural division tends to be increasingly clear-cut and agriculture has little prestige. The neglect of the agricultural sector in so many countries is in part a result of this lack of prestige.

So the omens were good and all seemed set to capitalize on the rural broadcasting experience of industrialized countries and to use radio as the main communication medium for rural development in the Third World, modifying the approach as necessary for local conditions. In the 1960s most countries had broadcasting service that covered the majority of the national territory, and today coverage is practically complete. True, radio receivers in the 1960s were relatively cumbersome and expensive, but this problem could be largely surmounted by organizing collective listening and providing each group with a receiver. Then as transistorized receivers became cheaper, smaller and lighter consumers of batteries, all of us involved in communication for rural development thought that the era of rural broadcasting in the Third World must be dawning. There were many technical assistance projects run by both bilateral and UN agencies such as Unesco and FAO, and for a while some improvement took place in rural broadcasting in some developing countries.

Situation today

Today, however, the general situation is abysmal. Rural broadcasting seldom, if ever, gets more than a fraction of total airtime. A survey a few years ago showed that in most countries it got from one to five percent of broadcasting time.

An FAO consultant recently visited four African countries to study the possibility of media campaigns that should help reduce post-harvest food losses, estimated at 12 per cent of all grain grown in Africa. The con-

sultant reported that in one country with well-developed broadcasting services and 90 per cent of the population living in rural areas, only 1.22 per cent of airtime is given over to rural broadcasting. The average for the four countries was 1.7 per cent. If such a situation were exceptional, the matter would not be so serious, but similar low priority for rural broadcasting is to be found almost everywhere.

Nor is it a question of airtime only. In most places programmes are uninspiring, if not outright boring. There is a shortage of portable recording equipment and transport, which means that very little field recording can be done, and rural broadcasters have far less prestige and fewer career prospects than do those involved in news and cultural programming. So rural broadcasts too often consist of studio talks by agricultural technicians, and little else, except perhaps repeats of the previous years' programmes, linked to the agricultural calendar.

The missed opportunities and unrealized potential of rural broadcasting can best be illustrated by a couple of examples of what radio has achieved in some countries. In Ecuador, a one-minute advertising spot on prevention of goitre, repeated several times a day over one year, increased the proportion of households using iodized salt from five per cent to 98 per cent.

In the late 1970s a disease threatened the vital cassava crop in the People's Republic of the Congo. An FAO-supported rural radio programme broadcast a warning that the crop should be harvested immediately. Harvesting cassava is exclusively women's work in central Africa, but the radio suggested that, in view of the crisis, the men should help. Reports soon began to arrive that a remarkable phenomenon was taking place in the villages: for the first time in memory, the men were helping the women to dig up cassava. They were doing so 'because the radio said to'.

Video technology

Let us take an example of another medium, that of portable video recording. In the last 10 years, video technology has made immense strides in becoming more convenient to use and relatively cheaper year by year. Portable closed-circuit video has characteristics that make it highly suitable for use in rural areas.

Its advantages over most other audio-visual systems include: its immediate playback facility; the fact that programmes can be made fairly easily and altered if necessary; its facility for incorporating more than one language version of the commentary on the same tape; and the fact that it can be battery-operated and does not need a blacked-out room for playback during daylight. It can be used for straightforward training, and it can also be used for provoking discussion and debate leading to self-awareness among people and to a clearer understanding of their situation and of the development options open to them.

The Canadian Film Board's *Challenge for Change* programme using film and video in the 1960s and 1970s pioneered this media-based approach to motivation and self-help among disadvantaged rural people, such as the Eskimos, and among isolated communities, such as those living on Fogo Island. The impact of media used in this way can be tremendous.

Latin American project

A few countries in Latin America have been assisted by the United Nations Development Programme (UNDP) and FAO to establish video-based training for people in rural areas. The methodology was painstakingly developed in the first country to receive assistance; the equipment was selected and tested over time to ensure its appropriateness, and many young national staff were trained to use the equipment properly and to make good educational programmes. This has so far taken more than six years and during that time there have been several evaluations which have established beyond doubt that video-based training is economical and much appreciated by rural people.

As one could have expected, in the early years the project ran into opposition from the more traditionally minded trainers who believed in 'chalk and talk' or even just 'talk'. The video-based approach was considered by many to be too sophisticated, and it was also said that to use it was to create long-term technological dependency on other countries. The various evaluations were precisely to find out whether these accusations were valid. They were found not to be.

Despite the painstaking approach and positive evaluations and the fact that about 80 per cent of peasants interviewed wanted more video-based training, the project has staggered from one crisis to another – and barely survived several of them. Among the problems has been international financing, even though the total amount required has not been enormous – some $2 million over a total period of eight years in a country that has received roughly $32 million form the UNDP in the same period.

National financing of the counterpart contribution, especially salaries for the national staff, has been another perennial problem, and many trained and capable national staff have left the project for better prospects elsewhere. The institutional framework for the project, that is, where it is placed in the Government's structure, has been debated and fought over at length. In summary, the project has survived and progressed and has generally proved the value of using video in rural areas in certain types of country, but has been a tooth-and-nail fight every inch of the way. And that fight continues today.

Political considerations

We cannot ignore politics in any serious discussion of communication for development. An anecdote may best highlight the problem.

A Latin American country decided to use

video for farmer training as part of its agrarian reform programme. With UNDP and FAO assistance, the methodology that had been developed in another country, as just described, was replicated. The head of the agrarian reform institution told the video team that he wanted maximum participation from the farmers, both in deciding what type of training programmes to make and during actual video production.

All went well for some time until a course on oil-palm production was being made. Some peasants began to discuss the wisdom or otherwise of turning over scarce agricultural land to this industrial crop when the country was unable to grow enough food to feed itself. Some sequences recorded from the discussion were left in the final video programmes. In the meantime, however, the progressive head of the agrarian reform institution had moved elsewhere and his place had been taken by a more conservative thinker. When he heard about the discussion sequence and then saw it, he accused the video specialists of undermining government policy. The ensuing recriminations and witch hunts stopped the video activities completely.

Need to accelerate progress

It must be admitted, despite the pessimism voiced so far, that progress is being made in applying communication to rural development. But it is slow. To accelerate the progress, we should draw conclusions from previous experience and look for ways of resolving or side-stepping the difficulties that have faced us so far in development communication.

The problem is most certainly not the technology. Certainly, solar-powered television receivers, for example, could be very useful in providing programmes to rural areas with poor electrification. But if we had them, would television programming for rural people improve? I believe not, at least judging by rural radio programming, which certainly has not improved in quantity or

quality since the arrival of the cheap and relatively widespread transistorized receiver. In sum, all our experience leads me to conclude that the mere availability of cheap and appropriate communication technology does virtually nothing to ensure its use for rural development.

Perennial poor relation

The real problems are of a different kind and are linked to rural development policies and to politics. For the fact is that although most governments state that agricultural and rural development is a priority, when it comes to budgetary appropriations and assignments of good staff, the rural sector remains the perennial poor relation. And within that sector, communication itself is often looked on as a peripheral activity, a sort of luxury that it is nice to indulge in if you can afford it, but not something as important as, say, agricultural research or irrigation.

Few governments sufficiently take into account the human dimension of rural development, the need to inform people and arouse them to participate and to find ways of transferring know-how to them effectively and economically. Nor do enough governments realize that communication is fundamental to these activities and should therefore be an integral part of development programmes. Until they do, and act accordingly, the availability of suitable electronic technology is irrelevant. Most countries are not using their existing, and in most cases quite adequate, communication facilities to more than a fraction of their potential effectiveness in rural development.

And nor is this statement confined to what are normally considered 'developing countries'. Even in Italy, a country that has undergone intensive industrialization since the Second World War, there is a serious problem of rural underdevelopment, of agricultural stagnation, and of massive food sector imports (they make up some 60 percent of the nation's large balance of payments deficit). In a relatively rich country like Italy, this is hardly the national disaster that it is in poorer countries. However, it is no accident that it is precisely the same development policies and priorities that have led to this rural stagnation, and to the failure to use the available communication media to help rectify the situation.

Problems for governments

On the political side, it is true that effective two-way communication programmes can easily cause problems to governments. As the rural people are stirred and are offered a channel of communication to the authorities, they begin to make their points of view and criticisms known. For example, farmers who have been advised by radio to use fertilizer and then find it is not available locally, will certainly be critical of the government's fertilizer distribution system and, if given a chance, say during an interview by a rural radio producer, will voice their complaints. The nub of the issue then is whether those in the government responsible for fertilizer distribution take such criticism constructively and try to ensure better service, or view it instead as a nuisance best ignored or even as a threat to their jobs.

The fact is that governments in the developing world are so beset by problems that to open up a dialogue would often seem to be a step that could only lead to further problems. It is easier to issue autocratic one-way commands and plan rural development in the comfort of the city than it is to communicate with rural people and plan with them. There is nothing more difficult than working with people. Building roads and dams and breeding high-yielding varieties is child's play by comparison. For proof of that statement, it is sufficient to look at the fine rural infrastructures built all over southern Italy in the last 30 years. They stand to a large extent unexploited while the people emigrate. The roads designed to bring physical communication to the villages, and thereby make life there more pleasant, have instead become routes by which people leave for the towns.

Need for training

A final factor of great importance is that of training people to use the tools of communication. One of the reasons that rural broadcasting is so dull in most developing countries is that the programme producers, apart from working in a low-prestige area, have not been trained in creative broadcasting. If the video projects discussed earlier have succeeded to a large extent, it is in good part due to the intensive training given to national staff.

If similar successes are to be achieved elsewhere, much more attention will need to be given to the training of people, not merely to use the technology but, even more important, in the conceptual aspects of applying communication technology to rural development problems. It is not easy to carry out successful village-level communication. It requires empathy, a real understanding of rural problems, a democratic approach, and above all creativity. Technology alone is not enough.

To sum up, experience thus far shows that even the existing communication technology is not being applied to rural development on more than a tiny scale. The reasons are manifold, but probably the most important are the general *de facto* neglect of the rural sector (whatever national development plans state), and that communication is still not seen as a powerful force for change and as a means of passing on know-how more economically and effectively than inter-personal communication alone. It is an aberration that communication media, used widely and successfully for political propaganda and commercial interests, are not used to help resolve what many consider to be the most pressing problem in the world today, that of hundreds of millions of people living in what Robert Mac-Namara described as a 'state of such misery as to be an affront to human dignity'.

About the Authors in Chapter 10

Augusto Varas is with the Facultad Latinoamericana de Ciencas Sociales (FLACSO) in Santiago, Chile. His edited volume, *Democracy Under Siege: A New Military Power in Latin America*, was sponsored by the Joint Committee on Latin American Studies of the Social Science Research Council and the American Council of Learned Societies and was published in 1989 by Greenwood Press of New York.

Fernando Bustamonte was an Ecuadorian sociologist at the Catholic University in Santiago, Chile in 1983. He has contributed extensively to a series titled "Documento de trabaja" of the Programa FLACSO, Santiago de Chile.

Jacques Perrin is with ECT (Economie des Changements Technologiques), a research team dealing with the economics of technical change at the University of Lyon in Lyon, France. His *Les transferts de technologie* (Paris, Editions La Decouverte), was published in 1983.

Lincoln W. Deihl is in the Department of Management, Kansas State University and is a Visiting Professor in the Graduate School of Business & Government Management at the Victoria University of Wellington in New Zealand. His article, "The Environmental Constraint on Certain Management Practices," appeared in the *Akron Business and Economic Review*, 12(4), Winter 1981.

Colin Fraser is Director of Social Communications, Extension, and Training at Agrisystems of Rome. He is the author of numerous articles and books including his 1989 volume, *Lifetimes: For Africa Still in Peril and Distress*, which was published in London by Hutchinson Education.

CHAPTER 11

Changing Health Patterns

Introduction

HEALTH IS A STATE of mental, physical, and social well-being. The better the health, the better the quality of life. As a quality, health is difficult to measure. Several indicators such as doctors and nurses per thousand population, per capita availability of hospital beds, and per capita health expenditures have been used as indicators of level of health services. In most countries in tropical Africa, or in Asian countries such as Afghanistan and Nepal, the availability of physicians ranges from two to three per 100,000 population. The number of hospital beds per 100,000 population is under fifty-five in Pakistan, Nigeria, and Ethiopia. These figures conceal the differences in the availability of health services between rural and urban areas. In rural areas there may be only one physician per 100,000 population.

Generally speaking, macro health figures often distort through underestimation the extent of the world's health problems (Escudero, 1980). Chossudovsky (1983) comments further on the inadequacy of per capita health measures and food consumption that do not represent the extreme heterogeneity of life conditions. And, as has been stated in other contexts in earlier chapters, patterns of ill health and malnutrition are distributed by socioeconomic status in developed and developing countries, more so in the latter. The material and social conditions of life in developing countries underlie health problems, which in turn impact further on income and adequate nutrition. The case of Chile, although relatively advanced in its development, is one in which the political and economic structure perpetuated low levels of nutrition among the poor (Solimano and Hakim, 1979).

Adequate health care in developing countries can be achieved without dramatic changes in the approach to the provision of health services. Immunization programs, mother and child health services, and diarrhea eradication programs are integral parts of the health campaign. These new technologies must be integrated into the local system of healing and cultural beliefs. A survey of health care and related programs based on a functional analysis of behavior (Elder, 1987), which simultaneously considers the structure of the society at the local level, concludes that there is some probability of success in changing individual behavior in developing areas. In providing inexpensive health care for the masses, it is necessary to perfect new health management and administration systems.

The question of medical health care vs. public health programs has also been a concern, particularly in countries where the medical profession controls policy, as Ugalde (1979) has described in Colombia. This is particularly a problem in areas where, " ... the medical profession has become a money aristocracy and has built powerful associations to retain its privileges when threatened by populations who consider access to medical services to be more a right than a privilege." The consequences of this are apparent in developing countries where morbidity and mortality are usually the consequence of living situations that call for preventive programs in sanitation, nutrition, immunization, and health education.

Unfortunately, programs, however laudable, require implementation. Models vary from country to country, all perhaps appropriate in their setting, but continuous evaluation is crucial (Orubuloye and Oyeneye, 1982). In addition, there is an immediate need for massive public education campaigns for controlling the epidemic of AIDS. Developing countries will need foreign aid to develop adequate health delivery systems but foreign aid alone will not do the job. The governments in developing countries must demonstrate a political will for making investments in health.

The Articles in Chapter 11

Per capita expenditures on health in developing countries exhibit a great deal of variation. *Evans, et al.,* indicate that the per capita per year public expenditures on health averages from U. S. $2.60 in the poorest countries to U. S. $469 in industrialized countries. The health of a population directly affects labor productivity and national wealth. The most important step toward development is to break the vicious cycle of poverty and poor health.

Evans, et al., also describe the stages in the evolution of health care systems and point out the differences in health care systems in developed and developing countries. The greatest returns to health investments are in maternal and child health services in rural and semirural areas. Going further, it is essential to build effective and well-organized health management systems that integrate the various levels of health care delivery.

The western medical system is most often used in providing health care to the masses in developing countries and the importance of indigenous medical systems is overlooked. Western practitioners find that it is very difficult for most people in developing countries to understand the importance of taking medicines before they become ill. The immunization program managed by the World Health Organization in developing countries, for example, often fails to consider cultural barriers to the diffusion of western ideas of disease.

Coreil describes the process of adoption of western medical technologies by practitioners of indigenous medicine. As an example, she describes the influence of gender, education, and traditional healer type on the use of oral rehydration theory (ORT) for childhood diarrhea among Haitian healers. Thus, it is important for development programs to keep in mind the cultural context (pluralistic health system) in which medical services are provided and received.

The epidemic of AIDS will considerably stretch fragile health systems in developing countries that are struggling to lower the number of deaths from preventable diseases such as measles and tuberculosis. *Hése* reports that the infection rates in some African cities are about 100 times higher than in the United States, a high prevalence of sexually transmitted diseases hastening the spread of AIDS. Unfortunately, the conditions of underdevelopment (poor hospital facilities, poorly equipped laboratories, and an inadequate supply of condoms) increase the likelihood of AIDS infection and death.

AIDS undermines economies. Studies from Kitwe and Chingola in Zambia suggest that a very large proportion of the miners are infected. The countries affected by the epidemic have been slow to react. Uganda has responded to the crisis by a massive public education campaign. Developing as well as developed countries must cooperate for a common cause, eradication of AIDS. This may bring about a new outlook toward development programs globally.

REFERENCES

Chossudovsky, Michael, "Underdevelopment and the Political Economy of Malnutrition and Ill Health," *International Journal of Health Services*, 13(1), 1983, pp. 69–87.
Elder, John P., "Applications of Behavior Modification to Health Promotion in the Developing World," *Social Science and Medicine*, 24(4), 1987, pp. 335–349.
Escudero, Jose Carlos, "On Lies and Health Statistics: Some Latin American Examples," *International Journal of Health Services*, 10(3), 1980, pp. 421–434.
Orubuloye, I. O. and O. Y. Oyeneye, "Primary Health Care in Developing Countries: The Case of Nigeria, Sri Lanka and Tanzania," *Social Science and Medicine*, Vol. 16, 1982, pp. 675–686.
Solimano, George and Peter Hakim, "Nutrition and National Development: The Case of Chile," *International Journal of Health Services*, 9(3), 1979, pp. 495–510.
Ugalde, Antonio, "The Role of the Medical Profession in Public Health Policy Making: The Case of Colombia," *Social Science and Medicine*, Vol. 13C, 1979, pp. 109–119.

Health Care in the Developing World: Problems of Scarcity and Choice

JOHN R. EVANS, KAREN LASHMAN HALL and JEREMY WARFORD

••••

In low-income countries, life expectancy at birth averages only 51 years, and in several it is less than 45 years (Table 1).

Mortality rates are 10 to 20 times higher for infants and for children aged one to four than in developed countries. Nearly half of all deaths occur in children under five years of age. The major causes are diarrheal diseases, respiratory infections, tetanus, and childhood infectious diseases such as diphtheria, measles, and whooping cough, all of which can be effectively and cheaply controlled by measures used in developed countries. Malnutrition is important as an associated – and even primary – cause of death in young children, and short birth intervals adversely affect the survival of infants. For those who reach the age of five, life expectancy is only eight to nine years less than in developed countries. The commonest causes of death are similar to those in industrialized countries: cancer, cerebrovascular disease, heart disease, respiratory disease, and trauma. However, in developing countries, tuberculosis ranks among the most common causes of death. These nations are also plagued with endemic diseases such as malaria, schistosomiasis, trypanosomiasis, onchocerciasis, and leprosy, which are major causes of serious morbidity and mortality in adults and children, but for which effective control measures have not been available or have proved difficult to implement or maintain.

Even in middle-income countries, more

Evans, Hall, Warford. *The New England Journal of Medicine* gave permission to reprint this article. It appeared in Vol. 305, 1981, on pages 1117–1127.

favorable national statistics in the aggregate disguise wide disparities between the conditions, on the one hand, of the rural and peri-urban poor that are typical of low-income countries and the conditions, on the other hand, of more affluent urban dwellers who are better educated and have better access to health services and whose health status closely resembles the profile in industrialized countries. Table 2 contrasts the high mortality rates for infectious and parasitic diseases in the less developed northeastern and frontier regions of Brazil with the high rates for cancer and cardiovascular diseases in the more affluent southeastern region of the country.

As economic development proceeds, the more prosperous regions of the country have the advantages of greater individual and collective wealth and greater political leverage. Consequently, national health policies give priority to their needs, and the limited resources of hospitals, equipment, drugs, physicians, and other health personnel are concentrated in the urban areas, widening the gap between urban and rural populations (Golladay and Liese, 1980).

In the push for development, particularly industrial and commercial development, protective measures for workers and the environment usually lag behind, as they did in the earlier stages of developed countries. These measures are often disregarded because they are initially expensive, and can generally be enforced only by firm legislation and inspection. Rapid development accelerates the appearance of new health problems such as traffic accidents, work accidents, accidental poisoning, and envi-

Table 1: Health-Related Indicators in Countries with Different Income Levels.[6]

INDICATOR	YEAR	LOW-INCOME COUNTRIES*	MIDDLE-INCOME COUNTRIES†	INDUSTRIALIZED COUNTRIES‡
Gross national product per capita (S)	1979	240	1420	9440
Crude birth rate (birth/1000 population)	1979	42	34	15
Crude death rate (deaths/1000 population)	1979	16	10	10
Life expectancy at birth (yr)	1979	51	61	74
Infant mortality rate (deaths/1000 live births)§	1978	(49–237)	(12–157)	13
Child mortality rate (deaths/1000 children 1–4 yr old)	1979	18	10	1
Per cent of population with access to safe water	1975	25	58	¶
Daily per capita calorie supply (% of requirement)‖	1977	96	109	131
Adult literacy rate (%)	1976	43	72	99

* Thirty-four low-income developing countries with a per capita income of $370 or less in 1979 (China and India are excluded from the low-income group in this table).
† Sixty middle-income developing countries with a per capita income of more than $370 in 1979.
‡ Eighteen industrial-market economies.
§ Weighted averages; figures in parentheses denote the sample range.
¶ Data not available but assumed to be close to 100 per cent.
‖ Requirements based on calories needed to sustain a person at normal levels of activity and health, taking into account age and sex distributions, average body weights, and environmental teemperatures, as estimated by the United Nations Food and Agricultural Organiztion.

Table 2: Regional Variations in Cause-Specific Mortality in Brazil, 1970*

CAUSE OF DEATH	REGION		
	NORTHEAST	FRONTIER	SOUTHEAST
	per cent of all deaths		
Infectious and parasitic diseases	24.5	26.6	11.2
Neoplasms and cardiovascular diseases	21.1	19.1	42.1

* Adapted from de Carvalho AVW, de Moura Ribeiro E. Estudo da Mortalidade proporcional, segundo Grupos de Idade e Causas de Obito, em algunas Capitais Brasileiras, em 1970. Revista Brasileira de Estatistica, 1976; 37(148):475 (as reported in World Bank. *Brazil: Human Resources Special Report*, Washington, D.C., October 1979).

ronmental pollution. Similarly, disruption of families and community, migration, and unemployment contribute to a variety of disorders of individual behavior – alcoholism, violence, promiscuity – each with attendant physical and mental risks, counterparts of those seen in industrialized countries.

Urban problems will increasingly dominate the health pattern of the developing world. According to United Nations projections, the urban population in developing countries will increase by 1.32 billion between 1975 and 2000; by 2000 it will average 43 per cent of the population of the less-developed regions overall, and 75 per cent of the population of countries in Latin America (Department of International Economic and Social Affairs, 1980). The primary-health-care approach for rural health problems may need to be modified to address different problems arising from life styles and diets in the urban setting. For example, recent analyses indicate that in several countries there are large numbers of malnourished urban dwellers, and that their numbers are increasing more rapidly than those of the rural malnourished (Austin, 1980).

Stages in the Evolution of Health Systems

The pattern of diseases in northern Europe and the United States evolved in stages over the past two centuries, and with each stage distinctive control measures were introduced.

The first stage, dominated by major and minor infectious diseases linked to poverty, malnutrition, and poor personal hygiene, responded slowly to improved food supply, housing, and literacy made possible by greater prosperity, and to public-health measures, particularly safe water supply, sanitation, and immunization campaigns. The steady decline in infant mortality and the reduction in child mortality as a percentage of all deaths may be attributed to these changes. As scientific advances provided a wide array of immunologic and therapeutic techniques to control acute bacterial and viral infections, life expectancy increased, and heart disease, cancer, and stroke replaced respiratory and gastrointestinal infections as the principal causes of death. For example, in the United States in 1900, the three leading causes of death (influenza and pneumonia, tuberculosis, and gastroenteritis) accounted for over 30 per cent of all deaths, whereas heart disease, cancer, and strokes were responsible for 18 per cent of deaths. By 1975, only influenza and pneumonia (3 per cent) ranked in the top 10 causes of death, whereas heart diseases (38

per cent), cancer (20 per cent), and stroke (10 per cent) together accounted for over two thirds of all deaths (National Academy of Sciences, 1979).

The second stage in the evolution has been dominated by chronic diseases, particularly cardiac and cerebrovascular diseases, cancer, diabetes, arthritis, and mental disorders. As the threat of infectious diseases receded, public-health measures were relegated to a regulatory role, and personal health services became the primary channel for prevention and treatment of health problems. The development of expensive and complicated technology for diagnosis and treatment has led to the transfer of care from doctors' offices to elaborate and expensive hospitals. Doctors and patients have looked to these curative techniques and facilities to provide striking improvements in health. Sadly, experience has shown that for many problems the benefits hoped for have not been realized. As Cochrane has noted, the massive public and private expenditures on health, now close to $1,000 per capita annually for capital and recurrent costs in the wealthier industrialized countries, have not produced commensurate improvement in the health status of the population (Cochrane, 1972). Only a small proportion of the interventions used are of proved effectiveness, and the benefits to be gained from the intensive services for terminal illnesses are at best marginal.

A third stage of evolution can now be defined. It reflects a shift from preoccupation with intrinsic disorders of structure and function of the body, to an awareness of the health hazards arising from environmental exposure to an increasing number of chemicals, drugs, and other toxic substances and from changes in the social conditions of the family, community, and workplace that influence behavior and lifestyle and are associated with absenteeism, violence, and alcohol and drug abuse of epidemic proportions. The personal health-care system concentrates on the consequences of such processes. New approaches are needed to encourage the healthy to avoid patterns of behavior that lead to disease, and to identify and treat the social and environmental causes of disease that originate in the community. Industrialized countries have recently recognized the importance of this third stage and the need to adapt their health systems to give greater emphasis to health promotion and preventive measures at individual and community levels (Ministry of National Health and Welfare, 1974 and United States Department of Health, Education, and Welfare, 1979). This stage is not new. These concerns provided much of the impetus for reform of industrial and other health practices for well over a hundred years. The meaning of the third stage is a return to the recognition that responsibility for health should not be exclusively the prerogative of the health professions – that protective and preventive measures have to be the responsibility of the individual and the society.

Industrialized countries have evolved through the three stages over the course of more than a century. In contrast, developing countries face the challenge of coping with all three stages simultaneously: the rural and peri-urban poor who constitute a majority of the population are in the first stage; the influential, more affluent urban dwellers are at the second stage; and manifestations of the third stage are already apparent because of environmental deterioration and the social disruption associated with massive urban growth and unemployment. Furthermore, developing countries must cope with just a fraction of the financial and human resources available to their industrialized counterparts. In any circumstances, but particularly in these, the strategy to improve health must be selective. Success will depend heavily on correctly identifying the most important problems in each population group, selecting the most cost-effective interventions, and managing the services efficiently. Uncritical accep-

tance of new and expensive high technology will not serve the purposes of developing countries. But developed countries do have much to offer through scientific and technical cooperation. Already, developing countries, by taking advantage of the innovations in the industrialized world (vaccines, microbiologic techniques, and antibiotics, for example) have achieved much faster rates of improvement in health status than those achieved in northern Europe and the United States. However, there are signs that this rate of progress in not being sustained. As Gwatkin and Brandel pointed out (unpublished data), life expectancy in the less-developed regions of the world, which had been rising by 0.64 year annually between 1950 and 1960, slowed to 0.40 year annually 15 years later. Several factors stand out as impediments to progress.

Obstacles to Progress

Uneven Distribution of Health Services

Access to health service is very uneven, and large segments of the rural population are not reached. Health facilities and personnel are concentrated in urban areas, and within the urban population the services are oriented to the middle-income and upper-income groups, neglecting the peri-urban poor. Political considerations may override all other priorities, and little progress can be expected unless there is a political commitment to apply resources where the need is greatest.

There is a shortage of skilled health personnel, particularly in the poorer countries. National averages for physician:population ratios are reported to be 1:17,000 in the least developed countries and 1:2700 in other developing counties, as compared with 1:520 in developed countries. The nurse:population ratios are 1:6500, 1:1500, and 1:220, respectively (World Bank, 1971). These national averages disguise the fact that in some rural areas there may be only one doctor serving 40,000 to 200,000 people. Furthermore, the pyramid of health manpower is inverted, particularly in the least developed countries. Instead of a broad base of inexpensively trained, less skilled personnel working at the community level, priority has been given to expensive training programs for "conventional" doctors, who expect sophisticated facilities and equipment, gravitate to practice in the cities, and have a propensity to emigrate. To achieve effective coverage of the population, large numbers of less skilled personnel need to be trained, and these health workers need to be part of a system that will provide supervision, drugs and supplies, and the support services necessary for their practice. Otherwise dissatisfaction will lead to high turnover of health workers and low utilization of their services as patients bypass the first level of care in the community in favor of higher-level facilities, which properly should function as referral centers. Doctors are key participants in the referral and supervisory systems; if they operate as primary-care workers, their expensive training is wasted and the cost of their practice may outweigh the benefits. The supervisory and managerial role of the physician in the health system must be addressed more directly in the process of medical education and in the career development and rewards for the physician in practice (Evans, 1981).

Lack of Appropriate Technology

A second obstacle to progress is the lack of appropriate technology to address Stage 2 and Stage 3 health problems and to cope with the serious endemic diseases prevalent in the developing world. For Stage 1 health problems, much of the technology needed is already available, and in the case of vaccines technologic advances that would reduce dependence on the cold chain are imminent. In contrast, for Stage 2 health problems, relatively few technologies for dealing with the serious diseases of the adult population are appropriate to the circumstances and financial resources of less developed countries. Most of the technologies that are being transferred from the developed world are expensive, and the equipment is often difficult to maintain. It is necessary to determine which interventions are effective and which yield large benefits at acceptable costs. The greater challenge is in the search for preventive measures to reduce the large burden of illness from cancer, hypertension, diabetes, respiratory, cardiac, and cerebrovascular disease. For Stage 3 health problems, we are still handicapped by inadequate understanding of behavior and the links between social and environmental hazards and specific diseases. We have much to learn about conveying health-education messages, motivating community participation, and using modern communications technology to circumvent the barrier of illiteracy.

The "tropical diseases" (e.g., malaria, schistosomiasis, filariasis, trypanosomiasis, and leprosy) are a particular problem for developing countries, in part because they generally have climates and ecologies conducive to disease vectors. Techniques for ecologic control of vectors or transmission routes are available but are expensive and require repeated application over wide areas. Treatment of patients is generally expensive, sometimes risky, and often delayed. Prophylactic measures such as vaccination are largely undeveloped. Knowledge of the biology of the diseases is far from complete. Research on these diseases has so far been largely neglected by the scientific community and the pharmaceutical industry, which have been preoccupied with cancer, cardiovascular disorders, and the other major diseases of the industrialized world. The Special Program for Research and Training in Tropical Diseases led by the WHO is an attempt to mobilize the health-science research community throughout the world to focus attention on these neglected tropical diseases in order to discover appropriate technologies for their control.

The scientific and development resources of the developing countries are limited, and their problems are difficult to solve. The most promising results will come from combining the scientific and technologic potential of the industrialized world with the local knowledge of scientists and professionals in developing countries who will have responsibility for applying the new technologies.

Pharmaceutical Policies

The most widely used technologies in health are drugs and vaccines. Shortages of supplies and failure to provide for the timely distribution of drugs and vaccines are serious problems that must be overcome for an effective health program. In looking to the future, however, the problems may be excessive and irrational use of drugs and unsustainable costs to the health system. Patients who consult health personnel expect to receive a prescription or, in some cultures, an injection. As access to health services broadens with the implementation of primary-health-care programs, a rapid increase in the consumption of drugs may be expected. Experience in less-developed countries supports this contention. In China, with nearly universal access to health care, curative medicine occupies 90 per cent of the time of "barefoot" doctors, and nearly all patients receive medication; there is evidence that drugs and traditional medicines account for two thirds of overall health expenditures. In countries with less complete coverage of the population, expenditures on drugs constitute about 40 to 60 per cent of the health budget (as compared with 15 to 20 per cent in developed countries [United Nations Conference on Trade and Development, 1980]) and over half of private health expenditures. In most developing countries, the majority of drugs are imported, and these outlays are a considerable drain on foreign exchange.

The importance of drugs to the quality of health care, to the credibility of community health workers, to the development of iatrogenic disease (for example, from toxicity or antibiotic-resistant microorganisms), and to the cost of health services makes it imperative that developing counties establish better mechanisms for assessing drug requirements and for purchasing, quality control, storage, and distribution of drugs. Experience in Tanzania and Ghana indicates that savings of up to 70 per cent of the budget for pharmaceuticals could be achieved by promoting generic alternatives and introduction of controls against overprescription (Yudkin, 1980 and Barnett, Creese, and Ayivor, 1980). The South Pacific Pharmaceutical Scheme projects cost savings of at least 25 per cent through limiting the availability of nonessential drugs and through bulk purchasing (Kumar, 1981). Without policies for national formularies, procurement, prescription, and pricing, this powerful and ubiquitous health technology could become more of a liability than an asset to the health system.

Management of Health Resources

One of the most difficult and pervasive problems to solve in the establishment of effective health services in developing countries will be deficiencies in management. The health sector presents a formidable organizational challenge. Some of its objectives can be achieved only with the cooperation of other sectors such as water supply and sanitation, education, agriculture, and community development. The delivery of health services involves widely dispersed facilities, numerous categories of personnel, general and specialized hospitals, vertically organized programs to control individual diseases such as malaria, tuberculosis, leprosy, or venereal disease – each with its own personnel and support services, community health-care programs with multipurpose workers, and a system of indigenous medicine with traditional healers and birth attendants. The different elements need to be organized to reduce conflict and duplication between programs and to provide a coherent system to screen and treat patients according to the level of care required and to refer patients with difficult problems. Supervision and continuous in-service education of health workers, improved logistics and supply to maintain credible services, institution of personnel policies and rewards to maintain the quality, distribution, and morale of staff, and policies and financial arrangements that encourage rational use of the health resources by the public are essential corollaries to enhance sector performance.

The weakest links in the administrative chain of most developing countries are institutions at district and local levels, which are usually poorly staffed, have inadequate authority or control of resources, and are unable to provide the necessary support and supervision of field staff. The development of planning and administrative capability at the district level is of special importance, since this is normally the lowest tier of the health-services organization still communicating directly with central government but also in contact with the villages, aware of their needs, and in a position to encourage community participation. It is at this level that matching of health needs and resource allocation is most likely to occur (Kaprio, 1979). Community-based non-governmental organizations active in health care may make an important contribution to the process of devolution of administrative responsibility.

The management of a system of health services is much more than the management of its facilities and support systems. It involves decisions about priorities and resource allocation that are based on the health needs of the population to be served. This epidemiologic perspective is missing from the training of many of those in positions of responsibility, and the information system on which to base such management decisions is typically inadequate. Management also involved gaining the cooperation and compliance of highly independent professionals and specialists who have their own constituencies and political support.

The medical profession is of special importance because of the profound steering effect of individual clinical decisions on the demand for expensive facilities and the consumption of resources for diagnosis and treatment. Most practicing physicians give relatively little weight to consideration of the efficacy of these procedures and almost no attention to the real cost and foregone opportunities in terms of resources used. Abel Smith (personal communication) has estimated that the consequential costs generated by the average medical specialist in Great Britain are on the order of £500,000 per year; if eliminating unnecessary procedures reduced expenditures by 10 per cent, the savings nationwide would be enormous. In developing countries, the secondary-health-system costs generated by physicians are smaller, largely because of the absence of much of the high-cost diagnosis and treatment modes, but the same problem exists as in developed countries, and the implications are more serious because of the much more limited resources available for health. To give priority to medical education and to a reward system for physicians is to place clinical decisions about the individual patient in the context of the health needs of the population and to promote more discriminating use of scarce resources for diagnosis and treatment based on evaluation of the effectiveness and the cost of these procedures. These decisions involve difficult ethical judgments. The concepts behind these decisions have only recently been introduced into medical education and health-services administration in developed countries (Evans, 1981).

Poverty

Money alone will not ensure good health.

However, in the opinion of most development specialists, the overriding constraint to improving health status in the least developed countries is the extreme poverty of most of the population and the low level of the gross national product per capita (below $400). Health must compete with other pressing developmental needs for extremely limited public resources.

The problem is made worse by the rapid growth in population, which averages 2.4 per cent per year among developing countries as a group and reaches nearly 4 per cent per year in Kenya; at this rate, the population of Kenya will double in 17 years. At current average annual growth rates, half the population will be under 15 years of age; and demands for employment, housing, and all basic services will increase rapidly. Public expenditures on health will have to increase commensurately just to "hold the line" on current levels of quality and coverage of services. Since population is the critical denominator of all development activities, with such limited resources reduction of fertility will be a decisive factor in attempts to improve services such as health care. At the same time, wider coverage of the population with effective services for maternal and child health and family planning is a necessary part of any strategy to reduce population growth.

Given the extremely limited resources and the rapid growth in population, several basic questions need to be addressed. First of all, what are the prospects for increased public expenditures on health, and to what extent are improvements in health dependent on economic progress? What other sources of financial support might be mobilized? Secondly, can existing resources be used more effectively? And thirdly, within these constraints is "Health for All" through primary health care feasible?

Financing of Health Services

Analysis of health expenditures in developing countries is hampered by a lack of satisfactory financial information on programs operated by different levels of government and the private sector. The available data indicate striking differences in the levels of current total public expenditures on health for capital and operating purposes, with average figures of $2.60 per capita per year in the poorest countries (1.1 per cent of the gross national product), $19 in middle-income developing countries (1.2 per cent of the gross national product), and $469 in industrialized countries (4.4 per cent of the gross national product). The combined public and private health expenditures in the United States and several northern European countries are close to $1,000 per capita per year – more than 100 times the level in the poorest group of countries. At the other extreme, a few of the poorest countries – Bangladesh, Ethiopia, Indonesia, and Zaire – have annual public expenditures on health of only $1 per capita. Since recurrent expenditures are concentrated in urban areas where hospitals and specialized manpower are located, it may be concluded that the resources available to operate health services for the rural population are very limited and in the poorest group of countries average substantially less the $1 per capita.

••••

In many countries the principal alternative to government financing has been official development assistance from bilateral and multilateral agencies and extensive local contributions by foreign nongovernmental organizations.

••••

In view of the economic difficulties facing industrialized countries, it seems unrealistic for developing countries to rely on any appreciable increase in external assistance for health in real terms to compensate for a shortage in public expenditures. Furthermore, care must be taken to avoid capital expenditures financed by external assistance if the recurrent cost obligations that they create are not in keeping with the priorities for use of the limited public funds available for health.

The tendency of governments to discriminate in budget allocations against programs with high recurrent costs in favor of capital-intensive projects is aggravated by the policy of many external donors not to support operating costs. In general, recurrent costs generated per dollar of capital investment are substantially higher for health than for other major public sectors, such as agriculture or transportation, and the ratios are particularly high for primary-health-care programs and rural health centers (Over, 1981 and Heller, 1979), in which expenditures are mainly for manpower and drugs. This makes these programs very vulnerable to budget cutting by government. In addition, even when general operating expenditures have been met, neglect of maintenance expenses leads to further capital expenditures for rehabilitation or replacement of facilities and equipment – a much more costly approach to sector development. An important consideration in the success of primary health care will be the willingness of governments and external donors to place appropriate priority on the financing of recurrent costs.

Efficiency and Effectiveness of the Use of Resources

National capability to plan and implement strategies and programs that make the best use of scarce resources is seriously deficient in most developing countries. The coexistence of subpopulations with different health needs requires programs that are designed for these groups and not based on national averages. The need to select from among a broad range of possible interventions the most appropriate mix of personnel, facilities, and technologies requires information on relative cost effectiveness, trade-offs between capital investment and recurrent costs, and assessment of the political and administrative feasibility of implementation – for all of these, data are seriously deficient.

••••

In the absence of cost-benefit analysis, unit costs of specific health improvements may be compared in order to identify the least-cost solution. To apply these epidemiologic and economic measurements when planning health programs requires much information and takes time. In many cases, detailed measurements cannot be made, but more vigorous review of available evidence on the health needs of different population groups and the consideration of cost effectiveness in selecting interventions offer the best hope for stretching limited resources to achieve maximum impact on health. In addition to encouraging better policies and practices in the health sector, this should enhance the acceptability of proposals by ministries of health to ministries of planning and finance.

••••

Financial Feasibility of Primary Health Care

Primary health care has been accepted by the member governments of the WHO as the key to achievement of universal access to health care by 2000. Assuming that the low-income countries will have no more than $3 to $4 per capita per year in public resources to devote to health by 2000, is it possible to achieve the goals envisaged in the primary-health-care approach with this financial constraint?

Evidence from six primary-health projects undertaken in the late 1960s and 1970s in developing countries indicates that marked health improvements can be demonstrated within five years through provision of basic services with annual operating costs ranging from about $0.50 to $3.50 per capita (Gwatkin, Wilcox, and Wray, 1980 and Berggren, Ewbank and Berggren, 1981). When corrected for inflation, these figures would be $1 to $7 per capita in 1981 prices. The results must be interpreted with caution since five of the projects were of a pilot nature; most involved very small populations; the cost data varied greatly. As a rule, they did not include capital investment, training, expenditures beyond the primary level of health care, or the value of expatriate and volunteer labor. The contribution of voluntary health workers is of special importance because they provide a large share of rural health services and because volunteerism may be difficult to sustain over the long term (Patrick, 1978). Although there should be economies in scaling-up to national programs, in fact higher marginal costs would be expected with expansion of primary health care to more widely dispersed populations. Furthermore, political and administrative problems involved in scaling-up would add costs for management, supervision, and support systems. Nevertheless, the results of the pilot projects, adjusted for inflation, are of the same order as the estimate of $1 to $3 by Joseph and Russell (1980) and $5 by Patel (unpublished data) for per capita recurrent costs of primary-health-care programs.

An alternative approach to estimating the cost of primary health care is to price the individual components of a model program designed to treat the principal causes of mortality in children in low-income countries, as outlined in a recent WHO discussion paper (World Health Organization, 1980). The model for a total population of 100,000 would try to provide basic care for children under five years of age (about 17,000), tetanus toxoid, iron and folic acid for pregnant women (about 4000), and contraceptive advice and supplies for fertile women (about 5100 at a 30 per cent level of coverage). On the basis of estimates of the need for immunization against common infectious diseases and for treatment of diarrhea, acute respiratory infections, malaria, and intestinal parasites, and assuming that all patients in need will be treated with the least expensive, effective treatment available, it is possible to calculate the annual cost of drugs and supplies for each condition. For example, to immunize the 4000 children under one year of age against measles, 3200 doses would be required to achieve 80 percent coverage (recognized as sufficient to halt transmission), which at $0.17 a dose would cost $544 each year. The annual cost of all the drugs, vaccines, and supplies for the model program was $35,000, or $0.35 per capita, for the population as a whole to cover the selected target groups.

The cost of commodities is, of course, only one component. It is necessary to add the cost of salaries of health workers, training, transportation, and maintenance. If these additional costs are in the same proportion to total primary-health-care costs as drugs are in national health budgets (drugs account for 25 per cent according to a conservative estimate), then the total annual recurrent costs for primary health care may be in the range of $1.40. Since annuitized capital costs for primary care are about one third of recurrent costs – $0.45 to $0.50 may be added to cover capital investments. The combined capital and recurrent costs of the primary-health-care program would be under $2 per capita per year, well within the financial reach of low-income countries.

••••

Conclusions

Developing countries face the challenge of coping with a heavy burden of illness that differs markedly in subgroups of the population at different stages of development. The greatest improvement in life expectancy from health investments can be expected in the rural and peri-urban poor through a program that provides maternal and child health services, including control of the major infectious and parasitic diseases of children under five. Effective technology for such a program is now available and affordable even within the financial constraints of the least developed countries. Two major problems remain: the first is the political will to allocate the necessary resources for the program, and the second is the management capability to organize and operate a system of services for the rural and peri-urban populations that use multi-purpose community-health workers.

No satisfactory strategy has been developed to meet the health needs of older children and adults within the financial means of most developing countries. There are relatively few simple, effective interventions to control the metabolic, vascular, degenerative, and malignant diseases of the adult population, and there is little understanding of the behavioral disorders. Without now technologies for control and prevention, it is unlikely that the poorer developing countries will be able to provide more than symptomatic care for most patients with these health problems. Furthermore, adoption of the expensive technologies now used for the diagnosis and treatment of these diseases in the industrialized world will divert the limited resources available for programs for the rural and peri-urban poor to sophisticated, hospital-based, urban services, which will have, at best, a marginal impact on health.

The search for health technology appropriate to the financial and organizational circumstances of developing countries must be seen as a high priority for the research and development community of the entire world. Existing technology must be critically evaluated, and new, simpler techniques developed for the control and prevention of common chronic diseases. Greater attention should be given to research and development on the "tropical" diseases, which are a major component of the disease burden of developing countries but have been largely neglected by the world's scientific community. Pharmaceuticals are of special importance since the timely supply of essential drugs is critical to the quality of health care and the credibility of community health workers. The dangers of excessive use or inappropriate choice of drugs necessitate the introduction of policies on procurement, prescription, pricing, and quality control to avoid health hazards and excessive costs.

Financial constraints will be an overriding consideration in the development of the health sector for the foreseeable future, particularly in the least developed countries. The poorest countries that now have public expenditures on health averaging only $2.60 per capita per year also have the least favorable economic prospects for the next decade. Greater efforts are required to mobilize resources for health from other sources, particularly the private sector, and to ensure that the limited resources available from all sources are used in the most cost-effective manner. Few developing countries have the institutional capability to select health interventions on the basis of expected health impact, least cost, and feasibility of implementation, and to integrate independent facilities, practitioners, and disease-specific programs into a more coherent, economical, multipurpose system. A high priority should be given to strengthening the capability of administrators, physicians, and other personnel in positions of leadership in the health system at central and local levels in order to develop a population perspective in the analysis of health problems, a cost-effectiveness attitude toward the use of resources, and management skills appropriate for a human-services organization. More efficient management of health services is only one aspect of the problem. It is equally important to mobilize communities and individuals to take a more active role in promoting health and in financing health services, rather than to rely passively on a government system.

Scarcity of money for health is a critical limitation on progress toward the goal of "Health for All by the Year 2000." More money alone, however, will not produce the desired outcome unless there is a political commitment to programs for those in greatest need, as well as the managerial capability to implement them. This is first and foremost a challenge for developing countries, but it is also a consideration in the investment policies of donor agencies. Progress toward the goal of "Health for All" can be accelerated if more external assistance can be provided for the areas of greatest need and if the unique scientific and technologic resources of the industrialized world can be made available to developing countries, to strengthen their institutions and to collaborate in the development of appropriate technology to meet their needs.

REFERENCES

World Development Report 1981. Washington, D.C.: World Bank, August 1981.

Golladay, F. and Liese, B. Health problems and policies in the developing countries. Washington, D.C.: World Bank, August 1980. (World Bank staff working paper no. 412).

Department of International Economic and Social Affairs. Patterns of urban and rural population growth. New York: United Nations, 1980. (Population studies report no. 68).

Austin, J. E. Confronting urban malnutrition: the design of nutrition programs. Baltimore: Johns Hopkins University Press, 1980:7. (World Bank staff occasional papers no. 28).

National Academy of Sciences. Science and technology: a five-year outlook. San Francisco: W.H. Freeman, 1979:384.

Cochrane, A. L. Effectiveness and efficiency: random reflections in health services. Abington, United Kingdom: Burgess, 1972.

A new perspective on the health of Canadians. Ottawa: Ministry of National Health and Welfare, April 1974.

United States Department of Health, Education, and Welfare. Healthy people: the Surgeon General's report on health promotion and disease prevention, 1979. Washington, D.C.: Government Printing Office, 1979.

Evans, J. R. Measurement and management in medicine and health services. New York: Rockefeller Foundation, September 1981.

United Nations Conference on Trade and Development, Trade and Development Board. Strengthening the technological capacity of the developing countries including accelerating their technological transformation: issues in individual sectors and other areas of critical importance to developing countries: technology policies and planning for the pharmaceutical sector in the developing countries. Geneva: UNCTAD, October 1980.

Yudkin, J. S. The economics of pharmaceutical supply in Tanzania. International Journal of Health Service, 1980; 10:455–77.

Barnett, A., Creese, A. L., Ayivor, E. C. K. The economics of pharmaceutical policy in Ghana. International Journal of Health Service, 1980; 10:479–99.

Kumar, V. Report on the establishment of the South Pacific Pharmaceutical Service. Manila: World Health Organization, Regional Office for the Western Pacific, 1981.

Kaprio, L. A. Primary health care in Europe. Copenhagen: World Health Organization, Regional Office for Europe, 1979.

Over, A. M. Five primary care projects in the Sahel and the issue of recurrent costs. Williamstown, Mass.: Williams College Department of Economics, 1981.

Heller, P. The underfinancing of recurrent development costs. Finance and Development, March 1979:38–41.

Gwatkin, D. R., Wilcox, J. R., Wray, J. D. Can health and nutrition interventions make a difference? Washington, D. C.: Overseas Development Council, 1980. (Overseas Development Council monograph no. 13).

Berggren, W. L., Ewbank, D. C., Berggren, G. G. Reduction of mortality in rural Haiti through a primary-health-care program. New England Journal of Medicine, 1981; 304: 1324–30.

Patrick, W. K. Volunteer health workers in Sri Lanka. Colombo, Sri Lanka: Ministry of Health, November 1978. (Health education series no. 4).

Joseph, S. C., Russell, S. S. Is primary care the wave of the future? Social Science Medicine, 1980; 14C:137–44.

Discussion paper: Selected primary health care interventions. Geneva: World Health Organization, 1980.

Innovation Among Haitian Healers:
The Adoption of Oral Rehydration Therapy

JEANNINE COREIL

Health planners began to take serious note of the various healers providing a large share of health care in the developing world when the World Health Organization formally endorsed a traditional medicine program in 1978 (WHO 1978; Velimirovic 1984). While structured efforts to integrate healers into modern health care programs are well documented (Harrison 1974; Pillsbury 1979; Maclean and Bannerman 1982), we know comparatively little about the unstructured adoption of modern medical practices by traditional and alternative healers (Cunningham 1970; Press 1971; Taylor 1976; Ferguson 1981; Van Der Geest 1982).

This paper reports findings from a study of the unplanned adoption of oral rehydration therapy (ORT) within the folk sector of Haiti's health care system. Based on survey and ethnographic data, the study examines differential knowledge and use of ORT among four categories of healers. The results are discussed in terms of general processes of innovation within pluralistic health systems.

Oral Rehydration Therapy and Anthropological Studies of Diarrhea

Oral rehydration therapy is a low-cost, simple, but life-saving technique for controlling body fluid loss due to diarrhea. It consists of the regular administration of a glucose-electrolyte solution to replace water and electrolytes lost in stools (His-

Coreil. The Society for Applied Anthropology, which publishes *Human Organization*, granted permission to use this article from the Vol. 47, No. 1, 1988, pp. 48–57, issue of the journal.

chhorn 1982). Originally developed in the early 1960s for treatment of cholera, in recent years the World Health Organization (WHO 1986a), the United Nations Children's Fund (1984), and the United States Agency for International Development (1986) and other organizations have supported major programs to promote the use of ORT for home management of childhood diarrhea in developing countries. The rapid spread of ORT programs, and the substantial reductions in child mortality (observed and projected) from these efforts have attracted much attention in the scientific medical community.

The standard composition for oral rehydration salts endorsed by WHO and UNICEF includes anhydrous glucose, sodium chloride, potassium chloride, and either sodium bicarbonate or trisodium citrate dihydrate. The salts are packaged for one-day use, and mixed with a liter of water to correct dehydration. An alternative to commercial packets is a simpler homemade solution of salt and sugar (SSS). The home preparation has the advantage of low cost and continual availability in most parts of the world, and it can adequately replace fluid losses due to non-cholera diarrhea. However, SSS cannot correct for hypokalemia or metabolic acidosis that sometimes accompany diarrhea (WHO 1986b). Instructions for measuring water in both packaged and homemade solutions are tailored to the readily available ("universal") containers used in different countries.

Ideally ORT should begin at the first signs of diarrhea and continue until the episode terminates. Early initiation prevents dehydration, but the technique can also restore fluid in cases of mild to moderate dehydration. The solution is administered by spoon or cup in small amounts (varying by age and stool losses) throughout the day. Usual feeding practices, including breast-feeding, are advised. The entire procedure can be handled by a family member without professional help. Educational programs do, however, instruct caretakers in how to recognize cases that need medical attention.

Anthropological studies of diarrhea management have taken a strong ethnomedical perspective. They have investigated herbal remedies used for enteric disorders (Logan 1973); the relationship between etiologic concepts and treatment choices (Nations 1982; Lozoff et al. 1975; de Zoysa et al. 1984); and the link between folk illness models and reactions to diarrhea intervention programs (Frankel and Lehmann 1984; Kendall et al. 1983; Bentley 1985; Hogle 1985). Other studies have demonstrated the utility of combining ethnographic and household survey data for program planning and community health assessment (Kendall et al. 1984; Scrimshaw and Hurtado 1984).

Most of the studies cited above included traditional healers as informants regarding the ethnomedical context of diarrhea. The potential role of healers as exponents of ORT in national programs has also been described by Nations (1984) and Green (1985), but the independent adoption of this new medical technology by folk practitioners has not been studied systematically.

The Haitian ORT Program. The investigation of healer innovation in Haiti was part of a larger study of community acceptance of oral rehydration therapy for diarrhea in children (Coreil 1985). A national campaign to promote the use of "Serum Oral" had been launched a year prior to the study (Rohde 1984; Allman et al. 1985). Promotional efforts included patient education in clinical settings, a mass media campaign, and outreach programs through community health workers. The campaign was aimed at the popular sector of health care, with the target focus on mothers and caretakers of preschool children who have primary responsibility fro therapy management.

In a few areas, some traditional healers had been supplied with ORT packets, but these were isolated cases. The official program did not include the training or utilization of unorthodox healers. The situation presented an excellent opportunity to study the independent adoption of the new technique by different practitioners. In addition, program officials were interested in finding out to what extent the healers had incorporated ORT in their practices in order to evaluate the possibility of using selected healers as disseminators of the technique.

Oral rehydration had been used in some Haitian institutions since the late 1970s. In the years prior to the official campaign, mothers were taught to use home preparation, since supplies of ORS packets were limited. In the early years some clinics taught a recipe that included salt and sodium bicarbonate (baking soda) in addition to sugar, and advocated boiling the water before mixing. Now the officially promoted home recipe consists of two tablespoons sugar, one teaspoon salt and three *kola* bottles of clean water. The addition of lime juice (for potassium) is taught as optional.

The national program advocates packaged mixes as the first choice of treatment, and home preparations as an alternative. Serum Oral packets are available primarily through medical institutions (hospitals, clinics, dispensaries and pharmacies). They are also sold in grocery stores, in some market centers, and by community leaders and girl/boy scouts. In locales served by a community health program, outreach workers are supplied with packets for their clients. The retail cost per packet averages $0.15 to $0.20 (U.S.).

The Haitian Study

The study was conducted in the coastal town of Montrouis and nine rural mountain communities located within a radius of 20 kilometers. The entire study area covered about 176 square kilometers. Located about 80 kilometers north of Port-au-Prince, Montrouis has a population of 5,500. About 60% of its residents subsist by farming, about 5% are fishermen, and the remainder work as merchants, craftsmen, laborers, teachers, civil servants, lottery operators or hotel employees. There are several tourist resorts along the coast not far away. The major market crops include rice, corn, plantain, sugar cane, tubers, beans, vegetables, fruits and coffee. However, agricultural productivity is poor due to the arid climate, low soil fertility and topographic problems with erosion.

Like other parts of Haiti, this region is very poor. Poverty is worse in rural areas, where 98% of the population are farmers. Agricultural productivity cannot provide enough food to support the very dense population. Families must sell much of their food to obtain cash for other living expenses. Malnutrition is widespread, particularly among young children. Diarrheal illness is the most common child health problem and cause of death, as in the rest of the country (Pape et al. 1984). The high rate of infant mortality, infectious diseases and other health problems reflect the general poverty of the country and the lack of resources available to cope with the situation.

In the town of Montrouis there was no shortage of modern medical facilities. Three outpatient clinics (two private, one state-owned) were in operation, and a fourth, private clinic was located a few kilometers to the north. In addition, a large government hospital and a smaller private hospital were available in the city of St. Marc 22 kilometers north. The quality of care provided at these facilities was good, but cost and distance (for the rural dwellers) were major limiting factors in utilization. Only one of the rural communities had a medical dispensary, where a nun with minimal training provided limited care.

A visit to one of these centers might cost between $1.50 and $5.00, depending on medications prescribed. The clinics stock their own drugs, and two of them charge a uniform fee that includes the cost of medicine. Pharmaceutical drugs can also be purchased at two pharmacies in St. Marc, and some nonprescription drugs are sold in the grocery stores of Montrouis.

The clinic that served the largest number of patients in the study area was a well-staffed facility operated by St. Paul's Episcopal Church. Open for more than 20 years, the clinic provided care to about 40 patients per day, six days a week. The staff included a full-time physician, a registered nurse, a laboratory assistant, and a pharmacy manager. In June 1983 the clinic expanded its operations to include an outreach community health program of preventive care. The activities of the program included immunization, prenatal care, family planning, health and nutrition education, growth monitoring, provision of vitamin A, and instruction on oral rehydration therapy.

The community health program was administered by a public health nurse, with the assistance of the clinic physician and a full-time record keeper. Program activities were implemented by 14 community health workers (*collaborateurs volontaires*), selected from the various communities served, and trained in the principles and practices of maternal-child health. Five of the geographic sectors were located in Montrouis, nine in the rural villages.

The health workers held regular meetings in their areas for mothers of children five years or younger. These "prevention days," as they were called, included teaching about the purpose and use of ORT. Mothers were told where packets could be obtained and how to prepare the solution from household ingredients. All of the clinics stocked packets, as did the two pharmacies. Three out of six grocery stores also sold packets, with two of these advertising the product through promotional posters.

About two months before the study took place the health workers also began to maintain their own supplies of ORS packets in their homes.

The number of practicing traditional and alternative healers in the study area was uncertain. However, we estimated that between 40 and 50 could be found in the town of Montrouis alone. However, most of these healers can be described as part-time practitioners, and all supplemented their income from therapy with sideline activities. Fairly equal numbers of shamans, midwives and herbalists were identified, but fewer numbers of injectionists were located. Clinic staff members had little knowledge of or contact with these healers.

A sample of traditional healers was surveyed to determine the extent to which different types of practitioners: 1) were involved in the treatment of childhood diarrhea, and 2) had adopted ORT in their own therapy and patient education. A total of 37 healers, identified through key informant networks, were selected for interview. For statistical purposes, an attempt was made to include equal numbers of the four types, and the final sample had 10 midwives, 10 herbalists, 10 shamans and 7 injectionists. Twenty-three of the healers were recruited from the town of Montrouis, and the other 14 were selected from the rural sectors. Informants estimated that the urban subsample represented about half the practicing healers in Montrouis. The 14 rural healers were selected on the basis of judgment and accessibility.

A 32-item questionnaire was pretested with six healers (including all four types) and revised. The questions covered information on demographic characteristics, clientele, management of diarrhea in children, etiologic concepts, knowledge and use of ORT, methods of ORS preparation, evaluation of the therapy's effectiveness, and interest in collaboration with health officials in the control of diarrhea.

The questionnaires were administered in Haitian Creole by the author or one of two trained interviewers. Before the interview, the healers were told that the purpose of the survey was to find out more about how the serious problem of child diarrhea was managed in the traditional healing system. After the questionnaire was completed, a series of unstructured, open-ended questions were posed regarding the causes and treatment of diarrhea to give the interviewees a chance to raise issues not covered in the written questions.

In addition to the healer survey, ethnomedical data were collected on popular beliefs and practices related to care for children with diarrhea. A total of 22 informants, mostly mothers and grandmothers of young children, were interviewed at length to determine the local definition of diarrhea, alternative etiologies recognized, and patterns of care and treatment. This paper also draws upon findings from a household survey of 320 mothers regarding diarrhea management (Coreil, in press).

••••

For the total sample, age ranged from 28 to 90 years, with a mean of 54 years. Forty-five percent had attended school, for an average of five years. Only 35% were literate. The healers had been in practice between 1 and 70 years, with an average length of 17 years. The number of patients treated in the previous month ranged from 0 to 25, with a group mean of 7.5 patients. Only three healers had taken a public health course in the past. An injectionist and a midwife had taken courses at one of the local clinics, and another midwife had been trained at the Isaie Jeanty Hospital in Port-au-Prince.

Sociologically, the injectionists were most different from the other healers. They were all male, tended to be younger, have higher school attendance and literacy, have been in practice for a shorter period, but have more patients than the others. This profile reflects the fact that injectionists make up a new class of health practitioners, who are not recruited to the healer role in the traditional manner of kinship association and divine calling. Nevertheless, with regard to involvement in the management of child diarrhea, injectionists and midwives appear to have much in common, while their roles differ considerably from those of herbalists and shamans.

Results

In this paper I follow the distinction proposed by Foster and Anderson (1978:257) regarding "traditional" and "alternative" healers. The term "traditional healers" refers to those specialists that existed prior to contact with scientific medicine (e.g., herbalists, midwives, magico-religious curers). In contrast, "alternative healers" include the newer specializations in which the therapeutic practices and ideological bases are derived almost exclusively from scientific medicine. The most common types of these "emergent" practitioners (Landy 1974) are injectionists and medicine vendors (Cunningham 1970), itinerant sellers of antibiotics and other drugs. Young (1983) refers to these unregulated "entrepreneurs" as the unofficial subsector of modern, allopathic medicine. While the process of recruitment and informal training of these practitioners is often more similar to the traditional model, they are legitimized by neither the professional nor the folk sector of health care.

Three classes of traditional healers (midwives, herbalists and shamans) and one type of alternative healer (injectionist) were included in this study. A fourth type of traditional healer, the bonesetter (dokte zo), was excluded because the limited range of therapeutic activities practiced in this specialty made it unlikely that its practitioners would have an interest in treating diarrhea. Midwives (fam saj, matronn) on the other hand, are frequently consulted for child illness, particularly in families where they have delivered babies. (The majority of births in Haiti are attended by traditional

midwives.) Herbalists (medsen fey) also treat children, and diarrhea is one of the most common illnesses for which they are consulted (Coreil 1983). Because of their specialization in supernatural misfortune which more often strikes adults, the vodou curers (boko, oungan, mambo), or shamans as they are referred to herein, see only a minority of child patients. However, many shamans also function as herbalists and treat natural illnesses as well. Finally, injectionists (pikiris) treat both children and adults, and specialize in the administration of commercial pharmaceutical products.

While the traditional healers acquire their skills through apprenticeship training, usually after a spiritual calling, most injectionists learn the basic techniques of injection through employment or other affiliation in a clinical setting. A large proportion of midwives receive additional formal training at hospitals and health centers. In terms of socioeconomic status, the vodou practitioners rank significantly higher than the other healer types owing to their higher fees, specialized skills, political power and the fear and respect commanded from the community. The fees charged by midwives for prenatal care and delivery are fairly uniform (about $2.00 U.S.), but for treating illnesses they vary. Likewise, herbalists and shamans charge variable fees depending on the difficulty of the treatment and the patient's ability to pay. The cost of an injection tends to be more standardized (about $.20 per shot). In some cases, healers will charge an initial consultation fee of less than a dollar, then base additional fees on the outcome of therapy.

A variety of treatment methods are used by traditional healers in Haiti. Most important are herbal preparations used in the form of teas, compresses and baths. There are also numerous dietary and behavioral prescriptions involving food taboos, social avoidances and ritual acts. Simple magical cures are used by all the healers, but it is the gifted shamans who are empowered to perform the complex healing ceremonies that may involve the invocation of spirits, singing and dancing, animal sacrifice and possession trance (see Coreil 1983 for a more detailed description of healer characteristics and intragroup diversity).

Midwives have received formal training in Haiti on a voluntary basis for about two decades. As an incentive, the government offers a token monthly salary to those who have taken an approved course. The training consists of instruction in basic concepts of hygiene, routine prenatal care, delivery techniques, and identification of high risk cases for referral to a health center. The trainees are supplied with metal childbirth kits containing essential equipment. Many rural clinics keep a list of practicing midwives from the area, maintaining contact and providing supplies regardless of whether the attendant is trained. In some programs, midwives have been taught methods for family planning.

Since 1977, public health officials have voiced increasing interest in the potential role herbalists might play in community health. Clinic directors have been encouraged to initiate a dialogue with the "leaf doctors" in their areas. In 1978 a pilot project was conducted in the Petit Goave district. A group of herbalists and midwives were trained in basic principles of scientific medicine and given monetary remuneration for attending classes (Clerisme 1979). The program received favorable evaluations but it had little impact on official policy. Herbalists still do not have a formal role in health service delivery. However, their healing techniques have received a measure of legitimation through scientific research on the therapeutic efficacy of certain plant remedies.

The existence of shamans is recognized, but no interest in collaboration or dialogue has been expressed. This can be generally attributed to the attitudes held on the part of the medical community which are ambivalent at best toward these influential

practitioners of *vodou*. The fact that some of these curers also practice sorcery, often through advanced knowledge of poisoning (Davis 1985), tends to cast the entire class of healers in a disreputable light. In addition, ideological incompatibilities severely restrict the possibility of practical communication.

Injectionists can be found in most urban areas where there are pharmacies. Some also make forays into rural areas, where, for example, they care for chronic patients unable to travel to a clinic. The medical establishment reluctantly acknowledges the presence of these practitioners, but prefers to downplay their significance. The injectionists are viewed as troublesome profiteers who lack legitimation in the traditional sector, and who rely on their vocational sideline because they cannot make a living otherwise. Also, some concern has been expressed about the possible role of unsanitary needles in the transmission of AIDS. Rather than encouraging their practical utility, officials would prefer if they were phased out of health care altogether.

Traditional healers play a significant informal role in the health system through the referral of patients with serious medical problems to hospitals and clinics. When indigenous therapy fails to help a patient, healers do not hesitate to advise consultation with a physician or clinic nurse. These healers recognize the limitations of folk remedies, and along with their families utilize modern medicine for many health problems. Like other Haitians, healers have a great respect for and confidence in scientific medicine. Health personnel likewise respect the skills of midwives and herbalists, and recognize their important function in filling the gaps in health care left by an understaffed and inadequately distributed official system. In some communities, health workers have gotten to know the local healers well, and regularly keep in touch with them.

From informant interviews, the term

"diarrhea (*diare*)" was found to correspond to both an illness category and a symptom of other disorders. The occurrence of watery stools (*poupou dlo*) was associated with intestinal worms (*ve*), tooth eruption (*dentisyon*), evil eye (*maldyok*), indigestion (*indijestyon*), and sunken fontanels (*tet fann*) (cf. Lozoff et al. 1975; de Zoysa et al. 1984; Kendall et al. 1984; Green 1985). Data from the household survey showed that the most common etiologies attributed to childhood diarrhea included food, teething, infection and heat. The last category often overlaps the others in that the notion of a hot-cold imbalance in the body may be associated with digestive problems, tooth eruption and fever. In fact, diarrhea is usually defined as a "hot" illness which is best treated by cooling the body with a number of refreshing teas (*rafrechi*). The excess body heat may result from hot weather, exertion or in the case of nursing infants, from mother's milk (*let manman*).

Foods may disagree with a child for several reasons. If the child is not accustomed to the food, if too much is eaten, or if it is consumed late in the day, diarrhea may ensue. These same factors may lead to a related condition best translated as "gaseous indigestion" (*gonfleman*), in which the predominant symptoms are abdominal swelling and discomfort. This digestive disorder is sometimes associated with diarrhea. The association of diarrhea with teething is a widely held belief. The perceived mechanism is the excessive ingestion of saliva, which is produced in larger quantities during teething. Often associated with fever, tooth eruption is believed to make a child overly hot, and therefore cooling remedies are administered. The causes labeled "infection" here include worms (*ve*), germs (*mikrob*), unclean water (*dlo sal*), eating dirt (*manje te*), and poor hygiene (*malpropte*). These causes are recognized by lay persons, but only minor importance is attributed to them in diarrhea etiology. Informants and household survey respondents identified food, teething and heat much more frequently than infection as causes of diarrhea.

Supernatural etiologies were recognized in several forms. For example, an episode of diarrhea which persists despite medical treatment or which has unusual symptoms may be suspected as supernatural in origin. Among children, evil eye (*maldyok*) is the most commonly recognized supernatural cause. Attributed to an admiring gaze upon a child, this folk illness is characterized by weight loss, weakness, decreased appetite and sometimes diarrhea. Midwives and herbalists can treat evil eye with relatively simple techniques. If sorcery or divine retribution is the source of the illness, however, a shaman must be consulted for ceremonial healing.

All but three healers said they at times provided care to children with diarrhea. On the average this amounted to only a few cases per month, with injectionists having the highest mean caseload of 7.4 per month. Also, unlike the other healers, all injectionists reported some cases of child diarrhea. The highest number of diarrhea cases (20 in the previous month), however, was reported by a shaman. More than half of all healers said they advise normal feeding during diarrhea.

Typical consultation fees ranged from 0 to 25 *gourdes*, with a mean of 8 *gourdes* ($1.60 U.S.). Midwives, herbalists and shamans had similar fee ranges, but injectionists charged less for consultations. The average fee for preparation of an herbal remedy was similar across health specialties ($1.50-2.00).

When asked what were some of the most common causes of diarrhea in children, healers of all types gave similar responses. In rank order by percent of respondents, these included food (30%), gaseous indigestion (22%), mother's milk (17%), teething (16%), germs (11%), and other illnesses (8%). Two respondents each mentioned worms, negligence, congenital problems, evil eye, and spirit or werewolf. Like the mothers interviewed in the household survey, healers assign great importance to food and teething in diarrhea etiology, and comparatively little importance to infection. Breastfeeding as a cause was mentioned more often among healers than among mothers.

Healers were asked to list up to three remedies they most commonly prescribe for diarrhea in children. More than 50 different plants were identified as sources of herbal remedies, but only a dozen were mentioned by more than one healer. The large variety of diarrhea remedies used in Haiti is also documented in Pierre-Noel (1974) where again more than 50 treatments are noted, and most are different from the ones named by the healers in this study. This finding is consistent with other studies which have found that medicinals for digestive disorders (particularly diarrhea and dysentery) make up a large percentage of the indigenous pharmacopoeia in preliterate societies (Logan 1973). This has been attributed to the high prevalence of digestive disorders in such societies and to the fact that many plants are empirically effective against gastrointestinal illnesses.

Nevertheless, there were several plants mentioned by more than one healer, and all of these had been noted by lay informants as well. Guava (goyav) leaves and fruit head up the list, followed by bahama grass (shyendan), spider flower (bwa dan), and bastard cedar (bwa dom). Others mentioned more than once were cotton (koton), wormseed (semenkontra), ti janvie, woman's tongue (tcha-tcha), plantain (masok), coconut (kokoye), thoroughwort (langishat) and tobacco (tabak).

The shamans described several features which distinguish natural from supernaturally caused diarrhea. In children, supernatural diarrhea is thought to be caused by werewolves (lougarou) or bad airs (move ze). Werewolves are said to get inside a child's body at night, drink his blood and inject poison water into the child. This foul water, drawn out of wild animals, causes the diarrhea. In the case of bad airs, the vapor also attacks during sleep, causing the child to have a seizure, cry out and defecate watery stools. One healer said supernatural diarrhea can be recognized by its white color. Others said diagnosis is made by examination, special vision and divination. Treatments involve various combinations of herbal remedies, charms and ceremonies.

Knowledge about ORT was lower among healers interviewed than in the maternal population. Whereas 74% of mothers had heard of the treatment for diarrhea, only 51% of healers were aware of it. However, similar proportions of mothers (40%) and healers (41%) knew the home recipe for ORS. Also, like mothers, the majority of knowledgeable healers (55%) had heard of ORT at a health center, 30% through radio, and 15% from other sources. About one-third of the healers (32%) taught mothers about ORT, and 27% had used it themselves. With regard to the perceived mode of action of ORT, the healers were fairly evenly divided among those who explain it as hydration maintenance and those who view it as a cure for diarrhea or a body fortifier.

The figures just presented for the total healer sample, however, obscure important differences among types of healers. Midwives and injectionists were significantly more knowledgeable about ORT and involved in dissemination of the technique than were herbalists and shamans. The proportion of healers who had prepared ORS themselves was 60% for midwives, 43% for injectionists, and 10% for herbalists. None of the shamans prepared the solution. Furthermore, whereas most herbalists and shamans who knew about ORT held a cure/fortify model of action, most injectionists described the effects in terms of hydration, and midwives were evenly divided between the two theories.

On injectionist from Montrious had used Serum Oral packets a number of times. He said he keeps a small supply of packets on hand, which he bought at one of the grocery stores for 50 centimes ($0.10 U.S.). When a parent brings in a child with diarrhea, he demonstrates how to prepare the remedy or, if the parent has used it before, he gives it to him or her to take home.

Statistical analysis of the relationship between healers' sociodemographic characteristics and their knowledge and use of ORT revealed few significant results. Age, literacy, school attendance and length of practice were not associated with the dependent variables. However, significant correlations were found between awareness of ORT and years of schooling (r= .40, p < .02), and between awareness and number of patients treated in the previous month (r= .39, p < .02). The more educated healers with heavier caseloads were most likely to have heard of ORT. However, no sociodemographic healer characteristics were associated with the use of ORT.

Among the healers who were aware of ORT (N=19), all said that the water used in its preparation should be boiled. Eleven out of fourteen (79%) who answered the question identified ORS as a "rafrechi." All but one, a midwife, evaluated the therapy as effective for diarrhea. Only four percent said they prescribed other remedies in conjunction with ORS. Six healers said there were conditions under which ORT should not be administered (when water loss is great; at night; during prolonged episodes; when child is very weak; with fever).

All but one healer, a midwife, said they would like to receive ORS packets for distribution to their patients. The exception was not interested because she planned to discontinue practice soon. All but three healers (two midwives, one injectionist) indicated that they would be in favor of working with public health officials in the control of diarrheal diseases. The reservations expressed by the three not in favor were related to their desire to know the terms of collaboration before giving an answer. When those in favor were asked how, in their opinions, such collaboration could be accomplished, all indicated it would be up to the health officials to propose a way.

Discussion

The fact that all but three of the healers were involved in diarrhea management suggest that there exists a potential interest among all classes of healers to learn about and to adopt the new therapy. Observed differences in knowledge and use of ORT, therefore, could not be attributed to variation in the opportunity to apply the innovation. However, in the case of injectionists, the heavier total caseload and higher number of pediatric diarrhea patients very likely confers a predisposition to accept new treatments for diarrhea.

In general, the perceived etiologies and most commonly prescribed remedies reported by healers were quite similar to those obtained from informants and survey respondents. That is, diarrhea is thought to be caused by food, gaseous indigestion, mother's milk, teething and germs, and is most often treated with a wide variety of herbal teas, most notably guava. That mothers and healers share a similar explanatory model of diarrhea suggests that in terms of ethnomedical beliefs, the healers are potentially comparable in receptivity to ORT as are members of the popular sector. Yet only about half the healers had heard of oral rehydration compared to three-fourths of survey respondents. Also, whereas about half the mothers had used the technique before, only a third of the healers had prescribed ORT for their patients and one-fourth had used it themselves.

These differences in innovative behavior between the popular and folk sectors are not explained by source of information about ORT, or place of residence. In fact, a higher proportion of the healer sample (62%) was selected from the urban area, while this proportion was close to 50% in the household survey. Because of greater exposure to mass media and accessibility to modern medical services, urban dwellers are usually quicker to adopt new medical practices, and this was confirmed in the survey of mothers.

The most compelling explanation for the differences appears to be sex role. The promotion of ORT has been geared primarily to that segment of the population responsible for the care of sick children, namely mothers and female caretakers. The greater involvement of women in therapy management creates a priori a heightened receptivity to innovations which apply primarily to children. Therefore, despite healers' substantial involvement in treating diarrhea, their basic gender roles (Banton 1965) influence exposure to the child care domain. This is reflected in the fact that midwives were quite knowledgeable about ORT, as were the herbalist and the shaman who were female. A good example of this gender influence was the case of an elderly male herbalist who had never heard of a serum for diarrhea, yet his daughter who lived with him, herself a grandmother, was quite knowledgeable about ORT and able to provide the correct home recipe.

The two healer types that participate actively in ORT, midwives and injectionists, appear to do so for very different reasons. In the case of midwives, as already noted, sex role orientation plays a part, and there is the additional fact that traditional birth attendants specialize in maternal and child health care. Therefore occupational specialization further predisposes midwives to learn about and accept a new pediatric therapy. Furthermore, one would expect that friends and health care professionals would be more inclined to communicate information about ORT during informal encounters to midwives than to other types of healers. Thus their exposure to information about the innovation is probably greater.

In the case of injectionists, occupational specialization also facilitated the adoption of the innovation, but in this instance the specialty relates to the use of commercial pharmaceutical products. Injectionists already have well-established connections with pharmacies, and tend to keep abreast of new drugs and techniques. Also, the injectionists treat a larger number of cases of diarrhea in children, which increases the potential utility of the technique in everyday practice. In fact, it was observed that a significant correlation exists between patient caseload of all ages and awareness of ORT in the total healer sample. Finally, injectionists have the added advantage of more years of schooling, on the average, than other healer types. Education has been shown repeatedly to predict adoption of innovations, and this study found significant correlations between education and awareness of ORT in both the household and healer surveys. The factors influencing adoption by injectionists, then, included occupational specialization, size of caseload, and educational attainment.

It might be argued that shamans were only minimally involved with ORT because they specialize in supernatural forms of illness and therefore have less need for technological therapies. Yet this would not explain the equally low participation of herbalists, who treat all types of diarrhea. In fact, one survey found that diarrhea ranked second to worms as the most common illness presented to herbalists for treatment (Coreil 1983). Also, shamans practice herbal medicine as well as magical curing. Since ORT promotion was not aimed at healers, low awareness and use of the therapy generally would be expected. It is the unanticipated higher utilization among midwives and injectionists which warrants explanation and this, therefore, has been the focus of discussion.

Among the healers who were aware of ORT, the majority had identified it with the traditional treatment for diarrhea. That is, they labeled it as a "rafrechi" which cools the body in the way that guava tea and other infusions help restore humoral balance. Yet none of the healers said they added guava leaves to their hydrating solutions, while 10% of mothers reported doing so. Furthermore, only four healers said they prescribed other remedies in addition to ORT. This suggests that the new remedy is viewed as a replacement for a traditional form, not as an adjunct therapy. This syncretic view is closer to the traditional model of diarrhea treatment as a specific cure for the illness itself. At the same time, half of the healer respondents espoused the model of fluid maintenance as the mode of ORT action, but here again, injectionists were overrepresented among them. Among the other healer types, the traditional curative model prevailed.

A brief note should be made on the question of potential collaboration between healers and health officials in the control of diarrheal diseases. While the response from healers on this issue was overwhelmingly positive, officials expressed many concerns. The notion of utilizing traditional birth attendants was expectedly well accepted, and by 1986 some community health programs had introduced ORT into their curricula for training midwives. However, no one spoke positively of the role of injectionists. For one thing, the medical community was surprised to learn that injectionists were so numerous and active in patient care. This alone was disturbing to officials, but even more so was the prospect of establishing a formal role for injectionists in health care delivery. Such an action would appear to confer a measure of legitimacy on an occupation which most officials feel should be discredited. Therefore, regardless of their current knowledge and practice of the new technique, these alternative healers are unlikely candidates for formal collaboration with the official health care sector.

The Haitian study illustrates several general points in understanding the process of innovation among traditional and alternative healers. Adoption of the new technique appeared to be influenced by role specialization within the population of healers, but also by more basic roles (i.e., gender) that transcend the domain of work. In other words, the social identities (Goodenough 1965; Keesing 1970) of healers separate from their therapeutic role can be of equal or even greater importance in this regard. Sociodemographic factors seemed to have limited influence on the process, and the effects were again mediated through role components (for instance, injectionists tended to have more schooling). The process seemed to operate differently among traditional and alternative healers. That is, different factors influenced adoption among midwives and injectionists, the pattern of syncretism varied between injectionists and the traditional practitioners, and official attitudes toward these two classes of specialists differed sharply. These differences underscore the need to keep traditional and alternative healers conceptually distinct in our analyses of medical diffusion and other problems.

As long as traditional healers in Haiti and elsewhere continue to practice and have exposure to modern medicine, they will continue to selectively incorporate the *materia medica* of Western therapy. Likewise, injectionists, medicine vendors and other types of alternative healers will continue to sustain an unregulated subsector of modern medicine, both in developing and industrial societies (cf. Salmon 1984). Yet we know very little about the process of medical innovation among folk healers. As a final note, I strongly reiterate Ferguson's (1981:124) observation that "Considerably more work needs to be done on how modern medications are integrated into the healing strategies of alternative curers."

REFERENCES

Allman, James, Gerald Lerebours, and Jon E. Rohde 1985. Lessons Learned in Implementing and Evaluating the National ORT Program in Haiti. Paper presented at the American Public Health Association Meetings, Washington, D.C., November 17–21.

Banton, Michael 1965. Roles. New York: Basic Books.

Bentley, Margaret E. 1985. Child Diarrhea: Illness and Intervention in Rural North India. Paper presented at the 84th Annual Meeting of the American Anthropological Association, Washington, D.C., December 4–8.

Clerisme, Calixte 1979. Recherches Sur la Medecine Traditionnnelle. Port-au-Prince: Fardin.

Coreil, Jeannine 1983. Parallel Structures in Modern and Professional Health Care: A Model Applied to Rural Haiti. *Culture, Medicine and Psychiatry* 7:131–151.

Coreil, Jeannine 1985. Community Acceptance of Oral Rehydration Therapy in Haiti. Unpublished report submitted to the Pan American Health Organization.

Coreil, Jeannine in press. Adoption of Oral Rehydration Therapy Among Haitian Mothers. *Social Science and Medicine.*

Cunningham, Clark E. 1970. Thai "Injection Doctors": Antibiotic Mediators. *Social Science and Medicine* 4:1–24.

Davis, Wade 1985. The Serpent and the Rainbow. New York: Simon and Schuster.

de Zoysa, Isabelle, Debbie Carson, Richard Feachem, Betty Kirkwood, Euan Lindsey-Smith, and Rene Loewenson 1984. Perceptions of Childhood Diarrhea and Its Treatment in Rural Zimbabwe. *Social Science and Medicine* 19(7):727–734.

Ferguson, Anne E. 1981. Commercial Pharmaceutical Medicine and Medicalization: A Case Study from El Salvador. *Culture, Medicine and Psychiatry* 5:105–134.

Foster, George M., and Barbara Gallatin Anderson 1978. Medical Anthropology. New York: Wiley.

Frankel, S. J., and D. Lehmann 1984. Oral Rehydration Therapy: Combining Anthropological and Epidemiological Approaches in the Evaluation of a Papua New Guinea Programme. *Journal of Tropical Medicine and Hygiene* 87:137–142.

Goodenough, Ward 1965. Rethinking Status and Role. *In* The Relevance of Models for Social Anthropology. Michael Banton, ed. Pp. 1–22. New York: Praeger.

Green, Edward C. 1985. Traditional Healers, Mothers and Childhood Diarrheal Diseases in Swaziland: The Interface of Anthropology and Health Education. *Social Science and Medicine* 20(3):277–285.

Harrison, Ira E. 1974. Traditional Healers: A Neglected Source of Health Manpower. *Rural Africana* 26:5–16.

Hirschhorn, Norbert 1982. Oral Rehydration Therapy for Diarrhea in Children – A Basic Primer. *Nutrition Reviews* 40(4):97–104.

Hogle, Janice 1985. Promotion of Oral Rehydration Therapy in Niger. Paper presented at the 84th meeting of the American Anthropological Association, Washington, D.C., December 4–8.

Keesing, Roger M. 1970. Toward a Model of Role Analysis. *In* A Handbook of Method in Cultural Anthropology. Raoul Naroll and Ronald Cohen, eds. Pp. 423–453. New York: Columbia University Press.

Kendall, Carl, Dennis Foote, and Reynaldo Martorell 1983. Anthropology, Communications and Health: The Mass Media and Health Practices Program in Honduras. *Human Organization* 42(4):353–360.

Kendall et al. 1984. Ethnomedicine and Oral Rehydration Therapy: A Case Study of Ethnomedical Investigation and Program Planning. *Social Science and Medicine* 19(3):253–260.

Landy, David 1974. Role Adaptation: Traditional Curers under the Impact of Western Medicine. *American Ethnologist* 1:103–127.

Logan, Michael H. 1973. Digestive Disorders and Plant Medicinals in Highland Guatemala. *Anthropos* 68:538–547.

Lozoff, Betsy, K. R. Kamath, and R. A. Feldman 1975. Infection and Disease in South Indian Families: Beliefs About Childhood Diarrhea. *Human Organization* 34(4):353–358.

Maclean, Una, and Robert H. Bannerman (eds.) 1982. Utilization of Indigenous Healers in National Health Delivery Systems. Special Issue, *Social Science and Medicine,* Vol. 16.

Nations, Marilyn 1982. Illness of the Child: The Cultural Context of Child Diarrhea. Doctoral Dissertation, University of California, Berkeley.

Nations, Marilyn 1984. Spirit Possession to Enteric Pathogens: The Role of Traditional Healing in Diarrheal Disease Control. *Proceedings of the International Conference on Oral Rehydration Therapy*, Washington, D.C., June 7–10, 1983, pp. 48–52.

Pape, Jean, Buffon Mondestin, Lambert Jasmin, B. H. Kean, J. E. Pohdo, and Warren D. Johnson, Jr. 1984. Management of Diarrhea in Haiti: Mortality Reduction in 8,443 Hospitalized Children. *Proceedings of the International Conference on Oral Rehydration Therapy*, Washington, D.C., June 7–10, 1983, pp. 87–89.

Pierre-Noel, Arsene V. 1974. Les Plantes et les Legumes d'Haiti qui Guerissent. Tome I. Port-au-Prince: Presses Nationales d'Haiti.

Pillsbury, Barbara L. K. 1979. Reaching the Rural Poor: Indigenous Health Practitioners Are There Already. A.I.D. Program Evaluation Discussion Paper No. 1. Washington, D.C.: AID.

Press, Irwin 1971. The Urban Curandero. *American Anthropologist* 73:742–756.

Rohde, Jon 1984. Accepting ORT: Reports from Haiti...Programming on a Shoestring. *Diarrhea Dialog* 19:4–5.

Salmon, J. Warren (ed.) 1984. Alternative Medicines: Popular and Policy Perspectives. New York: Tavistock.

Scrimshaw, Susan, and Elena Hurtado 1984. Field Guide for the Study of Health-Seeking Behavior at the Household Level. *Food and Nutrition Bulletin* 6(2):27–45.

Taylor, Carl E. 1976. The Place of Indigenous Medical Practitioners in the Modernization of Health Services. *In* Asian Medical Systems. Charles Leslie, ed. Pp. 285–299. Berkeley: University of California Press.

United Nations Children's Fund 1984. The State of the World's Children – 1985. London: Oxford University Press.

United States Agency for International Development 1986. Proceedings of ICORT II (International Conference on Oral Rehydration Therapy). Washington, D.C.: Agency for International Development.

Van Der Geest, Sjaak 1982. The Illegal Distribution of Western Medicine in Developing Countries: Pharmacists, Drug Peddlers, Injection Doctors and Others. *Medical Anthropology* 6(4):197–220.

Velimirovic, Boris 1984. Traditional Medicine is Not Primary Health Care: A Polemic. *Curare* 7(1):61–79.

WHO (World Health Organization) 1978. Promotion and Development of Traditional Medicine Technical Report Series No. 622. Geneva: WHO.

WHO 1986a. Fifth Programme Report 1984–1985. Programme for Control of Diarrheal Diseases. Geneva: World Health Organization.

WHO 1986b. Oral Rehydration Therapy for Treatment of Diarrhea in the Home. CDD Series No. 86.9. Geneva: WHO.

Young, Allan 1983. The Relevance of Traditional Medical Cultures to Modern Primary Health Care. *Social Science and Medicine* 17(16):1205–1211.

AIDS: New Threat to the Third World

LORI HEISE

Historically, epidemics have been as profound an agent for societal change as wars. The smallpox virus that Cortez loosed upon the Aztecs was largely responsible for Spain's conquest of this mighty empire. The plague that ravaged 14th-century Europe ruptured the bonds of feudalism, upsetting the power balance between peasant and lord.

Today a new disease, acquired immunodeficiency syndrome (AIDS), threatens to have an impact of equal measure in parts of the Third World. Unless brought under control, AIDS could undermine decades of progress toward improved health and sustained economic development.

AIDS kills by disabling the body's immune system, making its victim easy prey for certain opportunistic cancers and infections. Like syphilis – another disease endemic in much of the world – AIDS is transmitted through blood and body fluids during sexual intercourse. To a lesser but significant extent, it is also transmitted through blood transfusions, the sharing or reusing of contaminated needles, and from mother to child during pregnancy or birth.

Unlike syphilis, there is not known cure for AIDS. Once individuals become infected with the AIDS virus (known as the human immunodeficiency virus, or HIV), they remain at risk of developing the disease even though they may be symptom-free for years. Symptomless carriers are the invisible infectors who unwittingly fuel the AIDS epidemic.

Heise. We received permission from the Worldwatch Institute to reprint this article. It appeared in the Vol. 1, No. 1, 1988 issue of *World Watch* on pages 19–28.

Researchers estimate that for each reported AIDS case, 50 to 100 people may be infected with the virus. Present studies on the U.S. population suggest that of those infected, roughly 25 to 50 percent will develop full-blown AIDS within five years, and probably more will do so as time goes on. It is unclear, however, whether the disease will follow a similar course in developing countries.

By 1986, only five years after the virus was first identified, the World Health Organization (WHO) estimated that between 5 and 10 million people worldwide were HIV carriers. So rapidly is the infection spreading that by 1990 WHO projects 50 to 100 million people may be infected. If only 30 percent of these carriers develop AIDS within five years, 15 to 30 million people could be dead or dying of AIDS by 1995.

Assessing the scope of AIDS in developing countries is particularly difficult. Many Third World governments – given competing priorities and limited resources – lack the diagnostic equipment and funds necessary for AIDS surveillance. Others fear that acknowledging AIDS cases could jeopardize the tourist revenues and foreign investment upon which their economies depend.

Likewise, where only 30 to 35 percent of people are reached by modern health services, as is the situation in most African countries, many AIDS cases go undiagnosed. Consequently WHO statistics, which rely on voluntary government reporting, significantly underestimate the true impact of AIDS in the developing world.

African countries, for example, had

reported a total of 6,635 AIDS cases to WHO as of November 25, 1987; the United States had reported 45,436. Yet blood surveys measuring exposure to the virus confirm that HIV is more prevalent in urban areas of certain African countries than it is in the United States.

Studies from several African cities have documented a 2 to 20 percent rate of HIV infection among healthy adults, with women being exposed as often as men. This compares to a figure of 0.15 percent among U.S. military volunteers – the best comparable nationwide figure for Americans in the same age-groups – and a figure of 2.9 percent for volunteers from New York, New Jersey and Pennsylvania.

Thus the infection rate in some African cities is about 100 times higher than in the United States as a whole, and five times higher than in the New York region. And AIDS in Africa is no longer confined to the cities. In some rural areas, especially near main roads, from two to five percent of healthy adults and of pregnant women now test HIV positive.

Together these studies lead WHO to estimate that two million or more Africans carry the virus, making Africa the hardest hit continent in the world.

Yet no continent has escaped unscathed. Latin America and the Caribbean have reported a total of 5,366 cases with almost every country reporting some exposure. Haiti alone has 912. Bermuda and French Guiana have the highest infection rates in the world, roughly six times the U.S. level of 172 cases per million population. And Brazil reports 2,013 cases, although health officials fear that up to 400,000 Brazilians may already be infected with the virus.

To date, Asia has been the least affected, with the highest number of cases – 43 – being reported by Japan. There is concern, however, that AIDS could spread quickly in this region because of the prevalence in some countries of intravenous drug use and the prostitution associated with tourism.

AIDS Spreads in the Third World

Unlike the industrial world where AIDS is primarily communicated through homosexual intercourse and the sharing of needles between drug addicts, an estimated three-fourths of AIDS transmission in Africa occurs thorough heterosexual contact. The remaining transmission occurs from mother to child during pregnancy or birth, and through exchange of infected blood during transfusions or reuse of needles by health care providers.

It is thought that homosexual transmission predominates in the industrial world because the virus first infected the male homosexual population. Here it stayed until women began to contract the disease through intravenous drug use and bisexual men. As more and more women contract the virus, the role of heterosexual transmission in the industrial world is expected to rise.

Nonetheless, the overall rate of transmission is likely to remain greater in the Third World than in industrial countries because of certain realities of life there.

For example, researchers believe that the genital sores that commonly accompany other sexually transmitted diseases (STDs) increase chances of infection. Sadly, STDs are far more endemic in the Third World than in industrial countries and treatment is less accessible. During the early 1980s, the rate of gonorrhea per 100,000 people in Kampala, Uganda was 10,000, in Nairobi 7,000, and in India 5,000. By contrast, the rate in Atlanta, Georgia was 2,510 and in London, only 310.

Many Third World governments also do not have the equipment or the money necessary to test blood before transfusions, a form of HIV transmission largely eliminated in the United States and Europe. The United States spends $80 to 100 million a year ($6 to 8 per unit of blood) to protect its citizens from a relatively small risk of contracting HIV from transfusions. In

Africa today the risk to blood recipients may be as high as one in ten, yet in many areas blood is still not screened.

Unfortunately, conditions also conspire to make transfusions more common in tropical Africa than in industrialized nations. Severe anemias, long delays between obstetric or other bleeding and arrival at hospital, and many serious road accidents make the amount of blood needed by African hospitals as much as three times greater than that required by general hospitals in the industrial world.

Developing countries desperately need a quick, inexpensive blood test for HIV that is not sensitive to heat. There is hope that a test newly developed by Du Pont may be available for distribution this year.

In addition, underdevelopment promotes many forms of behavior that increase risks for transmission of the virus. For example, lack of economic opportunity in rural areas, political insecurity, famine, and war operate to increase the number of sexual partners of developing world citizens by displacing persons and separating families.

Likewise, medical overuse of transfusions in the absence of other remedies and the reuse of unsterile needles are practices of undeveloped or overtaxed health care systems that encourage the spread of AIDS.

Unhygienic conditions resulting from poverty may intensify the impact of AIDS in many developing countries. It has been proposed that Third World peoples – indeed poor people in general – may be more susceptible to AIDS because of prior and repeated exposures to other infections that overtax their immune systems.

Evidence suggests that chronic exposure to viral and parasitic infections (which are endemic in the Third World) leads to certain immunologic abnormalities that could increase susceptibility to HIV infection and to expression of the full-blown disease. More research is needed to confirm this relationship, but it is becoming increasingly clear that individuals differ in their prone-

ness to AIDS. Poverty, and the infections it breeds, may be one reason.

Indeed, the poor in developing countries – more at risk and less able to protect themselves from HIV infection – will likely be disproportionately affected by AIDS, just as poor, urban blacks and Hispanics are in the United States.

As Jon Tinker, president of the Panos Institute, observes: The global underclass, those who live in rural and urban shantytowns, who cannot afford condoms and are not reached by family planning advice, who cannot read and therefore are least likely to be reached by educational campaigns, who have little or no access to health clinics, who may have to sell their own blood to buy food – this global underclass will likely bear a disproportionate share of AIDS's misery.

In Africa, certain demographic and genetic characteristics may combine with poverty to make AIDS particularly difficult to control. Forty percent of the continent's population is in its sexually active years, a higher percentage than anywhere in the world. The proportion of African children moving from prepuberty into the years of sexual activity is likewise greater. Moreover, researchers have found a genetic trait that appears to facilitate AIDS transmission among its carriers; the frequency of this trait is three times higher in central Africa than in Europe.

In other developing regions, prevention campaigns will have to contend with "traditional" healers who administer folk remedies without medical supervision or properly sterilized equipment. Health authorities estimate, for example, that Haiti alone has between 10,000 and 15,000 "piquristes" (injectionists) who could potentially spread AIDS through reuse of needles.

A Matter of Triage

AIDS strains the ability of even the most organized and wealthy countries to respond effectively. But circumstances in the Third

World conspire to make an effective response to AIDS especially complicated.

Developing nations, for example, have even fewer options for treating the disease than countries in the West. Industrial world physicians largely respond by treating the secondary diseases, such pneumocystis carinii pneumonia, that accompany AIDS. It's an expensive ordeal that often involves long hospital stays. The only drug currently available to attack HIV infection directly – azidothymidine (AZT) – costs $10 to 20 a day and requires multiple blood transfusions, effectively eliminating it as an option for Third World patients.

Instead, the treatment for AIDS in Kashenye, Tanzania, is necessarily crude: "a few days in bed, some aspirin, and then home to die." With only one doctor for every 32,110 people, one hospital bed for every 900 people, and an abundance of patients with illnesses that can be cured, Tanzania must practice triage.

And in Zaire, providing treatment for 10 AIDS patients comparable to that delivered in the United States would cost more than the entire budget of Mama Yemo, the nation's largest hospital. Yet physicians at Mama Yemo diagnose up to 15 new AIDS cases each day.

Researchers do not anticipate a vaccine for AIDS within the next five years, so prevention in the near term will have to rely on protecting the blood supply and on changing behavior to restrict the spread of the disease. While changing behavior is difficult in any setting, once again the Third World will confront special challenges.

People must first be educated on the causes of the disease and how to prevent it. However, carrying out mass education in the Third World, is particularly difficult. First, education is expensive. President Ronald Reagan has requested $247.5 million in 1988 for AIDS education and information in the United States. Health budgets in the Third World cannot begin to achieve a comparable level of funding.

Second, fewer avenues of communication are available for reaching audiences. Many people in the Third World are illiterate and few have access to television. Although radio is widely available, it is most effective when used in conjunction with other communication channels. And even radio must contend with the Third World's many tongues: India alone has 16 major languages.

Nonetheless, changing conduct of the San Francisco gay community demonstrates that high-risk behavior – even sexual behavior – can be modified through education. It is on this hope that many Third World countries hang their future.

Indeed, some developing countries are moving energetically to control AIDS. Rwanda and Brazil already have government-run education campaigns, and the leaflets produced by Kenya Red Cross, which counsel "Spread facts not fear," are some of the best in the world.

Uganda's slogan, "Love Carefully," appears on posters in the nation's 22 languages, while radio announcers encourage Ugandans to practice "zero grazing." President Kaunda of Zambia, whose son died of AIDS, has given notable leadership. And prostitutes in Nairobi are now more likely to ask their clients to use condoms.

AIDS and the Multiplier Effect

Improving Third World health standards has been a major focus of development efforts for decades. But for struggling health systems, AIDS poses a multiple challenge that could undermine hard won health gains and threaten ongoing public health initiatives.

AIDS is an added drain on health care budgets already stretched too thin. In 1982, Haiti had $2.60 to spend on health care per citizen; the Central African Republic had $2.90. Rwanda's budget of $1.60 per person would not even buy a bottle of aspirin in the industrial world.

Yet these countries face epidemics of

frightening proportions. In Africa alone, malaria claims one million lives each year. Worldwide, over 1.5 million people die of measles. And across the globe, five million children succumb to chronic diarrhea. With health burdens like these, diverting funds for the treatment or prevention of AIDS becomes a question of trading lives for lives.

Not only does AIDS compete with other diseases for limited health budgets, HIV actually magnifies the problem of existing diseases. The virus weakens the immune system of its hosts, leaving carriers more susceptible to renewed attacks from microbes that may be lying dormant.

For example, individuals contracting tuberculosis (TB) often remain carriers of the TB bacteria even after their immune system conquers outward signs of the disease. Once suppressed, the individual's immune system may be overrun by a fresh attack of the TB bacteria, leading to the active and contagious form of TB. Thus an epidemic of tuberculosis may be initiated in an otherwise healthy population by an HIV carrier who has no symptoms of AIDS.

Evidence suggests that HIV is already having this multiplier effect on preexisting diseases. Tuberculosis is increasing in the United States, where until the mid-1970s its incidence had been declining. TB is also on the rise in Africa, where there is good reason to believe that HIV is the cause. In a study of TB patients tested in Kinshasa, Zaire, 40 percent were found to be HIV-positive. By contrast, only six to eight percent of healthy adults in the Zaire capital tested positive.

Doctors also wonder whether HIV may be activating latent syphilis infections through the virus's depressive effect on the immune system. There are an increasing number of cases where healthy people – previously treated for syphilis – are developing late-stage neurosyphilis after infection with HIV.

Physicians hypothesize that low levels of the bacteria that cause syphilis may be "hiding" in the body's central nervous system even after treatment with antibiotics (the syphilis bacterium can cross the blood-brain barrier, whereas most antibiotics cannot). By suppressing immune function, HIV infection may allow the syphilis virus to attack anew.

Women and Children First

It is in the area of maternal and child health that AIDS poses the most direct threat to development gains. In the last 20 years there has been a revolution in the way development organizations have approached Third World health. Shedding the West's preoccupation with hospitals and high-technology medicine, development organizations began to emphasize "primary health care" rather than "curative care."

Primary care stresses prevention of disease by encouraging immunization, oral rehydration therapy, nutritional education, and breast-feeding. Together with increased female literacy, education in hygiene, and improved access to clean water and family planning, primary health care strategies have inaugurated a "child survival revolution" that has cut infant deaths in the Third World from 20 percent of live births in 1960 to 12 percent today.

These gains, while impressive, are precarious: AIDS stands to undermine decades of struggle for mother and child health. When an HIV-positive woman becomes pregnant, evidence suggests that she becomes more likely to develop full-blown AIDS in the next few years.

A mother also has roughly a 30 to 50 percent chance of passing the infection to her child either in utero, during birth, or possibly through breast-feeding. Once infected, newborns experience an accelerated course of the disease; half will die before their second birthday.

AIDS may soon be a significant factor in the mother/child survival quotient. In some African cities – such as Kinshasa and Kampala – 8 to 14 percent of women attending prenatal clinics in 1986 were infected with the virus. Up to half the children born to these women may be doomed from birth. Another portion may die from neglect when their mothers succumb to AIDS.

In Zambia, medical officials predicted that they would have 6,000 "AIDS babies" in 1987. The United States, with more than 37 times Zambia's population, has had less than 600 since reporting began.

Also alarming is the threat AIDS could pose to beneficial interventions that today are saving the lives of millions of children each year. Immunization programs, for example, are the life preservers of one million Third World children each year. Immunization, however, has the potential to communicate AIDS if unsterile needles are used. There is no evidence that this is happening with immunization programs, but studies do indicate that HIV is being transmitted through other medical injections (for example, antibiotics and penicillin).

One study of infants aged one to 24 months showed that HIV- positive children born of uninfected mothers had received significantly more medical injections than children who were not infected with HIV. Another study confirmed that African mothers strongly believed that medication by injection was more effective than pills taken by mouth. These attitudes, along with the high incidence of childhood diseases requiring medication, account for the large number of injections received by African children.

Unfortunately, for financial and practical reasons, health workers often reuse syringes without proper sterilization, setting the stage for spread of HIV from child to child.

The study of infants did not, however, show a relationship between immunization and HIV infection. This lack of association probably reflects the wider use of properly sterilized equipment in immunization programs, the absence of traditional healers in vaccination programs, and the relatively small number of vaccinations received per child (less than one percent of all injections administered in the developing world).

Even though immunization programs are most likely safe, they run the risk of being shunned by mothers who, through experience with medical injections, fear HIV contamination from needles. Health workers already note this happening in Brazil. Ironically, unless greater vigilance is applied in medical injection programs, AIDS could undermine immunization indirectly through guilt by association.

Likewise, more research is needed to establish any relationship that may exist between breast-feeding and HIV transmission. Researchers have isolated the virus in breast milk and there have been between one and five cases of newborns apparently contracting AIDS through their mother's milk. World Health Organization experts doubt that breast milk is a significant route of HIV transmission, but evidence to confirm this belief is urgently needed.

Without such evidence, multinational companies and governments promoting infant formula have a ready-made selling point. It could set child health back decades if mothers again began substituting milk powder for breast milk out of fear of AIDS.

Because of contaminated water, overdiluting, and the absence of antibodies found in breast milk, bottle-fed babies in poor Third World communities are twice as likely to die as breast-fed babies.

AIDS Undermines Economies

As the development community contemplates Third World debt, AIDS is quietly changing the face of economics in the developing world. Because the disease attacks men and women in their prime, it has the potential to sabotage the future sustainability of entire economies.

Unlike other illnesses that cull the weakest

members of the population – the sick, the old, and the very young – AIDS eliminates the productive segment of the population. Approximately 90 percent of those with AIDS in industrial and developing countries alike are between 20 and 49 years of age.

The consequences of a fatal epidemic focused on this group will be immense. Children will be left without parents. And with little automation or mechanization to fall back on, societies will be without work forces. Zambia alone, with a population of under seven million, could have 700,000 people dead or dying of AIDS in the next decade.

Many of those lost will be the most educated and highly skilled of Zambia's first post-independence generation. Indeed, one study in the country's copper belt confirms that AIDS is already eroding the cornerstone of the Zambian economy: 68 percent of the men testing HIV positive in this region were the skilled laborers upon whom the mining industry depends.

The loss of such workers will have economic impacts that reverberate throughout society. Researchers at the Harvard Institute of International Development are attempting to quantify these impacts by modeling the indirect economic costs of AIDS in central Africa. According to their projections, by 1995 the annual loss to Zaire's economy due to premature deaths from AIDS will be eight percent of the country's gross national product (GNP), or $350 million if measured against Zaire's 1984 GNP.

Even though this figure does not include direct treatment costs or losses due to illness, it is still more than the $314 million Zaire received from all sources of development assistance in 1984.

Other countries will experience similar losses, and collectively the economic growth rate of the seven countries of the African AIDS belt – Tanzania, Uganda, Central African Republic, Burundi, Rwanda, Zambia and Zaire – will slow as people divert savings from investment to treatment. By 1990, the Harvard team projects the loss from AIDS due to economic slowing will be $980 million in this region.

These economic losses come at a time when Third World nations – especially African countries – are already laboring under severe economic hardship. Personal income is declining sharply, debt is mounting, and foreign aid is being cut back.

Against this backdrop, AIDS threatens to further complicate balance-of-payment problems. Foreign exchange will be lost as governments seek to import items necessary to combat the epidemic; tourist dollars will decline in response to travelers' fears; export revenues will fall as skilled labor becomes more scarce.

There is even evidence that AIDS may be scaring off foreign investors who are seeking to avoid the high medical costs associated with the disease. (In Africa, companies traditionally assume the cost of most medical benefits.)

These macroeconomic worries translate into a horrible reality for individuals. The true costs of AIDS are both economic and personal. Nowhere is this clearer than in the observations of correspondent Robert Bazell, who recently confronted the human dimensions of this frightening disease.

"A few months ago," Bazell recalls, "the town of Kytera in the Rakai district of southern Uganda was a busy center of commerce. Now it is almost deserted. Most of the merchants have either died of AIDS or fled from it. Most of those walking the dirt streets are children, orphans with both parents dead of AIDS.

"In the tiny houses and mud huts in the surrounding farm area it is unusual to find a home where AIDS has not struck...In the six years I have been reporting about AIDS," Bazell concludes, "I never imagined it could become so horrible."

What will be the economic impact of this reality? We can count up the direct costs and calculate the indirect cost of lost wages from disability and death. But what of the psychological toll on those left behind? What is the productive potential of a generation numbed by grief? Economic tally sheets cannot capture the potential lost when a society's members no longer feel in control of their destiny, when people no longer dream.

The International Response

Meeting the global challenge of AIDS will require unprecedented cooperation among nations. Unfortunately, parochial interests, along with overwhelming denial of the problem by some governments, have slowed the international mobilization against AIDS.

Also operative has been the persistent view that AIDS is someone else's problem: homosexuals, drug addicts, Haitians, Africans. It is only now, with AIDS threatening to infiltrate the Western mainstream, that resources have been loosed to combat the disease.

This egocentrism has allowed the virus to spread unchecked, making its ultimate control even more difficult. AIDS must be viewed as everyone's problem if an untold loss of human life is to be avoided.

••••

About the Authors in Chapter 11

John R. Evans is Chairman of the Board of Trustees of the Rockefeller Foundation. He was President of the University of Toronto from 1972 to 1978 and has been Director of the Population, Health, and Nutrition Department of the World Bank. His article, "Measurement and Health Services," was published by the Rockefeller Foundation in 1981.

Jeremy Warford is Senior Advisor to the Environment Department of the World Bank in Washington, D.C. In 1989 *Environmental Management and Economic Development*, edited by Gunter Schramm and Jeremy Warford, was published for the World Bank by the Johns Hopkins University Press of Baltimore.

Karen Lashman is Senior Country Officer for Chile with the World Bank in Washington, D.C. She has been involved in a major study of Social Development Programs in Chile over the last few decades and had contributed to numerous World Bank reports, including pharmaceuticals in the Third World.

Dr. Jeannine Coreil is an Associate Professor in the Department of Community and Family Health, University of South Florida. She and J. Dennis Mull recently edited *Anthropology and Primary Health Care*, which was published by Westview Press, Boulder, CO. in 1990.

Lori Heise was a researcher at the Worldwatch Institute when her article appeared. She was working on health issues in developing countries. *Reforesting the Earth*, by Sandra Postel and Lori Heise, was published in 1988 by the Worldwatch Institute of Washington, D.C.

CHAPTER 12

The Balance Between Environment and Development

Introduction

THE MARKETS FOR PERISHABLE and unperishable goods in northern urban, industrial countries have steadily expanded since World War II. The impact of this new consumerism is, to an extent, on developing areas where farmers switch from subsistence farming to cash cropping. Rain forests give way to new pastures and agribusinesses such as tobacco manufacturing increase the demand for wood fuel. The result of these activities is soil erosion and desertification. This has been a continuing problem in the Sahel, where mismanagement of natural resources has brought about increasing aridity and decreasing productivity. The Gambian case and other African countries in the Sahel have been used by Mann (1987) as an example of how deforestation, wind erosion, lack of rain, lower water tables, and inappropriate technology have combined to almost destroy livestock and field-crop production. The incentive to conserve decreases as the distance between producers and consumers increases.

But the Sahel is only one example of the fragile balance between development and ecological deterioration. The rapid increase in population growth in other parts of the world and consumerism have eroded the basis of life support systems such as arable lands, clean air, and water. In particular, the dramatic decline in the proportions of forest areas in developing countries is disturbing since forests play a crucial role in the production of life support systems. The destruction of forests for fuel-wood around urban areas has been a world-wide phenomenon in developing countries. The extent of the destruction of forests has been described in the Indian case by Bowander, Prasad, and Unni (1987).

Bandyopadhyaya and Shiva (1987, 1989) argue that market-oriented development plans in India that ignore damage to natural ecosystems have produced ecological movements (e.g., the Chipko Movement) that are sensitive to the limits of development. This is a move toward return to the indigenous culture of India rather than the resource-exploitative policies of colonial governments that have been continued in the name of "economic development."

By now the reader should be able to see that there are two sides to the coin, that development planning with a goal of removing poverty is commendable but that there are numerous pitfalls to which one should be alerted. The purpose of this chapter is to focus (1) on the extent of ecological deterioration, part of which may be assessed to development policy and (2) on the efforts now underway to reverse such processes as desertification and deforestation.

The Articles in Chapter 12

Watts suggests that trends toward internationalization of capital and industrial activities have increased the interpenetration of economic and social relations among nations at a global level, "the wheat trap," for example. One of the criticisms leveled against governments in developing countries is that they sometimes sponsor large scale wastage of scarce resources and, at times, invest in unprofitable ventures. In some instances developing nations are forced into unprofitable undertakings because they find themselves in subordinate positions and are unable to control the course of their national development.

In the presence of increasing commercialization the Sahel pastoralists, for example, were forced to maintain large herds to reduce the effects of market fluctuations or future droughts. Thus, crises in the developing countries are sometimes produced by a set of international social and economic relationships.

Collins describes the Transamazon colonization project, Ecuadorian colonization experiences, and coffee production in tropical Peru as examples of the impact of socioeconomic policies on environmental deterioration. Unfavorable market conditions created indebtedness, inattentiveness of the government to local conditions and an environment in which the small scale farmer was very likely to fail. Structural incentives to produce for short-term gain to avoid liquidation forced farmers to grow crops not necessarily suited to the land. Shortened fallows (times between crops) and monocropping led to soil erosion and declining yields. Thus, ecological deterioration and land loss became in part the product of institutional constraints favoring large scale farmers.

Schramm examines the sources of energy supply for Africa. At the present market rates, there is no incentive to replenish slowly declining wood supplies. If alternative sources of fuel such as kerosene are encouraged, the import cost of petroleum products would be unprofitably high for African societies. *Schramm* suggests that, as compared to the consumption of imported fuels, the use of domestic fuels has several advantages. First, wood is locally available, second, wood fuel manufacture generates local employment, and finally, technologies are available to generate efficient wood fuel supplies that cause low levels of environmental pollution. If indiscriminate destruction of natural forests by slash and burn methods is stopped and wood fuels are used properly, the environment can sustain the impact and the economy can prosper.

In the short term, energy policies should increase the efficiency of ongoing wood fuel production and in the long run, forests should be replenished. Cheap and environmentally safe energy supplies are necessary for economic development.

Myers describes the interconnections between beef consumption in the United States and the deforestation of Central America. Large scale ranchers play a large role in eliminating forest cover. The rain forests have been depleted by about 40 percent since 1960 and the forests have given way to pasture lands. About 60 percent of the entire beef production of

Costa Rica comes to the United States and the fast food industry is one of the biggest consumers of the imported beef. Cattle raising in Central America is very inefficient but, in spite of this, cattle raising continues to increase because of the involvement of elites in the cattle industry.

REFERENCES

Mann, Robert, "Development and the Sahel Disaster: The Case of Gambia," *The Ecologist*, 17(2), 1987, pp. 84–90.

Bandyopadhyaya, Janata and Vandana Shiva, "Development, Poverty and the Growth of the Green Movement in India," *The Ecologist*, 19(3), 1989, pp. 111–117.

_____, "Chipko: Rekindling India's Forest Culture," *The Ecologist*, 17(1), 1987, pp. 26–34.

Bowander, B., S. S. R. Prasad, and N. V. M. Unni, "Deforestation Around Urban Centres in India," *Environmental Conservation*, 14(1), 1987, pp. 23–28.

Conjunctures and Crisis: Food, Ecology and the Internationalization of Capital

MICHAEL J. WATTS

In Niger Republic, a landlocked Sahelian state in West Africa, the prolonged economic crisis since the late 1970s, and the austerity that has attended it, is widely referred to in cities and the countryside as "La Conjoncture." The conjuncture, the current constellation of global and national forces associated with economic recession, a Draconian debt burden, low commodity prices and an often quite radical restructuring of government activities, penetrates even the most remote rural communities. The pinch of stagnant export commodity prices, a sharp reduction of already Lilliputian state services and subsidies, a deterioration of basic infrastructure, and the price hikes of much-sought-after farm inputs are being felt.

The lineaments of this crisis can be traced to the sequence of events in the early 1970s: the collapse of the postwar financial order in 1971 with the devaluation of the US dollar, the OPEC-induced oil price increases of 1973, and the deep economic recession of 1974–1975. The major actors on the world stage – the multinationals (MNCs), the banks, the multilateral institutions such as the International Monetary Fund (IMF), and governments – have all been forced to adjust to the new atmosphere of heightened economic competition and the tentative birth of a new world order emerging from the ashes of the US-led postwar economic boom between 1945 and 1965.

Watts. The National Council for Geographic Education, publisher of the *Journal of Geography*, gave permission to reprint this article. It appeared in the November-December, 1987 issue of that journal on pages 292–299.

Understanding the shifting sands of the postwar system can be facilitated by acknowledging the domination of the advanced capitalist states in the world and the existence of an international economic order constructed by states as a framework for an international economic system constituted by patterns of trade, production, and profit (Pillay 1983). The international economic system refers to the structural relations of an expansionary capitalism and the processes of internationalization of production, finance, and services that underlie it. The international economic order refers to institutions such as those engineered at Bretton Woods at the end of World War II: The IMF, the World Bank and, subsequently, General Agreement on Tariffs and Trade (GATT) that required dismantling of trade and currency restrictions, that facilitated capital mobility, and that reflected US hegemony inscribed in the so-called "dollar shortage" system (Harris 1983). At any one moment, the world economy is dominated by one or more core states. The challenge to the postwar hegemony of the US by competing and rivalrous core states is a consequence of the crises of the 1970s.

The realignment of postwar order is a reflection of the intensification of competition at the global level and, as a corollary, three important developments: the increased movement of capital, the growing interpenetration of banking and industrial activities, and the extension of the industrial frontier into the Third World (Thrift 1986, p. 356). In the last twenty years, we have witnesses (1) the growth of an increasingly heterogeneous Third World characterized by quite rapid industrialization in such semi-peripheral states as Taiwan, Brazil, Mexico, and Hong Kong; (2) enhanced mobility and rationalization of multinational capital seen in mergers, acquisitions, industrial restructuring, the combination and division of production processes in innovative ways, and the deployment of radically new technologies and labor processes; and (3) the growing interconnection of productive, financial, and state operations. These changes have produced a global integration and internationalization of economic and social relations to an extent hitherto unknown, processes captured most dramatically in the "floating factory" and the "world car."

The anatomy of industrial capitalism is clearly changing; and the new architecture, which is in the process of emerging, is the outcome of global forces and tendencies. The fact that these changes are happening simultaneously throws up all sorts of tensions and contradictions. The result is that the nascent world economic order is anything but an ordered, coherent totality.

These new global realities – the interconnected, international, and global character of our lives – present important intellectual challenges for geographers, and it is the nature of this challenge that concerns me. In this paper, I argue that the color of geographical studies, most especially local and place-specific patterns of production and land use, must now appear on the larger canvas of what Nigel Thrift calls "international economic disorder" (Thrift 1986, p. 12). The analytic problem, therefore, is how to link our local geographies with a complex, internationalized, and shifting global political economy. I examine some of these problems in a discussion of resource questions located in the periphery of the world system: namely, questions of food and famine and of ecological degradation and population growth in parts of Africa and South Asia.

••••

The Wheat Revolution: Oil and Bread in Nigeria

In the Hausa village in which I worked in the mid-1970s, a large and vital district center located in the densely settled margins of Katsina town in northern Nigeria, peasant food consumption was characteristically dominated by the millets, sorghums, and cowpeas endemic to the West Africa savannas. A decade later, there are two mud ovens in Kaita village, which consume roughly 100 kilograms of flour apiece each day, that produce white bread for the local peasant market and surrounding rural hamlets. These new consumption patterns are suggestive of a "wheat revolution" currently underway in Nigeria, a movement that has enlisted many new partisans in the countryside. A rapid deepening of the wheat market, and the mushrooming of the flour-milling industry fed by wheat imports that grew by over fifteen percent per annum in West Africa during the 1970s, signals the extent to which US wheat surpluses have emerged as a central element in the postwar international food order. For example, Nigeria, a low-level importer of a paltry 3,500 tons of wheat in the early 1970s and which absorbed a little over 80,000 tons at independence in 1960, currently purchases over 1.5 million tons of wheat, ninety-five percent of which are hard wheats from the US. Bread has become, on the admission of a former Nigerian Head of State, Ibrahim Babangida, "the cheapest staple food of our people" (*Africa Economic Digest* 1984). Throughout the manufacturing districts of Kano City, industrial workers and large segments of a swollen informal sector subsist in large measure on a nightmarish diet of sweet, white bread and Carnation milk. It is the bread industry, which in all probability employs close to 10,000 people in Nigeria, that accounts for the largest private sector wage bill in Kano State.

Why is a country easily capable of self-sufficiency in staple foodstuffs currently importing 1.6 million tons of wheat during a major fiscal and foreign exchange crisis precipitated by the recent collapse of oil prices and, simultaneously through much nationalist rhetoric, calling for the support of local producers? Gunilla Andrae and Bjorn Beckman (1985) argued that Nigeria is caught in a "wheat trap" shaped both by international forces and those indigenous classes who have facilitated transatlantic wheat interests (i.e., import expansion) and who have benefitted directly from the milling, contracting, distribution, and production operations of the Nigerian bread complex. The wheat trap is a compelling example of how subordinated integration into a stratified world economy radically obstructs national development.

An understanding of the bread revolution must begin with the pattern of oil-based accumulation in Nigeria after 1973. The dramatic increases in crude oil prices in 1973 and 1979 generated a huge influx of oil rents directly into state coffers, windfall profits that financed an ambitious state-led industrialization project. Oil rents bolstered Nigerian federalism, underwrote an expansion and centralization of the Nigerian federal state (revenues quadrupled over two years), and simultaneously unleashed a spectacular import surge (both of intermediate and consumer goods) and an urban construction boom. The latter rapidly broadened the domestic food market because it drew labor from the rural sector. Labor shortage in agriculture, a labor market characteristically tight at certain moments of the growing season, produced inflated rural wages that coupled with low farm-gate prices generated a profit squeeze for producers.

Traditional export commodities (palm oil, groundnuts, cotton) collapsed under the additional burden of an unfavorable pricing policy for farmers, and the food output per capita almost certainly fell in the context of major intersectoral shifts of population and high natural fertility. A boom sector, therefore, produced severe lagged effects, the so-called "Dutch disease," which were papered over by the favorable commodity prices of the mid-1970s and the political instrumentalities at hand (viz., the deployment of foreign exchange surpluses to cover food staples acquired on the world market). The entrenchment of wheat must, then, be placed on the larger political-economic canvas of petrolic accumulation, the expansion of non-farm activities, the emergence of a food deficit, and the political means of taking care of the problem.

Why and how was wheat able to take hold of Nigerian markets? White bread emerges as the "Big Mac" of the Nigerian popular classes: fast, convenient, and compatible with the lifestyles of rapidly urbanizing and differentiating agrarian societies. But bread is also cheap. Cost, however, turns out to be a complex calculation because it reflects not only the different technical conditions of production between North America and Africa but also deliberate state policy. The Nigerian government controlled flour prices, which increased at only one-tenth the rate of other staples between 1975 and 1984, and the vanguard role of processors (flour mills and bakeries) that make bread so readily accessible. Bakers spearheaded the penetration of Nigerian markets, but bread is a highly segmented, flexible technology (village mud ovens and integrated electric bakeries in the cities) that allows for "maximum adaptability to market size, available investment funds and entrepreneurship" (Andrae and Beckman 1985, p. 3).

Baking has been a tremendous growth industry and also, at the most technologically complex levels, an important arena of state support (subsidies and loans) to indigenous capitalists. It is precisely the larger bakeries that have privileged access to the flour mills (guaranteed minimum prices) and institutional markets (schools, government institutions). Flour mills, on the other hand, are the "bridgeheads" of foreign capital. An aggressive policy of market expansion and taste transfer under the auspices of USDA, PL 480 and the major wheat dealers have been paralleled by the corporate capture of the processing industry. Multinationals are central to the Nigerian wheat industry; and Cargill, for example, has entered onto the Nigerian milling scene, and the eight major flour mills are all large-scale joint ventures between the state and foreign capital employing the most advanced forms of technology.

The intersection of state, class, and corporate capital at various points of the integrated bread industry also provides the backdrop for an analysis of wheat production schemes in Nigeria that were developed to quench the enormous demand for bread. The Kano, Bakalori, and South Chad schemes indicate a Chaplinesque story of failure and absurdity: enormous waste and cost overruns, technical problems at the point of production, huge environmental (downstream) externalities of dams construction, inadequacies of water supply, and the impossibility of double-cropping owing to impracticalities of farm mechanization and conflicts over household labor scheduling.

The three major wheat import-substitution schemes cost well over one billion US dollars; but if the enormous subsidies, overhead costs, and technical foulups are included, local production costs are currently between four and six times the cost of imported wheat! It may be argued that astronomical project cost also constitutes the major attraction of complex, high-tech irrigation schemes. These schemes constitute highly fertile terrain for political patronage through a venal contracting system and may, indeed, in spite of their technical inefficiencies be a source of considerable accumulation and profit to bureaucrats, the military, merchants, and civil servants who gain access to irrigated plots and monopolize the scarce but heavily subsidized inputs. The entire edifice is legitimated, of course, by the continued dependence on wheat imports; although the wheat schemes, by virtue of poor yields and low quality outputs, generate no forward linkages whatsoever. The schemes provide less than one percent of all wheat supplied to the local flour-milling industry.

Prosaic questions about what people eat can be illuminated by integrating levels of analysis from the global divisions of labor to local politics and patterns of state intervention. A starting point is what Harriet Friedmann (1982, p. 639) called the "postwar international food order," the principal features of which are surpluses of grain, especially wheat, sustained by American policies designed to dispose of such surpluses abroad, initially as food aid but of late through trade. Historically, the postwar dominance of the US economy and the centrality of the dollar underlay food aid as a critical mechanism of trade and price formation. Nonetheless, this food order and the gradual shift from aid to trade is only part of the mosaic. Nigerian "cheap food" policies and the political economy of its oil-led development, fused with local political forces and struggles with the state, produced a complex pattern of agrarian change, one manifestation of which is the wheat trap (Watts 1983).

Against the Grain: Famine and Ecology in the Sahel

In the early 1970s, a much-publicized famine devastated large parts of the semiarid savannas stretching from West Africa to Ethiopia, an area between 100 and 600 kilometers wide bracketed by the 100 and 600 millimeter isohyets. Covering some three million square kilometers across nine states, this thorn or scrub steppe is usually referred to as the Sahel. The countries of the Sahel (e.g., Chad, Mali, Niger, Ethiopia, Mauritania) fall into what may be called the Fourth World, the poorest of the poor. In 1972 the per capita income of Mali was less than US $100 and, by the time Malian citizens reached their mid-forties, there was a good chance that they were dead. The Sahelian states were and remain largely agro-pastoral. The peasants and pastoralists who perished during the famine, an estimated quarter of a million souls in West Africa alone (Franke and Chasin 1980), were those who also produced on the land. Already fragile economies were devastated, millions of animals died (i.e., eighty percent of all cattle and goats in Niger Republic), and historic forms of agro-pastoral production were threatened (Watts 1983). This tragedy occurred in the context of a great deal of debate on long-term secular changes in climate and ecological degradation along the desert edge. Poor rainfall, the lowest in sixty years, and expanding desert conditions had laid waste hundreds of thousands of square kilometers of the Sahel, according to the Director of the FAO. The fragility of Sahelian ecosystems was frequently seen to have been exacerbated by the willful overstocking of animals on Sahelian rangelands.

Ten years later, ironically in the aftermath of a very ambitious bilateral and multilateral foreign assistance program, the Sahel and indeed large parts of the continent faced another major food crisis. Emergency food aid to Africa in 1983–1984 amounted to 2.2 million metric tons, nearly three times the tonnage delivered to the Sahel during 1973–1974 (Watts and Bassett 1985). Once more drought and ecology reappeared as the central element in the analysis; according to Mustapha Tolba, Executive Director of the United Nations Environment Program, desertification was "accelerating [such that] millions of hectares of land are being lost every year" (Tolba 1982, p. 14).

How do we explain that those who produce food are those that starve or that billions of dollars of foreign assistance has evidently not changed the vulnerability of Sahelian states to famine? How do we explain that famine stalked a land in which

population density was quite low, in which land was widely available, and in which farm exports actually increased prior to and during the famine years?

Drought is not uncommon in the Sahel; rather, it is recursive and certainly not a climatic aberration. Accordingly, farmers and herders do not simply starve in the face of a drought; rather, they have a battery of social and technical strategies to try to mitigate its effects. Farmers have developed intercropping, and especially polyvarietal strategies (i.e., interplanting of different varieties of drought-resistant crops such as millet), as a means to enhance risk aversion in conditions in which biological survival is at stake. Farmers in northern Nigeria often exploit seasonally damp areas if rains are late or poor and simultaneously practice a series of water conservation measures. Herders diversify their herds as farmers diversify crops, and they maintain critical social relations including systems of animal loans to ensure that herds can be reconstituted; that is, they have breeding animals available for herd regeneration.

Drought is not mechanically linked to famine. Famines are no more acts of God than they are the products of nature; they can and have occurred without a decline in food availability. In other words, what matters is access to and control over food. As I discovered in northern Nigeria, throughout recent periods of famine and hardship, there was usually grain in the marketplace, but farmers did not have the means to acquire it; the problem was entitlement (Sen 1980).

A second point relates to the physical environment. In the same way that farmers are sensitive to risk, so are they knowledgeable about their environment. Farmers and herders are astute field ecologists: they experiment with crops and farming practices, and they exploit their own system of environmental knowledge. Why then would they overstock range or exploit their own farms, which is the basis of their reproduction and survival? Here a central concern is the nature of the constraints and risks that farmers and herders confront in the face of growing commercialization. Most Sahelian pastoralists are compelled to sell animals to buy grains from farmers in order to survive during the arduous dry season when forage is scarce and animal lactation rates (i.e., milk production) are low. But the volatile nature of grain prices and the fact that terms of trade can move sharply against herders has forced them to maintain larger herds to ward off the effects of future droughts or market fluctuations.

Farmers drawn into commodity production of export crops to generate cash for taxes and household needs have to change cropping strategies, often involving monocropping of export crops, with important implications for risk. Poor farmers in particular also feel the squeeze of price changes and changing terms of trade (e.g., pricing policies by governments anxious to acquire cheap commodities). In the face of limited assets, limited family labor, and few off-farm income sources, they may also have to squeeze more out of their small landholdings with deleterious ecological consequences. Environmental change may be important, though it is often exaggerated on the basis of flimsy evidence, but it occurs in quite specific places. Overstocking often results in great pressures around watering points, especially under conditions in which there is increasing privatization of communal wells and diminishing access to rangelands.

Farming and herding communities are not homogenous but are sharply differentiated in terms of wealth, access to resources, and life opportunities. When we say, therefore, that famines are not "natural," it implies that we must examine carefully the social relations of stratified farming and pastoral communities. During famines, food prices increase dramatically – by 100–200 percent in the case of Nigeria in 1973–1974 – but the effects are differentially experienced (Watts 1983). Some poor herders

have to sell most of their productive and most valued animals to purchase grain, but the livestock is frequently purchased by wealthy farmer-traders who then lease the animals back to herders. Poorer pastoralists can become effectively dispossessed. In the same way, poor and often heavily indebted peasants may have to borrow grain at usurious rates of interest or sell assets such as livestock, or even land, to withstand famine conditions. But such exchanges often occur at depressed prices because of an oversupply, and prize assets can be captured cheaply by well-to-do farmers. The transfer of livestock has, in fact, converted some pastoralists into wage workers or tenants, insofar as farmers now lease their animals back to dispossessed herders. The contracting arrangements themselves carry ecological implications, because the farmers who invest in cattle as speculative capital demand that herders limit their movements in order that animals can be sold at short notice (Little 1985). People and animals have become "boxed in," and these restricted dry season movements impose greater pressures on pastures (Livingstone 1986).

Conjunctional Explanations of Ecological Degradation

The Sahelian case is an example of degradation of common property resources (CPRs). The latter, embracing fishing rights, fuelwood tracts or communal pathways, are distinguished by individual use but not possession, by a multiplicity of users with independent rights, and by the collective regulation by users (Blaikie and Brookfield 1986). The basis of CPRs is collective regulation and the attribution of costs and benefits through indigenous institutions that are especially vulnerable in the context of expanding commodity relations. Lawrence Beck (1981), for example, traced the impact of the Shah of Iran's control of Qashqu'is pastoralists initially through CPR encroachment via land reform, large-scale irrigation development, and watershed protection.

The state disrupted principles and mechanisms of local reciprocity and dispute resolution by fixing the identity and number of households using sections of pastures, and by destroying the flexibility of local arrangements sensitive to a variety of migratory, ecological, and economic circumstances. Nigel Abel documented deteriorating CPR ranges in Ngwaketse District, Botswana between 1963 and 1982 (Abel et al. 1985). A doubling of herd size and subsidies for commercial off-take provided by the European Economic Community (EEC) eroded local communal and lineage-based reciprocities and management systems, and encouraged privatization of wells and ranges. Increased cattle reduced grass cover, increased soil erosion, and subsequently lowered biological productivity. In turn, the number and quality of fires was reduced allowing woody plants to invade and survive and to shade out high-quality grasses used for grazing. Faced with low biomass and reduced cattle productivity, local herders increased herd size to compensate for declining output. The vicious cycle of ecological impoverishment and privatization, the collapse of CPR systems, was complete.

These sorts of studies on ecological degradation confirm the great value of recognizing the interactive effects between political economy and society and the degradation of the physical environment. In their study of soil erosion in Nepal, for example, Piers Blaikie, John Cameron and Brian Seddon (1980) started with the intrinsic properties of landscape and ended with a discussion of the Nepalese state and its relations with the world economy. They showed dramatically how erosion occurs in quite specific locations and that local managers (e.g., peasants) who vary in their asset holdings are differentiated in their ability to manage ecological resources. Local use and management capacity is linked via other groups in society to the state, the market, and other avenues of surplus mobilization.

These causal chains ultimately rest at national and international termini. In such cases, however, the precise linkages – the means by which some groups may be marginalized ecologically, economically, and politically, and the manner in which some peasants may be driven to exploit their environment to compensate for their own exploitation by other forces – are highly conjunctural.

Suzanna Hecht (1985) showed how environmental degradation and deforestation in eastern Amazonia is best understood as a consequence of four broad conjunctural forces: (1) the role of land in an inflationary economy; (2) the function of livestock as a means for acquiring large and profitable land acreages; (3) the stimulating effect of opening agricultural frontiers on certain industrial sectors; and (4) the role of large government subsidies in creating speculative land markets in the Amazon. In other words, this conjuncture, one facet of the Brazilian development "miracle" in the postwar division of labor, rendered the quality of land resources of secondary consequence in the rapid conversion of forest to pastures. Land as a commodity became enormously valuable as a speculative asset, but in the process nature's capital was divested. As Hecht put it, "cautious land management becomes irrelevant and environmental degradation the inevitable result" (1985, p. 681). The "inevitability" of ecological degradation in countries such as Brazil, strapped by enormous external debt, is made yet more pressing by studies pointing to alternative, viable, sustainable farming systems that would improve the livelihood of marginal peoples (Redclift 1986).

••••

Conclusion

It is commonplace to observe that we are part of a single world, world citizens in a global system. A casual stroll through the pages of the *New York Times* reveals that South Korean workers built universities funded by Italian companies in Saudi Arabia, that Gambian peasants work on Atlantic trawlers off the Azores, that Japanese real estate interests beat out Californian developers in the battle for downtown development in Los Angeles. Yet as Erick Wolf (1982) pointed out, this arrangement holds true not only for the present but for the past. In the nineteenth century, Indian indentured laborers were shipped to South Africa, and in the seventeenth century the triangular trade created a new international division of labor. But in the postwar economic order, the world economy has become more integrated than ever. Links between MNCs, transnational banks, multilateral organizations and nation-states have been strengthened in new and complex ways. This great narrative of postwar internationalization should, however, no more confer total power to MNCs any more than it should suggest the collapse of national sovereignty or a predetermined world order shaped in the image of Western capitalism. As Thrift said, "the world economy is the outcome of a whole series of countervailing forces operating at a whole series of scales none of which makes sense without the other" (1986, p. 13).

The new empirical realities of the postwar order have analytical consequences for the way we understand problems of food, fertility, or ecology in an increasingly heterogeneous Third World. They will force us in our local studies of population, food, and resources to be less parochial, to cast our gaze beyond village boundaries to regional, state, and international forces as part of world economic order that is anything but an ordered and coherent whole! The internationalization of capital is as uneven, crisis-prone and jagged as it is messy. But as geographers, we should be especially sensitive to these characteristics and to their consequences, their conjunctural effects, on our local turf of resource use, environment, and agriculture.

REFERENCES

Abel, N. et al. 1985. *The Problems and Possibilities of Communal Land Management in Ngwaketse District*. Addis Ababa: International Livestock Centre.

Africa Economist Digest. 1984. 7 November.

Andrae, G., and Beckman, B. 1985. *The Wheat Trap*. London: Zed Press.

Beck, L. 1981. "Government policy and pastoral land use in southwest Iran." *Journal of Arid Lands* 4:253–67.

Blaikie, P., and Brookfield, H. 1986. *Land Degradation and Society*. London: Methuen.

Blaikie, P., Cameron, J., and Seddon, D. 1980. *Nepal in Crisis*. London: Oxford University Press.

Cain, M. 1983. "Fertility as an adjustment to risk." *Population and Development Review* 9: 688–702.

Franke, R., and Chasin, B. 1980. *Seeds of Famine*. Totowa, NJ: Allanheld.

Friedmann, H. 1982. "The political economy of food." In *Marxist Inquiries*, eds. M. Burawoy and T. Skocpol, pp. 639–52. Chicago: University of Chicago Press.

Harris, L. 1983. *Banking on the Fund – The IMF*. Third World Studies Case Study No. 9. Milton Keynes: The Open University Press.

Hecht, S. 1985. "Environment, development and politics: capital accumulation and the livestock sector in eastern Amazonia." *World Development* 13:663–84.

Little, P. 1985. "Absentee herd owners and part-time pastoralists." *Human Ecology* 13: 131–51.

Livingstone, I. 1986. "The common property problem and pastoralist economic behavior." *Journal of Development Studies* 23:5–20.

New York Times. 1984. 20 November.

Pillay, V. 1983. *Dimensions of World Integration*. Third World Studies Block 4. Milton Keynes: The Open University Press.

Redclift, M. 1986. "Sustainability and the market: survival strategies on the Bolivian frontier." *Journal of Development Studies* 23: 93–105.

Sen, A. 1980. *Poverty and Famines*. Oxford: Oxford University Press.

Thrift, N. 1986. "The geography of international economic disorder." In *Geography and the World Crisis*, ed. P. Dickens, pp. 12–67. London: Basil Blackwell.

Tolba, M. 1982. "Desertification." *Mazingira* 6:14–23.

Watts, M. 1983. *Silent Violence: Food, Famine and Peasantry in Northern Nigeria*. Berkeley: University of California Press.

Watts, M., and Bassett, T. 1985. "Crisis and change in African agriculture." *African Studies Review* 28:3–27.

Wolf, E. 1982. *Europe and the People Without History*. Berkeley: University of California Press.

World Bank. 1980. *Accelerated Development in Sub-Saharan Africa*. Washington, DC: International Bank for Reconstruction and Development.

Smallholder Settlement of Tropical South America: The Social Causes of Ecological Destruction

JANE L. COLLINS

Recent years have witnessed the emergence of a highly charged debate over the appropriate use of easily degradable tropical lands. As one observer has commented, tropical soils have either been represented as a "chimerical vision, liable to disappear in a puff the first time a spade is set into them, or a super-exploitation zone that can be mined constantly with little or no negative consequence" (Stouffer 1984:6). In the context of this debate, smallholder agriculture has alternately been promoted as the most efficient way to bring fragile lands into production, or has been downplayed as economically unsustainable.

Understanding of the ecological issues related to land use in the humid tropics has increased sufficiently in the past decade to allow us to move beyond such either/or propositions. Much has been learned about the variable properties of tropical soils and their relative susceptibility to deterioration. Research on cropping practices has revealed both the appropriateness and limitations of slash and burn agricultural techniques and has given rise to a growing concern for agro-forestry and other innovative cropping models that seek to work with, rather than against, the soil properties and productive characteristics of tropical environments. At the same time there has been a growing awareness that more sophisticat-

Collins. *Human Organization*, in which this article appeared in 1966 (Vol. 45, No. 1, pp. 1–10) is published by the Society for Applied Anthropology. Permission to include this article was granted by the society.

ed knowledge of a region's ecology and an increased repertoire of productive techniques do not guarantee sustained and successful resource management. Environmental deterioration cannot be understood without considering the ways in which land tenure, credit policies, titling and other institutional factors condition the resource management strategies of the producers who work the land.

The discussion that follows focuses on links between social processes and cycles of environmental decline in newly settled regions of tropical Latin America. It begins with the recognition that different land use patterns have different environmental impacts, and raises the question of how factors in the larger social environment affect these patterns. Examples from three areas are used to show how land tenure and related aspects of agrarian structure, access to capital and labor, market processes, technology, productive knowledge and a range of other variables affect the land use decisions of small producers in their new environment.

These examples reveal that unfavorable market integration, high levels of surplus extraction, and policies that engender indebtedness have double consequences. Not only do they perpetuate poverty and underdevelopment, but the strategies smallholders adopt to insure their survival under such circumstances are frequently incompatible with sustained, environmentally appropriate land use and lead to deterioration of soils and other natural resources.

Declining yields make it more difficult to meet external obligations and subsistence needs, and where competition for land is strong, may result in loss of holdings. In order to formulate adequate policies for land use and resource management in newly settled areas, the links between social and ecological dynamics must be made explicit, and social factors must be incorporated into models of ecosystem change in ways that go beyond simple descriptions of behavior and reflect a more sophisticated understanding of the contexts within which land use decisions are made.

Most recent anthropological work on peasants and small farmers has emphasized their rationality and adaptive behavior. While variability in knowledge and skills among local populations has been recognized, much attention has been given to the ways in which people alter their behavior to make best use of available social and ecological resources. Yet the destruction of tropical lands has often been attributed to the poor decisions of small producers. Colonists have been shown to pose a threat to the survival of indigenous populations (Whitten 1978; Vickers 1982). More frequently they have been accused of causing the wasteful and premature depletion of natural resources (Guppy 1984). A recent survey of development of lands in the humid tropics concludes that:

> The preference of most cultivators is to manage toward a steady state, but their trial-and-error means of adapting traditional agricultural practices in a gradually changing environment is inadequate to deal with the rapid environmental change brought about by increasing population and externally created market pressures (National Research Council 1982: 99).

Intensification of shifting cultivation, a frontier attitude toward new lands that leads to an ongoing pattern of exploitation and abandonment of fields, and failure to consider the long-term effects of cultivation practices are all problems that have been attributed to small farm colonists in new settlement areas.

In the following sections, explanations for what would seem to be poor and self-destructive management practices by small producers are sought in case studies of colonization areas where environmental degradation is occurring. The mechanisms of social and ecological change will be identified in published accounts of colonization efforts along the Brazilian Transamazon Highway, in northeastern Ecuador, and in research conducted by the author in a Peruvian valley on the eastern slopes of the Andes. In extracting these cases from their original presentations much detail is omitted and the full context of events cannot be conveyed. Growing numbers of well-documented local studies pose a challenge, however, to social scientists who wish to bring them to bear on policy decisions or social action. In comparing such studies, one can determine whether there are patterns in the interaction of variables in different cases. It becomes possible to ask whether the processes of environmental degradation, that almost without exception have accompanied the settlement of new regions, must be explained on the basis of idiosyncrasies of climate and culture, or whether significant patterns of interaction between the social context, producer decisions and environmental deterioration can be identified.

Social and Ecological Cycles in the Brazilian Amazon

The Brazilian Transamazon Highway, built in the 1970s, was one of the largest and most ambitious attempts ever made to open tropical lands to a variety of uses. It was widely viewed as a test of the proposition that the humid tropics of South America were a frontier for agriculture. In its initial stages it was also a test of a small farm model of colonization. Beginning in 1970, the Brazilian government provided support for homesteading programs directed toward small-to-medium-sized farmers. After four years, however, it reversed it s policy – proclaiming the failure of the small farm model and shifting its support to large-scale developers.

The successes and failures of the Transamazon colonization program have been the subject of an extensive literature contributed by scholars from a wide range of disciplines. Some have argued that the problems encountered are evidence that the skills and knowledge necessary to effectively exploit the Amazon are not yet available, with the implication that further attempts at agricultural development in the region should be halted until such knowledge is acquired (Goodland 1980). Detailed studies have revealed, however, that failure was related to the inadequacy of knowledge far less frequently than to the fact that the knowledge possessed was not implemented in particular settings.

Moran (1981) has provided a detailed analysis of the experiences of colonists along the Transamazon Highway. His research was conducted during the initial stages of the colonization in Altamira – a *municipio*, or county, of the state of Para. Moran suggests that the Brazilian government may have been premature in its declaration that small farm colonization was a failure. While he describes the difficulties encountered by many colonists, his analysis reveals that nearly 40% of the population he studied was able to achieve "respectable levels" of income and productivity during their first few years of residence in the zone (1981:224).

The soils in the region Moran studied did not conform to the popular image of the Amazon as characterized by easily degradable "laterite." While considerable variety existed within the region, there were significant areas of alfisols or *terra roxa*, which were high in nutrients, neutral in pH, and which possessed an excellent structure. Moran found that most of the problems that colonists encountered were related not to poor resources or an inability to sustain yields, but to their own poor management practices and an inattentiveness on the part of government agencies and other institutions to the local realities of the colonization context.

Moran gives numerous examples of these problems. Extension workers sent to the regions were frequently inexperienced, had little knowledge of the demands of local production, and could not seem to work effectively with individuals they perceived as being of lower social status. The bureaucracies of the Colonization Institute (INCRA – Instituto Nacional de Colonizacao e Reforma Agraria), the banks and other institutions were inflexible. This meant that it was frequently impossible to obtain inputs at the time they were required, or to acquire credit, tools, seed or extension services.

Moran (1981), Smith (1982), and Wood and Schmink (1979) all emphasize the failure of government agencies to provide services they had promised settlers as a factor affecting colonist performance in the initial colonization period. Jobs, food subsidies, housing and educational and health services never materialized in some cases, and were late or inadequate in others. These problems only exacerbated the difficulties of undertaking production in a new environment.

In discussing adaptation to the zone, Moran emphasizes the value of the knowledge of the *caboclos*, or Amazonian peasants, in suggesting effective patterns of resource use for the region (Moran 1974). The *caboclos* were particularly adept at recognizing the best soils of the area on the basis of the type of vegetation they supported, but they also possessed a wealth of knowledge about the exploitation of local game and wild products, the cultivation of native food crops, and medicinal practices. Smith (1982), whose work in the zone is contemporaneous and includes additional data from a later period, has questioned whether these skills were fully transferable to the demands of a cash-cropping, market-oriented agricultural system. He found that over time the incomes of *caboclos* declined relative to the income of migrants from other regions, a fact that he feels may have been related to their lack of management skills and their subsistence orientation.

Failure may also have been linked to the ways in which the exercise of the productive knowledge of the *caboclos* was constrained by credit and marketing policies. In particular, the maintenance of a diversified production system was made difficult by the active promotion of rice cultivation by government agencies and banks. Credit was not provided for traditional crops such as manioc, despite their high value on the local market. High costs of fertilizer for cacao and of transport for bananas made these crops somewhat risky. Knowledge of appropriate crops and diversified cropping strategies were effectively undermined by the sets of constraints and incentives provided by institutions associated with colonization.

Moran makes it clear that colonists did not enter the region with equivalent skills, experience and capital. He divided the colonist population of the initial colonization period into two groups: brokers and clients. Brokers were entrepreneurs or independent farmers who were able to generate their own capital and to reinvest in their enterprises. Clients depended on brokers for their access to cash and produced mainly for subsistence rather than reinvestment. Clients were subdivided by Moran into laborers and artisans depending on their antecedent economic activities.

This social differentiation was in part imported to the Amazon along with the migrants themselves. Brokers frequently possessed management experience and small but significant savings upon their arrival, while clients did not. Nevertheless, a system of patronage and class distinction quickly took root in the colonization con-text. Brokers emerged as market intermediaries and transporters; they moved into cattle ranching; they supplemented household labor resources with hired hands. Clients worked off-farm as well, but in wage labor, and became increasingly dependent on brokers and in many cases abandoned or sold their lands. The 40% of colonists Moran identified as successful were in the broker category. Even in the early period of the colonization covered by this study, the region appears to have been characterized by social groups standing in diverse relationships to productive resources and with differing capacities for capital accumulation.

Schmink (1982), Wood and Schmink (1979), Smith (1982) and Tendler (1980) all indicate that inequalities increased after the government's shift to an emphasis on larger enterprises in 1974. The indebtedness of farmers was exacerbated. Smith (1982) indicated that colonists in the late 1970s were often making payments on as many as four loans at the same time: they owed INCRA for their lots and frequently for the homes and the initial six-month start-up loans, the Banco do Brasil for short-term loans for rice cultivation and long-term loans for power saws, pumps, barbed wire, livestock and perennial crops. Those who could not earn enough to repay their loans and meet subsistence needs sold their plots to other colonists and left the region, or became hired workers on the lands of others. Land conflicts also became more prevalent. Violence increased in regions where large cattle ranchers began to establish claims (Schmink 1982; Foweraker 1981; Souza Martins 1980).

How was this process of social differentiation and land consolidation related to ecological occurrences? A partial answer is provided by Wood and Schmink's (1979) discussion of one particular type of land conflict that emerged in the colonization zone. In the years after 1974, numerous claims of "predatory burning" were brought against small producers by large landowners. These claims were based on the fact that official colonists were allotted 100 hectare plots by the government, on the condition that 50% of the land remain in forest reserve. This allowance was meant to include sufficient land for rotation and fallowing. When more than the prescribed amount of land was brought under cultivation, claims of predatory burning or predatory occupation could be brought against the landholder. Wood and Schmink note that there is little evidence that official colonists overstepped limits on clearing and suggest that this practice may have been more of a problem among spontaneous migrants who cleared land outside the officially allocated colonization areas. In any event, when proven, these claims usually resulted in a heavy fine being levied against the offender. If this could not be paid, the family had no alternative but to abandon their plot.

Clearly these claims were used by large farmers as a means of expanding their holdings. They provide an insight into colonist response to indebtedness, however, that might otherwise escape our attention. The pattern that emerges appears to be of more than local significance, since claims that small farmers clear too much of their land have also been used in this manner by ranchers in Bolivian colonization zones as well (Riviere d'Arc 1980).

Hecht (1981) provides information that helps to explain why the overexploitation of land by small producers may be an easy target for large landowners seeking to expand their holdings. In an article describing the impact of deforestation on Amazonian soils she makes the following point:

> Although small farmers could cultivate in a manner to reduce the environmental impact of agriculture (and possibly their own economic vulnerability), most titling and agricultural credit is linked to rice production. Rice yield declines without fertilizers are almost inevitable given current production technologies in the Amazon. The small holders

with few assets are usually highly leveraged either to official organs or informal money lenders. ... Given decreasing yields, the small colonist must often relinquish his land to richer, medium-sized farmers, *grileiros* (land grabbers), or ranchers when loans fall due, titles are contested or power clashes occur (1981:79).

Hecht notes that while the immediate causes of failure for the small farmer are soil nutrient changes and weed invasion, these phenomena are linked to credit policies that encourage rice production. The jeopardy in which they find themselves when yields begin to decline is a product of intensifying competition over land in the region. Ecological deterioration and land loss is not an inevitable feature of the ecology of the region, but is tied to institutional constraints and land economics.

The claims of predatory burning launched against small producers become easier to comprehend in the context of the ecological and economic pressures just described. Smallholders responded to indebtedness and the declining yields associated with a heavy emphasis on rice by intensification or expansion of their productive strategies. By shortening the fallow period, depleting forest reserves, or moving toward monoculture, families barter the short-term against the long. Predatory burning, to the extent that it existed and was not a fabrication of land-hungry enterprises, reflected this trade-off. Whether land was lost immediately, through legal proceedings in which small farmers could not effectively defend themselves, or came slowly through abandonment or foreclosure in the face of declining yields, the impact was the same. The social and ecological results, like the social and ecological causes, were intertwined.

The literature on agricultural intensification suggests that farmers will not intensify in the face of declining returns to labor unless faced with external pressures. Population growth and declining yields are processes that can induce such intensification. All evidence indicates that in the absence of significant inputs, yield declines are inevitable with the annual monocultivation of rice. In emphasizing this practice, the Colonization Institute virtually guaranteed that colonists would face this dilemma. The existence of heavy liens on production is an additional source of pressure that forces the smallholder to take some action. New land may be cleared to insure a good harvest undiminished by lowered soil fertility and weeds. There is no evidence that colonists intensified or expanded land area cultivated as a basis for accumulation. As Moran points out, most successful colonists accumulated on the basis of cattle or transport. It appears that in many cases smallholders engaged in environmentally destructive activities as a last resort in order to meet their obligations and to hold on to their lands.

Recent literature has reflected an increasing optimism about the potential role of agriculture in some parts of the Amazon basin. Moran, Smith and others make it clear that the ecological barriers once thought to preclude production in the region are not absolute. Low productivity and ecological deterioration along the Transamazon Highway are not so much the results of the exploitation of ecosystems that should not be used, but of the creation of incentives for improper use of land in an environment of strong competition. As Durham (1979) has pointed out for Central America, events that are profoundly tied to social structure – the accumulation or resources by one class at the expense of another – may be attributed to ecological causes. As the "soccer war" between El Salvador and Honduras was attributed to overpopulation, the failure of smallholding colonists in the Amazon has been called the inevitable result of exploitation of tropical soils. Closer analysis reveals that it was not inevitable, but a result of the interaction of social and ecological processes (a schematic version of these processes is presented in Figure 1). Whether this is an isolated case of resource mismanagement or one that has broader implications requires the analysis of other settings.

Credit, Titles and Social Differentiation in Northeastern Ecuador

Hiraoka and Yamamoto (1980) have described spontaneous and planned colonization schemes in northeastern Ecuador. They have focused on the area around Lago Agrio opened to colonization largely as a result of road building and a demand for labor resulting from petroleum exploitation activities. In the early 1970s approximately 10,000 workers were brought in the region to work on a variety of projects related to the oil boom. After the projects were completed, some 5 to 10% of the individuals chose to remain as farmers. At the same time the Ecuadorian Agrarian Reform Institute (IERAC – Instituto Ecuatoriano de Reforma Agraria y Colonizacion) began recruiting and transporting settlers to the region. While this planned resettlement was short-lived, the opening of roads attracted spontaneous migrants. At the time of the study conducted by Hiraoka and Yamamoto (1975–1978) some 37,500 people had settled in the zone.

Two farming systems competed for land in the region. A form of slash-mulch polyculture was practiced by most small farmers. Because there is no distinct dry season in this part of the Ecuadorian lowlands, felled vegetation is not burned, but allowed to remain as mulch for cultivated plants. Times for clearing and planting are not climatically determined and may be spread throughout the year. Annual crops (rice, maize and sweet potatoes) are intercropped with semi-perennials (*papa china*, plantains, bananas and yucca) and perennials such as coffee, cacao and citrus. Soil cover and shade are maintained in a way that is ecologically beneficial. Hiraoka and Yamamoto report that plots managed under such a system provide sustained yields for 10–15 years. The techniques of slash-mulch poly-

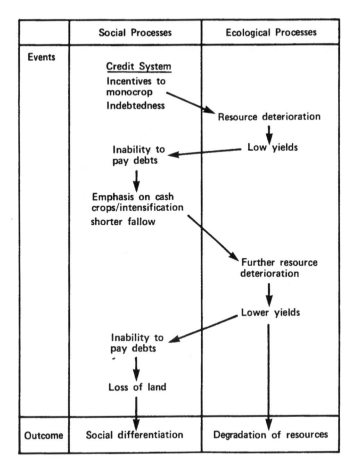

Figure 1: Social and Ecological Cycles in Brazil

culture represent an amalgam of the previous farming practices of migrants and of local practices.

The second major farming system in the region is cattle ranching. While most pastureland is controlled by large holders, Hiraoka and Yamamoto emphasize that ranching is an activity to which all colonists aspire. The climate of the region is favorable for year-round feeding, making it popular as a beef-fattening area. The advantages presented by cattle (their limited labor requirement, high value, relative lack of problems with overproduction, storage or

transport, and their relative price stability) create strong pressures for their production. There are no studies that indicate what the long-term impact of conversion to pasture will be on the soils of this area. Several pasture diseases have presented problems in recent years, and siltation of rivers has been cited as a major negative impact of pasture formation (Hiraoka and Yamamoto 1980).

As in the Brazilian case, however, Hiraoka and Yamamoto found that institutional rather then ecological factors posed the most immediate challenges to small producers. The costs of obtaining a plot were high, and included mandatory membership in an agricultural cooperative, and the surveying, mapping and registration of land, in addition to the cost of the land itself. While this amount could be amortized over as long as 25 years, settlers could not receive permanent title until the amount was paid in full. Without permanent title they could not obtain credit. Legal transfer was also impossible with provisional title so that those farmers forced to sell their lots before their debts were paid in full could only obtain a fraction of its real value.

All of these factors acted to impede capital accumulation among smallholders. Some impatient settlers converted their polycultural plots to pasture before they had amasses the capital to begin ranching. These partially formed grasslands were quickly absorbed by speculators, and those who were forced to dispose of their lots either left for urban centers, moved forward on the settlement frontier, or became part-time laborers for the ranchers, maintaining a small part of the former lot for subsistence purposes. Other colonists lost or abandoned their lands due to inability to make installment payments, inability to cover subsistence needs, or due to a drain on household labor resources as they found it necessary to seek alternate employment.

Hiraoka and Yamamoto identified three types of landowners in the period 1975–1978. Wealthy absentee owners held properties for appreciation and sale, bringing into production with hired labor only as much land as the law required. Landless farmers who had abandoned their plots for reasons beyond their control worked on the lands of others. A third group of small-to-medium-sized farmers had survived initial indebtedness and had established a foothold through cultivation or ranching. This third group faced pressures to expand their holdings to accommodate cattle, and significant land concentration was occurring on the part of larger ranching units at the expense of their smaller neighbors.

As in Brazil, the factors related to colonist loss of land in northeastern Ecuador were both social and ecological. The initial debts of colonists made short-term profits desirable, yet credit to improve perennial production or to invest in ranching was unavailable until permanent title was obtained. Frustrated colonists made first efforts at pasture formation or intensified production of perennials to meet their short-term needs. With land taken out of production or worked too intensively, yields dropped sharply. Worse off than before, colonists were often forced to sell their lands. Hiraoka and Yamamoto argue that left unchecked, this process will eventually lead to the recreation of the latifundia-minifundia pattern found in the Ecuadorian highlands (1980:444).

While it is true that the processes of accumulation in the Oriente are linked to class structure in Ecuador as a whole and the interests of national and international capital, a parallel with the processes that have generated inequality in the highlands cannot be too hastily drawn. First, the class interests involved in the colonization zone are quite different from those of the highland agrarian elite and must be interpreted in terms of the international flow of capital rather than simply as an extension of the power of the remnants of the highland oligarchy. Second, the ecological setting of the colonization zone alters the dynamics of social and economic change. The creation of minifundia and latifundia results from structural disincentives to sustained polyculture in a region where cattle ranching has increased competition for land, and from the rapid destruction of land resources that results when small producers attempt to overcome those disincentives by producing for short-term gain (see Figure 2). Socially created conditions of indebtedness and economic insecurity drive cycles of environmental decline, which in turn accelerate loss of land and social differentiation among settlers.

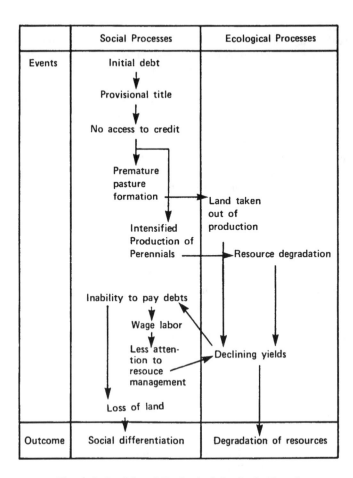

	Social Processes	Ecological Processes
Events	Initial debt ↓ Provisional title ↓ No access to credit ↓ Premature pasture formation ↓ Intensified Production of Perennials	Land taken out of production Resource degradation
	Inability to pay debts ↓ Wage labor ↓ Less attention to resouce management ↓ Loss of land	Declining yields
Outcome	Social differentiation	Degradation of resources

Figure 2: Social and Ecological Cycles in Ecuador

Seasonal Migration and Labor Constraints in Peru

The final example to be considered here is that of the Tambopata Valley of southern Peru. Lying in the lush rain shadow on the eastern slopes of the Andes, the valley has been the site of coffee cultivation by seasonal migrants from highland zones since the 1940s. Extremely steep slopes (rarely less than 40 degrees) make the region susceptible to erosion, and environmental degradation in the more accessible upper parts of the valley is already severe.

In addition to being ecologically fragile, the zone is also one of the most isolated coffee zones in Peru. A road did not reach the main settlement area until the early 1970s and the plots of many producers still lie several days beyond its reach. While national and international funds helped build a school and health center in the 1950s, lack of infrastructure is still a major impediment to economic activity in the region.

The case of coffee production in Tambopata challenges the traditional assumption of development theorists that labor is the most abundant resource for small producers in developing nations and the derived proposition that the opportunity cost of labor for colonists in new and fragile land areas is low. This proposition assumes that farmers are able to fully meet their needs with on-farm production, an assumption that no longer characterizes the majority of Latin American small farm producers. Thiesenheusen (1984) notes that semiproletarianization is the most important phenomenon affecting rural Latin American households over the past decade. Deere and Wasserstrom (1980) have argued that small farm resource management cannot be understood without taking into account that 50–75% of small farm income in Latin America is obtained off-farm. Posner and McPherson (1982) suggest that the need for alternate employment among members of small farm families reduces the labor available for investment in soil conservation and in productivity-improving technology.

Farmers producing coffee in the Tambopata Valley face a variety of production and marketing constraints, including a lack of access to credit and to inputs such as fertilizers and pesticides, poor transport, insecure titles, and a government-backed monopoly on the purchase of coffee. As a result of these constraints, it has not been possible for a family to obtain a sufficient return from coffee production to meet their year-round consumption requirements. The vast majority of coffee producers retain highland subsistence plots in order to make ends meet and to provide a measure of security against crop loss, price drops or loss of title. The need to maintain highland production has prevented permanent colonization of the valley, resulting instead in a prolonged pattern of seasonal migration that has lasted three generations.

Continued participation in both coffee production and highland subsistence agriculture places heavy demands on the labor resources of migrant families. Little or no wage labor is employed and these demands are met primarily by careful scheduling of productive activities, separation of family members into two "work-teams" for part of the year, and reliance on traditional highland mechanisms of labor exchange. Because labor is in short supply, little is available to be expended on the management of fragile valley soils.

Land is brought into production through slashing vegetation in June or July and burning it when it is dry – in August or September. Previously propagated, unimproved seedlings are set out in January or February and replanted about three meters apart in March. The coffee plot is weeded heavily in September and again in November or January. Weeding is performed more intensively than is advisable from the point of view of soil conservation, but this is felt necessary in order to get by with one or two weedings per year, thus minimizing labor inputs during the highland growing season.

Approximately three to four years after planting, the coffee trees produce their first cherries and they are usually in full production by the fifth year. Migrants report that by 10–15 years, yields have begun to decline markedly, and that after 20 years or so the plots must be abandoned. No fertilizers are used, nor are any significant efforts made to check soil loss by erosion. Despite the fact that land is not freely available and that new plots can only be opened in the lower part of the valley – a two to three day walk beyond the reach of the road – practices that could potentially extend the productive life of the trees are not implemented.

The median size of landholdings in the region is approximately two hectares. The smallest plots consist of less than a single hectare and the largest may reach 10–20 (Instituto Nacional de Planificacion 1980). Yields average 600 kg/ha, though new trees at the peak of production may produce up to 900 kg/ha and may drop to 300 kg/ha or less by 20 years. Based on 1980 coffee prices, a producer could expect net revenues of about $385 per 600 kg of coffee (Painter 1984). This income, with few exceptions, goes toward the consumption requirements of the migrant's family or is reinvested in subsistence production in the highlands.

Despite the degree of slope on which production is occurring in the valley, the potential for effective sustained-yield management exists. Coffee production in many parts of El Salvador and the Dominican Republic is sustained on lands equally precipitous. Permanent residence in the valley would permit intercropping and reduce heavy weeding, thus promoting the maintenance of soil cover, while current seasonal exploitation emphasizes heavy weeding. Introduction of crops such as plantains would improve the *Arabica* coffee by providing shade and would further reduce erosion. The farmers who grow coffee in the valley carefully manage their soil resources in the highlands, maintaining terraces and drainage systems, rotating and interplanting crops and using animal manure according to well-defined indigenous agricultural premises. The existence of archaeological remains of terraces in the Tambopata drainage system suggest that prehispanic civilizations applied many of the same principles to valley lands, and Peruvian agronomists and social scientists are currently involved in a number of projects to reconstruct such traditional land use practices. Introduction of more intensive practices is not possible as long as producers face heavy alternative demands on their labor, however. This in turn is unlikely to change until coffee production, or cropping systems that incorporate coffee production, become capable of producing income sufficient to make it possible for families to reside permanently in the valley (see Figure 3).

The failure to effectively manage fragile land resources due to alternative demands placed on labor is not unique to the Tambopata Valley. Participation in off-farm labor was listed as a factor in colonist loss of land by Hiraoka and Yamamoto. In any environment where off-farm employment is combined with mixed cropping systems and small-scale animal husbandry, excessive demands on labor may result. The impact of reduced investments in resource management will be felt in any context over time, but is likely to be more rapid and severe on tropical soils and steep lands where colonists do not have long experience in production.

The search for off-farm employment is directly related to the insufficiency of income that can be generated form the producers' holdings, a situation that may be the result of unfavorable price structures and commercialization systems as well as of the small or declining size of landholdings. Seasonal or temporary wage labor is also a frequent response to declining yields. As with the cycles of indebtedness, such a response sets up a positive feedback cycle with yields declining further due to reduced labor inputs. This link between lack of resources and poor management has been identified as a major cause of hill land destruction by Posner and McPherson (1982:347):

> Farmers who are less poor have less need to "mine" their farm land by emphasizing present consumption over future consumption. Second, being less poor, farmers will also have more resources, including labor time, to adopt soil conservation practices and invest in productivity-improving technology ... .

The initial poverty of small producers in settlement areas is an impediment to sound resource management, and government policies exacerbate this problem when they constrain small-scale accumulation and reinvestment by extracting surplus, or allowing it to be channelled to market intermediaries, and by reinforcing the differential access of large and small producers to credit and inputs. The semiproletarianization that increasingly affects small producers in Latin America challenges their ability to use traditional strategies for the

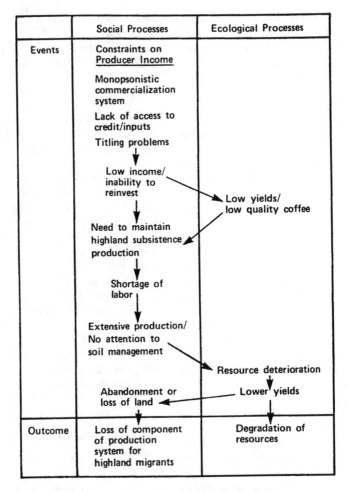

Figure 3: Social and Ecological Cycles in Peru

management of land and water resources (many of which require inter-familial cooperation). The demands that this process places on labor also reduce the time that producers have available to experiment with and adopt new practices.

Conclusions

Recent years have seen an increasing interest on the part of development agencies in the promotion of viable small farm sectors in developing nations. Governments throughout Latin America have promoted or permitted the colonization of new and easily degradable land areas by small producers. Yet as small farmers fail in these areas, losing their lands to larger interests or abandoning them in the face of declining yields, important questions are raised about the viability of small farm colonization of tropical lands.

Case studies of colonization areas reveal a consistency in the dynamics of such failure. It is tied to the kinds of constraints and incentives faced by small farmers – structural factors such as credit, titling, and commercialization networks that work against sustained-yield production systems. Small-scale accumulation for reinvestment is hindered by the inavailability of credit and technical inputs for such systems, or by marketing networks unfavorable to producers. Where they exist, credit policies discourage experimentation by focusing on crops such as rice in the Brazilian Amazon, and difficulties in obtaining title discourage investments. Further, once larger, more capital-intensive enterprises such as ranching enter a region, the most lucrative of mixed cropping systems find themselves at a relative disadvantage in terms of access to resources.

Faced with these constraints and incentives, producers are forced to orient production toward short-term gain. Whether farmers shift toward monocropping in order to benefit from credit and technical assistance available for certain crops, intensify production to repay credit obligations or expenses associated with claiming land, or fail to use appropriate management practices because insufficient revenues force them to work off-farm, the impacts are similar. Shortened fallows and monocropping on the one hand, or failure to use appropriate technologies and practices on the other, lead to soil erosion and deterioration, declining yields, increased economic pressures and almost inevitably, loss of land. Those who escape this cycle do so, not because they are necessarily better managers or make more appropriate choices, but primarily because they find ways to move into cattle ranching, marketing, or service activities. They must, in other words, "get big ... or get out" (Hecht 1981:82).

Development programs that seek to promote a viable small farm sector in colonization zones of the humid tropics must seek to alter the incentives provided to small producers and the constraints placed on small-scale accumulation and reinvestment in such enterprises. They must recognize that labor is not unlimited and that its

opportunity cost may not be low. Research is required that will provide an improved understanding of the ways in which credit, titling and factor and commodity markets affect the behavior of small producers in a variety of settings. Such insights can then be incorporated into models of the social and environmental cycles that characterize colonization of tropical lands and into policies designed to promote sustainable production, in keeping with environmental realities and the overall goals of agrarian policy.

It has been argued that in some contexts national and international development policies have created impediments to accumulation by small producers, perpetuating labor-intensive simple commodity production. Colonization zones are one context where such a strategy presents advantages to dominant classes since new lands can be opened by the intensive labor of peasants and then turned over to larger economic interests (Foweraker 1981; Wood 1983; Schmink 1982). In some instances the latter process has become institutionalized, as in the case of *troca pela forma* – the exchange agreement whereby a peasant family possesses land while hand-clearing and converting it to pasture for the rancher-owner in Brazil (Wood 1983). Where smallholder production is used as a lever for subsequent or simultaneous development of large farm enterprises, the failure of the small farm model as a viable option is predetermined. Questions about land use and ecology are tied to these kinds of policies and practices and the larger political economic context, and cannot be answered without reference to the differential interests of groups vying for land or without consideration of who benefits and who suffers as a result of the changes that occur.

Recognition of the links between structural incentives to produce for short-term gain, deterioration of resources, and loss of land by smallholders challenges the simple answers frequently provided to the question of how new tropical lands can best be brought into production. Assertions that these lands are simply unsuitable for agriculture, or that they require the superior management skills and capital resources of larger enterprises, are no longer tenable. Where a political commitment exists to support small farm production, and where available knowledge is relied upon to create incentives for sustainable resource management, small farm colonization should be able to succeed. Such a commitment, however, often comes at the expense of short-term economic benefits accruing to politically powerful interests. Perhaps for these reasons Latin America has not yet provided examples of such a strategy.

REFERENCES

Deere, Carmen Diana, and Robert Wasserstrom 1980. "Household Income and Off-Farm Employment Among Smallholders in Latin America and the Caribbean." Paper presented at the Seminario Internacional sobre la Produccion Agropecuaria y Forestal en Zonas de Ladera in America Latina, 1–5 December, Turrialba, Costa Rica.

Durham, William 1979. Scarcity and Survival in Central America: The Ecological Origins of the Soccer War. Stanford, CA: Stanford University Press.

Foweraker, Joe 1981. The Struggle for Land: A Political Economy of Pioneer Frontier in Brazil from 1930 to the Present. New York: Cambridge University Press.

Goodland, Robert 1980. "Environmental Ranking of Amazonian Development Projects in Brazil." Environmental Conservation 7 (1):9–26.

Guppy, Nicholas 1984. "Tropical Deforestation: A Global View." Foreign Affairs 62(4): 928–965.

Hecht, Susan 1981. "Deforestation in the Amazon Basin: Magnitude, Dynamics and Soil Resource Effects." Studies in Third World Societies 13:61–100.

Hiraoka, M., and S. Yamamoto 1980. "Agricultural Development in the Upper Amazon of Ecuador." Geographic Review 70:423–445.

Instituto Nacional de Planificacion (INP) 1980. Migraciones y Colonizacion en Puno. Puno, Peru (mimeo).

Moran, Emilio 1974. "The Adaptive System of the Amazonian Caboclo." In Man in the Amazon. C. Wagley, ed. Pp. 136–159. Gainesville: University of Florida Press.
_____ 1981. Developing the Amazon. Bloomington: University of Indiana Press.

National Research Council, Committee on Selected Biological Problems in the Humid Tropics 1982. Ecological Aspects of Development in the Humid Tropics. Washington, DC: National Academy Press.

Painter, Micheal 1984. "Changing Relations of Production and Rural Underdevelopment." Journal of Anthropological Research 40:271–292.

Posner, Joshua, and M. McPherson 1982. "Agriculture on the Steep Slopes of Tropical America." World Development 10:341–353.

Riviere d'Arc, Helene 1980. "Public and Private Policies in Santa Cruz, Bolivia." In Land, People and Planning in Contemporary Amazonia. F. Barbira-Scazzocchio, ed. Pp. 154–161. Cambridge, England: Center for Latin American Studies Occasional Publication No. 3.

Smith, Nigel 1982. Rainforest Corridor. Berkeley: University of California Press.

Souza Martins, Jose de 1980. "Fighting for Land: Indians and Posseiros in Legal Amazonia." In Land, People and Planning in Contemporary Amazonia. F. Barbira-Scazzocchio, ed. Pp. 95–105. Cambridge, England: Center for Latin American Studies Occasional Publication No. 3.

Stouffer, John 1984. Cattle, Coffee, Cocoa and Development in the Amazon. Unpublished manuscript, Department of Anthropology, State University of New York at Binghamton.

Tendler, Judith 1980. Shifting Agriculture, Land Grabbing and Peasant Organization on Brazilian Northeastern Frontier. Unpublished manuscript, Department of Agricultural Economics, University of California at Berkeley.

Thiesenheusen, William 1984. "The Illusory Goal of Equity in Latin American Agrarian Reforms." Paper presented to Land Tenure/Common Themes Workshop, USAID/University of Wisconsin Land Tenure Center, April 23–26, Annapolis, Maryland.

Vickers, William T. 1982. "Development and Amazonian Indians: The Aguarico Case and Some General Principles." In *The Dilemma of Amazonian Development*. E. Moran, ed. Pp. 25–50. Boulder, CO: Westview.

Whitten, Norman 1978. *Amazonian Ecuador: An Ethnic Interface*. In *Ecological, Social and Ideological Perspectives*. Copenhagen: International Work Group for Indigenous Affairs Document No. 34.

Wood, Charles 1983. "Peasant and Capitalist Production in the Brazilian Amazon: A Conceptual Framework for the Study of Frontier Expansion." In *The Dilemma of Amazonian Development*. E. Moran, ed. Pp. 259–278. Boulder, CO: Westview.

Wood, Charles, and Marianne Schmink 1979. "Blaming the Victim: Small Farmer Production in the Amazon Colonization Project." *Studies in Third World Societies* 7:77–93.

Managing Urban/Industrial Wood Fuel Supply and Demand in Africa

GUNTER SCHRAMM

Introduction

As can be seen from Table 1, use of biomass fuels, mainly fuelwood or derived charcoal and, to a lesser extent, crop residues and dung, account for between forty to over ninety percent of total energy consumption in the various countries of Sub-Sahara Africa. Rapid population growth, leading to accelerating land clearing for agricultural purposes as well as increasing woodfuel consumption, is resulting in drastic reductions of forest cover, with subsequent deleterious effects on the environment through increased run-off, erosion, siltation and flood damage. Increasing scarcity of wood supplies, particularly in and around areas of concentrated consumption such as cities and agro-industries (e.g., tobacco curing, tea drying), have led in many regions to sharply increasing real prices, as well as actual physical shortages. In most of them, substitutes such as petroleum fuels, coal, natural gas or electricity are not readily available, either because of a pervasive lack of foreign exchange needed to pay for additional imports, lack of the required supply infrasturcture, of suitable appliances for their use, or simply because of their costs relative to those of the more customary fuels.

The major driving force of increasing urban fuel demands is population growth. In 1960, the urban population accounted for 11 percent of the total; by 1980, this

Schramm. *The Annals of Regional Science*, published by Western Washington University, granted permission to use this article from Vol. 21, No. 1, 1986, pp. 60–77 of the Annals.

percentage had grown to 21 percent, an average annual growth rate of 5.9 percent. Projections for the year 2000 call for an urban share of 37 percent, or 234 million out of 639 million people (World Bank, 1981). Clearly, the pressures on spatially limited wood resources is immense, and without appropriate, long-term strategies that must be adopted now, resource exhaustion on a regional basis may well become the rule, rather than the exception.

Outside of the limited areas protected as national parks or forest reserves, uncontrolled exploitation of remaining forest resources is the rule, rather than the exception in almost all countries. Most of their governments have neither reliable data of, or control over this sector, nor do they collect significant revenues form it. This is in spite of the fact that urban/industrial firewood and charcoal sales represent a multi-million dollar business that employs tens of thousands of people. A major reason for the uncontrolled exploitation of the forest cover is the fact that the economic value of the standing stock of wood cannot be easily recovered from those that cut it down. In the majority of these countries, neither the land on which the wood is standing nor the wood itself belongs to those who cut it. Therefore, there is no incentive for long-term management that would lead to sustainable production of wood, nor is there for the maximization of yields. This is often due to the fact that the cutting itself as well as the related charcoal making is illegal, even though policing of these illegal activities is practically non-existent. There is no incentive for replenishing the dwindling supplies of wood through private efforts at replanting, because prevailing market prices reflect only the costs of production from standing stocks, but not the additional high costs of replacement.

There are several reasons why market prices do not reflect the growing scarcity. The first is related to the stock-flow problem. While in the past in most regions with little or no net population growth it probably was true that wood extraction was roughly balanced by regrowth within economic hauling distance to centers of demand, this is no longer true. When cutting starts to exceed regrowth, stocks necessarily must decline. However, with ratios of standing stocks to net incremental growth in the neighborhood of forty to seventy, this decline is slow and imperceptible at first. Catastrophe is approached incrementally, much like a malignant cancer that may take decades to develop, but then ravages its victim within weeks or months. Second, the competitive nature of the commercial firewood/charcoal business, combined with the common property nature of the resource base, assures that prices are kept low, reflecting only cutting, production and distribution costs until the local resource base essentially has disappeared. Third, in many countries the major sources of current charcoal supplies are agricultural land clearing operations, whose wood supplies are a waste product that would have to be burnt otherwise. In Kenya for example, it is estimated that land clearing accounts for some 80 percent of current urban charcoal supplies (UNDP/World Bank Energy Sector Management Assistance Program, 1981).

But while this wood has no alternative value, it represents a non-renewable resource. When land clearing operations come to an end, as ultimately they must when land with suitable soils for agriculture runs out, supplies will dry up practically overnight, shortages will occur and prices will rise drastically. Such price increases, in turn, would induce sharply increased poaching from remaining wood resources in protected, environmentally fragile areas (such as forest belts protecting important watersheds). It would also result in the overcutting of standing private tree stocks and single trees, leading to increased wind and water erosion.

The Rationale for the Continued Use of Woodfuels

With growing woodfuel scarcity, and the resulting environmental damages, the question is often asked why these countries do not follow the example of the rest of the world and convert rapidly to the use of so-called commercial energy sources instead, i.e., petroleum fuels, natural gas, coal or electricity. The answer to this question is quite complex. It has both macro and micro-economic dimensions.

First, it must be realized that few of the Sub-Saharan countries own readily usable domestic resources of these "commercial" fuels. Only a few have domestic crude oil resources (Angola, Cameroon, Congo P. R., Gabon, Nigeria, Zaire), and some of them have to export the crude and import all of their domestic requirements because of a lack of suitable refinery capacity. Even oil-rich Nigeria is a significant importer of certain types of petroleum products, because it cannot afford the high cost of developing a local refining industry capable of supplying all of its domestic product demands (UNDF/World Bank, 1983).

A few have coal (e.g., Botswana, Zimbabwe, Zambia, Tanzania, Swaziland, Mozambique), but deposits often are remote from centers of demand (e.g., Tanzania), and the costs of appliances for their use are far too high for households, given the low prevailing income levels. This is true for commercial uses as well. Tobacco curing, for example, is a prodigious consumer of woodfuels. But to replace wood with coal (as has been done in Zimbabwe when woodfuels became scarce) requires far

Table 1: Total Energy Consumption by Source of Fuel

Country	Urbanization % of population in urban areas (1980)	Fuelwood (%)	Charcoal (%)	Other Traditional Fuels 1/ (%)	Electricity (%)	Petroleum (%)	Natural Gas (%)	Coal (%)	Total 000's TOE 2/
Low Income									
Somalia	30	77	5	5	1	12	–	–	1,123
Niger	13	86	–	–	2	12	–	–	964
Ethiopia	15	37	1	55	1	7	–	–	8,016
Sudan	25	45	29	9	1	17	–	–	6,148
Zaire	34	75	5	7	4	7	–	2	8,598
Sierre Leone	25	81	4	–	2	13	–	–	911
Tanzania	12	88	4	–	1	7	–	–	9,025
Burkina		87	1	5	1	6	–	–	1,787
Burundi	2	46	2	–	13	38	–	1	906
Benin	14	78	1	8	1	11	–	–	847
Guinea	18	85	2	–	1	12	–	–	2,435
Ghana	36	59	10	5	3	23	–	–	3,068
Malawi	10	86	5	3	1	4	–	1	3,321
Togo	20	60	4	7	4	26	–	–	793
Uganda	12	90	4	–	1	6	–	–	4,513
Rwanda 3/	4	76	1	17	2	4	–	–	1,008
Kenya	14	65	9	–	2	24	–	1	8,070
Middle Income									
Senegal	25	57	7	–	3	33	–	–	1,679
Mauritania	23	44	6	3	4	43	–	–	289
Liberia	33	61	8	–	9	23	–	–	917
Zambia	38	25	6	1	39	18	–	12	3,604
Ivory Coast	38	52	4	9	5	31	–	–	2,765
Nigeria	20	60	1	–	2	32	5	1	22,016
Zimbabwe	38	25	–	3	29	11	–	32	5,874
Botswana	–	48	–	–	16	20	–	15	725
Congo	45	44	1	1	5	49	–	–	574

Sources: UNDP/World Bank
1/ Agricultural and animal residues.
2/ Tons of oil equivalent.
3/ Some of the "other fuels" refer to peat.

more sophisticated and costlier furnaces as well as electricity to drive the required fans. However, in most of the tobacco growing regions, electricity is not available, and the costs of making it available is usually prohibitive because of the small loads involved.

Electricity or natural gas (in the few countries that own gas deposits) are other options. Both, however, are very expensive relative to other energy resources. In most countries, fewer than twenty percent of urban households have access to electricity, and fewer still can afford the high costs of electric energy for cooking. Promotion of electric cooking would generally be undesirable for an electric utility because of the rather low load factor of ten to twelve percent involved (between two to three hours of cooking per day). The high costs of additional generating capacity needed to serve this type of load would make cooking either prohibitively expensive (if charged through capacity charges to users), or require substantial cross-subsidies from other users. The problem of high costs is even worse for natural gas. It has long been established that service connections to households are too expensive without winter heating or summer air conditioning loads (World Bank Energy Department, 1985). It is not surprising, therefore, that in none of the few gas producing countries in Sub-Sahara Africa domestic distribution systems exist. Where they do elsewhere in developing countries, domestic gas users are usually heavily subsidized (UNDP/World Bank, 1982).

This, then, leaves kerosene, and to a much lesser degree LPG[1] as the only practical fuels that could be readily used as a substitute for woodfuels. But in all of the Sub-Saharan countries, including oil-rich Nigeria, additional supplies of kerosene would have to be imported because of the imbalance between refinery outputs and demand. This would put a substantial strain on these countries' balance of payment position. Replacing all urban woodfuel

consumption by kerosene would increase overall petroleum import demands from a relatively modest five percent in Nigeria to as much as 74 percent in Tanzania. For most of these countries, the impact of such an increase on foreign exchange balances would be serious indeed. As can be seen from Table 2, petroleum imports already accounted for between 12 to 53 percent of total export earnings of these countries in recent years. With lower world market prices for petroleum at present, these percentages have declined, but still are formidable, particularly for interior locations, where transport costs from ports of entry can more than double delivered costs (Schramm, 1986 and UNDP/World Bank, 1986). Practically all of them incur substantial foreign exchange deficits year by year, and any increase, from any source, regardless of its magnitude, could only worsen their already precarious economic condition.

To take Malawi as an example of the potential impact: Replacing the approximately one million cubic meters of solid wood equivalent consumed by urban households in 1983 would have required additional kerosene imports of some 55,000 tons, costing about US$ 14 million in border prices (in January 1986 prices). This would have increased total petroleum imports by about forty percent, absorbed an additional five percent of the country's export earnings, and increased the balance of payments deficit by 18% (Malawi Government, 1986 and Malawi Ministry of Forestry and Natural Resources, 1984).

Given the heavy burden of oil imports, it is not surprising that in many of the countries petroleum products, and kerosene in particular, are in short supply. Recurring shortages are common. In countries with their own refineries (e.g., Kenya, Tanzania, Nigeria, Zaire, etc.) refinery outputs, usually geared to supply the major white products, diesel fuel and gasoline, do not produce enough kerosene and its twin, jet fuel, to serve local demands. Additional net imports would be needed. Lacking foreign exchange, such imports are not forthcoming. Furthermore, in the majority of countries posted kerosene prices are kept artificially low by government on the mistaken notion that kerosene is "a poor man's fuel." This makes distribution margins for petroleum distributors unattractive, so that they make no special efforts to secure additional supplies even in those countries where additional imports could be secured and paid for. The results are shortages, supply interruptions, and black market operations. Insecurity of supplies and high prices, in turn, make it unattractive for households to convert from woodfuels and charcoal to kerosene, even if, on the basis of posted prices, kerosene would appear to be the lower-priced fuel. As can be seen from Table 3, this seems to have been the case in at least some countries. After taking account of average efficiencies of kerosene versus charcoal stoves, the ratio of kerosene to charcoal prices was less than unity in eleven out of the eighteen countries shown, indicating that kerosene was lower-priced than charcoal. However, it is important to note that these comparisons are based on official prices only. For the two countries for which black market prices are also shown (Tanzania and Sierra Leone), the ratios are substantially higher. Furthermore, in most of the countries with apparently low kerosene to charcoal price ratios, currencies were grossly overvalued in the years shown in the table. Since then, devaluations of several hundred percent have taken place in several of them, e.g., in Zambia, Tanzania, Zaire, Uganda, among others.

This will have increased the relative cost of imported kerosene accordingly. In any case, proper shadow-pricing of the overvalued exchange rates of most of the countries would result in considerably higher kerosene prices.

Compared to the increased consumption of imported fuels, the use of domestic woodfuels has several distinct advantages. Being a domestic resource, the impact of their use on scarce foreign exchange resources is modest. It is limited largely to the costs of transport, i.e., the costs of imported petroleum fuels, trucks, and spare parts. Based on data form Kenya, with average hauling distances of about 200 km, transport costs accounted for about fifteen percent of the retail price of charcoal in Nairobi. Import costs of fuel, vehicles and spare parts accounted for about fifty-five percent of total transport costs. Hence imports accounted for only about eight percent of the delivered costs of charcoal (UNDP/ World Bank Energy Sector Management Assistance Program, 1987).

The second advantage is employment creation. Fuelwood and charcoal production are rather labor-intensive activities. Even more importantly, they utilize unskilled or semi-skilled labor, largely on a seasonal basis outside of peak agricultural activity periods. This type of employment is the one most urgently needed in these countries with their huge surplus of unskilled, seasonally unemployed labor. Properly shadow-priced, the real economic costs of this employment are far lower than the monetary earnings of the people employed.

Offsetting these advantages are the environmental costs of continued overcutting of existing wood resources. The question is: does continued use, and cutting in excess of regrowth, necessarily have to lead to environmental catastrophes? Mathematically, such consequences seem to be unavoidable. However, this assumes that current trends will continue indefinitely, that there will be no change in behavior, and no reaction by either policy makers or people. Here it will be argued that such an assumption is unrealistic, given current knowledge and current awareness of the problem by governments and people alike. If appropriate steps are taken, major environmental damages can be avoided in spite of further, significant reductions in forest covers and tree stocks.

Table 2: Petroleum Demand and Import Costs in Africa ('000s metric tonnes)

Country/Year	LPG	Gasoline	Kerosene a/		Jet Fuel	Diesel Oil	Total Petroleum Product Demand b/	Net Petroleum Import Cost (current US$ m.) in year shown	Ratio of Net Petroleum Import Cost to Total Earnings from exports (%) in year shown
Low Income									
Zaire/1983	0.3	89.4	38.7	(7%)	98.9	296.6	591.6	–	–
Uganda/1982	0.3	43.9	28.9	(18%)	17.3	50.3	156.7	100.0	30
Somalia/1984	0.1	42.0	13.5	(7%)	1.6	99.4	181.6	54.7	40
Kenya/1980	21.5	310.8	84.1	(5%)	347.9	451.1	1,677.5	297.5	36
Benin/1984	0.5	42.1	14.2	(12%)	15.3	37.0	119.3	48.0	20
Malawi/1980	–	39.5	5.7	(4%)	11.7	77.3	138.2	56.0	22
Togo/1982	0.6	45.8	13.9	(6%)	14.1	41.7	239.4	58.0	22
Ethiopia/1982	4.7	117.6	10.6	(2%)	75.4	240.0	526.0	185.0	53
Tanzania/1982	5.4	122.0	68.9	(11%)	37.7	294.9	638.0	289.0	–
Burkina/1983	0.6	46.1	11.0	(12%)	1.4	28.4	90.3	–	–
Sierra Leone/1984	0.9	38.2	27.7	(16%)	11.4	75.7	178.5	27.0	24
Rwanda/1980	–	24.3	6.7	(14%)	–	13.5	48.7	–	–
Burundi/1980	–	16.6	0.8	(3%)	–	15.2	32.6	–	–
Niger/1981	0.4	37.9	4.1	(3%)	16.2	89.8	151.2	34.0	26
Ghana/1985 c/	4.1	220.8	113.9	(16%)	24.4	308.9	699.7	166.0	26
Guinea/1984	–	70.4	3.1	(1%)	9.0	99.1	382.9	–	–
Sudan/1981	5.4	240.4	16.5	(2%)	43.1	529.0	967.1	–	–
Middle Income									
Mauritania/1983	2.2	27.2	1.4	(1%)	12.1	124.3	167.2	44.0	12
Nigeria/1981	48.0	3,620.0	900.0	(11%)	460.0	2,280.0	8,248.0	–	–
Zimbabwe/198c	5.3	192.8	20.4	(4%)	59.8	305.2	583.5	265.0	23
Congo/1985	3.9	53.3	21.1	(8%)	10.7	122.1	250.5	–	–
Botswana/1982	1.1	47.6	4.2	(3%)	0.8	87.0	141.1	91.0	22
Senegal/1981	10.4	102.9	10.7	(2%)	141.3	144.1	704.9	144.0	51
Liberia/1983	0.5	66.3	5.0	(1%)	27.9	123.3	402.1	115.0	24
Zambia/1981	1.0	120.0	30.0	(4%)	65.0	287.0	683.0	240.0	19
Ivory Coast/1983	16.4	203.7	63.3	(7%)	60.0	280.4	958.5	–	–

Sources: UNDP/World Bank

a/ The number in parentheses is the percentage of kerosene use relative to total petroleum demand.
b/ Total petroleum demand includes sum of products demand shown as well as for residual fuel oil (not shown).
c/ 61% of kerosene used in urban households, 31% in rural households and the remainder in industry/commerce.

Table 3: Retail Prices in Major Urban Centers for Kerosene and Charcoal US$ per MMBTU a/

Country	City	Year	Kerosene	Charcoal	Ratio of Retail Price of Kerosene to Charcoal	
					Unadjusted	Adjusted b/
Congo	Brazzaville	1986	14.9	16.7	0.89	0.38
Togo	Lome	1983	11.2	3.80–5.10	2.20–2.95	0.94–1.26
Somalia	Mogadishu	1985	15.1	4.90	3.08	1.32
Zambia	Lusaka	1982	14.2	8.80	1.61	0.69
Tanania	Dar-es-Salaam	1983	7.9 c/	7.90	1.00	0.43
			16.5 d/		2.09	0.90
Zaire	Kinshasa	1984	14.9	9.1	1.64	0.70
Sierra Leone	Freetown	1986	5.3 c/	7.40	0.72	0.31
			15.8 d/		2.14	0.92
Ghana	Accra	1986	3.6 c/	6.90	0.52	0.22
Niger	Niamey	1983	12.1 c/	5.4	2.24	0.96
Liberia	Monrovia	1984	19.0	5.2–8.1	3.02	1.01–1.57
Ivory Coast	Abidjan	1984	12.5	6.3	1.98	0.85
Benin	Cotonou	1983	8.3	4.9	1.69	0.73
Senegal	Dakar	1983	12.3	5.5	2.24	0.96
Ethiopia	Addis	1983	12.6 e/	13.6 e/	0.93	0.40
Kenya	Nairobi	1985	12.2	4.3	2.84	1.22
Burkina	Ouagadougou	1984	12.0	4.8	2.50	1.07
Mauritania f/	Nouakchott	1983	16.5 c/	5.0 c/	3.30	1.41
			20.2 d/	8.3 d/	2.43	1.04
Uganda	Kampala	1982	12.2 g/	3.9	3.13	1.34

Source: UNPD/World Bank

a/   Prices converted to US$ per million BTU at official rates of exchange, assuming − 1 metric ton charcoal = 27.4 million BTU; 1 metric ton firewood = 13.7 million BRU; and 1 barrel of kerosene = 5.2 million BTU.

b/   This is the ratio of prices after accounting for relative differences in efficiencies of use. Assumed efficiencies 35% for kerosene and 15% for charcoal stoves. A value equal to 1 implies equality of kerosene and charcoal prices.

c/   Official controlled price.

d/   Black market sales.

e/   Based on estimated shadow exchange rate of 2.7 Birr = US$ 1.00 compared to official rate of 2.07 Birr = US$ 1.00 in 1983.

f/   In Mauritania about 2/3 of charcoal supply is met from imports from Senegal.

g/   Exchange rate of 200 USh = $1.00 (end-1982).

There are a number of reasons for this cautious optimism. The first, and perhaps most important one, is that removal of trees as such does not cause damages. Damages occur only, if and when the trees are removed from specific locations in which they provided protection against damaging effects on soils by intense sunshine, wind and/or water erosion. Whether such damages occur in a given location depends on soil characteristics, on the slope of the land, on intensity, magnitude and duration of rainfall, on wind velocities, on the duration of dry and wet cycles, and on types of plant cover throughout the various seasons of the year. Many of these variables are subject to control by man. Sloping land can be protected not only by the roots of trees, but by contour plowing (if subsequently used for agriculture), by terracing, by grassy strips or hedge rows planted at regular intervals, by gully checkdams to reduce the velocity of water run-off (Schramm, 1979). Wind erosion damages can be greatly reduced or eliminated by the planting of wind breaks and the excessive siltation of reservoirs can be prevented by the design and protection of sufficiently large shelterbelts in the upstream watershed. This raises the troublesome issue of policing and prevention of encroachment for which there are no easy solutions, particularly in areas of strong population pressures and land scarcity.

There are, of course, some large and contiguous areas that should and must be fully protected, if severe damages are to be avoided. This forcefully applies to a number of tropical forest areas that contain large numbers of unique plant and animal specimens. It applies to key mountain watersheds that protect the headwaters of important rivers. It applies to areas with fragile soils, where removal of tree cover would destroy the thin layer of top soil underneath, leaving the land barren and infertile. Wide areas of the Amazon River Basin fall into this group (Browder, 1985). Protection must also be provided for Africa's unique wildlife parks and ranges which are a priceless heritage not only for Africans, but for the world as a whole.

Outside of these sensitive areas, however, the question whether in a given region of a country ten, twenty, or fifty percent, or alternatively, none of the land should be retained under forest cover is a question that can only be decided on the basis of some informed judgment about the importance and benefits from retention versus utilization and/or conversion to other uses. Nevertheless, if exploitation is found to be acceptable, the manner in which it proceeds can be of critical importance for future land use and the protection of the land's fertility and recuperative capacity. Hence, it is important that the current, indiscriminate destruction of natural forests for the purpose of extracting wood resources or for shifting agriculture by slash and burn methods, be reduced and eliminated, to be systematically replaced by less harmful practices, such as those discussed in the following section. Subject to these caveats, the utilization of existing forest resources to satisfy the growing demands for energy by rural and urban populations as well as industrial users is in the best interest of most African countries at their present stage of economic development. It will minimize energy costs to local industry as well as to those groups of society that can least afford it. It will utilize a domestic resource, minimize imports and provide domestic employment. Even if exploitation is depleting existing stocks, it will provide a breathing space in which scarce resources of foreign exchange and capital can be used to sustain economic development, rather than to pay for the import of alternative energy supplies.

Optimizing Production and Consumption of Woodfuel Supplies

In most countries, the major sources of woodfuel supplies to urban and/or industrial users, roughly in order of importance, are the following:

(a) Natural Forests;
(b) Land Clearing Operations
     (a sub-group of [a]);
(c) Woody savannah and range lands;
(d) Private lands;
(e) Man-made plantations.

Obviously, the importance of the respective sources varies by location.

For example in Kenya, land clearing is by far the most important source at the present time, accounting for about eighty percent of total supplies, followed by plantation and miscellaneous sources. Wood from land clearing, of course, is a depletable resource. Sooner or later its supplies will be exhausted, and alternative sources, or alternative fuels will have to take their place.

In larger cities, charcoal is by far the most important household fuel. Because of its higher energy density per volume (approx. 1.9 times that of wood), it can be transported over longer distances. Also, in densely populated urban areas, smokeless-burning charcoal is much preferable to smoky wood, which requires either outdoor cooking or the use of elaborate and expensive woodstoves equipped with appropriate chimneys. Industrial woodfuel uses, of which the most important ones are tobacco curing, tea processing and brick making, are almost exclusively based on the use of firewood. However, by their very nature, these industries are themselves located in rural areas and do not necessarily compete directly with woodfuel supplies to urban areas.

Optimizing strategies that should be adopted immediately to utilize the dwindling resource base should be directed at:

(a) Reduction of conversion losses from woodfuel to charcoal through systematic introduction of improved kiln technology;
(b) Minimization of transport costs to markets, thereby extending the potential areas of supply;
(c) Minimization of fuel losses resulting from charcoal breakage;

(d) Energy conservation through the use of more efficient appliances or furnaces in households and industry;
(e) Land use regulation and effective enforcement that would prevent overcutting, or encroachment on environmentally sensitive areas;
(f) Increased revenue collection from woodfuel production to finance an effective forest management and advisory service as well as the provision of services to woodfuel producers (roads, training, etc.);
(g) Improvements in the reliability of supply of alternative fuels such as kerosene, LPG or electricity, but with prices adjusted to fully reflect their economic costs to the economy.

Medium to long-term strategies to extend or replace existing wood stocks as needed to meet future demands should consist of the following:

(a) Establishment of a unit charged with regular updating of fuel demand forecasts by region and user group that would take into account projected prices as well as availabilities of substitute fuels;
(b) Regular monitoring of changes in remaining accessible forest stocks through spot surveys and satellite photography;
(c) Systematic identification of public, communal and private lands with low opportunity costs in terms of alternative use, suitable for the establishment of future fuelwood plantations;
(d) Development of a systematic program, backed by technical advisory services and appropriate credit facilities, to support and stimulate the establishment of private fuelwood plantations and wood lots to meet projected future demands that could no longer be satisfied form remaining resources.

Subject to the condition that at the time of planting the present value of the total supply costs of such plantations per unit of useful energy, supplied to the user's premises, has to be lower than the costs of alternative energy sources in both financial terms (including appropriate profit margins) and in economic terms (properly shadow-priced).

Overall, the immediate objective would be to increase as quickly as possible the efficiency of ongoing woodfuel production and charcoal conversion, as well as the efficiency of ongoing woodfuel use, subject to appropriate benefit-cost criteria. For the longer run, the objective would be to replenish the dwindling resource base by, first, providing access to more remote locations with un- or underutilized wood resources and, second, by providing new, man-made supplies from plantations, properly timed to be ready for harvesting when the existing resources become scarce enough that market prices have risen sufficiently to recover the wood replacement costs.

This longer-run strategy, quite clearly, involves some risks. Projections of supply, demand and prices will have to be made at the time of planting, when market prices presumably still are well below replacement costs. After the investment in new plantations has been made, the prices and availabilities of alternative energy resources (such as kerosene or natural gas) could change, making them more attractive to consumers than woodfuels from plantations planted long ago. Judicious decisions by governments and foreign donors, who currently are the major financiers of new investments, would be needed to support these activities, by accepting some of the inherent risks. It is for this reason that the need of careful forecasting of long-term supplies and demand, as well as of future costs and prices, is so important. Only if it can be shown that fuel resources from such plantations will have a high likelihood of being less, or at least not more costly than those of properly shadow-priced alternative sources of energy, should such forward strategies be adopted.

The immediate strategy of improving the efficiencies of production and of utilization is less risky. Today, almost all of the charcoal in Africa is produced by traditional earth kiln technology with conversion efficiencies from wood to charcoal on a weight basis form ten to twelve percent. While cases are known in which much higher rates were achieved, this requires a skill level which only a very few charcoal burners are capable of maintaining on a consistent basis. By contrast, the use of brick or steel kilns results in average efficiencies of between 28 to 35 percent, or about two and a half times higher. Improved earth kilns, such as the Casamance or the Subri Fosse kilns, achieve somewhat lower rates of twenty percent or more, but they are more flexible and less costly to build and move around. For a description and comparison of the various kiln types see: (Karch, Boutette and Christopherson, 1986). Clearly, the systematic use of such kilns would more than double the useful output of charcoal from a given volume of wood.

There are several reasons why these technologies are not being used now. The first is ignorance. Improved kiln technologies are new to Africa. Outside agencies, such as US AID or the German Technical Aid Organization GTZ, have long assisted African countries in adapting them to their particular circumstances. However, this was always done within the context of small-scale pilot projects, with no resources available for widespread introduction and dissemination. Charcoal production, however, is undertaken by a myriad of small-scale, oftentimes part-time charcoal burners, who generally can neither read nor write and have no financial resources of their own, nor access to credit sources. Without systematic outside help and systematic dissemination, these producers would not and could not adapt to these new technologies.

A second important part of this strategy is the need to develop and maintain proper wood utilization and conservation practices of existing and maintainable forest lands on the one hand, and to raise enough revenues from their exploitation on the other, in order to cover the costs of effective forest management and advisory services. At present, most of the forest lands in Africa are either owned in common by villagers or tribes, or by the Government. Well defined user rights are lacking. As a result, wood cutters or charcoal burners have no interest in maintaining or conserving the existing resource base. While stumpage fees may be levied by either local or central authorities, these are widely avoided because of the lack of proper policing. What is needed, instead, to bring about more efficient and less destructive utilization of natural forest stands, is the establishment of contractual user rights for individuals or communities, with stumpage fees or lease payments based on a realistic assessment of the netback (i.e., residual resource) value of the standing wood, and with enforceable rules of cutting regimes. If such leases or cutting rights are properly designed to provide the wood producer with a reasonable source of income, he in turn will try to protect his resource base against encroachment by others, substantially reducing or eliminating the need for public protection of the forest.

A Case Study: Malawi

Malawi is a land-locked country of close to seven million people in south-central Africa, bordering Tanzania in the northeast, Zambia in the northwest and Mozambique in the south. It stretches for about 520 miles from north to south along the Great Rift Valley and has a width of only five to one hundred miles, with about twenty percent of its area covered by Lake Malawi. Most of its economic activities and population are concentrated in the southern part of the

country. Apart from natural forests, several hundred megawatts of partially developed hydrosites and a few scattered coal deposits in the extreme north, it has no known energy resources of its own. All of its petroleum requirements and most of its coal, used by industry, have to be imported. Both are expensive. Because of the civil war in Mozambique, petroleum products have to be brought in from Durban, South Africa, with overland freight accounting for two-thirds of the delivered border price, more than tripling the cif price in Durban. Coal, formerly supplied from nearby Tete in Mozambique, now has to come from distant sources in Zambia or Zimbabwe at prices around $100/ton. Woodfuels, firewood in the rural areas and charcoal in the cities, account for about ninety percent of total energy consumption.

Woodfuels account for about ninety percent of total energy consumption. Almost one-third of this is used by the tobacco curing industry, the country's largest earner of foreign exchange. Rapid population growth, land clearing and the growing demand for woodfuels by households and industrial users have put substantial pressure on natural forest resources. In the densely populated southern parts of the country, deforestation of steep hill- and mountainsides has led to rapidly increasing erosion, threatening vital watersheds. Shortages of firewood and charcoal are becoming more and more frequent, particularly in the rainy season, when supplies to urban centers from more distant sources are cut off. On the other hand, there exist several large, Government-owned pinewood plantations in remote areas of the north and on mountain plateaus in the south that are basically unutilized, but costly to maintain. They were originally planted in the 1960s and early 1970s to support a hoped-for pulpmill operation. However, the mill never materialized for economic reasons.

The Government has recognized the threat of diminishing forest cover and resulting soil destruction and fuel shortages. Beginning in 1980, with assistance from the World Bank as well as bilateral donors, it began a systematic program of reforestation, both through direct Government plantations and a tree seedling distribution program to private landowners. However, experience showed that fuelwood plantations, established and maintained by the Forest Service, were extremely costly, with stumpage costs being almost five times as high as the current market prices for wood, which, however, reflect only the costs of cutting, transport and retailing, but not replacement costs. In 1986, roadside prices per stacked cu.m. of wood amounted to about $3, while replacement costs in industrial and government plantations were about $8 per cu.m. The original seedling distribution program only reached half its original target, largely because of the reluctance of farmers to purchase and plant the seedlings, because of the low prevailing market price of fuelwood and the easy access to free wood from customary land. After five years, it was quite apparent that cutting rates still far exceeded regrowth from both natural forest regeneration and reforestation efforts, posing a serious long-term threat to the environment, to fuel supplies and to the economy of the country.

Learning from this experience, a revised and more comprehensive program was developed. It consists of the following components:

(1) Sharp reductions in the direct Forestry Service planting program, restricting it to environmentally fragile areas;

(2) Phased increases in stumpage fees for wood, cut for commercial purposes (i.e., resale), to approach replacement costs over a period of ten years;

(3) Expansion of the area of fully protected forests in environmentally sensitive areas;

(4) Substantial increases in the number of foresters and forest guards to provide the necessary protection of forests under the above programs, and to collect stumpage fees, either directly from woodfuel producers or through a system of checkpoints on roads leading to commercial markets;

(5) Expansion of the tree nursery program, combined with systematic efforts at public education about the value of tree planting; seedlings to be sold at subsidized prices to farmers, who, after three years, will receive a cash payment of five times its original cost for each surviving seedling planted under the program;

(6) Establishment of pilot programs to test the technical, economic and financial viability of converting thinnings from pinewood plantations into charcoal for industrial, tobacco curing and household use;

(7) Systematic introduction of efficient charcoal kiln technologies to replace the customary earth kilns used;

(8) Pilot programs to establish the manufacture and dissemination of more efficient charcoal cookers (jikos) and woodfuel stoves;

(9) Test and demonstration programs to reduce fuel consumption in tobacco curing.

While most components of this program have only recently been established, some notable successes have already been achieved. The most outstanding one is the pinewood charcoal production program, based on the use of thinnings from the Viphya Plantation in the north, and several smaller plantations in the center and south of the country.

Systematic burn tests proved that, technically, pinewood charcoal could be used as fuel for a wide range of industrial applications, ranging from the kilns of the country's only cement mill to boilers of textile plants and hospitals. It was also found by extensive trials that charcoal could be adapted for use in the tobacco curing industry. Several charcoal production centers, based on the use of beehive brick kilns, were established. By the summer of 1987, only eight months after project startup, the total installed annual kiln capacity had already reached 6,000 tons. These kilns convert wood into charcoal at an efficiency rate (by weight) of about 32% under normal operating conditions. Production costs turned out to be very low. Including administrative overhead, plus stumpage rates based on replacement costs and appropriate profit margins, costs per ton of charcoal in 1987 prices amount to about $25/ton. Transport costs to the major industrial markets in the south add another $50/ton, for a total delivered price of $75/ton. This is quite competitive with the costs of imported or domestic coal, presently the major industrial fuels.

Thinnings from the Viphya Plantation, a waste product, are sufficient to support an average charcoal production of some 40,000 tons for a period of at least ten years. Wastewood and unusable timber from smaller plantations in the center and southern parts of the country could support the production of another 20,000 tons per year. Compared to this potential supply the total current market for pinewood charcoal has been estimated at 90,000 tons per year, of which some 32,000 tons would be used by industry, 1,000 as a replacement for industrial diesel fuel, 12,000 by tobacco producers in the central part of the country, and about 45,000 tons by households. Without encroaching on the very large, standing pinewood timber resources (for which, however, there are currently no markets), the utilization of wastewood from these plantations alone could supply two-thirds of the existing, potential charcoal demand in the country. Investment costs for a 60,000 ton/year production program would be very low, since the basic infrastructure (e.g., roads) already has been established. Kiln costs are only about $150 per unit of 100 tons of annual charcoal

capacity.

The full-scale development of the pinewood charcoal project will have a major impact on the forestry sector of the country. 60,000 tons of charcoal will save some two million cu.m. of wood from natural forests. The Government will gain net revenues from stumpage fees of some $0.3 million per annum, and will no longer have to pay the costs of the necessary thinning program in the plantations. Some 3,000 people will be employed, most of them in the economically depressed northern region. The country will reduce its import fuel costs by several million dollars and gain a much more secure and non-interruptible source of supply.

Another successful program component is the tobacco industry energy conservation program. Systematic trials have resulted in the development of new, low-cost furnace designs that reduce average fuel consumption from the country-wide average of 42 cu.m. per barn load to between 12 to 15 cu.m. under normal field conditions. This is a reduction of some 70%. The recently completed, successful charcoal trials, in addition, have provided access to another fuel formerly not available to the industry. Efforts are now underway to systematically re-equip the curing barns with the new furnaces, with charcoal to be introduced in producing regions close to sources of pinewood charcoal supply, or far away from suitable sources of firewood.

Tests of improved charcoal stoves and comparisons with customary appliances (mbaulas) used in Malawi have shown that average charcoal savings would range between 25 to 40%, with a pay-back period to users of less than three months. The program projects that within three years of the start-up of improved stove production some 85,000 improved stoves will have been sold, resulting in cumulative net savings to users of about $2.5 million, and a reduction in the need for wood, which is equivalent to the volume of standing timber of some 7,000 hectares of natural woodlands.

While it is too early to judge the success of the other program components listed above, the gradual increase in stumpage rates, together with the clampdown on illegal charcoal production, have had a noticeable effect on urban fuel markets already. Retail prices have increased somewhat, and recurring shortages of charcoal supplies from customary hardwood sources have created a strong demand for pinewood charcoal, even though so far no properly adapted, pinewood-charcoal stoves have been designed and marketed. Rising prices, of course, will provide an added inducement to farmers to participate in the seedling program, helping the overall supply situation in the long run.

Conclusions

Overall, it can be concluded that the Malawi woodfuel program represents an imaginative, thorough and multi-faceted response to the serious threat of overcutting and environmental degradation on the one hand, and the requirements of the economy for a reasonably priced and reliable source of fuel supplies on the other. It is designed to optimize the use of domestic woodfuel resources, both through measures on the supply and demand side. It proves that the use of wood fuels does not have to be destructive and environmentally damaging, but can form a vitally important part of a national strategy of economic development and growth.

Similar programs can be, and are being developed in other African countries, such as Ethiopia, Madagascar, Tanzania and Niger, to name but a few. For the short to medium term, standing wood from natural forests, many of them already subject to rapid depletion from land clearing operations, will have to provide the bulk of supplies. While current methods of exploitation are highly destructive, the systematic introduction of proper management of these activities can increase actual yields in the form of useful energy by factors of three to five, through a combination of more efficient charcoal production techniques, reduction in transport and handling losses, and the introduction and use of improved charcoal and/or woodfuel stoves and furnaces.

Careful management of the remaining resource base can minimize environmental damage, through regulation of cutting regimes that would enhance natural regeneration, the identification and protection of strips of land needed for shelter belts, or the protection against clearfelling of erosion-prone slopes. The granting of enforceable cutting rights in public forests to private woodcutters and charcoal producers, combined with proper regulations of their activities to minimize environmental damages, would provide the essential protection against the indiscriminate destruction of the forests by uncontrolled poachers. It could also provide a badly needed source of revenue to develop and support an effective, well-paid and properly equipped forest service that would be required to implement and manage these policies.

In the longer run, reforestation (mainly by farmers and private landholders and not by government because of costs), are likely to provide a cost-effective, long-term supply of needed fuels for the household sector as well as for industry. While woodfuel prices will have to increase in real terms over current levels in many locations to pay for the added costs of planting and maintenance, indications are that in most regions of Sub-Sahara Africa such plantations are likely to provide a competitive source of fuel either in the form of firewood or charcoal. Continued utilization of woodfuels will provide a significant source of domestic employment. It will also result in substantial balance of payments relief, reducing by substantial margins the quantities, and hence the total costs of imported fuels that would have to be used instead.

ENDNOTE

1. LPG is limited to countries with domestic refineries that produce LPG as a by-product of the refining process, usually a few percent only of the total quantity of crude processed. This limits LPG availability. High transport costs of the pressurized containers make imports generally too costly.

REFERENCES

Browder, J. "Subsidies, Deforestation, and the Forest Sector in the Brazilian Amazon," Paper prepared for the World Resources Institute, Mimeo, Washington, D.C. 1985.

Karch, E., Boutette, M., and K. Christophersen. *The Casamance Kiln*, University of Idaho Press, Nov. 1986.

Malawi Government. *Economic Report*, 1986.

Malawi Ministry of Forestry and Natural Resources, Energy Studies Unit. *Malawi Urban Energy Survey*, Lilongwe, Sept. 1984.

Schramm, G. "A Benefit-Cost Model for the Evaluation of On-Site Benefits of Soil Conservation Projects in Mexico," *The Annals of Regional Science*, Vol. XIII, No. 2, July 1979, pp. 19–28.

Schramm, G. "Regional Cooperation and Economic Development," *The Annals of Regional Science*, Vol. 20, No. 2, July 1986, Table 1.

UNDP/World Bank. *Bangladesh, Issues and Options in the Energy Sector*, Annex VI, Report No. 3873-BD, Washington, D.C., Oct. 1982.

UNDP/World Bank. *Nigeria, Issues and Options in the Energy Sector*, Washington, D.C., 1983.

UNDP/World Bank. *Zaire, Issues and Options in the Energy Sector*, May 1986, Table 4.7.

UNDP/World Bank Energy Sector Management Assistance Program. *Kenya, Urban Woodfuel Development Program*, Washington, D.C., 1987.

World Bank. *Accelerated Development in Sub-Sahara Africa*, 1981, Washington, D.C.

World Bank Energy Department. Energy Department Paper No. 22, *The Economic Value of Natural Gas in Residential and Commercial Markets*, Washington, D.C., March 1985.

The Hamburger Connection:
How Central America's Forests Become North America's Hamburgers

NORMAN MYERS

Rainforests are being steadily depleted in all three major regions of the tropics. If present rates of misuse and overuse persist (and they are likely to accelerate), the biome, now covering some 9 million square kilometers, could be reduced to remnant fragments within another half century.[1]

This would represent one of the greatest environmental impoverishments in the foreseeable future, and one of the greatest biological debacles to occur on the face of the earth.[2]

There are three main agents at work. One is the timber harvester, who degrades somewhere between 55,000 and 90,000 square kilometers each year, notably in Southeast Asia.[3] In addition to this legitimate logging, there is much illegal felling, possibly making the total twice as much. And the timber logger, with his negligent harvesting techniques and his clumsy equipment, grossly disrupts tropical forest ecosystems: he leaves the primary forests greatly impoverished, but he also damages as much as half of the residual forest beyond recovery.

Still more to the point the timberman, by laying logging tracks, opens up the forest to the second agent in the depletive process, the small-scale farmer, who plays a much more extensive part. Both the shifting cultivator of traditional type and the landless squatter of more recent form are penetrating deep into forest heartlands that have previously been closed to them. Overall the

Myers. Permission to reprint this article was received from the Royal Swedish Academy of Sciences, publisher of *Ambio*. It appeared on pages 3–8 of Volume 10, No. 1 of that journal in 1981.

forest farmer is probably damaging, if not destroying, 200,000 square kilometers of forest each year, primarily in Southeast and Southern Asia, in tropical Africa, and in parts of tropical Latin America.[4] The third agent represents a phenomenon that is confined to Latin America, and especially to Central America. This is the cattle raiser, who clears away a patch of forest entirely in order to establish artificial grasslands.[5] In rough terms, he can be reckoned to be eliminating some 20,000 square kilometers of forest per year, far less area than the other two main agents. But the stockman's impact is expanding more rapidly than the other two, and is by far the major factor in forest destruction in tropical Latin America.[6] In order to establish his pasturelands the cattleman clears the forest completely, by felling and burning it. True, he often converts a patch of forest that has already been subjected to shifting cultivation or "spontaneous settlement" by peasant farmers who serve as a "pioneer wave"; but it is the rancher, with his large-scale enterprise and operations, who is the prime agent in the final elimination of the forest cover.

The cattle raiser's activities are largely stimulated by consumerist lifestyles in affluent sectors of the global community. As beef produced in developed nations, and especially in North America, becomes more expensive, the rich-world consumer fosters the spread of cattle raising into the forest zones of the six Central American nations shown in the tables. He does not do it wittingly, and certainly not with wanton intent, but he does it effectively and increasingly. This link between materialist lifestyles in North America and forest destruction in Central America constitutes the theme of this article.

International Beef Trade

During the last two decades, consumers in the developed nations have revealed a virtually insatiable appetite for beef. In 1960, an average American consumed 38.7 kilograms of beef per year; by 1976 that total had risen to 61 kilograms. According to projects prepared by the Food and Agriculture Organization, the demand for beef will continue to rise more rapidly than for any other food category except fish, until at least 1990.[7]

At the same time, few items in the shopping basket have increased more in price during the past few years. In the United States, beef prices have been soaring far faster than the overall cost of living. Between 1975 and 1979, the price for a Montana steer at the packing plant rose from $0.63 per kilogram to $1.55; in the same period retail prices soared by 30 percent per year, until by 1980 they had topped $5 per kilogram.[8] At least another two years will pass before a US housewife will be able to confront hamburger in a supermarket without flinching.

Not surprisingly then, Americans have been seeking low-cost beef elsewhere, and Central America has proved to be a ready supplier. In 1978, the average price of beef imported from Central America was $1.47 per kilogram, compared with a wholesale price of $3.30 for similar beef produced in the United States.

Cattle in Central America are raised on grass rather than grain, so the beef is very lean. This makes it suitable for only one sector of the US beef market, the fast-food trade. According to the Meat Importers Council of America, virtually all the Central American beef makes its way into hamburgers, frankfurters, luncheon meat, hot dogs, and other processed meat products. As it happens, the fast-food trade is the fastest growing part of the entire food industry in the United States. Through much of the 1970s it grew at a rate of 20 percent per year, or two-and-a-half times faster than the restaurant industry overall[9] and Americans now spend $5 billion annually for fast food. One-fifth of the US food budget is spent dining out, and that proportion could rise to one-half by 1990; the demand for cheap lean beef is unlikely to slacken. Moreover it seems likely that as grain prices steadily increase, US cattle raising will shift toward more pastureland feeding, a change that may well reduce production of animal protein in the United States by 50 percent[10]; this in turn would further stimulate imports of foreign beef.

Faced with one inflationary price rise after another during the past several years, the US government has repeatedly stepped up beef imports. In 1960 the US purchased virtually no beef abroad; it now imports 800,000 tons each year, or around 10 percent of its total consumption. Of these imports, 17 percent come from tropical Latin America, three-quarters of them (just over 100,000 tons) from Central America. Additional imports in recent years have notably come from Central America, as well as from other sources such as Australia. And although the extra purchases from Central America contribute less that one percent of the US consumption of beef, the government estimates that they supply enough additional cheap meat to trim a nickel off the price of a hamburger each year. Food is the sector of the US economy most susceptible to inflation, and the greatest price increases have been for meat, and especially beef. It is believed that increased imports of cheap Central American beef have done more to stem inflation in the US than any other single government initiative. Indeed, the US government calculates that the additional imports save consumers at least $500 million a year.

The fast-food trade in the United States accounts for about 25 percent of all beef consumed, but not all the major chains acknowledge that they use imported beef. Burger King, the third largest chain in the fast-food business (after McDonalds and Kentucky Fried Chicken), admits that it does; so do Jack-in-the-Box, and the group of restaurants known variously as Roy Rogers, Bob's Big Boy and Hot Shoppes. But McDonalds, the largest fast-food enterprise and the largest buyer of beef in the world, denies that it uses beef from outside the United States. McDonalds sells 3 billion hamburgers per year, the equivalent of 300,000 head of cattle. The author made on-the-ground enquiries in Central America in late 1976 and early and mid-1979 and he heard on more than one occasion, during discussions with the Grupo Ganadero Industria de Costa Rica (a ranchers' organization), that Costa Rica beef does indeed find its way into McDonalds' hamburgers. In addition, a production engineer of the Guatemalan beef-packing plant Industria de Ganaderos Guatemalecos SA, and a supplier to McDonalds, stated in late 1979 that he was purchasing beef directly from the Guatemalan beef-packing plant in question.[11] Furthermore a spokesman of the Meat Importers Council of America has told the writer that meat imported into the United States is categorized, after it leaves its point of entry, as domestic beef: for wholesale and marketing networks, it is just "beef". So when McDonalds' spokesmen state that the company "obtains its meat within the United States", they may be speaking the truth as they see it, without recognizing that the beef originates from outside the country.

Cattle Raising in Central America

Since 1960 the area of man-established pasturelands and the number of beef cattle in Central America have both increased by two-thirds (Tables 1 and 2). The pasturelands have almost all been established at the cost of undisturbed rainforests, which have been reduced by almost 40 percent since 1960, apart from losses prior to that time. At present rates, all remaining forests will have been eliminated by 1990, according to information supplied privately to the author during discussions in Latin America in 1976 and 1979.

In terms of their biotic diversity, these rainforests constitute some of the richest ecosystems on earth. For example, Costa Rica, a country comprising slightly more than 50,000 square kilometers (hardly bigger than Denmark and a little less than West Virginia) has 758 bird species, 620 of them residents, or more than are found in all of North America north of the Tropic of Cancer.[12] Costa Rica likewise harbors over 8,000 plant species, with more than 1,000 orchids. The La Selva Forest Reserve, amounting to only 730 hectares, contains 320 tree species, 42 fish, 394 birds, 104 mammals (of which 62 bats), 76 reptiles, 46 amphibians and 143 butterflies – a tally that is, broadly speaking, half as many again as California's.

Costa Rica represents an extreme illustration of the "hamburger connection". In 1950, cattle-raising areas covered only one-eighth of the country; they now account for over one-third (Table 2). In 1960, the country's cattle herds totalled slightly over 900,000 head; by 1978 they had surpassed 2 million. During the 1960s and 1970s, beef production more than tripled. But during the same period, local consumption of beef actually declined to a mere 12.6 kilograms per head per year – less meat than a domestic cat received in the United States (Table 1). Almost all the extra output was despatched to foreign markets. Costa Rica now exports around 45 million kilograms of beef per year, more than 60 percent of its entire production; almost two-thirds of this beef goes to the United States (Table 3).

All in all, cattle production in Central America has risen 160 percent during the past 20 years, and beef exports have soared from 20,000 tons a year to more than 150,000 tons per year. The result is that

Table 1: Beef Production and Exports

COUNTRY	NO. OF CATTLE (000) 1961	1978	BEEF PRODUCTION (TONS) 1961	1978	NET EXPORTS (TONS) 1961	1978	BEEF CONSUMPTION PER CAPITA (KG/YEAR) 1978
Costa Rica	951	2,010	21,800	71,500	7,100	43,600	12.6
El Salvador	1,141	1,274	20,700	32,300	–	7,300	6.6
Guatemala	1,134	2,417	35,600	88,400	1,500	23,900	10.6
Honduras	1,411	1,740	17,600	51,300	3,300	29,300	5.8
Nicaragua	1,291	2,787	27,600	76,300	8,300	42,300	15.5
Panama	763	1,385	21,600	45,700	–	4,900	26.3
Total	**6,691**	**11,613**	**144,900**	**365,500**	**20,200**	**151,300**	
United States (for comparison)	97,700	116,000	7,425,800	11,197,000	454,100	970,000	55.9

SOURCE: Reference 8 and 9, and information gathered by the author during visits to Central America during 1976 and 1979.

Table 2: Central America: The Shift from Forests to Pasture

COUNTRY	AREA (KM²)	PASTURE (KM²) 1961	1978	FORESTS AND WOODLANDS (KM²) 1961	1978
Costa Rica	50,700	9,690	17,640	28,480	19,300
El Salvador	21,390	6,060	6,900	2,300	0
Guatemala	108,890	10,390	19,760	84,000	44,000
Honduras	112,090	20,065	23,700	71,000	39,000[1]
Nicaragua	130,000	17,100	28,200	64,320	44,000
Panama	75,650	8,990	14,300	41,000	32,000
Total	**498,720**	**72,295**	**110,500 (+ 65%)**	**291,100**	**178,300 (– 39%)**
United States (for comparison)	9,363,120	2,612,350	2,150,000	3,076,000	3,044,000

[1] This is the official figure. However, a recent land-use and resource survey in Honduras indicates that the true figure for forest cover may now be less than 20,000 km².
SOURCE: Reference 8 and 9, and information collected by the author during visits to Central America in 1976 and 1979.

while the region possessed some 400,000 square kilometers of moist forest before 1960 (and 500,000 square kilometers prior to white settlement 400 years ago), the forests have now declined to less than 200,000 square kilometers.

Ironically, cattle raising in tropical forest-lands is now recognized to be an exceptionally poor use of natural resources.[13] Stocking rates are absurdly low, only one head of stock to one hectare immediately following forest clearing, and only one animal for every five to seven hectares within five to 10 years, as the soil fertility and the nutritional value of grasses decline.

Steers require an average of four years to reach a weight of 450 kilograms for slaughter. In the year-round warm humid climate of Central America there is a problem with toxic weeds, which invade the pasturelands as the soil becomes compacted; as a consequence, some ranches lose one-fifth of their cattle within the first half dozen years. But to the wealthy stockman who obtains forestland for next to nothing (and may even receive tax incentives to develop it from its "unproductive" natural state), it matters little if he needs five or 10 times as much space to raise his beef as would be the case if he were to practice adequate management in the form of improved breeds of livestock, prophylactic drugs to counter epizootics, and the like.

Indeed, Central America could produce all the extra beef it wants without eliminating a single additional tree from the rainforests. But in addition to the economic inducements of the export trade, a local socio-cultural factor comes into play. The cattle raising industry in these countries tends to be dominated by a national oligarchy which traditionally views stock ranching as a prestige activity. Cattle herds represent social standing and political power, and many ranchers are professional persons who retire to their country estates on weekends, where they ride around on horseback and comport themselves as gentlemen stock-raisers. In contrast to the small-scale peasant, who of necessity must make the most intensive use of his small holding, the "prestige rancher" is often content to utilize his land in extensive fashion, which usually means an inefficient and wasteful fashion. Many of these large-scale landholders feel little incentive to intensify their beef-raising methods, especially when they believe there is still "plenty of virgin forest left".

At the same time these large-scale landholders control most of the land. Of approximately 400,000 farms in Central America, 90 percent are smaller than 50 hectares; but the remaining 10 percent account for three-quarters of all pasturelands and about two-thirds of all the cattle.[14] In Costa Rica, for example, the cattle industry is dominated by little more than 2,000 ranchers, who hold an average of 750 hectares each, and who control half of the agricultural land in use.

Table 3: US Imports of Beef

COUNTRY OF ORIGIN	1971 ('000s OF KG)	1978 ('000s OF KG)
Costa Rica	18,648	25,416
Honduras	15,066	18,430
Nicaragua	23,869	22,670
Guatemala	14,955	15,486
El Salvador	3,086	3,830
Panama	2,156	302
Total, from all countries	595,751★ (of which Austrialia and New Zealand 339,625)	750,883 (of which Austrialia and New Zealand 522,108)

★ Amounts to about 1 percent of US domestic production.
SOURCE: Information supplied by Dairy, Livestock and Poultry Division, Foreign Agricultural Service. US Department of Agriculture, Washington DC, January 1979.

In Guatemala, 2.2 percent of the population owns 70 percent of the agricultural land; in Honduras, the largest single landowner is United Brands (now diversifying out of bananas and into beef) with 810 hectares. While the concentration of land ownership in Central America is scarcely a new phenomenon, it has particular consequences: those who control the largest part of the land are those with the least incentive to use it efficiently, and in fact clearing the forest may bring them economic advantages. And because of their privileged position in the local political structure, they are unlikely to meet serious opposition.

Some Proposals to Resolve the Problem

Apart from the many opportunities the countries in question have to improve their beef production techniques, there are a number of initiatives available to the United States and to international aid agencies.

First, the United States could opt to import no more beef from Central America. This would mean that the US would have to reduce its beef consumption by a very marginal amount (or import more from non-tropical Latin America, or from other suppliers such as Australia). This would make more beef available in Central America for local consumption, and it would encourage the region to follow an agricultural track that is inevitable in the long run, one involving greater diversification into other agricultural products. It would be no great hardship for the United States to simply eliminate one percent of its beef intake – a trifling gesture compared with the five percent reduction in gasoline consumption during the past year.[15]

Secondly, both bilateral and multilateral aid agencies could support conservation activities in the countries concerned. Costa Rica, for example, while presenting a dismal record in forestland stockraising, has nevertheless achieved several first-rate measures in conservation. During the mid-1970s, President Daniel Oduber formulated a systematic strategy for his country's forests: he set up a Natural Resources Institute to conduct ecologic evaluation studies and to produce a program for integrated land-use planning of the entire country, and he expanded the national parks network until it now contains a greater proportion of land than is the case for any other Latin American country. Under the new President, Rodrigo Carazo, the parks network is scheduled to be expanded still further until it will cover about 10 percent of national territory, and the country is implementing a natural resource conservation program, with $9 million support from the US Agency for International Development (AID).

Third, along the lines of this AID support for Costa Rica, and a further AID gesture in the form of a $10 million contribution toward a $17 million project for watershed reforestation in the Panama Canal Zone, international aid agencies can do much to foster sustainable use of forests in Central America. To date the tendency has been for development agencies, notably the World Bank and the Inter-American Development Bank, to promote cattle raising in forestlands, a trend that should generally be reversed.

Conclusion

It is ironic that if Central America's forests disappear within the foreseeable future, not only local people will suffer by way of environmental degradation, decline of watershed services, and the like. (Already Costa Rica's hydropower dams are being silted up, and Honduras has undergone undue hurricane damage due to loss of forest cover.) Other human communities will suffer, notably North Americans. Central America's rainforests, with their exceptionally rich biotic diversity, contain many genetic resources of great value to modern agriculture, medicine and industry. For example, in 1978 a wild variety of perennial corn was discovered in a forest of southern Mexico. Not only could this new strain enable the corn-growing industry, through cross-breeding, to avoid the season-by-season cost of plowing and sowing, but the wild germplasm offers resistance to several viruses which attack commercial corn.[16] And according to a botanist from South Carolina, Dr. Monie S. Hudson, who specializes in medicinal applications of phytochemicals, a screening program to evaluate 1500 tree species in Costa Rica's forests has revealed that around 15 percent might have potential as a treatment for cancer.[17]

It is clear then that both Central Americans and North Americans are contributing to the "hamburgerization" of the rainforests, and that both will suffer from the loss of them. It is equally clear that both must cooperate if the problem is to be solved; either all will lose together, or all could gain together – a paradigm of interdependency resource relationships within the international community.

ENDNOTES

1. N. Myers. *The Sinking Ark* (Pergamon Press, Oxford and New York, 1979), and *Conversion of Tropical Moist Forests* (National Research Council, Washington, DC, 1980); G.O. Barney. *The Global 2000 Report to the President* (Council on Environmental Quality and US Department of State, Washington, DC, 1980); US Interagency Taskforce on Tropical Forests. *The World's Tropical Forests: A Policy, Strategy and Program for the United States* (Report to the President, US Department of State, 1980).

2. N. Myers. *The Sinking Ark* (op.cit.); National Academy of Sciences. *Research Priorities in Tropical Biology* (Report of the Committee on Research Priorities in Tropical Biology, P.H. Raven, Chairman, National Research Council, Washington, DC,1980).

3. N. Myers. *Environmental Conservation*, pp. 101–114, 7(2), 1980.

4. N. Myers. *op. cit.*, reference 1 and 3.

5. N. Myers. *op. cit.*, reference 1 and 3; W. M. Denevan, editor. *The Role of Geographical Research in Latin America* (Conference of Latin American Geographers, Publication No. 7, Muncie, Indiana, 1978); J. C. Dickenson. *Latin American Development Issues*, A. D. Hill, editor (Conference of Latin American Geographers, Publication No. 3, East Lansing, Michigan, 1973); J. D. Nations. *The Future of Middle America's Tropical Rainforests* (Centre for Applied Human Ecology, San Cristobal las Casas, Chiapas, Mexico, Mimeo, 1980); J. J. Parsons. *Revista de Biologia Tropicale*, pp. 121–138, 24, 1976; D. R. Shane, *Hoofprints in the Forest* (Office of Environmental Affairs, US Department of State, Washington, DC, 1980); J. R. Simpson. *Projections of Production and Consumption of Beef in Latin America for 1985* (Food and Resource Economics Department Staff Paper 88, Institute for Food and Agricultural Sciences, University of Florida, Gainesville, Florida, 1978); R. C. West. *Recent Developments in Cattle-raising and the Beef Export Trade in the Middle American Region* (Actes du XLII Congres International des Americanistes, I: 391–402, 1976).

6. J. D. Nations. *op. cit.*; J. J. Parsons. *op. cit.*; D. R. Shane. *op. cit.*

7. United Nations Food and Agriculture Organization. *Outlook for Agriculture: 2000* (FAO, Rome,1979), and *State of Food and Agriculture 1979* (FAO, Rome, 1980).

8. D. R. Shane. *op. cit.*; US Department of Agriculture. *Beef and Veal: US Imports by Country of Origin–Product Weight, Annual 1973–78* (Dairy, Livestock and Poultry Division, Commodity Programs, Foreign Agricultural Service, US Department of Agriculture, Washington, DC, 1979; US Department of Agriculture, *Livestock and Meat Situation* (Economics, Statistics and Cooperatives Service, US Department of Agriculture, Washington, DC, 1979).

9. US Department of Agriculture. *op. cit.* in reference 8; also *Business Week*, pp. 56–68, July 11, 1977; *Consumer Reports*, pp. 508–513, 44(9), 1979.

10. D. Pimentel, P.A. Oltenacu, M.C. Nesheim, J. Krummel, M.S. Allen, and S. Chick. *Science* 207: 843–848 (1980).

11. J.D. Nations. *op. cit.*; D.R. Shane. *op. cit.*; M. Boas and S. Chain. *Big Mac: The Unauthorized Story of McDonalds* (Mentor Books, New American Library, New York, 1976).

12. P. Slud. *Bulletin of American Museum of Natural History*, 121(2):49–148, 1960.

13. S.B. Hecht. *Some Environmental Effects of Converting Tropical Rainforests to Pasture in Eastern Amazonia* (Unpublished Ph.D. Dissertation, Department of Geography, University of California, Berkeley, California, 1980); J.M. Kirby. *Pacific Viewpoint*, 17 (2):105–132 (1976); E.E. Miller. *Journal of Tropical Geography*, 41:59–69 (1975); D.F. Osbourn. *World Review of Animal Production* 11(4):23–31 (1975); and P.A. Sanchez and L.E. Tergas, editors. *Pasture Produc-*

tion in Acid Soils of the Tropics (Centro Internacional de Agricultura Tropical, Cali, Colombia, 1980).

14. J.D. Nations. *op. cit.*; and information supplied privately to the author during three visits to Central America in 1976 and 1979.

15. D.R. Shane. *op. cit.*

16. Personal communication from Professor H.H. Iltis, University of Wisconsin at Madison and Dr. L.L. Nault, Ohio Agricultural and Research and Development Center.

17. Personal communications from Dr. M.S. Hudson in 1978 and 1980.

About the Authors in Chapter 12

Michael J. Watts is Associate Professor of Geography at the University of California-Berkeley. His volume, *Silent Violence: Food, Famine, and Peasantry in Northern Nigeria,* appeared in 1985 and was published by the University of California Press, Berkeley.

Jane L. Collins is at the State University of New York at Binghamton and is in the Department of Anthropology. She and Michael Painter co-authored *Settlement and Deforestation in Central America: A Discussion of Development Issues.* The book was published in 1986 by the International Development Program of Clark University, Worcester, MA, and the Institute for Development Anthropology, Binghamton, NY.

Gunter Schramm is Energy Advisor for the Industry and Energy Department of the World Bank, Washington, D.C. Among his publications (see Warford in Chapter 12 for another) is "Regional Cooperation and Economic Development," *The Annals of Regional Science,* 20(2), 1986.

Dr. Norman Myers is a Consultant in Environment and Development and is located in Oxford, England. His volume, *Deforestation Rates in Tropical Forests and Their Climatic Implications,* was published by Friends of the Earth, London, in 1989.

CHAPTER 13

Agricultural Development

Introduction

ABOUT 70 PERCENT of the world's population lives in developing countries in Africa, Asia, and Latin America. There is enough food to feed the global population today even though a large proportion of the food supply is produced in developed countries. Poverty and problems in the distribution of food are the two main causes of world hunger.

Agricultural technologies such as high yielding varieties of wheat, pesticides, and fertilizers have contributed toward dramatic increases in food production. However, in South Asia, Africa, and many other areas of the world, population growth has outpaced food production. Furthermore, the potential to grow more food in parts of Asia, Africa, and Latin America is diminishing due to environmental problems resulting from deforestation and loss of soil fertility. The spectre of massive starvation in many developing countries has to be resolved using new technological and organizational know-how. Fortunately, new approaches to rural development, farm organization, and forestation are emerging.

The green revolution of the 1970s, which introduced hybrid seeds to India, benefited a small fraction of the landed farmers by doubling the yield of food grains, but millions of other farmers have not benefited (Chakravarti, 1973). It also resulted in large regional disparities in production. Several obstacles limited the success of the green revolution. With an increase in oil prices came an increase in the price of input, including fertilizers. Unfortunately, in some instances, the new hybrids of wheat and rice were not liked by people. Finally, governments fixed market prices for grains at levels that were too low to motivate farmers to produce more. These lessons from the green revolution are slowly being accepted in developing areas. Countries such as Zimbabwe have encouraged free market policies and the results are beginning to show in terms of better-organized and more productive farmers' groups. While technologies are being introduced in many developing countries, their cultural context should be carefully considered.

Perhaps the most thorough summary of the literature on the effectiveness of programs designed to increase agricultural production has been presented by Ruttan (1986). In addition to describing the cyclical nature of emphasis on types of programs, he concludes that we seem to have neither learned from programmatic successes nor from failures. We have often thought this ourselves because so many of the dedicated, well-intended professionals or perhaps would-be professionals describe their efforts as though they have just invented the wheel. They have had such a limited background in the history of development experiences that the relationship of their successes or failures to the total picture is beyond their comprehension. As Ruttan goes on to point out, it has become increasingly possible to substitute social science knowledge and analytical experience for trial and error. Unfortunately, we must agree with Ruttan that this has not been done.

There is also an excellent literature on the diffusion of inventions, a literature that has developed in sociology over more than a 100-year period in the broader sense of diffusion of information. Agarwal (1983) has made an appropriate addition in describing a current experience with wood-burning stoves.

The Articles in Chapter 13

Bratton presents the key factors contributing to increased food production in Zimbabwe between 1980 and 1985. After Zimbabwe received independence in 1984, small farmers became more involved in the national economy and their share of national maize sales increased from 8 percent to 45 percent. These peasant farmers formed voluntary, self-managed organizations, leadership being drawn from among the farmers. Several types of organizations, such as production collectives, that pooled land and labor or engaged in bulk buying or selling came into being. In general, the farmers belonging to these organizations have a higher productivity than individual farmers. The success of farmers' organizations raises new hopes for food sufficiency and development in Africa.

Winterbottom and *Hazlewood* describe a new farming practice: agroforestry. It involves integrating trees and shrubs into traditional farming practices to increase productivity and sustainability of crops. The multiple outputs of this practice are seen in the use of trees in different ways that help to replenish soil fertility and to provide fuel, food, fodder, edible fruits, and other products. By using the trees for wood and non-wood products, households can also increase their incomes by selling to others who need these products and by not having to depend on an outside source for them.

The concluding article in this chapter and concluding article in the volume is undoubtedly one of the most thought-provoking; it is by *Ponna Wignaraja*, a person whose life has been devoted to consideration of the problem of how to organize people for development. *Wignaraja* has been concerned about the fact that, although most of the developing areas of the world are predominantly rural, they have had a model for development presented to them by the industrialized nations of the world based on the premise of one stock of knowledge. Thus far, the rich have gotten richer and the poor, poorer.

Wignaraja goes on to discuss the reasons for failure of rural development projects, criticizing central planning and control from the top, and provides a new model of rural development. *Wignaraja* concludes that before any new development can be successful in a rural area, the poor people living in the area must be united, and this cannot be legislated. Without the participation of the poor, a grass-roots approach, development cannot be achieved. For people to participate effectively in the change, they must create their own organization as well as become more conscious of the socioeconomic reality surrounding them, the forces that are keeping them in poverty. They must learn what they can do to improve their condition through collective action.

REFERENCES

Agarwal, Bina, "Diffusion of Rural Innovations: Some Analytical Issues and the Case of Wood-burning Stoves," *World Development*, 11(4), 1983, pp. 359–376.

Chakravarti, A. K., "Green Revolution in India," *Annals of the American Association of Geographers*, 63 (3), 1973, pp. 319–330.

Ruttan, Vernon, W., "Assistance to Expand Agricultural Production," *World Development*, 14(1), 1986, pp. 39–63.

Farmer Organizations and Food Production in Zimbabwe

MICHAEL BRATTON

1. Introduction

Independence in Zimbabwe brought about a dramatic upsurge in the involvement of small farmers in the national economy. Between 1980 and 1985, the share of national maize sales originating from the peasant sector registered a remarkable leap from 8 to 45%.

The reasons that smallholders chose to celebrate independence by growing and selling more maize are complex. To a large extent their reaction is attributable to a doubling of the producer price for maize and its maintenance ahead of inflation over the period in question. The government also distributed packs of hybrid seed and chemical fertilizer as a measure to reestablish farmers on the land in the aftermath of the independence war and the drought of the early 1980s. A conventional explanation would point to the effects of such prices and technologies in determining farmer performance.

But there is an additional element, often overlooked. Small farmers can take *organized collective action* to reach common agricultural goals. In 1980 people in Zimbabwe were keen for peace to return to the countryside. There were fresh political ideas abroad about social cooperation and new opportunities were available for small farmers to obtain government services and enter the marketplace. All these factors were expressed in a widespread grassroots impulse to create new farmer organizations

Bratton. This article appeared in *World Development*, 1986, 14(3), on pp. 367–384, from whom we received permission to use it. The journal is published by Pergamon Journals Ltd., Oxford, United Kingdom.

and to revive old ones. We can derive from this particular situation a point of general import. The explanation of production can be traced, at least in part, to the institutional arrangements that are made for practicing and supporting agriculture.

2. Markets, States and Collective Organization

In the past, official thinking about agricultural institutions in Africa has put the onus on *the state* as the responsible authority. Yet it is clear that "the span of control of even the most unitary government rarely extends in any complete way into the countryside" (Russell and Nicholson, 1981, p. 4). The organizational challenge is to reach a large number of small producers in scattered and remote locations and to deliver services at precise intervals across an agricultural season. Now the current orthodoxy in development policy is that *the market* "has been neglected or suppressed despite evident capacity to do many of the tasks (of) government" (Berg, 1984, p. 45). It is not immediately apparent, however, that private sector solutions are available for smallholder production problems. In many African countries, the capitalist market has even flimsier institutional foundations than the state. Moreover, because smallholdings are usually the least accessible of all production units, peasant farmers must always pay a premium for the delivery of any good or service priced by the market.

Because all types of central institutions enjoy limited competence in Africa – more limited, perhaps, than on any other continent – attention must turn to what small farmers do for themselves. Since the state and the market fall short, the alternative is to search within the rural social fabric for local organizations that have development potential. I am referring to voluntary associations of farmers that coalesce of their own accord on the basis of shared economic interests and cultural values.

The distinguishing feature of collective action among small farmers is that it is *"self-managed."* Local organizations of farmers, unlike institutions of the state and market, draw leadership and management from among their own ranks rather than from a cadre of professionals. This sets farmer organizations apart, for example, from cooperative societies that are regulated by a government department or which operate as commercial firms. The organizing principles of collective organization are voluntary membership, government by agreement and social control by peer pressure. When this kind of organization arises among farmers, it may take many forms: mutual aid parties, special interest clubs, primary cooperative societies. Whatever the form, however, all lie within the informal sector of popular local organizations, a field of enterprise which development studies has yet to comprehensively address.

The small but valuable literature on collective organization in rural development (Korten, 1980; Esman and Uphoff, 1984; Garcia-Zamor, 1985) draws heavily on case material from Asia and Latin America. Despite the need to understand the institutional dimensions of the current African food crisis, very little systematic empirical research has been done on self-help activity among dryland farmers in Africa. This paper summarizes findings from a study on the effect of farmer organizations on food production in Zimbabwe in the period 1980–85.

There are three main objectives:
(a) to propose a framework within which organization among smallholders can be analyzed;

(b) To describe the extent and social composition of farmer groups in the communal areas of Zimbabwe;
(c) to test three interrelated propositions, namely that farmer group membership is associated with:
(i) access to production assets,
(ii) access to production services, and
(iii) increased levels of food crop productivity.

3. The Context of Smallholder Agriculture

••••

I accept the general observation from public choice theory that the nature of the resource will influence the form that collective organization will take (Olson, 1965; Ostrom and Ostrom, 1979). But I do not agree that the nature of the resource can be fully captured by the common distinction between public and private goods. A further distinction seems to me to be needed, as follows.

In smallholder systems, production resources can be seen to emanate from either of two levels: the *level of production* or *the level of exchange.*

At the level of production, small farmers deploy *production assets* like land, draft power and farm implements. I also define family labor as an "asset," provided it includes only the work power of the family members who are permanently resident in the household and excludes temporary laborers. These assets can be thought of as the factor endowment that is vested in the household through membership, ownership or use rights. Taken together, they constitute the foundation on which the production potential of the household rests.

At the level of exchange, small farmers call upon *production services* from sources outside the village. It is difficult to see how agricultural productivity can be significantly enhanced without the introduction of scientific technology which in turn requires the household to enter into a transaction, usually using money, in a wider institutional arena. Production services include information, credit, chemical inputs and transport which are delivered by centralized public and private agencies. These resources are not intrinsic to the household, though they are purchased and consumed by it.

4. Types of Farmer Organization

The topography of the smallholder world, and the nature of the resources within it, give shape to the options for collective action and provide a basis for deriving a typology of small farmer organizations. At minimum, we would like to separately observe organizations that deliver public goods from those that deal only in private resources. Furthermore, we want to differentiate organizations that are designed to pool production assets among households – at the level of production – from those that exist to link members to central service institutions – at the level of exchange. Finally, we must leave room for farmer groups that attempt to straddle levels of organization and which undertake both to pool assets and to win services for their members.

This approach suggests that various patterns of collective action are possible, each expressed through a characteristic type of farmer organization.

(a) *Pooling land*. Where land is publicly owned, peasant farmers may organize, or be organized by the state, to undertake collective production. All agricultural operations are undertaken by the community in concert and no one is exempt from the obligation to participate. Surpluses are shared equally or according to work done. This type of organization is best described as a *production collective*.

(b) *Pooling labor*. Where land is privately held, smallholders may decide to work together or even contribute production assets into a common pool. In this case,

however, all proceeds go to the owner on whose land the crop is grown. The groups that arise are small – often limited to family neighbors and friends – and work contributions are voluntary. The most mobile household resource is labor, even though draft animals or implements may also be shared. For this reason, groups of individuals who choose to join together in some production tasks are here called *labor groups*.

(c) *Attaining knowledge.* Few agricultural services are public goods, if this is taken to mean that they are free, indivisible and accessible to all. The main exception is technical information which, in theory at least, can be obtained by any farmer without charge. When farmers assemble for the sole purpose of securing agricultural advice, whether from an agribusiness firm or from a government research and extension service, we can speak of *information groups.*

(d) *Bulk buying and selling.* Most agricultural services are private goods and are delivered to selected households that have the ability to pay a service fee. On a per household basis, smallholders can exert only limited and fragmented demand for services like credit, inputs and transport. To attract the attention of the market and to realize economies of scale, households may combine to make bulk purchases of inputs or bulk sales of produce. This type of collective action occurs in *market groups*.

(e) *Managing "the commons."* Certain production assets – like water, forests or grazing lands – belong to the community as a whole. But, unlike land, they can rarely be exploited without support services from agencies outside the village, for example to plan irrigation works or to fence and improve pastures. A democratic local organization is required to represent the interests of all community members and to ensure that the overexertion of these interests does not result in a "tragedy of the commons" (Hardin, 1972). For want of a better term, this type of organization is dubbed a *village assembly*.

(f) *Vertical integration*. Smallholders sometimes wish to engage in *both* pooling for production *and* bulking for exchange. For example, labor groups may decide to enter central markets in order to ensure a reliable and affordable flow of production services. Vertical integration is a strategy to expand the horizons of an organization to bring a larger portion of the environment under control. The type of organization which results in this context may be described as a *multipurpose group*.

It should be noted that two types of farmer organization do not occur in the communal areas of Zimbabwe with sufficient frequency to warrant inclusion in this study. First, as will be shown below, production collectives based on joint land holding are almost nonexistent. The main experiment with collective production in Zimbabwe is not in the peasant sector but on commercial farmland reallocated under the Mugabe government's land reform program. Second, there are very few cases of grazing or irrigation schemes managed by farmer organizations. Such activities collapsed during the independence war and have been slow to revive. This study will therefore focus on the types of collective organization which smallholders in Zimbabwe have shown themselves eager to initiate. I will discuss and compare information groups, labor groups, market groups and multipurpose groups.

A final theoretical point: the different types of farmer organization can be arrayed developmentally. Some groups are clearly more "complex," and others more "cooperative" than others. Analytically these organizational characteristics can be seen to constitute two development scales. The *scale of task complexity* refers to the number of tasks undertaken, the number of actors involved, and the extent to which procedures are bureaucratized. The *scale of member cooperation* refers to the frequency of contact among members, the amount of time each member contributes, and the value of personal assets contributed for group use.

It is now possible to propose how farmer organizations grow and change. The developmental relationship among the types of group is determined by the interaction of the two scales. According to this model, market groups are more complex than labor groups. They have more members, keep more formal records and must coordinate their activities with outside agencies. Labor groups, however, are more cooperative than market groups. Although they are smaller, member contact is more regular and intensive, and involves the commitment of assets. Multipurpose groups only come about when labor groups add supply and marketing to their repertoire of functions. They are the most complex and cooperative organizations of all.

5. Farmer Organizations in Zimbabwe

The scope of empirical inquiry in this study is the communal lands of Zimbabwe, formerly known as the Tribal Trust Lands. The majority of the country's population (about 55%) lives here and, however extensive the government's land reform program, will continue to do so. Because of population pressure and ecological degradation, the communal lands cannot offer every household an acceptable standard of living from agriculture alone. Many adult males (25–45%) migrate away in search of wage employment. Small-scale production in a mixed system of livestock herding and maize, millet, and groundnut cropping nonetheless remains the most common economic activity in Zimbabwe.

The data are derived from a survey of 464 randomly selected households and in-depth interviews with leaders and members of 50 farmer groups. Unless otherwise stated, all data refer to the 1981–82 agricultural season which was drier than normal but which preceded the devastating drought of 1982–83.

Four areas were selected for research which were widely dispersed and roughly representative of the diversity of the rural areas of the country, excepting Matabeleland:

(a) Chipuriro (Natural Region IIa, according to the standard agro-ecological classification of Zimbabwe; Vincent and Thomas, 1961) lies on prime agricultural land in the high rainfall belt. The district is well served with agricultural marketing infrastructure.

(b) Wedza (Natural Regions IIb and III) enjoys moderate rainfall and intermediate potential for mixed farming. Proximity to the capital city, however, has led to substantial male outmigration and reliance on wage remissions for farm capitalization.

(c) Gutu (Natural Regions III, IV and V) suffers from low and unreliable rainfall and susceptibility to drought. High population density is accompanied by landlessness and overworked soils.

(d) Dande (Natural Region IV) lies in the Zambezi valley. Land is plentiful, soils are fertile, and population density low. Exploitation of this potential is limited, however, by shortage of rainfall and lack of irrigation and other infrastructure.

I found that, in Zimbabwe as a whole, farmer organizations are *numerous and widespread*. In 1981–82, 44% of cultivators belonged to some form of voluntary agricultural association. This figure may be biased upward slightly by the large size of the Wedza subsample. Membership is most common in Wedza where more than half belong (56%) and least so in Dande where only one in five do so (21%). At minimum, however, the frequency of collective action in all districts calls into question the stereotype of peasants as fragmented, powerless and apathetic.

The propensity for farmers to organize is related to the extent of state and market penetration into a rural area. The four survey areas in Zimbabwe were classified according to whether state penetration (measured by the ratio of extension workers to farmers) and market penetration (measured by the distance from the furthest farm to the nearest grain marketing depot) were "high" or "low". Collective action by farmers is most common where the state and the market both have a strong presence and least likely where both are weakly represented. This implies that, while farmer groups are based upon local initiative and enjoy relative organizational autonomy, they are most likely to arise in a setting where agricultural support services are available from an administrative and commercial center.

••••

Because, in Zimbabwe, farmer organizations with nominally different labels perform similar functions I applied the typology which classifies them according to what they *do* rather than what they are *called*. I asked farmers "what activities does your farmer group engage in?" and – depending on whether they reported attaining knowledge, pooling labor, bulk marketing, or a combination of functions – assigned each group member to a particular type of organization.

This procedure revealed that:

(a) The attainment of knowledge is the most common activity and accompanies all other organized initiatives. Because it serves as a stepping stone to more complex or cooperative forms of organization, the *information group per se,* which assembles for educational purposes alone, is in fact the least popular type (17% of group households).

(b) *Labor groups* are the most common type of farmer organization (36%). Mutual work exchange, especially when seasonal labor requirements are at a peak is reported by a majority of group households. The practice is to form work parties (*zvikwata*) of 4–10 people to rotate around the fields of the group members. The pooling of labor (*majangano*) is a contemporary adaptation and substitute for the traditional practice of attracting labor with a beer party (*nhimbe*).

(c) *Market groups* and *multipurpose groups* occur in identical proportions (24%). Bulk purchases of inputs are more frequently undertaken than bulk sales of crops through market outlets.

Different types of groups predominate in different regions. The polar contrast is between Wedza, where labor and multipurpose groups are typical, and Guruve, where information and market groups hold sway. The reasons why farmers in one part of the country are inclined to more cooperative forms of organization and another to more individualistic forms is not easy to explain. Perhaps farmers form labor groups in Wedza because of the preponderance of female-headed households there with a shortage of family labor. Farmers may be more independent-minded in Chipuriro because the favorable soils and rainfall in that region permit households to make an income from farming on their own. The recent settlement history of Dande, and the absence of traditional ties of cooperation among "strangers," may partly explain why relatively few groups of any kind exist there.

6. Who Belongs?

Because organizations do not materialize in a vacuum – they are purposively constructed to serve particular economic interests – it is important to enquire into the social composition of small farmer groups. Because membership is voluntary and because they trade in private goods, one would not expect groups to be broadly representative. Who joins and who does not? How is membership distributed, say by wealth and sex? Do groups ever reach and involve the rural poor?

The best measure of economic differentiation in the countryside of the southern subcontinent of Africa is the household's assets in cattle. A herd provides a method of accumulating wealth and an insurance against hardship; equally importantly, it is a means of production for arable agriculture in the form of draft power and manure. Economists familiar with the peasant farming systems of Zimbabwe argue that the ownership of cattle is the greatest single determinant of a household's overall production potential (Collinson, 1982).

The data on cattle ownership indicate that collective organizations are composed of farmers who are more advantaged than average. In all districts, group members own slightly more cattle than individuals (on average, 8.3 animals versus 6.0). Farmer organizations are not immune from the universal tendency for power to accumulate in the same hands as status and wealth. This is not to say that voluntary groups merely reinforce the "law of big farmer dominance" that tends to hold wherever agricultural cooperatives are introduced from above as a government program. True, the very poorest generally find difficulty in joining. If group activities involve asset pooling or cash services they have nothing, except their labor, to contribute. But, by the same token, the richest farmers often also choose to stand back. For their part, they do not join groups because the scale of their farm enterprise is sufficiently large to be economic, or because they are reluctant to share assets with others who are less well endowed than themselves.

Instead, farmer organizations are liable to embrace "middle peasant" households. This stratum lies between the relatively "rich" individual farmers (18% of the population, own 13 cattle) and the "poor" individual farmers (38% of the population, own 2.5 cattle). Middle peasant households have undeveloped potential to raise productivity and income. They neither feel too impoverished to get involved, nor rich enough to go it alone.

Within these general parameters, the pattern of social mobilization varies considerably according to the type of farmer group. In brief, market groups and multipurpose groups tend to be elitist, whereas information and labor groups enjoy a more popular base. Whereas market groups take almost half their members (48%) from the top echelon of cattle owners, labor groups draw almost a third of membership (31%) from among the lowest. Of all the areas surveyed, only in Wedza, where labor groups predominate, do households entirely without cattle have a firm foothold in farmer associations.

The emerging pattern of membership by wealth is accentuated when the sex of respondents in groups is taken into account. Women most frequently belong to the poorer groups that pool labor; men, by contrast, dominate the market groups which specialize in bulk commodity transactions. Culturally, this reflects a division of labor in which women undertake the basic production tasks and men control the allocation of surpluses. Labor groups do, however, offer women a potential base from which to organize and accumulate wealth for themselves, providing they occupy the executive positions of leadership on group committees. Otherwise, the social composition of farmer organizations does not challenge traditional patterns of gender inequality. Indeed, in labor groups where a membership of female workers undertakes field operations under the direction of a committee of male farmers, group organization may actually reinforce the subordination of women.

7. Access to Production Assets

The important inquiry is whether small farmer organizations can make a contribution to food production. I ask first if group membership can help alleviate the basic resource constraints faced by households at the level of production. How much pooling of assets actually takes place? What effect does pooling have on the access of poor households to the means of production? In what ways, if any, do farmer organizations change the production practices of their members?

Land is a good place to start. In general, collective organization is likely to emerge where cultivators control their own land and where there is relative equity in the size of holdings (Esman and Uphoff, 1984, pp. 30 and 37). Both conditions prevail in the communal lands of Zimbabwe. Farmers have use-rights in land. There are gross disparities in the size of holdings between the commercial and peasant sectors, and within the communal areas, an average of 16% of the young men above school age have no land. Among landholders in the communal areas, however, land distribution is relatively even. The average holding is 3.2 hectares (ha) of arable land per household, exclusive of grazing, and few households have less than 2 or more than 4.5 ha. Nor is land universally in short supply. In only two of the four survey areas – Gutu and Chipuriro – do farmers cite land as their principal production constraint.

The first finding is that membership of a farmer organization has no discernible effect on the access to land for small farmers in Zimbabwe. From the outset, group members tend to hold slightly more land (3.4 ha) than individuals (2.8 ha), but the difference is not significant. I asked farmers whether they exchanged land among one another and very few reported lending (8%) or borrowing (12%). Most importantly, there was no difference whatever in the behavior of individual farmers and group members in this regard.

The effect of farmer organization becomes apparent when we consider collective plots in which the ownership of land and the proceeds of the crop are shared among members. A small number of cases occurred in only one district in the survey (12% of the households in Wedza). Interestingly, collective landholding was found almost exclusively (90%) within the ranks of farmer organizations, though none of these could be described as a true production collective. Certain types of groups – usually labor or multipurpose groups – typically operate small vegetable gardens located on wetlands or river banks and labor is rotated for the arduous task of bucket irrigation. Occasionally a field of from 1 to 10 ha will be planted with a cash crop like maize or cotton and the income used to finance group activities like trips to training courses or agricultural shows. But, even where group members have adjacent fields, the norm is for the land and the crop to be reserved as private property. Where collective fields have been established, they stand alongside, and are treated by members as ancillary to, the personal plots of individual households.

If access to land is not markedly affected by farmer organization, what about access to *labor*? Many households find themselves short of helping hands at peak moments in the agricultural season. In order of importance, extra labor is needed for weeding (69% of households), harvesting (52%) and plowing (44%), that is, for operations in which timeliness is a consideration. For activities like the shelling of maize or groundnuts, which can be spread out over several months and done whenever household members have a moment to spare, there is little demand for extra labor (10%).

Household labor resources can be supplemented in a number of ways. One common approach is to call upon nonresident relatives like townsfolk who visit the countryside on weekends or holidays (29% of all households). Alternatively, if the farmer can afford it, labor can be hired on a daily basis from among the large pool of rural residents who are anxious for opportunities for paid work (23%). The most common tactic, however, is to organize a reciprocal labor party (*chikwata*) among neighbors in the immediate vicinity (38%).

Because *chikwata* has roots in traditional practice, it is not exclusively a feature of modern farmer organization. I found some farmers who did not belong to a group but who nonetheless called labor parties in their fields. But, as expected, access to extra labor in work parties was significantly more likely among group members (46%) than among individuals (21%) (see Table 6). Not only are group members more likely to enjoy this kind of enhancement to the household labor supply, but work parties in the context of group organization are larger and more regular. Group members receive an average of four times as much extra labor per year from communal work parties than do individuals (28.4 extra person days compared with 7.3 extra person days).

A probable reason for better access to extra labor within groups is that the procedures for pooling are more institutionalized. Group members enter agreements to provide one another with standardized amounts of labor at specified times. Labor groups have a written roster of work assignments which is linked to a pattern of improved practices and which controls the rotation of work around the fields of each member. The group empowers its executive committee to supervise the implementation of the work plan and to discipline wayward members by fines or expulsion.

An anomaly that requires explanation is *the myth of majangano* by which farmers claim to engage in communal labor more often than they actually practice it. Even in labor groups the frequency of reciprocal labor (*majangano*) is lower than might be expected. I found, for example that only 57% of labor group members actually participated in a communal work party in the 1981–82 agricultural season, even though labor pooling was the reason they gave for joining a group. One possible explanation is that this was a dry year in which some crops were damaged and some lost entirely, thus reducing the demand for labor. I attempted, however, to check the reality of labor pooling by monitoring the labor use patterns of 12 households in Wedza at bi-weekly intervals over the course of the 1983–84 agricultural season. The results reveal that communal labor accounts for only a small proportion of the total labor deployed by the household. For those in groups only 17% of the sampled person days of labor expended on the household lands came from a work party. For individuals the same figure was less than 1%. While we can again note the superiority of access to labor that is associated with group membership, it is clear that, compared with the use of resident family labor, labor pooling is a relatively uncommon practice.

Access to draft power enables small farmers to undertake improved cropping practices. The extension service in Zimbabwe recommends that farmers prepare their fields by "winter plowing" in order to conserve moisture in the ground and finish heavy operations before oxen are weakened by the shortage of dry season grazing. They also recommend the early planting of maize immediately after the rains arrive in November in order to take maximum advantage of the limited moisture that falls in the short growing season. The findings on the adoption of these practices are as follows. "Draftless" households rarely plow in winter (18%). If they engage in draft borrowing, their ability to plow increases dramatically (48%), especially if borrowing is done through farmer groups (70%). The effect of group organization is not as marked for summer planting, though it is still worth recording. According to my data, "draftless" households who borrow oxen (60%) are no more tardy than the average individual (59%) in getting their maize seed in the ground. As for households that are merely "short of draft", only those in labor groups are able to plant as opportunely as households that have enough draft. Otherwise, even if they borrow, they fall behind.

All things considered, the activity of pooling has a rather limited effect on the mobilization of agricultural assets at the level of production. In some cases, as with land, group organization is unable to overcome the pressing resource constraints faced by the household. In other cases, as with draft power, group organization performs primarily to complement long-standing social obligations for reciprocal exchange. Group members enjoy a general advantage mainly in their capacity to mobilize extra labor from work parties. Even here, however, the tradition of communal work survives as much in myth as reality and is challenged by the values of individualism that accompany the insertion of peasant society into the modern world.

As confirmation, we can note that the pooling of production assets declines as groups develop. This is true partly by definition: market groups, for example, are formed for collaboration only at the level of exchange. But it is worth noting that multipurpose groups show lower levels of labor and draft pooling (47 and 48% of households, respectively) than the simpler type of organization from which they evolved, that is, the labor group (57 and 82%, respectively). From this we can propose a first paradox of rural organizational development: as farmer organizations begin to resemble modern forms of "cooperative," so they abandon or undermine traditional patterns of "cooperation" inherited from the past.

8. Access to Production Services

What then of the resources that small farmers try to attract from outside the village? In many African countries the peasant sector is secondary, if not residual, to the concern of agricultural service agencies. Since independence in Zimbabwe the government has made strenuous efforts to correct the colonial bias toward the white commercial farmer, but services like extension, credit and transport remain in short supply relative to demand from small farmers. Under these circumstances, it becomes important to consider how collective organization can facilitate the distribution of scarce services. By banding together, can a group of farmers create effective demand and attract central agencies to their locality?

Let us examine this question first with regard to agricultural *extension*. In 1982 in Zimbabwe, over half the farmers interviewed (55%) said they saw a government extension worker (EW) during the course of the agricultural season. Membership of farmer organizations is the major factor explaining this high level of contact. Whereas only 31% of individual farmers see the EW, a full 86% of group members do so. Group farmers also get advice more regularly and are more likely to express satisfaction with the applicability of the technical advice to their own farming situation.

Group organization for the consumption of technical advice has advantages for both the farmer and the extension service. The point of contact is a meeting called by the group chairman at a mutually agreeable place, sometimes on the fields of one of the group members. Farmers who otherwise would not receive a personal visit from an extension worker, or who feel inhibited from dealing face-to-face with a government official, are able to get exposure to new ideas. The field agent, for his or her part, can take advantage of the capacity of the group to organize an assembly, and thereby reach more clients with a lower expenditure of travel and time. Senior managers in the extension service in Zimbabwe have recognized the cost-effectiveness of a group approach and have launched several group extension experiments as a matter of policy.

Small farmers in Zimbabwe do not take all their technical advice from the government, but also from nongovernment educational programs run by missions or fertilizer companies. They also turn to other farmers, particularly those who have a formal qualification like a Master Farmer certificate. Group farmers are three times as likely as individuals (54% versus 16%) to use

a supplementary source of advice. As might be expected in a group setting, they are particularly active in interactions with fellow farmers. The diffusion of technical innovation, whether from scientific research or the accumulated experience of farmers themselves, is clearly heightened by the existence of voluntary organizations within a peasantry.

It follows that group farmers have most choice when obtaining knowledge about sound agricultural practices. Redundancy of sources may improve the reliability of service delivery for, if one channel fails, an alternative is available. Redundancy is problematic only if advice from different quarters is contradictory, or if the circulation of ideas among farmers propagates unfounded traditional beliefs. I have found that, as farmer groups develop, they tend to move from government extension services to alternative sources. The implication here is that collective organizations flourish and grow under conditions where there is pluralism in the channels for service delivery.

Credit is a scarcer service than technical advice. In 1982 in Zimbabwe, fewer than one in five smallholders (18%) had a loan from a financial institution. This proportion is well above the national average and is inflated by the inclusion in the sample of Chipuriro, a high-rainfall area in which the Agricultural Finance Corporation is willing to invest, and Wedza, where a mission-based credit program reaches many farmers. Of all districts, Gutu in the dry southeast quadrant of the country, has the lowest and most representative credit rating, with a mere 3% of farmers having loans.

Farmer organizations provide a gateway to services, even when such services are extremely scarce. In Zimbabwe, a far higher proportion of group members (32%) has access to credit than individuals (7%). When asked why they joined groups, farmers regularly mention the hope of getting credit, a reason cited second only to participation in communal labor. Farmers evidently seek material advantage from group membership and loans to purchase seasonal inputs are a powerful incentive to cooperation. In some cases, farmers join with others simply to be recognized by a credit agency, though "groups" formed in this manner may exist in name only and for no other common purpose. More often, credit is one function among many within groups first organized for communal labor or cooperative marketing. The strong and significant association between organizational membership and credit access is less interesting than at first apparent, however, since it results as much from policy as from probability. All credit agencies in Zimbabwe take advantage of the existence of voluntary associations among farmers for administration of small loans. While the government agricultural bank will lend to individuals, mission-based credit schemes require membership as a condition of eligibility. But since the vast majority of group farmers (84%) become members *before* they receive a loan, we can impute an organizational role in access to credit.

Beyond the initial issue of access to credit, group organization plainly influences the behavior of farmers in the use of borrowed money. I compared the repayment records of farmers who took short-term loans as individuals with those who borrowed as a group on terms of joint liability (Bratton, 1986). In seasons when the rainfall is within the range of normal variation (1980–81 and 1981–82 in Zimbabwe), the recovery rates from group farmers are significantly higher than from individual farmers (between 71 and 92%, depending on the exact terms of the joint liability, versus 54%). Only in seasons of extraordinary drought (as throughout Zimbabwe in 1982/83) do the legal provisions of group lending – that every member stand as financial guarantor for every other – encourage group farmers to default on loan repayment.

Peasant farmers in Zimbabwe live in relatively inaccessible parts of the country and face long lines of *input supply*. They nonetheless make intensive use of commercial inputs. Almost every maize grower (95%), for example, makes an annual purchase of certified hybrid maize seed. A substantial proportion also uses artificial fertilizers for cash crops of maize and cotton (61%), and chemical pesticides to protect maize stored in the household granary (66%). In the absence of subsidies or special production schemes, small farmers always pay top price for inputs and enjoy the least reliable supplies. Any organizational arrangement that can save money or guarantee timely delivery is therefore likely to attract support.

Do farmer organizations contribute here? As with other services, group farmers (77%) are significantly more likely than individuals (48%) to have access to an input like fertilizer. This organizational effect is not simply a function of the availability of credit to group farmers, since a statistical control for credit use does not diminish the difference between groups and individuals. Even if they have credit, farmers invest personal savings in fertilizer purchase. These savings, derived from produce sales or off-farm sources, are most likely to be mobilized if farmers belong to a "savings club" or "cash group" that bulks its money to make a single input order.

The most economical pathway for inputs is direct from factory to farm, sidestepping multiple handling and markups by middlemen. Group farmers (77%) are more likely than individuals (38%) to obtain fertilizer directly from an urban manufacturer. Depending on distance from the capital city, a bag of fertilizer may be 30 to 80% cheaper when purchased from this source. It is also more likely to be in stock than at a rural trading outlet. More group farmers (58%) than individuals (44%) place fertilizer orders between March and August each year and thus qualify for cash rebates for early delivery. When the time comes to transport inputs to the countryside, group farmers (59%) are again more likely than individuals (44%) to take on cheaper bulk road haulage rates and to avoid the expensive per unit cost of transporting fertilizer by methods such as public omnibus. The members of market and multipurpose groups are the most active in all aspects of the management of input supply, perhaps because their leaders had more business acumen than other cooperators. I found that in Wedza in 1984 group farmers ultimately paid an average of 13% less for a bag of compound maize fertilizer than their individual counterparts. In multipurpose groups in Zwimba communal land the savings were as high as 33%.

A major defect of bulk ordering that farmer organizations have been unable to overcome is timeliness of input delivery. Farmers throughout Africa have shown themselves willing to pay market price for fertilizer and to be more concerned with opportune availability than with price subsidy. Fertilizer which arrives after the first rains have fallen is of little use to the farmer. One might expect group organization to expedite delivery. The assumption is that suppliers and transporters attend more promptly to a large bulk order with a single delivery point than to small and fragmented orders from scattered individuals. In fact, this hypothesis cannot be confirmed from the Zimbabwe data. There is no difference whatever in the timeliness of fertilizer delivery between individuals and group members: in both cases, more than one out of four users (29%) gets their fertilizer late. Those who rely on bulk transporters (39%) – ironically, those in groups – are more likely to get tardy delivery than those who transport the inputs themselves (13%).

This suggests a second paradox of rural organizational development. While farmers achieve economies of scale from bulk ordering, they also encounter certain diseconomies associated with being the weakest actors in large central markets. Entering the market carries opportunities to increase

income but also exposes the small farmer to new risks and vulnerabilities.

The last of the production services to be considered are *market outlets*. Within the communal areas of Zimbabwe, particularly in the well-watered northeast, farmers regularly produce surpluses of food grains that exceed local demand. Farmers therefore seek out national marketing boards where a guaranteed sale at the best available price can be found.

The now-familiar pattern of farmer behavior prevails. Group farmers are more than twice as likely as individuals (57% versus 25%) to move their surpluses out of the communal lands to an official central market. This leads group farmers to incur higher transport costs, but because they get a better price for the product from the marketing board, the net return is generally higher. Timeliness is less of a critical factor in produce sales than in input supply, but because the bulk to be moved is so great, small farmers still encounter a transport bottleneck. This problem is most marked during bumper harvests (e.g. 1980–81, which coincided with a diesel fuel shortage, and 1984–85). While transporters attend to peasant farmers last, fewer of those marketing in groups complain of a transport problem (61%) than those marketing individually (77%).

To conclude the analysis of service access it is worth looking at the overall availability of *packages of services*. The usefulness of resources from state or market is additive. A single support service offered in isolation may have little impact; it is fully activated only when available in combination with other services. For example, extension advice to apply fertilizer may not be usable until the farmer has the credit with which to buy it and a reliable agent to supply it.

A desirable package for food crop production would seem to require a combination of at least three services: advice, fertilizer, and a market. This is a practical combination in Zimbabwe where remissions of urban wages or savings from other sources substitute for credit, and is the most common combination reported by farmers in the survey. The findings on access to service come through loudest and clearest for whole packages. Group farmers are four times as likely (57%) as individuals (14%) to get a full, complementary package of three services.

Moreover, as groups grow – from simple and individualistic to complex and cooperative – service access improves. There is a neat linear relationship between the development of farmer organization and the proportion of members receiving any given agricultural service. Members of market groups, for example, are more often able to obtain service packages than members of labor or information groups. Members of multipurpose groups do even better yet. The logical conclusion is that, as farmers organize to consolidate individual preferences into bulk demand, so they are able to win the agricultural services they need.

9. Food Production

We now know quite a lot about the farmers who participate in collective action in Zimbabwe's communal lands. They are largely middle peasants; on a limited scale they pool production assets; and they are becoming increasingly adept at organizing themselves to make use of the state and market. Accordingly, we would expect them to display a good production record.

I will present output data only for the 1981–82 season and only for maize, Zimbabwe's main food and cash crop.

The main finding is that, under every set of agro-ecological conditions, farmers in groups are *consistently more efficient* at maize production than individual farmers. The measure of efficiency is the productivity of land. In the 1981–82 season the average yields of group farmers were from 64% to 137% higher for each hectare under maize.

Farmers in groups also plant slightly larger areas to maize (1.38 ha versus 1.08 ha).

Consequently, the distinction between groups and individuals becomes more pronounced when total household production is considered. In the 1981–82 season, average total maize output was from 89 to 172% higher for group households, indicating that, even in a drier than average season, they *consistently outproduce* households working alone.

Farmer organizations also help members to convert their production into sales and, in turn, into incomes. Group members are likely both to *sell more maize* per household and to sell a higher proportion of their total crop. The effect of organization now becomes amplified. Group farmers sell between twice and seven times as much maize as individuals and at a higher average price.

The cultivation of maize as a cash crop, particularly if pursued in monoculture, can have negative repercussions on household food availability and child nutrition. There is no evidence, however, that group members retain fewer bags of maize per person for household consumption. Nor does the monoculture hypothesis stand, because group members are more likely than individuals to grow a variety – four or more – of crops.

We must be certain that the production record of group farmers is due to organizational initiatives and not simply to the fact that, as middle peasants, group members are relatively "well off" to begin with. I do this by comparing the production records of group farmers and the stratum of "richer" individuals that were identified earlier according to extensive holdings in cattle. If household resource endowment alone can predict production, then the richer individuals should perform better than the group farmers. In fact, the reverse holds true. Farmers in groups in every district are more productive, amass a greater total output and sell more maize than the rich individuals. By controlling for wealth, we are safe in assuming that food production performance is not attained solely by virtue of economic status, but to a large and measurable extent, from collective action in farmer organizations.

To complete the analysis, the production records of the various types of group must be examined. The close relationship between the growth of groups and service access is now broken. Only qualified support can be given to the assertion that, as collectivities of farmers develop into formal organizations, so their maize output rises. In overall ranking on productivity, production and sales, market groups score highest. This holds true even though market groups are not the most advanced organizations in terms of complexity and cooperativeness.

Two anomalies in the ranking of farmer organizations require explanation. First, why do market groups outstrip multipurpose groups when the opposite might have been predicted from the latter's better access to most assets and all services? Second, why do labor groups usually outperform information groups when their social composition and household resource base is virtually identical? Let us examine each type of farmer group in turn and try to explain these anomalies in organizational terms.

Information groups repeatedly rank at the bottom on indicators of maize output. This can be explained in terms of relatively low access to services by group standards. Member households receive advice from the extension service, but they do not necessarily have the basic factor endowment, or other supporting services, to put it into effect. They undertake farm operations and market transactions on their own and thus have no opportunities to supplement their meagre household resource base. I conclude that low levels of organizational involvement help to explain their poor performance.

Labor groups achieve a creditable record, being ranked third overall and second in total production. This is not the result of economic status – or the number of agricultural services received – for on both counts members are relatively deprived. I am led to infer that the pooling of draft power and communal work organization are explanatory factors.

Organizational analysis also casts light on why labor groups score high on production but lower on productivity. This type of group is more skillful at mobilizing local labor than at winning access to central supplies and services. Any gains in total output are therefore achieved by putting more land under cultivation (using communal labor) than on increasing the productivity of land (using technical innovation).

Market groups produce the most maize, whatever the measure. Only in one district (Wedza) do they fail to top the production and productivity rankings. But even here, they nonetheless sell the most, a fact attributable to the arrangements for bulk marketing in which the farmers of this type of group have chosen to specialize.

Multipurpose groups fail to produce up to expectations. Their members are well-endowed farmers who are better linked to support services than any other type of group. We would expect them to top the rankings yet in some places they come in a poor third in productivity and production.

A possible explanation is as follows. Multipurpose groups are the most complex and cooperative of the associations I have studied. The organizational requirements for successful operation are therefore considerable. The leaders of multipurpose groups have to meld two levels of organization: on the one hand the mobilization of assets at the level of production and, on the other, the coordination of services at the level of exchange. Each of these tasks requires management of a different style, skill and scale. For this reason, multipurpose groups often take on a two-tier "federated" structure. The top tier is a large and loose group managed by an overall area committee, and the bottom tier is composed of a number of smaller labor parties, each with their own tight neighborhood ties. To sustain a complex organization of this sort requires capable and flexible leadership.

The classic form of failure of collective organization is internal social conflict. As organizations expand to embrace a wider membership, so disputes arise for which rules of resolution have not been institutionalized. The challenge for the leaders of collective organizations is to simultaneously achieve the benefits of scale without losing the advantages of solidarity.

10. Conclusion

I have argued that the impressive expansion of peasant maize output in Zimbabwe between 1980 and 1985 is due in part to efforts by farmers to organize themselves. The process of development, whether in agriculture or any other field, rests squarely on the self-help initiatives of the protagonists. In the absence of collective organization, development by administrative fiat or price incentive is likely to have limited impact. The study and practice of "institutional development" must expand beyond a concern only with the capacity of central institutions. As I see it, collective organization at the local level is an essential complement to development strategies based on either state or market.

On the basis of the Zimbabwe data, I arrive at the conclusion that the incorporation of peasant producers into larger systems of authority and exchange does not always have a deleterious impact on household welfare. As states penetrate the countryside, political conflict will inevitably arise as the central quest for integration collides with the local urge to retain autonomy. This conflict is already manifest in Zimbabwe in disputes between farmer organizations on the one hand and the ruling party and cooperatives ministry on the other. And, as the scope of markets expands to embrace the rural hinterland, some households will invariably be better placed than others to take advantage. Zimbabwe does

not depart from the familiar tale of concentration of wealth among middlemen and big farmers during periods of capitalist transformation in peasant agriculture.

But I argue that collective organization can help to mitigate these negative effects, even if it cannot entirely overcome them. There are, it seems to me, patterns of institution-building in which central and local organizations can productively *articulate*. In this paper I have shown, for example, that access to support services by an organized mass clientele can address the needs *both* of the agricultural service agency *and* the peasant farmer. The task of institutional analysis is to identify mutualities and specify the conditions under which they are likely to pertain.

This is not to claim that a strategy of collective organization is a panacea to rural poverty any more than any other strategy has been. I will close by mentioning three general issues of development policy to which the performance of farmer groups in Zimbabwe gives rise.

First, collective organization *does not stand alone*. It is unlikely to arise and flourish in the absence of well-developed states and markets. Because farmer organization happens in part as a result of stimulation from outside, we would not expect to find much organized farmer action in parts of Africa where central institutions are weak. The nature of policy, rather than merely a crude institutional presence, is also important. Collective organization is likely to take root only under particular "regimes" of authority and price. States must permit independent centers of farmer power at local level and actively promote special programs to mobilize poor and women farmers. Markets must provide selective incentives, even subsidies, to correct for the uncompetitive position that all smallholders usually occupy.

The second general point is that collective organization works better at resolving problems of *efficiency* than at guaranteeing *equity* in the distribution of benefits. This shifts the conventional argument in favor of rural cooperativization from one of social justice to one of economic soundness. Productivity gains in food crops among group farmers in Zimbabwe are clear evidence of an efficiency effect. The involvement of middle peasants, rather than just the very richest, is evidence of some equity outcome, though in most types of farmer group the very poorest are still excluded. On this basis I infer that collective organization is best suited for articulation with bureaucratic organizations whose characteristic failure is inefficiency. It is less effective at overcoming the shortcomings of an unfettered market, the characteristic failure of which is to create and deepen inequality.

Third, and finally, the organization of small farmers takes place more at *the level of exchange* than at *the level of production.* "Bulking" for entry into the market is more of a distinctive characteristic of farmer organization than "pooling" of basic household assets. This latter activity survives from traditional or precapitalist societies and is not practiced exclusively within the boundaries of farmer groups. "The nature of the resource" around which farmers now organize for development is more likely to be a central service than a household asset.

The policy implications are far-reaching. It appears that in the African countryside the conditions are not ripe for a socialist transformation. Traditions of asset sharing do not imply a peasant preference for social ownership of the means of production. In Zimbabwe at least, small farmers want to retain control over family assets in land, labor and cattle. Governments that wish to promote production collectives (bulk access to services, pooled household assets) will have to make heavy investment in mass campaigns of persuasion or coercion. There are two apter and easier models for the future development of small farmer organization in Africa. One, the more likely, is the marketing cooperative (bulk access to services, no pooled assets), and the other

the production cooperative (bulk access to services, pooled labor on private plots). These are the working instruments of development that peasant farmers are building and operating for themselves. Governments with a genuine interest in alleviating hunger and promoting rural welfare would be well advised to acknowledge and support them.

REFERENCES

Berg, Elliot, "The Africa Report: An Overview," *Rural Africana*, Nos. 19–20 (Spring-Fall 1984), pp. 41–48.
Bratton, Michael, "Draft Power, Draft Exchange and Farmer Organization in Zimbabwe," *Working Paper No. 9* (Harare, Zimbabwe: University of Zimbabwe, Department of Land Management, 1984.
Bratton, Michael, "Financing Smallholder Production: A Comparison of Individual and Group Credit Schemes," *Public Administration and Development* (forthcoming 1986).
Butler, Richard, "A Transactional Approach to Organizing Efficiency: Perspectives from Markets, Hierarchies and Collectives," *Administration and Society*, Vol. 15, No. 3 (1983), pp. 323–362.
Collinson, Michael, "Demonstrations of an Interdisciplinary Approach to Planning Adaptive Agricultural Research Projects: Chibi District, Southern Zimbabwe," *Report No. 5*, (Nairobi, Kenya: CIMMYT Eastern Africa Economics Programme, 1982).
Esman, Milton and Norman Uphoff, *Local Organizations: Intermediaries in Rural Development* (Ithaca, NY: Cornell University Press, 1984).
Garcia-Zamor, Jean-Claude, *Public Participation in Development Planning and Management* (Boulder, CO: Westview Press, 1985).
Hardin, Garrett, "The Tragedy of the Commons," *Science*, No. 162 (1972), pp. 1242–1248.
Hyden, Goran, *No Shortcuts to Progress: African Development Management in Perspective* (London and New York: Heinemann, 1983).
Korten, David, "Community Organization and Rural Development: A Learning Process Approach," *Public Administration Review*, Vol. 40, No. 5 (1980), pp. 480–511.

Olson, Mancur, *The Logic of Collective Action* (Cambridge, MA: Harvard University Press, 1965).

Ostrom, Vincent and Elinor Ostrom, "Public Goods and Public Choices," in E. S. Savas (Ed.), *Alternatives for Delivering Public Services: Toward Improved Performance* (Boulder, CO: Westview Press, 1979).

Russell, Clifford S. and Norman K. Nicholson (Eds.), *Public Choice and Rural Development* (Washington, D.C.: Resources for the Future, 1981).

Vincent, V. and R. G. Thomas, *An Agricultural Survey of Southern Rhodesia* (Salisbury, Southern Rhodesia: Government Printer, 1961).

Agroforestry and Sustainable Development: Making the Connection

ROBERT WINTERBOTTOM and *PETER T. HAZLEWOOD*

Deforestation and unsustainable land use are causing extensive degradation of the natural resource base throughout the developing world. Every year more than 11 million hectares of tropical forests are lost through commercial and subsistence pressures (UN Food and Agriculture Organization, 1982). The loss of tree cover can set in motion a chain of events that leads to declining food production, land degradation, and, in extreme cases, desertification – a process of decline in the biological productivity of arid, semiarid, and subhumid lands. An assessment by the United Nations Environment Programme in 1984 states that some 1,300 million hectares of land in Africa, Asia, and Latin America are at least moderately desertified, and more than 300 million people live in areas at least moderately or severely desertified (Mabbutt, 1984).

As productive land becomes scarce, small farmers have been pushed into fragile upland forest areas and marginal lowlands that cannot support large numbers of people practicing subsistence agriculture. Declining forest area and rising population pressure have forced farmers to shorten field-fallow periods, degrading the productive capacity of the land and reinforcing the downward spiral of forest destruction.

Developing countries can ill afford to lose this land. A detailed study by the Food and Agriculture Organization of the United Nations (FAO) on the future world food situation concluded that, "by the end of the

Winterbottom and Hazlewood. *Ambio*, published by the Royal Swedish Academy of Sciences, granted permission to use this article. It appeared in 1986, 16(2–30), on pp. 100–110.

century, shortage of land will have become a critical constraint for about two-thirds of the population of the developing countries" (UN Food and Agriculture Organization, 1981). Developing country demand for food and agricultural products is expected to double during this time (Harrison, 1984).

The growing demand for food in developing countries will require bringing new land into production and improving the productivity of existing croplands. FAO estimates that cropland conversion will account for about one-quarter of the growth in food output from 1975 to 2000 (UN Food and Agriculture Organization, 1981). However, with much of the good agricultural land in developing countries already being farmed, further agricultural expansion will often be on sites of marginal productivity because of steep slopes, thin soils, and other physical constraints. Most of the needed increase in food production will therefore have to come from increasing the productivity of existing cropland primarily through the application of modern high-yield agricultural technologies. Yet, modern technologies based on costly inputs such as irrigation, fertilizers, and pesticides are not now applicable in many developing regions.

Developing countries thus face the critical challenge of expanding agriculture onto new, often marginal lands, and intensifying production on existing croplands, through land-use practices that are both sustainable and appropriate to the ecological, economic, and social constraints faced by small farmers. One response to this challenge that is receiving increasing attention worldwide is "agroforestry."

Agroforestry Systems

The term "agroforestry" encompasses both the traditional land-use practices that rely on trees and shrubs as part of crop and livestock production systems, and recently developed technologies which are aimed at integrating woody perennials into a variety of land-use systems in order to make these systems more productive and sustainable. Whether new or old, agroforestry systems all share a number of characteristics:

• The deliberate association of trees and shrubs with crops, livestock or other factors of agricultural production;

• Readily identifiable, yet often complex ecological and economic interactions between the woody plants and the other elements of the production system, and;

• At least two or more outputs from the system, with some production cycles extending beyond one year (Lundgren and Raintree, 1983; Nair and Fernandez, 1984).

A common aim of agroforestry technologies is to magnify positive interactions between trees, shrubs, ground cover, crops, livestock, soil and water so as to increase and diversify the total production from a given area of land. A related objective is to increase production to levels that can be maintained with available resources, and not force farmers to depend on inputs that are economically out of reach or simply unavailable in some rural areas.

As interest in agroforestry has grown, so has the recognition that many different types of agroforestry systems exist. A number of classification schemes have been proposed, and most distinguish three basic combinations: agroforestry systems with trees and annual crops (agrosilviculture); with trees and livestock on wooded pasture or rangeland (silvopastoralism); and with trees, crops and livestock (agrosilvopastoralism). These practices and others are more completely described in several publications

of the International Council for Research in Agroforestry (ICRAF), and in the rapidly expanding literature on agroforestry (Combe and Budowski, 1979; Nair, 1985; Vergara, 1985; and Mergen, 1986).

Bush Fallow and Shifting Cultivation

Agroforestry is usually defined to include systems that involve the sequential association of trees with crops, as well as the actual interplanting of the two. As the traditional practices of "bush fallow" and "shifting cultivation" involve the sequential association of trees and crops, they are in many respects precursors to more recently developed agroforestry systems. In these traditional systems, most of the woody vegetation is cleared from a patch of land and crops are planted for several years. Over time, declining soil organic matter and nutrient levels, and competition from weeds and resprouting vegetation, cause the farmer to move elsewhere to plant crops and allow the formally cultivated field to lie fallow. The bush or forest vegetation reestablishes itself and, given sufficient time, replenishes the lost soil fertility. In the process, the farmer gains a renewed stock of firewood, construction timber, fodder, and other useful products from the "forest fallow" areas.

Taungya

Some of the earliest recognized forms of agroforestry involved modifying the farming practices of shifting cultivators to include the planting of tree seedlings with food crops. In areas where foresters wanted to establish tree plantations, farmers were induced to clean around the seedlings by having access to the recently cleared land to grow food crops. As the tree canopy developed and began to shade the annual crops, the farmers would move to another area where the cycle was repeated. Using this system of "taungya," large areas of teak plantations have been established in Indonesia and Nigeria.

Home Gardens

Tropical "home gardens" are examples of a traditional agroforestry system which involves the simultaneous cultivation of trees and other crops. Home gardens are typically a very diverse mixture of trees, shrubs, food crops, medicinal plants, and livestock, tended within a multistoried structure around the homestead, and carefully managed over a period of generations. The gardens generally produce food, wood, fodder, and other subsistence goods, as well as cash crops. Some of the more carefully researched examples are found in Indonesia, Sri Lanka, and Tanzania.

Shade Trees

In Central America and Southeast Asia, a variety of different "shade trees" (*Erythrina poeppigiana, Cordia alliodora, Leucaena leucocephela*) are often associated with the cultivation of coffee and cacao. The trees themselves produce wood, and in the case of some leguminous trees, enrich the soil by fixing atmospheric nitrogen. The favorable influences on the microclimate beneath the shade trees, together with the addition of organic matter (and nitrogen) to the soil, result in higher sustained yields of the associated cash crop.

Fodder Trees

Livestock production can also be made more sustainable and productive through the association of trees and shrubs with either improved pastures or natural rangelands (Torres, 1983). Production from coconut plantations can be diversified by grazing livestock under the coconut canopy (Nair, 1983). In the semiarid regions of Africa, livestock rely on the protein-rich "aerial pastures" of woody shrubs and trees, which are the most nutritious forage available in the dry season (Okafar, 1980 and LeHouerou, 1978). In Nepal, over 80 percent of the fodder requirements of farm livestock are supplied by surrounding trees (Singh, Pandey, and Tiwari, 1984).

Dispersed Trees on Farmfields

In many parts of Africa, "farm trees" can be found dispersed throughout cultivated areas, both within and adjacent to farmfields. The trees are actively protected, harvested, and otherwise managed by farmers to yield construction poles, fuelwood, fodder, edible fruits, nuts and leaves, medicines, and a range of other products without unduly competing with associated annual crops. In the case of the sandy, relatively infertile soils of the Sahel, the presence of widely-spaced *Acacia albida* trees in fields of millet or sorghum actually increases crop yields up to 2.5 times (from 430 to 1,000 kg · ha^{-1}) over that obtained in open farmfields (Felker, 1978). In addition, the trees produce large quantities of nutritious seedpods that are highly valued for livestock feed; the wood is also used to make handles for farm tools and other household implements.

Twenty years of research on the effects of *Prosopis cineraria*, a farm tree commonly associated with the cultivation of millet in the arid, northwestern parts of India, has revealed its positive influence on soil fertility and crop yields. *Markhamia platycalyx* (a local species) and *Grevillia robusta* (an exotic) can be found in farmfields in several East African countries, where they are both valued for their wood and soil-enriching litter fall. The number and known uses or products of such multipurpose trees is rapidly growing, together with an understanding of how they can be incorporated into farming systems (Von Carlowitz, 1984 and Nair, Fernandez, and Wambugu, 1984).

Shelterbelts and Hedgerows

Apart from trees which may be dispersed within farmfields, there are many examples worldwide of agroforestry systems that use trees and shrubs planted in shelterbelts, windbreaks, living fences, and hedgerows. The positive influences of shelterbelts in terms of reduced wind erosion and a more favorable microclimate have resulted in increased crop yields (as well as wood and other by-products from the shelterbelt) in dozens of countries (Magrath, 1979). Trees or shrubs are planted as fences or hedgerows in many parts of the tropics. They serve to demarcate field boundaries, control livestock movement, and can be pruned to produce fuelwood and other products.

Alley Cropping

Over the past few years, the International Institute for Tropical Agriculture (IITA) in Nigeria has experimented with the hedgerow technique and developed a new system of "alley cropping" that involves the planting and intensive management of relatively close-spaced rows of nitrogen-fixing shrubs (such as *Gliricidia, Leucaena, Calliandra, Sesbania*), farming a crop like maize in the alleys between the rows. The shrubs are regularly pruned and the trimmings used to mulch the cultivated soil, replenishing its organic matter and nutrient levels. In areas where maize production is currently constrained by shortages of nitrogen, and where the added production of fuelwood is a recognized benefit, closely spaced rows of *Leucaena* can produce 3.5 cubic meters per hectare per year of fuelwood (enough to supply four persons) and sustain higher yields of maize with less reliance on chemical fertilizers (Torres, 1983).

Agroforestry and Sustainable Rural Development

The ultimate goal of agroforestry is to contribute to sustainable land-use systems that maximize total productivity and income while maintaining the productive capacity of the natural resource base. By serving both environmental and development objectives, agroforestry can contribute to sustainable rural development in a number of ways.

Helping to Control Deforestation

In many regions, the adoption of agro-forestry practices can relieve pressures on remaining natural forests by meeting local needs through farm and community tree resources. For example, farm trees are a significant source of fuelwood production in many farming systems. In eastern Java, 63 percent of the fuelwood consumed by farmers is produced on their farms (Salem and van Nao, 1981). In Kenya and other areas of East Africa with favorable growing conditions, farmers are able to meet virtually 100 percent of their fuelwood requirements from a combination of dispersed farm trees, hedgerows around the homestead and field boundaries, and small woodlots on soils that are too rocky or shallow for crop production (Van Gelder and Poulsen, 1982; Projet Agro-Pastoral de Nyabisindu, 1985). Traditionally, farm trees such as *Acacia albida* in Africa, *Prosopis* in India, *Erythrina* in Costa Rica, and poplars in the Near East are regularly pruned to provide fuelwood.

Another benefit of agroforestry is the possibility of establishing a permanent, sustainable land-use system in areas where traditional patterns of shifting cultivation and fuelwood gathering have broken down because of population growth and increasing land-use pressures. Faced with declining soil fertility, and increasing scarcity of fuelwood, fodder, and other necessities, farmers themselves have recognized the need to improve land use and intensify farm production. In many areas this recognition has resulted in an increased demand for seedlings and a "spontaneous" adoption of agroforestry practices.

The growing emphasis on involving farmers in tree planting is a rational response to the fact that in most developing countries governments lack the human and financial resources needed to carry out forest management and reforestation programs on a sufficient scale to counter current rates of deforestation. By mobilizing widespread support for tree planting at the farm and community level through agroforestry, tree stocks can be reestablished more rapidly and at lower cost than would be possible through reliance on centralized government programs (Arnold, 1987).

Increasing Agricultural Productivity

A growing body of evidence points to the physical benefits of incorporating trees into farming systems. The most significant contribution of trees may be their favorable influence on soil fertility. The evidence indicates that the added nutrients and organic matter from the presence of trees lead to favorable effects on soil fertility that more than compensate for any negative effects of trees from shading and competition for water.

With their deeper root systems, trees are thought to play an important role in "pumping up" nutrients from deeper soil horizons which would otherwise be inaccessible to annual crop roots. Trees also help to counteract the leaching of tropical soils under permanent cultivation, and renew both the nutrient and organic matter content of topsoils.

Nitrogen-fixing leguminous trees can directly contribute significant quantities of this important soil nutrient. Experiments in Nigeria by IITA indicate that *Leucaena* hedgerows intercropped with maize can fix 160 kilos per hectare per year of nitrogen, or enough to sustain maize yields at a level of 2 tons per hectare per year (Kang and Duguma, 1984). Enrichment of surface soil horizons under *Acacia albida* trees has been studied in a number of locations, with each study indicating substantial increases in both nitrogen and organic carbon in farmfields with widely spaced *Acacia* trees.

The increase in soil organic matter from leaf litter and tree roots improves soil structure, moisture holding capacity of soils, and cation exchange capacity, all of which contributes to improved production potential. Furthermore, trees can help reduce rainfall runoff, as well as increase infiltration and recharge of aquifers. This means more rainfall is captured and available for plant growth.

Windbreaks have repeatedly shown a favorable influence on crop yields by providing protection against wind and water erosion. In China, windbreaks or shelterbelts have reduced wind velocity 28–32 percent, increased air humidity 6–12 percent, reduced evaporation 15–20 percent, and increased soil moisture 15–25 percent. Crop yields have been increased by 16 percent for maize, 36 percent for soybeans, 43 percent for sorghum, and 44 percent for millet in fields protected by shelterbelts (Ministry of Forestry, 1985). An early evaluation of the effect of planting neem (*Azadirachta indica*) windbreaks in the Majjia Valley of Niger suggested a 23 percent increase in millet yields after allowing for the decreased production from the land occupied by the windbreak, about 6 percent of the farmfields (Bognetteau-Verlinden, 1980). Subsequent evaluations indicate a smaller increase in crop yields (15 percent) on the land cultivated between the rows of trees. The reduction in yield increases is most likely caused by the increased shading and competition from the larger, more mature trees in the windbreaks. Experiments are currently underway to evaluate different methods of harvesting the windbreaks and minimizing competition between trees and crops (CARE, 1986).

Farm trees can indirectly contribute to crop production by providing a readily available supply of fuelwood for cooking and heating. This enables farmers to apply dung and crop residues to their fields to improve the soil rather than having to burn them as a supplementary source of household energy. Studies in Nepal suggest that burning dung as a household fuel instead of using it to fertilize fields, leads to a decrease of 15 percent in grain yields, equivalent to 225 kg · ha^{-1} (The World Bank, 1984). Research in Ethiopia indicates that the burning of dung in areas where fuelwood has become scarce has substantially reduced annual grain harvests in those regions (Newcombe, 1984). Experience from a number of countries demonstrates that 2–5 percent of cultivated land can support trees for fuelwood production and other purposes without a loss in agricultural production (Salem and van Nao, 1981).

In developing countries, livestock supply half the nonhuman energy used in agriculture (UN Food and Agriculture Organization, 1983). Tree fodder is, in many regions, a very important source of livestock feed. As in the case of fuelwood production, agroforestry can contribute significantly to increased supplies of fodder, especially in areas where land-use pressures have led to the reduction of open rangelands. Research in Rwanda has demonstrated that the weight gain of stall-fed livestock can be increased from 14–16 grams per day to 20–30 grams per day by supplementing a ration of grasses with leaves from woody plants. The increased weight gain is largely a result of the higher protein content of the leaves from woody plants, which typically range from 20–26 percent of dry matter compared to less than 5 percent for grasses (Nyirahabimana, 1985).

Meeting the Needs Of Low-Resource Farmers

The majority of rural dwellers in developing countries are small farmers or landless people faced with a number of physical and socioeconomic factors that constrain their ability to move beyond the daily struggle for subsistence. Although the relative importance of these factors varies from one region to another, several common characteristics can be identified.

In many regions, physical factors pose a degree of environmental risk to which farmers must adapt. Examples of such factors are erratic rainfall and drought in arid and semiarid areas, and steeply sloping or relatively infertile soils in humid areas that depend on organic matter input to maintain their productivity and often cannot support continuous cropping. These physical constraints are frequently compounded by socioeconomic conditions prevailing in many rural areas. Lack of infrastructure is a common problem. Roads, where they exist, are often in poor condition, limiting transport and distribution. As a result, farmers are not well integrated into the market economy. They have low incomes, little if any cash reserves, and typically do not have access to credit. Government extension services are often weak, which severely constrains the dissemination of new technologies and innovative practices to the rural poor. Thus, small farmers and the landless generally have very limited access to outside inputs and technology, and must rely on locally available resources to meet a whole range of subsistence and cash needs.

Because agriculture is still based largely on traditional practices of low productivity, farmers are unable to produce a surplus that can be stockpiled as a hedge against environmental risk. Under these conditions, farmers take the rational course of adopting low-resource farming strategies that minimize the risk of failure. Any outside intervention to increase farm productivity must fit into this framework. That is, technologies must be low input, low risk, and provide high returns if poor farmers are to benefit. Agroforestry has several features that respond to the physical and socioeconomic constraints facing farmers.

By its very nature, agroforestry is a small-scale activity that is oriented to producing multiple outputs to meet local needs. By building on traditional agricultural practices with little or no reliance on outside inputs, agroforestry approaches are affordable, relatively easy to adopt, and widely replicable. Households and communities can determine their own priorities and grow the types and numbers of trees they choose (UN Food and Agriculture Organization, 1985). Trees are grown where they are accessible to those who need them, making households more self-sufficient. Finally, agroforestry can help farmers minimize risk by producing a more diversified and stable farming system. Agricultural production can be made more sustainable because of the physical benefits of combining trees with crops and livestock, and more flexibility exists to distribute the workload over the course of the year.

Generating Employment and Income

There is growing awareness that in many rural areas wood and nonwood products from forests and farm trees are an important source of off-farm employment and income. Agroforestry systems, by providing multiple outputs, have significant potential for generating employment and income opportunities for rural households.

In areas of wood scarcity, household income can be increased indirectly by producing forest products on-farm that would otherwise have to be purchased. With the growing commercialization of fuelwood in many areas, the cash or in-kind savings from on-farm tree planting can be substantial. The availability of on-farm fuelwood can also reduce the time that must be devoted to collecting fuelwood from distant sources, thereby allowing more labor time to be devoted to farming and other household activities. In Rwanda, recent agricultural surveys indicate that 20 percent of the farmland is currently allocated to pastures and woodlots; dispersed farm trees typically cover 2–10 percent of the farmland. With an average of 40 trees per hectare, rural households in Rwanda appear able to meet nearly 70 percent of their fuelwood requirements from farm trees (Winterbottom, 1985).

Agroforestry can directly increase household income through the sale of wood and nonwood products in areas where commercial markets exist. The adoption of cash-crop tree farming is increasing in many rural areas in response to emerging markets. In parts of India, for example, the market for poles has provided a strong incentive to farmers to take up cash-crop tree farming on a large scale. However, the

Indian experience has also demonstrated that there can be problems associated with commercial farm forestry with respect to the impact on small farmers and the landless. In the absence of adequate support services designed to reach this target group, the demands of cash-crop tree farming (such as the relatively long period of time required before earning a return) may place it beyond their reach. In addition, the use of more land for cash-crop tree farming and the diversion of wood supplies to commercial markets can further strain the ability of the poor to meet their needs. These potentially negative impacts must be taken into account in efforts to promote commercial farm forestry (UN Food and Agriculture Organization, 1985).

Finally, agroforestry systems can provide raw materials for traditional small-scale enterprises such as saw milling, carpentry, wood carving, and basket-making. An FAO survey found that forest-based small-scale enterprises account for a significant percentage of off-farm employment in many regions. In Jamaica, for example, forest-based enterprises account for more than one-third of total employment in the small-scale enterprise sector – the largest source of rural employment in the country (UNFAO, 1985).

••••

A Case Study of Successful Agro-forestry Experience

Agroforestry is increasingly recognized by developing country governments and the development assistance agencies as an appropriate and viable approach to addressing problems of land degradation and rural poverty. The following case studies present a sample of successful efforts to apply agroforestry solutions under varying social, cultural, and ecological conditions.

Agroforestry Outreach Project, Haiti

Charcoal and firewood satisfy 75 percent of the total energy demand in Haiti, and millions of rural farm families are completely dependent on fuelwood for cooking and heating. Between 1980 and 1985, consumption of wood was projected to increase from 4 to 5 million cubic meters per year, while estimated annual growth was expected to decline from 1.8 to 1.6 million cubic meters per year, creating a growing wood production deficit of more than 3 million cubic meters (The World Bank, 1982).

Deforestation from fuelwood harvesting and other causes is having a direct impact on the land's ability to retain moisture and regulate runoff, and has markedly increased the susceptibility of Haiti's farmers to both drought and flood damage. Erosion and other forms of land degradation associated with deforestation have caused agricultural production to stagnate; agriculture's share of Haiti's gross domestic product (GDP) decreased from 49 percent to 39 percent between 1970 and 1979 (The World Bank, 1982).

Despite the very obvious problems of deforestation, fuelwood scarcity and soil erosion, until recently forestry and soil conservation projects have had only limited success in Haiti. A major difficulty was the pattern of paying people to build erosion control structures or to plant trees, and a corresponding lack of incentives for the local population to maintain the structures or to take an interest in the survival of the trees.

In 1981, USAID funded a USD 8 million project aimed at exploring the social, economic, and technical feasibility of reforestation in Haiti (Smucker, 1986; Lowenthal; Stephens, 1984). Social scientists with considerable field experience in Haiti played a key role in designing the project. The project strategy included two major elements: a) provision of free seedlings and extension services to farmers to encourage them to grow trees as a cash-crop, producing charcoal and poles for the well-established urban markets; and b) provision of grants to two private voluntary organiza-

tions (PVOs) with established grassroots networks and working relationships with a large number of indigenous nongovernmental organizations involved in rural development in Haiti, and to a third PVO involved with seedling production technologies.

Between 1982 and 1986, the project has worked through more than 170 private voluntary agencies to supply over 27 million seedlings to 110,000 farmers, far exceeding the original objectives of the project. The prospect of increasing farmer income by planting trees, together with the availability of free seedlings and supportive extension services, has triggered an enthusiastic response. In the minds of the local farmers, the trees are increasingly seen as significant assets that can be harvested and the wood products either sold, consumed on the farm, or simply kept in reserve as a "savings account" that can be tapped when the need arises (as was the case with pig raising in Haiti before their numbers were reduced by African swine fever).

Rather than promote the adoption of a few specific planting techniques, the extension workers have played a less directive, but supportive role, distributing the seedlings to farmers who tailor the planting configurations and choice of species to their own particular needs and local site conditions. As a result, in addition to the production of poles and charcoal for cash, the trees have been used for field perimeter plantings, to demarcate farm plots, to enrich soils in fallowed fields, and to diversify and increase production in cultivated fields.

Although the initial interest focused on the faster-growing trees (*Azadirachta indica, Cassia siamea, Acacia auriculiformis*, and *Eucalyptus*), there is growing interest in some of the slower-growing and economically important local species (*Swietenia macrophylla, Columbrina arboresens, Cedrela odorata, Catalpa longissima*). Native species accounted for about one-third of the seedlings distributed in 1984–1985.

The diffusion of improved nursery techniques, including the use of a lightweight small container system for producing the tree seedlings, has proved to be an important contributor to the project's success. Survival rates of potted seedlings are much higher than bare-root planting stock, but the farmers had been reluctant to transport seedlings in heavier, larger plastic bags and prefer the small, compact container-grown seedlings because they are much lighter and less bulky. Also, the project has gradually moved from a reliance on a few large, central nurseries, to a greater number of smaller, decentralized nurseries. Many of the smaller nurseries were established with credit, materials, and other assistance from the project which were repaid by selling seedlings back to the project for subsequent distribution.

The project has recently been extended into a second phase, which includes an important research component aimed at evaluating the economics of farm forestry, and improved integration of treeplanting, soil and water conservation, and sustained agricultural productivity. A special effort is being made to systematically test and adapt the use of *Leucaena* hedgerows and alley-cropping techniques developed by IITA to conditions in Haiti.

Conclusions

Agroforestry is not a panacea for solving the problems of land degradation and poverty facing rural populations throughout the developing world. However, experience to date clearly demonstrates that agroforestry practices can be responsive to the particular constraints facing low-resource, poor farmers. Agroforestry can capitalize on the positive relationships among trees, forests, and agriculture – contributing significantly to sustaining or increasing agricultural productivity, increasing self-sufficiency, raising incomes and improving living standards, and slowing or reversing environmental degradation.

Although a number of successful efforts are underway to apply agroforestry approaches to rural development problems, they are relatively isolated and on far too small a scale. A review of past successful and unsuccessful experiences in agroforestry suggest a number of constraints and policy issues that must be more fully examined, and the means to alleviate them carefully evaluated, if the potential contribution of agroforestry to sustainable development is to be realized (UN Food and Agriculture Organization, 1985; Eckholm et al., 1984; Foley and Barnard, 1984).

• The lack of incentives for tree planting, such as inadequate access to seedlings, low confidence in the survival of planted trees, underpriced wood products, and inadequate access to markets;

• Inappropriate government policies or legislation that constrain tree growing and harvesting by farmers, particularly insecure land or tree tenure;

• Weak, poorly trained, and underfunded extension services;

• Inadequate communication and coordination among agriculture, forestry, and livestock development personnel;

• The absence of more site-specific research needed to adapt agroforestry principles to the wide range of social and ecological conditions encountered in developing countries.

In cases where these constraints have been identified and addressed, agroforestry practices are often enthusiastically adopted.

Agroforestry seems to be most successful when it builds on traditional practices, is developed in close cooperation with the local people who daily determine how resources will be used and managed, and when there is a sustained commitment to continued evaluation, experimentation, and innovation. This points to the need for greater involvement of nongovernmental organizations, which have a demonstrated ability to foster the participation of local communities and respond to their perceived needs through integrated, flexible, and long-term efforts.

REFERENCES

Arnold, J.E.M. 1987. *Farm Forestry*. Paper presented to the Seventh Agricultural Sector Symposium. The World Bank, Washington.

Bognetteau-Verlinden, E. 1980. *Study on Impact of Windbreaks in Majjia Valley, Niger*. Unpublished report for CARE, Niamey.

CARE. 1986. *The Majjia Valley Windbreak Evaluation Study*. Unpublished project brief prepared for CARE, New York.

Combe, J. and Budowski, G. 1979. Classification of agroforestry techniques. In *Proceedings of the Workshop on Agroforestry Systems in Latin America*. Centro Agronomico Tropical de Investigacion Y Ensenanza. Turrialba, p. 17–47.

Eckholm, E., Foley, G., Barnard, G. and Timberlake, T. 1984. *Fuelwood: The Energy Crisis That Won't Go Away*. Earthscan International Institute for Environment and Development. London/Washington, pp. 47–87.

Felker, P. 1978. *State of the Art: Acacia albida as a Complementary Permanent Intercrop with Annual Crops*. Report by the University of California, Riverside and the United States Agency for International Development, Washington.

Foley, G. and Barnard, G. 1984. *Farm and Community Forestry*, Technical Report No. 3. Earthscan International Institute for Environment and Development. London, pp. 61–124.

Harrison, P. 1984. *Land, Food and People*. UN Food and Agriculture Organization, Rome.

Kang, B.T. and Duguma, B. 1984. *Nitrogen Management in Alley Cropping Systems*. Paper presented at the International Symposium on Nitrogen Management in Farming Systems in the Tropics. International Institute of Tropical Agriculture, Ibadan.

Le Houerou, H.N. 1978. *The Role of Shrubs and Trees in the Management of Natural Grazing Lands (with Particular Reference to Protein Production)*. Paper prepared for the Eighth World Forestry Congress, Jakarta.

Lowenthal, I. United States Agency for International Development. Port au Prince. Personal communication.

Lundgren, B.O. and Raintree, J.B. 1983. Sustained agroforestry. In *Agricultural Research for Development: Potentials and Challenges in Asia*. ISNAR, The Hague.

Mabbutt, J.A. 1984. A new global assessment of the status and trends of desertification. *Environmental Conservation* 2, 106.

Magrath, W. 1979. *Shelterbelt Effect on Crops*. Unpublished Working Paper for the Agriculture and Rural Development Department. The World Bank, Washington.

Mergen, F. 1986. Agroforestry – An overview and recommendations for possible improvements. *Tropical Agriculture* 63.

Ministry of Forestry. 1985. *China's Forestry and Its Role in Social Development*. Paper prepared by the Ministry of Forestry, People's Republic of China for the Ninth World Forestry Congress. Mexico City.

Nair, P.K.R. 1983. Agroforestry with coconuts and other tropical plantation crops. In *Plant Research and Agroforestry*. International Council for Research in Agroforestry, Nairobi, pp. 70–102.

Nair, P.K.R. and Fernandes, E. 1984. *Agroforestry as an Alternative to Shifting Cultivation*. FAO Soils Bulletin No. 53.UN Food and Agriculture Organization, Rome.

Nair, P.K.R., Fernandes, E.C.M. and Wambugu, P.N. 1984. Multipurpose leguminous trees and shrubs for agroforestry. *Agrofor. Syst.* 2, pp. 145–163, Table 1.

Nair, P.K.R. 1985. Classification of agroforestry systems. *Agrofor. Syst.* 3, pp. 97–128.

Newcombe, K. 1984. *An Economic Justification for Rural Afforestation: The Case of Ethiopia*. Energy Department Paper No. 16. The World Bank, Washington.

Nyirahabimana, P. 1985. Les arbres fourragers et fruitiers au Rwanda. In *Compte-Rendu Journees d'etudes forestieres et agroforestieres du 9 au 12 octobre 1984*. Institut des Sciences Agronomiques du Rwanda, Ruhande.

Okafor, J.C. 1980. Trees for food and fodder in the savanna areas of Nigeria. *Int. Tree Crops J.* 1, pp. 131–141.

Projet Agro-Pastoral de Nyabisindu. 1985. *L'arbre et la Haie dans l'Exploitation Paysanne*. Fiche Technique No. 3, Nyabisindu.

Salem, B. and van Nao, T. 1981. Fuelwood production in traditional farming systems. *Unasylva* 33, p. 14.

Singh, J.S., Pandey, U. and Tiwari, A.K. 1984. Man and forests: A central Himalayan case study. *Ambio* 13, pp. 80–87.

Smucker, G. 1986. *Proje Pyebwa Annual Report 1985*. Pan American Development Foundation. Port au Prince.

Stephens, D. 1984. *CARE Northwest Agroforestry Extension Project: 1983 Annual Report.* CARE, Gonaives.

Torres, F. 1983. Potential contribution of leucaena hedgerows intercropped wtih maize to the production of organic nitrogen and fuelwood in the lowland tropics. *Agrofor. Syst.* 1, pp. 323–333.

Torres, F. 1983. Role of woody perennials in animal agroforestry. *Agrofor. Syst.* 1, pp. 131–163.

UN Food and Agriculture Organization. 1981. *Agriculture: Toward 2000.* UN Food and Agriculture Organization, Rome.

UN Food and Agriculture Organization. 1982. *Tropical Forest Resources.* FAO Forestry Paper No. 30, UN Food and Agriculture Organization, Rome 100 p.

UN Food and Agriculture Organization. 1983. *State of Food and Agriculture 1982.* UN Food and Agriculture Organization, Rome.

UN Food and Agriculture Organization. 1985. *The Contribution of Small-Scale Forest-Based Processing Enterprises to Rural Non-Farm Employment and Income in Selected Developing Countries.* FO:MISC/85/4. UN Food and Agriculture Organization, Rome.

UN Food and Agriculture Organization. 1985. *Tree Growing by Rural People.* FAO Forestry Paper No. 64. UN Food and Agriculture Organization, Rome.

Van Gelder, B. and Poulsen, G. 1982. *The Woodfuel Supply from Trees Outside the Forests in the Highlands of Kenya.* The Beijer Institute, Nairobi.

Vergara, N.T. 1985. Agroforestry systems: a primer. *Unasylva* 37, pp. 22–28.

Von Carlowitz, P. 1984. *Multipurpose Trees and Shrubs, Opportunities and Limitations.* Working Paper No. 17. International Council for Research in Agroforestry, Nairobi.

Winterbottom, R. 1985. *Rwanda Integrated Forestry and Livestock Project.* Report of the Phase II Rural Forestry PrePreparation Mission. UN Food and Agriculture Organization. The World Bank, Washington.

The World Bank. 1982. *Haiti: Issues and Options in the Energy Sector.* The World Bank, Washington.

The World Bank. 1984. *Economic Analysis Issues in Bank Financed Forestry Projects.* Draft technical note. Agriculture and Rural Development Department, The World Bank, Washington.

Towards a Theory and Practice of Rural Development

PONNA WIGNARAJA

The Model

Most of the Third World is predominantly a rural society. And yet, over a quarter century ago, when most Third World countries emerged as politically independent nations from centuries of colonial rule, they adopted a development model which was indifferent if not inimical to rural development. Support for this model, which essentially permitted continuation of existing international economic relationships, came from two external sources – the industrialized countries of the West and the industrialized centrally planned countries.

The framework that has influenced the development process in the past quarter century assumed that there were "developed" countries and "developing" countries and that if the experience of the former, along with some resources, were transferred to the latter the gap would be narrowed. The objectives and processes were viewed in economic terms and great reliance was placed on economic factors to achieve results. The framework assumed that rapid economic growth could take place if there was central planning and control of the economy as a "top-down" process, with emphasis on industrialisation, modernisation and urbanisation. Capital, the factor in short supply, was conceived as the main input into the process. Internal capital accumulation would be assisted by inflows of foreign capital and technology. The cumulative benefits of this kind of

Wignaraja. *Development: Seeds of Change* granted permission to use this article. It appeared in 1984 in Vol. 2 (pp. 3–11) of that journal.

growth in the modern sector were expected eventually either to "trickle down" automatically or at best be handed down in an administrative fashion or "delivered" to the large numbers of people who in Third World countries live predominantly in the rural areas. Material accumulation was expected to solve other human problems. Rural development was later added on a sectoral issue to this development model.

The widening gap between industrialised and Third World countries, the results of the "green revolution" which helped the rich get richer and made the poor poorer within Third World countries, the massive reverse transfer of resources from rural to urban areas, and from poor countries to rich confirms the irrelevance of this framework and indicated the limitations of this narrow "techno-economic" approach to development, even in its own terms.

Apart from the model's narrow orientation and its relevance for Third World countries, the realities of the quantity and quality of foreign aid and transfer of technology to supplement indigenous capital, the factor in short supply, and the weak internal mobilisation efforts made the assumptions regarding possibilities of rapid growth in the model of little operational value. There is sufficient evidence from U.N., World Bank and other studies to confirm that, by any standards, neither the quantum of aid nor its quality nor the kind of technology transferred from industrialised to Third World countries were sufficient or appropriate. Even as there is general apathy towards aid in most industrialised countries today, there is also a growing body of opinion which supports the view that the earlier kind of aid-giving and technology transfer is a thing of the past and may have helped to create "soft" societies, impoverish rural areas and increase the dependence of Third World countries. This is not an argument against aid or international development co-operation, as such, but it questions the way things have worked. Further, the transnational corporations, which control the stock of "modern" technology and which are still the main instruments for its transfer, extract high prices for their know-how and equipment: the "borrowed", highly capital-intensive, import-substituting technology which is continuing to be implanted in Third World countries has little relation either to real factor endowment, particularly labour, or to the existing technological stock. The entire process is wasteful and the contradictions too numerous.

Throughout the 1960s and early 1970s some token attempts have been made to modify these narrow techno-economic notions of development and to effect some reforms. The reformists argued that a modified framework of economic development could still be made to work "efficiently" if (a) redistributive or social justice were built into the objectives, (b) there were an element of popular participation in an essentially "top-down" planning process and (c) the U.N.'s New International Economic Order were to ensure a continuous process of transfer of an appropriate proportion of the income and technology from industrialised to Third World countries.

The reformist position continues to be based essentially on conventional development thinking. Even with social justice built into it, the development process is still considered mainly as an economic exercise, subject to allocation of scarce resources. Further, it assumes a conflict-free social framework for change. The vision of "one world" continues to pervade the climate of the New International Economic Order, as does the assumption that it will result under existing conditions and structures in an orderly and continuous process of significant amounts of income and technology transfer from industrialised countries to the Third World. Underlying all this are further assumptions: that the problem of development is still mainly in the poor countries; and that a consistent set of "policy packages" based on technocratic considerations ranging from structural changes to investment decisions to employment opportunities, can be evolved and can be carried out from "the top" with some consultation with the people and the good will and assistance of "developed" countries and the international community.

Premise of One Stock of Knowledge

To move from this (anti-rural) development model to a framework of rural development in wider human terms, it is not sufficient to merely critique the model in general terms. There are some specific elements which need to be demystified in the light of recent experience. A basic premise of the old framework of development was that there was one stock of knowledge i.e., modern technology, located in industrialised countries, which if transferred to the Third World would solve their problems. The technical assistance programmes and the extension worker concept are both part of this approach. It was assumed that this technology was value-free.

Today, it is clear not only that technology is not value-free but that it is also a carrier of cultural codes. Secondly, there is a greater technological choice for Third World countries. There are many stocks of knowledge located in different cultural settings, some of it half-forgotten, much of it able to stand the test of modern scientific validation, and there is also new knowledge being created by fragile R and D systems emerging in rural settings. There is also relevant knowledge in industrialised countries in response to "alternative ways of life" movements which may be less alienating when adapted to Third World conditions.

The following diagram presents the possibility of six different sources of knowledge and technology which can be drawn for rural development and which can be appropriate under different rural circumstances.

(i) The conventional growth model indicated that the "modern" stock in industrialised countries (1 in the diagram) should be transferred through "market" processes along with finance from rich to poor countries. This created islands of modernisation in Third World countries and left large numbers in rural areas uninvolved and without benefit. In fact the overall process resulted in a dual society, and an impoverishment of rural areas through a transfer of resources first from rural to urban areas and then into the industrialised countries.

(ii) The "intermediate" technology (1a) is a corollary of (1) and if transferred through the same processes would have the same effects.

(iii) Traditional technology (2) is another stock. Some of it can be used as it is.

(iv) Some traditional technology is half-forgotten and would need to be revived, some would also need to be upgraded in its own environment (2a).

(v) As a result of a two-way interaction between "experts" and the people in Third World countries, a new technology is gradually being created in Third World countries which does not exist in categories (1) and (2). The experience here differs from the concept of "experts go learn from the people" or "experts go tell the people". The new technology (3) results from a new and still fragile R and D system gradually being built up by committed experts and the people in Third World countries living and working together over time to evolve a more humane society using locally available resources and knowledge.

(vi) Likewise, in industrial countries, as a result of "alternative lifestyles" experiments resulting from the energy crisis, ecological concerns etc., individuals and groups are experimenting with technologies related to new values and new institutions which provide a glimpse of a different people/nature/technology mix. This technology may in the long run be more relevant for rural development than the conventional unadapted transfers from the modern sector. The diagram implies a two-way transfer as structural changes in industrial countries themselves take place.

The argument here is that there is a plurality of "stocks". This means there is a greater technological choice i.e., many more options in the selection of appropriate technology for rural development in Third World countries. This choice cannot any longer be left solely to the technocrats. The strategy of technological choice has to be related to a social philosophy, the local resource position, and factor distribution. The conventional approach to rural development has also glossed over the details of technological complexities, ruling out substitution possibilities, assuming there was only one primary factor of production and ignoring organisational, institutional, and psychological questions.

The Project Approach

A second element that requires demystification relates to the *project approach*. The old framework of development was supported at the micro level by a conventional technocratic approach to project development. Despite the fact that experience has shown the limitations of this approach, particularly in rural situations, it is deeply rooted in the current operations of most governments, donor agencies and the so-called integrated rural development programmes.

There is now a growing body of literature, some of it unpublished, which has evaluated newstyle integrated rural development projects that make use of the conventional micro level methodology for project development and are based on

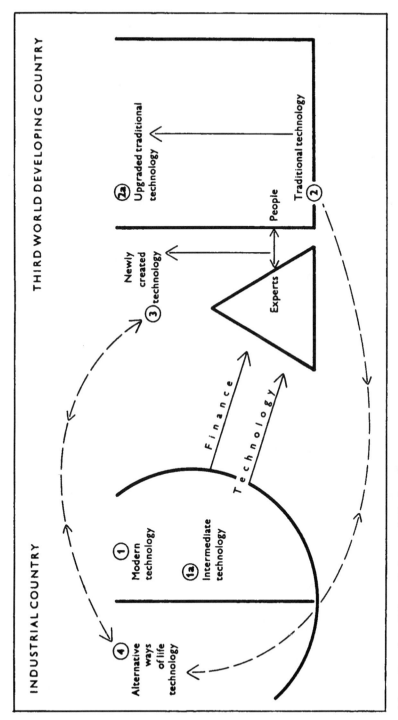

Many Stocks of Knowledge and Technology

cost-benefit analysis or minor variations of the same underlying principles. The evaluation indicate that a technocratically evolved package polarises the village, and the village rich get richer and the poor poorer. Even when this package is aimed at a "target" group identified as the rural poor, and is carried out with greater efficiency in the "delivery" mechanism, with some better co-ordination of bureaucratic procedures and with some attempt at consultation with the target group (often confused with real participation), it does not in itself ensure that the economic benefits reach the poor, let alone improve their condition in wider human terms.

It cannot any longer be contested that as long as the basic economic and social institutions in the village are controlled by the rich, a mere terminological separation of the poor from the rich does safeguard the interests of the former against the manipulations of the latter. A purely technocratic thrust cannot bring about the desired changes.

The problem of interdependence and linkages of several activities at the village level also seriously limits the project approach, which assumes that there is a beginning and a defined end to the "project", and that the inputs and outputs are quantifiable. The interdependent activities must evolve taking into consideration people's awareness, and cannot be formulated externally in a grand design or, in a predetermined fashion, supported by an aid package. One further point worth mentioning is that small-scale rural economic or social activity is guided mainly by considerations of minimising resource utilisation rather than maximising the benefits. This is very natural in a situation in which there is a lack of access to resources and a need to minimise waste. Such activity does not respond to normal investment criteria. Thus it is necessary to question the value of the conventional cost benefit analysis theory and the project approach under these circumstances either for designing rural development activities or

for evaluating them, particularly, when an alternative approach is available.

Any strategy of rural development involving the large numbers who are the rural poor (or any other oppressed group) has to begin by bringing about unity among the poor. Unity among the poor and a spirit of cooperation cannot be legislated into existence. Disunity among the poor arises from asymmetrical dependency relationships that tie the poor individually to the rich; this then generates dependency attitudes and a vicious circle is initiated with disunity built into it. Under these circumstances, before the poor can benefit, their dependency on the rich has to be reduced by giving them independent staying power in a conflict-ridden social environment.

The question then is how to break out of this vicious circle, and here is where *"another" approach to project designing and evaluation* comes into its own. It is really a process which should be understood in terms of an interrelated and varied set of activities which are undertaken in stages. The first stage of the initial activity is that which begins to unite the target group, or a part of it, and to set a positive spiral of activities in motion. It is becoming increasingly clear that positive interaction among people can be generated and sustained. The steps towards this end are as follows: (1) Separate out the target groups by understanding the contradictions in the social environment (the contradiction tree). (2) Work on their minds to actuate cooperative values, sensitising cadres for initiating and multiplication of activities. (3) Initiate cooperative activity among the target group or a subsector of the group (e.g., a women's group or a youth group starting with a non-confrontational activity), building organisations of the poor. (4) As the cooperative base of the activity progresses, further activities must be initiated to promote positive values in the minds of the target group, and critical village institutions that ensure participation of the poor have to be strengthened.

Together, the above steps constitute a movement towards the creation of a self-reliant base for the target group and a process which permits it to de-link from economic and psychological dependence, thereby building on its own creativity and self-reliance. Projects must evolve in the carefully staged manner and subsequent stages must be built on the collective experience of the previous stages. They cannot be formulated in a ready-made package, anticipating all the stages and assuming that all stages will proceed according to a pre-conceived technical plan designed from the "top" without involvement and understanding of the target group. Central to this process is the need for people to raise their level of consciousness and form their own organisations. Once this participatory self-reliant base has been built, external technical and financial inputs of one kind or another can be better absorbed and will not skew the benefits.

The process of building a participatory self-reliant base cannot at present be a spontaneous one. Given the deep-rooted dependency relationships, the poor lack the capacity to take initiatives individually for improving their lot. The intervention of a catalyst or initiator is necessary to break this vicious circle. Such change agents are fundamentally different from typical government rural development officers or extension workers or even the conventional rural volunteers. They need to be committed individuals who can identify with the rural poor, mobilize them, conscientise them and help them organise themselves for participatory self-reliant rural development. The identification and sensitisation of such change agents now become a critical part of launching rural development activities. Evaluation itself is built into the process in a continuous and participatory manner by those who are involved.

The "Harmony" Assumption

A last point that needs to be demystified relates to the concept of the "community" i.e., the harmony situation. Rural communities in the Third World are not homogeneous entities. Sometimes where land reform has occurred or in a tribal society in which land is communally owned and traditional societal values continue, the situation may be more harmonious. But even here a great deal depends on the extent of penetration of colonial systems and on other external interventions which have created contradictions, eroded communal bonds and values, and the equality of access to resources. By and large in most Third World villages there exist sharp contradictions among different groups with conflicts of interests. There are dominance/dependence relationships even at the village level which need to be understood. These relationships then give power to the dominant (the landlord, the trader, the money lender, the bureaucrat etc.,) to bring about a crisis of immediate survival for the poor. The divisions among the poor themselves and the inhibitions of the poor from taking economic, social and political initiatives individually to improve their lives further compound their difficulty and prevent them from benefiting from the technocratically evolved packages.

Under these circumstances any meaningful approach that will not benefit the rich at the expense of the poor must be a political approach. In some countries the "political space" exists for such an approach. In others the "political space" needs to be created or even a crack can be widened.

At this point in the discussion it is sufficient to state that despite the fact that a great many lessons have been learned from the workings of the old development model of what not to do at the macro/micro levels, it is nonetheless uncritically followed by large parts of the development establishment, both national and international. The current crisis in rich and poor countries – capitalist and socialist – and in the workings of the global system offers an opportunity to lay to rest the past faith in this simplistic framework for development thinking and action and establish the need for a new praxis on every aspect of development, including development in rural areas where the majority of people in the Third World live.

Participation and "Political Space"

Of central concern in any discussion of rural development in wider human terms is the issue of participation. It is a pretense to think that the crisis that the Third World is facing can be overcome and that the reshaping of its societies and the development of its rural areas can be undertaken without the participation of the people, particularly the large numbers who are poor. Perceptions of this complex question are varied, and a major debate relating to various aspects of participation is now taking place. Recently the Society for International Development published an issue of its journal on the theme "Participation of the rural poor in development" as an input into this debate.

Participation is democracy. Representative democracy as now practiced is a very limited form of participation. Participation means commitment to a more egalitarian society which permits equal access to resources – not only to land – but also to education, health, etc. Where formal power is in the hands of a few and their power is grossly misused, participation means building countervailing power which leads to a healthier democracy.

As has been mentioned earlier, people cannot be viewed as mere objects or targets of development – they are the subjects. Further, if development results from a process of releasing the creative energies of the people, particularly the poor, then *they* must be the final arbiters of their lives. Participation and self-reliance are thus two sides of the same approach. This goes beyond merely meeting the material needs of people and beyond considerations of equity. To participate people need to raise their level of consciousness and to form their own organizations. The rural poor need to become increasingly aware of the socio-economic reality around them, of the forces that keep them in poverty, and of the possibilities for bringing about change in their conditions through their own reflections and collective actions. This constitutes a process of self-transformation through which they grow and mature as human beings. In this sense participation is also a basic human need.

A truly participatory development process cannot be generated spontaneously, given the existing power relations at all levels and the deep-rooted dependency relationship referred to earlier. As has been mentioned it requires a catalyst. The catalyst or initiator who can break this vicious circle is a new type of activist who will work with the poor, who identifies with the interests of the poor and who has faith in the people. The interaction with initiators helps people to analyse their problems, to understand their problems better, and to articulate their felt needs. Their interaction sets in motion a process of reflection, mobilisation, organisation, action and further reflection among the poor. Through a process of awareness creation, initiators mobilise people into self-reliant action and assist in the building up of collective strength and bargaining among the poor.

Hence, identification, selection, and sensitisation of such initiators becomes a central task in launching an effective participatory rural development movement. Conventional training methodology (delivering a prepackaged basket of knowledge or skills through lectures and instruction) cannot be used for this purpose. It is a process of sensitisation rather than training. It is a process of self-learning through exposure to the dynamics of actual socio-economic situations rather than learning in the abstract. Observation, investigation, group interaction, sharing and comparing experiences, criticism and self-criticism, cultivating behavioural and social skills (particularly the capacity to analyse the political economy of poverty) are the central elements of this process of sensitisation. Without this awareness people cannot participate – they are merely manipulated with a pretense of consultation.

Finally, it is difficult for the poor to break away from the vicious circle of dependence and poverty individually. It is only through collective effort and organization that they can reduce dependence and initiate a course of participatory, self-reliant development. Thus participation implies mobilisation, conscientisation, and organisation – in that order.

The extent of participation will depend initially on the political space that is available for the participatory grass roots processes to start and for an intervention into the existing socio-economic system. In many Third World countries there is great potential energy and will to change. This energy needs to be harnessed, and change agents can be found in many areas to initiate the process. In various Third World countries there is strong support for people's causes from such groups as the radical church, various professions, students, and even members of the bureaucracy, the judiciary and the army.

The very nature of participatory self-reliant development activities is such that they eventually attract the attention of the power structure. Some activities are co-opted, others are exterminated, some are repressed, but survive. Those which survive, existing in isolation, do not add up to much in terms of social transformation. But if they are properly linked and multiply themselves through the process of mobilisation, conscientisation, organisation they can become a countervailing power in the societal context and help to widen the political space even further for participatory self-reliant rural development.

The crisis of rural mass poverty and human degradation in all countries of the Third World amidst affluence and minority power is generating various responses from different actor groups: spontaneous peasant struggles and initiatives by people's and workers' organisations, by non-governmental organisations made up of persons from different strata of society, and by political parties with different ideologies all trying to bring about a change in the power structure. Some of these will be illustratively identified in what follows.

Lessons from an Observable Reality – "Seeds of Change?"

Experience at the macro level

The elements outlined earlier are not abstract or the result of *a priori* theorizing. They are a reflection of an observable reality and lessons stemming from actual development experiments which provide a material basis for the generalisations. This reality can be analysed at two levels – the macro national level and the rural micro grass roots level.

The macro national level is where Governments have initiated transitional pathways to social change and rural development with elements of participation and self-reliance in different historical cultural settings. Selective illustrations include the attempt at mass mobilisation in China, the South Korean experience with Saemaul Undong (the New Community Movement) and Tanzania's Ujaama Movement.

In China after the revolution in 1949, and in continuation of the self-reliant progresses initiated in the liberated areas during the guerrilla war, a serious effort was made to restore the creative initiative of the masses and collective self-respect in the rural society. Using the creative energies of the people, local resources, and local knowledge, the worst forms of poverty and disease were mitigated for large numbers. China delinked from the global system during this period, set in motion several waves of mobilisation, and attempted to raise the consciousness of the people and organize them for this effort with minimum resource utilisation and waste. The course has not been smooth, and the more recent changes, involving relinking into the global system, trying to move to another level of technology, and introducing the "responsibility" system in the rural areas, merely raise new questions, and also underscore the dialectic of the development process and the unresolved ideological conflicts within the Chinese Communist Party. The important fact, however, is that evidence is emerging to indicate that the efforts at mass mobilisation for rural development in China may not be specific to its own historical course, which was in fact as dismal as any until conscious and determined human action altered it with a different people/nature/technology mix and a different process of mobilisation, conscientisation, and organisation of people and the use of resources. A question lingers on however, as to whether the conflicts of interest in some Third World rural societies are so sharp that the contradictions will first have to be resolved in a revolutionary manner before a common objective of rural development can be pursued.

In South Korea the problem was somewhat different. During the 1960s the South Korean economy grew at 10% per annum, supported by massive inflows of foreign aid and private foreign investment, which were concentrated in the modern urban, industrial, and mining sectors. This caused significant disparities in urban/rural incomes and led to a large migration from rural to urban areas with consequent social and political problems. The Saemaul Movement was initiated by the Government in 1970. There were a number of preconditions which served to provide a base from which the movement could be launched. These ranged from complete decolonisation from Japanese rule to the leveling effect after the Korean war, (which permitted the national reconstruction effort to start with a relatively clean state), massive external assistance, land reform, expansion of secondary education, and the establishment of an elaborate network of co-operative rural banking and marketing institutions. Thus the foundations had been laid for vigorous capitalist development under what may be called non-classical conditions. The Saemaul Movement brought considerable changes in rural South Korea. Land reform and the creation of co-operative and marketing institutions eliminated exploitation based on land, money-lending and marketing. The relative equality of the villagers has produced a more homogenous rural society with no sharp class conflicts and at the same time has provided an expanded domestic market in the rural areas for the industrial base. An important element in the movement was the orientation and training of elected local cadres, as well as, national political leaders and the bureaucracy, both groups being put through the same sensitisation process. Cabinet ministers, senior government officials, university professors, technical experts and other elites had to participate and exchange ideas with village leaders as part of the process of remolding the elite. The question that requires examination is how much effective political power is being shifted to the villagers through the movement, so as to give them increasing control over decisions which affect their lives. A second question relates to the terms of trade between the rural and urban areas to ascertain the extent to which the rural surplus is retained in the rural areas.

Experience at the Micro Level

Turning to the wide variety of micro grass roots experiments in the Third World, these represent a new factor in the rural development picture and also provide a wide range of experience from which to learn. There are the results of romantic and idealistic approaches taken by charitable institutions, religious organizations, the "small is beautiful" people, etc., which have tried to teach the people to do "good" things, often treating the village as a homogeneous entity or "community" to begin with. Secondly, there are ideas introduced by radical political parties looking for a political constituency. They have been able to mobilise poor people to anger at the workings of the exploitative system, but have not always been able to sustain a spontaneous people's movement and/or a grass roots experiment. Some of these represent "seeds of change" others are mere "bubbles".

At this stage it is important to make a distinction between a "seed" and a "bubble". A "seed" can be identified with such broad criteria as equality of access to resources; equality of social, political, cultural rights; real participation in all social decisions affecting work, welfare, politics etc.; the end of the division between mental and manual labor and the use of technology appropriate for this purpose. It is however, not merely a matter of stating these objectives; genuine participation, awareness creation and the effort to change social relations must be built into the process. One can keep adding to this list: local orientation, self-production and self-management, autonomy, solidarity and innovativeness. A "bubble" on the other hand is a "soft" process and also may not last for a variety of reasons. However, "bubbles" should not be dismissed too hurriedly; they may represent "entry points" to change and some of them can be transformed into "seeds" through additional sensitisation programmes, training of interveners and cadres. The essential point about a "seed" is that it is the outcome of a process of mobilisation, conscientisation, and organisation which leads to structural and social change.

The questions that need to be addressed at this juncture are: are these grass roots initiatives and experiments "seeds of change?" Can these "seeds" provide a material basis for an *alternative rural development strategy* which is responsive to the new compulsions for social change in most Third World

countries? Can this strategy reinforce the social transformation that is inevitable and is a part of a progressive response to a major challenge of our times? What needs to be done even in a modest way to reinforce this process which is already underway, and will gather momentum and cannot really be stopped in the long run?

Towards a New Praxis

So far this paper has raised a few basic questions that need to be addressed in an attempt at rethinking rural development. Much of the thoughts may not be completely new. Some of the elements, however, are at the margin of established thinking and practice and need to be given legitimacy. The assertions that follow may offer a guide to further thinking and action at the macro–micro, national or global levels.

(i) The basic issues raised by the lack of rural development, more than a quarter century after the problem was identified, are too fundamental to be resolved by the purely pragmatic approach and the marginal tinkering which has characterized the attempts at solutions by most governments, international organizations and some NGO's. *Some more coherent conceptual framework needs to be evolved to guide all this activity.* This framework when it emerges will not constitute a general "model", as each country and socio-cultural environment has its own specificity. Pluralistic perspectives will need to guide different approaches in different contexts. The new framework would depend on the nature of the social transition the country is going through, and on the need to be holistic and evolved with still inadequate inter-disciplinary analytic tools; it should reflect the perceptions of people who are both the subjects and objects. This is an extremely difficult intellectual exercise and all actors in the process have to be involved in a collective reconceptualisation, based on the emerging reality and the "seeds of change" which it contains, through a new social praxis.

(ii) The elements discussed essentially relate to aspects of social change in the Third World where countries are embarking on a variety of transitional pathways to growth and change. Since most of the Third World is predominantly rural or semi-rural, this social change and what is currently labeled "development" in these countries must essentially concern rural development in the widest sense. *Rural development is therefore not viewed as a sectoral issue, not is the approach to rural development viewed as being apolitical.* There should be no attempt to obfuscate the real issue, which is one of political power and which manifests itself even at the village level.

(iii) The depth of the current development crisis in both industrialised and Third World countries – "capitalist" and "socialist", the failure of the post-war pattern of development, and the emergence of new global problems have made it eminently clear that *development problems – let alone rural development problems – cannot be solved by means of the prescriptions of the past thirty-five years* (the "imitation" the "trickle down" etc.). Given the similarity of the crisis of confidence in the industrialised countries – in regard to the welfare state and socialist experiments – and in the Third World with its dehumanising poverty and alienation, both groups of countries need to find alternative driving forces for growth and social change. For the large number of people in the Third World the driving forces for growth and change that pertain to the industrialised countries no longer offer a viable road to accumulation, let alone to fulfillment in wider human terms; they need to find it through a different people/nature/technology mix.

(iv) At the international level, the problem of rural development in the widest sense must enter into the North-South dialogue and global negotiations. The North-South dialogue in recent years has dealt for the most part with specific changes in the manner in which existing international organisations function and the rules of the current and emerging international game. It is not focused on an optimal world, with different rules and a different people/nature/technology mix for which a new international order is required.

The North-South dialogue is needed more than ever before as the crisis intensifies, but its substance must have a basis in the reality at the village and local levels in all countries. It cannot be based on *a priori* theorizing on how the global order should work and let this perception inform people's responses at the local level. The best the current North-South dialogue is able to offer is "more of the same" and offers no real alternatives. In fact, for the most part, the prescriptions amount to a little more aid or trade, a little more efficiency in the delivery mechanism or the addition of another sectoral institution. All this can lock the Third World back into the very framework of thinking and action which is anti-rural development and which needs to be changed.

As far as Third World is concerned, this whole approach represents a continuation of the attempt to incorporate it into an inequitous, unmanageable and contradictory global system without first changing that system. *If rural development in wider human terms is to result, a flexible global system needs to be evolved to supplement national rural development efforts and be mutually reinforcing.* This would require structural changes within countries and at the global level, as well as, the initiation of a de-linking process with an orderly re-linking into a New International Order. A New International Order by itself means little unless alternative development strategies are pursued in both industrialised and Third World countries – capitalist and socialist alike. The alternatives must themselves find legitimacy in activities in which the people who are now uninvolved have participated. As has been said earlier the intellectual underpinnings for this cannot be provided by *a priori* theorizing as in the past.

(v) Those who claim to be working on rural development problems must have *a basic commitment to and identity with the following minimum valuational framework* – irrespective of whether they are policy makers, researchers, grass roots activists:

• equality of access to economic resources;

• equal rights for all: political, social and cultural;

• real participation in all social decisions: work, welfare, politics, etc.;

• end of the division between mental and manual labor and the use of technology appropriate for this purpose.

There should be no ambiguity about this. This commitment is a prerequisite for a progressive response to a deep-seated human problem, which has already assumed crisis proportions. It requires committed actors to use whatever power they have – political power or power of ideas – to bring about the necessary changes and a solution to the real problems of rural development which have now been clearly identified.

(vi) The grass roots experiments that are in evidence do not constitute a monolithic movement inspired by a single unifying ideology – though most of them, even rhetorcally, emphasise people's participation and self-reliance. They are located mainly in political and economic spaces in pre-capitalist or semi-feudal structures which are locked into a global system in a dependency relation. There is a great deal of isolation among these activities so that even when the political or economic space exists or suddenly widens through fortuitous circumstances or the emergence of a charismatic leader committed to this kind of change, they are unable to move beyond the narrower confines of their immediate activity and relate to the wider macro social processes.

To be part of a wider social process these grass roots experiments need to be selectively *linked*, first within countries – horizontally among themselves and then even vertically with committed individuals and groups, wherever they may be, to build new alliances and coalitions – then between groups in similar or neighboring countries.

Since there are positive and negative aspects of linkage to these isolated activities, the process has to be evolved slowly, so that any attempt to link by an external (meaning outside the activity or movement) vanguard, must be sensitively undertaken to ensure that the negative aspects do not outweigh the mutual benefits from the exchange of experiences and information by these groups which would result from linkage.

Groups that consider themselves involved in promoting social change for the benefit of the masses in the Third World, must link with each other in order to become a countervailing power; otherwise an isolated experiment which may be interesting in itself will not become a social force.

A grass roots movement may continuously advance in an upward spiral towards participatory self-reliant rural development for a particular group, in a particular location, but, apart from linking with each other for the reasons mentioned above, these activities must also *multiply* and cover larger and larger numbers of people and geographical locations. The key element in multiplication is the training of the catalysts; first, the training of vanguard groups who can initiate the process then of local level rural development activists whose leadership capabilities can be developed.

Since Paulo Freire first enunciated conscientisation methodologies for political struggle, a great deal of experimentation and refinements have been undertaken in training methodologies for rural development cadres and activists, and effective training/sensitisation programmes are in operation. This training is completely different from the training imparted in training center, by pre-packaged lecture methods as in the case of most extension workers and other rural development personnel. The training implies sensitisation to develop an identity with and commitment to resolving the rural development problematique with an awareness of why the problem exists. The new training methodology is a part of the praxis and cannot be separated mechanistically from the reflection and action research which are also part of the same process.

A great deal of action research guided by the perspectives enunciated in this paper is currently underway. This is not the sectorally oriented, fragmented single-discipline activity of the past. It is interdisciplinary with more holistic perspectives and is collectively undertaken using the methodology of participatory action research. Much of this work and the research results are presently at the margin of the debate and action of rural development. If this action research is to have an impact on the current crisis in development/rural development it has to be protected, supported and allowed to mature. In bringing it out of the cold, however, it should not merely be co-opted. The ILO for instance through its work in the Rural Employment Policies Branch has carried out research which can feed into ILO's technical co-operation and advisory services in the field of rural development.

As was mentioned earlier a great deal *more conceptual work* also needs to be done. Research at the broader level is necessary to understand the micro-macro linkages and give greater coherence to the elements mentioned in this section. There is also a need for the study of the entire political economy of pre-capitalist social formations – both feudal and tribal – in different cultural settings. For instance, as has been mentioned earlier, the work of Prebisch and Amin at the macro global level must be integrated with the initial work of Wahidul Haque et al of the micro political economy, which in itself needs further refinement in the light of the better understanding of the emerging micro reality.

To conclude, no society is following a pre-determined historical pathway. No society can any longer lay claim to ideological purity. Some of the labels are much abused and have constituted "blinkers" to the understanding of reality. As a result of the interpenetration between capitalist and socialist formations in different historical cultural settings, new conditions pertain. The different pathways and transitions to social change call for new perspectives and analysis, and the elements mentioned in this paper only constitute the beginning of a new intellectual process of social change.

REFERENCES

An Approach to Evolving Guidelines for Rural Development. Discussion Paper Series n. 1. Bangkok: United Nations Asian Development Institute, 1975.

Bhaduri, A. and Md. A. Rahman. *Studies in Rural Participation*, World Employment Programme. ILO, Oxford: IBH Publishing Co. and Oxford Press, 1982.

Bhasin, K. and R. Vimala, eds. *Readings on Poverty, Politics and Development*. Freedom from Hunger Campaign/Action for Development. Rome: Food and Agriculture Organization of the United Nations, August 1980.

De Silva, G.V.S. "Social Change". Unpublished manuscript. Colombo, 1978.

GRIS NOTES. Newsletter of the SID's Grass Roots Initiatives and Strategies Programme, Nos. 1 and 2. Rome: Society for International Development, 1981.

Haque, W., N. Mehta, Md. A. Rahman, and P. Wignaraja. "Towards a Theory of Rural Development". *Development Dialogue*, 1977:2.

Mehta, N., Md. A. Rahman, G.V.S. De Silva, and Wignaraja. "Bhoomi Sena: Struggle for Peoples Power" *Development Dialogue*, 1979:2.

"Participation of the Rural Poor in Development". *Development: Seeds of Change, Village through Global Order*, 1981:1.

P. Wignaraja, "From the Village to the Global Order". *Development Dialogue*, 1977:1.

Unpublished manuscripts of:

1) Participatory Institute for Development Alternatives (PIDA). Sri Lanka, 1981–82.

2) Peoples Institute for Development and Training (PIDIT). India, 1979–82.

3) Centre of Human Development (Proshika). Bangladesh, 1976–82.

About the Authors in Chapter 13

Michael Bratton is an Associate Professor in the Department of Political Science at Michigan State University. The University Press of New England (Hanover, NH) published his book, *The Local Politics of Rural Development*, in 1980.

Robert T. Winterbottom, Director of the Forestry and Land Use Program of the World Resources Institute in Washington, D.C., is the author of "Rwanda Integrated Forestry and Livestock Project." This was a Report of the Phase II Rural Forestry PrePreparation Mission, U.N. Food and Agriculture Organization, World Bank, in 1985.

Peter T. Hazlewood was an associate in the Tropical Forests and Biological Diversity Program of the World Resources Institute when this article appeared. He is author of *Expanding the Role of Non-Governmental Organizations (NGOs) in National Forestry Programs: The Report of Three Regional Workshops in Africa, Asia, and Latin America*, Washington, D.C.: World Resources Institute, 1987.

Ponna Wignaraja is with the South Asian Perspectives Project, Sri Lanka, and was formerly Secretary General of the Society for International Development and Chairman of the Participatory Institute for Development Alternatives (PIDA) in Sri Lanka. Wignaraja's *Women, Poverty, and Resources* was published in New Delhi, India and Newbury Park, CA by Sage Publications in 1990.

Index